ANALYZING COMPLEX APPRAISALS FOR BUSINESS PROFESSIONALS

ANALYZING COMPLEX APPRAISALS FOR BUSINESS PROFESSIONALS

SHANNON P. PRATT AND JOHN LIFFLANDER

McGraw Hill Education

New York Chicago San Francisco Athens London
Madrid Mexico City Milan New Delhi
Singapore Sydney Toronto

1 2 3 4 5 6 7 8 9 DOC 21 20 19 18 17 16

ISBN 978-0-07-181293-1
MHID 0-07-181293-8

e-ISBN 978-0-07-181294-8
e-MHID 0-07-181294-6

This publication is designed to provide accurate and authoritative information in regard to the subject matter covered. It is sold with the understanding that neither the author nor the publisher is engaged in rendering legal, accounting, securities trading, or other professional services. If legal advice or other expert assistance is required, the services of a competent professional person should be sought.

—From a Declaration of Principles Jointly Adopted by a Committee of the American Bar Association and a Committee of Publishers and Associations

Library of Congress Cataloging-in-Publication Data

Pratt, Shannon P., author.
Analyzing complex appraisals for business professionals / by Shannon Pratt and John Lifflander.
pages cm
ISBN 978-0-07-181293-1 (alk. paper) — ISBN 0-07-181293-8 (alk. paper)
1. Valuation. 2. Business enterprises—Valuation. I. Lifflander, John. II. Title.
HG4028.V3P677 2016
657'.73—dc23 2015006812

Contents

Preface

This book was written to combine many appraisal subjects into one text that could help business professionals better understand how to read and review them. It occurred to Dr. Pratt and me that, to our knowledge, nothing like this book was available, and this was the beginning of our collaboration to write it. The challenge was to determine how much information should be included—if there was too much, then readers might get bogged down and not be able to quickly find the information they were seeking. If it did not include enough, then readers might lack the knowledge necessary to determine the credibility of appraisals that they might encounter in their work as bankers, lawyers, accountants, real estate brokers, and other professionals.

Our hope is that we found the correct middle ground, and those who need more information can consult texts that treat the specific appraisal subject they are reviewing with more depth, and those who need less will be pleased that they can find what they need with a minimal effort because there is not an overload of material. All in all, we hope this book fills a need for those who deal with appraisals in the course of their daily business.

John Lifflander, July 2016

SECTION 1

REAL ESTATE AND MACHINERY AND EQUIPMENT APPRAISALS

Chapter 1

Introduction to Appraisal Theory and Terms

The basis of most appraisal theory is the concept of substitution. People use this theory in everyday life to some extent, as they are confronted with choices in purchasing various items. In its most basic distillation, they compare the same product or similar products that are offered at different prices. The question that often arises is this one: Can a less expensive product be substituted for a more costly one without a loss in quality?

A generic medicine may be cheaper than its brand-name competitor, but is the substitute for the name brand just as effective, safe, and reliable? Given the choice of various automobiles with similar characteristics, a buyer might wonder if it is worth saving money by buying a less popular brand. Will the cheaper car be as reliable and have the same resale value? Is it worth the risk of buying it to save several thousand dollars? Perhaps without realizing it, people use appraisal principles in their lives on a regular basis.

The appraiser is generally not the buyer, so he or she uses the substitution principle from the perspective of a professional analyst. This means appraisers should not impose their own likes and dislikes and other biases about the property under valuation. Rather, they should, to some extent, put themselves in the position of a buyer, as they seek to determine the value of the subject property. For instance, an appraiser might never even think of buying a house next to the freeway because of the constant noise. Nevertheless, to determine the value of the property, the appraiser must consider other sales with a similarly noisy environment and base the value conclusion on what those properties have sold for. Essentially, the appraiser must play the part of a buyer who doesn't mind the noise and who would be shopping for similar properties.

Likewise, an industrial appraiser may think that a particular paper mill is not a good investment because of various economic factors that suggest that demand for the type of paper that the mill produces is waning and, to add to the difficulty, there is more production coming online in the future. For this reason the appraiser, if acting as a buyer, would never consider purchasing the mill. Nevertheless, that personal view should not influence the appraiser's value conclusion. The conclusion should include the knowledge of the industry and consideration of the economic issues for the mill that that appraiser has, but the estimate of value should not be influenced by the appraiser's subjectivity.

The bias that the appraiser must avoid in order to get an accurate value conclusion is the bias that is typical of most buyers who are making purchasing decisions. In other words, many buyers have an inherent bias due to their personal taste and requirements. For instance, a family is looking for a home, but they eliminate all homes with two-car garages because the father is adamant that he must have a three-car garage. The extra garage may add only $8,000 in value when adjusted for in an appraisal, but the family will not even consider a two-car-garage home, so they may pay a premium to get what they want—probably more than the adjustment the appraiser would have made in comparing properties. Shopping in this manner is common, but it also means that the buyer may pay more than market value due to circumstances that an appraiser would not normally consider in a market-based analysis. Another example would be a foreign industrial manufacturer looking for a counterpart in the United States to avoid certain exporting restrictions. That buyer may pay more than market value for a facility to get exactly what is needed in a coastal location to reduce tariffs and shipping costs.

Understanding these concepts is important, and they are more easily explained with simpler appraisals, such as the valuations of houses, before applying them to commercial, industrial, and other types of appraisals. For this reason this book begins, as previously noted, with the appraisal of residences and more common real estate and then builds toward more complicated issues of valuation.

Three Approaches to Value

For real property, there are three approaches to value, and they all are based, to some extent, on the substitution principle. Appraisers are supposed to utilize all three approaches if they are applicable to the subject property. If all of the approaches are not used, a statement should be made explaining why. The Uniform Standards of Professional Appraisal Practice (USPAP) regulates real estate appraisals, and it directs appraisers to make certain statements about their methodology. The USPAP will be discussed later in the book, but the definition the USPAP uses for market value is as follows:

> **Market value** means the most probable price which a property should bring in a competitive and open market under all conditions requisite to a fair sale, the buyer and seller each acting prudently and knowledgeably, and assuming the price is not affected by undue stimulus.

Implicit in this definition are the consummation of a sale as of a specified date and the passing of title from seller to buyer under conditions whereby:

1. Buyer and seller are typically motivated.
2. Both parties are well informed or well advised and acting in what they consider their own best interest.
3. A reasonable time is allowed for exposure in the open market.

4. Payment is made in terms of cash in U.S. dollars or in terms of financial arrangements comparable thereto.
5. The price represents the normal consideration for the property sold unaffected by special or creative financing or sale concessions granted by someone associated with the sale.[1]

The three approaches to value are the *sales comparison approach* (also known as the *market data approach* or the *comparable sales approach*), the *cost approach*, and the *income approach*.

The *sales comparison approach* is the approach that is most directly related to the principle of substitution. The appraiser finds sales that are similar (comparable) to the subject property and then adjusts the sales for dissimilarities to determine a value estimate. This follows a simple formula:

Sale price of comparable property ± adjustments = property value

Market Value of Subject Property

The *cost approach* requires the appraiser to separate the land value from the improvement value (buildings, fences, and so on) of the subject property. The value of the land must be found using the sales comparison approach. The value of the improvements is calculated by estimating the replacement or reproduction cost (more on this in Chapter 7). The appraiser then deducts any loss in value due to depreciation of the property. Depreciation can take various forms, but essentially it is a loss in value for any reason. The formula for the cost approach is as follows:

Replacement or reproduction cost of improvements
− depreciation on improvements + site value
= property value

The *income approach* for real estate should not be confused with the *business valuation approach*, which is used to value a complete business. The income approach for real estate is generally an *income capitalization approach*, which is based on net income, or the investment return that a buyer expects to receive from the property. In other words, the price the buyer pays will be based on how much income the buyer estimates will be yielded from the investment. The income approach uses a basic formula, which is known as IRV:

$$\frac{I}{R} = V$$

where

I is the net income

R is the capitalization rate

V is the property value

Two variations of the formula would be these:

$$\text{Rate} = \frac{\text{Income}}{\text{Value}}$$

$$\text{Income} = \text{Rate} \times \text{Value}$$

Relationship of the Three Approaches

The three approaches to value are used together to determine market value, but generally one approach is the primary approach in an appraisal and the other two buttress the valuation estimate. As previously stated, for some properties not all of the approaches are applicable, and where two or more approaches are utilized, the weight put on each approach may vary according to the significance the appraiser places on it. The values determined by the three approaches are normally never averaged; rather, the appraiser assigns a final value estimate by relying on the approach deemed most relevant for the subject property. This is all determined in the reconciliation portion of the appraisal, where the appraiser lists the estimate of value for the different approaches and then states the final value conclusion.

Generally, the sales comparison approach is the most accurate for single-family residences. For special-purpose properties, especially those that are non-income producing, the cost approach may be the best choice. And, for income producing properties, the income capitalization approach is generally the best approach.

As previously mentioned, the income approach for valuing real estate is different from a business income approach used to value a whole business, which may or may not include real estate. An income approach for valuing a business may incorporate any of the various methods, such as a *capitalized future economic method*, or a *discounted future economic income method*, sometimes known as a *discounted cash flow method*. A business valuation may also use a *market approach* by comparing publicly traded companies or sales of private companies and adjusting them to reach a value conclusion. The *cost approach* might be used in conjunction with other approaches, particularly where there are business assets that can be valued by cost minus depreciation, and then considered as a portion of the total value conclusion. This might be necessary to determine what portion of a business is depreciable for IRS reporting purposes.

Terminology

As one reads an appraisal, there is some terminology that can be easily misunderstood. The following are a few examples and clarifications.

Price, Cost, and Sales Price

Price, *cost*, and *sales price* are not interchangeable. The *price* typically refers to the asking price of the property when it is offered for sale (the *asking price*). Anyone can ask any price for anything that is for sale, so price does not always carry much weight in appraisals, with the exception of the fact that the lowest asking price of a property similar to the subject property may give the appraiser an understanding of the highest value for the subject property.

In other words, in a simplified example, a tract home is for sale for $300,000, and the same builder in the same subdivision has duplicated it. Other houses with the exact same floor plan, similar location, and condition are being offered for $320,000, $310,000, $290,000, $292,000, and $295,000. Before any sales are found, it is obvious that the highest value of the house, in the absence of other characteristics that are not known, would be in the low $290s. So the listings of other properties tend to reveal the high end of value for the home, but not the value, which could be lower and probably is lower since sellers often sell for less than list price in most markets.

Cost is the amount paid for something. It may be different from the price, or it may be the same if the buyer was willing to pay the full price. It is differentiated from price in that it is the exact expense for a good or service. The cost to buy a home would also be the sales price that it sold for.

Sales price (or *sale price*) is what the property actually sold for. Appraisers generally use only those sales that are arm's length transactions, which is essentially what is meant by the previously quoted definition of *market value* found in the USPAP. There are sales that are between relatives, or sales that are made under duress because the seller is going bankrupt or the property is in foreclosure, and those types of sales are normally excluded as comparable sales. However, there is an exception to that rule, which is when there are many sales of distressed properties and it becomes the market, and a seller cannot expect to get a higher price due to the competition of a plethora of distressed sales that are available.

An example would be a financial crisis in an area where many homes are in foreclosure and there are so many that they have saturated the market and become the norm. For an industrial example, at one point the wood products industry in the Northwest was in such poor financial condition that many sawmills were closed and were selling in foreclosure. No buyer would pay the premium for a mill that was not in that condition because the price would be much higher. Foreclosure prices were, in that case, the market.

Different Types of Appraisal Values

There can be a variety of appraisal values and circumstances, and the following are a few. The important thing to remember in reviewing an appraisal is that the appraiser must state what type of appraisal the report is, and in analyzing it, one must be careful to read what has been stated.

Retrospective and Hypothetical Appraisals

An appraiser may be given an assignment to value a property under special circumstances. There is no limitation as to the types of value that may be used, but the criteria will be determined by the request of the client, and the appraiser must clearly state them. For instance, a valuation is often made for property for a date in the past because of a divorce decree or a buyout agreement for a facility that was written at a certain time but not completed at that time. If the valuation was to be as of a date three years in the past, then a *retrospective appraisal* would be performed, and the appraiser would generally use only data that was available as of the requested historic date of the valuation. A retrospective valuation can be complicated by the fact that the market may have changed drastically in the ensuing years, which might make objectivity more difficult.

A *hypothetical appraisal* would be based on circumstances that don't exist. For instance, an appraiser might be hired to value a parcel of land as if it were improved with an apartment complex. Again, the USPAP requires that the appraiser must clearly state in the appraisal what the hypothetical circumstances are.

Liquidation Appraisals

The appraiser may be instructed to value the property as an *orderly liquidation.* This method of sale is one in which the seller may be compelled to sell, or voluntarily wants to sell, by a specific date, but the deadline allows a reasonable amount of time to market the property. A *forced liquidation sale* occurs when the property must be sold rather quickly, typically by means of an auction. Depending on the property and the economic circumstances at the time, the value may vary a great deal from a fair market value appraisal to an orderly liquidation or other type of appraisal.

Liquidation sales are often implemented because there is pressure to sell due to a bankruptcy, foreclosure, or some other distress situation. Because there are time constraints, there is typically a deadline for selling that a market value sale would not entail, and the price may be much lower than a market sale. Sale prices from liquidation sales are generally not usable for a fair market appraisal, but there are some exceptions.

With the sale of a facility with machinery and equipment, an appraiser might be asked to perform a valuation as a going concern (meaning the facility is functioning) or as a nonfunctioning facility.

Value in Use and Value in Exchange

For some appraisals, distinguishing between these two terms is important to understand. *Value in use* means the value according to how the property is being used. It is normally the value to the owner as opposed to the value on the open market. Often this will be a principle in an industrial valuation because industrial facilities are often specialized. Consequently, *value in use* typically refers to the value of property dedicated to a specialized use. If there is no specialized use, then often *value in use* and *value in exchange* are the same.

Value in exchange is the value agreed upon between a willing buyer and a willing seller in the open marketplace. This type of value may differ from value in use depending upon the circumstances of the particular property. A factory that is not functioning but is being purchased for a different use other than that for which it was originally built would fall into this category.

Exposure Time and Marketing Time

Appraisers make estimates in appraisals for exposure time and marketing time, but these terms often confuse the reader. Here is an explanation of them.

Exposure time happens prior to the effective date on the report. It is the time the appraiser estimates it would have taken for the subject property to sell if it had been for sale. For instance, an appraisal for an apartment complex may state that the exposure time is 18 months, meaning that if the property had been for sale 18 months before the effective date of the appraisal, it would have sold on that date. This estimate is normally made by the appraiser based on sales of similar properties. Otherwise, if the subject property is being appraised due to a sale, the actual time it was on the market would be primary evidence for the estimate if it was marketed normally. To reiterate, if the subject property was not for sale, then the estimate is based on the length of time it would have been offered if it had been for sale and on the market, prior to a hypothetical sale of the property on the appraisal date.

Marketing time refers to the time it would take to sell the property after the effective date of the appraisal. The appraiser estimates this time based on the current sales of other properties, the economic outlook for those properties, the amount of time comparable properties are staying on the market, and the supply and demand for comparable properties. The exposure time may have been 18 months, but now the real estate market has slowed down, and the appraiser estimates the marketing time to be 24 months. Conversely, if the market has become more active, the marketing time might be 12 months.

Both of these times are estimates, but the marketing time is more prone to inaccuracy since the prognostication of any market is inherently problematic. Consequently, this bit of information, which is required by the USPAP for most real estate appraisals, should not be greatly relied upon.

Highest and Best Use

Appraisers must determine the *highest and best use* of a property, which means considering alternative uses of the property to see if a different use would be more valuable than the current use. For instance, a five-acre property that is zoned for apartments has an old mobile home on it. The highest and best use might be to build an apartment complex on the land.

There are four criteria for highest and best use:

1. **Legally permissible.** What are the zoning and building restrictions?
2. **Physically possible.** Can it be constructed on the site?
3. **Financially feasible.** Is it cost effective?
4. **Maximally productive.** Is it the most financially rewarding use?[2]

Typically an existing improvement would be the highest and best use as long as it contributed more to the market value in monetary return than a new improvement would, taking into consideration the expense of demolishing the existing improvement and constructing the new one.

Reading the Appraisal

Narrative appraisals often contain a lot of information that is not specific to the particular property under valuation. The reader may get bogged down in this information when looking for the pertinent information. Certain disclaimers and other explanatory information are required by the USPAP, but other things in a report might be superfluous and may have been added to make the report more voluminous.

Forms are generally easier to read through, but they are used mostly for residential appraisals and smaller residential income properties such as duplexes, triplexes, fourplexes, and small apartment buildings.

Many narrative appraisals begin with what might be called an *executive summary*, which contains the highlights of the appraisal and often has salient information that can be read quickly. The summary, if the appraisal has one, is an important starting place, but it does not explain to the reader how the appraiser reached the valuation conclusion. It simply states general information about the property. The summary may be similar to Exhibit 1.1.

From this summary, perhaps the most important items noted are the appraised value, land size, improvement type and size, zoning, and highest and best use. But after the summary, there may be a lot of information that the reader might want to avoid because it will not help in determining the accuracy of the appraisal. Some of that information will be *standardized text*, which is more informally known as *boilerplate*. This text includes disclaimers and explanations about the appraisal, some of which may be required by the USPAP or simply added as filler by the appraiser, as previously noted. Large, voluminous reports often appear impressive to clients, but they may be difficult to sift through to get to the pertinent information.

Exhibit 1.1
Executive Summary

Client and intended user	Hometown Bank 56789 Walker Street Medford, OR 97504
Subject location	12345 Smith Street Klamath Falls, OR 97601
Assessor's parcel	Map 4 Tax lot 1
2010–2011 assessed value	$509,270
Gross site area	3.70 acres
Zone	IL: Light industrial
Special hazards	None
Flood zone designation	Zone C: No flooding FEMA FIRM 410109 1205B 12-18-84
Improvements	1 mobile home space and 4,000- square-foot metal shop building with concrete floor
Highest and best use	
As vacant	Industrial development
As improved	Interim use "as is" until more intensive industrial development is feasible
Market value estimates	
Cost approach	N/A
Sales comparison approach	$623,000
Income capitalization approach	N/A
Total market value conclusion	$623,000
Interest appraised	Fee simple
Date of inspection	September 26, 20XX
Date of value	September 26, 20XX
Date of report	September 29, 20XX
Appraiser	David Smith, MAI

The appraisal will typically include statistical data about the geographic location, with population estimates, economic statistics, and other things one would normally find from the local chamber of commerce. It may also have explanations about appraisal methodology, with definitions of the various approaches and the reasons why they were or were not used. The reviewer of the appraisal should keep in mind the distinction between specific data that pertains to the valuation and information that is irrelevant to the value conclusion.

Chapter 2

Analyzing the Single-Family Residential Appraisal

The Sales Comparison Approach

In the ideal single-family residential appraisal, if the appraisal had three comparable properties, one would be slightly higher, one slightly lower, and one exactly the indicated value for the subject property. In reality, a range of comparable sales like this is rarely found, so the appraiser must do the best job with the sales that are available.

Exhibit 2.1 is the sales comparison approach sheet for a typical single-family residential appraisal, which is on what is called a Fannie Mae Form 1004. Most residential appraisals use this form because it is the one needed to sell loans to the Federal National Mortgage Association (Fannie Mae) and Federal Home Loan Mortgage Corporation (Freddie Mac), which purchase most of the residential mortgages in the United States. The form uses codes for certain entries such as quality of construction and condition. The codes are part of a program called the Uniform Mortgage Data Program, which standardizes entries so that appraisers will use the same reference for various descriptions of the characteristics of houses.

For many years, instead of a code, the appraiser would enter a word. For instance, under "condition," the appraiser might enter "average" for

Exhibit 2.1

Sales Comparison Sheet for a Typical Single-Family Residential Appraisal (Fannie Mae Form 1004)

FEATURE	SUBJECT	COMPARABLE SALE # 1		COMPARABLE SALE # 2		COMPARABLE SALE # 3	
Address 1911 NW 110th St. Vancouver, WA 98685		1905 NW 110th St. Vancouver, WA 98685		11409 NW 14th Ave Vancouver, WA 98685		2015 NW 110th Street Vancouver, WA 98685	
Proximity to Subject		0.02 miles E		0.40 miles NE		0.04 miles SW	
Sale Price	$		$ 429,000		$ 360,000		$ 410,000
Sale Price/Gross Liv. Area	$ sq.ft.	$ 203.51 sq.ft.		$ 179.73 sq.ft.		$ 194.50 sq.ft.	
Data Source(s)		RMLS/Driveby;DOM 18		RMLS/Driveby;DOM 0		RMLS/Driveby;DOM 298	
Verification Source(s)		County Records				County Records	
VALUE ADJUSTMENTS	DESCRIPTION	DESCRIPTION	+(-) $ Adjustment	DESCRIPTION	+(-) $ Adjustment	DESCRIPTION	+(-) $ Adjustment
Sales or Financing Concessions		ArmLth Conv;0		ArmLth Conv;0		ArmLth Cash;0	
Date of Sale/Time		s09/11;c08/11	-6,425	s10/11;c08/11	+3,600	s12/11;c12/11	
Location	N;Res;Res	N;Res;Res		N;Res;Res		N;Res;Res	
Leasehold/Fee Simple	Fee Simple	Fee Simple		Fee Simple		Fee Simple	
Site	8077 sf	14,384 sf	-13,000	6534 sf	+3,000	7634 sf	0
View	N;Res;Res	N;Res;Res		N;Res;Res		N;Res;Res	
Design (Style)	Ranch	Ranch		Ranch		Ranch	
Quality of Construction	Q2	Q2		Q3	+20,000	Q2	
Actual Age	1	1		1		1	
Condition	C1	C1		C1		C1	
Above Grade	Total / Bdrms. / Baths	Total / Bdrms. / Baths	0	Total / Bdrms. / Baths		Total / Bdrms. / Baths	0
Room Count	6 / 2 / 2.0	7 / 3 / 2.0	0	6 / 3 / 2.0		7 / 3 / 2.0	0
Gross Living Area	1,994 sq.ft.	2,108 sq.ft.	-6,840	2,003 sq.ft.		2,108 sq.ft.	-6,840
Basement & Finished Rooms Below Grade	0sf	0sf		0sf		0sf	
Functional Utility	Average	Average		Average		Average	
Heating/Cooling	FWA Gas & AC	FWA Gas	+3,000	FWA Gas & AC		FWA Gas & AC	
Energy Efficient Items	Std Items	Std Items		Std Items		Std Items	
Garage/Carport	3 Att. Garage	3 Att. Garage		2 Att Garage	+10,000	3 Att. Garage	
Porch/Patio/Deck	Porch/Patio	Porch/Patio		Porch/Patio		Porch/Patio	
KITCHEN EQ.	Std Appl	Std Appl		Std Appl		Std Appl	
Fireplace	1 Fireplace	1 Fireplace		1 Fireplace		1 Fireplace	
Net Adjustment (Total)		☐ + ☒ -	$ -23,265	☒ + ☐ -	$ 36,600	☐ + ☒ -	$ -6,840
Adjusted Sale Price of Comparables		Net Adj. 5.4 % Gross Adj. 6.8 %	$ 405,735	Net Adj. 10.2 % Gross Adj. 10.2 %	$ 396,600	Net Adj. 1.7 % Gross Adj. 1.7 %	$ 403,160

the subject and "inferior" for one of the comparable sales. Since individual appraisers used different words and methods, a standardized system of codes (Exhibits 2.2 and 2.3) was introduced, as is seen in Exhibit 2.1. However, because these codes must be looked up to understand them, for the rest of this book the older system that used words rather than codes will be used to save the reader the trouble of looking up the codes.

Exhibit 2.2 shows the quality (Q) of construction ratings and definitions. Exhibit 2.3 shows the condition (C) ratings and definitions. Exhibit 2.4 shows the standardized abbreviations. These exhibits come from the Uniform Appraisal Data Specification, which is a product of the Federal Housing Finance Agency (FHFA) that regulates Fannie Mae and Freddie Mac. The full manual can be found on the Fannie Mae website: https://www.fanniemae.com/singlefamily/uniform-appraisal-dataset.

Exhibit 2.2

Quality of Construction Ratings and Definitions

Q1

Dwellings with this quality rating are usually unique structures that are individually designed by an architect for a specified user. Such residences typically are constructed from detailed architectural plans and specifications, and they feature and an exceptionally high level of workmanship and exceptionally high-grade materials throughout the interior and exterior of the structure. The design features exceptionally high-quality exterior refinements and ornamentation and exceptionally high-quality interior refinements. The workmanship, materials, and finishes throughout the dwelling are of exceptionally high quality.

Q2

Dwellings with this quality rating are often custom designed for construction on an individual property owner's site. However, dwellings in this quality grade are also found in high-quality tract developments featuring residences constructed from individual plans or from highly modified or upgraded plans. The design features detailed, high-quality exterior ornamentation and high-quality interior refinements and detail. The workmanship, materials, and finishes throughout the dwelling are generally of high or very high quality.

Q3

Dwellings with this quality rating are residences of higher quality built from individual or readily available designer plans in above-standard residential tract developments or on an individual property owner's site. The design includes significant exterior ornamentation and interiors that are well finished. The workmanship exceeds acceptable standards, and many materials and finishes throughout the dwelling have been upgraded from "stock" standards.

Q4

Dwellings with this quality rating meet or exceed the requirements of applicable building codes. Standard or modified standard building plans are utilized, and the design includes adequate fenestration and some exterior ornamentation and interior refinements. Materials, workmanship, finishes, and equipment are of stock or builder grade and may feature some upgrades.

Q5

Dwellings with this quality rating feature economy of construction and basic functionality as main considerations. Such dwellings feature a plain design using readily available or basic floor plans featuring minimal fenestration and basic finishes with minimal exterior ornamentation and limited interior detail. These dwellings meet minimum building codes and are constructed with inexpensive, stock materials with limited refinements and upgrades.

Q6

Dwellings with this quality rating are of basic quality and lower cost; some may not be suitable for year-round occupancy. Such dwellings are often built with simple plans or without plans, often utilizing the lowest-quality building materials. Such dwellings are often built or expanded by people who are professionally unskilled or possess only minimal construction skills. Electrical, plumbing, and other mechanical systems and equipment may be minimal or nonexistent. Older dwellings may feature one or more substandard or nonconforming additions to the original structure.

Source: Federal Housing Finance Agency (FHFA) Uniform Data Appraisal Specification.

Exhibit 2.3

Condition Ratings and Definitions

C1

The improvements have been recently constructed and have not been previously occupied. The entire structure and all components are new, and the dwelling features no physical depreciation.

Note: Newly constructed improvements that feature recycled or previously used materials and/or components can be considered a new dwelling provided that the dwelling is placed on a 100 percent new foundation and the recycled materials and the recycled components have been rehabilitated and/or remanufactured into like-new condition. Improvements that have not been previously occupied are not considered new if they have any significant physical depreciation (that is, newly constructed dwellings that have been vacant for an extended period of time without adequate maintenance or upkeep).

C2

The improvements feature no deferred maintenance, there is little or no physical depreciation, and they require no repairs. Virtually all building components are new or have been recently repaired, refinished, or rehabilitated. All outdated components and finishes have been updated and/or replaced with components that meet current standards. Dwellings in this category are either almost new or have been recently completely renovated and are similar in condition to new construction.

Note: The improvements represent a relatively new property that is well maintained with no deferred maintenance and little or no physical depreciation, or they may represent an older property that has been recently completely renovated.

C3

The improvements are well maintained and feature limited physical depreciation due to normal wear and tear. Some components, but not every major building component, may be updated or recently rehabilitated. The structure has been well maintained.

Note: The improvement is in its first cycle of replacing short-lived building components (appliances, floor coverings, HVAC, and so on) and is being well maintained. Its estimated effective age is less than its actual age. It also may reflect a property in which the majority of short-lived building components have been replaced but not to the level of a complete renovation.

C4

The improvements feature some minor deferred maintenance and physical deterioration due to normal wear and tear. The dwelling has been adequately maintained and requires only minimal repairs to building components and/or mechanical systems and cosmetic repairs. All major building components have been adequately maintained and are functionally adequate.

Note: The estimated effective age may be close to or equal to its actual age. It reflects a property in which some of the short-lived building components have been replaced, and some short-lived building components are at or near the end of their physical life expectancy; however, they still function adequately. Most minor repairs have been addressed on an ongoing basis resulting in an adequately maintained property.

C5
The improvements feature obvious deferred maintenance and are in need of some significant repairs. Some building components need repairs, rehabilitation, or updating. The functional utility and overall livability are somewhat diminished due to condition, but the dwelling remains usable and functional as a residence.

Note: Some significant repairs are needed to the improvements due to the lack of adequate maintenance. It reflects a property in which many of its short-lived building components are at the end of or have exceeded their physical life expectancy but remain functional.

C6
The improvements have substantial damage or deferred maintenance with deficiencies or defects that are severe enough to affect the safety, soundness, or structural integrity of the improvements. The improvements are in need of substantial repairs and rehabilitation, including many or most major components.

Note: Substantial repairs are needed to the improvements due to the lack of adequate maintenance or property damage. It reflects a property with conditions severe enough to affect the safety, soundness, or structural integrity of the improvements.

Source: Federal Housing Finance Agency (FHFA) Uniform Data Appraisal Specification.

The following are comments on each entry on the sales comparison approach portion of the form, in order of how they appear starting at the top of the page. Beside information for each category, red flags are noted where errors or inaccurate information might be an issue.

Location and Proximity

As is taught in real estate brokerage, the location is perhaps the most important characteristic for comparable properties. The sales should be in the same area as the subject property or at least in an area equal in quality to the subject. For most residential appraisals located in urban or suburban areas, lenders prefer to see sales that are within a mile of the subject property. With rural properties, which are often on large acreages, distances may be much greater. Moreover, rural properties tend to have more diverse characteristics, meaning that more adjustments are often necessary. In other words, some subdivisions have "cookie-cutter," or at least somewhat similar, houses, as compared to large-acreage properties that are rarely similar. Larger luxury homes also often require more adjustments.

Exhibit 2.4
Standardized Abbreviations

Abbreviation	Full Name	Appropriate Fields
ac	Acres	Area, Site
AdjPrk	Adjacent to Park	Location
AdjPwr	Adjacent to Power Lines	Location
A	Adverse	Location & View
ArmLth	Arm's Length Sale	Sale or Financing Concessions
ba	Bathroom(s)	Basement & Finished Rooms Below Grade
br	Bedroom	Basement & Finished Rooms Below Grade
B	Beneficial	Location & View
Cash	Cash	Sale or Financing Concessions
CtySky	City View Skyline View	View
CtyStr	City Street View	View
Comm	Commercial Influence	Location
c	Contracted Date	Date of Sale/Time
Conv	Conventional	Sale or Financing Concessions
CrtOrd	Court Ordered Sale	Sale or Financing Concessions
DOM	Days on Market	Data Sources
e	Expiration Date	Date of Sale/Time
Estate	Estate Sale	Sale or Financing Concessions
FHA	Federal Housing Administration	Sale or Financing Concessions
GlfCse	Golf Course	Location
Glfvw	Golf Course View	View
Ind	Industrial	Location & View
in	Interior Only Stairs	Basement & Finished Rooms Below Grade
Lndfl	Landfill	Location
LtdSght	Limited Sight	View
Listing	Listing	Sale or Financing Concessions
Mtn	Mountain View	View
N	Neutral	Location & View
NonArm	Non-Arm's Length Sale	Sale or Financing Concessions
BsyRd	Busy Road	Location
o	Other	Basement & Finished Rooms Below Grade
Prk	Park View	View
Pstrl	Pastoral View	View
PwrLn	Power Lines	View
PubTrn	Public Transportation	Location
rr	Recreational (Rec) Room	Basement & Finished Rooms Below Grade
Relo	Relocation Sale	Sale or Financing Concessions
REO	REO Sale	Sale or Financing Concessions
Res	Residential	Location & View
RH	USDA -Rural Housing	Sale or Financing Concessions
s	Settlement Date	Date of Sale/Time
Short	Short Sale	Sale or Financing Concessions
sf	Square Feet	Area, Site Basement
sqm	Square Meters	Area, Site
Unk	Unknown	Date of Sale/Time
VA	Department of Veterans Affairs	Sale or Financing Concessions
w	Withdrawn Date	Date of Sale/Time
wo	Walk Out Basement	Basement & Finished Rooms Below Grade
wu	Walk Up Basement	Basement & Finished Rooms Below Grade
WtrFr	Water Frontage	Location
Wtr	Water View	View
Woods	Woods View	View

Source: Federal Housing Finance Agency (FHFA) Uniform Data Appraisal Specification.

Red Flag

If the comparable properties are more than a mile away in an urban or suburban location, the appraiser may have ignored closer comparable sales because the appraiser was trying to reach a certain value. Or the appraiser may have had a legitimate reason. For instance, in a slow market, there may have been a need to go farther out from the subject property for sales because there were few sales to choose from.

Red Flag

Typically, a location map is included in a residential appraisal, and it shows where the subject and comparable sales are located. This map should be looked at because an appraiser may stay within the mile of the subject and still go into another neighborhood that is not comparable to the subject's neighborhood. This situation might be difficult to determine in a review, but phone calls to a real estate agent who knows the area might reveal if there is a problem.

When the location map shows that the comparable sales are on another side of a freeway, major artery, river, or similar boundaries, there might be a problem with the appraisal. For example, Exhibit 2.5 shows the location map for the Exhibit 2.1 appraisal. If the appraiser had chosen a sale on the west side of NW Lakeshore Avenue, which changes to NW 31st Avenue, the sale might be suspect because there is a lake just west of that which cannot be seen in this location map. Being closer to the lake would normally make that comparable sale property more valuable, and it might improperly increase the value of the subject property if no adjustments were made for it.

Exhibit 2.5
Location Map for Exhibit 2.1 Appraisal

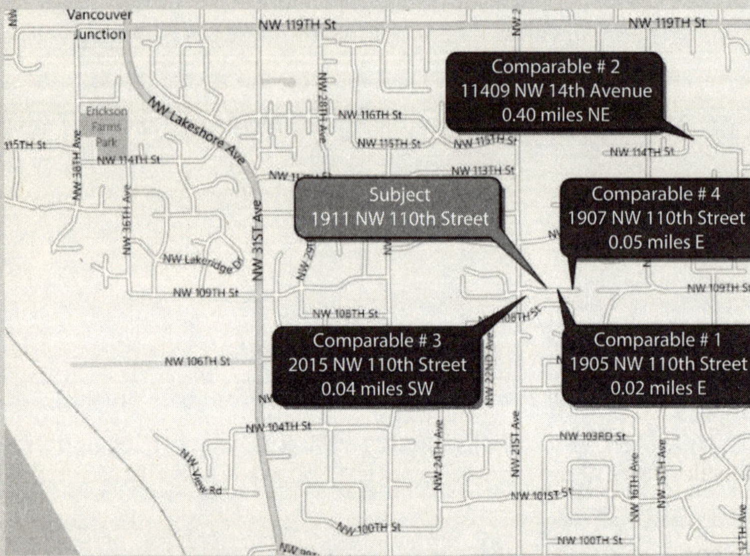

Sales and Financing Concessions

The type of financing may make some difference that requires an adjustment, but it will probably be minor. There should be no adjustments between Veterans Administration (VA), Federal Housing Administration (FHA), and U.S. Department of Agriculture (USDA) and conventional financing. However, there might be a warranted adjustment for owner financing depending on how different the terms were from these other financing instruments. If a sale was made for 2 percent interest amortized for 40 years and the typical financing was 6 percent interest with a 30-year amortization, then an adjustment would be needed. Essentially, the value of the under-market financing would need to be calculated to determine the savings compared to typical financing to deduce the amount of the adjustment.

More commonly, a sale will have a sales concession, which should be adjusted for in the sale price, because the effect of a concession is to reduce the sale price of the property. In other words, concessions make the sale price artificial compared to sales without concessions because the seller is giving up something of value to sell the property, even though the price may remain the same. Concessions are often made with the intention of getting more financing than would normally be allowed. For instance, if a lender were requiring a 10 percent down payment on a $200,000 house, the buyer would need to have $20,000 for the transaction. However, if the buyer and seller agreed to a sale price of $210,000 with the borrower getting a $10,000 sales concession in escrow, then the down payment would be $21,000, but the buyer would need only $11,000 for the down payment. In reality, it would be the lender who would carry more risk because instead of financing 90 percent of the value of the home, the lender would now be financing $189,000, or 94.5 percent of the actual home value.

Therefore, if the subject property has concessions or the comparable sales have them, the concessions should be subtracted from the sale price to get the actual sale price. Some appraisers may state that the concessions are customary for the area, but that is irrelevant. An adjustment should be made for any concessions because they effectively reduce the sale price.

Date of Sale

The date of the sale becomes exceedingly important in a fluctuating economy where property values are changing. With residential real estate the typical requirement and/or preference is that the sales have sold within six months. However, when the market is changing quickly, a six-month-old sale may be obsolete and unrepresentative of the current value of the subject property, and sales less than three months old may be more appropriate. In any event, the comparable sales used in appraisals need to be considered in light of the current economic situation, particularly when recent changes have occurred in the economy.

It is also important in a fluctuating market for the appraiser to examine listings and include them as well as comparable sales because they will give an understanding of the current market asking prices for similar properties. Listings are only valuable in showing the high end of the market, and sometimes there are no reasonably priced listings that exist. If the appraiser does not show listings, then the reviewer, in analyzing the appraisal, might look at properties for sale on websites such as www.realtor.com to see listings that might help in the analysis of the appraisal.

Site

Adjustments are normally made for sites that differ from the subject property by over 1,000 square feet, although that is not the case for some locations. If the subject has a particularly small lot for the region it is in, such as 2,500 square feet where most homes have a minimum of 5,000 square feet, a more sizable adjustment is normally required than if the subject had 5,000 square feet and the comparable sale had 7,500 square feet. The differential of 2,500 feet is not as significant for the larger parcels because for the area they are still within the norm, whereas an unusually small lot may have a major effect on the market value.

Consequently, in valuing the home with a 2,500-square-foot lot, it would be important for the appraisal to have at least one and preferably two comparable sales with the same size lot to alleviate any concern that there is a detrimental effect due to the size differential.

Red Flag

An extremely small site size, such as 2,000 or 2,500 square feet, might diminish the value of a home significantly, and the appraisal should have comparable sales with similar sizes. If all the sites are larger than the subject, the final value may be inaccurate.

View

The view is often not a major adjustment, if it is a matter of a certain type of street view compared to another. However, an ocean view, in some areas, and a city light view for a high-rise condominium are exceptions, and they can make a huge difference in the price of a property.

Red Flag

If the appraiser uses a comparable property with a view and the subject does not have a view, this might be a ploy to inflate the value of the subject property.

Design (Style)

There may be an adjustment in this category if it is warranted, but often there is no measurable difference in design styles. However, a basic example might be that an adjustment might be required between a ranch style and a two-story home, if the market data shows that there is a continuous pattern of buyers paying more for ranch-style homes. This decision can be very subjective, so the reviewer might want to examine it carefully if the appraiser has made a substantial adjustment, particularly if there are no comments explaining why the adjustment was made in the summary of sales comparison approach below the adjustment grid.

Quality of Construction

The differences in the quality of the construction should be explained if they are not obvious. Photographs of the subject home and the comparable sales might be important to look at in determining if the appraisal is accurate. Adjustments here might be for something as small as the difference between metal windows and updated vinyl windows, or they may be as significant as the difference between a luxury custom home and a tract home with basic construction and amenities.

Red Flag

If a custom-built home is used as a comparable sale for the valuation of a tract home, the adjustment might be difficult to determine. Appraisers rarely go inside a comparable sale, and using the sale price of a custom-built home may inflate the value of a tract home. To be accurate, the appraisal should include at least two comparable sales that are also tract homes.

Actual Age

Since the form asks for the actual age, that should be entered here. However, often appraisers will also enter what is called the *economic age*. By entering a number for the economic age, the appraiser is denoting that, for instance, a home that was built 60 years ago is only 30 years old economically. The typical reason would be that it has been updated and maintained to approximate a younger age than the original construction date. If this information is entered, it should have the original age (O) and then the economic age (E), which might be entered as O – 60, E – 30 or in some similar format.

Condition

One of the largest areas of inaccuracy is in comparing the condition of the comparable sales to the subject. Looking at photographs in the appraisal can help, but the appraiser should also comment on the differences if there is an adjustment. The appraiser often depends on the listing information from the sale of a comparable property, and that information may not be accurate.

Red Flag

If the condition of all the comparable properties is vastly superior or inferior to the subject property, then the reviewer should look for a comment by the appraiser as to why there were no comparable sales at the other end of the spectrum. Appraisals can be inflated by using all comparable sales that are superior to the subject property. However, it may be that the subject is a "fixer" and is in need of repair in a neighborhood where properties are typically well kept, and this might be an adequate explanation.

Above-Grade Room Count

Normally bedroom differences do not require an adjustment, but the exception might be if a home had only one bedroom and it was compared to homes with more than one bedroom. The reason is that a one-bedroom home is unique, and it is often considered deficient, and therefore worth significantly less since most home buyers want at least two bedrooms. There should always be adjustments for the number of bathrooms if the comparables differ from the subject property. However, the adjustment between a one-bathroom home and a two-bathroom home might be larger than an adjustment between a home with two bathrooms and one with three because a home with only one bathroom might be a lot less marketable than a home with two.

With larger homes with many bathrooms, the law of diminishing returns is applicable. Adjustments for bathrooms may decrease with large homes that have more than three bathrooms. For instance, the difference between a home with two bathrooms and three bathrooms might require a larger adjustment than the difference between a five-bathroom home and six-bathroom home.

Gross Living Area

Often the location and size of a home are the most important characteristics affecting the price. Appraisers measure homes from the outside of the home with the exception of attached properties such as condominiums, which are measured based on the inside dimensions. The appraiser generally uses the square footage for the comparable sales that is reported in the multiple listing service or other data service and does not personally measure them.

The appraiser is supposed to adjust for square footage differences based on market evidence. This means that the appraiser should look at the sales of homes that are similar to the subject but vary in size to determine the square foot value differential. The price per square foot that is computed is noted at the top of the form and labeled "Sale Price/Gross Liv. Area" will normally not be the same number as the adjustment for the price per square foot. The "Sale Price/Gross Liv. Area" is the price of the home divided by the size, which includes the land, but the adjustment for size is based on what the appraiser thinks the market recognizes for the differential, and it does not have a linear relationship with the sale price divided by the gross living area. They are two different numbers and should not be confused.

Red Flag

If all of the comparable properties or most of them are significantly larger than the subject property, the appraiser may be attempting to inflate the value. Normally the sizes of the comparable sales may vary by a few hundred square feet, but if they vary by 400 or 500, there may be an accuracy problem. There is also often a nonlinear increase in value with homes that are much larger. For instance, homes that are in the range of 2,700 to 2,800 square feet may not be equivalent to sales in the range of 3,400 to 3,500 square feet because between these sizes, prices often take a jump in the price per square foot.

Exhibit 2.6 is an example of an appraisal that has been inflated by using sales that are larger than the subject property. In this example, the subject property is 2,809 square feet, and the comparable sales are 3,622, 3,822, and 3,450. The adjustment for the square footage is $40 per square foot for the size, which is questionable for homes of this size because they are generally more expensive and luxurious than homes the size of the subject, making them more expensive to construct. Since there are no smaller properties, there is no way to know the value of the subject from these comparable sales.

The adjustment for the bathrooms may also be low since larger homes often have luxury bathrooms that can be quite expensive. The example here is a very obvious one. However, an appraiser might have also searched for a very high sale that was close to the size of the subject and then used it as well as two of the larger sales, which would make the appraisal more acceptable but might still inflate it if the appraiser

Exhibit 2.6

Residential Appraisal Inflated by Using Sales That Are Larger Than the Subject Property

FEATURE	SUBJECT	COMPARABLE SALE # 1		COMPARABLE SALE # 2		COMPARABLE SALE # 3	
Address	20421 SE Deerfern Loop Camas, WA 98607-9470	510 NW View Ridge Street Camas, WA		2425 NW Iris Court Camas, WA		1450 NW Ilwaco Court Camas, WA	
Proximity to Subject		0.94 miles E		0.90 miles NE		0.86 miles E	
Sale Price	$ Refinance		$ 501,000		$ 530,000		$ 490,000
Sale Price/Gross Liv. Area	$ sq.ft.	$ 138.32 sq.ft.		$ 138.67 sq.ft.		$ 142.03 sq.ft.	
Data Source(s)		RMLS/Drive-By		RMLS/Drive-By		RMLS/Drive-By	
Verification Source(s)		County Records		County Records		County Records	
VALUE ADJUSTMENTS	DESCRIPTION	DESCRIPTION	+(-) $ Adjustment	DESCRIPTION	+(-) $ Adjustment	DESCRIPTION	+(-) $ Adjustment
Sales or Financing Concessions		Conventional Not Reported		Conventional Not Reported		Conventional Not Reported	
Date of Sale/Time							
Location	Average	Average		Average		Average	
Leasehold/Fee Simple	Fee Simple	Fee Simple		Fee Simple		Fee Simple	
Site	9200	9,583		9500		9430	
View	River/Territorial	River/Territorial		River/Territorial		River/Territorial	
Design (Style)	2 Story	Tri Level		2 Story		2 Story	
Quality of Construction	Average	Average		Average		Average	
Actual Age	10	9		13		12	
Condition	Average	Average		Average		Average	
Above Grade	Total Bdrms. Baths	Total Bdrms. Baths		Total Bdrms. Baths		Total Bdrms. Baths	
Room Count	8 4 2.5	8 5 4	-6,500	8 4 4	-6,500	9 4 3	-3,000
Gross Living Area	2,809 sq.ft.	3,622 sq.ft.	-32,520	3,822 sq.ft.	-40,520	3,450 sq.ft.	-25,640
Basement & Finished Rooms Below Grade		None None		None None		None None	
Functional Utility	Average	Average		Average		Average	
Heating/Cooling	FWA Gas & AC	FWA Gas & AC		FWA Gas & AC		FWA Gas & AC	
Energy Efficient Items	Std Items	Std Items		Std Items		Std Items	
Garage/Carport	3	3 Att. Garage		3 Att. Garage		2 Att Garage	+10,000
Porch/Patio/Deck	Porch/Pat/Deck	Porch/Deck		Porch/Deck		Porch/Deck	
KITCHEN EQ.	Std Appl	Std Appl.		Std Appl.		Std Appl.	
Fireplace	2 Sided Fpl	3 Fireplaces	-3,000	2 Fireplaces		1 Fireplace	+1,500
Net Adjustment (Total)		☐ + ☒ -	$ -42,020	☐ + ☒ -	$ -47,020	☐ + ☒ -	$ -17,140
Adjusted Sale Price of Comparables		Net Adj. 8.4 % Gross Adj. 8.4 %	$ 458,980	Net Adj. 8.9 % Gross Adj. 8.9 %	$ 482,980	Net Adj. 3.5 % Gross Adj. 8.2 %	$ 472,860

was trying to reach a certain value. In such a situation a reviewer might ask the appraiser why only larger homes were used and what evidence the appraiser used to determine the $40 per square foot adjustment amount.

Nevertheless, the appraiser does not make the comparable sales, and there are instances where finding more comparable sales is not possible because they don't exist. The appraiser may have had no motive in using larger properties, but the result is the same—the value has not been adequately proven. In such a case, the appraiser may be asked to expand the search for sales to include similar neighborhoods that are farther away, use sales that are older and adjust them for age, or use sales that are smaller to counter the larger sales.

Basement and Finished Rooms Below Grade

This category is for basements, and the amount of adjustment can vary greatly due to the finish of the basement (finished, unfinished, partially finished) and the type of basement. Types range from *daylight basements* that are finished as well as the rest of the house is finished to basements that have no windows and are completely unfinished. Adjustments should be made accordingly. Values might be inflated if too much credit is given for a basement that has little value due to its level of finish.

Functional Utility

This category rarely has adjustments because most homes do not have significant functional problems. A simple example of a home that might need an adjustment would be one in which a bedroom could be accessed only by walking through another bedroom.

Heating and Cooling

Adjustments in this category vary with the type of heating and cooling systems a home has, and the adjustments will be greater in certain parts of the country depending on the variance of the weather. For instance, in a very warm climate in the South, the adjustment for the lack of air-conditioning might be substantial, but for a property in the Northwest, it might be much less.

Energy-Efficient Items

This could include solar panels and other efficiency amenities.

Garage or Carport

Adjustments for this category vary. In some larger houses, less than a three-car garage can be a deficiency that reduces the salability of the home if the smaller garage is not typical. After three or four garages, the adjustment will diminish per additional garage space.

Porch, Patio, and/or Deck

Often the adjustment for these items is small, and it varies according to size and quality.

Kitchen Equipment

Adjustments for kitchen equipment would be for only built-in appliances. Appliances that can be moved are considered personal property, and they are normally not part of the house appraisal. The value of such equipment depreciates very quickly, and if an adjustment were warranted, it would likely be very small.

Fireplace and/or Woodstove

Generally adjustments for these features are relatively small.

Outbuildings

Small sheds are often movable and require no adjustment. Larger outbuildings are typically on properties that are on acreage, but they rarely add the value of what they cost to construct, so the adjustment for these might appear small.

Adjusted Sale Price of Comparable Properties

These boxes show the percentages of the net and gross adjustments. The *net adjustment* refers to the final total amount of the adjustments, which is the addition of all the adjustments negative and positive. For instance, if an adjustment for inferior condition was made for +$10,000 and an adjustment was made for the same property for superior location for −$12,000, the net adjustment would be the difference, or $2,000.

The *gross adjustment* is the total of all the adjustments without consideration of whether they are positive or negative amounts. Therefore the gross adjustment for this example would be $22,000. Most lender guidelines want the gross adjustment to be no more than 25 percent, and the net adjustment to be no more than 15 percent of the sale price. Additionally, some want no adjustment to a single item to be more than 10 percent of the sale price.

These requirements are generally realistic for tract homes, but for homes with acreage and high-end homes, they often cannot be met. The reason is that as homes become more expensive, they become more dissimilar and require more adjustments. Acreage properties also often have various characteristics, such as different sizes of acreage, barns, shops, and other amenities for which it is difficult to find similar comparable sales.

Another situation that tends to skew the percentage of adjustment is when the subject or some of the comparable sales have basements and others do not. Since the basement adjustment is considered separate from the main square footage, a large adjustment must be made, which increases the net and gross adjustment totals. For instance, if the subject has 1,000 square feet at street level and 1,000 square feet of daylight basement, and a comparable sale has 2,000 square feet all at street level, a large adjustment must be made to the comparable sale since street-level and basement square footage must be entered separately. The adjustments will total a high percentage, but in reality the homes are the same size, except that they are configured differently and the daylight basement footage will probably be worth less than the street-level footage.

There are different levels of appraiser licenses, and not all residential appraisers can value high-end properties over a certain amount of value. Multi-million-dollar homes often become complex appraisals because of the dearth of similar comparable sales and the difficulty in making accurate adjustments for the variance of amenities between the subject and the comparable sales. For this reason, lenders often want more than one appraisal for high-value homes. Many appraisers can value typical low-end tract homes, but it requires an experienced, advanced appraiser to value high-value homes.

Sales Comparison Approach Tips

The following are some guidelines to keep in mind in analyzing the comparable sales comparison approach.

Adjustments

In the sales comparison approach, adjustments are always made to the comparable sales and never to the subject. If the comparable sale is inferior to the subject, it requires an upward adjustment or a plus to the starting point, which is the sale price. If the sale is superior, the adjustment is downward and is subtracted from the sale price. Even experienced appraisers sometimes make mistakes and add instead of subtracting an adjustment or vice versa.

In some locations, some amenities do not require the same amount of adjustments as others—the adjustments are market driven, and the market is local. For instance, in the Northwest, a large, $60,000 exterior in-ground swimming pool may get only a $10,000 adjustment because the weather does not permit much usage, and there is little demand for pools. Conversely, in a warm state like Florida, the lack of a swimming pool in an upper-end neighborhood where most houses have them may require a large adjustment because the marketability of the house may be severely affected.

Some amenities may be considered a superadequacy, which will be discussed in more detail in the industrial section of this book. A *superadequacy* may be defined as an excessive amenity that is not typically found in properties similar to the subject and for which there is normally no need. An example of a superadequacy would be the foundation of a house that is built with twice the support that is actually necessary. Buyers would typically not pay more for that construction, so an adjustment would not be warranted since the market does not recognize this as a value-adding asset.

Explanation of Adjustments

Some adjustments are self-explanatory. For instance, when lot sizes vary, the adjustments for size are obvious. However, any adjustments that are not obvious should be explained, especially if they are large adjustments that have a significant effect on the value of the subject property. For instance, a large adjustment for functional utility or location should be explained in the comments section or somewhere in the appraisal. If the location of one of the comparable sales is next to a noisy freeway, the appraiser should state that this was the reason for the adjustment.

Red Flag

If the reason for a significant adjustment is not clear, the reviewer should ask for the justification for it. Without it, the accuracy of the appraisal is questionable.

Dissimilar Comparable Sales and Complex Single-Family Residential Appraisals

Although it might seem oversimplistic, it is important to remember that the appraiser does not make the comparable sales. The appraiser finds only what exists. Nevertheless, reviewers sometimes want to see better comparable sales. That may not be possible, however, if the appraiser has performed accurate market research and he or she has already utilized the most similar sales. When the market is slow, or when the property has special features or is nontypical in some way, comparable sales may be difficult to find, and the ones that are found may require large adjustments. In such cases, there are good reasons for large adjustments, and they do not necessarily mean that the appraisal has not been performed properly.

Assessment Information

Assessment information typically includes the square footage of the home and land in the assessment records. As previously mentioned, the size of a home is one of the major characteristics that affect the value, which means the accuracy of the measurement is of paramount importance. The appraiser does not measure the comparable properties, but the appraiser should measure the subject property. If the size of the house in the appraisal varies a great deal from the size shown in the assessment records, this can mean one of several things.

It could mean that the appraiser made a mistake measuring the home, or it could mean that the appraiser from the assessor's office made a mistake measuring the house. Rarely do two people get the exact same size when measuring a home, especially if it is a home with a lot of angles. A difference of 100 square feet or less would not be considered substantial, and it should not cause concern for the reviewer. In fact, because of variances due to human errors, many appraisers do not adjust for square footage differences of less than 100 square feet. But if the difference is larger than 100 square feet, the appraiser should have determined where the problem lies and made a note in the appraisal explaining it.

Another reason for the difference in size might be that the house was added on to, and the assessor's records are not up to date. Normally when a building permit is granted, the assessor is notified and the record is changed to show the change in square footage, which also generally increases the property taxes. The assessor could have overlooked the permit, or the addition might be too new for the record to have been changed. Note that even if there has been a lag in reporting the addition, there should still be a record at the home showing that the building inspector approved the addition.

Red Flag

If the size of the home is larger in the appraisal than in the assessor's records, it is possible that the owner of the property built an addition without getting a building permit. Nonpermitted space diminishes the value of the addition, and it should not be given the same value as permitted space. In some cases, it might even require dismantling the addition if the construction is substandard and does not meet building codes.

Whatever the reason may be, the appraiser should explain why there is a difference in a clear and concise way. Furthermore, the appraisal should be considered inaccurate until the explanation is given.

Nonconforming Property

Sometimes a property does not conform to current zoning, and it cannot be rebuilt if it is destroyed by a fire or some other calamity. Since this can adversely affect the value, the appraiser, if aware of this, should explain the situation. Sometimes a letter stating that the property can be rebuilt may be required by a lender to finance a property with this issue. However, it is not the appraiser's responsibility to produce such a letter, and there may be an expense in procuring one from the building department. The reviewer will want to do more research if this is an issue in an appraisal.

Examples of Complex Single-Family Residential Appraisals

The following are examples of appraisals that are complex due to the difficulty of finding comparable sales that were similar to the subject. When comparable sales vary significantly from the subject property, adjustments are always a high percentage of the original sale price and are difficult to estimate. Not all complex appraisals are of high-value properties. The appraisal in Exhibits 2.7 and 2.8 was difficult because of the large amount of land the subject has.

Exhibit 2.7

Residential Appraisal That Is Complex Due to Land Size

FEATURE	SUBJECT	COMPARABLE SALE # 1		COMPARABLE SALE # 2		COMPARABLE SALE # 3	
Address	9900 NE 174th Street Battle Ground, WA 98604	22806 NE 67th Avenue Battle Ground, WA 98604		18606 NE 182nd Avenue Brush Prairie, WA 98606		9701 NE 425th Street Woodland, WA 98674	
Proximity to Subject		3.3 miles		7.6 miles		19.3 miles	
Sale Price	$ N/A		$ 187,100		$ 280,000		$ 285,000
Sale Price/Gross Liv. Area	$ sq.ft.	$ 104.41 sq.ft.		$ 253.62 sq.ft.		$ 101.32 sq.ft.	
Data Source(s)		Realtor/Drive-By		RMLS/Drive by		Realtor/Drive-By	
Verification Source(s)		County Records		County Records		County Records	
VALUE ADJUSTMENTS	DESCRIPTION	DESCRIPTION	+(-) $ Adjustment	DESCRIPTION	+(-) $ Adjustment	DESCRIPTION	+(-) $ Adjustment
Sales or Financing Concessions		Cash Not Reported		Cash Not Reported		Conventional Not Reported	
Date of Sale/Time		5/29/2012		4/17/2012		11/15/2011	
Location	Average	Similar		Superior	-30,000	Inferior	+10,000
Leasehold/Fee Simple	Fee Simple	Fee Simple		Fee Simple		Fee Simple	
Site	34.01 acres	20.01 acres	+98,000	20.34 acres	+98,000	22.7	+84,000
View	Average	Similar		Similar		Similar	
Design (Style)	Ranch	Ranch		2 Story		2 Story	
Quality of Construction	Average	Average		Average		Average	
Actual Age	37	61		74		10	
Condition	Fixer	Fixer		Fixer		Very superior	-40,000
Above Grade Room Count	Total 3, Bdrms. 2, Baths 1	Total 4, Bdrms. 3, Baths 1.1	-1,000	Total 6, Bdrms. 4, Baths 2	-3,000	Total 6, Bdrms. 3, Baths 2.1	-4,000
Gross Living Area	924 sq.ft.	1,792 sq.ft.	-30,380	1,104 sq.ft.	-6,300	2,813 sq.ft.	-66,115
Basement & Finished Rooms Below Grade	0 0	0 0		695/Unfinished 0	-14,000	0 0	
Functional Utility	Average	Average		Average		Average	
Heating/Cooling	FA / None	FA/None		FA/None		FA/None	
Energy Efficient Items	Std Items	Std Items		Std Items		Std Items	
Garage/Carport	1 Carport	2 Detached	-8,000	None	+2,000	2 Attached	-8,000
Porch/Patio/Deck	None	Por/CV Patio		Porch		Porch/Deck	
KITCHEN EQ.	Std Appl	Std Appl		Std Appl		Std Appl	
Fireplace/Woodstove	1 Fireplace	1 Wood		None		2 Fireplaces	-2,500
Outbuildings	1600 SF Poor	None	+4,000	Outbldg/shop	-7,000	Shop, barn	-10,000
Net Adjustment (Total)		☒ + ☐ -	$ 62,620	☒ + ☐ -	$ 39,700	☐ + ☒ -	$ -36,615
Adjusted Sale Price of Comparables		Net Adj. 33.5 % Gross Adj. 75.6 %	$ 249,720	Net Adj. 14.2 % Gross Adj. 57.3 %	$ 319,700	Net Adj. 12.8 % Gross Adj. 78.8 %	$ 248,385

Exhibit 2.8

Partial Notes for Comparable Sales for Appraisal in Exhibit 2.7

Summary of Sales Comparison Approach Adjustments are made to reflect the effect or contribution to resale market value of each amenity or difference.
No square footage adjustments under 100 SF. Gross living area adjustment was $35. No time adjustments were made as market has not changed
significantly in sale time period. Adjustments are large for this appraisal but that could not be helped - no sales closer in land size and / or
improvement size could be found. Subject land is larger than all comparable sales and was adjusted at $7,000 per acre, based on the differential
in prices of parcel in this size range. Consideration for VOR easement (radio ground station for aircraft) was given (1000 Ft radius unbuildable
while easement is valid). Subject land may have wetlands, but there is no delineation to prove it, nor does the county show wetlands on its
environmental map. Land is very flat without trees which limits its value. Home is in fair to poor condition as is the storage building
next to it.
Indicated Value by Sales Comparison Approach $ 250,000

Properties on acreage are often difficult to appraise because the appraiser has to find sales that are similar in acreage size, as well as similar in building characteristics. In this case, the subject had 34.01 acres, but there were no other sales that could be found that were that large. Consequently, the appraiser found the largest parcels he could, and he adjusted them upward to make up for the size. Further complicating this valuation is the fact that the subject house is small—and is in fact half the size of sale 1 and one-third the size of sale 3. The adjustments are huge in this example, with gross adjustments over 75 percent for sales 1 and 3. Sale 3 is also 19.3 miles away, but according to the appraiser's notes, there were no closer sales. There is also an easement for a very high frequency omnidirectional range (VOR) facility, which is a short-range radio navigation system for aircraft. The VOR easement affected the subject's land value since nothing could be constructed within 1,000 feet of it.

Exhibit 2.9 is an example of an appraisal for a high-value home. In this example, note that all the sales had to be large, oceanfront properties, which limited the choice of sales. One of the sales is over 60 miles away, but it is located in an area the appraiser deemed similar to the subject's location. The percentage of adjustments is high, but this is to be expected with a property of this type. The appraiser's notes shown in Exhibit 2.10 state that the comparable properties are newer and that the condition adjustment and the age adjustment have been combined. The subject property is an older home, but it has been remodeled and it is in good condition, although not comparable to the newer homes. To bolster the appraisal, the appraiser has included listings. In Exhibit 2.11, the appraiser explains some of the specifics about the subject home that affect its value in comparison to the comparable sales.

Exhibit 2.9

Residential Appraisal That Is Complex Because the Subject Is an Oceanfront Property

FEATURE	SUBJECT	COMPARABLE SALE # 1		COMPARABLE SALE # 2		COMPARABLE SALE # 3	
Address	12345 S. Ocean Avenue Gearhart, OR 97138	2030 N. Ocean Avenue Gearhart, OR 97138		89211 Pinehurst Road Gearhart, OR 97138		44480 Sahhali Drive Neskowin, OR 97149	
Proximity to Subject		1.10 miles NW		2.33 miles N		61.42 miles S	
Sale Price	$		$ 1,750,000		$ 1,350,000		$ 1,135,000
Sale Price/Gross Liv. Area	$ sq.ft.	$ 421.59 sq.ft.		$ 335.40 sq.ft.		$ 348.37 sq.ft.	
Data Source(s)		Realtor/Drive-By		Realtor/Drive-By		Realtor/Drive-By	
Verification Source(s)		County Records		County Records		County Records	
VALUE ADJUSTMENTS	DESCRIPTION	DESCRIPTION	+(-) $ Adjustment	DESCRIPTION	+(-) $ Adjustment	DESCRIPTION	+(-) $ Adjustment
Sales or Financing Concessions		Cash Not Reported		Conventional Not Reported		Cash Not Reported	
Date of Sale/Time		01/16/2011	-145,833	12/16/2011	-123,750	07/08/2012	-56,749
Location	Ocean Front	Similar		Similar/ Gated	-10,000	Similar	
Leasehold/Fee Simple	Fee Simple	Fee Simple		Fee Simple		Fee Simple	
Site	14,375 sq. ft.	55,321 sq. ft.	-200,000	43,646 sq. ft.	-150,000	19,134 sq. ft.	-10,000
View	Ocean	Similar		Similar		Similar	
Design (Style)	2 Story	2 Story		2 Story		2 Story	
Quality of Construction	Good	Similar		Similar		Similar	
Actual Age	104	2	-200,000	7	-180,000	10	-160,000
Condition	Average	Superior/inc age		Superior/inc age		Superior/inc age	
Above Grade	Total / Bdrms. / Baths	Total / Bdrms. / Baths		Total / Bdrms. / Baths		Total / Bdrms. / Baths	
Room Count	14 / 10 / 10	10 / 4 / 3.5	+30,000	10 / 3 / 4.5	+25,000	10 / 5 / 6.5	+15,000
Gross Living Area	5,911 sq.ft.	4,151 sq.ft.	+176,000	4,025 sq.ft.	+188,600	3,258 sq.ft.	+265,300
Basement & Finished Rooms Below Grade	1,140 sf. 1-rec/1-bd/2-ba	1,796 sf. 2-bd/util/1-ba	-45,920 +5,000	119 sf. 1-wine cellar	+71,470 +10,000	1,956 sf. 1-fr/3-ba/3-ba	-57,120 -5,000
Functional Utility	Average	Average		Average		Average	
Heating/Cooling	FA / None	FA/None		FA/None		Rad/None	
Energy Efficient Items	Std Items	Std Items		Std Items		Std Items	
Garage/Carport	None	3	-50,000	3	-50,000	3	-50,000
Porch/Patio/Deck	Porch/Patio	Porch/Patio		Porch/Patio		Porch/Patio	
KITCHEN EQ.	Std Appl	Std Appl		Std Appl		Std Appl	
Fireplace/Woodstove	1	2	-8,000	4	-20,000	3	-12,000
Other							
Net Adjustment (Total)		☐ + ☒ -	$ -438,753	☐ + ☒ -	$ -238,680	☐ + ☒ -	$ -70,569
Adjusted Sale Price of Comparables		Net Adj. 25.1 % Gross Adj. 49.2 %	$ 1,311,247	Net Adj. 17.7 % Gross Adj. 61.4 %	$ 1,111,320	Net Adj. 6.2 % Gross Adj. 55.6 %	$ 1,064,431

Exhibit 2.10

Partial Notes for Comparable Sales for Appraisal in Exhibit 2.9

Summary of Sales Comparison Approach The adjusted values present a range of value supported with market data from within the subject's market
area. Adjustments are made to reflect the effect or contribution to resale market value of each amenity or difference. No square footage
adjustments under 100 SF. Gross living area adjustment was $100 for above ground, $70 for basement. Adjustments for time due to declining
market are figured at 10% from 30 days before COE. Older sales had to be used due to lack of ocean front sales, which are rare. Adjustments are
also based on specific area research. A search had to made along the coast line because the subject property is located on the ocean and there
are few sales similarly located. The listings are also ocean front with the exception of listing 1, which has private beach access and an ocean view,
but is not ocean front. Subject's condition is good for its age, but is inferior to newer homes. That condition adjustment is included in the age
adjustment. As bathrooms increase, the value of each diminishes as they become a superadequacy, as do fireplaces - thus nonlinear adj.
Indicated Value by Sales Comparison Approach $ 1,200,000

In Exhibit 2.12, the listings, as opposed to sales in Exhibit 2.9, show the top of the market. In other words, there is no way to know what they will sell for, but they do establish the highest price they may sell for, although not the lowest. From this information the appraiser can get an idea of what the upper end of the market is, and in a market that is changing quickly, the listing information is particularly important. For instance, if the market is declining and the sales are six months old or older, in that six-month time period, prices may have dropped by 5 or 10 percent.

Exhibit 2.11

Partial Notes Relating to the Subject Property in the Appraisal in Exhibit 2.9

The average marketing time varies a great deal depending on how properties are priced. If they are priced well, they may sell in 180 days, if not it could take years, particularly for high value properties such as the subject.
The subject has the following drawbacks which greatly affect it marketability and therefore reduce its value:
1. Although located on the ocean, the lot is narrow and the neighbors are very close to each side.
2. There are gated communities with high value homes nearby, which are generally preferred by buyers seeking properties in this price range.
3. The house is 104 years old, which is a detriment when compared to the newer homes.
4. This house is very large, but because it is older, it was built with small bedrooms and it also lacks a larger master bathroom. These items make it functionally obsolete for today's market.
5. For many, this sprawling home might be a "white elephant" because to heat and maintain it the costs are high.
6. The subject has no garage, which is extremely unusual for a home of this size and caliber. Moreover, there appears to be no place to build one, which is a major deteriment to value.
These things were taken into consideration in this appraisal. In today's market, many properties are selling for much less than their list price, and adjustments were made for the listings that are also included. Because the property is located on the ocean, a search for sales had to be made along the coastline.

Exhibit 2.12

Residential Appraisal for High-Value Beach Property Listings Comparable to the Subject Property in Exhibit 2.9

FEATURE	SUBJECT	LISTING # 1		LISTING # 2		LISTING # 3	
Address	12345 S. Ocean Avenue Gearhart, OR 97138	48 NW Lincoln Shore Star R Lincoln City, OR 97367		33112 Malarkey Lane Warrenton, OR 97146		89500 Ocean Drive Warrenton, OR 97146	
Proximity to Subject		74.88 miles S		4.56 miles N		3.53 miles N	
List Price	$		$ 799,000		$ 1,595,000		$ 1,350,000
List Price/Gross Liv. Area	$ sq.ft.	$ 154.49 sq.ft.		$ 330.50 sq.ft.		$ 423.99 sq.ft.	
Last Price Revision Date		11/18/2011		09/03/2011		09/28/2011	
Data Source(s)		Realtor/Drive-By		Realtor/Drive-By		Realtor/Drive-By	
Verification Source(s)		County Records		County Records		County Records	
VALUE ADJUSTMENTS	DESCRIPTION	DESCRIPTION	+(-) $ Adjust.	DESCRIPTION	+(-) $ Adjust.	DESCRIPTION	+(-) $ Adjust.
Sales or Financing Concessions		N/A		N/A		N/A	
Days on Market		313		90		485	
Location	Ocean Front	Not ocean front	+350,000	Similar		Similar	
Leasehold/Fee Simple	Fee Simple	Fee Simple		Fee Simple		Fee Simple	
Site	14,375 sq. ft.	19,166	-10,000	54,450	-200,000	149,846/50K usabl	-250,000
View	Ocean	Similar		Similar		Similar	
Design (Style)	2 Story	2 Story		2 Story		2 Story	
Quality of Construction	Good	Similar		Superior/Stucco	-30,000	Similar	
Actual Age	104	6	-200,000	27	-150,000	2	-200,000
Condition	Average	Similar		Similar		Similar	
Above Grade	Total / Bdrms. / Baths	Total / Bdrms. / Baths		Total / Bdrms. / Baths		Total / Bdrms. / Baths	
Room Count	14 / 10 / 10	9 / 3 / 5.5	+20,000	8 / 3 / 8	+10,000	8 / 3 / 3.5	+30,000
Gross Living Area	5,911 sq.ft.	5,172 sq.ft.	+73,900	4,826 sq.ft.	+108,500	3,184 sq.ft.	+272,700
Basement & Finished	1,140 sf./Finished	2,576 sf./Unfinish	+3,000	1,272 sf./Finished	-9,240	1,152 sf./Finished	
Rooms Below Grade	1-rec/1-bd/2-ba	None	+10,000	3-ba	-5,000	1-bd/1-ba/1-utility	+5,000
Functional Utility	Average	Similar		Similar		Similar	
Heating/Cooling	FA / None	FA / None		FA / None		FA / None	
Energy Efficient Items	Std Items	Similar		Similar		Similar	
Garage/Carport	None	2	-33,000	3	-50,000	2	-33,000
Porch/Patio/Deck	Porch/Patio	Similar		Similar		Similar	
Listing to sale adjustment		Listing to Sale Adj.	-50,000	Listing to Sale Adj.	-150,000	Listing to Sale Adj.	-150,000
Net Adjustment (Total)		☒ + ☐ -	$ 163,900	☐ + ☒ -	$ -475,740	☐ + ☒ -	$ -325,300
Adjusted List Price of Comparables		Net 20.5 % Gross 93.9 %	$ 962,900	Net 29.8 % Gross 44.7 %	$ 1,119,260	Net 24.1 % Gross 69.7 %	$ 1,024,700

Note that the appraiser has included a "listing to sale adjustment," which is an estimate of how much the property may ultimately sell for after negotiations. In an accelerating market, houses may be selling for list price or close to it, or in some cases more than list price.

However, in a declining market, which is the type of market this appraisal was performed in, the reduction from list price (asking price) may be large. This will probably be especially true for large beach homes because they are typically vacation homes. And in a declining market, the demand for homes that are not primary residences often drops more quickly because they are considered a luxury in deteriorating economic conditions.

The Income Approach

For single-family home residential properties, the income approach is rarely used. However, if the property is being purchased as a rental home, an income approach analysis might be utilized. It would also be used for the purchase of rental homes by an investment entity, which might include multiple single-family residential properties owned in a portfolio. In such a case the income would be a primary consideration. A discussion of the income approach can be found in Chapter 5 on commercial appraisals.

Chapter 3

Analyzing the Land Appraisal

The sales comparison approach is the only method that can be used for land appraisals unless the land is leased or in some other way produces income. Land is sometimes leased for grazing, parking, or other uses. However, when it is leased for structures, the lease is generally long term—often for 20 years or more—and leases of this type are more common in other countries than in the United States.

With long-term leases, the lessee may build a structure, and generally the ownership of the structure goes to the lessor at the end of the lease. A typical lease for land in the United States would be for a cell tower. Depending on the agreement, the lease may require the lessee to remove the tower at the end of the lease or the tower may become the lessor's property when the lease terminates.

The income approach for appraising leased land will not be covered here because Chapter 5, the commercial appraisal chapter, will go over it, and the same principles are applicable. The example in that chapter applies to any income stream, whether it comes from a lease or another source.

Complex Issues for Land Valuation

Land valuations can be relatively simple if the valuation is for a lot in a subdivision where others that are similar have sold. However, for many land appraisals, there are myriad aspects that must be considered that are specific and often unique for each parcel under valuation. And, like the proverbial snowflake, the more closely comparable land sales are examined, the more apparent their differences become. Moreover, the complexity of land sales seems to rise relative to the land regulations of the state in which they occur. The more environmentally active states tend to have more rules limiting development, and they allow more avenues of recourse for those organizations and state agencies that challenge development.

Some of the issues the appraiser has to consider are wetlands, protected species, environmental contamination, noise and pollution, drainage, traffic restrictions (also known as *concurrency*), building moratoriums, and citizen pressure. All of these issues are set against a backdrop of dealing with various echelons of government—federal, state, and local—some of which are redundant in the areas they regulate and may use different yardsticks in their determinations.

For this reason, the fact that land is zoned for a particular use does not mean that its development is realistic or cost effective. For instance, a small parcel of land that is two acres in size may be zoned for 6,000-square-foot lots. However, once the easements for access are considered, and the engineering and other development fees are calculated, in addition to the time that the property must be held to get the permits approved, there may be no profit in the venture.

For this reason, developers pay a premium for *prime land*, which normally means land that has been approved for construction and has already been through the permitting process.

Land values can also change quickly and significantly depending on hearings that may be held regarding potential usage in various tribunals, or by local politicians. (For more information, also see the segment on land valuation in Chapter 7 on industrial building appraisal.)

Land Values in a Quickly Changing Market

When development is at low ebb due to economic conditions or other circumstances that have lessened demand, there may be very few buyers for land, and prices may fall precipitously. However, the appraisal may not reveal this clearly because sales may be used that are older, and adjustments for those sales may not have kept up with the diminished demand. Listings also may not reveal the extent of the drop in value because they often stay higher than market value as compared to other real estate. The reason for this is that landowners often own their property free and clear and are under less pressure to sell than the owners of other types of real estate.

Red Flag

In a declining market, land appraisals can be inflated because often landowners are not under the same compulsion to sell as homeowners who need to move, perhaps because of lost employment. This means land listings may be much higher than actual market values, and if older sales are used due to a lack of current sales, those transactions may not reflect the current market. Consequently, if proper adjustments are not made for the elapsed time from the date of sale for the comparable sales, the appraisal may be higher than market value. The lack of recent sales may also portend a market that has become stagnant.

However, in an appraisal in a declining market, the appraiser may not be attempting to inflate the value. The appraiser works only from the data that is available. If there are few sales and they are older, the indicated value of the subject property may be inaccurate only because there have been no recent sales that reflect the change in values, and the appraiser has no other valuation evidence to use.

Conversely, when values are climbing because demand has increased, even sales that are six-months or a year old may not reflect the current value. Appraisers may know that values are increasing in such a market, but they must work from actual sales as evidence of the value, and higher listings do not provide evidence that can be used in the appraisal to prove a value. Essentially the appraiser's hands are tied in such a market, and the value may come in lower than the sale price due to the rapidly increasing market.

Summary Appraisal Report

PROPERTY

Vacant residential land

Parcel number 216888-000

20-acre parcel

May 11, 2012

PREPARED FOR

Department of Parks

Attention: Mr. Ralph Jones

Administrator

230 Acacia Avenue

Olympia, WA 98642

PREPARED BY

Expert Appraisals, Inc.

John Smith, ASA

702 NE 19th Circle

Ridgefield, WA 98642

(360) 111-1111

1

Dear Mr. Ralph Jones:

At your request, I have prepared an appraisal of the Ridgefield land identified by the assessor as parcel number 216888-000, which is currently a 20-acre parcel. The purpose of this appraisal is to estimate the **subject's as-is fee simple market value,** for the possible purchase of the property. The market value conclusion is predicated on an **18-month exposure period**.

This report has been prepared in conformance with the Uniform Standards of Professional Appraisal Practice (USPAP) as formulated by the Appraisal Foundation. Further, this report is prepared in conformance to the Appraisal Standards for the American Society of Appraisers.

Please refer to the Assumptions and Limiting Conditions section of the attached report for an explanation of the basis on which the value conclusion is predicated. The signatory of this report is qualified by experience and education to competently appraise the subject property. The values reported in this appraisal are not contingent on the approval of a specific loan amount or any other circumstance. This appraisal was not performed to reach a predetermined value or predetermined value range.

I conclude, based on the analysis contained in this report, the subject property had an **as-is rounded fee simple value**, as of May 11, 2012, of

FOUR HUNDRED TWO THOUSAND DOLLARS ($402,000)

The basis for this value conclusion will be explained in the contents of the attached appraisal report.

Sincerely,

John Smith, ASA
Washington State
Certified General
Appraiser 1100000

2 Summary Appraisal Report

Table of Contents

Executive Summary

Client and intended user	Department of Parks, Olympia, WA
Subject location	Acreage on Hillhurst Road Ridgefield, WA 98642
Assessor's parcel	216888-000
2010–2011 assessed value	$258,779
Gross site area	20 acres
Zone	RLD-4 (4 units per acre)
Special hazards	None noted
Flood zone designation	Zone C FEMA 5300240161C 8/19/1986
Improvements	None. Old barn has no value.
Highest and best use	
As vacant	Single-family development
Sale price for pending sale	$400,000
Market value estimates	
Cost approach	N/A
Sales comparison approach	$402,000
Income capitalization approach	N/A
Total market value conclusion	$402,000
Interest appraised	Fee simple
Date of value	May 11, 2012
Date of report	May 11, 2012
Appraiser	John Smith, ASA

4 Summary Appraisal Report

Maps of Subject Property

Map of Subject Property—Approximate, Not Actual, Address

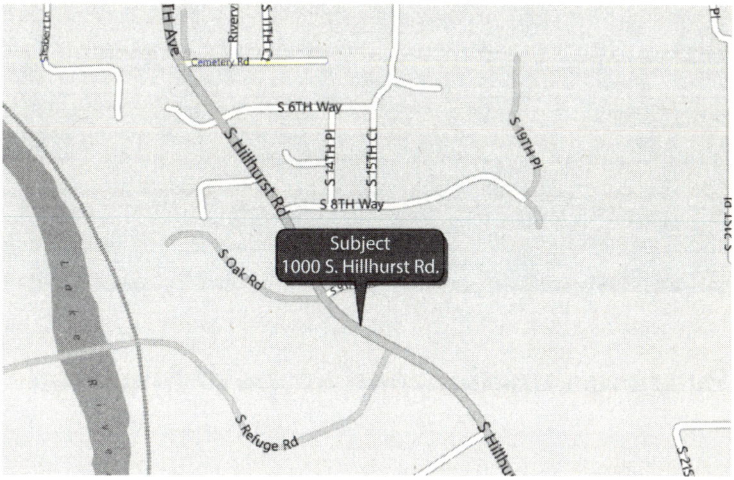

Map of the Subject Property, Parcel Number 216888-000, on Record with the County Assessor

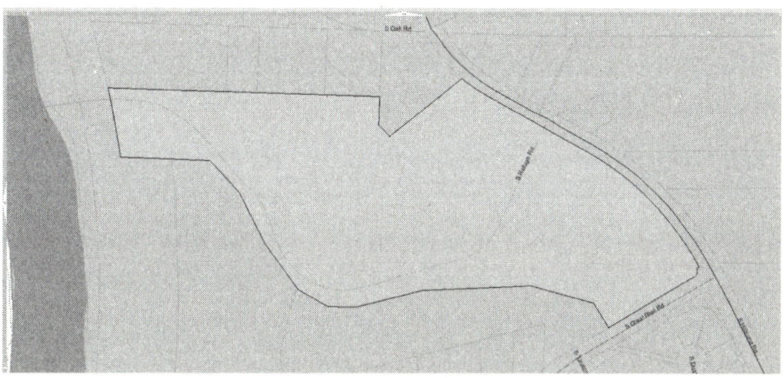

Summary Appraisal Report **5**

Aerial Map of the Subject Property, Parcel Number 216-888-000, on Record with the County Assessor

Purpose, Function, and Scope of Appraisal

This is a *summary appraisal report*, which is intended to comply with the reporting requirements set forth under Standards Rule 2-2(b) of the Uniform Standards of Professional Appraisal Practice for a Complete Appraisal presented in Summary Form. As such, it presents summary discussions of the data, reasoning, and analyses that were used in the appraisal process to develop the appraiser's opinion of value. The depth of discussion contained in this report is specific to the needs of the client and for the intended use stated below.

I have appraised this property previously, and that appraisal is in the possession of my client. The appraiser is not responsible for unauthorized use of this report. This report is the result of a full appraisal process. The sales comparison approach is the only applicable valuation approach for this assignment. The value opinion is based on current understanding of the market and market trends.

6 Summary Appraisal Report

Client	Department of Parks
Intended User	The client
Appraiser	John Smith, ASA
Subject	Vacant land 20-acre parcel Ridgefield, WA 98632

Purpose of the Appraisal

The purpose of this appraisal is to provide the appraiser's best estimate of the subject's as-is fee simple market value. The use of this appraisal is to aid the Department of Parks to determine the price the Department may want to pay for the land.

Market value is defined by the federal financial institutions regulatory agencies as follows:

> *Market value* means the most probable price which a property should bring in a competitive and open market under all conditions requisite to a fair sale, the buyer and seller each acting prudently and knowledgeably, and assuming the price is not affected by undue stimulus. Implicit in this definition is the consummation of a sale as of a specified date and the passing of title from seller to buyer under conditions whereby:
>
> 1. buyer and seller are typically motivated;
> 2. both parties are well informed or well advised, and acting in what they consider their own best interests;
> 3. a reasonable time is allowed for exposure in the open market;

4. payment is made in terms of cash in U.S. dollars or in terms of financial arrangements comparable thereto; and
5. the price represents the normal consideration for the property sold unaffected by special or creative financing or sales concessions granted by anyone associated with the sale.

(*Source:* Office of the Comptroller of the Currency under 12 CFR, Part 34, Subpart C-Appraisals, 34.42 Definitions [F].)

Intended Use of Report

This appraisal is intended to assist the client, the Department of Parks, in decision making concerning a possible land purchase. The use of this report is restricted to the client only, who is the intended user. The depth of discussion contained in this report is specific to the needs of the client and for the intended use stated herein. The appraiser is not responsible for unauthorized use of this report. Regardless of who pays for this appraisal, the intended user is the client only.

The scope of work in this appraisal has been customized for the intended user. It may be inappropriate for other users and put them in jeopardy. Therefore, regardless of the means of possession of the report, this appraisal may not be used or relied on by anyone other than the stated intended user. The appraiser, appraisal firm, and related parties assume no obligation, liability, or accountability to any third party. If you are not the stated intended user, please contact my office to have an appraisal customized for your needs.

There is currently an offer of $400,000 on the subject property, and the sales contract was analyzed by the appraiser.

8 Summary Appraisal Report

Interest Valued

The appraiser has valued the fee simple ownership interests in the subject property. The subject is a 20-acre parcel.

Effective Date of As-Is Value

May 11, 2012

Date of Report

May 11, 2012

Appraisal Development and Reporting Process

In preparing this appraisal, the appraiser:

- Inspected the subject site and walked on the land.
- Gathered and confirmed information on comparable improved sales. The appraiser considered all three approaches and applied all applicable approaches to arrive at an indication of value.

Methodology

Three basic approaches are typically used to estimate market value: (1) the cost approach, (2) the sales comparison (market) approach, and (3) the income capitalization approach.

Assumptions and Limiting Conditions

1. As agreed on with the client prior to the preparation of this appraisal, this appraisal conforms to the Uniform Standards of Professional Appraisal Practice (USPAP) and the Financial Institutions Reform, Recovery, and Enforcement Act of 1989 (FIRREA).

Summary Appraisal Report 9

2. This is a summary appraisal report, which is intended to comply with the reporting requirements set forth under Standards Rule 2-2(b) of the Uniform Standards of Professional Appraisal Practice for a summary appraisal report. As such, it might not include full discussions of the data, reasoning, and analyses that were used in the appraisal process to develop the appraiser's opinion of value. Supporting documentation concerning the data, reasoning, and analysis is retained in the appraiser's file. The information contained in this report is specific to the needs of the client and for the intended use stated in this report. The appraiser is not responsible for unauthorized use of this report.
3. No responsibility is assumed for legal or title considerations. Title to the property is assumed good and marketable unless otherwise stated in this report.
4. The property is appraised free and clear of any or all liens and encumbrances unless otherwise stated in this report.
5. Responsible ownership and competent property management are assumed unless otherwise stated in this report.
6. The information furnished by others is believed to be reliable. However, no warranty is given for its accuracy.
7. All engineering is assumed to be correct. Any plot plans and illustrative material in this report are included only to assist the reader in visualizing the property.
8. It is assumed that there are no hidden or unapparent conditions of the property, subsoil, or structures that render it more or less valuable. No responsibility is

10 Summary Appraisal Report

assumed for such conditions or for arranging for engineering studies that may be required to discover them.

9. It is assumed that there is full compliance with all applicable federal, state, and local environmental regulations and laws unless otherwise stated in this report.
10. It is assumed that all applicable zoning and use regulations and restrictions have been complied with, unless a nonconformity has been stated, defined, and considered in this appraisal.
11. It is assumed that all required licenses, certificates of occupancy, or other legislative or administrative authority from any local, state, or national governmental or private entity or organization have been or can be obtained or renewed for any use on which the value estimates contained in this report are based.
12. Any sketch in this report may show approximate dimensions and is included to assist the reader in visualizing the property. Maps and exhibits found in this report are provided for reader reference purposes only. No guarantee to accuracy is expressed or implied unless otherwise stated in this report. No survey has been made for the purpose of this report.
13. It is assumed that the utilization of the land and improvements is within the boundaries or property lines of the property described and that there is no encroachment or trespass unless otherwise stated in this report.
14. The appraiser is not qualified to detect hazardous waste and/or toxic materials. Any comment by the appraiser that might suggest the possibility of the

Summary Appraisal Report **11**

presence of such substances should not be taken as confirmation of the presence of hazardous waste and/or toxic materials. Such determination would require investigation by a qualified expert in the field of environmental assessment. The presence of substances such as asbestos, urea-formaldehyde foam insulation, or other potentially hazardous materials may affect the value of the property. The appraiser's value estimate is predicated on the assumption that there is no such material on or in the property that would cause a loss in value unless otherwise stated in this report. No responsibility is assumed for any environmental conditions, nor is any responsibility assumed for any expertise or engineering knowledge required to discover them. The appraiser's descriptions and resulting comments are the result of the routine observations made during the appraisal process.

15. Unless otherwise stated in this report, the subject property is appraised without a specific compliance survey having been conducted to determine if the property is or is not in conformance with the requirements of the Americans with Disabilities Act. The presence of architectural and communications barriers that are structural in nature that would restrict access by disabled individuals may adversely affect the property's value, marketability, or utility.
16. Any proposed improvements are assumed to be completed in a good workman-like manner in accordance with the submitted plans and specifications.
17. The distribution, if any, of the total valuation in this report between land and improvements applies only

under the stated program of utilization. The separate allocations for land and buildings must not be used in conjunction with any other appraisal and are invalid if so used.

18. Possession of this report, or a copy thereof, does not carry with it the right of publication. It may not be used for any purpose by any person other than the party to whom it is addressed without the written consent of the appraiser, and in any event, only with proper written qualification and only in its entirety.
19. Neither all nor any part of the contents of this report (especially any conclusions as to value, the identity of the appraiser, or the firm with which the appraiser is connected) shall be disseminated to the public through advertising, public relations, news, sales, or other media without the prior written consent and approval of the appraisal.
20. This report must be used in its entirety. Reliance on any portion of the report independent of the report as a whole may lead the reader to erroneous conclusions regarding property values. No portion of this report stands alone without express written approval from the author.
21. The liability of Expert Appraisals, Inc., and its employees is limited to the client only and only up to the amount of the fee actually received for the assignment. Further there is no accountability, obligation, or liability to any third party. If this report is placed in the hands of anyone other than the intended users, the client shall make such party aware of all limiting conditions and assumptions of the assignment and related

Summary Appraisal Report **13**

discussions. The appraiser is in no way responsible for any costs incurred to discover or correct any deficiency in the property. The appraiser assumes that there are no hidden or unapparent conditions relating to the property that render it more or less valuable.

22. The subject property in this appraisal is identified primarily by the assessor's map and tax lot as put forth in the body of this report or by other descriptions found in the body of this report if the assessor's map and tax lot are not applicable. Any other legal description found in the body or addenda of this report has been placed there as a courtesy and should not be viewed as the primary identifier of the property. These descriptions have been provided by the client or a title company and have not been prepared or verified by this office. I am not a surveyor, and it is beyond the scope of this appraisal to verify metes and bounds legal descriptions.
23. Due to various considerations including timing and distance, some photographs and maps and drawings in this report may have been taken or made by others. Typical sources include multiple listing services, real estate agents' marketing brochures, county assessor's records, LoopNet, Google, Oregon Water Resources Department, USDA web Soil Survey, FEMA, OrMap, county planning departments, and other sources. In all cases the comparables were investigated by this appraiser and inspected and investigated adequately, either in person or through published sources, and/or personal verifications to provide the appraiser a good understanding of the comparability of the property comparable to the subject.

14 Summary Appraisal Report

Special Assumptions and Limiting Conditions

This valuation is based on an existing 20-acre parcel that may have wetlands or other environmental issues. The appraiser was not given any reports, analyses, studies, or wetlands delineations regarding these matters, and the appraiser assumes no responsibility for the amount of usable land for the subject property, or the potential use for dividing or building on the subject property, and will be held harmless regardless of the final determinations by government officials and others regarding the usability of the subject property.

Compliance and Disclosures

This report complies with USPAP requirements as well as Interagency Appraisal and Evaluation Guidelines. It is a full appraisal assignment.

Disclosure of Competency

I am aware of and knowledgeable about the Competency Provision as set forth by the USPAP. The firm of Expert Appraisals, Inc., and John Smith, ASA, more specifically, has performed appraisals of comparable properties in recent years.

Market Value

The definition of *market value* as used in this report is given in the Purpose of the Appraisal section of this report.

Summary Appraisal Report **15**

Written Appraisal Form

This appraisal is a summary report stating the appraiser's opinion as to the fee simple value of the subject property. The report format presents the data and analysis that contributed to the value conclusions, and additional data and analysis are retained in my files.

Revenues, Expenses, and Vacancy

This is not applicable to the subject property because it is vacant land.

Market Exposure

Market exposure has been estimated based on current market data. I estimate a market exposure for the subject property of approximately 18 months.

Trend Analysis

The current state of the national and state economy is such that sales of real estate have been very slow, and as a result overall real estate values are in state of decline.

Prior Sales of the Subject Property

In the last five years, only quit claim deeds without a value indicated have been recorded on this parcel, from the county records.

Legal Description

A legal description of the subject property has been found from the assessor's records, but I assume no responsibility

16 Summary Appraisal Report

for matters legal in character, nor do I render any opinion as to the title, which is assumed to be good. I have not surveyed the property and assume no liability for such matters. If any metes and bounds description or other legal description of the subject appears in the body or addenda of this report, it appears as a courtesy and should not be relied upon for legal purposes. I am not a surveyor and cannot determine the accuracy or sufficiency of metes and bounds legal descriptions or of the assessor's legal descriptions.

Deductions and Discounts

The property does not require specific discounts or deductions in the valuation process. No deductions or discounts were used to arrive at a final value conclusion with the exception that the cost to remove the mobile home according to my client's suggestions has been taken into account.

Prohibited Influences

This appraisal includes a signed certification page from John Smith, ASA, certifying that he meets the current appraisal standards mandated by federal law and the USPAP. None of the value conclusions presented in this appraisal were based on a requested valuation. In my opinion, they are true, unbiased market values. I have taken into consideration the information, concerns, and opinions given me by the client. However, I have not altered or skewed my opinion of value to favor any individual or group of people.

Summary Appraisal Report **17**

Personal Property, Fixtures, and Intangible Items

This appraisal does not include personal property, freestanding equipment, rolling stock, inventories, mobile homes, or any intangible items such as business value.

Use of Recognized Appraisal Procedures

This appraisal follows a reasonable valuation method that employs the sales comparison approach as applicable to value the subject property. Neither the cost approach nor the income capitalization approach is applicable to this appraisal.

Subject Description

Neighborhood Description

The subject is located in Ridgefield, Washington, which is a bedroom community to Vancouver, Washington. The community includes subdivisions and residential properties on acreage, as well as retail, commercial, and industrial sections.

Site Description

The subject is a 20-acre parcel. The subject is rolling terrain, mostly dry from appearance, and it borders Hillhurst Road. The shape is irregular. Zoning is RLD-4 which allows four units per acre.

This appraisal assumes no hazardous materials are in the subject property. Prior to further development, the potential for hazardous materials should be fully explored by a qualified engineering firm. I am not qualified to detect hazardous materials and make no affirmation as to the presence or absence of such in regards to the subject property.

18 Summary Appraisal Report

Improvement Description Real Property

There are no usable improvements on the subject property, and for development purposes, utilities would have to be brought in.

Area Analysis

Note to Reader: Typically an area analysis does not need to be read by the reviewer, unless the reviewer is not familiar with the subject's geographical location. Often appraisals will be filled with statistics and other chamber of commerce type of information that can be skimmed over or ignored.

General: Vancouver Area

The subject is located in Ridgefield, Washington, in Clark County. It is close to the Interstate 5 and is in the north end of the county, and it is convenient to the major freeways I-5 and I-205. The Clark County area is part of the larger Portland/Vancouver primary metropolitan statistical area (PMSA).

This area comprises various counties including Multnomah, Clackamas, Washington, and Yamhill Counties in Oregon and Clark County in Washington. Many of the residents of Clark County have employment in the Portland, Oregon, area, and some Oregon residents also work in Clark County. The Portland/Vancouver PMSA is the largest population center on the West Coast between Seattle and San Francisco, and it is rated as the thirty-first largest metropolitan area in the United States, and the eighth largest in the northwestern and western portion of the United States.

The population of Vancouver, according to the Clark County 2010 estimate, is 161,791. The area has been known for low unemployment until about 2007, when property values declined and unemployment increased into the double digits. Ridgefield's 2010 population was 4,763 in 2010.

Exposure and Marketing Time

The property sales indicate that *exposure time* (that is, the length of time the subject property would have been exposed for sale in the market had it sold at the market value concluded in this analysis as of the date of this valuation) would have been from 6 to 18 months. The estimated *marketing time* (that is, the amount of time it would probably take to sell the subject property if exposed in the market beginning on the date of this valuation) is estimated to be 18 months if marketed at the value as concluded in this report.

Because of the current declining market, the client should be aware that if the subject marketing period is extended, the sale price could reasonably be expected to be below this appraised value even within the one-year typical marketing period.

Assessment Review

Note to Reader: Assessment information should be included in the appraisal, although it is not required. It is not unusual for the assessor's value to differ significantly from the appraiser's value, and it does not necessarily indicate an error in the appraisal. The reason is that assessors often use mass appraisal techniques that are not specific to the property, and they generally lack the staff to keep the values current.

The 2011 values for 2012 taxes from the assessor's office show a total value of $258,779.

Summary of Analysis and Valuation

Sales Comparison Approach

Value Not Attributable to the Real Property

To my knowledge, unless stated, none of the comparable sales included personal property, business value, goodwill, or other non–real estate goods. Unless otherwise noted, the sale price of each comparable is attributable to the real property only. See comments in the sales narrative concerning adjustments made to some sales. I have considered this factor qualitatively in my analysis.

Property Rights Conveyed

Each sale involved the transfer of fee simple interest from grantor to grantee. No adjustments for property rights were necessary.

Financing Terms

Adjustments for financing are sometimes necessary depending on the terms of a contract. Sellers sometimes inflate the sale price and offer attractive atypical contract terms. Also conversely, contract terms, which are above market rates, may reduce the cash equivalent sale price of a property. However, buyers are often protective of the terms of sale and are unwilling to release this information. Of the comparable sales used in the sales comparison, all were sold for cash or for terms I deemed as cash equivalent. Because of this, no cash equivalency adjustment was necessary.

Summary Appraisal Report **21**

Conditions of Sale

Based on my research, the sales appear to be arm's-length transactions in which neither the buyer nor the seller was under undue influence to consummate the sale.

Market Conditions

A market conditions adjustment is best supported by a general market analysis and a paired-sales analysis. However, a paired-sales analysis is effective only when at least two sales are similar in nearly all respects, except for the date of sale. A difference between the unit values can be attributed to changes in the marketplace during the time between the two sales. My conversations with real estate brokers, county officials, and other appraisers have led me to believe that the market for property such as the subject has decreased approximately 10 percent annually over the time span of the comparable sales execution dates to the present. One of the problems in this adjustment is that there have been so few sales of similar properties in Ridgefield and the surrounding area.

Adjustments

The sales were weighted accordingly for differences as needed. For instance, the land sales were adjusted quantitatively for size, zone, and location as well as market conditions and for its being a listing because listings often sell for less than their listed prices.

The sales comparison approach was used exclusively for this property because it is vacant land. The following show the sales used in the appraisal, as well as listings of properties that are for sale. Please note that listings indicate the

22 Summary Appraisal Report

highest value a property would sell for and that in the current market, which has been declining for several years and has not yet recovered, the list price for many properties may be well over the final actual sale price. A listing-to-sale adjustment has been made for the listings, which is the appraiser's opinion of the likely sale price that may be received.

Because the market is very slow, there were few sales to use for this appraisal, and an expanded search included sales in Vancouver and nearby areas. The subject is zoned for development, but because of current economic conditions, land has been selling for less than its normal development value. Some sales are not developable, and others are dividable only into two parcels. Therefore, appropriate adjustments were made under the zoning adjustment on the grid.

Sales Comparable to Subject Property

Sale	1	2	3	4
Location	27713 NW 31st Ave	3557 S 15th St.	NE 107th Ave	NE 232nd Ave
City/State	Ridgefield, WA	Ridgefield, WA	Battle Ground, WA	Vancouver, Wa
Sale Price	$ 382,500	$ 351,000	$ 500,000	$ 650,000
Sale Date	May-12	Feb-11	Aug-11	Mar-12
Imp Size	17.67	6.27	40.00	25.00
Price per acre	$ 21,646.86	$ 55,980.86	$ 12,500.00	$ 26,000.00
Zoning	RLD-6	R1-7.5	AG-20	R-5
Comments	Bank owned	Financed sale	Cash sale	Cash sale
Notes on property	Pre. appr. for 64 lots		Wtr rights creek	Five 5 acre lots
Zoning Adj.	0.7	1	1.7	1.3
Location/ Land Adj.	1	1	1.4	0.9
Topo Adj.	1.3	0.8	0.8	0.8
Size Adj.	1	0.5	0.8	0.9
Net Adj'mnt	0.91	0.40	1.52	0.84
Adj'd Sale Price	348,075.00	140,400.00	761,600.00	547,560.00
Time Adj.	100%	90%	98%	100%
Final Adj'd Price	$ 348,075.00	$ 126,360.00	$ 746,368.00	$ 547,560.00
Adj. SP/SF Time	**$ 19,698.64**	**$ 20,153.11**	**$ 18,659.20**	**$ 21,902.40**
Adj. Comments	Bank owned; adj for 64 lot pre appr.	Small size is more accurate for subj.	40 acres but can divide 20 acre	Creek waterfront
Subject Lot Size	20.0	20.0	20.0	20.0
Value SF X Subj.	**$ 393,973**	**$ 403,062**	**$ 373,184**	**$ 438,048**

Listings Comparable to Subject Property

Active Listings	1	2	3
Location	Carty Rd	6019 NW 269th St.	132nd ave
City/State	Ridgefield, WA	Ridgefield, WA	Ridgefield, WA
List Price	$ 487,000	$ 199,000	$ 349,900
Imp Size	25.03	15.91	24.29
Price per acre	$ 19,456.65	$ 12,507.86	$ 14,405.10
Zoning	R5	R1-7500	AG
Comments	5 acre parcels	Hilly, much	One home only
Notes on property		not useable	
Zoning Adj.	1.2	1	1.7
Location/ Land Adj.	1	1	1.2
Topo Adj.	1	1.8	0.8
Size Adj.	1.1	1	1.1
Net Adj'mnt	1.32	1.80	1.80
Adj'd Sale Price	$ 642,840.00	$ 358,200.00	$ 628,140.48
Listing-to-Sale Adj.	80%	88%	80%
Final Adj'd Price	$ 514,272.00	$ 315,216.00	$ 502,512.38
Adj. SP/SF Time	**$ 20,546.22**	**$ 19,812.45**	**$ 20,688.04**
Adj. Comments	Has stream	No more than 4 lots - adj in zoning	No trees adj. in location
Subject Lot Size	20.0	20.0	20.0
Value SF X Subj.	**$ 410,924**	**$ 396,249**	**$ 413,761**

Discussion and Conclusions of Value

The land comparables vary in location, size, and timing, but all are generally helpful in estimating the subject value.

After a qualitative and quantitative analysis of these sales, I believe that a value of $20,100 per acre for the land as if vacant is supported and reasonable. The total land value would therefore be as follows:

$$20 \text{ acres} \times \$20{,}100 = \$402{,}000$$

Note to Reader: It is common for the appraiser to discuss each of the comparable sales as part of the analysis, but that was not done in this appraisal. The lack of a discussion does not necessarily mean the appraisal is lacking, but it would have been preferable to get a little more information about each sale to understand the appraiser's reasoning for the adjustments for the sales.

Sales Comparison Approach Value Conclusion

Based on the data and analysis presented, I therefore conclude the sales comparison approach yields a **fee simple market value**, as of May 11, 2012, of:

$402,000

Reconciliation

Cost approach	Not performed
Sales comparison approach	$402,000
Income capitalization approach	Not performed

The vacant lot is valued by the sales comparison approach only, and that is the only applicable approach for this lot.

The cost approach was inapplicable to this assignment.

The sales comparison approach is closely tied to the marketplace, and there was adequate data to support the land value and improved value conclusions by this approach.

The income capitalization approach was not performed in my valuation because the subject is not primarily an income producing property and because the client has requested a land-only appraisal. Therefore, I have placed all weight on the conclusion of the sales comparison approach.

Summary Appraisal Report **25**

Real Property Value Conclusion

I therefore conclude the subject property has an as-is **fee simple market value**, as **of May 11, 2012**, of:

Four Hundred Two Thousand Dollars

Photographs of Subject Property

The following are photographs of the subject property from different perspectives.

Property from Southeast Corner of Easement

Looking West from South End of Property (South Great Blue Road)

Looking South, Land on Right

Looking North, Land on Left

Hilly Portion of Land, Looking Southeast

Looking Down on Land, Southeast

Looking East, Old Barn

Looking North from Great Blue Road (South End of Land)

Looking West, Middle of Parcel

Looking North from the South End of Land

Certification

The undersigned does hereby certify that, except as otherwise noted in this appraisal report, to the best of my knowledge:

1. The statements of fact contained in this report are true and correct.
2. The reported analyses, opinions, and conclusions are limited only by the reported assumptions and limiting conditions, and they are my personal, unbiased professional analyses, opinions, and conclusions.
3. I have no present or future interest in the property that is the subject of this appraisal, and I have no personal interest or bias with respect to the parties involved.

Summary Appraisal Report **31**

4. My compensation is not contingent on an action or event resulting from the analyses, opinions, or conclusions in, or the use of, this report.
5. My analyses, opinions, and conclusions were developed, and this report has been prepared, in conformity with the requirements of the Code of Professional Ethics and the Standards of Professional Practice of the Appraisal Institute.
6. The use of this report is subject to the requirements of the Appraisal Institute relating to review by its duly authorized representatives.
7. As of the date of this report, I, John Smith, have completed the requirements under the continuing education program of the American Society of Appraisers.
8. I have made a personal interior and exterior inspection of the property that is the subject of this report. I have inspected the exterior and investigated all comparable sales used in this report.
9. No one provided significant professional assistance to the persons signing the report.
10. I do not authorize the out-of-context quoting from or partial reprinting of this appraisal report. Further, neither all nor any part of this appraisal report shall be disseminated to the general public by the use of media for public communication without my prior written consent.
11. This appraisal is prepared in conformance with the Uniform Standards of Professional Appraisal Practice (USPAP) as promulgated by the Appraisal Standards Board of the Appraisal Foundation. The departure provision does apply.

32 Summary Appraisal Report

12. My employment was not conditioned upon the appraisal producing a specific value or a value within a given range. Future employment is not dependent upon reporting a specified value. Neither employment nor compensation is dependent upon the approval of a loan application.
13. I have acquired through study and practice the necessary knowledge and experience to complete this assignment competently.
14. I have appraised a portion of this property previously.

John Smith, ASA
WA Certification No. 1100000

Appraiser's Qualifications

John Smith, ASA
Certified General Appraiser

Professional Experience

Jacobs and Company Appraisers and Consultants
Vancouver, WA
2000 to 2010

Clark County Assessor
Commercial Appraiser
Vancouver, WA
1991 to 2000

Summary Appraisal Report 33

Education

- Oregon State University
- BA degree in economics
- Numerous appraisal courses

Licensing and Designation

- Certified General Appraisal, licensed in Washington and Oregon
- Accredited Senior Appraiser, American Society of Appraisers

Chapter 4

Wetlands, Contaminated Property, and Eminent Domain Land Appraisals

In-depth treatment of these issues is beyond the scope of this book, but the following is an introduction. The effect that environmental issues can have on the value of land should not be underestimated, and wetlands are one of the more prevalent environmental detriments to land development.

Contamination is another environmental issue that can not only diminish the value of land but due to liability issues may actually render it worthless.

Eminent domain valuations for partial takings of land require a special type of government-mandated valuation process. That process can result in a value that is much different from other market value appraisals.

Wetlands

Wetlands can be a major obstacle to development, and hence the valuation, of all types of land. For this reason, the appraiser should be familiar with wetlands and have experience in valuing them if they are part of the appraisal under review. One legal definition of wetlands can be found in the Emergency Wetlands Resource Act of 1986, which states:

> **Wetland:** Land that has a predominance of hydric soils and that is inundated or saturated by surface or groundwater at a frequency and duration sufficient to support, and under normal circumstances does support, a prevalence of hydrophytic vegetation adapted for saturated soil conditions.

To understand the basis that the government uses to intervene in the wetlands issue, the act goes on to say this:

> **Overview**
>
> The purpose of the Act is to promote wetlands conservation for the public benefit and to help fulfill international obligations in various migratory bird treaties and conventions. The Act authorizes the purchase of wetlands from Land and Water Conservation Fund monies. The Act also requires the Secretary of the Interior to establish a National Wetlands Priority Conservation Plan, requires the states to include wetlands in their Comprehensive Outdoor Recreation Plans, and transfers funds from import duties on arms and ammunition to the Migratory Bird Conservation Fund.
>
> **Findings/Policy**
>
> Congress finds that: wetlands play an integral role in maintaining the quality of life; wetlands provide essential habitat to a major portion of migratory and resident fish and wildlife; migratory bird treaty obligations require federal protection of wetlands; wetlands, and the fish, wildlife, and plants dependent on wetlands, provide recreational and commercial benefits, including contributions to a commercial marine harvest valued at over $10 billion annually, support for the nation's annual fur and hide harvest,

and wetland-related recreation activities that generate billions of dollars annually; wetlands enhance water quality and supply by serving as groundwater recharge areas, nutrient traps and chemical sinks; wetlands provide a natural means of flood and erosion control by retaining water during periods of high runoff; wetlands are only a small percentage of the U.S. and continue to disappear; certain activities of the federal government have altered or assisted in the alteration of wetlands; existing federal, state, and private cooperation in wetlands conservation should be strengthened.[1]

Based on the act, there are essentially three characteristics necessary to categorize land as wetlands. However, it should be noted that biologists and others often disagree about what constitutes a wetland and that frequently there are legal disputes regarding them. And the reason for these legal disputes is clearly understood in light of the fact that land can lose a huge amount of its value if it is classified as wetlands. Often the fact that wetlands exist on a property is not in dispute, but the extent of the wetlands, and consequently the boundaries of them, bring about litigation.

The three basic characteristics that lead to land being classified as wetlands are evidenced by the following:

1. **Hydrology.** *Hydrology* refers to the presence of water on land.
2. **Hydric soils.** These are soils that show evidence of water saturation. When soil is underwater for prolonged periods, the lack of oxygen produces anaerobic conditions that often change its color. The wetlands biologist will dig a hole in the ground to examine the soil underneath and examine it for signs of saturation.
3. **Wetlands plants.** Also called *hydrophytic vegetation*, these are plants that grow in the soil and conditions found on land that is periodically inundated with water.[2]

Types of Wetlands

According to Cowardin et al., there are five basic types of wetlands environments: palustrine, lacustrine, marine, estuarine, and riverine.[3] The following are brief and noncomprehensive definitions of these types of wetlands.

Inland properties are generally considered *palustrine wetlands* because they are swamps and bogs and other wet areas that are not connected to the wetland systems.

Lacustrine wetlands are generally associated with lakes and dammed bodies of water such as reservoirs.

Marine wetlands are found along ocean shorelines.

Estuarine wetlands are found between marine wetlands and uplands; they are generally marshy areas and swamps near the ocean.

Riverine wetlands, as the name implies, are found near rivers, creeks, and manmade waterways.[4]

Permits Required for Wetlands Development

Requirements for permits are quite complex, and they also are constantly changing. The information supplied here is very superficial and should not be relied upon except as a general introduction.

Basically, there are two different permits that one must obtain to fill wetlands, but the permits can vary according to agricultural and other aspects. The *nationwide permit* is necessary if areas as small as one-tenth of an acre are to be filled. An *individual permit* is necessary for filling larger areas. The amounts that trigger the need for permits have changed over the years, and the restrictions keep getting tighter.[5]

Mitigation

In order to develop a property with wetlands, it is sometimes possible for a developer to mitigate some of the wetlands. In other words, if the developer wants to build on an area that is wetlands, he or she might mitigate the area by creating new wetlands or restoring or enhancing existing wetlands. This might occur on the same property that is under development. For instance, if the property is a five-acre parcel and one acre is wetlands but that acre is in the most usable portion, the developer might create wetlands on other acreage to mitigate for it.

The rules are constantly changing, and mitigation ratios may also vary according to whether the developer is creating, restoring, or enhancing the mitigated areas. The ratio could be up to 1:8, or some other number. In the past, mitigation could be performed on a distant site, but with the newer rules, property has to be mitigated with property in the same watershed, the borders of which are generally outlined by the Army Corps of Engineers.[6]

Mitigation banks have been established in some areas where developers can purchase mitigation credits for their property. Sometimes, banks are started by developers for their own projects, or they may be established by entrepreneurs who sell the credits for a profit. The sale prices from mitigation banks can be helpful in determining the value of wetlands. However, sales of this nature can be complicated, and if they are used in the appraisal, they should be reviewed carefully.

Valuation of Wetlands

There are various theories regarding the best valuation methods for wetlands, but the sales comparison approach is generally the most accurate. Wetlands that can be further enhanced are usually sold for mitigation purposes, and the price of those sales should have been considered and examined by the appraiser to determine the value of the wetlands under valuation. The circumstances of the sale are of paramount importance. Supply and demand can vary depending on what is available at a given time.

If land is purchased to create wetlands, then the value of the land in such a situation may not be usable as a wetlands comparable because it was purchased as uplands. If there are enough wetland sales in a certain area, a pattern should develop that should form a range for valuing the subject property. The appraiser will probably use a sales grid, which will be constructed as it would be for any other land sale analysis, and a conclusion should be drawn after the sales are analyzed and reconciled.

Contaminated Property

Appraisers normally have a statement in their appraisals that protects them from liability regarding contaminants on the property they are appraising. It might be similar to this:

> The appraiser is not qualified to detect hazardous waste and/or toxic materials. Any comment by the appraiser that might suggest the possibility of the presence of such substances should not be taken as confirmation of the presence of hazardous waste and/or toxic materials. Such determination would require investigation by a qualified expert in the field of environmental assessment. The presence of substances such as asbestos, urea-formaldehyde foam insulation, or other potentially hazardous materials may affect the value of the property. The appraiser's value estimate is predicated on the assumption that there is no such material on or in the property that would cause a loss in value unless otherwise stated in this report. No responsibility is assumed for any environmental conditions, or for any expertise or engineering knowledge required to discover them. The appraiser's descriptions and resulting comments are the result of the routine observations made during the appraisal process.

Properties Likely to Be Contaminated

For industrial properties, certain industries tend to be contaminated with chemicals associated with the products they produce. For instance, trichloroethylene (TCE) was used for many years as a degreasing agent, and it may be present at certain types of plants, such as paper mills. A company under valuation may not want to know if contamination exists because that knowledge can force them to clean it up. Consequently, property can be contaminated, making it a risk for a lender, and the lender may never know about it. The reviewer would be wise to ask questions if the appraisal is for an industrial facility.

Residential and commercial sites may also have contamination. Gasoline stations may have buried tanks that have leaked. Dry cleaning establishments may have used chemicals that have polluted the ground, and homes with buried heating oil tanks may also have issues.

If a company's property is possibly contaminated, the reviewer might want to ask it to conduct an *environmental assessment report* to determine if it is contaminated, and if so, to what extent the contamination exists. The American Society for Testing and Materials (ASTM) has set certain standards for different phases of testing. The following is an example of what is performed for a typical Phase I through IV report. Please note that the following information is introductory and basic. More detailed information is required for an in-depth understanding of these reports.

Phase I

The first phase is an initial review to determine whether there is a reason to suspect contamination. This environmental assessment is a due diligence screening tool designed to make a basic assessment, using research and observation, to determine potential environmental contamination associated with real property. It usually includes the following activities:

- Inspection of the property, including all structures, to identify possible sources of contamination, such as asbestos, electrical equipment containing polychlorinated biphenyl (PCB), and/or chemical spills
- Inspection for leaking storage tanks, old waste disposal areas, chemical containers that have been stored on the property, and other visible sources of potential contamination

- Investigation of past chemical spills or disposal of hazardous substances, legal or illegal, by observing soil stains or disturbed vegetation
- Contact with people familiar with the property and data sources so the investigator can discover its history to identify past events or uses that may have contaminated the property
- Search of available government records on the property to identify possible sources of contamination on or near the site; search of databases that reveal properties in the vicinity that have been identified as contaminated
- A 50-year or longer title search for previous owners and uses of the property, which may reveal usage that could have caused contamination
- Search for historical aerial photographs of the site to determine past uses and evidence of contaminating activities such as waste disposal

Phase II

The second phase is a physical investigation to determine whether there is contamination. This phase differs from Phase I in that the site is actually tested. It generally follows Phase I if Phase I reveals a need for further testing. It is also aided by Phase I since Phase I directs what is tested and what tests need to be performed:

- **Surface and subsurface soil sampling.** This may require boring holes and taking samples at different levels in the soil.
- **Groundwater sampling.** Drilling wells may be required to determine whether water is contaminated at any level. Monitoring wells are often installed on sites that are contaminated.
- **More extensive testing of the site depending on conditions.** The chemical constituents chosen for analysis should correspond with the potential contaminants for the site. In other words, it is

difficult to test for every type of chemical, so the testing should be for chemicals related to the use of the land.

Phase III

This phase is to determine the type and extent of the contamination. Studies need to be conducted before the cleanup process can begin:

- Before the cleanup process can begin, studies need to be conducted to find the geographic location of the contamination.
- It must be determined whether the contamination is still spreading (through groundwater, for instance). A remedial action plan (RAP) must be developed, studied, and approved by the controlling regulatory agencies.

Phase IV

In this phase, the process of cleanup and remediation begins. This is the actual cleanup of the toxic material. It may not rid the property of all contamination because doing so may be impossible. Rather, the goal is to clean up the site to the extent that the governmental regulatory agencies' requirements are met.

Remediation may be *in situ* (within the site) or *ex situ* (outside of the site). In situ cleanups are generally less expensive, but they may be less successful than ex situ. An example of an in situ cleanup is treating the soil to rid it of a toxic chemical. In an ex situ cleanup, the soil is taken from the site and dumped in an approved toxic waste disposal site.

Changes in technology have had a mixed effect on the detection and remediation of contamination. Micro-technology—micro-separation devices with micro-sensors—can now be used to detect contamination plumes. This means that contamination that might have escaped detection in the past can now be identified. This adds to the burden of remediation, but it also allows for more precise cleanup, which can save costs because noncontaminated areas can be more easily distinguished. The point is, as technology changes, the cleanup process is affected.

Types of Contamination

Different types of contamination affect property values differently. There are many types of chemicals that can contaminate a property, as well as various ways in which a property can become contaminated. For instance, chemicals such as arsenic can be found at aluminum plants, and trichloroethylene (TCE), a degreasing agent, can be found in paper mills. Chemicals vary in their toxicity, and some are easier to clean up than others. The more dangerous chemicals can be more expensive to clean up, depending on their molecular structure and other properties.

The diminution in value depends on how the contamination affects the site. For instance, the presence of asbestos in a building may entail the removal of it or the sealing and containment of it, and when that is accomplished, the contamination issue should be resolved. The expense of the work may not be certain, but it will be within a range of cost that can be reasonably estimated, and when the cleanup is accomplished, the property will not be stigmatized.

In comparison, a site with contaminated soil has more risk because the extent of the contamination is not known until the cleanup begins. Estimates can be made, but they will not be as certain as those for an asbestos cleanup. Moreover, the site may continue to suffer from the stigma of contamination because there may be a lingering question about whether the cleanup was complete. Soil testing has its limits, and it is possible to miss an area that needs cleaning.

A site with contaminated groundwater poses an even higher risk. Water is difficult to clean, and it can travel to other sites, increasing the liability aspect of a cleanup. Monitoring wells may help to determine the condition of the groundwater, but no one knows the exact route that water takes under the earth, so contamination can seep into areas that cannot be anticipated. Remedial work is also more questionable with groundwater contamination because methods vary in expense and effectiveness. The property may continue to be stigmatized for a long time into the future because of the seriousness of this type of contamination.

Cost to Cure

The results of the report investigations will determine if there is contamination, but it will not necessarily be accompanied by a cost to cure. An environmental engineer typically makes this estimate, and it will probably state cleanup costs based on the assumed amount of contamination. If groundwater is the issue, the estimate will likely include projected future costs, including monitoring wells and other expenses. In any event, often the full extent of the contamination cannot be known until the cleanup begins, so a specific estimate is rare at this stage.

If there is a cost-to-cure estimate, the figure that results when that amount is subtracted from the market value of the property as clean will not necessarily be the market value for the property as contaminated. The time and effort to clean the property and the cost of borrowing the funds to clean it will also have to be considered. Moreover, accurate estimates can rarely be made for cleanups, and they often cost more than anticipated.

Stigma

There is another aspect of the contamination issue that should be considered in reviewing the appraisal, even if the property has been cleaned: stigma.

Stigma is defined by *The Dictionary of Real Estate Appraisal* as "an adverse public perception regarding a property; the identification of a property with some type of opprobrium (environmental contamination, a grisly crime), which exacts a penalty on the marketability of the property and hence its value."[7] *Merriam-Webster's Collegiate Dictionary* defines it as follows: "1 (a) archaic: a scar left by a hot iron; brand. (b) a mark of shame or discredit; stain. (c) an identifying mark or characteristic; specifically: a specific diagnostic sign of a disease."[8]

Stigma as it relates to real estate is defined as follows: a characteristic of real property that is detrimental to its market value, based on perceptions about the property. Stigma includes, but is not limited to, the following items:

- Fear of current and future liability
- Concern that the cleanup is not complete
- Inability to finance property (Lenders are leery.)
- Problems for public relations (For instance, does the company want to be known as being located on a previously contaminated site, even if it is now clean?)

The reviewer should understand that stigma, in the case of environmental contamination, should be separated from the specific cost to cure. The cost to cure can be more easily measured than stigma, and stigma is an additional loss in value that is not inherent in the cost to cure.

Illegal and Legal Contamination

The stigma affecting a site, and the potential liability due to the ramifications of the contamination, may be affected by the circumstances of the contamination. Many sites became contaminated with chemicals that were legal to use years ago but have since been banned. Some chemicals may still be in use, but they are now subject to strict methods of disposal, whereas in the past they were simply dumped on the ground or into a river.

Sites with contamination from such uses, where the law was not broken, may be less prosecutable and less risky regarding liability claims than sites that have become toxic due to illegal conduct. For the same reason, the stigma associated with a legally contaminated site is often diminished compared to that associated with a site subject to criminal activity.

Summary

Property may be contaminated without that problem being noted in the appraisal. In fact, most appraisals specifically state that the subject property is being appraised as if it is free of contamination and that the appraiser is unqualified to detect contamination and will be held harmless of any liability should the site prove to be contaminated. There are certain properties that are more likely to be contaminated than others, such as gasoline stations, dry cleaners, and most industrial plants, and specific chemicals may be associated with certain industries. To determine if a site is contaminated, an environmental assessment should be conducted.

Sites that are certified to be clean but were previously contaminated may still suffer from a loss in value due to the stigma associated with the property. Stigma is not the only issue with these sites. Often there is uncertainty that a site has been thoroughly cleaned, even if it has been certified as such. There may be significant risk and liability associated with a contaminated site or with a site that has been cleaned up, and the valuation of it requires an appraiser who is a specialist.

Red Flag

Wetlands and other environmental issues can exist on a property unbeknownst to the appraiser. In fact, most appraisals have a hold harmless clause in their limiting-conditions section that states the appraiser is not responsible for such issues. If there is a question about hazardous waste or wetlands, it is important to have a specialized professional inspect the property.

Land Values and Eminent Domain

An in-depth treatment of eminent domain valuations is beyond the scope of this book, but the following is an explanation of how eminent domain appraisals differ when compared to typical market value appraisals. *Eminent domain* is the right of the government to take private property for public use. It is further defined in *The Dictionary of Real Estate Appraisal*, as follows:

> The right of government to take private property for public use upon the payment of just compensation. The Fifth Amendment of the U.S. Constitution, also known as the takings clause, guarantees payment of just compensation upon appropriation of private property.[9]

Eminent Domain Rules

Eminent domain rules for takings for the federal government may vary from the rules for state governments. The federal government publishes a document titled *Uniform Appraisal Standards for Federal Land Acquisitions*, which is often referred to as the Yellow Book. It is a guide to appraisers on how eminent domain property should be valued. The definition of *market value* from the federal book is as follows:

> Market value is the amount in cash, or on terms reasonably equivalent to cash, for which in all probability the property would have sold on the effective date of the appraisal, after a reasonable exposure time on the open competitive market, from a willing and reasonably knowledgeable seller to a willing and reasonably knowledgeable buyer, with neither acting under any compulsion to buy or sell, giving due consideration to all available economic uses of the property at the time of the appraisal.[10]

However, in comparison, the definition of market value for eminent domain takings for the state of California is this:

> The fair market value of the property taken is the highest price on the date of valuation that would be agreed to by the seller,

> being willing to sell but under no particular or urgent necessity for so doing, nor obliged to sell, and a buyer, being ready, willing, and able to buy but under no particular necessity for so doing, each dealing with the other with full knowledge of all the uses and purposes for which the property is reasonably adaptable and available.[11]

Consequently, it is extremely important for the appraiser and reviewer to know what laws the eminent domain takings fall under. If a property is being taken in California by the federal government, the definition will be different than if the same piece of property is being taken by the state of California. The main difference here is that the federal government pays based on the most probable sale price, whereas the state of California pays on the highest sale price.

The Larger Parcel

The differences between the federal rules and the rules of each state should be understood and quoted in the appraisal. The federal government requires that the definition for *market value* be included as well as other statements, and state governments also require this information.

However, a major difference that may not be apparent, or stated clearly enough to understand for a reviewer not familiar with such appraisals, is the requirement that the appraiser find the *larger parcel.* This is extremely important if the taking is for a partial acquisition—that is, if the government is taking only a portion of a parcel of private land and not the whole parcel. The following is a quote from the federal book that explains this requirement in regard to ownership:

> B-11. **Partial Acquisitions.** When the United States acquires only part of a unitary holding, federal law requires that compensation be made not only for the property interest acquired but also for the diminution, if any, in the value of the remainder directly

> caused by the acquisition and/or by the use to which the part acquired will be put. This diminution in the value of the remainder is often and "somewhat loosely" referred to as *severance damage*. When the remainder is specially benefited as a result of the government's project, the value of the remainder will reflect that fact, which will result in a lessening of the compensation paid to the landowner.
>
> It is essential to a partial taking and to the application of the rules on severance damages and special benefits that the land acquired be part of a unitary holding (a "whole"), commonly referred to as the *larger parcel*. It is often difficult to determine what constitutes the whole property comprising the part acquired and the remainder, in particular when there are vast acreages or non-contiguous parcels involved. Because of this difficulty, tests have been established to determine the larger parcel. First, there must be a unity of ownership in all parts of the whole. Second, there must be a unity of highest and best use for all parts of the whole.[12]

Note that at first these paragraphs may seem to refer to extra compensation only when there is damage to the remaining property with a partial taking. However, special attention should be paid to the statement, "When the remainder is specially benefited as a result of the government's project, the value of the remainder will reflect that fact, which will result in a lessening of the compensation paid to the landowner." This means that in a partial taking, if the remainder is benefited in the appraiser's judgment, the compensation will be diminished. But it is also applied in another manner, and this is why the determination of the larger parcel is so important to the government: the compensation will be based on the total value of the parcel from which the land is taken.

For example, if land is being taken by the government to widen a freeway, and there are two landowners who are both giving up two acres of land, the compensation may be different for each landowner even if the land being taken is essentially the same in value.

Let us suppose that landowner 1 has 200 acres and landowner 2 has 4 acres. If the total value of land for landowner 1 is $400,000, then landowner 1 would get $4,000 for the 2 acres, or $2,000 per acre. If the total value for landowner 2 is $40,000, then landowner 2 will get more than landowner 1. The reason is that the appraiser may figure that a 4-acre parcel will sell for $40,000 or $10,000 per acre. Therefore, if landowner 2 is diminished by 2 acres, the loss would be $20,000. Consequently, landowner 1 will get $2,000 for the 2 acres being taken, whereas landowner 2 will get $20,000.

That is the explanation as to why there is a vast difference between the compensation for these two landowners. However, the value could be more drastic in another scenario. If the government finds out that the landowner with 200 acres also has a contiguous tract with 800 acres, the compensation might then be determined based on the market value of a 1,000-acre tract. That amount might be $800 per acre, so now the compensation to landowner 1 totals $1,600, compared to landowner 2, who is getting $20,000.

The key to this is how the appraiser determines what the larger parcel is because, in a partial taking, that factor can have a significant effect on the value of the taking. This determination is complicated by various rules, which are beyond the scope of this book, but suffice it to say, it is important for the reviewer to know and understand the basic concept. The larger parcel issue is a consideration for an eminent domain appraisal that would not be an issue in a typical appraisal.

In a normal sale, if a neighbor wanted to buy 2 acres from landowner 1, the landowner would research prices and sell it for the going price for 2 acres, and would not base the sale amount on the amount of land that he or she already owns. Likewise, an appraiser hired to value the 2-acre parcel would not consider what the 2 acres were being taken from; the appraiser would be concerned with only the value of the property being sold.

The process is explained in a slightly different way in the following instructions for the appraiser from the *Uniform Appraisal Standards for Federal Land Acquisitions.* In this note, the appraiser finds that the 10-acre parcel is the larger parcel and not the 200-acre parcel:

> For instance, if an appraiser determined that the larger parcel was a 10-acre tract out of a total ownership of 200 acres, the unit (e.g., per square foot; per acre) value may well be different for the smaller tract, and the appraiser would utilize comparable sales similar in size to the 10-acre larger parcel, rather than sales similar in size to the entire 200-acre ownership.[13]

Since these rules can be complicated, it is advisable for the reviewer to get professional help from an appraiser and/or an attorney who specializes in eminent domain if there is a question about the valuation. It should be remembered not only that the federal rules are complex but also that the state rules may vary from the federal rules.

Red Flag

In an eminent domain appraisal, if there is a partial taking, there may be an error over what was determined by the appraiser to be the larger parcel, and that error can have a significant effect on the final valuation. If the reviewer has a question about this, it is advised that an appraiser and/or attorney who is an expert in eminent domain be retained.

Chapter 5

Analyzing the Commercial Appraisal

Commercial appraisals include a wide range of income-producing properties, such as apartment complexes, retail strip centers, shopping centers, office buildings, medical buildings, and hotels and motels. The income approach to value is the predominant and normally the most reliable approach to use for appraising income-producing commercial properties.

The Income Approach

The income approach is based on the principle of *anticipation* that can be defined as follows:

> The perception that value is created by the expectation of benefits to be derived in the future.[1]

This concept of anticipation might also be understood in considering what buyers and investors normally seek in purchasing income property: the highest profit for their investment. Consequently, an investor might be willing to pay a certain amount for a property based on the present worth of what the buyer perceives will be future benefits.

To determine this, the buyer will most likely use the most basic income approach, which is called *direct capitalization*.

Direct Capitalization

Direct capitalization is a tool investors use to determine how much income a property will make in a year, and an understanding of this is necessary to properly review a commercial appraisal. It is defined by *The Dictionary of Real Estate Appraisal* as follows:

1. A method used to convert an estimate of a single year's income expectancy into an indication of value in one direct step, either by dividing the income estimate by an appropriate rate or by multiplying the income estimate by an appropriate factor.
2. A capitalization technique that employs capitalization rates and multipliers extracted from sales. Only the first year's income is considered. Yield and value change are implied, but not identified.[2]

It may also be defined, in its most basic sense, as a method to convert the income of a property into an indication of value.

The Concept

Another way of looking at direct capitalization is with the simple concept that if a buyer has a choice between two assets that are alike, the buyer will pay more for the one that makes more money. As previously stated, the premise that investors will pay a certain amount of money for an investment based on the expected profits they hope to receive from that investment is the foregone conclusion. And when comparing investment opportunities, direct capitalization is the standard method used by investors and appraisers to determine which investment yields the most profit.

Just as a person chooses the best interest rate from a variety of banks offering savings accounts, the real estate investor considers the rate of return offered by income-producing properties by calculating the capitalization rate. However, with savings accounts that are FDIC insured funds, the saver will probably have to consider only the rate, whereas the real estate investor will have other considerations besides the capitalization rate. Moreover, the way the rate is computed—that is the underlying information on which the rate is based, is an important aspect of determining the validity of the rate and, hence, the value of the property.

The primary advantage, then, of the direct capitalization income approach is that it approximates the thinking of the typical investor. The approach measures income for only one year, but the investor will often extrapolate that to consider what the income might become in future years. Direct capitalization is a starting point for many investors because the first question they may have is, "What is the cap (capitalization) rate?"

The disadvantages of the approach stem from the fact that there are many aspects to consider, including how the income data is analyzed and interpreted by those who compute the rate. It is also subject to manipulation, and a slight change in data may effect a major change in the value conclusion.

Market Extraction Method

The reliability of the rate also diminishes when the method used to compute the rate does not come from the market. In other words, appraisers typically look at other sales to determine the capitalization rate to use, and that method (the *market extraction method*) is the only one that many reviewers would consider reliable because it is based on the actions of buyers and sellers in the marketplace. It is also the only one discussed in detail in this book.

Other methods are considered to be more susceptible to manipulation and subjectivity. It is highly recommended that if another method is encountered in an appraisal, the reviewer should question why that method was used rather than the market extraction method. The explanation of how the other methods are used is beyond the scope of this book, but the following is a brief explanation of some of them.

Buildup Method

In the *buildup method* (sometimes called the *built-up method*), a rate is determined by analyzing components of the rate. The two basic components are the *recapture rate* and the *interest rate*. This method is based on the concept that the investor for the property expects to get a *return of the investment*—that is, the sales price at the end of the term of ownership, which is also called *capital recapture*. The investor also expects a *return on the investment*, which is the investor's profit on the money used to buy the property, and it is referred to as the *return on rate*, as well as some other names.

Band of Investment Method

In the *band of investment method*, the appraiser considers the financial components or bands of debt and equity capital required to support the investment. It takes into account the rate required by the lender and the rate necessary for the equity investor's desired pretax flow.

Yield Capitalization Method

In the *yield capitalization method*, the real estate investment return is separated into two components. One is the income flow for a specified number of years, and the other is a capital change (gain or loss) that results at the end of the multiyear investment period from an assumption that the property will be sold then. It is computed on a cash account basis from the investor's point of view.

There are also other methods such as the *annuity method*, *building residual technique*, and *land residual technique*. However, to reiterate, none of these methods are considered as reliable as the market extraction method, and it is advised that the reviewer consider the use of these methods questionable for properties for which comparable sales are available from which rates can be extracted.

The Formula

The formula for direct capitalization is often referred to as the *income, rate, value* (IRV) *formula* because it is calculated as follows, depending on what is sought:

To Find the Capitalization Rate

$$\text{Rate} = \text{income divided by value, or } R = \frac{I}{V}$$

To Find the Income

$$\text{Income} = \text{rate times value, or } I = R \times V$$

To Find the Value

$$\text{Value} = \text{income divided by rate, or } V = \frac{I}{R}$$

A simple example would be an investment that costs $1 million and has an income of $100,000 a year:

$$\begin{aligned}\text{Rate} &= \text{income divided by value, or } \frac{I}{V}\\ &= \frac{\$100{,}000}{\$1{,}000{,}000}\\ &= 10 \text{ percent}\end{aligned}$$

The Income Factor

The income used in this formula is what is called the *net operating income* (NOI). However, there are several steps needed to get to the net operating income. To begin the process, the appraiser must start with the property's *actual gross income*, which might be defined as the property's total income from all sources for one year. Using the example of an apartment complex, this income would include rent, as well as income from other sources such as laundry services, vending machines, parking fees, and interest earned on security deposits held in the bank. The rents for the apartments should be confirmed by ledgers that show what the current rents are. In some cases, if it is possible, tenants might be interviewed to confirm the ledger amounts. If the complex is large, then a sampling of tenants might be sufficient if there is a lack of other verifiable evidence. If there is a question about the veracity of the stated income, the reviewer might want to ask for further information.

An example might be a 24-unit apartment complex. The complex has 20 units that are two-bedroom apartments and 4 that are one-bedroom apartments. The actual gross income (also called *contract rent*) for the property might look as it is shown in Exhibit 5.1.

This spreadsheet shows the actual gross income for one year, but it is not the income the appraiser will use to determine the value. The appraiser will examine the rents for the units to determine if they are at market or not. Normally, they will be at market or below market, and most likely the latter because landlords are rarely able to keep increasing rent right up to the market rent. Moreover, leases are often signed that limit the rent until the lease expires, although some rental agreements include escalators, which build in increases at certain times during the lease. If the rent is above market, it could be the result of escalators that are higher than market. Otherwise, if the rents are above market, the veracity of the reported rents might come into question.

Exhibit 5.1
Rent Schedule

RENT SCHEDULE										
No of	Room Count			Total	Sq. Ft.	Vacant	SCHEDULED RENTS		
Units	TOT	BR	BA	Rooms	per Unit	Units	Unf	Furn	Total Rent
20	4	2	1	80	710	0		$ 515	$10,300
4	3	2	1	12	598	0		$ 460	$1,840
Laundry Income									$1,540
Interest Income									$ 345
Total Gross Monthly Income									$14,025
Total Gross Annual Income									$168,300

Red Flag

If the income for the subject property is inaccurate, the final value in the appraisal will also be inaccurate. It is important for the reviewer to have credible evidence of the actual income, especially if it seems significantly lower or higher than incomes for similar properties.

The appraiser will seek to determine what is called the *potential gross income* (PGI), which will include estimates for *economic rent* or *market rent*. These two terms refer to the amount of rent the apartments could rent for if the rents were current. A savvy investor will consider what the maximum rents might be and may plan to raise them after the purchases, providing there are no leases that prevent an increase. In the spreadsheet in Exhibit 5.2, the economic rent has been estimated.

In addition to the economic rent as listed in Exhibit 5.2, there is also a price per square foot and per room for the apartments. It appears from this information that the scheduled rents are significantly lower than the economic rent. Because there is such a difference, it would be important to know the reason why, which may be stated in the appraisal. It may be that the landlord has kept rents low because he or she has good tenants and the landlord does not want them to have a reason to vacate, which is often the case. Nevertheless, whatever

Exhibit 5.2
Rent Schedule with Economic Rent

RENT SCHEDULE														
No of	Room Count			Total	Sq. Ft.	Vacant	SCHEDULED RENTS			ECONOMIC RENTS				
Units	TOT	BR	BA	Rooms	per Unit	Units	Unf	Furn	Total Rent	Unf	Furn	Total Rent	Per S.F.	Per Rm
20	4	2	1	80	710	0	$ 515		$10,300	$ 700		$14,000	$ 0.99	$ 175
4	3	2	1	12	598	0	$ 460		$1,840	$ 600		$2,400	$1.00	$200
Laundry Income									$1,540			$1,600		
Interest Income									$ 345			$ 240		
Total Gross Monthly Income									$14,025			$18,240		
Total Gross Annual Income									$168,300			$218,880		

the reason is, it should be understood by the reviewer because it will have a major effect on the final value conclusion.

The appraisal will most likely include a rent survey that has a compilation of rents for similar properties. The appraiser will probably quote the source for this survey, and it might be a secondhand survey. The term *secondhand*, in this case, means a survey that was conducted by a third party, such as a local real estate company. This type of information may look official, but it is actually much poorer evidence of the market rent than a firsthand survey conducted directly by the appraiser. One of the reasons is that rent surveys are often more general surveys and may include rents from properties that are not similar to the subject property. They also normally include very large apartment complexes because real estate companies can more easily track rents with these types of properties.

In our example, the subject property is a small complex, and rents should be derived from similar properties. Small apartment complexes may have fewer amenities than large ones, but they may also be preferred because many renters do not like large complexes. Therefore, one cannot conclude that rents would be higher or lower between the two types of properties. However, one can conclude that there is enough dissimilarity that the rent survey may not be accurate when rents from large complexes are applied to a smaller complex, and vice versa.

There is a relatively easy way for the reviewer to check the rent survey for accuracy. Even if the reviewer is in a different part of the country, local rents can be found using the Internet to search the area where the property is located. A search on Craigslist or a similar website that advertises rentals can give the reviewer a good idea of what apartments are renting for that are similar to the subject. The appraiser may also have used this source, but the reviewer can verify the accuracy of the appraiser's research with a minimal investment of time.

Leases are another issue to consider. The appraiser may not be aware of leases that exist on the property and may be using a potential gross income that is not reachable for several years due to lease commitments. This is often more of an issue with retail and other commercial properties than it is with apartments because businesses often sign long-term leases. If the appraiser discusses the leases in the report, the reviewer may want to confirm what is said or request a copy of the leases if that is possible. The reviewer should not assume that the appraiser's information about the leases is accurate unless the leases are included in the report or the source is given with contact information. Mistakes in this area are often made, and sometimes erroneous information is given to the appraiser. A brief discussion with the owner or manager might have been the only source for the information, and if it was erroneous, the value conclusion can be skewed.

Effective Gross Income

Once the potential gross income is determined, the next step for the appraiser is to adjust it to get the *effective gross income* (EGI). Exhibit 5.3 gives the formula and calculation to compute the effective gross income for our example.

As demonstrated in Exhibit 5.3, the effective gross income is calculated by subtracting the vacancy rate and collection losses from the potential gross income. To get an accurate estimate for these two numbers, it is important to have historical rental data on the subject property. The appraiser may have a survey showing that the vacancy rate is 5 percent, but that number assumes certain things that may not apply to the subject property. For instance, if the subject property is located adjacent to a busy freeway and there is a lot of traffic noise, the vacancy for the subject property may be much higher than

Exhibit 5.3
Calculating the Effective Gross Income

CALCULATING EFFECTIVE GROSS INCOME			
	POTENTIAL GROSS INCOME		$218,880
MINUS	Vacancy Rate	5%	$ 10,944
MINUS	Collection Losses	0.7%	$ 1,532
EQUALS	Effective Gross Income		$206,404

5 percent. There could be other issues that might diminish or increase the vacancy factor that are specific to the subject property but not common to most properties.

If a survey provided by others is used, the appraiser should explain the source and how it was conducted. Often surveys track only certain properties. If the subject is an office building, a national real estate company may track several office buildings in the subject's city. If it is an apartment complex, there may be several complexes that are tracked. Understanding the source of the survey will help the reviewer determine how similar, and hence applicable, the other properties are to the subject property.

The other item to subtract is *collection losses*. In most appraisals, the vacancy percentage and the collection losses will be combined into one percentage. Often 5 percent is the lowest one might see, but there are cases in which the vacancy factor can be lower.

With some retail spaces, generally in shopping malls, tenants might be allowed to stay for free. They pay no rent because the mall does not want empty spaces that would cause more tenants to leave, which in turn would cause fewer people to shop there. In such cases, the free rentals must be considered as vacant. Moreover, with such a property, the future viability of its continuing to function is problematic and should be considered by the appraiser.

The free rent should not be confused with *concessions*, which are given to renters of apartments or commercial properties. Concessions such as one month's free rent might be used to entice a new tenant, but they do not necessarily mean the complex is in financial trouble. With commercial retail and office space, there are often concessions that might include a remodel of the space based on a fairly long term lease. In such cases, the actual rent can be calculated by dividing the cost of the concession or free rent by the term of the lease, as shown in Exhibit 5.4.

As seen in the spreadsheet, whether it is actual rent that is not charged or some modification of the space, the value of the concession is $12,000. Over the five-year lease period, the rent would then be $3,800 per month rather than $4,000 per month. Appraisals may show concessions in

Exhibit 5.4

Adjustment for Rent Concession

ADJUSTMENT FOR RENT CONCESSION							
Rent per Month	Annual	Lease Term Years	Rent for 5 Years	Concession Value	5 Years Minus Concession	Annual Minus Concession	Monthly Minus Concession
$ 4,000	$ 48,000	5	$ 240,000	$ 12,000	$ 228,000	$ 45,600	$ 3,800

different ways, but if concessions are the norm for renting the spaces, they should be considered in any projection of potential rents.

Income Information Accuracy

The income information that is used for the appraisal may also be sullied by the fact that the owner may not have audited financial information. Another problem could be that the owner may produce income tax returns, but he or she may have erroneously deducted some expenses for the property as a way of reducing the income taxes. In the first situation, the profits for property may be exaggerated, but in the second situation the actual expenses would be less than what was reported.

In other words, the source of the income information is always in question when the income approach is used; therefore, the reviewer of the appraisal should consider its fallibility. In the appraisal, the appraiser has probably made estimates for expenses in addition to considering the actual reported expenses, and those estimates should be considered and compared to typical percentages for similar properties. For instance, it may be that expenses generally run around 40 percent for most apartment complexes similar to the subject property, but the subject is reporting expenses of only 30 percent. If the appraiser is also using 30 percent, and that figure is not supported by expense ratios for other properties listed in the report, the report should state the reason why.

The Internet can also be a good source for expense ratios as can reports compiled by major real estate brokerages, which may often be obtained for free by asking. These reports are usually composed of averages and are not specific to a particular property, but if the reviewer can get this data, it will provide a benchmark for comparison against the expense ratio in the appraisal.

Red Flag

If the income information is inaccurate, then the entire income approach will be inaccurate. Therefore, if the source of the information cannot be verified, or it cannot be trusted for some reason, the value estimate for the income approach is immediately questionable. The sales comparison approach may be used to corroborate the value reached by the income approach if there is a question about the income data.

Expenses

The operating statement is an important part of the income approach. It should be modified for different types of accounting and for personal or nontypical expenses.

The Operating Statement

The operating statement will supply most of the information to the appraiser. It can be prepared in one of two ways. The first method is the *cash basis*, in which cash income is recorded when it is received, and expenses are recorded when they are actually paid. The other method is the *accrual basis*, in which income is reported in a certain period even if it has not been actually received in that period, and expenses are reported in the same period regardless of whether they were actually paid in that period. It is often the case that businesses use the accrual basis, whereas individuals use the cash basis.

The appraiser has to know which method was used to modify the statement for the appraisal. Consequently, the operating statement will be modified for the type of accounting used and for the items that are not applicable to the appraisal. It will also be modified to take out expenses that would not be applicable to the typical buyer.

Excluded Expenses

When buyers consider purchasing income-producing properties, they normally also look at costs and benefits that relate to their personal situation, but these items would not be part of the appraisal. Some of these are expenses that would be used for accounting purposes, and the appraiser should take these out of the operating statement in reconstructing it for appraisal purposes. The following is a list of such items.

Financing Costs

The appraisal is performed without considering what the financing expenses or the interest rate might be. (There is an exception to this, which would be the *mortgage equity capitalization method*, but it is not considered a particularly reliable method, and it is beyond the scope of this book.) However, in using comparable sales, financing is considered by the appraiser because certain types of favorable financing may influence the sale price of the property. This may seem like a contradiction, but it is not: essentially the appraiser considers that the financing for the subject property will be typical in competing with other properties that have sold, so it is only the anomalous sale that would require an adjustment. As previously stated, adjustments are always made to the comparable sales and not the subject property.

An example would be an owner-financed sale with an interest rate 2 percentage points below the current lending rate from lending institutions. In such a case, the lower rate would require an adjustment to the selling price (reflected in a financing adjustment made to the comparable sales), which would effectively raise the price of the sold property as a counterbalance to the extremely favorable financing.

Income Taxes

Buyers will calculate the depreciation for the property, and that is part of their financial planning. One buyer might consider a *cost segregation study* (a breakdown of items in the building that can be depreciated more quickly under IRS rules) to increase depreciation, whereas another will take the standard depreciation for the whole building. In any event, the personal income tax situation of the buyer will unquestionably influence the buyer's behavior, *but this relates to the buyer and not to the property, so it would not be considered in the valuation.*

Included Expenses

Management expenses are expenses that the appraiser will consider, but with smaller properties or properties with triple net leases (leases are explained in Chapter 7), the buyer may decide to self-manage. The appraiser will use typical management expenses, so if the owner self-manages, there would be a savings to the owner but not one that would be reflected in the appraisal.

The exception to this might be for very small income properties. Sometimes an appraiser will leave out a management fee if owner management is considered the norm. Since this will affect the final value, the appraiser should state how this factor correlates to the compilation of sales from which the capitalization rate was estimated. The appraiser should have clear evidence that the comparable sales did not include a deduction for management fees. Management fees are normally in the range of 3 to 10 percent, depending on the duties required.

Reserves for Replacements

This is also called a *replacement allowance*, and it is defined in *The Dictionary of Real Estate Appraisal* as follows:

> **Replacement allowance:** An allowance that provides for the periodic replacement of building components that wear out more rapidly than the building itself and must be replaced during the building's economic life.[3]

The idea behind this is that there should be an adjustment for money needed for improvements such as new carpeting, roofing, flooring, appliances, hot water heaters, HVAC items, parking lot asphalt, and painting. Instead of subtracting the whole amount for these items, the appraiser estimates what will be needed for them and amortizes the expense over the years of the life of the item. For example:

Cost of new roof	$10,000
Life of roof	20 years
Annual reserve allowance for roof	$500

There has been some debate about using reserves for several reasons because of the way it affects the capitalization rate. When appraisers get rates from other properties, there is no certainty as to whether the rate was computed using reserves, and if it was, the question arises as to how the estimate was made. In an apartment complex, was there a reserve for each appliance, and if so, what life was assigned to them? Was it 3 years for a dishwasher or 8 years? Was it 20 years for the roof or 30 years? Was resurfacing of the parking lot considered or not? Was there a reserve for the sidewalks, and how many years were estimated for tearing them out and installing new concrete? It is easy to see why it is important in reading an appraisal to understand how these calculations may affect the value conclusion.

Red Flag

Estimates for reserves and replacements can vary a great deal between appraisers, and the amount of the estimates can make a significant difference in the final value. The variance can be found in the cost and life expectancy of the appliances, carpet, and other items, and the estimate of the cost for reroofing and other anticipated maintenance. Appraisals can be inflated or deflated based on these estimates.

Exhibit 5.5 is a full list of expenses that one might find in an appraisal for an apartment complex. It comes from a commonly used appraisal form: Freddie Mac Form 71A.[4]

Exhibit 5.5

List of Expenses for an Appraisal of an Apartment Complex

ANNUAL EXPENSE ANALYSIS

ITEM	☐ ACTUAL ___ (yr.) ☐ PROPOSED	APPRAISER'S FORECAST	APPRAISER'S CALCULATIONS OR COMMENTS
FIXED EXPENSES:			
1. Real Estate Taxes	$	$	☐ Actual ☐ Est. Total Assessment Value $ % of Value Tax Rate Per $100 $
2. Other taxes or assessments			
3. Insurance			
4. Licenses			
5. Unsubordinated ground rent			
OPERATIONAL EXPENSES:			
6. Fuel	$	$	
7. Gas			
8. Electricity			
9. Water & sewer			
10. Trash removal			
11. Pest control			
12. Building maintenance & repairs			
13. Interior & exterior decorating			
14. Cleaning expenses			
15. Supplies			
16. Elevator maintenance			
17. Pool maintenance			
18. Parking area maint. & snow removal			
19. Gardening			
20. Nonresident management			
21. Resident manager's salary (No._____)			
22. Resident manager's apt. allowance			
23. Custodian's salary (No. _________)			
24. Custodian's apt. allowance			
25. Engineer's salary (No. __________)			
26. Elevator operator's salary (No.________)			
27. Telephone operator's salary (No._______)			
28. Security personnel's salary (No._______)			
29. Other salaries (No.__________)			
30. Payroll taxes			
31. Advertising			
32. Telephone			
33. Legal & audit			
34. Leased furniture			
35.			
36.			
REPLACEMENT RESERVES:			
37. Carpeting & drapes	$	$	
38. Ranges & refrigerators			
39. Dishwashers & disposals			
40. Individual heating & AC units			
41.			
42.			
TOTAL EXPENSES & REPLACEMENT RESERVES	$	$	

Comments (identify items by number): ____________________

INCOME APPROACH

Total Gross Annual Economic Income (See Rent Schedule) .... $ __________

Less Forecasted Vacancy and Collection Loss .... (_______%) .... $ (__________)

Effective Gross Annual Income .... $ __________

Less Forecasted Annual Expenses and Replacement Reserves (_________% of Total Gross Annual Economic Income) .... $ (__________)

Net Annual Income from Total Property .... $ __________

Less Return on and Recapture of Depreciated Value of Furnishings ($__________ @ _________%) .... $ (__________)

Net Annual Income from Real Property .... $ __________

Detail clearly method and mathematics of capitalizing Net Annual Income from Real Property __________

INDICATED VALUE BY INCOME APPROACH .... $__________

Rounded to .... $ __________

Freddie Mac Form 71A (04/2004), Page 7 of 8

Source: Adapted from the Freddie Mac Form 71A that can be found at http://www.freddiemac.com/multifamily/mf_forms/pdf/f71a.pdf.

Chapter 6

Commercial Appraisal Excerpts

The following are excerpts with some related commentary from the appraisal of an apartment complex, which used a form rather than a narrative format. Exhibit 6.1, the first portion of the form, shows the entries for expenses, followed by the income approach information.

Note that the appraiser has made some notes explaining why the forecast may differ from the actual expenses. Here the forecast is about $11,000 lower than the actual expenses. The explanations for the reason that the forecast is lower are important. It appears that the appraiser has adequately explained them in the comments.

In order to estimate the rent for the subject property, the appraiser has researched other rentals and has found three comparable properties, as shown in Exhibit 6.2, from which to determine the market rent for the subject. Note that the property is located in a small town outside Portland, Oregon, and since there were few rentals in the area, rents from Portland are being used. The appraiser also notes that asking rents in the specific city were researched on Craigslist.

Since rents are rarely negotiated for apartments, the asking rent range is good evidence for the market rent estimate, which is shown in Exhibit 6.3. However, the rents from a more highly populated area

Exhibit 6.1
Annual Expense Analysis

ANNUAL EXPENSE ANALYSIS			
ITEM	☒ ACTUAL 2011 (yr.) ☐ PROPOSED	APPRAISER'S FORECAST	APPRAISER'S CALCULATIONS OR COMMENTS
FIXED EXPENSES:			
			☒ Actual ☐ Est. Total Assessed Value $
1. Real Estate Taxes			varies % of Value Tax Rate Per $100 $
	$ 14,800	$ 20,301	Taxes paid were from call to assessor. Measure 50
2. Other Taxes or Assessments	425	425	taxable assessed value from becoming market
3. Insurance	7,191	7,191	value. Property is under appeal to have taxes
4. Licenses			lowered according to owner.
5. Unsubordinated Ground Rent			
OPERATIONAL EXPENSES:			
6. Fuel	$	$	
7. Gas			
8. Electricity	2,555	2,600	
9. Water & Sewer	4,634	4,700	
10. Trash Removal	3,375	3,400	
11. Pest Control			
12. Building Maintenance & Repairs	24,511	24,000	Many repairs previous year - this may be high.
13. Interior & Exterior Decorating			
14. Cleaning Expenses			
15. Supplies	1,220	300	
16. Elevator Maintenance			
17. Pool Maintenance			
18. Parking Area Maint. & Snow Removal			
19. Gardening	11,207	6,000	Appears high - notes say plants bought 2011
20. Nonresident Management	16,799	17,000	
21. Resident Manager's Salary (No.____)	6,116	6,200	
22. Resident Manager's Apt. Allowance			
23. Custodian's Salary (No.____)			
24. Custodian's Apt. Allowance			
25. Engineer's Salary (No.____)			
26. Elevator Operator's Salary (No.____)			
27. Telephone Operator's Salary (No.____)			
28. Security Personnel's Salary (No.____)			
29. Other Salaries (No.____)	600	600	Workman's comp
30. Payroll Taxes	2,064	1,000	Based on current payroll
31. Advertising		300	
32. Telephone	2,289	2,100	
33. Legal & Audit	8,921	2,500	Special legal issue for 2011 increased actual
34. Leased Furniture			
35. Training Expense	1,230	0	Not necessary in typical cases
36. Other admin. exp.	2,080	1,500	
REPLACEMENT RESERVES:			
37. Carpeting & Drapes	$	$	
38. Ranges & Refrigerators			
39. Dishwashers & Disposals			
40. Individual Heating & AC Units			
41. Reserve, replacements	5,991	5,500	
42.			
TOTAL EXPENSES & REPLACEMENT RESERVES	$ 116,008	$ 105,617	

Comments (identify items by number): Actual management expenses appear high for a conventional value. This property operates under USDA standards, which requires audits the complex would not need normally. Training expense was also deemed unneeded for a typical property. Expense ratio is high compared to typical apartments.

would normally be suspect without the Craigslist information because often rents are lower in less urban areas. In this appraisal, the rents on the apartments are restricted, and this is noted in the comments. The value is therefore hypothetical.

Exhibit 6.2
Comparable Rental Data

COMPARABLE RENTAL DATA												
Comparables selected are the most recent rentals, similar and proximate, known to the undersigned, that a tenant of subject property would have given consideration to renting.												
ITEM	COMPARABLE NO. 1				COMPARABLE NO. 2				COMPARABLE NO. 3			
Address or location	2345 SE 135th Ave. Portland OR 97233				38620 Pleasant Ave. Sandy, OR 97055				6739 SE Woodstock Blvd Portland, OR 97206			
Proximity to Subject	21.99 miles W				1.03 miles N				21.4 miles W			
Map Code												
Date of Rental Survey	2/12/2013				2/12/2013				2/12/2013			
Brief Description of Property Improvements	No. Units: 28 No. Vac.: N/A Yr. Blt.: 1972 Closer in than Sandy				No. Units: 8 No. Vac.: N/A Yr. Blt.: 1972				No. Units: 10 No. Vac.: N/A Yr. Blt.: 1960 Closer in location, older apartments than subject. Size for apartment is estimate for this one - could not get info.			
Quality & Condition	Quality Avg Condition Avg				Quality Avg Condition Avg				Quality Avg Condition Avg			
	Unit Rm Count	Size	Monthly Rent		Unit Rm Count	Size	Monthly Rent		Unit Rm Count	Size	Monthly Rent	
	Tot. BR B	Sq. Ft.	$	per sq. ft.	Tot. BR B	Sq. Ft.	$	per sq. ft.	Tot. BR B	Sq. Ft.	$	per sq. ft.
Individual Unit Breakdown	12 1 1	600	605	1.01¢	4 2 1	700	630	0.90 ¢	2 2 1	750	695	0.93¢
	4 2 1	900	758	0.84¢	4 3 1.1	900	730	0.81 ¢	7 1 1	600	650	1.08¢
	14 3 1.1	1100	880	0.80¢				¢	1 1 1	600	425	0.71¢
				¢				¢				¢
				¢				¢				¢
				¢				¢				¢
				¢				¢				¢
				¢				¢				¢
Utilities, furniture and amenities included in rent	Water/Sewer/Trash				Water/Sewer/Trash				Water/Sewer/Trash Not certain why one of the apartments is such low rent compared to other seven.			
Comparison to Subject	Closer in to Portland. Older than subject which was built in 1988.				Is also comp 2 for sales. Older than subject which was built in 1988. Rents appear low on this property due to existing leases, but it was used because of the location. Survey of Sandy/Gresham of rents on Craigslist show most 1BR 600 +, 2BR 700 +				Older than subject which was built in 1988.			
General comments (including any rental concessions) if applicable: Some of these rents could increase in some cases, as leases keep rents lower and there has been a recent increase in rental demand, thus rent prices are rising.												

Red Flag

If the estimated economic rent is much higher than the actual rent, it is important that the comparable rents back up the conclusion. There may also be a specific reason for the difference, such as rent restrictions that exist on the property.

Exhibit 6.3

Monthly Rent Schedule

MONTHLY RENT SCHEDULE–SUBJECT PROPERTY

Rental schedule is shown by type of units. Scheduled rents are actual rentals for an existing property, or projected rents for a proposed or incomplete building. Economic rents are forecasted rents to indicate the fair market rental the subject units would command if available for rent on the open market.

No. of Units	Unit Rm. Count Tot.	BR	B	Total Rooms	Sq. Ft. Area Per Unit	No. Units Vacant	SCHEDULED RENTS Per Unit Unfurn.	Per Unit Furn.	Total Rents	ECONOMIC RENTS Per Unit Unfurn.	Per Unit Furn.	Total Rents	Per Sq. Ft. or Room	
4	4	2	1	16	710		$ 515	$	$ 2,060	$ 700	$	$ 2,800	0.99¢	$ 175
24	3	1	1	72	598	0	460		11,040	600		14,400	1.00	200
28	←TOTAL→			88					$ 13,100			$ 17,200		

OTHER MONTHLY INCOME

	Scheduled	Economic
Parking	$	$
Laundry Income	$ 3,756	$ 167
Commercial Space	$	$
Tenant Charges	$	$
Interest income	$	$
Total Gross Monthly Income	$ 16,856	$ 17,367
Total Gross Annual Income	$ 202,272	$ 208,404

Utilities Included in Scheduled (actual) Rents: ☒ Water ☐ Gas ☐ Heat ☐ Electric ☐ Air Conditioning ☒ Sewer, Trash

Utilities Included in Economic Rents: ☒ Water ☐ Gas ☐ Heat ☐ Electric ☐ Air Conditioning ☒ Sewer, Trash

If proposed project or project under construction, the rent up time necessary, after completion, to lease 80% of the units at the projected economic rents is estimated to be ________ months.

Comments (including any rental concessions in scheduled rents, or anticipated in economic rents; if none, so state). Rents may be declining in this market and conservative estimates were used. THIS IS A HYPOTHETICAL VALUE - IT WAS VALUED AS IF THERE WERE NO RENT RESTRICTIONS. No income from laundry - machines are from vendor. Survey of Sandy/Gresham of rents on Craigslist show rents begin at: 1BR $600 + and 2BR $700 +. Lowest 1BR in Sandy was $595 - everything else was higher. Note: Income for laundry, etc. average $2,000 per year for 2009, 2010 and 2011. Appraiser put average in for current appraisal.

The final value for the income approach on the form in Exhibit 6.4 shows the impact of the expense ratio, vacancy rate, and collection loss percentage.

The form in Exhibit 6.5 shows the market approach, also called the *comparable sales approach*. (The one-page form is shown over two pages for easy viewing.) Exhibit 6.6 provides the appraisal reconciliation.

Exhibit 6.4

Income Approach

INCOME APPROACH

Total Gross Annual Economic Income (See Rent Schedule)		$ 208,404
Less Forecasted Vacancy and Collection Loss	(3 %)	$(6,252)
Effective Gross Annual Income		$ 202,152
Less Forecasted Annual Expenses and Replacement Reserves (50.68 % of Total Gross Annual Economic Income)		$(105,617)
Net Annual Income from Total Property		$ 96,535
Less Return on and Recapture of Depreciated Value of Furnishings ($ 0 @ 0 %)		$( )
Net Annual Income from Real Property		$ 96,535

Detail clearly method and mathematics of capitalizing Net Annual Income from Real Property Capitalization rate is based on similar properties and takes into consideration condition and location of subject property. THIS IS A HYPOTHETICAL VALUE - IT WAS VALUED AS IF THERE WERE NO RENT RESTRICTIONS OR SUBSIDIES. Vacancy is currently zero and demand appears to be increasing or staying the same, thus the 3% vacancy. 6.7% cap rate equals a value of $1,441,000 rounded. Well adds value of about $10,000. Total is $1,451,000 rounded.
Cap rates for other sales are: 1. **3803 SE Cesar Chavez, Ptld sold 2/2/2012 6.56%, 6110 SE 52nd Ave, Ptld, sold 12/20/2012 6.59%, 12730 SE Mcloughlin Blvd, Ptld, sold 7/1/2011 7%, 2717 SE Courtney Ave., Milwaukie, OR 7.29%.** ***Note that rates have declined on later sales in 2012 into the 6 range where as older sales are in the 7 range.*** **Cap rate range is 6.5 to 7.**

INDICATED VALUE BY INCOME APPROACH	$
Rounded to	$ 1,451,000

Exhibit 6.5

Market Approach

MARKET APPROACH

The market data selected are the most recent sales of properties, similar and proximate to subject, known to the appraiser, that a buyer of subject property would have given consideration to purchasing. In the absence of actual sales, listings of comparable properties may be used but an explanation must be included in the "Comments" section below.

ITEM	SUBJECT	COMPARABLE NO. 1	COMPARABLE NO. 2	COMPARABLE NO. 3
Address	39665 Albert St. Sandy	252 NE Kane Dr. Gresham OR 97030	38620 Pleasant Ave Sandy, OR 97055	12424 SE River Rd Milwaukie, OR 97222
Proximity to Subject		11.2 miles NW	1 mile N	24.3 miles W
Map Code	See attached map			
Lot Size	1.6 acres	1.11	14,000 SF Est.	25,000 SF Est.
Brief Description of Building Improvements	No. Units: 28 No. Vac.: Year Built: 1984 2 story, 4 buildings	No. Units: 25 No. Vac.: N/A Year Built: 1978 2 story	No. Units: 8 No. Vac.: N/A Year Built: 2 story	No. Units: 13 No. Vac.: N/A Year Built: 1977 2 story
Quality	Average	Average	Average	Average
Condition	Average	Average	Average	Average
Recreational Facilities	None	None	None	None
Pool	No	No	No	No
Parking	Adequate	Adequate	Adequate	Adequate
Tenant Appeal	Average	Average	Average	Average
Gross Bldg Area	19,402 (rentable 18,996)	21736	8144	11,730

Unit Breakdown	SUBJECT No. of Units	UNIT ROOM COUNT Tot.	BR	b	COMP. NO. 1 No. of Units	UNIT ROOM COUNT Tot.	BR	b	COMP. NO. 2 No. of Units	UNIT ROOM COUNT Tot.	BR	b	COMP. NO. 3 No. of Units	UNIT ROOM COUNT Tot.	BR	b
	2	3	1	1	4	5	3	1	4	4	2	1	13	4	2	1.5
	16	4	2	1	12	4	2	1	4	5	3	1.1				
	6	5	3	1.5	8	3	1	1								
					1	2	0	1								

ITEM	SUBJECT	COMPARABLE NO. 1	COMPARABLE NO. 2	COMPARABLE NO. 3
Util. Paid by Owner	Water, Sewer, Trash	Water, Sewer, Trash	Water, Sewer, Trash	Water, Sewer, Trash
Data Source	Management, Inspection	MLS and/or Loopnet	MLS and/or Loopnet	MLS and/or Loopnet
Price	$ N/A ☒ Unf. ☐ F	$ 1,525,000 ☒ Unf. ☐ F	$ 440,000 ☒ Unf. ☐ F	$ 960,000 ☒ Unf. ☐ F
Sale--Listing--Offer	N/A	1,725,000	499,000	975,000
Date of Sale	N/A	5/2/2012	8/17/2011	5/11/2011
Terms (Including conditions of sale and financing terms)		Cash sale. Cash tends to drive the price down since the seller does not have to wait for an appraisal and loan approval.	Conventional. Sold in 21 days - very quick sale which may have been underpriced. Older sale, and market has improved since then.	Conventional On market 196 days. Land for 4 more units. Older than subject by 10 years.

(Continued)

Exhibit 6.5
Continued

	Subject			
Gross Annual Income	$208,404	$191,031	$62,016	$101,831
Gross Ann. Inc. Mult. (1)		7.98	7.09	9.43
Net Annual Income	$Subject	$88,850	$34,906	$63,455
Expense Percentage (2)	Subject %	40.16 %	43.17 %	38.00 %
Overall Cap. Rate (3)	%	5.83 %	7.93 %	6.61 %
Price Per Unit	$	$61,000	$55,000	$73,846
Price Per Room	$	$23,828	$9,167	$12,632
Price Gross Bldg. Area	$ /sq. ft. bldg. area	$ 70.16 /sq. ft. bldg. area	$ 54.03 /sq. ft. bldg. area	$ 81.84 /sq. ft. bldg. area
COMMENTS		Ten years older than subject but closer in to Portland. Gresham, however if a less desirable area than Sandy.		
COMPARISON TO SUBJECT	See comments below.	Similar condition Different location but not better	Inferior condition Similar location	Similar condition Superior location

VALUE INDICATORS FOR THE SUBJECT PROPERTY		
	Indicated Gross Income Multiplier 8.00 X Gross Annual Economic Income $ 212,060	$ 1,696,480
	Indicated Value Per Unit $ 60,000.00 X 28 Units	$ 1,680,000
	Indicated Value Per Room $ 16,000.00 X 100 Rooms	$ 1,600,000
	Indicated Value Per Sq. Ft. of Gross Bldg. Area $ 65 X 18,730 Sq. Ft. Bldg. Area	$ 1,217,450
	Indicated Overall Capitalization Rate	6.7%

(1) Sale Price ÷ Gross Annual Income (2) Total Annual Expenses ÷ Total Gross Annual Income (3) Net Annual Income ÷ Price

RECONCILIATION: Sales were chosen that were in outlying areas which are considered somewhat comparable to the subject property. However, no other comparable sales could be found in the Sandy, the city where this property is located. It has a very small population. 39501 Evans (Firwood Apts) sold for $1,210,000 on May 25, 2012. This property could not be used as a comparable because it had subsidized rents from USDA and was also not marketed with MLS or Loopnet with normal market exposure. Even though the subject is USDA subsidized, the comparables in this appraisal are required to be market sales. Firwood was also in inferior condition to the subject property and had significant deferred maintenance.

INDICATED VALUE BY MARKET APPROACH	$ 1,550,000
Rounded to	$ 1,550,000

Exhibit 6.6
Reconciliation and Value Conclusion

RECONCILIATION AND VALUE CONCLUSION

Indicated Value by the Cost Approach	$
Indicated Value by the Market Approach	$1,550,000
Indicated Value by the Income Approach	$1,451,000

FINAL RECONCILIATION This property is in an outlying area, which in some ways is a detriment, in that the pool of potential renters is smaller. It will not draw from Portland, unless people have a particular reason to live in Sandy and commute. On the other hand, for those who wish to rent in Sandy, it competes only with other properties in that specific area, which is a benefit in that there are not many one bedroom apartments in the area, and the current vacancy rate is zero. A small 3% rate was used due to current strong demand for apartments, particularly one bedroom apartments. This property has a well that has some value as a back-up water supply. Because cap rate range is 6.5 to 7, and the market approach showed a higher value, weight was given to both approaches that stayed within the cap rate range. Bank interest rates are the lowest in decades and FDIC insured funds now bring less than 1% interest. Therefore, the demand for apartments with yields that are in this cap rate range has increased, as investors seek to get a better return.

Chapter 7

Analyzing the Industrial Building Appraisal

Industrial facilities that are functioning are often valued with a business income approach that captures the total value of the property, including buildings, land, machinery and equipment, and the value of intangibles such as goodwill, workforce in place, customer lists, and contracts.

However, if the appraisal does not utilize this approach, it will typically value the buildings, land, and machinery and equipment separately and then combine the estimates for a total value. If the property is valued in this manner, it will exclude intangible values, and it will use the methods discussed in this chapter to value the buildings.

Two Basic Categories of Industrial Buildings

Industrial structures typically fall into two basic categories: *general use* and *special use*. *Special-use properties* are normally built for a specific use and that use only, and they are therefore not easily adaptable or modified for alternative uses. In fact, to convert a special-use building to another use is normally neither cost-effective nor feasible. Conversely, *general-use properties* can be used for multiple purposes. These properties are generally of such a size, shape, and configuration that they can be used for different manufacturing processes or as warehouses, with relatively little or no modification.

Special-Use Buildings

Special-use buildings are normally buildings that were constructed (or modified) for a certain type of manufacturing. A paper mill is a good example of a special-use property because the buildings and structures are constructed specifically to house machines for the production of paper. If the facility were to close down, it would be possible to utilize the buildings for an alternative use, but it probably would not be cost-effective for several reasons. First, removing the equipment would be a major obstacle. Papermaking machines are huge, and the expense of taking one apart, even to sell for scrap metal, may not be worth the effort. Second, even if the machines were removed, the configuration and design of the buildings used for most paper mills make their utilization for another industry difficult without expensive modifications.

Chemical refineries are another example. They are generally built for a specific production or refining process, and the design precludes other uses. The value of special-use properties lies in the continued use of the property for the special purpose for which they were constructed.

Red Flag

If the appraisal is of a special-use building and the future of that industry is in question, the value of the building might drop significantly if the special use is not continued. The reviewer should consider this and question the appraiser about it if there is no mention of it in the appraisal.

If that use will not be continued for some reason—for instance, there is no longer a market for the item the company produces—the value should be based on an alternative use if there is one. But that alternative use will probably involve major modifications to the building, and an estimate for that conversion would be essential in determining the potential change in value should the use change.

General-Use Buildings

The category for general-use buildings includes buildings that can be used for many types of manufacturing or other business activities. General-use buildings are usually rectangular and range in height from 16 to 30 feet. They are the types of buildings that can also be used as warehouses or even large retail establishments. Plants that manufacture plastics, cut metal, or assemble parts to make a product are often general-use structures. What differentiates general-use from special-use buildings is that general-use buildings can be leased and sold for different uses, and a new tenant or owner could move in without a great amount of expense for modification. For general-use buildings, changes for a different use typically involve things like adding to the building's electrical power system, installing a bridge crane, or adding concrete foundations for heavy machinery while the building shell remains intact.

A general-use building can become a special-use building when improvements are made to the interior that will cost more to dismantle than the effort will be worth. For example, an underwater cable company that has built many large, aboveground concrete tanks in which to test its cables could operate in a building that would normally have multiple uses. However, in order to prepare the space used by the cable company for an alternative use, its tanks would have to be broken up and taken out. After that, the floor damage would have to be repaired. This might make conversion impractical because it would not be cost-effective.

Different Valuation Methods for the Two Categories

It is important for the appraiser to recognize the difference between these two types of buildings because it will be used to determine the valuation method for the subject property. The cost approach often will be the appraisal method used to value special-use buildings. The sales comparison or income approach will often be the appraisal method used to value general-use buildings. The term *income approach* is used here to denote a direct capitalization method that values the building and land only. It is not a business income methodology that would be used to value the whole plant. As previously mentioned, the business income approach would encompass not only the building and land but also the machinery and equipment and intangible values.

Building Characteristics That Should Be Included in the Appraisal

For either type of building, the appraisal should supply information about the construction of the building, which would include the type of structure, the height, and other aspects of the building's physical characteristics. If the plant is a special-use building, more data will probably be required than if it is a general-use building because typically the building will be more complex, and the special construction might increase the expense of building compared to a general-use structure. The following is some of the information the appraisal should include.

Type of Construction. Industrial buildings are generally concrete tilt-up, concrete block, poured concrete, or pre-engineered steel. Concrete tilt-up buildings are constructed by tilting up the walls from the ground. Older buildings constructed of wood may have a limited use because of their susceptibility to fire hazards.

Height and Other Measurements. There should be data not only on the square footage of the building but also on the cubic square footage. There are several heights that should have been measured, and they are typically taken from the floor of the building. If the roof has a slope to it, there is a distinction between the *ridge height*, which is the highest point in the middle of the roof, and the *eave height*, which is the edge and lowest point in the roof. The most important is the *clear height* because it defines the available operating area. It should have been measured from the floor to the bottom of the closest rafter or any other permanent obstruction. The reason this is important in valuing the building is that companies often need certain clear heights in order to store inventory with forklifts or to install a bridge crane to lift items from the floor for assembly. If the building has a lower clear height than is typical, the value may be diminished because the use is limited.

Characteristics of Concrete Floors. The thickness of floors varies from about 4 inches of concrete and up. Many buildings have 6-inch-thick concrete floors. Floors that are thinner limit the use and value of the building because they support less weight. For heavy machines, thicker concrete is often poured. For instance, a machine might have 12 to 36 inches of concrete under it, while the rest of the floor around it is 6 or 8 inches thick. A *super-flat floor* is an improvement that affects the value. This type of floor allows forklifts to travel faster and with more stability, which helps them operate in higher buildings. They are typically installed at the time that a building is constructed, but they can also be a modification in an older building.

Width of Bay. *Bay width* is the distance between supporting columns. Two measurements are often made. One is the distance from the center of one column to the center of another, and the other is the *clear span*, which is the distance between the columns. Older buildings may have narrower distances, which diminish usability and value.

Loading Docks. The number of loading docks should be noted. General-use buildings with too few loading docks may have less value.

Insulation. This feature can be expensive in a large building, and it may be more important in cold climates than in warmer climates.

Heating, Ventilation, and Air-Conditioning (HVAC). In reviewing the appraisal, note the type of HVAC system and whether it is typical for the area. In some climates, it is not unusual for manufacturing facilities to not have heating systems. Often, the heat from the machines and employees is sufficient. Suspended gas heaters are common for those that do have heat. Certain manufacturing processes require special ventilation, and these systems may become a superadequacy for another user of the building. Cooling systems, although rare, may be found in extremely hot climates or for manufacturing processes that produce high temperatures.

Amount and Quality of Office and Manufacturing Space. The ratio of the office to manufacturing space can affect the value, but this might be something the appraiser does not realize. In a typical general-use building the size of the office space is considerably less than the size of the manufacturing space. A normal amount of office space might be 10 to 15 percent of the size of the total facility. The exception to this would be if the facility is also the company headquarters, in which case the office space could be any size and may exceed the size of the manufacturing space. In the latter case, the property may be less marketable because the buyer or lessee would also have to want the large amount of office space, and there are fewer potential users for such properties.

Transportation Services. Does the building have rail service, or is it located on a waterway that has access to water transportation? Is it near major freeways, and does it have easy ingress and egress for large trucks? The appraiser should address any transportation services issues that may exist.

Utility Services. The appraiser should note the existing electric power capability of the building. Some manufacturing processes require more than others, and the more power that is available, the more potential buyers and lessees there may be.

Most industrial properties are on a sewer system. Rural industrial properties that are not served by a sewer system have very limited uses, which can drastically reduce the market value of the property.

An adequate water supply is also important. Some manufacturing processes, such as semiconductor manufacturing, paper manufacturing, and certain types of food processing, use huge quantities of water. Water may be limited in some areas, or the quality of water that is available may be an issue for some processes. Some facilities may have wells.

Unavailable or higher-than-average costs for utilities may exclude certain industrial uses and raise costs.

Fire Prevention Sprinklers. There are *wet* and *dry fire prevention sprinkler systems*—meaning that the sprinkler head will either have water in it already or it will be dry and water will be sent when needed. *Early suppression fast response* (ESFR) *systems* are able to respond more quickly to fires and put them out faster with less water damage, which can increase the value of the building. Older buildings that do not have sprinklers may be out of compliance with local codes, which will render them completely unusable or will limit the uses for the building. Lacking sprinklers, therefore, can greatly reduce the value of a property.

Yard Improvements. Yard improvements include items such as fencing, asphalt paving, gravel, concrete paving, a guard shack, and retention ponds. In addition, hidden items such as underground storage tanks, wells, water/oil separation systems, pipelines, gas pumps, and weigh stations need to be noted.

Condition of Improvements. The age and condition of any improvements should be clearly stated, and there should be sufficient photographs to back up the estimate by the appraiser. Any deferred maintenance should be commented on.

Red Flag

A lack of photographs of the building—such that the reviewer cannot determine the building's condition—is a good reason to require that the appraiser produce more photographs. Most appraisals should have complete photographs of the interior and exterior of the buildings, yard improvements, street scenes, and deferred maintenance issues.

Functional Problems. Examples of functional issues might be poor ingress and egress for trucks to access the property, inadequate parking for employees, and lower clear height than is typical for the type of building. Another consideration might be if the subject is surrounded by residential properties—in some cases subdivisions spring up after a plant has been built. This might make doing business for the manufacturer difficult, due to complaints by residents about noise, odors, and traffic.

Highest and Best Use Market Analysis

There are four criteria for highest and best use determinations, which are also listed in Chapter 1 but are repeated here:

1. **Legally permissible.** What are the zoning and building restrictions?
2. **Physically possible.** Can it be constructed on the site?
3. **Financially feasible.** Is it cost-effective?
4. **Maximally productive.** Is it the most financially rewarding use?

The criteria used for less complex properties are also applicable to industrial properties, but determining whether the criteria have been met may require more insight and consideration. This assessment by the appraiser will normally not be an issue for the reviewer unless the appraiser states that the highest and best use is something other than the current use. This criterion can be evaluated in two ways. First, it may apply to the use of the building. It would be rare if a building were being used for something less than its highest and best use, but is it possible. One example would be a building that has *flex spaces* that will bring in more rent when leased as individual units but is currently rented to one tenant.

Second, it may apply to the land. This would rarely be a factor because generally the land upon which an industrial property is constructed represents only a small fraction of the value of the total factory.

Consequently, with profitable manufacturing plants, the highest and best use is typically "as improved." Exceptions to this might include plants that are closed down or obsolete and near the end of their economic life, especially if they are located on rivers or other bodies of water or in residential communities that have grown up around them.

In any event, if the appraiser has speculated on a different use for the property than what it is currently being used for and he or she has valued it accordingly, it would be wise to make certain that the alternative use is actually viable. In the former example of the flex space leased to one tenant, the appraiser would have to prove that there is a market for smaller spaces, that those smaller spaces rented separately would bring in higher rent, and that the increased expense to manage and lease them as a collection of separate units would be cost-effective. Any change in the use of the land or buildings that requires approval at any echelon of government should be considered extremely speculative because there are often many legal, environmental, and other obstacles that preclude use changes. Appraisers are not always aware of such potential difficulties, nor do they always understand the expenses involved.

Red Flag

If the highest and best use for a property is determined by the appraiser to be a use other than the current use, it is important for the appraiser to document the likelihood of an actual change being effected due to the potential obstacles that government approvals may present. Moreover, the appraiser should notate the expense of changing the use in a way that proves that it is cost-effective.

To reiterate, regulations for land use have become exceedingly complex and ambiguous in some cities, placing many financial, political, and especially environmental obstacles in the path of those who would seek to develop property or change the use of it. Therefore, utmost care must be taken in predicting and estimating the value of any property based on an alternative use. Unless the appraiser is certain that a change is not only possible but also highly probable—and perhaps imminent—and also understands all of the fees involved (for example, brokerage fees, legal fees, engineering fees, or holding costs), a value based on a speculative alternative use might prove to be inaccurate.

The Cost Approach for Industrial Buildings

The cost approach is based on the *principle of substitution* in that it is predicated on the premise that a buyer will pay a certain amount for a used property as compared to building a new one. The *cost approach* is used to find the cost to replace (or reproduce) the property after depreciation is subtracted. The concept revolves around the understanding that an existing structure is worth what a new structure would cost to build, diminished by any value-reducing characteristics inherent in the existing property.

The approach starts by calculating the cost for a new building. Once that value is estimated, the appraiser should subtract from it everything that reduces its value—that is, every aspect of depreciation. Depreciation generally takes three forms, as described below. Although discussed elsewhere in this book, it will be explained here in its application specifically to buildings.

First, depreciation can take the form of *physical depreciation*, which is essentially wear and tear from all sources on the property from age and use. This would include deterioration from the elements, such as the rain, sun, and wind.

Second, depreciation can take the form of *functional obsolescence*, which generally is related to an inefficient design or to materials that are obsolete. This type of depreciation renders the property less valuable because its utility is limited as compared to that of a new structure. For instance, assume that a building was constructed 15 years ago with an extremely high roof to allow the manufacture of a certain product. However, at the time of appraisal, the building is empty, and the high roof is useless to most prospective tenants. The high roof also increases expenses because it increases heating costs. Consequently, the function of this building is to some extent obsolete due to this superadequacy.

Another example would be the opposite of this situation. A building may have a roof that is only 15 feet high, whereas the typical height for an industrial building might be 24 feet. This would limit the users for the building and reduce its value accordingly.

Third, depreciation can take the form of *economic obsolescence*, which is depreciation that impairs the property because of detrimental influences outside the property. It is sometimes referred to as *external obsolescence*. Economic obsolescence can occur when the market for a structure decreases because the market for the product it has been specifically constructed to manufacture has declined or collapsed. Another example might be if it has become cheaper to produce the product overseas. Foreign producers may be undercutting sales for domestic production, reducing the need for specialized structures for this type of manufacturing facility. The building may have been expensive to build, but the use for it is limited. Thus the lack of demand for such a building has resulted in a diminution in its value.

The term *technological obsolescence* is used by some appraisers to denote depreciation that has diminished value because of the advances in technology that have occurred since the subject property was built. Technological obsolescence may include a mix of both functional and economic obsolescence since both factors can fall under this category. Technological obsolescence is often used in regard to machinery and equipment, but it is not limited to that application. If the design of a facility is so integrated into a specific method of production that it limits the newest technology from being implemented, a building's value could suffer from this type of obsolescence.

Has the Appraiser Used the Correct Approach?

If the appraiser has used only the cost approach for a general-use building, this could be a major error. The reason is that for a general-use building, the cost approach may be the least accurate approach if the building is older than one or two years. A building that can be used for multiple purposes may not depreciate with age but may actually appreciate due to inflationary cycles and increased demand. By the same token, it may decline in value when the market is in decline—for instance, if vacancy rates are very high and demand lessens. In either scenario, simply estimating depreciation and applying it to the replacement or reproduction cost does not accurately measure the value because the value of the building is market driven—that is, it is subject to the market pressures of supply and demand.

For special-use buildings, however, the cost approach may be the primary approach for valuation if adequate comparable sales do not exist and there is no rental data to determine the income stream for the building. The cost approach will render a value for the specific use the building was constructed for. So if the appraisal is for the value of a special-use property but the property is not being used in that way, either because it is, for example, vacant or in foreclosure, the appraisal should state the likelihood of the building continuing in its specialized use, or the appraiser should value the building according to its possible alternative uses.

Where Does the Cost Data Come From?

There are several well-known national costing services that may be utilized to value industrial buildings and structures. From these services a replacement cost can be determined, based on the type and quality of the building construction. Trends are also available from costing services, but they would be based on the reproduction cost of the property, not the replacement cost, because they take the original cost and adjust it for inflation and depreciation. However, the dependability of trends diminishes as one moves further away from the acquisition date. In other words, a building that was constructed 10 years ago will be more accurately valued using this approach than a building that is 40 years old because it is more difficult to estimate inflation and depreciation as time periods become more distant. Trends are discussed in Chapter 9 in greater detail.

After the appraiser determines a cost new for the subject property, he or she must apply depreciation to that cost to get the estimated value. Depreciation estimates may be offered by the cost service, or they may be calculated in other ways, perhaps from the appraiser's collected data on other properties. Two major cost services are Marshall & Swift Valuation Service and R.S. Means Company.

Methods the Appraiser Uses for the Cost Approach

Typically, the new cost of a building is calculated by a calculator method, a segregated cost method, or a quantity survey method.

Calculator Method

The *calculator method* is the fastest and the easiest method to use, and it requires the least experience. The appraiser uses the manual from the costing service to choose the type of building under appraisal. The type chosen is determined by the quality and type of construction. After the base price per square foot is found, other multipliers are utilized depending on additional amenities or fees. Local cost modifiers are also applied depending on what part of the country the building is located in.

In its most simplistic form, an example would be that the building could be constructed for $110 per square foot. That amount is then changed according to quality and location, and perhaps it ends up at $130 per square foot. That amount is then multiplied by the size of the building to get the value.

The appraiser might also use estimates from local builders to get the price per square foot. The latter information is generally more accurate than the costing service because it is more specific.

The appraiser should document how the information was derived. Exhibit 7.1 is an example of a costing service calculator, courtesy of Marshall & Swift Valuation Services.

Exhibit 7.1

Example of a Costing Service Building Appraisal Calculator

SwiftEstimator

MARSHALL & SWIFT® THE BUILDING COST PEOPLE

SAMPLE REPORTS TUTORIALS LOG OUT HELP

Commercial Estimator

General Info
Sections
Building Data
Occupancies
Components
Additions
Remarks
Adjustments
Reports/Calc
Save
Save As
Close Estimate

Reports / Calculate — **Acme Iron Works**

Report Type Summary — Format HTML — Download — Print — Calculate

Marshall & Swift - SwiftEstimator Commercial Estimator - Summary Report

General Information

Estimate ID:	Acme Iron Works	**Date Created:**	1-2-2014
Property Owner:	Acme Corporation	**Date Updated:**	
Property Address:	NE 5th St. Battle Ground, WA 98604	**Date Calculated:**	01-02-2014
Local Multiplier:		**Cost Data As Of:**	12-2013
Architects Fee:		**Report Date:**	using default

Section 1

Area	75000	**Overall Depreciation %**	20
Stories in Section	1	**Physical Depreciation %**	
Stories in Building	1	**Functional Depreciation %**	
Shape	rectangular	**External Depreciation %**	
Perimeter	(auto-calc)		
Effective Age	10		

Occupancy Detail

Occupancy	%	Class	Height	Quality
495 Industrials, Heavy Mftg.	100	A	38	2.5
Occupancy Total Percentage	100			

System : Exterior Walls

	%/Units	Quality	Depr %	Other
865 Exterior Walls : PE.-Metal Sandwich Panels	100	Occ.		
Total Percent for Exterior Walls:	**100**			

System : HVAC (Heating)

	%/Units	Quality	Depr %	Other
606 HVAC (Heating) : Space Heater	100	Occ.		
Total Percent for HVAC (Heating):	**100**			

System : Land and Site

	%/Units	Quality	Depr %	Other
61 Land and Site : Land	4000000	Occ.		
62 Land and Site : Site Improvements	400000	Occ.		
7001 Land and Site : Paving, Asphalt	10000	Occ.		
7117 Land and Site : Fence, Chain Link	1000	Occ.		

System : Mezzanines

	%/Units	Quality	Depr %	Other
763 Mezzanines : Mezzanines-Storage	5000	Occ.		

System : Miscellaneous

	%/Units	Quality	Depr %	Other
764 Miscellaneous : Fire Alarm System	75000	Occ.		

System : Sprinklers

	%/Units	Quality	Depr %	Other
682 Sprinklers : Dry Sprinklers	100	Occ.		
Total Percent for Sprinklers:	**100**			

Calculation Information (All Sections)

	Units	Unit Cost	Total Cost New	Less Depreciation	Total Cost Depreciated
Basic Structure					
Base Cost	75,000	$208.61	$15,645,750	$3,129,150	$12,516,600
Exterior Walls	75,000	$20.81	$1,560,750	$312,150	$1,248,600
Heating & Cooling	75,000	$1.99	$149,250	$29,850	$119,400
Sprinklers	75,000	$3.31	$248,250	$49,650	$198,600
Mezzanine	5,000	$41.12	$205,600	$41,120	$164,480
Fire Alarm System	75,000	$1.95	$146,250	$29,250	$117,000
Basic Structure Cost	**75,000**	**$239.41**	**$17,955,850**	**$3,591,170**	**$14,364,680**
Extras					
Site Improvements - Depreciated			$400,000	$80,000	$320,000
Replacement Cost New	**75,000**	**$244.74**	**$18,355,850**		
Less Depreciation					
Physical & Functional	20.0%			$3,671,170	$14,684,680
Depreciated Cost	**75,000**	**$195.80**		**$3,671,170**	**$14,684,680**
Miscellaneous					
Land			$4,000,000		$4,000,000
Paving, Asphalt	10,000	$2.56	$25,600		$25,600
Fence, Chain Link	1,000	$3.25	$3,250		$3,250
Lighting High Inten w/o Pole	100	$1,318.50	$131,850		$131,850
Total Cost	**75,000**	**$300.22**	**$22,516,550**	**$3,671,170**	**$18,845,380**

Except for items and costs listed under "Addition Details," this SwiftEstimator report has been produced utilizing current cost data and is in compliance with the Marshall & Swift Licensed User Certificate. This report authenticates the user as a current Marshall & Swift user.

MARSHALL & SWIFT
THE BUILDING COST PEOPLE

Cost data provided by Marshall & Swift

Source: Copyright © 2014 Marshall & Swift/Boeckh, LLC, and its licensors.

Segregated Cost Method

The *segregated cost method* is more detailed than the calculator method in that different segments of the construction cost are calculated separately. For example, the foundation might be calculated as one cost segment, and the walls and roof as other cost segments. This method may or may not be more accurate than the calculator method, but it requires more steps and more experience with cost factor books. This estimate will be harder to understand and verify for the reviewer, but the reviewer can still determine the cost per square foot from the total calculated cost.[1]

Quantity Survey Method

The *quantity survey method* is rarely used by appraisers for market value appraisals. Instead, it is more commonly used by cost engineers who are estimating building costs. This method measures virtually every component that goes into the structure in order to get the cost. It requires knowledge of structural components that might surpass that of the average appraiser. Appraisers that use this method are probably doing so to estimate a rebuild cost for insurance purposes rather than market value appraisal purposes.

Costs That Should Be Included in the Appraisal Estimate

The following costs should be included in the appraisal estimate. Costs are normally divided between direct and indirect costs, as follows.

Indirect Costs

Indirect costs, also called *soft costs*, are expenses that are not categorized as labor and building material costs. They include, but are not limited to, fees for the following services:

- Engineering
- Architectural
- Accounting
- Appraisal
- Administrative
- Consulting
- Legal
- Interim construction financing
- Interim construction insurance
- Title and escrow services
- Sales commissions and marketing costs
- Due diligence services
- Building permits, licenses, and associated fees
- Property taxes during construction
- Holding costs during construction

Direct Costs

Direct costs are expenses for labor and materials used in construction. They should include contractor profit but not entrepreneurial profit:

- Labor
- Materials
- Contractor profit
- Overhead
- Workers' compensation
- Liability insurance
- Unemployment insurance
- Utility installation
- Temporary structures and fences
- Security expenses
- Sales tax

Entrepreneurial profit is not included in either of these lists. It might be defined as the measure of all the costs combined, subtracted from the market value of the property.

The Dictionary of Real Estate Appraisal defines *entrepreneurial profit* as "a market-derived figure that represents the amount an entrepreneur receives for his or her contribution to a project and risk; the difference between the total cost of a property (cost of development) and its market value (property value after completion), which represents the entrepreneur's compensation for the risk and expertise associated with development."[2]

Entrepreneurial profit should not be confused with *contractor profit*. Contractors are paid to build structures, but the expense of employing them is normally not considered part of the entrepreneur's profit. Entrepreneurs can also be contractors, or they may hire contractors. Nevertheless, the increment does not change the final market value of the finished property.

If the company builds the facility itself, there is typically no entrepreneurial profit to measure because the project has not been built for another user. However, if it can be proved from comparable sales that the costs to build leave an increment of value that is not accounted for, that gap may be representative of entrepreneurial profit. For example, the Acme Company builds a warehouse to store its inventory. Once it is completed, the costs of the land and building are lower than the typical market sales of similar buildings. The difference might be attributed to entrepreneurial profit. The appraiser should have stated in the appraisal if entrepreneurial profit is part of the cost approach calculations.

Company Supplied Costs

The appraiser may have used new costs from the company under valuation. If the company is national, there is a chance that it has costs for the construction of new facilities from green field. *From green field* means that the costs include everything it will take to build the plant, starting with a green field, which indicates undeveloped land. Depending on what the appraisal is for, it may or may not be appropriate to rely on costs from the company. Nevertheless, whether or not there may be a conflict of interest in the company supplying the costs, it still should not be the only source of cost data that the appraiser has relied on. Instead, the appraiser should provide figures corroborated by other data.

Replacement Versus Reproduction Costs

It is important to know the starting point the appraiser used, and the type of cost is a major part of this. *Replacement cost* can be defined as the cost to rebuild a building of equal utility to the one being replaced. The materials and even the configuration might be different, but the building should provide the same effective functionality as the existing structure. Understanding replacement cost is important, especially for special-use structures, because with new technologies and methods of production, the replacement structure may be significantly different from the original structure, although it is constructed to manufacture the same product.

Reproduction cost is the cost to build an exact replica or duplicate of a building using the same materials. It is rarely used in the cost approach because it requires an estimate of an exact copy of the subject property. Not only is it difficult to achieve this exactness, but it is also needed only in exceptional circumstances. Technology continues to progress, and this affects not only engineering and methods of production but also building materials. Therefore, the replacement cost typically is lower than the reproduction cost. Since this is generally the case, the appraiser may have made a comparison between the two in order to measure economic obsolescence because in most cases the difference between the replacement cost and the reproduction cost is excess cost that can be attributed to economic obsolescence. This might also be a way to determine the accuracy of a trend that is being used for an industry. Except for these types of special circumstances, the appraiser generally utilizes the replacement cost rather than the reproduction cost.[3]

The Income Approach for Industrial Buildings

If the appraisal is for a general-use building, in most circumstances the appraiser should have used the income approach to value it.

The income approach is the preferable approach for valuing general-use buildings because buyers normally purchase income producing properties based on the income they produce.

These purchases reveal the actions of buyers and sellers in the actual marketplace, which has been deemed a significant indicator of value in many court decisions in which the value of income producing property has been disputed. Nevertheless, the validity of this approach is subject to the amount of sales and rental data that are available in the subject's area. In order to use this approach, the appraiser would have to have searched for comparable properties to extract the necessary rates and other information. It would be helpful for the appraiser to also note listings for sale or lease in the vicinity of the plant.

The Source of the Data

In most locales, certain real estate agents specialize in the sale or lease of industrial properties, and the appraiser may have contacted them. The appraiser most likely used websites such as LoopNet to get information about listings and sold properties. Because Internet sites exist that publish this information, the reviewer can access these sites in the course of determining the accuracy of the appraisal (however, some may require payment for certain information). In addition, in areas that have access to waterways, there may be municipally owned industrial ports that lease buildings, and those port authorities can also be a source of information.

In larger cities, *published information* (also called *third-party information*) might have been used by the appraiser. However, this type of data is usually more general and therefore less useful than specific data that can be obtained through agents. Published data may look more impressive to some, but it generally takes second place to specific information gathered locally.

If the appraiser received information from real estate agents or other local experts, that information may have been verified by another source as well. The appraiser may have spoken to the buyer, seller, listing and selling agent, leasing agent, or someone else to get firsthand information about the market. Sales of industrial facilities tend not to be as simple as residential or even commercial sales, so the depth to which the appraiser researched the sales and leasing information can have a significant effect on the quality of the appraisal. For instance, if the appraiser found capitalization rates from Internet posted sales, it would be hard for the appraiser to know how they were calculated without discussing the sale with one of the parties involved.

Possible Problems with the Data

Sometimes the circumstances of a sale or a lease invalidate the transaction for use as a comparable. Perhaps a lease was contingent on some work that the lessor agreed to do for the lessee, which constitutes a substantial adjustment compared to other leases. A sale may have been influenced by the fact that the owner's family had just inherited the property and it was liquidated quickly in probate. Another sale may be higher than market because the company wanted a building proximate to its headquarters. Finding none for sale, the buyer approached the owner of a property who was not eager to sell, but the owner acquiesced because the offer was higher than a normal market price.

The more complex the property is, the more complex and involved the transaction of its sale or lease typically is, which increases the importance of getting all of the details regarding the transaction. As the appraiser's research continued, a pattern should have emerged that showed the appraiser a value range for sold and leased properties. If that range cannot be determined by the reviewer from reading the appraisal, then the value may be questionable. If the reviewer has access to the appraiser, it might be appropriate to ask for backup notes that are not in the appraisal. The appraiser is required to keep this backup information for a number of years (depending on the use of the appraisal and circumstances in which it was made).

Expenses

The level of expenses can make a major difference in the final value conclusion, and it is an area where errors in actual information and estimates are common. Careful attention should be paid to the derivation of the data for expenses by the reviewer.

Vacancy and Debt Collection Loss

The appraiser needs to estimate the expense of vacancy and debt collection loss. The *vacancy factor* is generally figured by determining the typical amount of time that the subject property may be vacant; this often is estimated by comparing it to other properties in the area. Because industrial tenants are generally long-term tenants, the appraiser needs to consider the potential vacancy over several years. Industrial vacancies may occur less frequently than residential vacancies, but when there is a vacancy, it tends to last for a longer time. In many markets a large, single-user industrial building may stay vacant for a year or more until it is leased. The reason is that the characteristics of the building must line up with the needs of the user, and the chances of this occurring quickly are not always good, even if the real estate market, in general, is active.

Moreover, a new tenant often needs to spend a significant sum to remodel or modify the building for the specific manufacturing and office requirements of the company. The expense of moving and reinstalling equipment can be hundreds of thousands of dollars, and the downtime that the company experiences due to the move also is expensive. Consequently, such decisions are normally not made without careful consideration.

An appraiser may calculate a vacancy loss by looking only at published information from some commercial real estate companies that track certain buildings and report the current vacancy for them. However, the reviewer should be aware that there are several problems inherent in relying solely on published information for an industrial appraisal. First, the buildings being tracked may include vacancies for new buildings that have only just begun to lease up or for older buildings at the end of their economic life that are being shunned by many potential lessees for that reason. Second, the vacancy rate at the time of a survey for a particular geographical location may not directly relate to the subject property. Third, the buildings tracked may not be similar in location, size, and desirability, among other things, when compared to the subject property.

Nevertheless, the reviewer should consider the published vacancy data, but normally that data should be augmented with research on buildings that are considered comparable to the subject property. The vacancy history of the subject property should also be noted in the appraisal and researched as a key element in estimating future vacancies. Knowledge of past vacancies may or may not be relevant, depending on the situation; if market conditions have changed a great deal, that information might have minimal value.

The reviewer should put himself or herself in the position of a potential buyer. What sort of allocation for loss of rental income for vacancy would a knowledgeable buyer make in projecting future income streams? Does the vacancy history portend that a vacancy may occur one year out of five because this has occurred in the past, or are there different economic factors that nullify this prediction? Single-user industrial buildings generally rent with long-term leases, but if the tenant is having financial problems or is in bankruptcy, the tenant may be on the verge of moving out of the facility. If this information is available, the reviewer should consider it in trying to determine the accuracy of the appraiser's estimate.

Debt collection loss is often mixed into the vacancy rate percentage, and the appraiser rarely segregates it from the vacancy estimate, so the reviewer cannot know what portion of that rate it makes up. However, it is normally not a big expense for large industrial properties because corporate tenants usually pay their rent and do not present the collection problems that residential properties may experience. The exception would be the previously noted scenario of a company that is in a financially precarious position. Industrial flex space may also be an exception, particularly in complexes where a variety of tenants rent smaller areas, perhaps 3,000 to 5,000 square feet. Smaller companies that rent spaces such as these present more risk, and the chances of rent loss are much higher than with a large corporate tenant. Therefore, the reviewer should consider the financial stability of the single large tenant or the several small tenants that occupy the buildings.

Types of Leases

It is important for the reviewer to understand the difference between types of leases because the type of lease guides the appraiser in the allocation of expenses.

A *gross lease* is a lease in which the landlord (lessor) is required to pay most of the operating expenses associated with the property, including maintenance and property taxes. A gross lease might also include utilities in some situations, but this is more likely the case for office buildings than for large, single-user industrial properties. However, the utility charges for the common areas often are paid by the lessor for multi-tenant, flex-space industrial parks, although sometimes a surcharge is added to the rent for this expense. For industrial properties, it would be very unusual for the landlord to pay utilities for the manufacturing operation because machinery and equipment often use a large amount of power, and the amount may vary greatly from one operation to another.

A *net lease*, or *single net lease*, is a lease in which the tenant (lessee) pays one of the major expenses. For instance, the tenant pays for property taxes in addition to rent, and the landlord pays for all other expenses.

A *net net lease*, or *double net lease*, is one in which the tenant pays for any additional major expense that the landlord would have paid for under the net lease. For example, the tenant pays for property taxes and property maintenance, and the landlord pays for everything else.

A *net net net lease*, or *triple net lease*, is one in which the tenant assumes responsibility for all of the operating expenses. In some triple net leases the exception to this lease agreement might be structural repairs, such as roof repairs, but this is not always the case. A triple net lease for which the tenant pays for structural repairs is also called an *absolute net lease*. Triple net leases for very long rental periods, for instance, 20 years or more, are more likely to require the tenant to pay for structural repairs than shorter-term triple net leases. Larger, single-user industrial buildings are generally leased under triple net leases, whereas small industrial parks and flex-space parks are more likely to be less than triple net.

A caveat regarding terminology: The meaning of terms such as *triple net* can vary from one area of the country to another and even between leasing agents. Therefore, when terms such as these are used, it is important to ask what is specifically meant, if it is an issue that affects value in the appraisal. And, as previously stated, two different properties, both of which are leased on a triple net basis, can have different terms. One lessee may have the responsibility for absolutely all maintenance, whereas the other may be responsible for all maintenance with the exception of major components of the site, such as the asphalt in the parking area or the roof of the buildings. These exceptions are generally spelled out in the lease and can vary according to whatever agreement is reached between the lessor and the lessee.

A typical triple net lease is normally at least five years in length and can range up to 30 or 40 years or longer. Therefore, if the building stands alone and the tenant is taking care of most of the expenses, often there is little need for management, and the expense for management will be quite small.

With a triple net lease, part of the lessor's expenses will probably include insurance, although the lessee may also carry it and may be required by the lessor to do so. Both parties may carry insurance for various reasons, including liability issues and mortgage requirements. The allocation for maintenance expenses should include reserves for remodeling expenses that the lessor may incur after the lease is fulfilled. These expenses would not be applicable if the lease required the tenant to return the building in the same condition as it was originally leased.

The reviewer should understand that there is a difference between the expenses associated with a large, single-tenant building and the expenses of a multitenant industrial park comprising smaller spaces. The management expenses on the latter type of building are considerable, whereas the management expenses for a single-tenant building are minimal. The appraiser should have noted in the appraisal the typical fees that leasing agents are receiving for handling the type of building under valuation. Their compensation is typically based on a percentage of the lease amount.

Another consideration is that at times a lease may be inflated because "build-to-suit" improvements have been amortized over the life of the lease, reflecting a reduction in rent that diminishes the value of the lease. If these improvements are specialized for the specific tenant, they may not add to the building's value because neither another tenant nor the owner would pay more for them. However, if they are general in nature, they may improve the overall value of the property.

For example, in negotiating a lease, the tenant may request that the existing office space be increased in size and that all the offices be remodeled. For the manufacturing portion of the building, the tenant may want some walls moved, the electrical power increased, and several larger access doors installed. The office remodeling may increase the overall value of the property because it would be valuable to any new user, whereas the walls and the additional electrical power may not add value. This is particularly true if the electrical power for the building was adequate for most manufacturing uses to begin with.

The expense of these items may be included in the rent, so the actual rental rate has been inflated to cover this. In other words, the lessee might agree to pay the asking rent but require that this work be performed as part of the transaction. Consequently, the actual rental rate could be extrapolated by deducting the expense of these improvements from the amount of rent to be received over the life of the lease. These details should have been stated in the appraisal and factored into the financial analysis of the building, so that the actual rent was determined and an inflated figure is not mistakenly used, which would skew the final value. Exhibit 7.2 is an example of an analysis of the effect of a rent concession.

Exhibit 7.2

Analysis of Rent Concessions for an Industrial Building

Analysis of Rent Concessions for an Industrial Building		
Total building size, square feet	200,000	Total space, footprint
	20,000	Office area
Asking rent:	$ 0.35	manufacuring per S.F.
	$ 0.65	Office space surcharge
Rent totals:	$ 840,000	Manufacturing
	$ 156,000	Office
	$ 996,000	Total annual rent
RENT BEFORE CONCESSIONS:		
Blended rent per S.F. per year:	$ 4.53	
Blended rent per S.F. per month:	$ 0.38	
Term of Lease:	5	Years
Modification cost to lessor:	$400,000	
Lease total (times 5 years)	$ 4,980,000	
Concession cost	$400,000	
Lease minus concession:	$ 4,580,000	
Annual amount of concession:	$80,000	
RENT AFTER CONCESSIONS:		
Blended rent per S.F. per year	$ 4.16	
Blended rent per S.F. per month:	$ 0.35	

Leaseback Contracts

Companies often buy a building under the name of a different business entity and, using a *leaseback contract*, lease the building back to themselves. Tax laws require them to rent back to themselves at fair market rates, and sometimes an appraiser is hired to determine the rental amount. Nonetheless, rental rates from leasebacks should not be used for the valuation of buildings because they are not arm's-length transactions. The reviewer should be aware of this in case the appraiser used the leaseback rent without confirming that it is also the market rent. Also, comparable rentals should not be used if they are leaseback properties.

Property Tax Expenses

The appraiser should note the actual tax rate for the property and also the projected rate. Property taxes can change for various reasons, and those changes can affect the income enough to change the value derived using the income approach. Considerations for these extra expenses should be noted when the expenses are calculated.

Another issue is the effect of any *special tax assessments*. With regard to comparables, the appraiser should note whether some of the properties are located in areas where special tax assessments will increase the rate of taxes as compared to the subject property. A special assessment might be additional property taxes due to the expansion of available utilities in the area where the subject property is located, which voters specifically approved to promote industrial development.

Maintenance

The estimate for maintenance varies according to the financial responsibilities the lessor assumes in the lease (see discussion of leases earlier in this chapter). An allocation should be made for reserves and replacements depending on the projected costs for covered maintenance items the lessor assumes responsibility for. Sometimes, inexperienced appraisers overestimate the expenses for triple net or absolute net leases because they do not realize that most of the maintenance burden is on the lessee.

Separating Manufacturing Assets and Determining Superadequacies

It is important that the appraiser clearly identifies what actual assets are being valued when the income approach is utilized. The estimated rental of the building under appraisal would typically be for the shell of the building, and it would not include the infrastructure necessary to accommodate the specific manufacturing process or processes of the company. Special foundations, electrical wiring, plumbing, and bridge cranes, among other things, that are above and beyond what is typically found in the standard manufacturing building shell should be segregated and valued as a company asset and not as part of the building. Otherwise, the building value will be skewed. If the reviewer has a question about what has been valued, it should be answered by reading the description of the assets the appraiser has in the report.

If the subject property is a building that is vacant and for lease and it contains special items such as those listed—that is, items that are left over from the previous owner or tenant—it should be determined whether or not the items add value. If it is unlikely that the typical tenant would pay extra for their use, these items have then lost the value they had to the previous user. Therefore, they should be assigned little or no value in the appraisal, and they should be considered superadequacies. As mentioned elsewhere in this book, but repeated here for convenience, a *superadequacy* could be defined as a feature in a property that is in excess of what it needs to function. The determination of that is whether the market recognizes the special item as something that would typically add value.

An example of a superadequacy for an industrial building might be excessive ceiling height. Perhaps the typical height is 24 feet and the subject's height is 48 feet. The question the appraiser should have considered was whether a typical tenant would pay more for the higher ceiling. It should be understood that there might be a tenant somewhere who would pay more for the high ceiling, but the likelihood of finding such a tenant would be remote. In the same way, a building wired with more power than is typically needed will probably not bring more rent or a higher sales price than one with the normal amount.

There is a significant difference, however, between these two examples. In the latter case, a building wired for more power than is needed does not diminish the value of the building—it may simply not add any more value than one without the excessive power. In the former situation, a building with high ceilings may be a detriment because the cost of heating and/or cooling the building may reduce the potential lease value. In other words, a tenant that is faced with paying more to heat and cool a building for a ceiling that is too high may expect the rent to be reduced proportionately. The ceiling height in this example is incurable functional obsolescence, and it also reduces the value of the property.

From these examples it is clear that there are some superadequacies that do not affect the value of a building and others that have a detrimental effect and lower the value of a building. The appraiser should state what effect any superadequacy that was noted in the appraisal has on the valuation of the subject property.

Rental Data and Analysis

Considering the quality of rental data is of paramount importance in reviewing an appraisal that is relying predominantly on the income approach. If the data is significantly flawed, then the value conclusion will be skewed.

Rental Data

The appraiser must collect rental data to determine the income stream for the subject property, which will in turn reveal its value as an income-producing property. Please refer to Exhibit 7.3 as an example of a format that the appraiser may have used to record rental data on comparable properties to estimate the rental income for the subject property. The appraiser will probably have a similar spreadsheet in

Exhibit 7.3

Comparable Rental Property Rents

COMPARABLE RENTAL PROPERTY RENTS			
CHARACTERISTICS:	**Rental 1**	**Rental 2**	**Rental 3**
Address:	8409 Parker St.	99123 Weldon Ave.	4402 Donner Rd.
City/State:	Vancouver, WA	Vancouver, WA	Vancouver, WA
Verification:	J. Smith	J. Smith	J. Smith
Lessor:	Roger Harris	Seal Holding, Inc.	Advanced Realty
Lessee:	BLM Corp	Aztec Corp.	Esco Corp.
Total Size:	58,000	74,000	62,000
Percent Office Space:	9%	15%	10%
Year Built:	1970	1994	1995
Land Size in Acres:	5	4.9	8
Land-to-Building Ratio:	3.76	2.88	5.62
Excess Land:	No	No	3 acres
Ceiling Height:	24	26	24
Type Construction:	Conc. Tilt-up	Metal	Conc. Tilt-up
Condition:	Average	Average -	Average +
Zoning:	Light Ind.	Light Ind.	Light Ind.
Sprinklers:	Yes	Yes	Yes
Misc:	None	Insufficient Parking	None
LEASE INFORMATION:			
Current Lease Date:	Oct-06	Mar-05	Dec-06
Length of Lease in years:	3	5	10
Current Blended Lease Amount S/F:	0.42	0.38	0.45
Lease amount manufacturing:	N/A	N/A	N/A
Lease amount Office:	N/A	N/A	N/A
Lease amount warehouse:	N/A	N/A	N/A
Lease concessions:	None	None	None

his or her backup files, but it would be unlikely for this to be in the appraisal. It is shown here to help the reviewer understand the method of collection and recordation.

Theoretically, the optimum appraisal includes some rental data from properties that are superior to the subject, some that are inferior, and some that are virtually equal. If that can be achieved, then within that range of rents the middle or median rents should apply to the subject. Realistically, this may not be possible, especially if the subject property is a high-end or low-end structure. If that is the case, then the comparable properties that best match the subject should be applied by the appraiser. Averaging is not acceptable because when an average is used, the most weight is not put on the comparable properties that are most like the subject, and this makes the valuation less accurate.

Red Flag

If the appraiser used rents on the high or low end of the range of rents, and the comparable sales that were given the most weight are not properties that appear to be the most similar to the subject property, look for an explanation of why more weight was put on those properties. If there is not an adequate explanation, then the resulting value may be inaccurate. A suggestion would be to ask the appraiser for the reason if that is possible.

Income Multipliers

The appraiser may have used a *gross income multiplier* (GIM)—*also called a gross rent multiplier* (GRM)—which is one way of valuing the property based on income. To get the GIM, an income multiplier is derived by dividing the sale price by the gross rent. This can be done on an annual or monthly basis, but using the annual income is the predominant method. However, the *gross income multiplier*, as the name implies, measures only the gross income and not the net income. It also does not consider expenses, so the actual income of the property is not taken into consideration, affording very little information on which to base a valuation analysis. A simple example of a GIM would be as follows:

Sale price of property	$420,000
Gross annual income for property	$36,000
Gross income multiplier (GIM), annual	11.66
Gross income multiplier (GIM), monthly	140

The GIM can be refined for more accuracy by using an *effective gross income multiplier* (EGIM), which is the income of the property after an allowance is made for vacancy and collection losses. Nevertheless, with most appraisals, this method can be misleading because of the variance of expenses between comparable sales.

Direct Capitalization

Note: For more details on this approach, please see "The Income Approach" section of Chapter 5, "Analyzing the Commercial Appraisal."

Direct capitalization can be defined in its most basic sense as a method to convert the income of a property into an indication of its value. The premise is that investors will pay a certain amount of money for an investment based on the expected profits they will receive from their investment. A simple example would be an investment that costs \$200,000 and that has an income of \$20,000 a year. The formula to convert the relationship between the cost and income into a rate would be as follows:

$$\begin{aligned} \text{Rate} &= \frac{\text{income}}{\text{value}} \\ &= \$20{,}000/\$200{,}000 \\ &= 10 \text{ percent} \end{aligned}$$

The variations on this formula are as follows:

$$\text{Income} = \text{rate} \times \text{value}$$

$$\text{Value} = \frac{\text{income}}{\text{rate}}$$

Direct capitalization generally considers the value of the property based on one year's income. However, the anticipation is not that the property will produce income for one year only but that the income will continue into the future. The rate that is used is often called the *overall rate* because it is used to determine the overall property value.

The income used in the direct capitalization method is not gross income. It is net operating income, which begins with gross income. The *gross income* encompasses income from all sources, although rent is typically the predominant source. From that amount, vacancy and collection losses are subtracted to get the effective gross income, and from that amount, all other expenses are subtracted to get the *net operating income* (NOI). Alternatively, other income may be added after the effective gross income is calculated if it needs to be segregated. Exhibit 7.4 is an example of a spreadsheet used for direct capitalization. This type of spreadsheet probably will not be in the appraisal, but

Exhibit 7.4

Direct Capitalization for the Income Approach

DIRECT CAPITALIZATION FOR THE INCOME APPROACH				
OWNER/OCCUPANT:	Plastic Fab Building			
LOCATION:	Houston			
VALUATION DATE:	Jun-14			
USE:	Office/Manuf/Warehouse			
POTENTIAL GROSS INCOME				
		SF AREA	(NNN) RENT PER SF	(NNN) RENT
	Manufacturing/Warehouse	200,000	0.35	$840,000
	Executive Offices	5,000	1.20	$72,000
	Production Offices	2,000	0.60	$14,400
	Lunchroom	3,000	0.80	$28,800
TOTAL				$955,200
EFFECTIVE GROSS INCOME				
POTENTIAL GROSS INCOME				$955,200
less VAC./COL. LOSS			5.00%	($47,760)
EFFECTIVE GROSS INCOME				$907,440
EXPENSES				
EFFECTIVE GROSS INCOME				$907,440
less MGMT, MAINT, & INSURANCE			5.00%	($45,372)
NET OPERATING INCOME				$862,068
IMPROVEMENT VALUE				
NET OPERATING INCOME				$862,068
CAPITALIZED AT AN OVERALL RATE			8.00%	
TOTAL CAPITALIZED VALUE:				$10,775,850
less NORMAL LAND VALUE:				($500,000)
IMPROVEMENT VALUE:				$10,275,850
SURPLUS LAND:				
TOTAL IMPROVEMENT, LAND, AND SURPLUS LAND VALUE:				$10,775,850

it is shown here to give the reviewer an understanding of how the value may be derived mathematically. Something of this type should be in the appraiser's notes.

Note in the example that there are different rent amounts for the basic shell of the building, the executive offices, the production offices, and the lunchroom. The appraiser should have segregated these rents; they should be shown either in a spreadsheet or somewhere in the appraisal. It is important for the reviewer to understand that the additional rent for the office areas is added as a *surcharge* (a rent charge on top of the basic shell rent). In other words, the basic shell rents for 35 cents per square foot, but the production offices rent for 60 cents per square foot. However, because the rent listed at 35 cents per square foot covers the complete footprint of the building, the additional charge, or surcharge, is 60 cents, making the total rent for the office 95 cents per square foot.

If the production office structure is two stories within the shell, the bottom story square footage would be listed as 60 cents per square foot, but the top story would be listed as 95 cents per square foot because the shell rent has already been taken into consideration for the lower area, but not for the top. Some buildings have office structures outside the main building. Therefore, an interior office most likely is quoted as a surcharge on top of the shell rent, whereas an exterior office rent quote stands alone.

In this example, the expense for management, maintenance, and insurance is 5 percent of the gross income, and it could be as low as 2 or 3 percent depending on the lease. This being a triple net lease, the maintenance expenses may be very small because, as previously noted, most of the maintenance costs are the tenant's responsibility. The exception might be that major maintenance expenses, such as roof repairs, would be the lessor's responsibility. Even if this is not the case, there may be a large expense such as to refurbish the offices when the tenant leaves, which should be considered over the life of the lease. If the appraiser did not have specifics of each lease, and estimates were made based on what is considered typical or average for the area, the appraiser should have stated that this was the case.

How the Appraiser Extracts Capitalization Rates

For this income method to be accurate, the appraiser must choose the correct capitalization rate. This is normally determined by researching other sales that are similar to the subject, called the *market extraction method.* The appraiser may have used different methods, such as the buildup method (see Chapter 5 for more details), but those other methods are not considered as reliable because they do not capture the local market situation that reveals actions of buyers and sellers.

Unlike most commercial properties, industrial buildings often sell from one user to another, so there may be no rental data for the appraiser to use to determine the capitalization rate for the comparable sale. Moreover, even if the property sold with a tenant, often the lease that was in effect at the time of the sale does not reflect current market rents because leases for industrial properties are often long term. The lease may have escalators built in that increase the rent at certain intervals, but these rarely reflect what actually occurs in the market because they are estimates that were made at the time of the signing of the lease.

For example, a 25-year lease may have an escalator that increases the rent every 5 years. This increase may be tied to a certain index, or it may be a percentage increase. If the lease is 10 years old and has experienced two increases, it would be coincidental if the lease amount turned out to be in line with current market rents.

Because of this, the appraiser may have estimated a market rent for the comparable sale to get the capitalization rate. This should have been practiced only if there was a lack of sales that have current rental data from which a rate may be extracted. If the appraiser utilized this

Exhibit 7.5
Example of a Capitalization Rate Deduction

CAPITALIZATION RATE DEDUCTION				
SALE NUMBER:	1			
LOCATION:	8820 Marcy Road			
SALE DATE:	Jan-13			
USE:	Manuf/Office			
POTENTIAL GROSS INCOME				
		SF AREA	(NNN) RENT PER SF	(NNN) RENT
Manufacturing	Actual rents:	77,400	0.34	$315,792
Office	Actual rents:	12,600	0.85	$128,520
TOTAL		90,000		$444,312
EFFECTIVE GROSS INCOME				
POTENTIAL GROSS INCOME				$444,312
less VAC./COL. LOSS			5.00%	($22,216)
EFFECTIVE GROSS INCOME				$422,096
EXPENSES				
EFFECTIVE GROSS INCOME				$422,096
less MGMT, MAINT, & INSURANCE			5.00%	($21,105)
NET OPERATING INCOME				$400,991
IMPROVEMENT VALUE				
NET OPERATING INCOME				$400,991
SALE PRICE				$4,222,200
CAPITALIZATION RATE				9.50%

method, the appraiser should have noted in the appraisal how the rates were computed and should give less weight to those comparables with estimated rental rates than to sales in which the property was currently leased. The appraiser may have used a format such as the one in Exhibit 7.5, but it will probably not be part of the appraisal. It is included here to help the reviewer understand how the capitalization rate may have been deduced by the appraiser. Exhibit 7.6 shows a

Exhibit 7.6
Summary of Comparable Building Capitalization Rates

SUMMARY OF COMPARABLE BUILDING SALES - CAPITALIZATION RATES									
No.	Location	Age/ Sale Date	Land/Bldg Ratio	Building Size	Office Percent	Wall Height	Price	Price/SF	Cap Rate
1	9820 SW Lerner Rd.	1980 Oct-13	3.86:1	90,000	14	20	$4,222,000	$46.91	9.5
2	20497 SW Junction Rd.	1991 Jun-13	2.63:1	41,072	9.06	24	$1,875,000	$45.65	9.3
3	9650 SW Tyler Rd.	1996 Apr-13	2.8:1	59,003	10	20	$2,550,000	$43.22	10.5
4	15757 SW Apple St.	1978 Mar-13	2.94:1	129,434	9.19	24	$5,200,000	$40.17	10.2
5	SW 94th Ct.	1980 Dec-13	3.5:1	60,000	10.8	24	$2,752,000	$45.87	9.8
6	11006 NE 95 Ct.	1991 Feb-13	2.53:1	80,747	8	24	$3,700,000	$45.82	9.7

typical list of sales and their capitalization rates. This type of list may be in the appraisal.

Land Value Extraction

For some appraisals, such as insurance appraisals for which the building value alone is needed or ad valorem (property tax) appraisals for which the land must be separated from the building for taxation purposes, the land value must be extracted from the total value. The land value estimate should be made based on land sales that have been researched. This process is analyzed in Chapter 3 and also, briefly, at the end of this chapter.

It is important for the reviewer to understand that the total value does not change if the land value is increased or decreased—only the allocation of value between the land and improvements changes. Exhibits 7.7 and 7.8 illustrate this point. The exhibits describe the same property, but in Exhibit 7.7 the land value

Exhibit 7.7

Example of the Effect of a Change in Land Value, Income Approach: Land Value of $800,000

LAND VALUE CHANGE, INCOME APPROACH				
OWNER/OCCUPANT:	Steelco Building	Land at $800,000 value		
LOCATION:	Rochester, NY			
VALUATION DATE:	November 2013			
USE:	Office/Manuf/Warehouse			
POTENTIAL GROSS INCOME				
		SF	(NNN) RENT	
		AREA	PER SF	(NNN) RENT
	Manufacturing/Warehouse	200,000	0.35	$840,000
	Executive Offices	5,000	1.20	$72,000
	Production Offices	2,000	0.60	$14,400
	Lunchroom	3,000	0.80	$28,800
TOTAL				$955,200
EFFECTIVE GROSS INCOME				
POTENTIAL GROSS INCOME				$955,200
less VAC./COL. LOSS			5.00%	($47,760)
EFFECTIVE GROSS INCOME				$907,440
EXPENSES				
EFFECTIVE GROSS INCOME				$907,440
less MGMT, MAINT, & INSURANCE			5.00%	($45,372)
NET OPERATING INCOME				$862,068
IMPROVEMENT VALUE				
NET OPERATING INCOME				$862,068
CAPITALIZED AT AN OVERALL RATE			8.00%	
TOTAL CAPITALIZED VALUE:				$10,775,850
less NORMAL LAND VALUE:				$800,000
IMPROVEMENT VALUE:				$9,975,850
SURPLUS LAND				
TOTAL IMPROVEMENT, LAND, AND SURPLUS LAND VALUE:				$10,775,850

is $800,000 whereas in Exhibit 7.8, it is $500,000. The total value remains the same.

To reiterate, when using direct capitalization, the total property value does not change when the land value is changed. The importance here is that the appraisal can be accurate for the total value for the property, even if the land is not accurately valued.

Exhibit 7.8
Example of the Effect of a Change in Land Value, Income Approach: Same Property as in Exhibit 7.7 but with a Land Value of $500,000

LAND VALUE CHANGE, INCOME APPROACH				
OWNER/OCCUPANT:	Steelco Building	Land at $500,000 value		
LOCATION:	Rochester, NY			
VALUATION DATE:	November 2013			
USE:	Office/Manuf/Warehouse			
POTENTIAL GROSS INCOME				
		SF AREA	(NNN) RENT PER SF	(NNN) RENT
	Manufacturing/Warehouse	200,000	0.35	$840,000
	Executive Offices	5,000	1.20	$72,000
	Production Offices	2,000	0.60	$14,400
	Lunchroom	3,000	0.80	$28,800
TOTAL				$955,200
EFFECTIVE GROSS INCOME				
POTENTIAL GROSS INCOME				$955,200
less VAC./COL. LOSS			5.00%	($47,760)
EFFECTIVE GROSS INCOME				$907,440
EXPENSES				
EFFECTIVE GROSS INCOME				$907,440
less MGMT, MAINT, & INSURANCE			5.00%	($45,372)
NET OPERATING INCOME				$862,068
IMPROVEMENT VALUE				
NET OPERATING INCOME				$862,068
CAPITALIZED AT AN OVERALL RATE			8.00%	
TOTAL CAPITALIZED VALUE:				$10,775,850
less NORMAL LAND VALUE:				$500,000
IMPROVEMENT VALUE:				$10,275,850
SURPLUS LAND				
TOTAL IMPROVEMENT, LAND, AND SURPLUS LAND VALUE:				$10,775,850

Excess and/or Surplus Land

An adjustment needs to be made if there is excess land because only the amount of land necessary to support the structures under appraisal should be included in the income approach. Excess land should be valued separately and then added back to the value, as the example in Exhibit 7.9 indicates. Generally, a price per square foot is found for industrial land, and that amount can be used to determine the value of the excess land. To determine whether there is excess land, the

Exhibit 7.9

Value of Excess Land, Income Approach

VALUE OF EXCESS LAND, INCOME APPROACH				
OWNER/OCCUPANT:	Aviation Plastics			
LOCATION:	Duluth, MN			
VALUATION DATE:	November 2014			
USE:	Office/Manuf/Warehouse			
POTENTIAL GROSS INCOME				
		SF AREA	(NNN) RENT PER SF	(NNN) RENT
	Manufacturing/Warehouse	100,000	0.35	$680,000
	Offices	7,000	0.70	$58,800
TOTAL		107,000		$738,800
EFFECTIVE GROSS INCOME				
POTENTIAL GROSS INCOME				$738,800
less VAC./COL. LOSS			5.00%	($36,940)
EFFECTIVE GROSS INCOME				$701,860
EXPENSES				
EFFECTIVE GROSS INCOME				$701,860
less MGMT, MAINT, & INSURANCE			4.00%	($28,074)
NET OPERATING INCOME				$673,786
IMPROVEMENT VALUE				
NET OPERATING INCOME				$673,786
CAPITALIZED AT AN OVERALL RATE			7.30%	
TOTAL CAPITALIZED VALUE				$9,229,945
less NORMAL LAND VALUE	7 acres needed for 3:1 ratio requirement			$914,760
SURPLUS LAND	3 acres excess land, @ $3 per foot.			$392,040
TOTAL IMPROVEMENT VALUE WITHOUT EXCESS LAND				**$8,837,905**

appraiser needs to research what ratio of land to structures is required by the governing authority (normally the county or city building code). In many localities, it is a 3:1 ratio, but that may vary.

It is important for the reviewer to understand that the value of the excess land depends on whether or not it is usable and developable. If the land is not usable, in most cases the value will be severely diminished. It may also be that the configuration of the structures may preclude further development, even though the ratio of land to buildings would appear to allow development. If this is the case, the excess land generally adds minimal value to the property.

Buildings and Structures: The Sales Comparison Approach

Much of the same data used to value a building with the income approach is utilized in the sales comparison approach. In this approach, the sales are compiled and a cost per square foot (or sometimes the cost per cubic foot) is calculated by dividing the sale price by the total square footage. The appraiser will have most likely made adjustments to the price per square foot based on an understanding of how the differences affect the value.

For instance, if one facility lacks adequate parking and the appraiser knows that a certain amount of rent is being paid for parking space across the street to augment this shortcoming, a corresponding adjustment might be made based on that additional expense. In another scenario, a building might have a low clear height, which limits its use, and an adjustment might be estimated for this functional problem.

In some cases, attempting adjustments may not be realistic because of the diversity of the comparable sales. Nevertheless, even without adjustments a range of value should have been established, based on prices paid per square foot, and that may corroborate the figures reached by the other approaches to value. This method might have been used as another way to analyze the same buildings that have been used for comparison in the income approach, if there is appropriate similarity. The reviewer should understand that as the diversity of the properties increases, the accuracy of the sales comparison approach decreases.

Sales that are on the extreme high or low side of the normal range of value would probably not have been used by the appraiser because they would be considered anomalies. Sometimes reviewers mistakenly think that the appraiser made an error if they find that such sales were not used. However, it is proper procedure to exclude them if there are enough sales in the typical value range. The reason is that these outlier sales often have special circumstances that preclude them from being good indicators of value, which makes it inappropriate to use them as comparable sales.

Elements of Comparison

The elements of comparison the appraiser will have chosen should have been based on the effect they would have on the market value of the property under valuation. In other words, the appraiser should have been familiar enough with the marketplace for industrial properties to determine what property characteristics were value significant to buyers. The reviewer can check this by talking to real estate brokers who specialize in industrial properties.

The following list suggests some elements of comparison. It is by no means exhaustive, and it includes items that do not apply to every valuation, but it gives the reviewer some insight into what characteristics might be considered. As previously stated, comparable properties are always adjusted to the subject—the subject is never adjusted to the comparable properties.

Property Rights Conveyed

Most sales are *fee simple*. It is the most common type of ownership, and it is defined as follows:

> **Fee simple:** The greatest possible estate in land, wherein the owner has the right to use it, exclusively possess it, commit waste upon it, dispose of it by deed or will, and take its fruits. A fee simple represents absolute ownership of land, and therefore the owner may do whatever he or she chooses with the land. If an owner of a fee simple dies intestate, the land will descend to the heirs.
>
> The term *fee* used independently is an adequate designation of this type of estate in land. The term *simple* is added to distinguish clearly this estate from other interests in real property.[4]

Red Flag

If the subject is in fee simple ownership, the comparable sales should also be in fee simple ownership. If they are not, adjustments for different types of ownership are problematic and may be inaccurate because the value difference between ownerships is difficult to determine.

Financing Terms

Special financing terms are sometimes offered by government entities as incentive programs. Sellers sometimes finance at below-market rates to attract buyers. In such cases, the appraiser should have adjusted the terms to a cash equivalency by researching the market rates for financing. In other words, if financing typically would cost a buyer 8 percent and the special financing is at 3 percent, the present value of the difference of 5 percent should be calculated for the adjustment.

Time Adjustments

The appraiser should have made time adjustments only if the comparable properties were sold when the market was considerably different from the time of the appraisal. Time adjustments should be based on a study of more current sales. If the appraiser has a property that has been resold and that shows a change in the market, it may offer excellent evidence of appreciation or depreciation since the time of sale.

An example of a resale would be a building that sold twice in the period of time that the sales comparables sold in. For instance, if sales were used that sold in the past three years, a property that resold in that time period might be good evidence of how the market changed. However, the appraiser should have disclosed whether research was conducted on the resale to determine if modifications were made to the building, which would increase its value and are not attributable to a market increase. Another issue may be the circumstances of the sales, which should all be arm's-length transactions.

Red Flag

A property that has been resold may have been modified between the first and second sales. If it was, the change in sale price between the two sales may not accurately reflect an increase or decrease in the market. Comparable sales may also have been modified subsequent to the purchase of them, which may require an adjustment.

Modifications to Comparable Sales

The reviewer should be aware of an issue that can invalidate a comparable sale, or at least require an adjustment for it. For instance, the appraiser may have used a comparable sale that had improvements that were made after the sale transpired, unbeknownst to the appraiser. Often industrial buildings are purchased and vastly improved, but if the appraiser was not aware of this, an appropriate adjustment may not have been made. Improvements may also be made as a condition of a sale, and the expense of these modifications may affect the value and warrant an adjustment.

For example, a company may buy a building contingent on the movement of interior walls because that company desires a particular configuration. However, that change may not increase the value for another user. Therefore, it does not warrant adjustment because the market value has not been increased. Conversely, if the sale was contingent on improving the building by putting on a new roof, remodeling the offices, and installing a new HVAC system, those improvements would increase the market value, and an adjustment to the price should have been made accordingly.

Business and Personal Property Values

The reviewer should be aware that buildings are sometimes sold as part of a business that is a going concern. The value of the building may be allocated, but an allocated value is not accurate enough to allow the sale to be used in the sales comparison approach. There may also be personal property included in the sale, which should be deducted if the value is known. It is generally difficult to segregate the costs on sales of this type.

Condition and Other Improvement Characteristics

Often the largest adjustments will be made for size, age, and condition of the improvements. The size of the comparable properties is normally adjusted based on a square footage or cubic footage basis. The age of the property and the condition of the property are major characteristics that also normally need adjustments.

Some properties have deferred maintenance issues, and if they are purchased, there may be considerable expenditures involved to bring them up to optimum condition. If the subject property is in inferior condition, adjustments should be made to the superior comparable properties. Age should be considered on two levels: chronological age and economic age. Some facilities may be older than others, but because of excellent maintenance and/or remodeling, they have as much or more value.

Office Space

For typical industrial buildings, office space is often 10 to 15 percent of the total size of the facility. Properties that are company headquarters often have more office space, and they range from about 30 to 50 percent. If the facility is a company headquarters, the office space is often of a higher quality than for manufacturing offices because the space is used for executives. However, the marketability of the facility may be lessened because there are normally fewer buyers for buildings with this much office space. If the appraiser used sales that vary a great deal from the office percentage of the subject, the result might be a skewed valuation.

Floor Thickness

For industrial property, the thickness of floors varies from about 4 inches of concrete up. Many buildings have 6-inch-thick concrete floors. Floors that are thinner limit the use and value of the building because they support less weight. Often the thickness of the floor is matched to the type of machines or vehicles that utilize it. If heavy equipment is being used, the floor can be much thicker, and often foundations for heavy equipment can be around 18 to 36 inches thick, depending on the weight of the equipment.

Width of Bays

If the appraiser used older buildings to compare to a newer building or vice versa, there may need to be an adjustment for the width of the bays. Older buildings generally have narrower widths, and that would diminish usability and value.

Loading Docks

Adjustments for loading docks vary depending on the type of building and the use. If the property is a distribution warehouse, the number of docks would be an important factor in determining value. However, if it is a manufacturing facility, the number of docks may not be an issue unless the lack of loading docks is deleterious to its function. More docks than are needed would be considered a superadequacy and would not add value.

HVAC Systems

The appraiser may have made adjustments for heating, ventilation, and air-conditioning (HVAC) systems. These systems vary in efficiency, sometimes because of the type and quality of the units and sometimes because of the types of fuel. For instance, natural gas heating is more efficient than electric heating in most areas. Some buildings may lack heating systems, relying instead on the heat from the machines and employees, particularly in warmer parts of the country. The appraiser should have made adjustments for only those differences that affect marketability.

Utility Services

The reviewer should note if the appraiser has stated if the comparable sales have the same level of utilities as the subject. Sometimes adjustments should be made for differences if they affect the market value. However, if a building has a great amount of electrical power, which would normally not be needed by other users, this would constitute a superadequacy. In such a case, no adjustment is warranted because no value would be added. Other aspects of this are the availability of utilities. For instance, if the subject is located in an area where more power is available but a comparable sale is not, an adjustment might be needed, depending on the needs of a typical manufacturer. This also applies to other utility needs such as natural gas, water, and sewerage.

Rural or suburban industrial properties that are not served by a sewer system are typically less valuable than those that have sewer system service. If sewer system service is available, even if it is not installed, its availability alone can ameliorate the situation and reduce the size of the adjustment. The distance from the sewer line and difficulty of installation are issues that should be considered. Users of buildings often do not wish to deal with the aggravation of having to get access easements from other properties in order to bring in sewer service.

Red Flag

The value of rural or suburban industrial buildings may be greatly diminished if they lack sewer connections or if the availability of electrical power is minimal.

Yard Improvements

Typically there is a minimum adjustment for yard improvements, with the exception of major installations of fencing and paving that may be needed for the operation of certain industrial facilities.

Functional Problems

Functional problems would include inadequate parking or inadequate space for large trucks to access the facility or turn around. Industrial buildings in urban areas sometimes lack parking, and the building owners lease nearby parking lots for the employees. The appraiser should have considered these issues and adjusted the appraisal accordingly.

Location and Freeway Access

The reviewer may be able to determine if there is a problem with this aspect of the building by looking at photographs and maps included in the appraisal. Most industrial properties have raw materials shipped in and finished goods shipped out. Shipping may be more expensive and less convenient if the site is distant from major freeways and arterials. In some cities, larger trucks are not allowed to use certain roads, which may be a further obstacle for convenient trucking.

Workforce Availability

If the appraiser compared buildings that are a long distance from the subject property, workforce availability could be an issue. Geographical areas that have employment statistics that differ from the subject property's area might be a reason for an adjustment. Certain locations may also have built-in recruitment problems such as long commuting times.

Commercial Value

From photographs and from a little Internet research about the street or area where the industrial facility is located, the reviewer can determine if there is commercial value for the subject or the comparable properties. When seeking comparable properties, the appraiser should have considered not only the industrial value of the subject and the comparable sales but also the commercial value.

Some industrial sites have frontage in heavily traveled areas, which adds commercial value to the site. Companies may want this exposure to sell products directly to the public, perhaps as a factory outlet store, or they may consider it useful to heighten their profile in the community. This is particularly important for flex-space industrial parks because they often have tenants that are engaged in retail activity.

Zoning and Use Restrictions

In most geographical locations, there are various levels of industrial zoning that dictate the potential use of the property, and the differences between these levels can significantly affect the value of a building.

For instance, a property that is zoned for light industrial use can obviously not be used for an industry that is categorized as heavy industrial. Value differences among the various strata of zoning ordinances can occur depending on the supply and demand in the area under appraisal. In other words, if there is a dearth of heavy industrial property available, a property already zoned for heavy industrial use may be worth a lot more than a property zoned for light industrial, or vice versa. If the appraiser did not find comparable properties with zoning the same as the subject property, adjustments should have been made accordingly.

Incentives from Government Entities

A variety of property tax incentives and other types of incentives are sometimes offered in certain locations by government entities. Some are offered to bring businesses in to develop land, but some are available for existing structures. These may include various programs such as enterprise zones, tax credits, utility discounts, tax-exempt industrial bonds, property tax credits or abatements, special financing, employment training incentives, and employment credits.

Incentives of this type can affect the value of a property, but since they are often temporary and conditional, an adjustment may not have been made. Nevertheless, if the reviewer is aware of such incentives, it is important to consider what their impact may be on the value.

Transportation Services

The appraiser may have adjusted for transportation services depending on the situation. The availability of docks for shipping, as well as railroad spurs and private airports, can have a major effect on value. Conversely, it may be found that although a property has some of these alternatives, they add little or no value because there is little demand for them.

For instance, in one geographical location the majority of companies may ship by truck, so the presence of a rail spur on or near the property may not add significant value. In another area where shipping by rail is common, the lack of a rail spur may severely diminish the value of a property.

Additional Size Issues

The reviewer should note if the appraiser stayed within the size range of the subject property. Buildings that are 70,000 or 80,000 square feet in size generally do not trade at the same price per square foot as buildings that are 10,000 or 15,000 square feet. There are exceptions to this, but even so, the general rule is that one should not try to prove a value using comparable sales that are dissimilar in size to the subject.

Another type of building to distinguish is a flex-space building. One building may be 150,000 square feet in size, but it may be leased out in smaller areas, such as 5,000- or 10,000-square-foot segments, to different tenants. These types of buildings usually do not rent as triple net buildings, and the rent is normally much higher on a per-square-foot basis. Consequently, the price per square foot for a large flex-space building is normally higher because the value of small spaces leased for higher rents increases the total worth of the building. When a large single-user building is vacated, the owner may attempt to build walls and make flex space out of it. However, the cost often is prohibitive—that is, the project is not cost-effective because the cost to construct walls and separate the spaces and electrical meters is too high to recover in a reasonable amount of time.

Red Flag

The appraiser should not have mixed flex-space industrial buildings with single-user-space industrial buildings. Flex-space buildings generally rent and sell for more per square foot.

Extremely Large (Jumbo) Buildings

The reviewer should understand that buildings that are extremely large often sell or lease for a much lower price per square foot than moderate-sized buildings. However, *jumbo* is a relative term that may be interpreted differently depending on the location of the building. In some parts of the country a 200,000-square-foot building may not be considered excessively large, whereas in another part of the country, it may be. However, buildings that are close to or over the 1,000,000-square-foot size should be considered jumbo buildings regardless of the location.

Often, very large buildings stay on the market for a long time, and generally buyers are companies that want their headquarters as part of the facility. Buildings of this type can at times be difficult to value. If there is a specific buyer who needs a lot of space, there may be very few options for that buyer, whereas there may also be very few buyers for this type of building. The point is that although a building of this kind may be on the market a long time, when the right buyer comes along, the buyer may be willing to pay a relatively high price because of scarcity. On the other hand, since there are very few buyers, buildings like this may be listed at a certain price, but they may sell for much less than the listed price because the seller is susceptible to a lower offer due to the lack of interest among potential buyers. Therefore, the resulting sale price may have a lot to do with whether or not the owner wants to hold the property for a long time to wait for the particular buyer who needs this type of property.

Essentially, an oversized building may be considered a superadequate structure. The gist of this is that the reviewer needs to realize that the more specialized or atypical a building is, the fewer buyers there will be for it, and the more it may suffer from economic obsolescence because it is nonstandard.

In other words, when a building exceeds a certain size, it often becomes less marketable, and the price per square foot may decrease, sometimes dramatically. For instance, buildings smaller than 100,000 square feet might sell for $50 a square foot, whereas a building with 500,000 square feet may sell for $30 per square foot. The size of the city, the amount of industry in the city, and the economic conditions in the area will have a bearing on the marketability of larger buildings.

Variation in Sale Prices

Sometimes, the reviewer may note that there are rather extreme variations in the sale prices of buildings, and the reasons may not be apparent. One possible explanation can be found in understanding the motivations of corporate sellers. Manufacturers typically are not real estate investors, and when they have excess property that is costly to maintain, they may accept a lower offer for the property in order to get rid of it. The manufacturers' income is based on making and selling products, not leasing or selling real estate.

There are also other reasons why a sale might be less than other comparable sales if a manufacturer is the seller. In some instances, there is great pressure on companies by shareholders to produce high short-term profits, and holding assets such as vacant buildings drags on those profits. Also, the pay structure for management is often linked to the company's profitability. The sale of a closed facility at below-market value hurts profitability, but if the property is sold quickly, only one year's profitability is affected. However, if the property stays on the books as a fixed asset year after year, it continues to increase investment and reduces the rate of return, which in turn reduces executive incomes and also decreases the company's return on investment.

For these reasons a manufacturer might be more susceptible to a lower offer for a building than would be an owner in the business of leasing industrial property. The former does not want to be in the real estate holding or leasing business, but the latter is specifically in that business and will probably be much more patient in waiting for a buyer.

Exhibits 7.10 through 7.12 are examples of grids used for adjusting comparable properties. In Exhibit 7.10, the sales are put into a grid without adjustments. Exhibits 7.11 and 7.12 demonstrate two of the

Exhibit 7.10
Summary of Comparable Building Sales—Unadjusted

SUMMARY OF COMPARABLE BUILDING SALES—UNADJUSTED

No.	Location	Age/ Sale Date	Land/Bldg Ratio	Building Size	Office Percent	Wall Height	Price	Price/SF
1	1402 Barker Rd.	1980 Feb-13	3.86:1	90,000	14	20	$4,222,000	$46.91
2	84229 Whelen Ln.	1991 Mar-12	2.63:1	41,072	9.06	24	$1,875,000	$45.65
3	8402 Cartright St.	1996 Jan-13	2.8:1	59,003	10	20	$2,550,000	$43.22
4	20044 Everly Rd.	1978 Jun-12	2.94:1	129,434	9.19	24	$5,200,000	$40.17
5	NE 284th St.	1980 Dec-13	3.5:1	60,000	10.8	24	$2,752,000	$45.87
6	8719 Pagonia Rd.	1991 Apr-13	2.53:1	80,747	8	24	$3,700,000	$45.82
	SUBJECT PROPERTY COMPARISON:							
	Widget Machinery Co.	1990	3:1 (adj.)	104,000				
	Unadjusted price per square foot:			$ 44				
	Indicated unadjusted value:			$ 4,576,000				
	Add adjusted excess land:			498,840				
	Total site:			5,074,840				

Exhibit 7.11

Summary of Comparable Building Sales—Adjusted

SUMMARY OF COMPARABLE BUILDING SALES—ADJUSTED															
No.	Location	Age/ Sale Date	Land/Bldg Ratio	Building Size	Percent Office	Clear Height	Price	Price/SF	Econ. Age	Con-dition	Office Qual/%	Const. Type	Misc.	Net Adj.	Adj. S/F
1	1402 Barker Rd.	1980 Feb-13	3.86:1	90,000	14	20	$ 4,222,000	$ 46.91	3	2		-6	-4	-5	$ 41.91
2	84229 Whelen Ln.	1991 Mar-12	2.63:1	41,072	9.06	24	$ 1,875,000	$ 45.65			-4		2	-2	$ 43.65
3	8402 Cartright St.	1996 Jan-13	2.8:1	59,003	10	20	$ 2,550,000	$ 43.22	-2	-3		4	2	1	$ 44.22
4	20044 Everly Rd.	1978 Jun-12	2.94:1	129,434	9.19	24	$ 5,200,000	$ 40.17	5	1			-4	2	$ 42.17
5	NE 284th St.	1980 Dec-13	3.5:1	60,000	10.8	24	$ 2,752,000	$ 45.87	3		-4		-2	-3	$ 42.87
6	8719 Pagonia Rd.	1991 Apr-13	2.53:1	80,747	8	24	$ 3,700,000	$ 45.82			-2		-3	-5	$ 40.82
	SUBJECT PROPERTY COMPARISON:														
	Widget Machinery Co.	1990	3:1 (adj.)	104,000											
	Adjusted price per square foot:			$ 43											
	Indicated adjusted value:			$ 4,472,000											
	Add adjusted excess land:			498,840											
	Total site:			4,970,840											

Exhibit 7.12

Additional Adjustment Information

COMP SALES DATA	SUBJECT	COMP 1		COMP 2		COMP 3	
Sale Price:	N/A	3,900,000		4,300,000		4,400,000	
Address:	883 Arrow Rd.	4209 NW Alvin Rd.		8219 Hwy 99		29001 84th St.	
City/State:	Vancouver, WA	Vancouver, WA		Vancouver, WA		Vancouver, WA	
Assessor Parcel Number:	223994000	243986000		299001000		244918000	
Ownership Type:	Fee Simple	Fee Simple		Fee Simple		Fee Simple	
Verification:	N/A	J. Smith		J. Smith		J. Smith	
Grantor:	N/A	Herring Corp.		Acme Mfg. Corp		John and Jane Doe	
Grantee:	N/A	Adam Rogers		Wellborn Corp.		Sealy Corp.	
Total Size:	67,000	58,000		74,000		62,000	
Price per SF:	N/A	67.24		58.11		70.97	
ADJUSTMENTS:			**ADJ.**		**ADJ.**		**ADJ.**
Financing:	N/A	Cash to seller		Cash to seller		Cash to seller	
Sale Contingencies:	N/A	remodel office	-40,000	Typical		Typical	
Personal Property:	None	None		None		None	
Built in M & E:	None	None		None		Bridge crane	-30,000
Sale Date:	N/A	10/05/13		12/15/2013		1/30/2013	
Location:	Average	Similar		Similar		Similar	
Year Built:	1992	1970	30,000	1994		1995	
Commercial Value:	No	No		No		No	
% Office	12%	14%		12%		11%	
% Manufacturing	75%	77%		74%		75%	
% Warehouse	13%	9%		14%		14%	
Total:	100%	100%		100%		100%	
Mezzanine	No	No		3,000 square feet	-15,000	No	
Land Size in Acres:	5	5		4.9		8	
Land Size in Square Feet:	217,800	217,800		213,444		348,480	
Land to Building Ratio:	3.25	3.76		2.88		5.62	
Excess Land:	No	No		No		Yes - 3 acres	-260,000
Ceiling Height:	24	24		26		24	
Type Construction:	Conc. Tilt-up	Conc. Tilt-up		Metal	100,000	Conc. Tilt-up	
Condition:	Average	Inferior	20,000				
Zoning:	Light Ind.	Light Ind.		Light Ind.		Light Ind.	
Sprinklers:	Yes/ dry	Yes/ wet		Yes/ dry		Yes/ dry	
Misc:	None	None		Insufficient Parking	100,000	None	
Gross Adjustments:			90,000		115,000		290,000
Net Adjustments:			-10,000		185,000		-290,000
Adjusted Sale Price:			3,890,000		4,485,000		4,110,000
Adjusted Price Per SF:			67.07		60.61		66.29
VALUE CONCLUSION							
$ Per S. F.Estimate:	$ 65.00						
Size of Subject Building:	67,000						
Value Conclusion:	**$ 4,355,000**						

more common ways of making adjustments. In Exhibit 7.11, the same sales are adjusted, and the adjustments are made as a dollar amount per square foot. In Exhibit 7.12, another method is utilized in which the top portion of the grid is without adjustments, and the bottom portion includes them. Each adjustment is made as an estimate of an actual dollar value. Exhibit 7.12 also includes more information than shown in Exhibits 7.10 and 7.11. Although not shown here, adjustments can also be made as a percentage of the sale price of the comparable property.

Chapter 8

Industrial Building Appraisal Excerpts

The following are excerpts from an example of an industrial facility appraisal with some related commentary. It includes office space as well as manufacturing space. Most industrial facilities will have both.

Valuation of Real Property—Buildings and Structures

Real Property Description

The subject was constructed in 1997, with some additions made up to 2004. The buildings are mostly engineered steel construction, which are classified by the Marshall Valuation Service as a standard Class S heavy industrial manufacturing construction. This type of structure includes construction materials and characteristics common among industrial buildings. The improvements consist of a heavy steel I-beam frame, steel panel walls, a steel roof frame, and a steel panel roof.

The main manufacturing facility includes crane runways for 12 cranes ranging in capacity from 6 to 55 tons. The crane bridges and hoists are valued with the personal property. The facility includes rooms of various dimensions and wall heights, and it has been labeled by Prosteel based on the operations conducted in those areas.

We have utilized Prosteel's nomenclature in discussing the subject improvements.

The subject consists of 472,334 square feet of improvements that are owned by Prosteel, and an additional 37,510 square feet of buildings leased from the Port. The leased buildings include a 5,010-square-foot office building and a 32,500-square-foot warehouse that are not part of this appraisal.

The main production facility is 434,506 square feet, and there is a freestanding two-story office building of 29,640 square feet. In addition, there is a freestanding training center of 1,848 square feet, a freestanding paint room of 4,830 square feet, and a freestanding paint intermix building of 1,510 square feet. The site improvements include concrete and asphalt paving, areas that have been graded and gravel covered, rail spurs, perimeter fencing, and so on.

Current Use

The current use is for heavy industrial manufacturing that processes steel coils.

Date of Construction

1997 for most of the facility.

Condition

Average to good. This property is in average to good condition by observation, but we have not inspected the property for hidden defects and cannot warranty or guarantee the condition. Our estimate of condition is based simply on basic observation.

Number of Floors

Mostly one. The Administration Building and one of the electrical equipment rooms have two floors. This represents only a small percentage of the overall floor space. The Cold Mill Building also includes a basement area of approximately 10,865 square feet.

Exhibit 8.1
Details of the Office Area

Area No.	Building	Square Feet
1	Administration	29,640
2	Training Room	1,848
3	Cold Room	5,334
4	Paint Line	5,334
5	Workshop	3,060
Total		45,216 square feet, or 10% of the gross building area

Dimensions

The dimensions of the entire complex are irregular. The dimension of each of the individual buildings is fairly regular.

Area

472,334 square feet.

Ground Floor Area

440,433 square feet, or 93 percent of the gross building area.

Office Area

45,216 square feet, or 10 percent of the gross building area. See Exhibit 8.1.

Heated Floor Space

51,556 square feet, or 11 percent of the gross building area. See Exhibit 8.2.

Exhibit 8.2
Details of the Heated Floor Space

Building	Square Feet
Cold Roll Mill Office	5,334
Paint Line Office	5,334
Workshop Office	3,060
Administration Office	29,640
Training Room	1,848
Paint Store	4,830
Intermix	1,510
Total	51,556 square feet, or 11% of the gross building area

Exhibit 8.3
Details of the Wall Height

Area No.	Building	Wall Height, Feet
1	Export Coil Handling	62
2	Zincalume Line	100
3	Finished Product Storage	42
4	Paint Line	72
5	Zincalume	24–45
6	Zinc Storage	27
7	Utilities	45
8	Pickle Line	41.5
9	Pickle Line	28.5
10	Raw Acid Storage	34
11	Cold Roll Mill	62
12	Cold Roll Mill	48.5
13	Cold Roll Mill Office	20
14	Paint Line Office	21
15	Workshop	34
16	Cold Mill Motor Room	56
17	Paint Line	28.5
18	Cut-to-Length Line	26–31
19	Administration Office	9
20	Training Center	8
21	Paint Storage	18
22	Intermix	10

Wall Height

8 to 100 feet. See Exhibit 8.3.

Fire Sprinklered Area

49,708 square feet, or 10 percent of the gross building area. See Exhibit 8.4.

Exhibit 8.4
Details of the Fire Sprinklered Area

Building	Square Feet
Cold Roll Mill Office	5,334
Paint Line Office	5,334
Workshop	3,060
Administration Office	29,640
Paint Storage	4,830
Intermix	1,510
Total	49,708 square feet, or 10% of the gross building area

Loading Facilities

Truck-height docks: 1

Drive-in doors: 36

Rail doors: 2 (Export coil building has a pass-through rail line.)

Rail docks: 2

Crane Capacity

6 to 55 tons. See Exhibit 8.5.

Construction and Finish

The construction and finish details of the subject are described in Exhibit 8.6.

Deferred Maintenance

Deferred maintenance causes physical depreciation that is curable when repaired. A cursory inspection of the subject property did not reveal any deferred maintenance requirements. This facility appears to be adequately maintained.

Functional Utility

The functional utility of the improvements affects the performance and usability of a building, and it is an important factor that will be

Exhibit 8.5
Details of the Crane Capacity

Crane No.	Building/Area	Craneway Capacity
1	Pickle Line	11 Tons, 58′ Wide
2	Cold Mill	50 Tons, 90′ Wide
3	Export	55 Tons, 110′ Wide
4	Export	55 Tons, 110′ Wide
5	Zincalume Line	22 Tons, 72′ Wide
6	Finished-Product Storage	33 Tons, 72′ Wide
7	Paint Line	11 Tons, 55′ Wide
8	Recoil Slit Line	33 Tons, 72′ Wide
9	Zinc Storage	11 Tons, 21′ Wide
10	Workshop	11 Tons, 60′ Wide
11	Zinc/Alum. Storage	6 Tons, 21′ Wide
12	Cold Mill	33 Tons, 95′ Wide

Exhibit 8.6

Details of the Construction and Finish

Building Number	1	2	3	4	5
Building Name	Bldg 1 - Export Coil Handling	Bldg 2 - Zincalume Line	Bldg 3 - Finished Product Storage	Bldg 4 - Paint Line	Bldg 5 - Zincalume Line E.E.R.
Year(s) of Construction	1997	1997	1997	1997	1997
Condition	Good	Good	Good	Good	Good
# of Floors	1	1	1	1	1
Dimensions	115 x 475	86 x 364.5	86 x 776.5	64 x 706	80 x 145
Area	55,373	31,374	66,779	45,184	11,600
Ground Floor Area	55,373	31,374	66,779	45,184	11,600
Office Area (Sq. Ft.)	0	0	0	0	0
Air Conditioned Area (Sq. Ft.)	0	0	0	0	11,600
Heated Area	0	0	0	0	0
Wall Height	62	100	42	72	24 - 45
Fire Sprinklered Area (Sq. Ft.)	0	0	0	0	0
Truck Docks	0	0	0	0	0
Drive-In Doors	1	3	4	5	0
Rail Docks/Doors	2	0	0	0	0
Effective Age	9	9	9	9	9
Economic Life	45	45	45	45	35
Functional Utility	Average	Average	Average	Average	Average
Construction Characteristics	Class S	Class S	Class S	Class S	Class S
Exterior Walls	Pre-Engineered Steel Panel	Pre-Engineered Steel Panel	Pre-Engineered Steel Panel	Pre-Engineered Steel Panel	Pre-Engineered Steel Panel
Foundation	Poured Concrete	Poured Concrete	Poured Concrete	Poured Concrete	Poured Concrete
Roof Deck	Pre-Engineered Steel Panel	Pre-Engineered Steel Panel	Pre-Engineered Steel Panel	Pre-Engineered Steel Panel	Pre-Engineered Steel Panel
Roof Shape	Single-Pitched	Double-Pitched	Single-Pitched	Double-Pitched	Single-Pitched
Frame	Steel I-Beam And Column	Steel I-Beam And Column	Steel I-Beam And Column	Steel I-Beam And Column	Steel I-Beam And Column
Roof Additions	Gutters And Downspouts	Gutters And Downspouts	Gutters And Downspouts	Gutters And Downspouts	Gutters And Downspouts
Insulation	Vinyl-Backed Fiberglass Batt	Vinyl-Backed Fiberglass Batt	Vinyl-Backed Fiberglass Batt	Vinyl-Backed Fiberglass Batt	Vinyl-Backed Fiberglass Batt
Floor	Finished Poured Concrete	Finished Poured Concrete	Finished Poured Concrete	Finished Poured Concrete	Finished Poured Concrete
Ceiling	Pre-Engineered Steel Panel	Pre-Engineered Steel Panel	Pre-Engineered Steel Panel	Pre-Engineered Steel Panel	Pre-Engineered Steel Panel
Lighting	Sodium Vapor	Sodium Vapor	Sodium Vapor	Sodium Vapor	Sodium Vapor

Building Number	6	7	8	9	10
Building Name	Bldg 7/8 - POT Equip/Zinc Storage	Bldg 17 - Utilities	Bldg 20 - Pickle Line	Bldg 21 - Pickle Line E.E.R.	Bldg 22 - Raw Acid Storage
Year(s) of Construction	1997	1997	1997	1997	1997
Condition	Good	Good	Good	Good	Good
# of Floors	1	1 with mezzanine	1	1	1
Dimensions	80 x 101	90 x 248	70 x 436	42 x 81.5	42 x 53
Area	8,080	22,320	30,876	3,423	2,226
Ground Floor Area	8,080	22,320	30,876	3,423	2,226
Office Area (Sq. Ft.)	0	0	0	0	0
Air Conditioned Area (Sq. Ft.)	0	0	0	3,423	0
Heated Area	0	0	0	0	0
Wall Height	27	45	41.5	28.5	34
Fire Sprinklered Area (Sq. Ft.)	0	0	0	0	0
Truck Docks	0	0	0	0	0
Drive-In Doors	3	3	4	0	0
Rail Docks/Doors	0	0	0	0	0
Effective Age	9	9	9	9	9
Economic Life	35	45	45	35	35
Functional Utility	Average	Average	Average	Average	Average
Construction Characteristics	Class S	Class S	Class S	Class S	Class S
Exterior Walls	Pre-Engineered Steel Panel	Pre-Engineered Steel Panel	Pre-Engineered Steel Panel	Pre-Engineered Steel Panel	Pre-Engineered Steel Panel
Foundation	Poured Concrete	Poured Concrete	Poured Concrete	Poured Concrete	Poured Concrete
Roof Deck	Pre-Engineered Steel Panel	Pre-Engineered Steel Panel	Pre-Engineered Steel Panel	Pre-Engineered Steel Panel	Pre-Engineered Steel Panel
Roof Shape	Single-Pitched	Double-Pitched	Double-Pitched	Single-Pitched	Single-Pitched
Frame	Steel I-Beam And Column	Steel I-Beam And Column	Steel I-Beam And Column	Steel I-Beam And Column	Steel I-Beam And Column
Roof Additions	Gutters And Downspouts	Gutters And Downspouts	Gutters And Downspouts	Gutters And Downspouts	Gutters And Downspouts
Insulation	Vinyl-Backed Fiberglass Batt	Vinyl-Backed Fiberglass Batt	Vinyl-Backed Fiberglass Batt	Vinyl-Backed Fiberglass Batt	Vinyl-Backed Fiberglass Batt
Floor	Finished Poured Concrete	Finished Poured Concrete	Finished Poured Concrete	Finished Poured Concrete	Finished Poured Concrete
Ceiling	Pre-Engineered Steel Panel	Pre-Engineered Steel Panel	Pre-Engineered Steel Panel	Pre-Engineered Steel Panel	Pre-Engineered Steel Panel
Lighting	Sodium Vapor	Sodium Vapor	Sodium Vapor	Sodium Vapor	Sodium Vapor

(*Continued*)

Exhibit 8.6

Continued

Building Number	11	12	13	14	15
Building Name	Bldg 23 - Reversing Cold Mill	Bldg 24 - Roll Mill E.E.R.	Bldg 31 - CRM/Pickle/Prod. Office	Bldg 32 - ZAL/Paint/Prod. Office	Bldg 34/41 - Workshop/Maintenance Stores
Year(s) of Construction	1997	1997	1997	1997	1997
Condition	Good	Good	Good	Good	Good
# of Floors	1, with 10,865 Sq. Ft. Basement	2	1	1	1
Dimensions	103 x 453	42 x 148	63.5 x 84	63.5 x 84	93 x 263 (Irregular)
Area	57,524	12,432	5,334	5,334	22,259
Ground Floor Area	46,659	6,216	5,334	5,334	22,259
Office Area (Sq. Ft.)	0	0	5,334	5,334	3,060
Air Conditioned Area (Sq. Ft.)	0	12,432	5,334	5,334	3,060
Heated Area	0	0	5,334	5,334	3,060
Wall Height	62	48.5	20	21	34
Fire Sprinklered Area (Sq. Ft.)	0	0	5,334	5,334	3,060
Truck Docks	0	0	0	0	1
Drive-In Doors	2	0	0	0	2
Rail Docks/Doors	0	0	0	0	0
Effective Age	9	9	9	9	9
Economic Life	45	35	35	35	35
Functional Utility	Average	Average	Average	Average	Average
Construction Characteristics	Class S	Class S	Class S	Class S	Class S
Exterior Walls	Pre-Engineered Steel Panel	Pre-Engineered Steel Panel	Pre-Engineered Steel Panel	Pre-Engineered Steel Panel	Pre-Engineered Steel Panel
Foundation	Poured Concrete	Poured Concrete	Poured Concrete	Poured Concrete	Poured Concrete
Roof Deck	Pre-Engineered Steel Panel	Pre-Engineered Steel Panel	Pre-Engineered Steel Panel	Pre-Engineered Steel Panel	Pre-Engineered Steel Panel
Roof Shape	Single-Pitched	Single-Pitched	Single-Pitched	Single-Pitched	Double-Pitched
Frame	Steel I-Beam And Column	Steel I-Beam And Column	Steel I-Beam And Column	Steel I-Beam And Column	Steel I-Beam And Column
Roof Additions	Gutters And Downspouts	Gutters And Downspouts	Gutters And Downspouts	Gutters And Downspouts	Gutters And Downspouts
Insulation	Vinyl-Backed Fiberglass Batt	Vinyl-Backed Fiberglass Batt	Vinyl-Backed Fiberglass Batt	Vinyl-Backed Fiberglass Batt	Vinyl-Backed Fiberglass Batt
Floor	Finished Poured Concrete	Finished Poured Concrete	Finished Poured Concrete	Finished Poured Concrete	Finished Poured Concrete
Ceiling	Pre-Engineered Steel Panel	Pre-Engineered Steel Panel	Suspended Acoustical Tile	Suspended Acoustical Tile	Pre-Engineered Steel Panel
Lighting	Sodium Vapor	Sodium Vapor	Recessed Fluorescent	Recessed Fluorescent	Sodium Vapor and Fluorescent Strip

Building Number	16	17	18	19
Building Name	Bldg 39 - CM Motor Room	Bldg 40 - Paint Line E.E.R.	Bldg 49 - Cut to Length Line	Bldg 9 - Administration Office
Year(s) of Construction	1997	1997	2003	1997
Condition	Good	Good	Good	Good
# of Floors	1	1	1	2
Dimensions	66 x 123	42 x 78	103 x 398 (Irregular)	65 x 228
Area	8,118	3,276	42,994	29,640
Ground Floor Area	8,118	3,276	42,994	14,820
Office Area (Sq. Ft.)	0	0	0	29,640
Air Conditioned Area (Sq. Ft.)	0	3,276	0	29,640
Heated Area	0	0	0	29,640
Wall Height	56	28.5	26 - 31	9
Fire Sprinklered Area (Sq. Ft.)	0	0	0	29,640
Truck Docks	0	0	0	0
Drive-In Doors	2	0	4	0
Rail Docks/Doors	0	0	2	0
Effective Age	9	9	3	9
Economic Life	35	35	45	45
Functional Utility	Average	Average	Average	Average
Construction Characteristics	Class S	Class S	Class S	Class C
Exterior Walls	Pre-Engineered Steel Panel	Pre-Engineered Steel Panel	Pre-Engineered Steel Panel	Stucco and Metal Panel
Foundation	Poured Concrete	Poured Concrete	Poured Concrete	Poured Concrete
Roof Deck	Pre-Engineered Steel Panel	Pre-Engineered Steel Panel	Pre-Engineered Steel Panel	Pre-Engineered Steel Panel
Roof Shape	Single-Pitched	Single-Pitched	Single-Pitched	Hip Style
Frame	Steel I-Beam And Column	Steel I-Beam And Column	Steel I-Beam And Column	Steel Column and Web Truss
Roof Additions	Gutters And Downspouts	Gutters And Downspouts	Gutters And Downspouts	Gutters And Downspouts
Insulation	Vinyl-Backed Fiberglass Batt	Vinyl-Backed Fiberglass Batt	Vinyl-Backed Fiberglass Batt	Fiberglass
Floor	Finished Poured Concrete	Finished Poured Concrete	Finished Poured Concrete	Tile and Carpeting
Ceiling	Pre-Engineered Steel Panel	Pre-Engineered Steel Panel	Pre-Engineered Steel Panel	Suspended Acoustical Tile
Lighting	Sodium Vapor	Sodium Vapor	Sodium Vapor	Recessed Fluorescent

(*Continued*)

Exhibit 8.6
Continued

Building Number	20	21	22
Building Name	Bldg 10 - Training Center	Bldg 14 - Paint Store	Intermix
Year(s) of Construction	1997	1997	2004
Condition	Good	Good	Good
# of Floors	1	1	1
Dimensions	33 x 56	46 x 105	30 x 35 (Irregular)
Area	1,848	4,830	1,510
Ground Floor Area	1,848	4,830	1,510
Office Area (Sq. Ft.)	1,848	0	0
Air Conditioned Area (Sq. Ft.)	1,848	0	460
Heated Area	1,848	4,830	1,510
Wall Height	8	18	10
Fire Sprinklered Area (Sq. Ft.)	0	4,830	1,510
Truck Docks	0	0	0
Drive-In Doors	0	2	1
Rail Docks/Doors	0	0	0
Effective Age	9	9	2
Economic Life	35	40	35
Functional Utility	Average	Average	Average
Construction Characteristics	Class S	Class C	Class S
Exterior Walls	Pre-Engineered Steel Panel	Concrete Block	Pre-Engineered Steel Panel
Foundation	Poured Concrete	Poured Concrete	Poured Concrete
Roof Deck	Pre-Engineered Steel Panel	Pre-Engineered Steel Panel	Pre-Engineered Steel Panel
Roof Shape	Double-Pitched	Double-Pitched	Double-Pitched
Frame	Clear-Span Pre-Engineered Structural Steel	Load-Bearing Concrete Block	Clear-Span Pre-Engineered Structural Steel
Roof Additions	Gutters And Downspouts	Gutters And Downspouts	Gutters And Downspouts
Insulation	Vinyl-Backed Fiberglass Batt	None	Vinyl-Backed Fiberglass Batt
Floor	Finished Poured Concrete	Finished Poured Concrete	Finished Poured Concrete
Ceiling	Suspended Acoustical Tile	Pre-Engineered Steel Panel	Pre-Engineered Steel Panel
Lighting	Recessed Fluorescent	Explosion Proof Lights	Explosion Proof Lights

considered by prospective purchasers. *The Dictionary of Real Estate Appraisal* defines *functional utility* as "the ability of a property or building to be useful and to perform the function for which it is intended according to current market tastes and standards; the efficiency of a building's use in terms of architectural style, design, and layout, traffic patterns, and the size and type of rooms." Items that limit functional utility have what is often referred to as *functional obsolescence.* Features and components that have *functional obsolescence* are generally those that result from deficiencies or superadequacies in the structure.

The subject was built for the manufacturing process that it employs, and the buildings are generally functional for this utilization. However, it does suffer from some functional obsolescence due to the superadequacy of the ceiling heights, which are excessive. Heavy industrial, crane-served buildings typically have wall heights that range from 40 to 60 feet. However, there are two sections of the subject building that have wall heights of 100 and 72 feet, respectively.

The salability of the property will probably not be hampered by this superadequacy because the building is unheated and the added maintenance attributable to the additional wall area would be insignificant. However, the costs to construct the building would be lower if the heights were lower, which would be considered in a cost approach. Nevertheless, this has been noted, but it is not adjusted for in the appraisal because the cost approach has not been utilized in this appraisal except in regard to trending, and the difference would be hard to estimate in the sales comparison approach adjustments.

Zoning

According to the Clarkdale County Planning Department, there is no zoning for the subject site, but the county recommends a heavy industrial use for the land. Consequently, to obtain permits the use must still be approved by the county.

Highest and Best Use

The four criteria the highest and best use must meet are legal permissibility, physical possibility, financial feasibility, and maximum profitability.

The conclusion is that the current use is the highest and best use and, alternatively, that another manufacturing use would be a possible highest and best use. However, since the building is somewhat specialized, it would not lend itself to every manufacturing use. And because the property is encumbered with the facility it now has, demolishing and rebuilding something different would not be financially feasible. In any event, the manufacturing facility on the subject property is presently the one that meets each of the highest and best use criteria.

As If Vacant. The site does not appear to have any drainage problems. Soil and subsoil conditions appear stable and suitable for development compatible with other properties in the area.

There appear to be no topographical problems that would hinder development of the site.

The subject has access to all utilities typically found in this location.

Since the site qualified for heavy industrial use, this use appears to be the one that best meets all four highest and best use criteria for this property. Therefore, any industrial use that would meet the highest and best use criteria and need this amount of land would be the highest and best use for this land if it were vacant.

As Improved. The subject is currently improved with a large industrial building and office space. The location is near Route I-5, and it is functioning profitably as a steel processing facility.

Because the highest return on investment appears to be a continued industrial use, its current use is considered its highest and best use.

Exposure and Marketing Time

The improved property sales indicate that exposure time (that is, the length of time the subject property would have been exposed for sale in the market had it sold at the market value concluded in this analysis as of the date of this valuation) would have been from 24 to 48 months. The estimated marketing time (that is, the amount of time it would probably take to sell the subject property if exposed in the market beginning on the date of this valuation) is estimated to be about 24 to 48 months.

Valuation Methodology for Buildings and Structures

Three basic approaches are typically used to estimate market value for buildings and structures. The approaches have been previously mentioned in conjunction with the machinery and equipment, but they are explained a little differently here, as they apply to real property. The approaches are these:

1. Cost approach
2. Sales comparison (market) approach
3. Income approach

The **cost approach** involves deducting accrued depreciation from the cost new of the improvements. *Cost new* is estimated on the basis of current prices for components of the improvements. Depreciation is computed after analyzing any disadvantages or deficiencies of the improvements. Land value and entrepreneurial profit are added to improvement cost new. Land value is developed using sales of similar sites. Entrepreneurial profit is the difference between the market value of the subject and the cost to develop (cost of the improvements plus land value).

The **sales comparison approach** involves gathering data on sales of comparable properties and analyzing the nature and condition of each sale and providing logical adjustments for differing characteristics. Typically, a common denominator is found. For land value, this is usually a price per square foot (SF) or price per acre; for improved properties, it may be the price per square foot, price per unit, or a gross income multiplier. The market approach can be a good value indicator when sales of similar properties are available.

The **income approach** is predicated on the assumption that there is a definite relationship between the income a property will earn and its value. The anticipated annual net income is computed to an indication of value. *Net income* is the income generated before payment of any debt service. The process of converting it into value is called *capitalization.* Net income is then divided by a capitalization rate to get an indicated value. Factors such as risk, time, interest on the capital investment, and recapture of the depreciating asset are considered in the rate. Applying a capitalization rate based on indications from comparable sales reflects expectations and actions of buyers and sellers in the market.

Cost Approach: Not Utilized

Since the subject property is 10 years old, the cost approach was not used for this appraisal because it would not have provided good evidence for the value. If the cost new of the property were estimated, the depreciation would need to be market driven to be accurate, which would render it irrelevant since it would be derived from the same information that was used for the market approach. The appraisal process therefore involved no departure from Standards Rule 1-4.

Income Approach: Not Utilized

Because of the large size of the main building and the specific configuration of the buildings, the income approach was not utilized. Buildings of this size are generally not rented or leased, and no income data could be found that could be used to value this property utilizing this approach. The appraisal process therefore involved no departure from Standards Rule 1-4.

Comparable Sales Approach: Utilized

The comparable sales approach was considered to be the only approach applicable to the subject. The subject is around 472,000 square feet, and buildings of this size are not common, so a wide search was made. Some buildings were found in the Northwest, and a national search was also performed. Buildings found nationally are only presented to buttress the value determination that was made from the more local sales; therefore, adjustments were not made to the national sales.

The Northwest sales were mostly in Oregon, with one in Washington. Most of them were within 100 miles of the subject. Generally, the smaller the property, the higher the price per square foot, and some of the sales were smaller than the subject. Consequently, the smaller properties would typically represent the upper end of value. Exhibits 8.7 and 8.8 show the comparable sales, and they are followed by a discussion of the sales.

Comparable Sales Approach: Discussion

National Sales

The national sales show a range of value from $7.71 to $37.36 per foot before an estimate for the land value is deducted from the price per square foot, with the exception of one property that was also on leased land. The deduction for the land is an estimate of 30 percent, which was derived from the percentage of land value noted in Exhibit 8.8, which shows the jumbo sales for the Northwest. Those sales show an average of about 36 percent for the land, and it was rounded down to 30 percent for the national sales. Other than the land adjustment, adjustments have not been made for the national sales because they are included to buttress the Northwest sales, and the Northwest sales are considered the primary evidence for the building value.

Exhibit 8.7

Sales of Jumbo Industrial Buildings Nationally

NATIONAL SALES OF JUMBO INDUSTRIAL BUILDINGS								
Sale	City/State	Sale Price, $	Sale Date	Bldg Size, SF	Land Acres	Year Built	Price Per SF, $	Minus Land
1) 5851 N 51st Ave.	Glendale, AZ	3,700,000	Aug-06	371,403	21.75	1952	9.96	6.97
2) 8110 Kempwood Dr.	Houston, TX	8,900,000	Jun-06	435,168	20	1986	20.45	14.32
3) 2130 Refugee Rd.	Columbus, OH	4,000,000	Aug-06	519,000	0	1970	7.71	7.71
4) 2305 Mount Vernon Ave.	Pomono, CA	9,178,855	Jul-06	442,910	12.01	1980	20.72	14.51
5) 8001 US 64 E	Knightsdale, NC	12,450,000	Jul-06	411,595	60	1972	30.25	21.17
6) 3501 Corporate Dr.	Joliet, IL	13,125,000	Aug-06	408,932	19	1999	32.10	22.47
7) 5765 N. Green Point Dr.	Groveport, OH	13,401,500	Aug-06	358,760	19.5	2000	37.36	26.15
8) 3710-3720 N. River Rd.	Franklin Park, IL	10,000,000	Jul-06	500,000	23	2002	20.00	14.00
9) 5820 Opus Dr.	Groveport, OH	12,800,000	Dec-06	406,694	27 est.	2006	31.47	22.03
10) 600-6005 Freeport Ave.	Memphis, TN	19,789,455	Jan-07	550,000	32.39	2000	35.98	25.19
11) 2801 River Rd.	Yakima, WA	8,150,000	Mar-06	501,270	21.14	1983	16.26	11.38
12) 6400 SE 101st Ave.	Portland, OR	11,400,000	Mar-06	423,379	70.21	1952	26.93	18.85
13) 10793 W County St.	Somerton, AZ	9,250,000	Oct-06	610,412	35.9	1998	15.15	10.61
14) 3765 Sunnybrook Rd.	Kent, OH	6,700,000	Dec-06	580,693	93.26	1985	11.54	8.08
15) 1127 Vaugh Dr.	Portland, TN	13,087,561	Sep-06	500,000	40	2005	26.18	18.32
16) 175 Bearfoot Rd.	Northborough, MA	14,000,000	Dec-06	495,809	55.13	2001	28.24	19.77
							$ 370	$ 262
			Subject Size SF Avg	Indicated Value Per Average				
	Subject Size:	472,334	16.34	$ 7,720,173				

Exhibit 8.8

Sales of Jumbo Industrial Buildings in the Northwest

SALES OF JUMBO BUILDINGS IN NORTHWEST					
Sale	1	2	3	4	5
Address	1600 NE 181st Ave	3950 Fairview Industrial Dr. SE	5555 N. Channel Ave	7920 SW Hunziker	219 C St.
City	Portland, OR	Salem, OR	Portland, OR	Tigard, OR	Washougal, WA
Sale Price	$ 13,375,000	$ 13,320,000	$ 7,750,000	$ 5,040,000	$ 2,297,050
Sale Date	Aug-05	Jul-06	Oct-06	May-04	Nov-05
Price per SF	$ 31.70	$ 25.98	$ 26.36	$ 33.39	$ 25.34
Imp Size	421,975	512,666	293,978	150,952	90,660
Yr Blt	1960/1983 renov	1982	1943	1965	Various
Site Size SF	746,618	2,394,450	625,957	701,315	348,480
In acres	17	55	14	16	8
L:B Ratio, X:1	1.77	4.67	2.13	4.65	3.84
Office %	8 est	5 est	5 est	5 est.	N/A
Adjustments					
Location	0.8	1	0.8	0.75	1.1
Const Type	1	0.95	1	1	1
Quality/Cond.	1.1	1	1.25	1.1	1.1
Net Adj'mnt	0.88	0.95	1.00	0.83	1.21
Adj'd SP/SF	27.89	24.68	26.36	27.55	30.66
Adj'd Sale Price	$ 11,770,000	$ 12,654,000	$ 7,750,000	$ 4,158,000	$ 2,779,431
Comments		85K of clean room 2 campuses	Older up to 50' ceiling ht.	Mix of steel frame and concrete tilt-up	Steel Bldg includes 6 structures
Land Deduction	$ 2,228,199	$ 7,145,971	$ 1,868,099	$ 2,092,997	$ 1,040,000
Final Value	$ 9,541,801	$ 5,508,029	$ 5,881,901	$ 2,065,003	$ 1,739,431
Price per SF	$ 22.61	$ 10.74	$ 20.01	$ 13.68	$ 19.19
Subject Bldg. Size	472,334	472,334	472,334	472,334	472,334
Value SF X 472,3345	$ 10,680,531	$ 5,074,706	$ 9,450,441	$ 6,461,465	$ 9,062,345
% of Land Value	17%	54%	24%	42%	45%

The national sale that is on leased land is Sale 3, and it also has the lowest value per square foot. Although it is not in the exhibit, the average adjusted price per square foot before the land is deducted is $23.14, which would indicate a value of $10,930,000 for the subject. With adjustments, the final value is $7,720,173, which is the indicated value from the national sales for the subject building.

We deducted the land value from the comparables for the national and Northwest properties. However, please note that a larger reduction for the land value for the subject could be justified because it has a much higher percentage of land, at 75 acres, than most of the comparable properties. That is the case because the manufacturing process requires a long building and because the extra land is needed for storing metal outside that is kept as inventory for production. An analysis of the land value follows this section.

Northwest Sales

The Northwest properties were mostly within 100 miles of the subject property. Sale 5, in Washougal, Washington, was smaller than the other sales, but it was included due to the lack of jumbo sales in the area. The land value for the sales was computed based on comparable land sales (see Exhibit 8.8).

Sale 1. This sale consists of five buildings on 181st Avenue and Morrison Street in Portland. This is a location superior to the subject location, which is not located in or near a metropolitan area. Morrison Street is a busy area in Portland, and this property also has commercial value as well as industrial value. The buildings are older—they were built in 1960 and renovated in 1983, and they were adjusted for condition due to their age.

These buildings vary from 22 to 26 feet in height, which is a typical height for industrial buildings. However, the fact that there are several buildings increases their value in at least one way: it is easier to lease smaller buildings, and they would bring more money per square foot than larger buildings. They were adjusted down for location and up for quality and condition because even though they are masonry buildings, the older age warranted the adjustment.

Sale 2. This is a multiproperty sale that consists of nine buildings in the same complex. This property was once owned by Mitsubishi Silicon America, and the appraiser has toured this facility. The construction date is 1982, but the construction is superior to the metal construction of the subject. These buildings would be categorized as Class B, instead of C and S for the subject.

The buildings are heavy concrete, but because of age have been adjusted for condition compared to the subject, which was built in 1997. This property is in Salem, Oregon, and it is the farthest away of all the sales. It may have more commercial value than the subject, but the location is rated as similar because the Salem area is not a strong manufacturing area.

Sale 3. This property was built in 1943. It has some deferred maintenance, and it was adjusted for condition. This building varies in height from 14 to 50 feet, making it similar in that characteristic to the subject. It is composed of one 293,978-square-foot building, and the building is a Class C structure. It is located on Hayden Island in Portland, which is superior to the location of the subject property.

Sale 4. This is a sale of the Coe Manufacturing plant. The building has 105,952 square feet and 701,315 square feet of site area, which would allow additions to the building. It is a mix of steel frame and concrete tilt-up construction. This is an older sale, and it was weighted accordingly. The building was started in 1965, but it was added on to since that time. The condition is considered average.

Sale 5. This is a sale of the Hambleton Brothers Lumber Company in Washougal, Washington. The buyer was Washougal Investors II LLC. It includes several tax lots covering 8.08 acres of land. The 90,660 square feet of improvements includes six structures of mixed construction that were built over many years. The average age is estimated to be about 1977 to 1985. These buildings are mostly metal.

Analysis of Land Lease

Although not the subject of this appraisal, the land lease that Prosteel pays annual rent on was analyzed to determine how it affects the building value. We adjusted for the land values for each of the Northwest comparable sales, which reduced those sales to make them more comparable to the subject's buildings. However, the subject has more land than the typical industrial facility, and it has more land than most of the comparable properties that we could find. The largest comparable property in terms of land size was national Sale 14, which had 93.26 acres of land, and the next largest were national Sale 16 and Northwest Sale 2, both of which had 55 acres. National Sale 3 was on leased land, and its square footage was very close to the subject's size.

Chapter 9

Analyzing the Machinery and Equipment Appraisal

Generally only two approaches are used to value machinery and equipment: the cost approach and the sales comparison approach. The income approach might be used to value a machine based on its production and efficiency, but it is so rarely used that this book will concentrate only on the first two approaches. But before they are examined, the reviewer needs to gain an understanding of the information the appraiser should have to utilize the approaches.

The Asset List

When appraisers begin a machinery and equipment assignment, the asset list is normally their starting point. Companies maintain asset lists for a variety of reasons, including inventory records, property tax records, and income tax records. Some companies keep very good records, while others do not, and equipment that is retired or newly added may not appear on the asset list. Therefore, the accuracy of the list can be an issue in the valuation of a company, particularly if it's a large company with a lot of machinery and equipment. The asset list may be called the *fixed asset list*, which generally means that items consumed in a year or less are not on the list.

Although it may seem simplistic, knowing what is actually at the industrial site where the equipment is supposed to be is one aspect of any machinery and equipment appraisal that should be considered when the appraisal is analyzed. Nevertheless, it is often the case that the majority of the value will reside in certain major pieces of equipment, and if those pieces are inventoried, the absence of less expensive equipment may not have a substantial effect on the value.

The appraiser might perform a sample inventory on the equipment and compare it to the asset list to determine the accuracy of the list. This exercise may begin with a check of 5 or 10 percent of the assets, which are chosen randomly. If these show the asset list to be accurate, the appraiser may stop there, but if the asset listing is unreliable at this point, the appraiser may take a larger percentage and, in some cases, may perform a detailed audit. Normally every piece of equipment will not be audited, unless the company is very small, because the value of spending time looking for smaller assets that have depreciated in value is questionable.

The appraiser may decide on a cutoff point in value for the assets that he or she will definitely examine, and this will vary according to the size of the company and the value of the assets. For example, only items over $100,000 in value may be physically examined for one company, whereas only items over $500,000 in value may be examined for another company.

Accounting Principles and the Asset List

Companies generally carry a *book value*, which is the value of their assets after depreciation for accounting purposes. Property is booked at a certain value according to the depreciated value, which is not the fair market value, and it is important to understand the difference. Under *generally accepted accounting principles* (GAAP), property owned by corporations is either *capitalized* or *expensed*. If the item is capitalized, it will be depreciated for income tax purposes over a certain number of years. If it is expensed, it will be depreciated fully in one year.

Capitalizing Equipment

For an example of capitalized equipment, consider the following example. The purchase price of a machine (normally including installation, transportation, and interest to finance it) is $1 million. It would typically be capitalized, and the company accountant would depreciate it according to IRS guidelines, generally for the maximum allowable depreciation. (*Note:* There are exceptions. For some calendar years, the IRS may allow accelerated depreciation.)

The IRS has industry classifications, and the allowed amount of depreciation correlates to the classification. With the $1 million example, if the equipment had an IRS designated life of seven years, the depreciation for each year would be as follows based on *straight-line depreciation*, which means each year gets the same amount of depreciation:

$1,000,000 / 7 = $142,857 per year (rounded)

The company is allowed by the IRS to deduct this amount each year for seven years, which reduces its taxes and results in higher profits. For a simplified example, assume the company made $3 million in gross income, and after expenses were paid, the company made a net profit of $400,000 before income taxes were paid. The spreadsheet in Exhibit 9.1 shows the difference in profits with and without the tax savings.

This also means that the value of the machine, as it is computed for book value, follows the seven-year cycle, as seen in Exhibit 9.2. In reality, this machine may be worth $300,000 in year 7, or $400,000 or $100,000 or even $50,000, but according to the IRS depreciation rules, it is depreciated to zero value in the seventh year.

Depreciation for Buildings

Although this chapter is about machinery and equipment, accounting methods for buildings will be briefly discussed since they are similar. Depreciation for buildings is also determined by what the IRS allows, and for commercial and industrial buildings the current "life" for buildings in these categories is 39 years. Land is not depreciated but instead

Exhibit 9.1
Machine Depreciation Example

Example: Machine Depreciation		
Cost of Machine:	IRS Life (Years):	Annual Depreciation:
$ 1,000,000	7	$ 142,857
Profit Without Depreciation:		
$ 3,000,000	Gross income	
$ 2,600,000	Expenses	
$ 400,000	Net profit	
34%	Tax rate	
$ 136,000	Taxes to pay	
$ 264,000	Profit for company without depreciation	
Profit with Depreciation:		
$ 3,000,000	Gross income	
$ 2,600,000	Expenses	
$ 400,000	Net profit	
$ 142,857	Depreciation for machine	
$ 257,143	Net profit including depreciation	
34%	Tax rate	
$ 87,429	Taxes to pay	
$ 312,571	Profit for company with depreciation	
Tax Savings with Depreciation:		
$ 48,571	Tax savings with depreciation	

Exhibit 9.2
Seven-Year Straight-Line Depreciation

Changes in Value: Seven-Year Straight-Line Depreciation		
Cost of Machine:	IRS Life (years):	Annual Depreciation:
$ 1,000,000	7	$ 142,857
Value of machine in year 1:		$ 857,143
Value of machine in year 2:		$ 714,286
Value of machine in year 3:		$ 571,429
Value of machine in year 4:		$ 428,571
Value of machine in year 5:		$ 285,714
Value of machine in year 6:		$ 142,857
Value of machine in year 7:		$ —

is segregated from the building based on its market value (often accountants will use the property tax assessment estimate for the land value). For example, if the building was purchased for $3 million, and the land is worth $300,000, the depreciation would be calculated as follows:

$$\$3,000,000 - \$300,000 = \$2,700,000$$

$$\$2,700,000 \, / \, 39 \text{ years} = \$69,231$$

Therefore, the company can deduct a depreciation expense of $69,231 per year, which will result in tax savings that increase profits for the company.

The depreciation for the machine may or may not have equaled the true yearly value diminution—if it happened to equal it, then that would be a coincidence. The machine may actually last for 10 or 15 years instead of 7 years. Or the machine may have become obsolete in 3 years and is no longer very useful to the company. In the latter case, there are ways to accelerate depreciation if it can be proven to the IRS.

With the building, depending on the economy of the area and the type of building it is, the value may have actually increased instead of decreased, and the chances that the value will correlate to the 39-year depreciation table is even less likely than with the machine.

Accounting Depreciation Not Used for Appraisal Purposes

As demonstrated thus far, the book value does not correlate to the fair market value, liquidation value, or any other value that the appraiser will be estimating. Depreciation used in accounting does not measure the fair market value of the equipment being depreciated. It is only an allocation of the annual depreciation for tax purposes. Therefore, the net book value of the plant, or of the machinery and equipment of the plant, is the sum of depreciated original costs, which is an artificial value based on IRS depreciation tables and not an appraised value.

Expensing Equipment

If the equipment is not capitalized by the company accountant, it will be *expensed.* When it is expensed for IRS purposes, it is depreciated in one year. Another way to say this is that it is "written off" in the same year it was purchased. Generally, a company will have a policy that sets a threshold at which the property it owns is either capitalized or expensed. For instance, a company may decide to expense every item under $2,500 and capitalize items over that amount.

Consequently, by examining the list, the appraiser should have noticed that nothing over $2,500 is on it, indicating that the list is a fixed asset list only and does not have expensed items on it. If that is the case, the appraiser should have asked the company for a complete listing of equipment, which would include the expensed items, because they are still counted in valuing the assets of the company. In analyzing the appraisal, the reviewer could also make the same determination if the asset list is part of the appraisal or if it can be requested. Adding expensed items that still have value may not amount to a lot, but it will make the appraisal more accurate.

It should also be noted that with some asset-based lending, the appraiser, at the direction of the lender, will list only those items over a certain threshold amount, regardless of accounting policy, because the potential lender cannot realistically use smaller assets for lien collateral.

Reconciling to the General Ledger

It is helpful to know if the appraiser has had the asset list reconciled to the general ledger. This is something that the appraiser cannot do—it must be done by the company's accountant. The reconciliation to the general ledger accounts for all the expenditures and validates the list as accurate in the company's accounting records.

Double entries and other mistakes are normally discovered in the process, as well as other accounting errors. Whether or not this has been done may not be stated in the appraisal, but depending on the level of review of the appraisal and the authority of the reviewer, it is an important step in confirming the accuracy of the asset list.

Classifications for the Asset List

Normally, the appraiser, upon receiving the asset list, will sort out the assets according to classifications. The company will likely have assigned cost center numbers and/or classification numbers that will help in gathering like-kind equipment into categories. The appraiser will need to do this to accurately *trend* the property, about which more will be discussed later in this chapter. The following is a typical classification table:

1. Buildings
   a. Production buildings
   b. Office buildings
   c. Small support structures
2. Land
   a. Utilized land
   b. Excess land buildable
   c. Excess land not buildable such as wetlands
3. Yard improvements
   a. Fencing
   b. Concrete
   c. Asphalt
   d. Guard shack or other small buildings
   e. Detention ponds
   f. Bone yard
   g. Storage areas—gases, chemicals, and so on
   h. Electrical equipment area
   i. Miscellaneous
4. Mainline production machinery—that is, mainline machinery used to produce goods. This category could include *computer numerical control* (CNC) *machines*, plastic injection mold machines, paper machines, baking ovens, wafer steppers, or other equipment depending on the industry.

5. General support equipment (nonintegrated). This category would include machines that are peripheral but necessary to the production process, such as brake presses, cutting machines, and polishing machines.
6. Process support equipment (integrated). This category includes support equipment that is integrated into the infrastructure. Semiconductor fabrication plants, for example, have a lot of this type of equipment because their buildings are constructed for the processes that are utilized.
   a. Piping for chemicals and gases
   b. Electrical power equipment beyond what is necessary for the building to operate; includes motor control centers (MCCs)
   c. Special foundations to support machinery and equipment but not necessary for the building
7. Computers and related equipment
   a. Personal
   b. Mainframe
   c. Network
   d. Printers
   e. Software (not taxable in some jurisdictions)
8. Furniture, fixtures, and office equipment
   a. Desks
   b. Chairs
   c. File cabinets
   d. Office machines
   e. Facsimile machines
   f. Intercoms
9. Research and development (R&D) and testing
   a. Testing equipment
   b. Laboratory equipment

10. Tools
    a. Short-life tools
    b. Larger mobile tools
    c. Molds, jigs, dies, patterns, templates
11. Transport equipment (rolling stock)
    a. Licensed vehicles
    b. Unlicensed vehicles
    c. Forklifts
12. Noninventory supplies
    a. Supplies used for operations but not part of the final product
    b. Fuels—gasoline, diesel fuel, oil, and so on
    c. Cleaning agents
    d. Spare parts
    e. Hardware
    f. Electrical components to maintain machinery and equipment
13. Pollution control equipment
    a. May include equipment that burns gaseous pollutants before release
    b. May include equipment that neutralizes acids or other dangerous chemicals
    c. May include equipment that cleanses process water before discharging it
    d. Equipment may have shortened life if new laws change to require stricter environmental controls

Noninventory Supplies

These supplies are used to maintain the machinery and equipment and the facility. They are not inventory—that is, they do not become the product or part of the product. Rather, they are used to service and support the facility and the machines in the facility. They include such things as fuels for forklifts, office supplies, spare parts for equipment, hardware to maintain the building, fluids for the machines, and other things of this sort.

These items should be considered by the appraiser if the valuation is for all the machinery and equipment in the plant, unless the client has stated that they should be excluded. If the appraisal is, for instance, for a company buyout and these items are not noted or valued in the report, this oversight might constitute an error of incompleteness in the appraisal. In such a case, the reviewer might want to read the instructions for the appraiser, which is generally in a letter in the appraisal, to see what the appraiser was contracted to value.

Inventory

Inventory is generally not part of a machinery and equipment appraisal, but it can be, depending on what the appraiser is asked to value. If it is part of the valuation, there are several important aspects to consider. First, is the inventory constantly changing? This is normally the case in a going concern, and the effective date of the appraisal would be of paramount importance if that were the case. If the plant is shut down, the value of any unsold product may be questionable because selling it would be difficult without an active system of salespeople, distributors, and retailers.

The appraiser may be experienced with machinery and equipment, but valuing inventory is a complex task that requires specific knowledge of the marketing part of a business. Therefore, any value put on unsold inventory needs to be scrutinized carefully, and the type of value (fair market, liquidation) also needs to be explained in the report. Inventory that retails for a certain price for a going concern may sell for a small fraction of that amount when a company closes down.

Process Support Equipment

This is equipment that is integrated into the building to support the larger machinery and equipment. It is often built into the infrastructure if the building was constructed for a specific use, or it may have been added to an existing building. It typically includes special electrical wiring, piping for gases, water, and other liquids, concrete supports, drains and gutters for the equipment, and other items necessary to install and run machines. Semiconductor manufacturing is an example of an industrial sector that normally designs buildings with process support infrastructure. Buildings for this industry normally have a lower level that contains the gases, chemicals, and electrical power that are fed to the next level for use in production.

The appraiser needs to separate these items from the shell of the buildings to value them. An aid to this would be a cost segregation study, if one is available. A *cost segregation study* is a listing of items that according to the IRS depreciate more quickly than the building shell. These items must be segregated from the shell and categorized according to their respective depreciation schedule for the IRS to allow the faster depreciation. If this study does not already exist, the appraiser may segregate these items to value them for an appraisal of the facility.

In reviewing an appraisal of this type of industrial facility, particularly if it is not functioning, it is important to understand that the process support items may be rendered valueless if the building is sold for another use. The reason is that it is improbable that a different type of manufacturing would require the same infrastructure. Moreover, in the example of a semiconductor building, rarely do two companies use the same setup of process support equipment. This means that the value of what exists in a shutdown facility, even if it is sold to a company with similar manufacturing, may be a fraction of the original cost.

Red Flag

If a manufacturing facility under appraisal is not functioning, the process support infrastructure may be worth much less than it would be in a going concern.

Source Documents

A question often arises as to what costs are included in entries on the asset list that the appraiser has. This question can also have significance in the review of the appraisal, particularly for asset-based lending. The reason is that the lender needs to know what is included in the event of a default. Capitalized equipment normally includes the costs listed in Exhibit 9.3.

Without seeing the source documents, the amount for just the machine is not known although the amount for the whole project is known but not confirmed. In a buyout of a plant, the total cost might be all that is requested. However, in asset-based lending, if there is a default and the property must be liquidated, only the value of the used machine would be recoverable. The appraiser may have checked source documents for some of the machines or none of them. If they were checked, the documents may be in the appraiser's files but not in the report. Appraisers are required by the USPAP to keep in a file all the information regarding the appraisal.

It is also possible that the entry amount on the asset list could be inflated (there are several reasons this might have occurred), and an investigation of the source documents would be the only way to detect the problem.

Exhibit 9.3
Machine Project Cost

Machine Project Cost		
$	1,100,000	Machine cost
$	70,000	Sales tax
$	12,500	Transportation cost
$	192,000	Installation cost, electrical, plumbing, concrete, etc.
$	84,560	Engineering, debugging, software configuration
$	102,134	Interest on financing expense for project
$	12,300.00	Training for employees
$	**1,573,494**	**Total entry on asset listing**

Note: The actual machine cost $1,100,000, but the entry is for $1,573,494. The difference is $473,494.

Understanding Labels and Nomenclature[1]

The appraiser's files should also include nomenclature on the machinery and equipment. This information is rarely in the appraisal, but the reviewer may want to request it if there are questions about certain high-value machines in the appraisal or if the reviewer needs to determine how thorough the appraiser's work was. This is particularly important if the sales comparison approach was used because misidentifying a machine can lead to an inaccurate valuation. Terminology in the valuation is also often misunderstood, and the following definitions can help the reviewer.

Original Acquisition Cost. This is what the company paid for the item. It is not the current value. As previously mentioned, this number probably includes everything that was capitalized for the item, such as transportation of the item to the factory, installation costs, engineering and debugging costs, training, and sales tax.

Year Acquired. This is the date on which the item was purchased. It may or may not be the date that it was manufactured.

Year Manufactured. This is the year in which the item was made. It may differ from the year acquired because the item may have been purchased used.

Description. The items should be described adequately. Often, companies use a type of shorthand for a description that is not understandable to outsiders. The appraiser may have described the item so that it is more easily identified.

Asset Number. The asset should have a number that identifies it for the company's accounting system.

Cost Center. Sometimes a cost center is assigned to assets according to their function, location, or the specific project they are related to.

Manufacturer's Name. Generally this would be in the description, or the appraiser may have taken it from the nameplate.

Proprietary Equipment. This is equipment that is manufactured specifically for the company and is used exclusively by the company. Certain companies may make the equipment themselves, whereas others might have it made by an outside source. It is important that the appraiser state in the appraisal what equipment is proprietary because the value of such equipment is often diminished by the fact that it either cannot be sold to others or it has no value in the marketplace of manufacturing equipment because it has been customized for only one company.

If the equipment was built in house, the appraiser may have estimated the value based on the cost of materials and the man-hours used to construct it. This information would have come from the company because it would be necessary as a basis to capitalize the equipment for accounting depreciation purposes.

Serial Number. The serial number is assigned by the manufacturer, not by the company under appraisal. It helps the manufacturer identify the item if the appraiser needs more information.

Model Number. This is a number that identifies the machine for the manufacturer. It may also denote the size, capacity, and other attributes of the machine. It usually provides more general information about the particular model, whereas the serial number may provide more specific information. In some cases, the serial number may also include the model number.

Motor. The size of the motor may be rated in horsepower or electrical power.

Capacity. Many machines are rated by the amount of product they can process. For instance, presses come in various sizes and pressing capabilities. Plastic injection mold machines come in various capacities, and paper machines produce different widths and types of paper. The capacity can be one of the most important aspects in determining the value of a machine, so in reviewing an appraisal that uses the sales comparison approach, the capacity should be considered a major characteristic of the comparison.

Special Aspects and Customization. Machines are often ordered with special equipment or are customized for a particular use, which can greatly affect the value. Customized machines are not necessarily proprietary equipment. A *customized machine* is typically a standard machine that has been modified, whereas a *proprietary machine* is especially built or modified for the company from inception, to the extent that it is virtually unusable by other manufacturers.

History. The history can reveal the amount or hours of past usage, reconditioning, rebuilding, and repair work, all of which may affect the current value.

Estimated Useful Life. This estimate is related to the condition. The appraiser may have to estimate how many years the machine has until it must be rebuilt, becomes technologically obsolete, or no longer functions profitably. Most machines lose their tolerances and become less effective as they age. These judgments are based on a number of estimates, such as the current condition, years since overhaul or reconditioning, anticipated life based on other machines in the factory, and past reinvestment record for similar types of machines. Typically, this is rated in terms of "percent good." A machine that is considered "30 percent used up" would be considered "70 percent good." If the total life is 10 years, this means that the machine has 7 years of life left.

Running Time. Some machines have meters that show how many hours they have been run. In some plants, machines are run 8 hours a day, and in others they are run 16 or 24 hours a day. Some machines are used only intermittently because they are utilized for only certain production orders. This information is helpful in estimating the current value because the value is related to the condition.

Level of Maintenance. Even as individuals vary in the way they maintain their automobiles, companies vary in how well they maintain their equipment. Companies have different philosophies regarding this. Some companies prefer to have a large maintenance crew, and others use outside sources for maintenance. Often, the former types of companies maintain their equipment better because they are paying for the crew to be on site and can utilize their services daily.

Some companies invest heavily in maintenance, whereas others run their machines hard and replace them more often. Sometimes a company determines that its business is diminishing, so it decides to run the plant with minimum maintenance in anticipation of closing it once the equipment is worn out. For instance, this can happen in an area where the cost of raw materials or energy has increased for a particular product, or demand for the product has simply decreased. The company may figure that a profit can still be made for a certain amount of time if expenditures for optimum maintenance are not made. Exhibit 9.4 is a part of an asset list for a company.

The Cost Approach

The *cost approach* for machinery and equipment is based on the principle of substitution. The value of a used piece of equipment may be estimated by determining the cost of substituting a new piece of equipment that can perform the same function with equal utility and efficiency. Once the value of the new piece of equipment is found, it is then diminished by an appropriate percentage of depreciation to get the fair market value. Depreciation is an integral part of using the cost approach for machinery and equipment, and it is important to understand it in reviewing appraisals.

Exhibit 9.4

Example of Part of a Company's Asset List

Asset Number	Sub Ass No	Cat	Sub Asset Description	Asset Class Code	Date Capitalized	Distr. Code	Capital Cost Opening Balance (201302)	Capital Cost Movement	Capital Cost Closing Balance (201302)	Accumulated Depreciation (201302)	Net Book Value (201302)
030120000100	001	it	EMPIRE PIT VOICE / DATA WIRING	01	01 Nov 2003	1412	$ 30,835.00	$ 0.00	$ 30,835.00	$ 30,697.83	$ 137.17
030120000200	001	it	EMPIRE PIT PHONE SWITCH	01	01 Nov 2003	1412	11,275.69	0.00	11,275.69	11,225.68	50.01
030130000100	001	it	EMPIRE HIGH SPEED NETWORK CONNECTION	01	01 Dec 2003	1412	36,040.74	0.00	36,040.74	36,040.74	0.00
040134000200	001	it	CMMC TERMINAL SERVER - EMPIRE	01	30 Dec 2004	1412	38,728.19	0.00	38,728.19	38,728.19	0.00
050124100100	001	elec	DCS OPERATING LEASE BUYOUT - EMPIRE	01	27 Jun 2005	1412	89,940.12	0.00	89,940.12	89,940.12	0.00
050134000200	001	it	EMPIRE CITRIX EXPANSION	01	26 Jul 2005	1412	37,068.46	0.00	37,068.46	37,068.46	0.00
050190000100	001	pr	SURVEY GPS SYSTEM UPGRADE	01	28 Feb 2005	1412	25,010.28	0.00	25,010.28	25,010.28	0.00
060290000200	001	it	INFOCASTER INFORMATIONAL BORADCAST SYS	01	27 Nov 2006	1412	28,752.00	0.00	28,752.00	24,597.19	4,154.81
070190000100	001	pr	PIT SURVEY GPS UPGRADE	01	29 May 2007	1412	49,160.00	0.00	49,160.00	49,160.00	0.00
110120000100	001	it	COMMUNICATIONS INFRASTRUCTURE UPGRADE	01	27 Dec 2011	1412	439,028.00	0.00	439,028.00	177,984.30	261,043.70
030270010100	001	crane	MOTORIZED BRIDGE CRANE EMP COMPRESS ROOM	02	30 Dec 2004	1412	17,127.88	0.00	17,127.88	15,099.81	2,028.07
040225000201	001	me	04-<$100K PLANT LUBE CARTS	02	27 Jun 2005	1412	40,962.00	0.00	40,962.00	34,935.54	6,026.46
050220000100	001	TLSE	PIT - GAS WELDER REPLACEMENT	02	30 Jun 2005	1412	19,885.50	0.00	19,885.50	18,158.39	1,727.11
050220000300	001	TLSE	LOVA 16 REFRACTORY GUNNING MACH	02	28 Oct 2005	1412	11,363.00	0.00	11,363.00	10,132.87	1,230.13
050265000100	001	pr	TRUCK SHOP SYSTEM IMPROVEMENTS	02	28 Feb 2006	1412	58,838.51	0.00	58,838.51	58,838.51	0.00
050290000100	001	pr	CONCENTRATOR SCREEN REPAIR AREA	02	28 Oct 2005	1412	23,381.51	0.00	23,381.51	20,747.25	2,634.26
060220000200	001	misc	CRUSHER TRAM CARTS	02	27 Feb 2006	1412	44,626.50	0.00	44,626.50	36,095.94	8,530.56
060220000300	001	TLSE	CONC - TORQUE WRENCH	02	30 Mar 2006	1412	13,652.50	0.00	13,652.50	13,652.50	0.00
060220000400	001	pe	PPLT - HOPPER CAR GATE OPENER	02	24 Jul 2006	1412	12,900.00	0.00	12,900.00	11,338.11	1,561.89
070220000100	001	pe	PPLT - HOPPER CAR GATE OPENER	02	21 Jun 2007	1412	11,400.00	0.00	11,400.00	9,662.24	1,737.76
070225000100	001	me	'2007 MAN LIFT REPLACEMENT 30' REACH	02	28 Sep 2007	1412	55,942.00	0.00	55,942.00	52,035.31	3,906.69
070225000200	001	me	'2007 MAN LIFT REPLACEMENT 60' REACH	02	28 Sep 2007	1412	90,291.00	0.00	90,291.00	83,985.57	6,305.43
070225000400	001	me	'2007 MAN LIFT PIT WELDERS UNIT #5650	02	29 Nov 2007	1412	13,820.00	0.00	13,820.00	12,482.12	1,337.88
070225000500	001	me	'2007 MAN LIFT TRUCK SHOP UNIT #5666	02	29 Nov 2007	1412	13,820.00	0.00	13,820.00	12,482.12	1,337.88
070230000100	001	TLSE	VERTICAL BAND SAW	02	25 Mar 2008	1412	74,121.26	0.00	74,121.26	53,876.35	20,244.91
071660000100	001	me	30' MAINTENANCE TRAILER	02	28 Dec 2007	1412	13,925.00	0.00	13,925.00	10,242.17	3,682.83
080220000200	001	TLSE	BELT VULCANIZER- 36 INCH	02	31 Dec 2008	1412	22,815.15	0.00	22,815.15	15,481.95	7,333.20
080220000300	001	me	KONI LIFTS	02	30 Jun 2008	1412	38,500.00	0.00	38,500.00	27,694.16	10,805.84
080220000400	001	me	DOZER POWER STEPS	02	30 Jun 2008	1412	9,871.04	0.00	9,871.04	7,209.59	2,661.45
080220000410	001	me	DOZER POWER STEPS TD62	02	30 Jun 2008	1412	12,039.04	0.00	12,039.04	8,793.03	3,246.01
080220000420	001	me	DOZER POWER STEPS TD63	02	30 Jun 2008	1412	11,479.04	0.00	11,479.04	8,383.97	3,095.07
080220000430	001	me	DOZER POWER STEPS TD64	02	30 Jun 2008	1412	9,681.04	0.00	9,681.04	7,070.78	2,610.26
080220000440	001	me	DOZER POWER STEPS TD65	02	30 Jun 2008	1412	11,511.04	0.00	11,511.04	8,407.39	3,103.65
080220000450	001	me	POWER DOZER LIFT TD66	02	30 Jun 2008	1412	10,338.04	0.00	10,338.04	7,550.59	2,787.45
080220000460	001	me	DOZER POWER STEPS TD67	02	30 Jun 2008	1412	9,860.04	0.00	9,860.04	7,201.49	2,658.55
080225000300	001	me	FLOOR SWEEPER #4380	02	31 Dec 2008	1412	38,279.00	0.00	38,279.00	32,537.14	5,741.86

Understanding Depreciation

The definition of *depreciate* in *Merriam-Webster's Collegiate Dictionary* is, "to lower the price or estimated value of" and "to fall in value." *Depreciation* is a loss of value for any reason and from all causes. It is measured by comparing the item under appraisal to its *replacement* or *reproduction cost new*.[2]

Reproduction and Replacement Cost

The difference between these two terms is as follows: *reproduction cost* means the cost to reproduce an exact replica of the machine under valuation, whereas *replacement cost* is the cost to purchase a machine that provides the same utility and function. Since technology is constantly changing, it is unrealistic to use reproduction cost in most cases. However, there is a large exception to this that will be discussed later in the chapter.

Often the replacement for a machine is more efficient than the original machine. These new efficiencies may mean that the replacement machine is superior to the old machine in a number ways, for any of the following reasons:

- It is less expensive.
- It is more expensive but more efficient; thus the savings outweigh the initial cost.
- It uses less energy.
- It is easier to operate.
- It needs fewer personnel to operate.
- It is smaller and perhaps lighter, taking up less space and being easier to transport.
- It functions with more precision.
- It keeps its tolerances and settings longer.
- It has more automatic features.

- It produces more product per hour (or other measurement unit).
- It requires less maintenance.
- It lasts longer.
- It does not last as long, but it is less expensive to buy and operate.

Although it is most always the case that a machine loses its value as it ages, it is also possible for a machine to increase in value since it was purchased due to inflation or other causes, and this will be discussed in the upcoming section on *trending*. The typical machine will lose value from one or more of the three forms of depreciation: *physical*, *functional*, and *economic* (*economic* is sometimes called *external*).

Physical Depreciation

Physical depreciation (PD) involves deterioration of the item. Even if a machine is set up correctly when it is new, it will never again run as well because as it ages, tolerances are lost, and the result is a diminution in the quality of performance. Even a machine that is not used or is rarely used eventually deteriorates. Metal rusts and corrodes, and metal fatigue occurs simply from the stress produced by the forces of atmospheric pressure and gravity. If the machine is outside, the sun, rain, and wind cause erosion and other damage. As equipment is used, it continues to wear out, until eventually the equipment is no longer usable. Machines can be rebuilt, but they still have components that are not new, making them less valuable than new machines.

Physical depreciation can be determined in different ways. Observation is one way. Often the appraiser inspects the equipment as a first step in determining an estimate for physical depreciation, but it is not wise to base everything on the exterior appearance for obvious reasons. Large machines often have an hour meter that shows how many hours the machine has been run. Also, the company may have maintenance records that should reveal two things. First, the overall level of maintenance should be apparent from these records, which should give the appraiser an indication of how the company maintains all of its equipment. Second, the specific machine's history should be recorded, giving the appraiser knowledge of when it was last rebuilt and how often it has broken down, among other things. In reviewing the appraisal, the reader should look for comments by the appraiser about the extent of his or her research and inspection of the equipment.

As a machine ages and is less productive, it generally requires maintenance at more frequent intervals. This maintenance may shut down a production line, slow down overall production, and become a drag on the production line. The expense of these problems can be called *excess operating costs*, which can be translated into a percentage of depreciation.

Functional Obsolescence Depreciation

The second form of depreciation is *functional obsolescence* (FO), which is a loss in value because of an inadequacy or inefficiency in operation, as compared to a replacement machine, or as compared to the subject machine when it was new. A machine with this type of obsolescence may have symptoms such as inutility (that is, its usefulness is lessened), undercapacity, or excess operating costs. A machine that requires additional manpower to operate, as compared to a newer, more automated machine, is a good example of functional obsolescence that is manifested in excess operating costs.

Economic Obsolescence Depreciation

The third type of depreciation is *economic obsolescence* (EO), which is depreciation that impairs the property because of detrimental influences outside the property. For this reason it may also be called *external obsolescence.* This is obsolescence over which the owner has no control and that also affects others in the same industry if they are in a similar location. An increase in the price of raw materials or utilities or rising labor costs would be applicable factors.

Other factors that could contribute to this type of obsolescence are the increased expense of, or imposition of, environmental regulations or diminished demand for the product manufactured. An example of environmental regulations causing economic obsolescence would be new clean air and water requirements for an industry such as papermaking or oil refining. The expense of meeting the new requirements, especially for an older facility, may be great enough to force the company to close the plant.

Technological Obsolescence Depreciation

Technological obsolescence diminishes value because of advances in technology that render a machine obsolete. This type of obsolescence can occur to a new machine that has been warehoused but never used. Technological obsolescence is a form of functional obsolescence and is sometimes referred to as *functional obsolescence.* It may also be economic obsolescence because changes in technology are often external to a facility. The definition from the American Society of Appraisers says this:

> Some appraisers draw a distinction between functional obsolescence and technological obsolescence. They define *functional obsolescence* as a loss in value resulting from differences in capability between a new machine and the appraised machine, and *technological obsolescence* as a loss in value resulting from the difference between design and materials of construction used in present-day machines compared with those used in the machine being appraised.[3]

Understanding How the Appraiser Applies Depreciation

There are three basic methods for applying depreciation, the *market extraction method,* the *age-life method,* and the *direct dollar,* or *cost-to-cure, method.* The market extraction method requires finding comparable sales, whereas the other two methods are applied to the estimated current cost (*cost new*) of the machine.

Market Extraction Method. The *market extraction method* requires finding comparable sales prices of similar equipment to extract depreciation. This method combines all the different forms of depreciation together because they are inherent in the sale price of the item used for comparison. Essentially, the market extraction method is a form of the sales comparison approach, and its accuracy is tied to the quality of comparable sales that are utilized. Adjustments may need to be made to the sales to compare them to the subject.

A simple example of market extraction is as follows. Machine A is being appraised. It is seven years old and cost $100,000 new. A search for comparable sales has been made, and three machines have been found that are similar to machine A—machines B, C, and D. These machines are six, seven, and eight years old, respectively. They have sold for $60,000, $55,000, and $52,000. The percentage of depreciation of the cost new for each machine would be 40 percent, 45 percent, and 48 percent, respectively. A choice in this range should be made for the subject's depreciation—perhaps 45 percent since machine C is the same age as the subject. This example does not take into consideration installation, freight, and other costs, nor does it consider condition as compared to age. It is, rather, a starting point, used only to illustrate the theory behind the market extraction method.

Age-Life Method. This method of estimating depreciation is based on a ratio of the economic life to the effective age. All machines have a *chronological age*, which is the actual age of the machine, based on the date it was manufactured. A machine also has an *economic age*, or *effective age*, which is an age assigned by the appraiser to represent the condition of the machine.

Typically this age is greatly affected by the level of maintenance, overhauls, and amount of usage, among other things, that pertain to the machine. For instance, a machine may have a chronological age of 15 years. Because of excellent maintenance, its economic, or effective, age may be 7 years. If its total *economic life*, which is the time period the machine may be used for what it was intended to do, is 20 years, then a formula can be used to determine the percentage of depreciation that can be applied to it. That formula can be applied based on years of economic life or on hour usage:

$$\text{Use/total use} = \text{percentage of depreciation}$$

Therefore

$$7 / 20 = 35\%$$

When this formula is applied to the property, the balance, which is 65 percent, is the percent good. The remaining economic life is 13 years. If the measurement of the machine is by hours run, then the same formula can be used based on the hours, rather than the years. However, it should be noted that simply using the hours of a machine does not take into consideration the condition of the machine, unless the hours are adjusted in conjunction with the maintenance and other upkeep. In the following example, the total hours of economic life assigned to the machine is 500, and it has been run 100 hours:

$$500 / 100 = 20 \text{ percent depreciation}$$

The remaining economic life is 400 hours, which does not equate to years, unless the number of hours per year is estimated. For instance, if the machine will be operated for 40 hours a year, the remaining economic life will be 10 years.

Direct Dollar, or Cost-to-Cure, Method. The *direct dollar method*, also called the *cost-to-cure method*, involves estimating the actual expense of curing the value loss caused by the depreciation. Some elements may be curable, and others may not be. The appraiser estimates the curable elements and then translates that dollar figure into a percentage that is subtracted from the replacement or reproduction cost new.

For example, a machine may need two new motors to operate optimally. The reproduction cost for the machine is $800,000. The replacement cost new (RCN), as shown in Exhibit 9.5, for a machine that is equal in utility but is not the exact machine, is $600,000. Therefore, the machine has incurable technological obsolescence of $800,000 divided

Exhibit 9.5
Adjustment for Replacement Cost

Adjustment for Replacement Cost		
	$800,000	Reproduction Cost New
	$600,000	Replacement Cost New
25%	$200,000	Incurable Technological Obsolescence
Adjustment for Economic Age		
	$600,000	Replacement Cost New
50%	$300,000	Incurable Physical Depreciation
	$300,000	Residual Value
Adjustment for Curable Physical Obsolescence		
	$300,000	Residual Value after Depreciation
16.6%	$50,000	Curable Physical Depreciation (cost to replace motors)
	$250,000	Final Value after Depreciation

by $600,000, or 25 percent. The machine also has a total economic life of 20 years and has been used for 10 years, so the economic life adjustment for obsolescence is 50 percent, leaving a value of $300,000 for the machine.

The motors cost $50,000 to replace. This number is subtracted last because its specific cost represents the diminution of value due to curable obsolescence. In other words, when the motors are installed, the value should be $300,000. The percentage for this amount is 16.6 percent, and the resulting value is $250,000. Exhibit 9.5 shows this in a different format.

Order of Depreciation

There is an order of depreciation that should be followed. Using this method also helps the appraiser avoid double-counting the various forms of depreciation. It is as follows:

Replacement cost new (RCN) – physical depreciation (PD)
RCN – PD – functional obsolescence (FO)
RCN – PD – FO – economic obsolescence (EO)
RCN – PD – FO – EO = final value

Excess Operating Costs

Excess operating costs can be caused by physical depreciation when, for a variety of reasons, a machine becomes more expensive to operate than a new machine would cost to operate. Economic obsolescence can cause excess operating costs if, for instance, the source of energy necessary to operate a machine becomes too expensive. An example would be a machine that operates on electricity in a situation in which electricity increases in cost but natural gas decreases in cost and is an option with a different machine. Functional obsolescence can cause excess operating costs due to the expense of manufacturing with a machine that is not optimum for the task.

The typical methods used to determine the amount of functional obsolescence are the income approach or used-equipment approach. With the used-equipment approach, the value of the machine is found by comparing it to other, similar machines. For the income approach for a specific machine, the appraiser should have obtained operating costs from the company under appraisal. Sometimes costs can be obtained from equipment manufacturers, but they are neither as accurate nor as specific as information from the company under valuation. The optimum situation would be a company that has a new machine and an older one because then the costs can be compared.

These costs might represent savings in efficiency of the machine, including a requirement of less energy for operation, less manpower to operate, less maintenance, and faster production. The amount of the difference should then be adjusted for income taxes because the company realizes tax savings for the expenses that are incurred.

After that amount is subtracted, the savings are projected into the future, based on the remaining useful life of the equipment or the date the equipment is scheduled for replacement. A discount rate must then be chosen, and a present value factor must be utilized to get the value of the projected future savings.

To determine the excess operating costs for the whole plant, several methods can be used. If the appraiser can find sales for plants that are more modern or in some other way lack the obsolescence issue for the subject property, then he or she can use a sales comparison approach, just as the used-equipment approach (sales comparison approach) would be used for a specific machine, as previously mentioned.

Exhibit 9.6
Method for Finding Economic Obsolescence

Method for Finding Economic Obsolescence	
Income Approach Value	$23,000,000
Land Value	$3,000,000
Income Approach Value without Land	$20,000,000
Cost Approach Value	$24,000,000
Amount of Economic Obsolescence	$4,000,000

If comparable sales are not available, comparing the income approach to the cost approach is another method. The difference in the two values, after land is deducted, will to some extent be the economic obsolescence amount. Exhibit 9.6 is a simple example of this method.

In some situations, economic obsolescence can also be estimated using an *income shortfall analysis*. The concept is that the earnings produced by the plant do not justify the investment made in the plant. The following formula is an example:

(Expected return on investment − actual return on investment) / expected return on investment = economic obsolescence

There are other methods as well such as the *gross margin analysis* and *return on capital analysis*, but all of these methods are essentially measures of the performance of a company compared to what is or was expected of the company.[4]

Other Aspects of Depreciation

Depreciation is often foundational to any industrial appraisal, and the main point that the reviewer should keep in mind is that the accuracy of the applied depreciation will affect the accuracy of the final valuation.

Chapter 10

Machinery and Equipment Appraisal Excerpts

The following is a portion of the machinery and equipment (M&E) part of an industrial appraisal with some related commentary. To save space, only the pertinent parts of the appraisal have been included. The first part that is included is an overview of the industry that is under appraisal. The fictional company name is Prosteel.

Overview of Industry

Understanding the steel market today helps if one understands a little about its recent history. In the early 1990s the steel industry was failing in the United States. The dollar was strong, and many overseas producers were dumping steel at a price that had U.S. mills desperately asking the government for regulatory relief and for penalties against importers. There was a question as to whether the industry would survive, and many steel companies went out of business.

Since that time there has been a rebound in steel, and in the last six years prices have been increasing steadily. World demand has increased, and the surge in the construction industry has increased demand domestically for the products that Prosteel produces. And for most of 2006, production was strong, and profits were good for the company. However, in the last quarter of 2006, demand suddenly dropped, and as of January 1, 2007, production was waning. It turned out that 2007 would result in a loss of $13.3 million for the company.

In a forecast in January 2007, Standard & Poor's Equity Research Services stated that several factors were expected to contribute to a decline in demand for steel. It cited a 2 to 3 percent decrease in demand from the U.S. auto industry and a decline in shipments to distributors and original equipment manufacturers (OEMs). That forecast dealt with the steel industry as a whole, but S&P's statements also related somewhat to Prosteel's position in the industry.

Prosteel markets most of its steel to the domestic construction industry. Rain gutters and metal siding are two products that top the list, and it is well known that the construction industry had been in a boom for many years until it began to decline in 2006, and it was in a decline as of January 1, 2007, the date of this appraisal. Moreover, a history of the industry has shown a roller coaster of production and profits that has caused instability. The profitable years have been good, but the unprofitable ones have been dire, and the cycles of these extremes make investments in the industry risky.

As of January 2007, with the advent of diminishing construction activity, rising unemployment, a steep increase in the cost of energy, and the economic problems with the mortgage and real estate industry, the future for steel products, particularly the ones that Prosteel manufactures, appears to be less lucrative than in recent years.

Red Flag

The appraiser is explaining the condition of the industry and the forecast, and it is not optimistic. This should be noted by the reviewer because it insinuates that the value of this plant and its machinery and equipment may be declining.

Valuation of Machinery and Equipment

Production Capability

Prosteel has machinery and equipment that produces metallic coated and painted steel coils for the construction industry. The Spokane Division handles every major stage of the secondary steel processing and coil coating processes, including pickling, cold rolling, zinc coating, painting, slitting, and sheeting. The coatings range from being painted, passivated, oiled, and/or resin coated. The Spokane Division can also process steel in a wide range of thicknesses, widths, grades, and coatings. Prosteel can also process customer-owned products.

Prosteel manufactures ProZinc galvanized steel, which is a corrosion-resistant coating of zinc that can be used for many different products. ProZinc steel can also be used in conjunction with a wide range of forming and welding processes. The factory can also add a clear resin coating on line, which produces a product called ProZinc Plus Steel. In addition to these capabilities, applications of other coatings and/or paint of any color can be applied by its dual paint rollers and payoff reels. The metal can also be embossed and slitted to custom specifications. The following are the range specs for the Spokane plant's capabilities:

Thickness range: 0.010 to 0.036 inches

Width range: 24 to 50 inches

Coil inside diameter: 20 inches

Output coil weight: 33,000 pounds

Coatings: zinc, (ProZinc), paints, resin and/or oil coatings, and cold rolled

Fabricating: slitting and sheeting to specifications

Description of Machinery and Equipment

The following is a description of the main production lines and the processes that are applied to the steel coil that comes into the plant.

Pickle Line

The first stage of the process is normally the pickle line. This line removes surface rust from the hot rolled coil and cleans it. Coils are welded together to enter the continuous four-stage cleaning process. They pass over a tension leveler that breaks up the surface rust and improves the flatness of the coil. The next stage of treatment is entry into a series of acid tanks, which remove rust and other impurities. After the acid bath, the coil is rinsed in hot water to remove the remaining acid. The sides of the coil are then trimmed to the final width. The coil is then sheared to approximately its original length. The coil can be coated on both sides with a protective film of oil, if desired. The tension reels rewind the coil so it may be sent to the customer or further processed in another step.

Cold Reversing Mill

The second step is the cold reversing mill, which reduces the thickness of the steel to the customer's desired specifications. The band or coil passes back and forth, reducing the thickness or gauge until it reaches the proper specification. The steps in the process include a dual coil payoff section, which unwinds the coil. The second stage is the entry tension reel, which controls the tension in the process. The coil passes over a thickness gauge, which measures the thickness with each pass through the mill.

The press section uses two work rolls, which are in contact with the steel coil. They apply pressure to reduce the thickness. These work rolls are supported by two backup rolls, which support the enormous pressure placed on the work rolls. Both sets of rolls need to be changed frequently to ensure that product quality and specifications are maintained. The coil is then rewound on a delivery tension reel. If it has not reached its finished gauge, it reverses the process and sends it back through the mill in the opposite direction for another reduction. If it is at its final gauge, the coil is removed, and it is either shipped to a customer, or it goes on to the next step in the process, which is the coating line.

Zinc Coating Line

The third step is a metallic zinc coating line that takes a finished coil of steel (pickled and rolled) and places a zinc coating on all sides. This process consists of unrolling the coil of steel and submerging the steel in a bath of molten zinc. As the steel emerges, various means are used to level and control the thickness of the zinc coating to achieve a specific coating weight.

The reason for the zinc coating is to protect the steel sheet from corrosion by acting as a barrier to exclude air, water, and other corrosion promoters from contact with the steel substrate. In addition to barrier protection, zinc and zinc alloys have the ability to react to scratches and other damage through an electrochemical (galvanic) action between steel and zinc. This galvanic action makes it possible for the zinc to protect breaks in the coating and prevent further damage. In this galvanic process, zinc actually fills in the crack or other breakage, which protects and maintains the structural integrity of the steel. This well-established characteristic of a zinc coating on steel is known as *sacrificial protection*. This sacrificial, or galvanic, protection is provided by zinc, zinc-iron, and zinc-aluminum coatings.

The beginning of the coating process starts at the zinc coating lines' entry or dual payoff reels. This allows for the efficient handling of a second coil while the first coil is in process. Since the process is a continuous one, the end of one coil is welded to the start of the second one to keep the process moving. The coil enters an accumulation section, which expands and contracts to allow for coil changeovers. The coil is cleaned in a caustic bath, rinsed, and dried. The coil enters a furnace to clean the surface and develop the proper technical properties to accept the zinc coating. The coil then enters the coating pot where it is immersed in a liquefied zinc coating.

After exiting the pot, high-pressure air knives strip off the excess coating. The thickness of the coating is monitored by a computer-controlled gauge. The coil then passes through a cooling tower, which reduces it to near room temperature, after which the coil passes into the surface conditioner section, which, at the customer's option, can be used to create a smooth surface for painting. The coil then goes through a series of tension levelers that control slack and improve the flatness of the coated coil. Coils that are not going to be painted can then go through a chemical coating section, which protects the surface against deterioration during storage. Also, depending on application, the next step in the process is to apply an optional resin coating to enhance the performance of the steel in certain applications. The coil then enters the exit accumulator, which provides slack in the process to allow for the changeover of coils on the exit end of the line while in continuous operation. The last main step is the dual exit tension winders, which rewind the coil. The coil is then either sent to a customer or to the painting, slitting, or sheeting lines for further processing.

Paint Line

The metal is painted in the paint line, to protect it and to beautify it for a variety of applications. The paint line applies a number of different painted coatings based on the intended use of the steel. The process begins from dual payoff coils, which allow for the continuous operation while reloading the next coil. Coils are joined at a stitcher station just after the payoff reels. There is a front-end accumulation section to allow time in the continuous process for coil changeovers. The steel is then cleaned in a caustic bath, rinsed, and dried. The next step in the process is a roll-on pretreatment of the initial coating of the paint systems. A drying oven cures the pretreatment coating.

The next step is for the prime coater to apply a prime coat of paint to both sides of the coil. This then goes into a prime curing oven to cure. The coil then travels through the finish coaters where the final coat of paint is applied. From there, it then goes into the finish curing oven to dry. The coil then goes into a water quench where the temperature is lowered to near room temperature. The coil then enters the exit accumulator, where it is rewound on a tension coiler. From there, the product is either sent to a customer or is sent for further processing to slitting and sheeting, if desired.

Slitting Line

The slitting line has a standard machine used to slit coils to desired widths.

Cut to Length Line

In this process the sheets are cut into the desired size.

Other Machinery and Equipment

There are other assets including a roll grinder and various support equipment, but this is the basic process, most of which was installed in 1997.

Condition of Machinery and Equipment

The machinery and equipment at this plant are considered to be in average condition for their age, with some items in good condition, as defined in Exhibit 10.1. The division's major processing machinery was installed in 1997, so as of the retrospective date of the appraisal, it was 10 years old. It appears to be well maintained, but the asset list also shows that there have been very few replacements. That means that because of the age of this plant, maintenance costs will be higher in the future than they have been for the past 10 years. Exhibit 10.1 has been adapted and modified from materials published by the American Society of Appraisers. We have used these descriptions in this appraisal to identify the condition of the assets.[1]

The machinery and equipment were only visually inspected, and some of it was not in operation during the plant visit. It appeared to be in the condition noted, but this is not guaranteed because the appraiser did not test or closely inspect it and suggests an inspection by a qualified technician or engineer for a more certain assessment of the condition of the equipment. The age of the equipment, and the fact that it appeared to be functioning properly, was the basis for the

Exhibit 10.1
Machinery and Equipment Classifications

Classification	Description
New	Property that is new and not used; may be installed or uninstalled.
Very Good	Close to new condition, slightly used, capable of full utilization. No repairs or modifications needed.
Good	Used; will operate at full or near specified capacity; may have undergone repairs as part of regular maintenance.
Average	Used; has probably had repairs and replacement of parts. Does not perform at level of initial specifications.
Fair	Used; operates below specified capacity and/or below original tolerances. Requires increased maintenance and has limited life left.
Poor	Used; operates well below specified capacity and needs new parts and/or rebuilding to operate optimally. May have some features that are not working.
Broken	Used; out of service and needs major or minor repair, but has operational value and is worth repairing.
Scrap or salvage	Used; no longer serviceable and not economically feasible to repair. Value is in metal or other parts or reusable components only.

Source: Adapted from American Society of Appraisers, *Valuing Machinery and Equipment: The Fundamentals of Appraising Machinery and Technical Assets*, 2d ed., American Society of Appraisers, Herndon, VA, 2005, p. 68.

assessment done by the appraiser. As this is a retrospective appraisal, it is assumed that the equipment was in a condition at least as good, if not better, on the appraisal date.

Machinery and Equipment Valuation Approaches Defined

The American Society of Appraisers has defined three basic valuation methods that are generally used in the valuation of machinery and equipment. They are the *cost approach*, *sales comparison approach*, and the *income approach to value*:

Cost Approach Defined

The appraiser adjusts the replacement cost (new) of the asset being appraised for the loss in value caused by physical deterioration, functional obsolescence, and economic obsolescence. The cost approach is based on the principle of substitution: a prudent buyer will not pay more for an asset than the cost of acquiring a substitute property of equivalent utility.

***Sales Comparison Approach* Defined**
The appraiser adjusts the prices that have been paid for the assets comparable to the asset being appraised, equating the comparables to the subject.

***Income Capitalization Approach* Defined**
The appraiser determines the present value of the future economic benefits of owning the property.[2]

Machinery and Equipment Valuation Approaches Discussed

Income Approach: Not Utilized

The income approach was not developed for the valuation of the machinery and equipment assets. This is sometimes a method used in appraisals, but "it is not usually applied to individual items of machinery and equipment unless they are leased."[3] An assembly of assets is generally a better candidate for this approach, but as was previously noted, there is no income information for this division as a whole, let alone income information that could be applied to the machinery and equipment. Consequently, this method was not used for valuing the M&E assets.

Sales Comparison Approach: Utilized

In this approach used equipment is researched to find sales of similar machinery and equipment that has sold. These sales are then analyzed, and adjustments to the sale prices are made to compare differences between the sales and the subject. This approach focuses on the actions of buyers and sellers in the marketplace.

As is typical, adjustments were made for the sales comparison approach. However, besides the adjustments that are made for the differences between the subject property and the comparable sales, generally there has to be an estimate of the cost to transport and install the machinery. A more detailed list of these costs is noted in the next section, which explains the cost approach.

In this appraisal, it was difficult to find used equipment that was similar to the subject's equipment because of several factors. First, when mills of this sort are built, bids are placed by companies to install whole lines of equipment, without a specific breakdown of the costs of each piece of equipment. Raytheon is one of the main contractors that built the Spokane plant, and it is no longer doing this type of work, and it does not have specific invoices that delineate the costs between installation and the actual machinery and equipment.

Second, since this is specialized equipment, it is very difficult to find used machines that match it. Nevertheless, enough equipment sales were found to adequately perform this approach, and sales for three main lines of equipment—the slitter line, banding line, and cut-to-length line—were found.

Other machinery and equipment for which sales were found include the facility generator, a stitcher, and an uncoiler. This mix of specific pieces of equipment and whole lines yielded a valuable balance of comparable sale information that was then used to determine a ratio of cost new to cost used for the rest of the equipment. That ratio resulted in a trend that was then applied to similar equipment that was purchased in 1997 only. This approach was used in conjunction with a trended investment cost method approach, which is explained in more detail in the "Trending" section later in this chapter.

Red Flag

The appraiser made up trends based on the equipment that he or she valued and surveyed costs for. Since the trends did not come from a costing service such as Marshall & Swift Valuation Services, special attention should be given to the method and basis for the trending that was used.

Whole Plant Sales: Not Utilized

Comparable sales for the machinery and equipment were used, but comparable whole plant sales were not used. The first reason is that none could be found that were truly comparable. All of the sales of plants that process steel that were considered have so many differences that the adjustments would have been too large to render a relevant valuation of the subject. If more similar sales could have been found, there would still be, in any event, myriad issues that make whole plant sales difficult to utilize.

The only sales found, after an extensive search, varied so much in design, location, type of manufacturing, capacity, product mix, age, condition, and circumstances of sale, as compared to the subject, that they cannot be realistically adjusted to derive a value. It should also be noted that plants that are operating entities can actually sell for less than those that are closed due to factors such as union agreements that inflate labor costs. Another issue can be contractual obligations made in the past to make products for prices that are no longer profitable, due to the increase in costs for raw materials and other aspects of production.

Cost Approach: Utilized in Conjunction with Sales Comparison Approach

The cost approach to value is based on the principle of substitution. The value of a used piece of equipment will depend on the cost of a new piece of equipment that can perform the same task with equal utility and efficiency. Once the value of the new piece of equipment is discovered, it is then diminished by an appropriate percentage of depreciation to get the fair market value. That depreciation can be defined as a loss in value for any reason and from all sources. It includes physical deterioration and functional and economic obsolescence.[4]

The starting point for the cost approach is to estimate the current installed replacement cost new (RCN) or reproduction cost (RC) of the property under valuation. Included in this estimate of cost new will be the following direct and indirect costs.

Direct Costs. These include costs of the item, labor to install it, transportation of the item, and other costs incurred to buy the item and get it into the production line:

1. Cost of the item
2. Transportation (freight costs)
3. Sales tax (not assessable in some jurisdictions)
4. Installation costs
   a. Foundation work
   b. Electrical wiring
   c. Plumbing
   d. Rigging

Indirect Costs. These are expenses that are normally not part of the initial purchase or invoice but are incurred in the process of the total project of utilizing the equipment for the company:

1. Overhead
   a. Administration and management
   b. Accounting

2. Consultants
3. Engineering and architectural fees
4. License and permit fees
5. Temporary structures and enclosures
6. Legal fees
7. Construction and installation insurance
8. Security expenses related to installation
9. Rental equipment for installation
10. Debugging and ramp-up costs

These costs are added together to utilize a method called the *summation method*. After they are totaled, the various forms of depreciation are subtracted from them.

Depreciation

The following are the different types of depreciation that must be deducted.

Physical depreciation is loss of value due to wear and tear from all sources on the property from age and use. *Functional obsolescence* is a "loss in value because of an inadequacy or inefficiency in operation, compared to a replacement machine." *Economic obsolescence* "is depreciation which impairs the property because of detrimental influences outside the property."[5]

Another form of depreciation is called *technological obsolescence*, which "denotes depreciation that diminishes value because of advances in technology that render machinery obsolete. Technological obsolescence is a form of functional obsolescence and is sometimes referred to as *economic obsolescence*. Technological obsolescence may also be economic obsolescence since changes in technology are often external to a facility."[6]

Trending

Trending was utilized in this appraisal in two ways. First, trends were applied from Marshall & Swift Valuation Services. Second, specific trends were developed by the appraiser from the sales comparison approach, and they were applied to the machinery and equipment. Information and direction regarding trending is quoted as follows from the book *Fundamentals of Industrial Valuation*:

> *Trending* is a cost approach method of estimating the current value of used assets by adjusting their historical costs with trend factors. It is the most common approach for appraising industrial properties for assessment purposes, and is also used frequently in the private sector. This process may be referred to by several names, including: trended investment technique, trended investment cost method, trended investment cost approach, trended cost approach, etc. The trends utilized may come from a national costing service, or they may have been calculated by a government entity, or by the appraiser.

And this:

> Trending is one of the fastest ways to value industrial property, and it is also the easiest. Another advantage of trending is that it is entirely objective. . . . Nevertheless, the lack of personal judgment can also become a pitfall in trending—for the trend is blind to circumstances specific to a company whose property may suffer from devaluation for some reason, such as a higher than average rate of use. Additionally, trends may or may not take into consideration all the economic aspects of the industry under appraisal. Some industries, which are subcategories within a certain general category of industry, may be affected by negative economic influences that are specific to them only.[7]

Fast-Track Costs

Fast-track costs are the expenses associated with expedited building or machine installation. They are additional costs that are not realized in the sale of the asset, and they are above and beyond the normal costs for building or installing equipment.

These costs should generally be deducted from the listed costs for the asset, and they have been deducted from a few items on the original asset list for the subject property. This was done after consulting with the plant personnel who pointed out the items that were installed or built with fast-track methods. An estimate for the deductions was made based on the appraiser's experience and the interviews with plant personnel.

Methodology Applied to Deriving Value for Machinery and Equipment

The sales comparison approach was used in conjunction with the cost approach to derive a final value for the machinery and equipment (M&E). Trending was the aspect of the cost approach that was used, and it was based on the ratio of cost new to cost used determined from the analysis of used-equipment sales. Exhibits 10.2 through 10.5 show the implementation of the sales comparison approach for the machinery and equipment.

The equipment used for comparison to the subject was discussed with knowledgeable plant personnel to confirm the similarities and consequent appropriateness to be used in this approach to value. In addition to the charts in Exhibits 10.2 through 10.5 are information sheets (the sections "Loopco Slitting Line Sale" through "Pro-Eco Slitting Line") about some of the equipment, which is then followed by a discussion about the comparable equipment. Please note that at the bottom of the charts in Exhibits 10.2 through 10.5 is an item called "subject cost," which is the amount of the acquisition cost of the subject, including all installation, freight, and other direct and indirect costs as previously detailed in the "Cost Approach" section.

Exhibit 10.2

Comparable Listings and Sales for Items 1 Through 3

COMPARABLE LISTINGS AND SALES						
COMPARABLE SALES DATA	**ITEM 1**	**ADJ.**	**ITEM 2**	**ADJ.**	**ITEM 3**	**ADJ.**
Type:	Slitting Line		Slitting and Banding Line		Slitting Line	
Comparable Brand:	Loopco		Pro-Eco		Paxson	
Subject Brand:	Stamco		Stamco		Stamco	
Sale Price:	$ 220,000		N/A		$ 175,000	
Asking Price:	N/A		$ 957,000		N/A	
List to Sale Adj.:	N/A			$ (95,000)		$ (15,000)
Freight Cost:		$ 30,000		$ 30,000		$ 30,000
Installation Cost:		$ 500,000		$ 600,000		$ 500,000
De-installation Cost:		$ -		$ 35,000		$ -
Seller:	Perfection Machy Sls, Inc.		Machinery Int. Corp		Accurate Machinery	
Location - City/State:	Elk Grove, IL		North Branford, CT		Lindenhurst, NY	
Sale Date:	Dec-07		Listing		Listing	
Condition:	Older	$ 550,000	Older	$ 350,000	Newer	$ (100,000.00)
Year Manufactured:	Est 1982		1985 upgraded		2002	
Status:	Uninstalled		Installed		Uninstalled	
Capacity:	Similar		Similar		Slightly lower	$ 200,000
Misc:	None		None		None	
Net Adjustments:		$ 1,080,000		$ 920,000		$ 615,000
Adjusted Sale Price:		**1,300,000**		**1,877,000**		$ 1,230,000
Subject Cost:	3,930,000		5,882,903			3,930,000
Percent of Subject Cost:	27%		32%			31%
Comments:			Includes banding line		6 years newer	

Exhibit 10.3

Comparable Listings and Sales for Items for Items 4 Through 6

COMPARABLE LISTINGS AND SALES						
COMPARABLE SALES DATA	**ITEM 4**	**ADJ.**	**ITEM 5**	**ADJ.**	**ITEM 6**	**ADJ.**
Type:	Slitting Line / Some Banding		Slitting Line		Slitting Line	
Comparable Brand:	Yoder		Loopco		Yoder	
Subject Brand:	Stamco		Stamco		Stamco	
Sale Price:	$ 365,000		N/A		N/A	
Asking Price:	N/A		$ 195,000		$ 169,500	
List to Sale Adj.:	N/A			$ (20,000)		$ (15,000)
Freight Cost:		$ 35,000	$ 25,000	$ 30,000		$ 30,000
Installation Cost:		$ 600,000	$ 550,000	$ 600,000		$ 550,000
De-installation Cost:			$ 35,000	$ 35,000		$ 30,000
Seller:	Sunbelt Machinery		Ray Jacobs Machinery		Accurate Machinery	
Location - City/State:	Marietta, GA		Farmington Hills, MI		Lindenhurst, NY	
Sale Date:	Approx. June 2008		Listing		Listing	
Condition:	Older	$ 550,000	Older	$ 400,000	Older	$ 600,000
Year Manufactured:	Est 1984 upgraded		1985 Upgraded		Est. 1975	
Status:	Uninstalled		Installed		Installed	
Capacity:	Similar		Similar		Slightly lower	$ 100,000
Misc:	None		None		None	
Net Adjustments:		$ 1,185,000		$ 1,045,000		$ 1,295,000
Adjusted Sale Price:		**$ 1,550,000**		**$ 1,240,000**		**$ 1,464,500**
Subject Cost:	$ 3,930,000		$ 3,930,000			$ 3,930,000
Percent of Subject Cost:	30%		32%			37%
Comments:			Currently running			

Exhibit 10.4

Comparable Listings and Sales for Items 7 Through 9

	COMPARABLE LISTINGS AND SALES					
COMPARABLE SALES DATA	**ITEM 7**	**ADJ.**	**ITEM 8**	**ADJ.**	**ITEM 9**	**ADJ.**
Type:	Cut to Length Line		Stitcher		Generator	
Comparable Brand:	Pro-Eco		Behlen		Cummins 1250 KW	
Subject Brand:	Alcos		Behlen			
Sale Price:	N/A				N/A	
Asking Price:	$ 365,000		67,500		98,000	
List to Sale Adj.:	N/A	$ (30,000)		-15,000		$ (5,000)
Freight Cost:		$ 20,000		3,000		$ 3,000
Installation Cost:		$ 400,000		4,000		$ 3,000
De-installation Cost:		$ 25,000		$ -		$ -
Seller:	H.E. Phipps Co., Inc.		H.E. Phipps Co., Inc.		Accurate Machinery	
Location - City/State:	Roxboro, NC.		Roxboro, NC		Lindenhurst, NY	
Sale Date:	Listing		Listing		Listing	
Condition:	Older	$ 300,000			Similar	
Year Manufactured:	1988		N/A		1993	5000
Status:	Installed		Uninstalled		Installed	
Capacity:	Similar		Inferior	$ 3,000	Exact	
Misc:	None		None		None	
Net Adjustments:		$ 715,000		$ (5,000)		$ 6,000
Adjusted Sale Price:		**$ 1,080,000**		**$ 62,500**		**$ 104,000**
Subject Cost:	$ 1,913,485		149,394			336,904
Percent of Subject Cost:	37%		42%			31%
Comments:			Told price soft—make offer		Like new, only 142 hours	

Exhibit 10.5

Comparable Listings and Sales for Items 10 Through 12

	COMPARABLE LISTINGS AND SALES								
COMPARABLE SALES DATA	**ITEM 10**		**ADJ.**	**ITEM 11**		**ADJ.**	**ITEM 12**		**ADJ.**
Type:	Uncoiler			Slitting Line			Slitting Line		
Comparable Brand:	Paxson			Stamco			Pro-Eco		
Subject Brand:	Pro-Eco			Stamco			Stamco		
Sale Price:	N/A			$	269,000		$	825,000	
Asking Price:	$	94,500		N/A			N/A		
List to Sale Adj.:	N/A		$ (20,000)			$ (20,000)			$ (50,000)
Freight Cost:			$ 2,500			$ 30,000			$ 30,000
Installation Cost:			$ 3,000			$ 400,000			$ 400,000
De-installation Cost:			$ -			$ 30,000			$ -
Seller:	Sunbelt Machinery			USA Machinery Corp			USA Machinery Corp		
Location - City/State:	Marietta, GA			Allison Park, PA			Allison Park, PA		
Sale Date:	Listing			Listing			Listing		
Condition:	Older		$ 10,000	Some older, some newer		$ 300,000	Some older/newer		$ 300,000
Year Manufactured:		1973		1986-2006 Upgraded			1980s with Upgrades		
Status:	Installed			Installed			Uninstalled		
Capacity:	Similar			Wider		$ (50,000)	Superior		$ (100,000)
Misc:	None			None			None		
Net Adjustments:			$ (4,500)			$ 690,000			$ 580,000
Adjusted Sale Price:			**$ 90,000**			$ 1,380,000			$ 1,160,000
Subject Cost:		235,453				$ 3,930,000	Has turnstyle and		$ 3,930,000
Percent of Subject Cost:		38%		SCR drives installed 2006		35%	eveler subject lacks		30%
Comments:	Price soft—make offer			Excellent condition			eveler new is 500K		

General Comparable Information

Most of the comparable machinery and equipment are listings and not sales, and listings generally represent the upper end of value. Because of this, an estimate was made (noted as a "listing-to-sale adjustment") as to what the sale price might be, based mainly on discussions with the sellers and/or brokers about the typical ratio of sale to listing price, as well as specifics about each piece of equipment, if that was available.

For instance, a broker may have told us that the price was firm, or that it was soft and a low offer would be considered. We were able to find sales and/or listings for three complete lines: the slitting line, the banding line, and the cut-to-length line. These lines represent a good portion of the manufacturing process. From this research, it appears that in this industry and at this time, complete lines sell for a lower price than individual pieces of equipment.

Many other sales were researched, but most of them were not similar enough to be considered comparable. Most of the equipment was older than the Spokane facility equipment, but some was newer or the same age. It was hard to find newer equipment because it is generally auctioned off when a plant goes up for sale, and auction prices are normally not recognized as typical market value sales that can be used to determine fair market value.

Therefore, none of the sales were distress sales or auction sales, nor were any of the listings. Much of this equipment has not changed too much over time, with the exception of the electronics and software, and adjustments were made accordingly. We also found a price on a piece of equipment that is not specific to the steel industry: a large backup generator. We found the exact model with barely any usage, and the ratio to the price new lined up with the ratio range of the sales of the industry-specific equipment.

Installation costs were estimated based on discussions with plant personnel who have overseen the construction and installation of this particular equipment. When a range of expenses was given, we used the highest range because of the recent inflation for labor that we have researched. For example, a range of $500,000 to $750,000 was given as an estimate to install the slitting and banding lines, and we used $750,000.

Red Flag

The appraiser says the top of the range was used based on inflation for labor to install. The reviewer might ask for some backup information to confirm that this was appropriate.

Loopco Slitting Line Sale. This is a sale that took place in December 2007. This line is older than the subject property, but it is in good condition. It was not installed, so there was no need to estimate the cost of uninstalling it. Included in the freight cost is the cost to load the machinery on the truck, as well as the cost to ship it. Shipping costs are varying a great deal with the recent fluctuation in the cost of diesel fuel, and the estimates are subject to a variation of about 15 percent. However, this amount is small enough that it should not affect the percentage of value that is estimated. The seller for this property is Perfection Machinery, out of Elk Grove, Illinois.

Pro-Eco Slitting and Banding Line. This is a listing and not a sale. This line was installed, and we got a specific cost to uninstall it, load it on trucks, and ship it. With both lines, we were told it would take 12 trucks. This line was functioning well and in operation, and it could be observed before the purchase if a buyer wanted to see it working. It was manufactured in 1985, but it had upgrades, which most likely include the electronics.

Paxson Slitting Line. This is a listing and not a sale. The slitting line is six years newer than the subject line, and it was manufactured in 2002. It appears from the price that this newer equipment is not selling for a lot more than the older equipment. This was the newest equipment we could find to use for a comparable, and it looks to be in excellent condition from the photographs we were sent of it. This line has a slightly lower capacity than the subject line and was adjusted accordingly.

Yoder Slitting Line with Some Banding. This is a sale that took place in 2008, but we could not get the exact time. It appears to be around June 2008. This is a line that is in very good condition, and it was manufactured in 1984 with upgrades since that time. It was not installed, so there was no estimate to take it apart. The seller was Sunbelt Machinery located in Marietta, Georgia. Although this is a newer sale, we consider it close enough in time to be comparable with the subject.

Loopco Slitting Line Listing. This is a listing and not a sale. This line was built in 1985 and has been ungraded since that time. It is installed, and an estimate was made for the expense of uninstalling it. An adjustment was also made for age, but this unit has been upgraded to the point where it is very usable as is.

Yoder Slitting Line. This equipment is quite a bit older than the subject property and has been adjusted by a large amount, $600,000, to make up for the difference in condition. It is also slightly lower in capacity and has been adjusted accordingly. The seller is Accurate Machinery from Lindenhurst, New York.

Pro-Eco Cut-to-Length Line. This line is very comparable to the subject because it is in very good condition, as is the subject. It is presently installed and running so a potential buyer can see how it performs. It is a smaller line than the slitter line, and the uninstallation cost is less. It was manufactured in 1988, it has been well maintained, and it is similar to the subject cut-to-length line. The seller is H.E. Phipps Co. in Roxbury, North Carolina.

Behlen Stitcher. This machine is for sale for what appears to be a fairly high amount, and the sellers say that they will look at all offers, which suggests the sale price will be considerably lower than the listing price, and an adjustment has been made accordingly. It appears from this asking price and other research we have done that the cost for individual pieces of equipment is generally higher than the purchase of a whole line of equipment. The capacity of this stitcher is slightly less than the subject.

Cummins 1,250-Watt Generator. This generator has only 142 hours on it, which makes it like new, even though it was manufactured in 1993. The subject generator was installed only a few years after this one, making this almost an exact match. It is the same wattage, 1,250 kilowatts, and the same brand—it is an Onan with a Cummins diesel engine. The ratio of cost new to used cost for this piece of equipment, which is not specific to the industry, falls into the same range as the industry-specific equipment.

Paxson Uncoiler. There are two Pro-Eco uncoilers in the Spokane plant, and they both sold for about $235,000. This one is older, but uncoilers have been about the same for many years, and there is not much in the way of new technology with them. However, an adjustment of about 14 percent was made for age. The price was quite soft, so an adjustment was made for the listing to sale adjustment.

Stamco Slitting Line. This is the same brand as the line that is installed at Spokane. It is older, as it was manufactured in 1986, but there have been many upgrades as recently as 2006. One upgrade is the installation of new SCR drives. The machine is reported to be in excellent condition. It has wider capability than the subject. This is offered by USA Machinery Corporation in Allison Park, Pennsylvania.

Pro-Eco Slitting Line. This is also offered by USA Machinery Corporation in Allison Park, Pennsylvania. It is very similar to the subject line, but it has two other machines that the subject does not have—a turnstyle and a leveler. The leveler alone sells for about $500,000 new. Adjustments were made for age and for the additional equipment.

Summary of Comparable Sales

The comparable sales show a range of percentage of original acquisition cost from 30 to 42 percent, and the average is 36 percent. In other words, the used-equipment sales show us that the existing equipment is worth between 30 and 42 percent of the original cost of that equipment.

The majority of the equipment was purchased in 1997, when the plant opened, so most of it was 10 years old as of the assessment date of January 1, 2007. Some of the sales are past that date, but just as older sales are used in appraisals, newer sales were used in this case because of a lack of available comparable sales.

Even though this is a retrospective appraisal, the sales are within a time period that is close enough to the valuation date to provide reasonable accuracy. The ratio average here was applied to the rest of the equipment as discussed in the next segment on trending.

Two Types of Trending

Marshall & Swift Trends Applied

Because trending is by far the most widely used method for valuing machinery and equipment for assessment purposes, it was utilized in this appraisal in two ways. First, the equipment was trended according to the trending tables that Marshall & Swift Valuation Service provides for a fee.

These trends were used to get an idea of the value that would typically be assigned to the property if no further appraisal work was done for the specific machinery and equipment that subject has.

Specific Trends from the Used-Equipment Approach Applied

In addition to trending the property using trends supplied by Marshall & Swift, the second way used was the ratio derived from the used-equipment approach (sales comparison approach). We believe that the trends from this ratio are much more accurate than the trends from Marshall & Swift because they were derived from actual sales and listings in the marketplace, which are specific to the exact equipment used in the subject's facility. The trend average is 36 percent, which is further explained in the "Summary of Comparable Sales" section.

However, we used a percentage in the higher range (which translates into a higher value for the property), which was 40 percent and which was applied only to the machinery and equipment property that was purchased in 1997, which was when the plant began. For equipment other than the machinery and equipment, such as computers, office equipment, and software, Marshall & Swift was used. To reiterate, equipment purchased after 1997 used the Marshall & Swift tables, regardless of the category, because the ratio was established using the 1997 equipment, and not newer equipment, and it was thought the Marshall & Swift tables were accurate for the newer equipment, after checking prices for it.

Final Value

The value for the machinery and equipment using only trends from Marshall & Swift was $89,004,387 including noninventory supplies. This amount is shown for information purposes, and it is not the value conclusion for this appraisal.

The final value for the machinery and equipment using the trends from the used-equipment approach, including noninventory supplies, is $73,500,000.

> **Red Flag**
>
> This is a significant difference, so the trends computed from the sampling of comparable sales for the larger machines from 1997 or earlier should be looked at carefully. Also, if this appraisal is for asset-based lending, a decision should be made as to whether or not the installation and other associated costs would be recoverable, if the plant closes. The question arises as to whether the plant would be sold as a package or if the equipment would be sold piecemeal. This decision might depend on the type of industry and the economic forecasts for it.

Chapter 11

How Government Policies Can Affect Property Values

In basic economics, supply and demand are typically the primary drivers of prices, and with less expensive items that do not require financing, this is the predominate principle. However, with purchases that are typically financed, the interest rate of the debt instrument becomes another major factor. The purchases of real estate and businesses are normally financed, and interest rates fluctuate mostly based on the discount rate set by the Federal Reserve (the Fed) in the United States. The *discount rate* is the rate at which banks borrow money from the Fed. They may also borrow from other institutions at the Fed, and that rate is known as the *federal funds rate.* Those trades often occur overnight between *depository institutions*, which are the institutions with surplus balances that lend to those that need funds.

Low interest rates effectively raise the cost of real estate, so when interest rates rise, values can be expected to drop. For a proper perspective on this, two extremes can be considered. At one extreme, if there were no loans to purchase it, the value of real estate would drop significantly. Under that scenario, if every piece of real estate could be purchased only in cash, there would be very few people who could afford it, and those who had to sell would eventually have to lower their prices to that new paradigm.

At the other extreme, if loans had an interest rate of zero percent, if they required no down payment, and if they were available to everyone regardless of credit rating or income, values would rise because demand would increase. New buyers with bad credit and without funds for a down payment would be able to buy a home rather than rent.

It's the Monthly Payment, Not the Price

What would prices be under each scenario? Because the U.S. economy is credit driven, most buyers of real estate look at the monthly payment rather than the total cost. Thus, prices would plummet in the first scenario and skyrocket in the second. For instance, as shown in Exhibit 11.1, a $500,000 mortgage amortized for 30 years would have a monthly payment of $2,358 at 3.9 percent. That same mortgage would have a monthly payment of $4,023 at 9 percent, which was a normal rate for many years in the past. Therefore, price fluctuations are based on the interest rate paid (also known as the *cost of money*) and the availability of credit, both of which are to a great extent controlled by the government and, more specifically, the Federal Reserve Bank. To reiterate, the Fed indirectly causes mortgage lending rates to go up or down by setting the interest rate that banks are charged for borrowing from it.

Exhibit 11.1
Mortgage Payment on a $500,000 Loan Amortized over 30 Years

Mortgage Payment $500,000 Loan Amortized for 30 Years		
Amount	Rate	Payment
$500,000	3.9%	$2,358
$500,000	9.0%	$4,023
Payment almost doubles (71% increase).		

Exhibit 11.2
Interest Rates from 1962 Through 2012

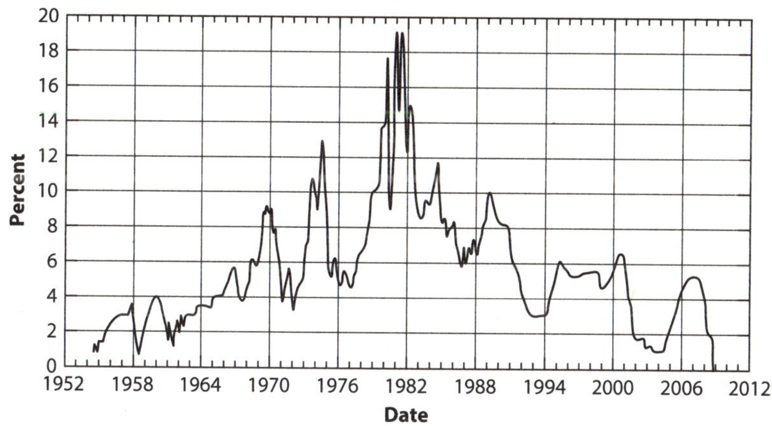

Source: Federal Reserve.

Historically, the last time rates were pushed to an extreme was under President Jimmy Carter in the late 1970s and early 1980s. At that time the United States was experiencing increasing inflation, and to stem it, the Fed raised rates until a mortgage might cost 18 percent or more. This rate increase did limit inflation, but it also slowed real estate sales and business loans, and lending slowed to a dribble, causing financial failure for many business entities and throwing the country into a recession. The spike in that time period is shown in Exhibit 11.2, which is a chart showing the history of interest rates over the period of 1962 through 2012.

Unintended Ramifications of Low Interest Rates

Another result of low interest rates is the effect it has on savers. People who rely on income from savings see their incomes drop drastically when rates plummet. For instance, a person who has $1 million in the bank will see a substantial change in income when rates are low. One of the most risk-free investments is an FDIC insured fund. As shown

Exhibit 11.3
Rate of Return on a $1 Million CD

Rate of Return on a $1 Million CD		
Amount	Rate	Return
$1,000,000	0.7%	$7,000
$1,000,000	5.0%	$50,000
$1,000,000	9.0%	$90,000

in Exhibit 11.3, when an FDIC insured certificate of deposit (CD) or money market rate is about 0.7 percent, it will return an annual yield of $7,000. When the rate is 5 percent, the yield will be $50,000 a year. When the rate is 9 percent, the yield will be $90,000.

As the rates decrease, more savers seek riskier investments to keep the yield up, and this is where real estate is affected. Historically, when significantly better returns are available for investment real estate than for savings, property prices are driven up, only to come down when the bubble in value bursts. And this is particularly true for single-family houses. In the bubble that burst around 2006, 25 percent of the homes bought were for investment purposes.

Another by-product of the low rates is overborrowing—particularly in the business sector. When money is cheap, businesses tend to spend more and expand when they might not have otherwise. The consequence of this is that many companies that invest in expanding production in an overheated economy later find demand falling and rates going up simultaneously. They continue to have higher fixed operating costs as the demand for their goods is diminishing. This is why in some industries, when there is overexpansion, factories and machinery and equipment can drop precipitously when the economy enters a recession. One example is the solar industry, which at one point was expanding production just at the time the economy was ebbing.

Moreover, many government subsidies for solar installations around the world diminished or were terminated, making the product so noncompetitive that it lost its appeal in the marketplace.

Another aspect of this phenomenon is that most business loans are not long-term loans, and when rates increase, many lenders will not renew current loans, which can put even a viable business in a predicament. Commercial loans are similar in that they are normally made with a renewal period of every 3 to 5 years, but they are amortized over a longer period, generally 20 to 25 years. Lenders generally tell commercial borrowers that renewal will not be a problem when the loan is made, but things can change when real estate values decrease.

Government programs that essentially subsidize real estate purchases or certain industries can produce an artificial market that may collapse. Federal Housing Administration (FHA), Veterans Administration (VA), and U.S. Department of Agriculture (USDA) real estate loans generally require a lower down payment than conventional loans, and because of this, they tend to drive values up. They may also set up buyers for failure by allowing them to buy with such little equity that the market has to decrease only slightly to put these buyers "upside down" with their mortgage—which means they owe more than the property is worth. In the same way, programs to finance certain industries, such as the example of solar power, can induce overproduction and riskier investments than would normally be considered prudent.

If certain government policies are having an impact on the market of the subject property being reviewed, the reviewer needs to understand how these properties are affected in determining if the appraisal is accurate. *Appraisal* has been defined as the present worth of future benefits, and in many cases those potential benefits will be determined by the status of government programs and subsidies.

Chapter 12

USPAP: The Rules Under Which Appraisers Work

The Uniform Standards of Professional Appraisal Practice (USPAP) have promulgated what might be called the "generally accepted standards for professional appraisal practice in North America." The complete manual for the USPAP can be read at www.uspap.org.

The manual is long, and it can be read at that website, but the basic 10 standards are as follows:

- *Standards 1 and 2* set the requirements for the development and reporting of a real property appraisal.
- *Standard 3* sets the requirements for development and reporting of an appraisal review assignment for a real or personal property appraisal.
- *Standards 4 and 5* set the requirements for real property consulting in line with the USPAP.
- *Standard 6* sets the requirements for mass appraising, which in general pertains to assessors (ad valorem assessment).
- *Standards 7 and 8* set the requirements for personal property appraisals.
- *Standards 9 and 10* set the requirements for the valuations of businesses and intangible assets.

There are also *advisory opinions*, which may be used as guidelines for appraisers in that they may give scenarios of how the appraisal standards may be applied. However, advisory guidelines do not carry the weight of the actual standards, and they are not binding on the appraiser.

Compliance with the USPAP

The following are 12 of the basic requirements that should be covered in the appraisal to comply with the USPAP. For a complete list, it is recommended that the reader read the USPAP.

1. *Identify the client and intended users.* There can be more than one client and/or intended user. Only those listed are legally allowed to use the appraisal.
2. *State the intended use of the appraisal.* If the appraisal was written for a particular user and the client wants to also use it for another purpose, the appraiser should be contacted to get written permission. For instance, the appraisal may have been performed to list a property for sale, but if owners also wanted to use it for a tax appeal, they would need to secure the permission of the appraiser.
3. *Describe the property that is being appraised and the characteristics relevant to the assignment.* This might be accomplished by using the legal description, address, survey, maps, and so on.
4. *Describe the real property interest that is being appraised.* This will normally be fee simple, but it could also be leased fee or some other type of ownership.
5. *State the purpose of the appraisal and include the definition of the value being determined.* This purpose is normally to establish the fair market value, but it could be something else such as the liquidation value.
6. *State the date of the appraisal report and the effective date of the valuation.* The effective date notes the time period for which

the value was estimated for the subject property. It may be a retrospective date, or it may be a current or prospective date. The date of the report notes when the report was completed.

7. *State the scope of work the appraisal entails.* This statement should stop confusion over the assignment. The reviewer should be able to understand exactly what was valued and how it was valued from reading the scope of work. It should also state if the appraiser had significant assistance from others in developing the report.
8. *State assumptions, limiting conditions, and hypothetical conditions that affect the development of the report and the value conclusion.* There are normally limiting conditions that might state, for example, that the property is being appraised as a clean site. In that case, if there is hazardous waste contamination found on the site later, the appraiser will not to be held liable for not detecting it. There may also be extraordinary or special assumptions or limiting conditions. An example would be a hypothetical condition for the property.
9. *Summarize the information collected and analyzed and the reasoning behind opinions and conclusions.* This summary should also include any current sales contracts, options, listings, prior sales, and the like.
10. *Include a highest and best use analysis, a statement concerning the use of the property on the appraisal date, and a rationale for the appraisal's assumed highest and best use of the subject property.* The reasons for the highest and best use conclusion should be understandable to the reviewer or the requirement has not been satisfied.
11. *Explain any departures from Standard 1, and provide valid reasons for excluding any of the valuation approaches.* When there is a departure, the appraisal becomes a limited appraisal, and it must contain a section explaining the reason for the departure.
12. *Include the required signed certification.*

SECTION 2

BUSINESS VALUATIONS

Chapter 13

Defining Value in the Relevant Context: Definitions of Value

Business valuation normally occurs in context: a specific value or range of values in a given set of defined parameters that, among other factors, include the legal universe in which the value is being considered, the organization of the business, and the particular rights and responsibilities of the ownership stake within that business, all as of the date of the valuation.

Identifying the correct definition of value in the legal context is a crucial beginning step in an appraisal. The belief that "value lies in the eye of the beholder" is not helpful when there is a legal need for a definition of value. Value is defined differently in different legal contexts, and the quest for the appropriate definition in any particular legal context can be difficult.

The lawyer and appraiser should agree on the definition of value at the outset, and the definition should be included in the written assignment. It is best to define and cite the source of the definition and, if appropriate, to include those details in a buy-sell or arbitration agreement. The valuation practitioner can bring experience to bear in helping the lawyer at this step. However, ultimately the definition of value is a legal question must be based on the law that pertains to the specific valuation.

It is often a shock to some lawyers and their clients to learn that there may be multiple definitions of value for the same property at the same time and that one definition may legitimately lead to an amount more than twice as much as another definition. For example, the phrase "fair market value of these shares" is frequently found in buy-sell agreements. Usually, the minority parties assume that "fair market value" means a proportionate share of the value of the enterprise as a whole. When the triggering event occurs, they are surprised to find that the term implies discounts for minority interest and lack of marketability, and those discounts sometimes total as much as 50 percent.

If an expert's report, methodology or testimony does not follow the pertinent legal definition of value, the judge may disallow them.[1]

Commonly Used Definitions of Value[2]

The two most common expressions of value found in U.S. statutes are *fair market value* and *fair value*. Other significant terms are *market value, true value, true cash value, intrinsic value, investment value,* and *marital value* as well as other definitions. Often opinions will not define the term as it is used or include authority or precedent for its use.

Other than *fair market value* and *fair value*, business appraisers and investment bankers will also frequently use *investment value* and *intrinsic*, or *fundamental, value.* These two terms are often found in court opinions but, again, usually without definition.

Fair Market Value

In the United States and Canada, the most widely recognized and accepted standard of value is *fair market value*. It is the standard that applies to most U.S. federal and state tax matters, including estate taxes, gift taxes, inheritance taxes, income taxes, and ad valorem taxes. It is also the legal standard of value in some other valuation situations, primarily in those involving taxes. The Treasury regulations define the fair market value of a business interest as "the net amount which a willing purchaser, whether an individual or a corporation, would pay for the interest to a willing seller, neither being under any compulsion to buy or to sell and both having reasonable knowledge of relevant facts."[3]

There is general agreement that the definition implies that the parties have the ability—as well as the willingness—to effectuate this hypothetical cash transaction. The "market" in this definition can be thought of as all the potential buyers and sellers of like businesses or professional practices.

In the legal interpretations of fair market value, the willing buyer and willing seller are hypothetical persons, dealing at arm's length, rather than any particular buyer or seller. In other words, a fair market value price would not be influenced by special motivations not characteristic of a typical buyer or seller. (In Canada, however, fair market value may include the value of synergies with a particular buyer.[4])

However, while the fair market value concept assumes an open and unrestricted market, it does not preclude identifying groups of willing participants. On the contrary, the valuer should be able to identify categories of willing purchasers. The analyst also cannot ignore the position of the seller, who is assumed to be willing to sell under conditions that exist as of the valuation date.

Fair market value also assumes prevalent economic and market conditions at the date of the particular valuation. The concept of fair market value means the price at which a transaction could be expected to take place under conditions existing as of the valuation date. In other words, the fair market value buyer is looking for the best risk/reward relationship available in the market at a given time.

The terms *market value* and *cash value* are sometimes used interchangeably with *fair market value*. Real estate appraisers generally use the term *market value* rather than *fair market value*. The Appraisal Foundation gives the most useful definition of *market value*; as defined by the Uniform Standards of Professional Appraisal Practice (USPAP), *market value* is virtually synonymous with *fair market value* as defined in the Treasury regulations.[5]

Judge David Laro, in a U.S. Tax Court decision, articulated the following as some guiding principles regarding the estimation of fair market value:

1. The willing buyer and the willing seller are hypothetical persons, rather than specific individuals or entities, and the characteristics of these hypothetical persons are not necessarily the same as the personal characteristics of the actual seller or a particular buyer.
2. Fair market value is determined as of the valuation date, and no knowledge of unforeseeable future events that may have affected the value is given to the hypothetical persons.
3. Fair market value equals the highest and best use to which the property could be put on the valuation date, and fair market value takes into account special uses that are realistically available due to the property's adaptability to a particular business. Fair market value is not affected by whether the owner has actually put the property to its highest and best use. The reasonable, realistic, and objective possible uses for the property in the near future control the valuation thereof. Elements affecting value that depend upon events or a combination of occurrences which, while within the realm of possibility, are not reasonably probable, are excluded from this consideration.[6]

It is generally understood that *fair market value* is a value in cash or cash equivalents (as indicated in the Appraisal Foundation definition of *market value*) unless otherwise stated.

Fair Value Under State Statutes

The expression *fair value* is an excellent example of ambiguous terminology used in commercial appraisal. Context is crucial to understanding the concept. In the context of a standard of value in business valuation, *fair value* is a term found in state statutes governing dissenting stockholder and minority oppression actions. Its meaning is quite different from the term as used in generally accepted accounting principles (GAAP), where until recently *fair value* and *fair market value* were used almost interchangeably.[7] Courts have given very different interpretations to the term *fair value* as a statutory business value standard.

Courts apply a fair value standard in cases in which the aggrieved party alleges he or she is being forced to accept less than adequate consideration for stock following a merger or sale of the business. Here, the aggrieved party seeks to enforce his or her right to have his or her shares appraised and to receive fair value in cash.[8]

Revisions made to the Model Business Corporation Act of 1950 and adoption of the same, in part or in full, by 35 states has led to uniformity before the 1984 revision and to its being called the Revised Model Business Corporation Act (RMBCA). Prior to 1999, the RMBCA defined *fair value* as follows:

> The value of the shares immediately before the effectuation of the corporate action to which the shareholder objects, excluding any appreciation or depreciation in anticipation of the corporate action unless exclusion would be inequitable.

In 1999, the definition changed to the following:

> "Fair value" means the value of the corporation's shares determined:
> (i) immediately before the effectuation of the corporate action to which the shareholder objects;
> (ii) using customary and current valuation concepts and techniques generally employed for similar businesses in the context of the transaction requiring appraisal; and
> (iii) without discounting for lack of marketability or minority status except, if appropriate, for amendments to the articles.

Although a majority of states adopted the pre-1999 RMBCA definition,[9] only a few of the states have adopted the 1999 version.[10] A minority of states that adopted the pre-1999 definition did so without the "unless exclusion would be inequitable" phrase[11]; other states omit this phrase but, in addition, add a clause that states that all relevant factors should be considered in determining value.[12] Florida and Illinois use a hybrid of the pre-1999 and 1999 definitions.

There is no clearly recognized consensus about the definition of fair value in the context of dissenting shareholder statutes.[13] However, the judicial precedents of most states certainly have not equated it to fair market value. When a situation of actual or potential stockholder dissent arises, it is important to carefully research the legal precedents applicable to each case and to take note of the date.

The term *fair value* is also found in the dissolution statutes of those states that have such statutes (for example, California Corporations Code Section 2000). An increasing number of states have enacted such statutes in recent years. Under these statutes, stockholders can trigger a corporate dissolution under certain circumstances. The company can avoid dissolution by paying the stockholders the fair value of their shares. Even within the same state, however, a study of case law precedents does not necessarily lead one to the same definition of fair value under a dissolution statute as under that state's dissenting stockholder statute.[14] The term *fair value* in the context of state statutes is more extensively discussed in the chapter on shareholder partner disputes.

In summary, *fair market value* is a willing buyer/willing seller standard, whereas *fair value* does not necessarily assume a "willing" seller and/or a "willing" buyer.

Fair Value for Financial Reporting[15]

The Financial Accounting Standards Board (FASB) has another definition of *fair value*. Here, the term is used for financial reporting purposes—specifically, to report the fair values of certain assets and liabilities appearing on financial statements.

The fair value definition was promulgated in the Statement of Financial Accounting Standards (SFAS) 157.[16] It is effective for financial statements issued for fiscal years beginning after November 15, 2007, and for interim periods within those years.

The SFAS 157 definition is as follows:

> The price that would be received to sell an asset or paid to transfer a liability in an orderly transaction between market participants at the measurement date.

The important feature of this definition is that it is an *exit* price, *not* the price that would be paid to acquire the asset or to assume the liability (an *entry* price). SFAS 157 emphasizes that assets should not be valued at cost (an *entry* price) unless they can be disposed of at cost.

The "market" referred to in this definition is "the market in which the reporting entity would transact for the asset or liability, that is, the principal or most advantageous market for the asset or liability." Thus, the definition specifies an orderly transaction in the most advantageous market. Market participants are buyers and sellers in the principal (or the most advantageous) market for the asset or liability. These market participants are (1) unrelated, (2) knowledgeable about factors relevant to the asset or liability and the transaction, (3) able to transact (that is, have the legal and financial ability to do so), and (4) willing to transact (that is, motivated but not forced or otherwise compelled to transact). SFAS 157 clarifies that the term *fair value* is intended to mean a market-based measure, not an entity-specific measure.

The fair value premise for an asset is the asset's highest and best use, from the perspective of market participants, that would maximize a company's future cash flows. A company's intended use of an asset is not necessarily indicative of the highest and best use of that asset as determined by a market participant; the fair value measure is *not* an entity-specific measure that reflects only the company's expectations for the asset. SFAS 157 requires fair value measures consider the perspectives of market participants and the assumptions those participants would use to price an asset or a liability.

The market price on the valuation date is fair value if there is an active market for the subject asset or liability but not if the market is thin. The FASB identifies three levels in the hierarchy of measurements to quantify fair value, with the highest level available to be used:

- **Level 1** (highest-priority) inputs are quoted prices in active markets for identical assets or liabilities.
- **Level 2** inputs are those other than quoted prices included within Level 1 that are directly or indirectly observable.
- **Level 3** inputs are unobservable inputs that reflect assumptions about what market participants would use in their pricing analyses.

This implies that, if there is an active market for the subject asset, the quoted price on the valuation date applies. For assets for which there is not an active market but for which there is an active market for close comparables, the prices for the comparables, with appropriate adjustments for differences, could be used as inputs. The standard clearly favors observable market data. For other subject assets (Level 3 assets), other valuation methods, including a discounted cash flow (DCF), could be used as inputs. The company may use its own assumptions, but Level 3 inputs must be adjusted if information is available that indicates that market participants would use different assumptions.

Although the FASB emphasizes "market participant assumptions at the measurement date," there are differences between "fair value" for financial reporting purposes and "fair market value." For example, SFAS 157 apparently makes a (perhaps unintended) distinction between legally imposed restrictions on sale (for example, restricted stock, which normally *should* be discounted) and market-imposed restrictions (for example, blocks of stock that are too large to be sold without depressing the market, which *should not* be discounted for what the market refers to as *blockage*). Blocks of stock are to be valued at the price multiplied by the quantity, with no discount applied for the size of the block. However, there is the contrary opinion that no discounts are applied for SFAS 123R.[17] The FASB says that it did not adopt the definition of fair market value because it did not want the definition of fair value to be saddled with the nuances of court interpretations of fair market value.

Investment Value

The primary distinguishing characteristic of *investment value* is that it denotes *value to a particular owner or investor*. This is in contrast to *fair market value*, which is a concept of value in exchange, assuming hypothetical and typically motivated buyers and sellers. In other words, investment value is the value to a particular individual or entity, considering that individual's or entity's situation, perceptions, and motivation, but not necessarily value in the marketplace. This is also essentially the same way that investment value is defined in the context of real estate appraisal.[18]

Investment value is generally a "subjective" value, whereas fair market value is an "objective" value.

Valid reasons for the investment value to one particular owner or prospective owner to differ from the fair market value include the following unique factors:

1. Synergies with other operations owned or controlled—for example, a buyer has a particular use for the particular property
2. Relationships with other owners
3. Differences in estimates of future earning power and/or perception of degree of risk
4. Differences in aversion to or willingness to accept degrees of risk
5. Differences in income tax status

Whether or not the term *investment value* is actually used, the concept is found frequently in business valuations for marital dissolution. That is, the courts often focus on value to the spouse who operates the business as opposed to value that could be realized in the market.

Finally, investment value has a slightly different meaning in the context of dissenting stockholder suits. In this context, it means a value based on earning power. However, the appropriate present value discount rate or the direct capitalization rate is usually considered to be a consensus rate rather than a rate singularly appropriate for any specific investor.

Intrinsic or Fundamental Value

Financial analysts that follow and report on publicly traded stock commonly use *intrinsic value* (sometimes called *fundamental value*) to report value. Intrinsic value differs from investment value in that it represents an analytical judgment of value based on the investment characteristics perceived by a financial analyst rather than on how the characteristics comport to the circumstances of a particular investor.

Concurrence on the meanings of intrinsic value and fundamental value is found in the following definitions from an authoritative reference in the accounting field:

> *Intrinsic value:* The amount that an investor considers, on the basis of an evaluation of available facts, to be the "true" or "real" worth of an item, usually an *equity security*. The value that will become the market value when other investors reach the same conclusions. The various approaches to determining intrinsic value of the *finance* literature are based on expectations and discounted cash flows. See *expected value; fundamental analysis; discounted cash flow method.*[19]
>
> *Fundamental analysis:* An approach in security analysis which assumes that a security has an "intrinsic value" that can be determined through a rigorous evaluation of relevant variables. Expected earnings is usually the most important variable in this analysis, but many other variables, such as dividends, capital structure,

> management quality, and so on, may also be studied. An analyst estimates the "intrinsic value" of a security on the basis of those fundamental variables and compares this value with the current market price of this security to arrive at an investment decision.[20]

In securities analysis, intrinsic value is generally considered the appropriate price for a stock according to the perspective of an analyst who has completed a fundamental analysis of the company's assets, earning power, and other factors. Two University of Chicago professors comment on the notion of intrinsic value as follows:

> The purpose of security analysis is to detect differences between the value of a security as determined by the market and a security's "intrinsic value"—that is, the value that the security *ought* to have and will have when other investors have the same insight and knowledge as the analyst.[21]

Typically, if the market value is below what the analyst concludes is the intrinsic value, the analyst considers the stock a "buy." If the market value is above the assumed intrinsic value, the analyst suggests selling the stock. It is important to note that such "buy" and "sell" assumptions are both predictive and predicated on the notion that at some point in the future the market can and will be made to realize the same level of knowledge and insight about the stock as the analyst.

It is important to note that the concept of intrinsic value cannot be entirely disassociated from the concept of fair market value. This is because the actions of buyers and sellers based on their *specific* perceptions of intrinsic value eventually lead to the *general* consensus market value in the course of the constant and dynamic changes in market value over time.

Case law often refers to intrinsic value. However, almost universally, such references do not define the term other than by reference to the language in the context in which it appears. Such references to intrinsic value can be found both in case opinions in which there is no statutory standard of value and also in case decisions in which the statutory standard of value is specified as fair value or even fair market value. When references to intrinsic value appear in the relevant case law, the court usually is referring to notions such as those discussed in this section. It is also common to find court cases that use the term *intrinsic value* to mean the inherent worth of the stock to the owner—in other words, to equate the term to investment value, as defined earlier.

Other Terms Referring to Value

Acquisition Value

Acquisition value means the value to a particular acquirer. It is very similar to *strategic value* (see below). In this sense, it falls within the concept of investment value, as described in the previous section. The term may also be used to denote the actual price at which a transaction occurred. In this sense, it would be the same as transaction value, described more fully below.

Book Value

The term *book value* is an accounting term, not a financial term, and it is not necessarily, or even usually, indicative of any of the definitions of value discussed in the previous section. It is not related to any concept of economic value.

The term represents historical costs of assets owned by the entity, less any depreciation or amortization deducted in the accounting system used by that entity. The American Society of Appraisers defines book value as follows:

> With respect to assets, the capitalized cost of an asset less accumulated depreciation, depletion, or amortization as it appears on the books of account of the enterprise. With respect to a business enterprise, the difference between total assets (net of depreciation, depletion, and amortization) and total liabilities of an enterprise as they appear on the balance sheet.[22]

Many of a company's most valuable assets, especially if goodwill and other intangible assets are developed internally rather than purchased,[23] may not appear on the balance sheet at all. Similarly, there may be liabilities, especially those of a contingent nature, that do not appear on the balance sheet.

Going-Concern Value

The term *going-concern value* has two separate and distinct meanings, depending on the context in which it is used.

In one sense, it refers to the premise of the total value of the operations of the company on an ongoing basis.

The other concept of going-concern value is that of an intangible asset. In that context, it means the value of having a system of operating assets, systems, and personnel in place, with the ability to operate. It can be thought of as the difference between merely a set of physical assets and a "turnkey" operation ready to do business. For example, in a marital dissolution case, the Pennsylvania Supreme Court, in addressing the value of a professional practice, distinguished between the personal goodwill of the professional (not part of the marital estate) and the value of having support staff, systems, and other operating systems in place (the "going-concern value," to be valued and included as part of the marital estate).[24] Other courts have differed on this question, and, as always, it is critical for the lawyer and appraiser to refer to the appropriate case law.

Enterprise Value

A term that causes much confusion is *enterprise value*. Sometimes it is used to mean the market value of the company's entire capital structure (all equity and long-term debt). Other times it is used to describe market cap plus interest-bearing debt plus preferred stock minus total cash and cash equivalents. At other times, it refers to the total value of the company's common stock on a control basis. When this term is encountered, one should carefully try to interpret its meaning from the context in which it is used.

Liquidation Value

Liquidation value means the net amount that can be realized (after liquidation expenses) in either an orderly or a forced sale of the business assets or some portion of them.

Strategic Value (Synergistic Value)

A *strategic* or *synergistic value* reflects added benefits to a particular acquirer because of synergies with the acquiree. That is, it is a price or potential price reflecting all or some portion of the value of synergistic benefits created through the combination of the respective entities for which a buyer might be willing to pay. Such benefits could include, for example, increasing market share, reducing costs by combining operations, particularly in the form of either staff reductions, sale of redundant assets or economies of scale, and/or raising prices by eliminating a competitor, to name a few.

Synergistic value generally reflects some added value above fair market value. Because it reflects the value of benefits available to a particular buyer, it is usually considered to fall within the concept of *investment value*, as discussed previously.

Transaction Value

Transaction value is the price at which an actual transaction occurs, either in the form of an asset sale or a stock sale. The International Business Brokers Association's *Business Brokers Glossary* defines the term as follows:

> The total of all consideration passed at any time between the buyer and seller for an ownership interest in a business enterprise and may include, but is not limited to, all remuneration for tangible and

intangible assets such as furniture, equipment, supplies, inventory, working capital, noncompetition agreements, employment, and/or consultation agreements, licenses, customer lists, franchise fees, assumed liabilities, stock options, stock or stock redemptions, real estate, leases, royalties, earn-outs, and future considerations.

Some definitions exclude the value of noncompetition agreements and/or employment agreements on the basis that payments for these intangibles often are contingent on future personal performance.

Transaction value specifically refers to *price* as opposed to *value*. It is empirical (historical) in nature; it is not a legal standard of value. *Price* is the *face value* (the amount shown on the transaction documents) at which a specific transaction occurred, without any adjustment to cash equivalent value to reflect special terms. The price may or may not represent an arm's-length negotiation. It may be arrived at by negotiation, by contract, by court order, or by some other means. It may or may not comport to any of the definitions of value discussed in the previous section. The use of transaction prices in the market approach to appraisal is further discussed in Chapter 16.

Sources of Authority for Definition of Value

The search for the appropriate definition of value usually proceeds in approximately the following hierarchy:

- Statutory law
- Legally binding rules and regulations
- Contractual definitions of value
- Non-legally binding administrative rules
- Precedential court decisions
- Direction from the court
- Direction from the lawyer
- Use of IRS authority in non-tax situations.
- Opinions of other lawyers and appraisers

Statutory Law

Our experience has been that statutes have the advantage of having the greatest force of law and the disadvantage of being the least explicit of all sources in defining value.

The relevant statutes may be either federal or state. For example, federal statutes require that valuations for tax purposes will be at fair market value.[25] Most state statutes governing dissenting stockholders require that valuations will be at fair value and most (if using the Revised Model Corporation Act or a close variation of it) add that the valuation date will be the day before the event to which the shareholder dissents, without considering the effect of that event. Most state statutes governing marital dissolution are silent about definitions of value other than some language about valuation dates.

Specifics of statutory law are discussed in considerable detail in the various chapters relating to the purposes of the valuation, such as gift and estate tax, shareholder disputes, marital dissolution, and so on. The purpose of this chapter is simply to make the point that statutory law usually is the first stop in the quest for the proper legal definition of value. Some examples of statutory law include the following.

Federal Statutes

- Internal Revenue Code (IRC), especially Section 2031 on estate taxes, Section 2512 for gift taxes, and Subsection 2701–04 on intra-family transfers
- Employee Retirement Income Security Act (ERISA), 29 USC Section 1002 (26)
- U.S. Bankruptcy Code, 11 USC Section 522(a)(2) ("value" means fair market value as of the date of filing the petition, or with respect to property that becomes property of the estate as of a certain date.)[26]
- Securities and Exchange Act

State Statutes

- State revenue codes
- State securities codes

- Business Corporations Act (often the Uniform Business Corporation Act), usually addressing dissenting stockholder valuations
- Statutes granting oppressed minority shareholder relief, including an appraisal option (in a growing number of states)
- Marital dissolution statutes, which generally do not address valuation matters

Legally Binding Rules and Regulations

Many legislative bills authorize rules and regulations that have the force of law, with implementation delegated to an administrative authority. Examples include the following:

- Treasury regulations
- Federal Rules of Evidence and Civil Procedure
- Various state revenue regulations
- Department of Labor (DOL) proposed regulation 29 CFR Part 2510,[27] Definition of Adequate Consideration for Employee Stock Ownership Plan (ESOP) Stock
  - DOL issued the proposed regulation in 1988, it has never been finalized.
  - Despite lack of finalization, it provides guidance, and most ESOP appraisers consider compliance with it important.

Contractual Definitions of Value

Parties sometimes are bound by contractual definitions of value in documents governing certain types of transactions. Such documents may include the following:

- Articles of organization
- Articles of incorporation or partnership
- Bylaws

- Shareholder or partnership agreements
- Prenuptial agreements
- Agreements entered into specifically for the purpose of settlement of the instant dispute, such as arbitration agreements

Such agreements may be very helpful in defining value for the purpose at hand, or they may be the source of another element of controversy:

- **Is the definition of value legally binding in the instant case?** Even if it is not, it *may* be accorded some weight, especially if it has been used in other transactions with some similar characteristics.
- **Is the definition of value clear and unambiguous?** Unfortunately, documents intended to provide guidance all too often are drafted with ambiguous language that leaves the interpretation open to controversy. We recommend that an appraiser be consulted to review draft language relating to value to be sure that the lawyers and all parties to the agreement understand the value implications in the document.

Non-Legally Binding Administrative Rulings

Many government agencies issue rulings containing their interpretations of definitions of value. Courts usually give consideration to such rulings, but a court will not necessarily accept them if it feels that they are not consistent with the law.

For example, the IRS issued Revenue Ruling 81-253, which states that a minority discount should not be applied to gifts of minority shares of stock if other members of the family control the company. IRS Revenue Rulings represent the position of the IRS, but they are not the law. The position taken in Revenue Ruling 81-253 lost every time it was challenged in court,[28] and finally (after 12 years) the IRS reversed its position with Revenue Ruling 93-12, recognizing that shares were to be valued on the basis of the size of the block transferred, irrespective of attribution of family control value.

Precedential Court Decisions

By far the richest source of specific guidance as to definitions of value in almost any legal context is interpretation found in precedential case decisions. This book contains many annotations to decisions on valuation issues in many legal contexts (for example, tax, dissent, and divorce) and in various jurisdictions. Careful study of precedential case law is a very important step in understanding the relevant legal definition of value.

Nevertheless, it is also important to examine the many challenges and pitfalls inherent in using precedential case law as a source of guidance for definitions of value.

- **Lack of precedent.** There are valuation issues for which no precedent exists in many state jurisdictions. Courts tend to then cite precedent from other states that have similar statutes governing the issue. Each lawyer, of course, seeks out precedents in other jurisdictions that support his or her position.
- **Ambiguous language.** Most judges are not experts in financial language, and financial language itself has many ambiguities. For example, an opinion may use the term *fair market value* and then accept valuation methods that reflect factors that are not consistent with most courts' and financial analysts' understandings of the definition.
- **Distinguishable facts and circumstances.** Lawyers and appraisers may sometimes identify facts and circumstances in the case that may lead to an interpretation of the definition of value different from that found in a seemingly on-point precedential decision.
- **Sweeping generalizations.** Opinions sometimes contain broad statements that, if read literally, would apply to a broader set of cases or circumstances than the court may have intended. It usually is preferable that the lawyer, rather than the appraiser, originate the discussion of such distinctions in court.

- **Changing and contradictory precedents.** Precedential positions on issues sometimes change as a result of revisiting an issue. Be sure to rely on the latest case decisions. Precedents within a jurisdiction sometimes seem to contradict each other. In such a case, one might look for possible differentiation in facts and circumstances to distinguish them. When relying on a U.S. Court of Appeals decision, remember that it is controlling only in the circuit that issued the opinion, and it is not uncommon to find different circuits holding contradictory opinions.

Direction from the Court

Sometimes, it is possible for the lawyer to request and get a ruling from the court on the definition of value and/or the applicable valuation date before the appraiser prepares the report. This can save a great deal of expense in preparing reports under different definitions of value.

Direction from the Lawyer

Sometimes the lawyer has a clear-cut concept of the legal theory of the case, and that theory dictates a definition of value that the lawyer directs the appraiser to use. If the source of the definition of value is the lawyer rather than some quotable statutory or regulatory language, the appraiser is still responsible for its use, and must be in agreement to adopt it.

Use of IRS Authority in Nontax Situations

It is not uncommon for appraisers to cite IRS authority, such as Revenue Rulings, when describing the nuances of the definition of fair market value. If this is done for a valuation other than for federal taxes, it is important that the IRS standard be appropriate for the valuation.

Opinions of Other Lawyers and Appraisers

From time to time one may gain points of view on definitions of value from experienced lawyers or appraisers. These may come from either writings or discussions.

For example, one leading California corporate lawyer has published clear-cut ideas about the definition of fair value under California Corporations Code 2000. This attorney adds that "the cases provide only a patchwork of insights, only some of which are consistent with the basic purpose of Section 2000."[29]

Value to Whom? Levels and Premises of Value

"Levels of value" deal with both control and marketability, which may have a significant effect on the value of any business entity.

Levels of Value

By *levels of value*, we mean the varying degrees of control it is possible for an investor to hold in relationship to a particular business entity. The degrees of responsibility and freedom in such relationships are integral to determining specific value.

The attorney and the appraiser should decide at the outset what level of value the appraisal will represent. Exhibit 13.1 is a schematic depiction of the basic levels of value. The relative dollar amounts and percentages used are strictly for example purposes. Each situation is analyzed on a fact-specific basis.

The typical levels of value to be appraised in a closely held company are either control or minority nonmarketable. "Nonmarketable" means that the shares cannot be sold to the general public because they have not been registered with the Securities and Exchange Commission.

The level above control is "strategic acquisition value," which is the price that a company that has a specific reason for wanting to purchase a company might pay, often because the purchase will create a synergy with its existing businesses. This level could be appropriate if the purpose of the appraisal was to estimate a price that a synergistic buyer might pay. However, unless there is a group of synergistic buyers that creates a market, fair market value reflects the value of the company on a stand-alone basis and does not include possible synergies with other companies.

Exhibit 13.1

Levels of Value in Terms of the Characteristics of Ownershp

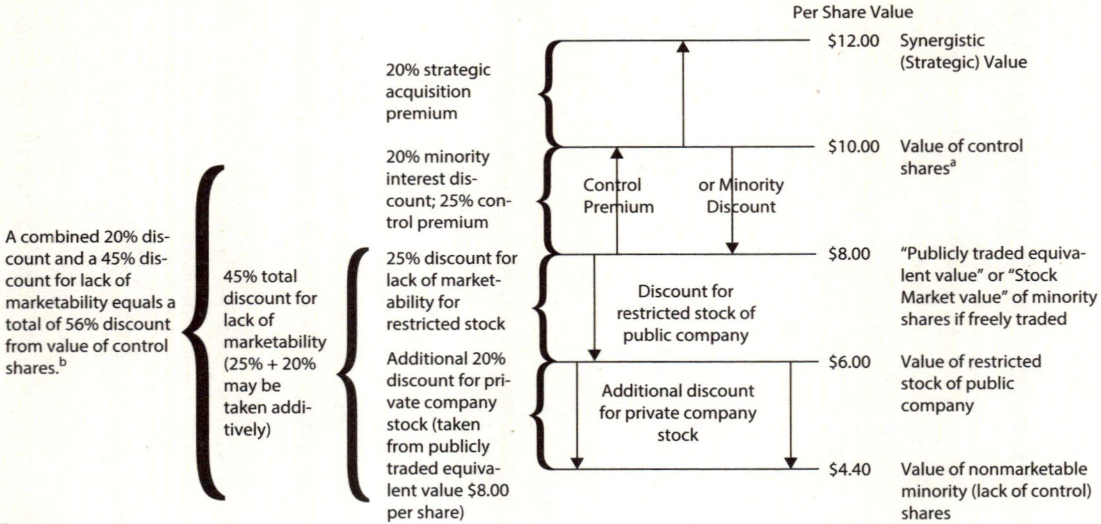

Notes:

[a] Control shares in a privately held company may also be subject to some discount for lack of marketability but usually not nearly as much as minority shares.

[b] Minority and marketability discounts normally are multiplicative rather than additive. That is, they are taken in sequence:

$	10.00	Control value
–	2.00	Less: minority interest discount (0.20 × $10.00)
$	8.00	Marketable minority value
–	3.60	Less lack of marketability discount (0.45 × $8.00)
$	4.40	Per share value of nonmarketable minority shares

Source: Jay E. Fishman et al., *PPC's Guide to Business Valuations*, 18th ed.

The line below control, "minority marketable," reflects an estimate of what the minority shares might trade for in a public market. When valuing minority shares in a private company, it may not even be necessary to estimate what the company as a whole would be worth—one might simply find guideline companies in the public market, estimate the value if publicly traded, and deduct a discount for lack of marketability from that. However, there is a school of thought that, although publically traded stocks are clearly minority interests, their prices are tantamount to prices of controlling interests.

The next level down is "restricted stocks of public companies." Some publicly traded companies may not have all their shares registered for public trading (they might issue unregistered shares for an acquisition, for example), but they can sell blocks of unregistered shares to qualified investors. These blocks are usually sold at a discount compared to the same day's public trading price.

Until the 1990s, these discounts averaged about 35 percent, and the restricted stock discounts were sometimes used as a proxy for the discount for lack of marketability for closely held stocks. Around 1990, the SEC started to loosen restrictions on sales of restricted stocks, and, accordingly, the discounts started to come down. But the loosening of SEC regulations for restricted stocks of publicly traded companies did nothing to enhance the marketability of closely held stock, for which there is little or no market. So the lower line reflects the fact that closely held stocks are much less marketable than restricted stocks of public companies.

These varying levels of value can have a significant impact on the eventual value because they will determine the extent of the discounts for lack of marketability or control, if any.

Premises of Value

By a *premise of value*, we mean an assumption as to the status of the business under which a transaction would be expected to take place. That is, would it be as a going concern or in liquidation, or some variation or combination of going concern or liquidation value? The selection among alternative possible premises of value obviously can have a major impact on value.

In some situations, the premise (or premises) of value is mandated as part of the definition of value by controlling documents or the purpose of the valuation. In other situations, the premise of value is left to appraiser judgment. For example, it may be left to the appraiser to determine what premise of value represents the highest and best use of the business or property.

Virtually all businesses or interests in businesses may be appraised under any of the following four alternative premises of value:

1. **Value as a going concern.** Value in continued use, as a mass assemblage of income-producing assets, and as a going-concern business enterprise.
2. **Value as an assemblage of assets.** Value in place, as part of a mass assemblage of assets, but not in current use in the production of income, and not as a going-concern business enterprise.
3. **Value as an orderly disposition.** Value in exchange, on a piecemeal basis (not part of a mass assemblage of assets), as part of an orderly disposition; this premise contemplates that all the assets of the business enterprise will be sold individually and that they will have normal exposure to their appropriate secondary market.
4. **Value as a forced liquidation.** Value in exchange, on a piecemeal basis (not part of a mass assemblage of assets), as part of a forced liquidation; this premise contemplates that the assets of the business enterprise will be sold individually and that they will have less than normal exposure to their appropriate secondary market.[30]

Each of these alternative premises of value may apply under the same standard, or definition, of value. For example, the fair market value standard calls for a "willing buyer" and a "willing seller." Yet the willing buyer and seller have to make an informed economic decision as to how they will transact with each other with regard to the subject business. In other words, is the subject business worth more to the buyer and the seller as a going concern that will continue to operate as such, or as a collection of individual assets to be put to separate uses? In either case, the buyer and seller are still "willing." And in both cases, they have concluded a set of transactional circumstances that will maximize the value of the collective assets of the subject business enterprise.[31]

If left to the judgment of the appraiser, the premise of value selected may depend on whether the interest is being valued on a controlling interest or minority interest basis. In a controlling interest valuation, the selection of the appropriate premise of value typically is a function of the highest and best use of the collective assets of the subject business enterprise. The appraiser might value the operations of the business on a going-concern basis and the assets not necessary to operations on a liquidation basis.

If valuing on a minority interest basis, the appraiser is more likely to value on the assumption of "business as usual"—that is, as a going concern. In other words, the appraiser normally would not assume a liquidation of any assets unless there was an indication that such a liquidation was imminent. This treatment has been met with acceptance by courts.[32]

Chapter 14

Overview of Approaches, Methods, Procedures, and Terminology

Approaches and Methods

The classification of business appraisal methodology is somewhat arbitrary because the methods are not totally discrete. Nevertheless, organizing the classification of methodologies can be helpful in both implementing and reviewing the appraisal process. The classification of methodology as presented in this chapter, while not followed universally, is representative of a growing consensus on the taxonomy of business appraisal. The balance of this book is generally organized to follow this classification.

Business appraisers usually try to use two or more appraisal methods to maximize the reliability of the final result. They may give different relative weights to different methods or conclude that one appraisal method is dominant in a given situation.

When business appraisers implement different methods, they usually try to make the data and procedures used in each method as discrete as possible from those used in the other methods, in order to reach the different indications of value as independently as possible.

There is, however, necessarily some interrelationship among the methods. Each method is based on some form of economic income, and/or asset values, and all depend to some extent on market data. For instance, the income approach uses expected economic income while the market approach may use both historical and expected economic income. The asset approach uses adjusted asset values for all assets, while the income and market approaches may use asset values for excess or nonoperating assets. The income approach derives its discount and capitalization rates from data extracted from the market. The market approach uses market-derived multiples of some form of economic income variables and/or asset values.

Business appraisers capitalize income in both the market and income approaches, but they develop their capitalization rates in different ways. In the market approach, capitalization rates come from direct observation of specific market transactions. In the income approach, capitalization rates are developed through a cost-of-capital model using broad market data. The asset approach develops its adjusted asset values from market data.

In reviewing descriptions of different appraisal methods, the reviewer should think about the extent to which each method is really an indication of value independent of another method, or whether the appraiser is simply presenting the same data in different formats. For instance, the use of a market multiple of book value of equity in the market approach and the use of the book value of equity in the asset approach as separate indications of value are actually one and the same method.

Hierarchy of Approaches, Methods, and Procedures

The professional business valuation community has generally adopted a hierarchy of the terms to complete an appraisal. They are: *approach, method*, and *procedure*:

- *Approach* is, in the broadest sense, an accepted means of achieving a valuation result.

- *Method* refers to general ways of implementing the approaches.
- *Procedure* means the specific calculations, data used, and other details involved in a specific method.

Basic Appraisal Approaches

The three approaches recognized in business valuation are essentially analogous to the three approaches used in real estate appraisal:

1. **Income approach.** Valuing the business or business interest on the basis of some form of expected economic income stream—in real estate appraisal, usually called "capitalization"
2. **Market approach.** Valuation of the business or business interest by reference to other transactions—in real estate appraisal, usually called the "comparable sales approach," or "sales comparison approach"
3. **Asset-based approach.** Valuation of the business on the basis of assets and liabilities—in real estate appraisal, usually analogous to something like the "cost approach"

Methods Used Within Appraisal Approaches

Within each of the three approaches, there is reasonably broad consensus on the terminology used to denote the methods employed.

Income Approach Methods

Discounting. Projecting the expected economic income over the life of the investment and discounting each increment of that expected income back to a present value at a rate of return is known as a *discount rate.* This method is also known as the *discounted cash flow* (DCF) *method.* (The procedures are similar to the method known as *yield capitalization* in real estate appraisal.)

Capitalizing. Observing or estimating a single period's economic income and dividing it by a rate of return known as a *capitalization rate.* This method is also known as the *capitalization method.* (The term is almost analogous to direct capitalization in real estate appraising, except that it is adjusted for the growth rate.)

Market Approach Methods

Guideline Public Company Method (Sometimes Called the Comparable Company Method*).* This method involves deriving valuation multiples from prices and financial data for company stocks traded in the public market and applies the multiples to the appropriate financial data of the subject company. No counterpart exists in real estate appraisal because there is no organized market for fractional interests in real estate.

Guideline Transaction Method. This method involves deriving valuation multiples from prices and financial data of public or private companies that have been sold and applying the multiples to the appropriate financial data of the subject company. This method is analogous to the *comparable sales approach* in real estate appraisal. (Some might further subdivide this method based on whether the company was public or private before the sale.)

Past Transactions Method. This method uses multiples of financial data from the company's own past transactions:

- Past change of ownership of 100 percent or a controlling interest in the subject company
- Past transactions of minority interests in the subject company
- Past acquisitions made by the subject company
- Past offers (but must examine whether the offers were bona fide and arm's length)

Buy-Sell Agreements. This method has been placed arbitrarily under the market approach with the idea that someone negotiated and agreed to the buy-sell terms for the subject at some point in the past. Depending on the purpose of the valuation and the terms of the buy-sell agreement, its valuation provisions may range all the way from completely controlling to irrelevant. The weight, if any, to be accorded to the valuation terms of the agreement is often a critical decision.

The agreement may be controlling for some valuation purposes and not for others. Sometimes, the degree of weight may depend on the extent to which the agreement was arm's length when negotiated. Often the appraiser and/or the court decides that the terms of the buy-sell agreement are a factor to be considered, but they are not controlling.

Rules of Thumb. Ballpark ranges of possible values are derived from simple formulas used in an industry. Sometimes classified under the market approach because the rules are allegedly market derived, the rules of thumb are generally applied without support from any body of underlying market data.

Asset Approach Methods

Adjusted Net Asset Value (ANAV) Method. The appraiser adjusts all of the company's assets (both tangible and intangible) and liabilities to their current value, usually fair market value, and subtracts the liabilities from the assets based on the following premises:

- **Going-concern premise.** All assets and liabilities are adjusted to the current fair market value in continued use, and the liabilities are subtracted from the assets.
- **Liquidation premise.** All assets and liabilities are adjusted to fair market value on a liquidation premise of value, and all the liabilities and liquidation costs are subtracted from the assets.
- **Hybrid premise.** Assets are valued with the expectation that they will be in continuing operation on a going-concern basis and non-operating assets will be valued on a liquidation basis. This could involve more than one operating unit of the business, where each operating unit is valued on a going-concern basis

and non-operating assets are valued on a liquidation basis. This latter version is sometimes called a *breakup method* or *disaggregation method.*

Excess Earnings Method. The appraisal adjusts only the company's tangible assets to current value—again, usually fair market value in continued use—and subtracts the liabilities to obtain a net tangible asset value. The appraisal estimates the amount of income needed to support the net tangible assets. If there is income over and above that amount, the excess income is divided by a capitalization rate to estimate the value of the company's intangible assets. The appraisal adds the estimated value of the intangibles to the value of the tangible assets.

This method is classified under the asset approach because, in theory, it adds the values of the tangible and intangible assets. Because it involves the capitalization of excess income, some appraisers prefer to call it a *hybrid method*, and some may even classify it under the income approach.

Summary of Business Appraisal Approaches and Methods

A schematic diagram of this classification of business valuation approaches and methods is presented as Exhibit 14.1

Business Appraisal Procedures

The "procedure" is a more detailed step used in implementing an appraisal method. For example, as we will see in Chapter 15, there are several accepted procedures to develop discount and capitalization rates within the discounting and capitalizing methods. These procedures are often referred to as *methods*, and the reader can think of them as methods within methods or the different ways that a method can be carried out.

For example, the discounted cash flow method, or the discounting method, is a major valuation method within the income approach. However, that same term is commonly used to describe a procedure for

Exhibit 14.1
Schematic Diagram of Business Valuation Approaches and Methods

Approaches	Methods
Income	Discounting (discounted cash flow, DCF)
	Capitalizing (capitalization)
Market	Guideline public companies
	Guideline transactions
	Past transactions
	Buy-sell agreements
	Rules of thumb
Asset based	Adjusted net asset value • Going-concern basis • Liquidation basis • Hybrid basis
	Excess earnings (sometimes classified as *hybrid*)

estimating the discount or capitalization rate to be used within either the discounting or capitalization methods in the income approach.

Invested Capital Versus Equity

Another important example of different procedures is the choice of either valuing the equity directly or valuing the firm's total invested capital (common stock [common equity] plus any preferred stock and long-term debt) and then subtracting the debt to arrive at a value for the equity.

This choice of procedures can be available within most of the valuation methods. For example, within the market approach, using either the guideline public company or the guideline transaction method, one could value the equity directly by using a price-to-earnings multiple. Alternatively, one could use the multiple of market value of invested capital to earnings before interest, taxes, and depreciation (MVIC/EBITDA) to estimate the value of the firm's invested capital, and then subtract the debt from that value to estimate the value of equity.

Some businesses have more than one class of equity, usually preferred equity and common equity. The preferred equity is senior to the common equity, and from a financial analysis point of view, it usually has more of the characteristics of debt than equity. Therefore, the term *equity* typically is used to mean only the common equity, and the value of preferred equity would be subtracted along with the debt in the invested capital procedures to arrive at the common (or residual) equity value.

Exhibit 14.2 summarizes procedures commonly used within various valuation methods.

Exhibit 14.2

Value of Invested Capital and Direct Valuation of Equity Procedures

Valuation Method	Valuation Procedures
Income approach: either discounting or capitalizing	**Invested capital.** Discount or capitalize the expected returns (usually measured as cash flows) available to holders of all components of invested capital, and then subtract the debt to get the value of common equity.
	Direct to common equity. Discount or capitalize only those returns available to common equity.
Market approach: using guideline public companies, guideline transactions, or other market approach methods	**Invested capital.** Use the market value of invested capital in the numerator of the ratio used to compute the multiple, and use the returns available to all invested capital in the denominator. Apply the multiple to the returns available to all invested capital, and subtract the debt to get the value of the equity.
	Direct to common equity. Use only the value of the equity in the numerator of the ratio used to compute the multiple. Use the returns available to common equity in the denominator.
Asset approach: adjusted net asset value	By definition, the assets on which all invested capital has claims are valued, and the debt is subtracted to get net asset value (value of equity).
Excess earnings method	This method values equity directly because the method requires subtracting the debt to get the net tangible asset value.
Buy-sell agreement	May be useful depending on the terms and viability of the agreement.
Rules of thumb	Rules of thumb are generally intended to value all of the invested capital. Therefore, the debt, if any, would have to be subtracted to get the equity value (although the exact procedure may vary from one rule of thumb to another).

Business Valuation Terminology

Unfortunately, the terminology found in the literature of financial theory and corporate finance is fraught with ambiguities, and these carry over into the literature of business appraisal and business appraisal reports. We have addressed the problem in this book by defining each term within the context of the discussion where it is used. To find these definitions, we suggest that readers use the index.

Many appraisal reports contain definitions of terms employed. These definitions should be read carefully because different appraisers may use the same term differently.[1] Consequently, the reader of an appraisal may be left to try to figure out the intended meaning, and this becomes even more problematic when interpreting court case decisions.

This chapter includes both accounting and financial terms. Many of the numbers represented by the accounting terms can be read directly from financial statements. Numbers representing other accounting terms and numbers for most of the financial terms must be computed. This chapter will define the terms and, where necessary, illustrate how to compute amounts for each. However, this is only the most perfunctory primer; other resources will be necessary for illustrations of more complex financial statements.

With the information shown in Exhibit 14.3, it is possible to extract or compute most of the financial variables that are typically used in the various approaches to business valuation. This chapter necessarily involves numbers and computations. However, it would be impossible to simplify things much more without omitting concepts that one is almost certain to encounter within the scope of reviewing valuation reports. Therefore, we suggest that the reader might want to peruse it fairly quickly the first time through and thereafter use it for reference.

The Basic Financial Statements

The two most commonly used financial statements are the *balance sheet* and the *income statement*. The balance sheet presents assets, liabilities, and owner's equity at a point in time, all at *book value*. Book value generally represents original, historical cost less depreciation and other noncash charges in accordance with accounting principles.

The income statement presents revenues, expenses, and income over a period of time (fiscal period), usually a year. Sometimes (generally if the valuation date is not close to the end of a company's fiscal year), it may be necessary to use *interim financial statements*—that is, those prepared as of a time other than the company's fiscal year-end.

Exhibit 14.3
Widget Corporation Financial Data

Widget Corporation Balance Sheet

Assets	
Current assets	
Cash	$ 500,000
Accounts receivable	1,000,000
Inventory	1,500,000
Total current assets	$3,000,000
Plant and equipment	
At cost	$5,000,000
Less: accumulated depreciation	3,000,000
Net plant and equipment	$2,000,000
Total assets	$5,000,000
Liabilities and Equity	
Current liabilities	
Accounts payable	$1,000,000
Long-term debt	3,000,000
Total liabilities	$4,000,000
Preferred stock	0
Common equity (1,000 shares outstanding)	$1,000,000
Total liabilities and equity	$5,000,000

Widget Corporation Income Statement

Sales	$10,000,000
Cost of goods sold	6,000,000
Gross margin	$ 4,000,000
Selling, general, and administrative expenses	2,700,000
Operating income, before interest and taxes	$ 1,300,000
Interest expense	300,000
Income before taxes	$ 1,000,000
Income taxes	300,000
Net income	$ 700,000

Widget Corporation Other Financial Data

The following data are derived from the statement of cash flows, footnotes to financial statements, and company books and records:

1. The interest rate on the long-term debt is 10%.
2. The selling, general, and administrative expenses include depreciation of $250,000.
3. The selling, general, and administrative expenses include compensation for the president (who owns 100% of the stock and both manages the company and maintains all the key customer contacts) as follows:

Salary	$500,000
Bonus	200,000
Retirement plan contribution	100,000
Health and life insurance	50,000
Discretionary entertainment expenses (golf club, yacht, and so on)	100,000
Total owner's compensation	$950,000

4. The capital expenditures average about $300,000 per year.
5. The company's sales are growing at about 10% per year.
6. The company maintains net working capital at about 20% of sales, typical for its industry.
7. No changes in the level of long-term debt are contemplated in the foreseeable future.

There are three levels of preparation of financial statements, in descending order of their degree of detail (and, usually, their reliability): audited, reviewed, and compiled. Definitions of each are shown in Exhibit 14.4. The appraiser's report should indicate which level of financial statement preparation was used and also who prepared the statements. This may be different for different dates, and, if so, the correct information should be listed for each date.

The balance of this chapter defines the terms used to describe the most important components of the context of these statements. Analysis of the statements is covered in subsequent chapters.

Balance Sheet Concepts

Please refer to the balance sheet shown in Exhibit 14.3. as the concepts are explained.

Exhibit 14.4
Levels of Financial Statement Preparation

- **Audited statements.** In *audited statements*, the independent auditor expresses an opinion or, if circumstances require, disclaims an opinion, regarding the fairness with which the financial statements present the financial position, the results of operations, and the changes in financial position, in accordance with generally accepted accounting principles.
- **Reviewed statements.** The independent accountant expresses limited assurance in *reviewed statements* that there are no material modifications that should be made to the statements in order for them to be in conformity with generally accepted accounting principles. A review does not provide assurance that the accountant will become aware of all significant matters that would be disclosed in an audit.
- **Compiled statements.** Finally, the *compiled statements* are management's representations presented in the form of financial statements, but the accountant has not undertaken any efforts to express assurance on the statements. Sometimes statements are prepared internally by management without the services of an outside accountant.

Common Equity

Common equity (at book value) is paid in capital plus retained earnings. In Widget Corporation, the common equity is the following:

$1,000,000 from the balance sheet

Invested Capital

The *invested capital* is the equity plus interest-bearing debt. For Widget Corporation, the invested capital at book value is the following:

Long-term debt	$3,000,000
Common equity	1,000,000
Book value of invested capital*	$4,000,000

* Some analysts deduct cash when computing invested capital. Also, some deduct cash that they consider to be in excess of the company's cash requirements for operations. The important thing is that the analyst be consistent. For example, if cash is deducted when computing invested capital for the subject company in the market approach, it must be deducted when computing invested capital for the guideline companies as well.

If the company had preferred stock, that would be shown as a separate item in the capital structure and would be included in the MVIC. (Some define invested capital to include only long-term debt, excluding short-term interest.)

Capital Structure

The *capital structure* is the relative proportions of the various elements of invested capital. In this case, at book value the capital structure is the following:

Long-term debt	$3,000,000	75 percent
Equity	1,000,000	25 percent
	$4,000,000	100 percent

Book Value

With respect to assets, the *book value* is the capitalized cost less the accumulated depreciation. For Widget Corporation, for example, the book value is the following:

Plant and equipment	$5,000,000
Less: depreciation	3,000,000
Net book value of plant and equipment	$2,000,000

With respect to the business as a whole, the book value is the difference between the total assets (net of depreciation, depletion, and amortization) and the total liabilities. This is also the book value of the equity. For Widget Corporation, this is as follows:

Total assets	$5,000,000
Total liabilities	4,000,000
Book value of equity	$1,000,000

Book Value per Share

On a per share basis, the book value is the value of common equity divided by the number of shares outstanding. For Widget Corporation, the book value per share is the following:

$$\frac{\$1,000,00}{1,000 \text{ shares}} = \$1,000 \text{ per share}$$

Tangible Book Value Versus Total Book Value

The *tangible book value* reflects only the company's tangible assets. The *total book value* reflects both the tangible and intangible assets, such as copyrights, patents, and many other items. If a company buys its intangible assets, those assets generally are on the balance sheet and thus are part of book value.

On the other hand, if the company creates its own intangible assets, those assets usually are expensed and do not appear on the balance sheet. Therefore, for comparative consistency, analysts usually prefer to work with only the tangible book value rather than the total book value. In any case, to completely understand the financial statements being analyzed, the reviewer of the report should know whether or not there are any intangible assets included in the book value if that figure is used for any computations in the valuation report.

Net Working Capital

The *net working capital* is the current assets minus the current liabilities. For Widget Corporation, net working capital is the following:

Current assets	$3,000,000
Less: current liabilities (accounts payable)	1,000,000
Net working capital	$2,000,000

Miscellaneous Expense Concepts

Miscellaneous expense concepts include noncash charges and other items that vary from company to company.

Noncash Charges

Noncash charges are items that are charged as expenses on the income statement but do not require a cash outlay. Examples would include depreciation, depletion, amortization, and deferred taxes. For Widget Corporation, the only noncash charge is the following:

Depreciation: $250,000 from other financial data

The noncash charges are added back to the net income to arrive at either the gross or net cash flow, and they are added back to the operating income to arrive at the earnings before interest, taxes, depreciation, and amortization (EBITDA).

Owner's Compensation (Including Disclosed or Hidden Perks)

The *owner's compensation* includes all elements of compensation, including salary, bonuses, retirement benefits, life and health insurance benefits, discretionary expenses, and the value of stock options. For Widget Corporation, the owner's compensation is the following:

$950,000 from other financial data

Levels of Economic Income

One of the most crucial and yet highly ambiguous concepts used in business valuation is that of income, also sometimes referred to as *earnings*. It is common to see one or the other of these two terms used without further definition. So many different levels of income are used in various business valuation methods and procedures that the term *income* is virtually meaningless until the level of income intended is clearly specified.

In recent years, the business appraisal profession has embraced the broad term *economic income* to mean some level of income (any level) that needs further specific definition before it can be used meaningfully in a business valuation method or procedure. All of the following levels of economic income are commonly used in business appraisal practice:

- Sales
- Discretionary earnings
- Earnings before interest, taxes, depreciation, and amortization (EBITDA)
- Earnings before interest and taxes (EBIT)
- Gross cash flow (net income plus noncash charges)
- Debt-free net income (DFNI)
- Debt-free cash flow (DFCF)
- Pretax income
- Net income
- Net earnings
- Net cash flow to invested capital
- Net cash flow to equity

Sales (Net Revenues)

The terms *sales* and *net revenues* are generally used interchangeably. For Widget Corporation, the sales amount to the following:

$10,000,000 from the income statement

A multiple of sales is often used in the market approach when valuing invested capital. It is less frequently used (and potentially very misleading) when valuing equity directly because sales are based on the assets supported by the entire capital structure.

Discretionary Earnings (Also Called Seller's *Discretionary Cash Flow* [*SDCF*] and *Owner's Cash Flow* [*OCF*])

Discretionary earnings are those that may be defined, in certain applications, to reflect the earnings of a business enterprise prior to the following items: income taxes, nonoperating income and expenses, nonrecurring income and expenses, depreciation and amortization, interest expense or income, and owner's total compensation for those services that could be provided by a sole owner-manager.[2] For Widget Corporation, discretionary earnings are the following:

Pretax operating income (before interest expense) from income statement	$1,300,000
Plus: depreciation	250,000
Plus: owner's compensation	950,000
Discretionary earnings	$2,500,000

Discretionary earnings are used in the transaction method in the market approach usually only when valuing small companies.

Earnings Before Interest, Taxes, Depreciation, and Amortization (EBITDA)

EBITDA is computed as earnings before interest, taxes, and *all* noncash charges, including depreciation, amortization, depletion, and deferred taxes. Widget Corporation's EBITDA is the following:

EBIT (operating income)	$1,300,000
Plus: depreciation	250,000
EBITDA	$1,550,000

EBITDA is one of the most commonly used variables in the market approach *when valuing invested capital.*

Earnings Before Interest and Taxes (EBIT) (Also Called *Operating Income*)

For Widget Corporation, the EBIT is the following:

$1,300,000 from the income statement

EBIT is one of the most commonly used variables in the market approach *when valuing invested capital.*

Gross Cash Flow

When the term *gross cash flow* is used, it almost always means *gross cash flow to equity,* sometimes just called *cash flow.* It is defined as net income plus noncash charges. For Widget Corporation, the gross cash flow is the following:

Net income	$ 700,000
Plus: depreciation	250,000
Gross cash flow	$ 950,000

Debt-Free Net Income (DFNI)

Debt-free net income (DFNI) refers to what the net income would be if there were no debt. It is computed by adding the interest expense, net of the tax effect (income taxes saved because the interest is a tax-deductible expense) to the net income. For Widget Corporation, the DFNI is the following:

	Net income	$700,000
+	Interest expense, net of pro forma income taxes $300,000 × (1 − 0.30) (taxes of $300,000 on $1,000,000 pretax income, or 30%)	210,000
	Debt-free net income	$910,000

The same result is obtained by the tax-affecting EBIT, or the operating income:

Operating income, before taxes	$1,300,000
Less: 30% of taxes	390,000
Debt-free net income	$910,000

When debt-free net income is used, it is in the context of the market approach *when valuing invested capital.*

Debt-Free Cash Flow (DFCF)

Debt-free cash flow (DFCF) means *gross* debt-free net cash flow. It is debt-free net income plus noncash charges. For Widget Corporation, the DFCF is the following:

Debt-free net income	$ 910,000
Depreciation	250,000
Debt-free cash flow	$1,160,000

When debt-free cash flow is used, it is in the context of the market approach *when valuing invested capital.* The "debt-free" measures are used to make companies with significantly different capital structures more comparable to each other. However, since they are artificial in the sense that they create a comparison that doesn't actually exist, they are losing some favor among analysts.

Pretax Income

Pretax income is income after all expenses except income taxes. For Widget Corporation, the pretax income is the following:

$1,000,000 from the income statement

Pretax income is often used in the market approach when valuing equity directly. It is sometimes used in the excess earnings method, sometimes as a proxy for net income in a small company, sole proprietorship, or partnership that does not pay any income taxes.

Net Income

Net income is income after all expenses, including interest, owner's compensation, noncash charges, and income taxes. For Widget Corporation, the net income is the following:

$700,000 from the income statement

The net income is used in the market approach when valuing equity directly. It is sometimes used in the excess earnings method as well.

Primary Versus Diluted Net Income per Share

On a per share basis, net income can be stated as either primarily *net income per share* or *diluted net income per share.* Primary net income per share is computed on the basis of the number of shares actually outstanding. Diluted net income per share is computed on the assumption of convertible debt being converted to common stock, preferred stock being converted to common stock, and warrants and options to buy stock being exercised. When doing comparative analysis, it is important to be sure that any figures used for comparison are computed on the same basis.

Net Cash Flow to Invested Capital

The *net cash flow to invested capital* is the amount of cash available to distribute to owners of all components of the capital structure (preferred and common equity and interest-bearing debt) after leaving enough for the capital expenditures and working capital necessary to sustain projected operations. The computation is as follows:

Net income (after taxes) to common equity	
+	Noncash charges (depreciation, amortization, deferred taxes, and so on)
–	Capital expenditures*
–	Changes in net working capital†
+	Interest expense, net of the income tax effect (interest expense × [1 – tax rate])
+	Preferred dividends, if any
=	Net cash flow to overall invested capital

* Assumes that these amounts are those necessary to support projected business operations.

† Some analysts deduct cash when computing invested capital. Also, some deduct cash that they consider to be in excess of the company's cash requirements for operations. The important thing is that the analyst be consistent. For example, if cash is deducted when computing invested capital for the subject company in the market approach, it must be deducted when computing invested capital for the guideline companies as well.

For Widget Corporation, the net cash flow to invested capital is the following:

Net income		$700,000
+	Depreciation	250,000
−	Capital expenditures	300,000
−	Additions to net working capital	200,000
+	Interest expenses, net of pro forma income taxes*	
	$300,000 × (1 − 0.30)	210,000
	= Net cash flow to invested capital	$660,000

* Taxes of $300,000 on $1 million pretax income, or 30 percent.

The net cash flow to invested capital is the measure of economic income that tends to be preferred by the professional financial community when using the income approach to value a company's invested capital. From the valuation of invested capital, the debt and preferred equity are subtracted to get to the value of common equity.

Net Cash Flow to Equity

The *net cash flow to equity* (sometimes called the *free cash flow to equity* or even the *net free cash flow to equity*) is the amount of cash available to equity owners to withdraw from or distribute from the business after leaving enough for the capital expenditures and working capital necessary to sustain projected operations. The computation is as follows:

Net income (after taxes)	
+	Noncash charges (for example, depreciation, amortization, deferred income taxes)
−	Capital expenditures*
−	Changes in net working capital†
+	Net changes in long-term debt
=	Net cash flow to equity

* Assumes that these amounts are the levels necessary to support projected business operations.

† Assumes that these amounts are those necessary to support projected business operations.

If there are preferred dividends, they must be subtracted. The objective is to estimate net cash flow available to common equity holders. For Widget Corporation, the net cash flow to equity is the following:

	Net income	$700,000
+	Depreciation	$250,000
−	Capital expenditures	$300,000
−	Additions to net working capital	200,000
=	Net cash flow to equity*	$450,000

* If the company is growing, it may increase long-term debt, or, if highly leveraged, it may decrease long-term debt. Increases in long-term debt would be increases in net cash flow to equity, and payoffs of long-term debt would decrease net cash flow to equity.

The net cash flow to equity is the measure of economic income that tends to be most preferred by the corporate financial community when using the income approach to value equity. Sometimes it is also used as the economic income variable in the excess earnings method.

Variables Affecting Net Cash Flow

Capital Expenditures

The *capital expenditures* are amounts paid for assets expected to have a long-term economic life (usually more than one year), recorded on the balance sheet at the amount paid and usually depreciated (or depleted or amortized) over time as expenses on the income statement and reductions to book value on the balance sheet. For Widget Corporation, the capital expenditures are as follows:

Approximately $300,000 per year from other financial data

The expected capital expenditures must be estimated as a component in computing net cash flow in the income approach since the capital expenditure requirements represent a portion of the gross cash flow that must remain in the business to support the projected operations.

Changes in Net Working Capital

The *changes in net working capital* are amounts added to or subtracted from the net working capital needed to support the operations of the business:

Expected sales growth:		
	10% × $10,000,000 =	$1,000,000
Percentage of sales needed as additional net working capital (the percentage of incremental sales, from other financial data)		20%
Expected additions to net working capital		$ 200,000

Changes in net working capital must be estimated as one of the components in computing the net cash flow in the income approach, since it represents an amount of cash flow that must remain in the business to support projected operations

Changes in Debt

If the company increases long-term debt, the increase is an addition to net cash flow to equity. Conversely, repayments of long-term debt are a deduction when calculating the net cash flow to equity.

Cash Versus Accrual Basis Accounting

Most companies record their accounting on an accrual basis in accordance with generally accepted accounting principles (GAAP). However, some companies, especially smaller ones, prepare their financial statements on a cash basis. Some companies prepare financial statements on an accrual basis and tax returns on a cash basis. Other companies do not prepare financial statements separate from their tax returns, in which case it should be ascertained whether the tax returns are on a cash or accrual basis.

Accrual Basis Accounting

In *accrual basis accounting*, revenues and expenses are recorded when they are earned or incurred. For example, if a company renders services and bills the customer for later payment, the revenue is shown on the income statement when it is earned, and the account receivable becomes an asset on the balance sheet. This is based on the accounting principle of matching costs with related revenues.

Cash Basis Accounting

In *cash basis accounting*, revenues and expenses are recorded when they are received or paid. For example, if a company renders services and bills the customer for later payment, the revenue is shown on the income statement when it is collected, and the account receivable is not shown on the balance sheet at all.

Conversion from Cash to Accrual Basis

Valuations usually are performed on accrual basis data. For example, once a service has been performed, the revenue and profit are usually considered part of the income stream, and the related receivable is usually considered an asset of the company.

Therefore, if the subject company accounts on a cash basis, the valuation analyst usually adjusts the financial statements from a cash to an accrual basis for the purpose of valuation. Of course, there can be exceptions, such as when a buy-sell agreement requiring valuation using cash basis accounting data is determined to be controlling for the valuation purpose at hand.

All data that have been presented in this chapter have been assumed to be on an accrual basis.

Summary

While business valuation approaches and methods are not totally discrete, there is broad consensus on three generally accepted approaches: the income approach, the market approach, and the asset-based approach.

Within each approach, there are two or more generally accepted methods. Within the income approach, the basic methods are *discounting* and *capitalizing*. Within the market approach, there is the *guideline public company method*, the *guideline transaction method*, the *past transactions and/or offers method*, *buy-sell agreements*, and *rules of thumb*. Within the asset-based approach, there is the *adjusted net asset method* and the *excess earnings method*.

Within each method there is a variety of accepted procedures for its implementation. Two of the most important (either of which may be used with most methods) are the *invested capital procedure* (valuing the entire capital structure and subtracting the senior obligations to arrive at the residual common equity value) and the *direct equity valuation procedure* (using techniques that value the equity directly).

Business valuation is fraught with ambiguous terminology. This book attempts to define each esoteric term in the context in which it is used. This chapter has provided a rudimentary guide to the terms most often encountered with respect to financial statements as they are used in business valuation. It should make a handy reference for any term with which the reviewer is unfamiliar or for any term about which the reviewer is unsure of the definition commonly used in the context of valuation.

Chapter 15

The Income Approach

The income approach is presented first because, in theory, it is the dominant approach in business valuation (although Revenue Ruling 59-60 and many investment bankers also put heavy emphasis on the market approach). The discounted cash flow (DCF) method is the most conceptually correct method because it captures the driving principle of valuation: value is the present worth of future benefits. Capitalizing is merely a shortcut method that hopes to produce a similar result, as it considers only one year of income, whereas the DCF method projects income into the future. A basic corporate finance text articulates this critical point:

> Value today always equals future cash flow discounted at the opportunity cost of capital.[1]

Not only is discounted cash flow the most theoretically correct valuation method but it is also the most widely practiced valuation method in the world of corporate finance. Furthermore, the method is increasingly used by valuation experts and increasingly accepted by the courts. For example, in the family law area, the DCF method has been accepted in some cases[2] (even though, as in other areas, it has at times been rejected where the data to support the method were insufficient[3]).

In both *discounting* and *capitalizing*, we are converting an expected stream of income into a present value. In other words, we are estimating what someone would pay today (or as of the effective valuation date) for an expected stream of future economic income.

For those not familiar with the arithmetic formulas and notations used in business valuation, this will be a very technical chapter, but hopefully the explanations of commonly used terminology in Exhibit 15.1 will be helpful.

Exhibit 15.1

Terms and Notations Commonly Used in the Income Approach

The notation system used in this book is the Pratt notation system, which is used in the courses of the American Society of Appraisers and the American Institute of Certified Public Accountants. No matter what notation system is used in an appraisal report, each term should be defined.

PV = **present value**
In appraisal terms, this is the estimated value as of the specified appraisal date.

D = **dividend**
This is usually the expected annual dividend, although it could be the actual dividend for the past 12 months or some other time period.

c = **capitalization rate**
This is a percentage, expressed as a decimal (for example, 20% = 0.20), which is used as a denominator to divide into some amount of income (for example, dividends, earnings, cash flow) to arrive at an indication of value.

k = **discount rate (cost of capital)**
This is the total expected rate of return that the market requires to attract investment into the business or securities of the type being valued, reflecting investment risk and other characteristics of the investment.

g = **growth**
This is the average compound annual rate at which a financial variable (for example, the dollar amount of dividends, earnings, cash flow) is expected to increase in the future. As used in the income approach formulas, this usually is a long-term rate, technically in perpetuity.

E = **expected economic income**
This is a generalized variable used in an income formula without specifying the definition of income. Income in this formula could be dividends, earnings cash flow, or some other income variable.

WACC = **weighted average cost of capital**
This is the weighted discount rate for each type of security in the company's capital structure (for example, common stock, preferred stock, long-term debt), each component weighted by its percentage of the market value of the company's total invested capital that is represented by the respective capital component.

W = **weight**
This is the percentage of each component of the capital structure out of the total, with each measured at market value.

t = **tax rate**
This is the company's combined federal and state corporate tax rate.

Subscripts denoting time periods:

0 = **the base period**
This is usually the time period immediately before the effective valuation date (for example, D_0 would be the dividends for the last year).

1,2,3,etc. = **future time periods**
This is usually the first time period following the valuation date, etc. (For example, D_1 would be expected dividends for the coming year.)

n = **the last period**
In the income approach, *n* is usually the last period for which specific projections of expected future benefits are available. (For example, D_n would be projected dividends in the last year for which a specific dividend projection is available.)

Subscripts denoting type of capital component:

e = **equity**
This represents common stock or partnership interests without any senior priority. (For example, k_e would be the cost of equity; that is, the discount rate or market-required rate of expected return for an equity investment in the company.)

d = **debt**
This represents borrowed capital. (For example, k_d would be the cost of the company's borrowing.)

***d*(pt)** = **debt, pretax**
This represents debt, not reflecting the tax deductibility of interest cost. (For example, $k_{d(pt)}$ would be the company's gross cost of borrowing, not adjusted for the tax deductibility of the interest.)

The Concept of Discounting

In discounting, we are specifically estimating each future period's expected income and reducing each period's expected amount by a *discount rate*, which is the market's required rate of return for investments of comparable risk and other characteristics. This discount rate is a present value (PV) rate, or present value (PV) factor.

Discounting is exactly the opposite of *compounding*. In compounding, we invest a certain amount of money at some expected, annually compounded rate of return. Assuming that the expected rate of return is achieved and that each year's return is added to the principal to continue to compound, we can compute what that investment will be worth any number of years into the future. In discounting, we do just the opposite. We start with an expected payment at some specified time in the future. In effect, we discount the value backward for the length of time until we expect to receive it, at the required rate of return reflecting the risk (degree of uncertainty) of realizing the payment at the time and in the amount expected.

We discount the amount of each individual increment of expected future return to a present value, and then we add the present values of each increment to get the value of the investment. An example is shown schematically in Exhibit 15.2.

The Concept of Capitalizing

In capitalizing, instead of projecting each future increment of income and dividing it by the discount rate compounded for some number of years into the future, we select a single expected number and simply divide that number by a rate of return that we call a *capitalization rate*. We are really using a procedure that is a shortcut form of discounting. It is still our objective to estimate the present value of an expected future income stream. However, we are making some implicit assumptions to simplify the procedure.

The assumption that is implicit in the capitalization method in the income approach is one of the following:

1. The amount of income being capitalized will remain constant each year in perpetuity.

Exhibit 15.2
Discounted Present Value of an Annuity

Today's Value (Present Value)	**Amount to Be Received at End of Each Year**		
	Year 1	Year 2	Year 3
	$1,000	$1,000	$1,000
$ 925.93	1 year @ 8%		
$ 857.34	2 year @ 8%		
$ 793.83	3 year @ 8%		
$ 2,577.10	Total present value of 3-year annuity of $1,000 per year with a compound rate of return of 8% per year.		

Note how this is just the opposite of compounding: If you invested $925.93 for a year at 8%, it would be worth $1,000 at the end of the year. If you invested $857.34 for 2 years at 8% compounded annually, it would be worth $1,000 at the end of 2 years, and so forth.

$$\$925.93 \times 1.08 = \$1,000$$
$$\$857.34 \times 1.08 \times 1.08 = \$1,000$$
$$\$793.83 \times 1.08 \times 1.08 \times 1.08 = \$1,000$$

2. The amount of income being capitalized will either increase or decrease at some constant annually compounded rate in perpetuity.

In capitalizing, as in discounting, we are converting expected future income into a value. However, in capitalizing, instead of projecting all the future expected benefits, we are using only a single period's expected benefit—often, for example, next year's expected return. We divide that return by a *capitalization rate.*

As will be explained in more detail, the capitalization rate, as used in the income approach, is a function of the discount rate; that is, it is derived by starting with the discount rate. In the unique situation of assumption 1 above (constant income), the capitalization rate and the discount rate are equal. Under assumption 2 above (reasonably constant growth or decline in the income stream), the capitalization rate equals the discount rate less the long-term sustainable rate of growth, or plus the long-term rate of decline.

The capitalization procedure may also be used in the context of the market approach in either the guideline public company or the transaction method. In the market approach, however, capitalization rates are developed by direct observation in the market, rather than as a function of the discount rate, and implied assumptions 1 and 2 above do not necessarily apply. Also, for the capitalization method in the income approach, the income variable that is preferred is *net cash flow*, as discussed later. However, in the market approach, net cash flow is rarely used, and other economic income variables, such as net income and earnings before interest and taxes, are capitalized.

The Basic Capitalized Cash Flow Model

In this section, we will explore the different capitalization models and formulas which are used depending on the value that is being estimated.

The Constant Income Capitalization Model

The simplest form of the constant income capitalization model found in the market, and familiar to most people, is the *perpetual life (noncallable) preferred stock.*

Preferred stock is technically equity, but from a financial viewpoint, in some ways it is much more like debt. The dividends normally are at a fixed dollar amount for the life of the stock, which in many cases is in perpetuity. Payment of the dividends is senior to any dividends on common stock, but junior to debt service requirements. If, as in the case of the perpetual life preferred stock, the expected income stream is the same every year and expected to last forever, the procedure is simply to divide the amount of the annual dividend or cash distribution by the capitalization rate.

The constant income capitalization formula is as follows:

Formula 15.1

$$PV = \frac{D}{c}$$

Where:

PV = present value
D = dividend (or distributions, in case of a partnership)
c = capitalization rate

For example, assume the following:

Dividend:	$5 per year
Capitalization rate:	10%

Inserting these numbers in Formula 15.1 gives us the following:

Formula 15.2

$$\begin{aligned} PV &= \frac{\$5}{0.10} \\ &= \$50 \end{aligned}$$

(The choice of the capitalization rate is just as important as the amount of income being capitalized. Proper procedures for developing capitalization rates are discussed in a later section.)

The Income Capitalization Growth Model (Gordon Growth Model)

In many business enterprises, the cash flow or other income stream is expected to increase over time. If one accepts the assumption that growth in the income stream can be predicted at a reasonably steady rate and for a very long period of time, then the expected rate of growth in the returns can be impounded into a capitalization model that takes account of that expected growth.

The procedure for the capitalization growth model is as follows:

1. In the numerator of the capitalization equation, multiply last year's economic income by a growth factor.
2. In the denominator, subtract the rate of growth from the discount rate.

The capitalized income formula under the assumption of a constant rate of growth is as follows:

Formula 15.3

$$PV = \frac{E_0(1+g)}{k-g}$$

where

PV = present value

E_0 = economic income in the year immediately preceding the effective valuation date

g = growth rate in expected income level, sustainable into the indefinite future (theoretically in perpetuity)

k = discount rate (cost of capital)

The discount rate represents the *total* required rate of return (dividends or distributions plus capital appreciation). Development of discount rates is presented in a later section.

For an example of the application of the above formula, assume the following:

Last year's payout	\$10
Expected annually compounded growth in amount of payout	3%
Discount rate	13%

Inserting those numbers in Formula 15.3 gives us the following:

Formula 15.4

$$\begin{aligned} PV &= \frac{\$10(1+0.03)}{0.13-0.03} \\ &= \frac{\$10.30}{0.10} \\ &= \$103.00 \end{aligned}$$

Of course, if the starting point were next year's expected return (E_1 instead of E_0), then we would not need to multiply by the growth factor in the numerator. We would still subtract the growth rate from the discount rate (total required rate of return) to get the capitalization rate in the denominator.

In using this growth model, it is very important that the long-term sustainable growth rate be realistic. If one uses a long-term growth rate close to the discount rate, then the capitalization rate is extremely low, and the calculated indication of value will be materially overstated.

The Basic Discounted Cash Flow Model

In this section, we will explore the different models and formulas which are utilized in the discounted cash flow method.

The Discounted Cash Flow Model for a Limited Life Investment

The simplest form of a limited life investment model found in the market, and familiar to most people, is a bond with no special features. The bond pays a fixed amount of interest each year, and the holder expects to receive a fixed amount when the bond matures.

The discounted cash flow formula for the value of a limited life investment is the following:

Formula 15.5

$$PV = \frac{E_1}{(1+k)} + \frac{E_2}{(1+k)^2} + \ldots + \frac{E_n}{(1+k)^n}$$

where

PV = present value

$E_1 \ldots E_n$ = expected economic income in each of periods 1 through n

k = discount rate (cost of capital)

For example, for a bond that matures in three years, assume the following:

Annual interest payment*	\$80
Value at maturity	\$1,080 (\$1,000 plus the last year's \$80 interest payment)
Yield to maturity on bonds of comparable risk as of the effective valuation date	10%
n, the number of years to maturity	3

* Most bonds pay interest semiannually, but for the sake of simplifying the illustration, we will assume that this bond pays interest only at the end of each year.

In other words, the yield to maturity available on comparable bonds today (in the above example) is greater than the rate of interest on the face value of the subject bond (8% = \$80/\$1,000). In this case, the value of the bond is less than its face value.

Inserting these numbers in Formula 15.5 gives us:

Formula 15.6

$$PV = \frac{\$80}{(1+0.10)} + \frac{\$80}{(1+0.10)^2} + \frac{\$1{,}080}{(1+0.10)^3}$$

$$= \frac{\$80}{1.100} + \frac{\$80}{1.210} + \frac{\$1{,}080}{1.331}$$

$$= \$72.73 + \$66.12 + \$811.42$$

$$= \$950.27$$

Note that in the above computations, each year's return is reduced to a present value by a calculated divisor. This divisor can easily be converted to a multiplier by dividing each divisor into 1. For example, the divisor for the first year's payment is 1.100. Dividing that into 1(1 ÷ 1.100) equals a multiplier of 0.909. Similarly, the multipliers for years 2 and 3 are 0.826 and 0.751, respectively. It is common to see these multipliers presented as discounting "factors." Such a presentation of the above data would appear as follows:

Year	Amount	PV Factor	Present Value
1	$80	0.909	$ 72.72
2	$80	0.826	$ 66.08
3	$1,080	0.751	$811.08
			$949.88

The small differences between this tabular presentation and the formula presentation above are due to rounding.

The Discounted Cash Flow Model Using a Terminal Value

Most businesses are expected to have an indefinite life. However, it is usually not possible to make reasonably accurate forecasts of expected returns on a year-by-year basis for very many years into the future.

Appraisers deal with this dilemma by using specific forecasts as far into the future as reasonably reliable, and then they assume a value for the business at the end of the specific forecast period. This value is called a *terminal value* or a *residual value.*

The procedure preferred by most appraisers for developing the estimate of the terminal value is to use the capitalization model, usually the *constant growth capitalization model* (also known as the *Gordon growth model*). In other words, the implied assumption is that, after the specific forecast period, the business's net cash flow will continue to grow at some average annual compound rate.

The formula for the discounted cash flow model, using a terminal value calculated by the constant growth capitalization model, is the following:

Formula 15.7

$$PV = \frac{E_1}{(1+k)} + \frac{E_2}{(1+k)^2} + \ldots + \frac{E_n}{(1+k)^n} + \frac{\frac{E_n(1+g)}{k-g}}{(1+k)^n}$$

where

PV = present value

$E_1 \ldots E_n$ = expected economic income in each of the periods 1 through n

k = discount rate (cost of capital)

g = growth rate in economic income beyond year n (expected sustainable annually compounded rate)

Note that the above formula is an exact combination of Formula 15.5, the limited life discounted cash flow model, and Formula 15.3, the income capitalization growth model. In Formula 15.7, the terminal value is $En\ (1 + g)\ /\ (k - g)$ and is estimated using the Gordon growth model.

What projection period should be used (that is, how many years) before using the terminal value factor? The analytically correct answer is, until the company is expected to reach a steady growth state. The specific forecast period typically runs from 3 to 10 years, with 5 years being common.

To make our example as simple as possible, we will assume only a three-year specific forecast period. Assume the following forecasts:

Net cash flow year 1	$100
Net cash flow year 2	$130
Net cash flow year 3	$150
Required rate of return (discount rate)	20%
Annually compounded growth in net cash flow beyond year 3	5%

Inserting these numbers in Formula 15.7 gives us the following:

Formula 15.8

$$PV = \frac{\$100}{(1+0.20)} + \frac{\$130}{(1+0.20)^2} + \frac{\$150}{(1+0.20)^3} + \frac{\dfrac{\$150(1+0.05)}{0.20-0.05}}{(1+0.20)^3}$$

$$= \frac{\$100}{1.200} + \frac{\$130}{1.440} + \frac{\$150}{1.728} + \frac{\dfrac{\$157.50}{0.15}}{1.728}$$

$$= \$83.33 + \$90.28 + \$86.81 + \$607.64$$

$$= \$868.06$$

Each year's expected return, plus the terminal value, has been reduced to a present value by a divisor. Note that the terminal value divisor is based on the same number of years into the future as the expected return in the last year's specific forecast period. That is because the last period's return is expected to be received at the *end* of year 3, and the capitalized value in the terminal value calculation represents the value as of the *beginning* of year 4, essentially the same moment as the end of year 3.

If we were to convert the divisors used in Formula 15.8 to multipliers and present the results in tabular form, we would have the following:

Year	Amount	PV Factor	PV
1	$100	0.833	$ 83.30
2	$130	0.694	$ 90.22
3	$150	0.579	$ 86.85
Terminal value	$1,050	0.579	$607.95
Total present value			$868.32

(The figures differ slightly due to rounding.)

Another important item to note is that the shorter the specific forecast period, the greater the impact of the terminal value on the indicated present value. That is, the shorter the specific forecast period, the more the discounting method approaches the equivalent of the capitalizing method. Because of this, the assumed long-term growth rate following the specific forecast period takes on great significance, and the reviewer should consider whether the growth rate into the long-term future seems reasonable.

In other words, the shorter the specific forecast period, the more important the terminal value becomes as a percentage of the total present value. To illustrate this point, assume growth rates in income beyond year 3 in the above example from zero to 15 percent, still assuming a discount rate (total cost of capital) of 20 percent. These varying assumptions would have the following impact on the figures in the above example:

Assumed Growth Rate After Year 3 (%)	Terminal Value	Present Value of Terminal Value (PVTV)	Total Present Value (TPV)	PVTV as a % of TPV
0	$750	$434	$694	63%
1	$797	$461	$721	64%
2	$850	$492	$752	65%
3	$909	$526	$786	67%
4	$975	$564	$824	68%
5	$1,050	$608	$868	70%
6	$1,136	$657	$917	72%

Assumed Growth Rate After Year 3 (%)	Terminal Value	Present Value of Terminal Value (PVTV)	Total Present Value (TPV)	PVTV as a % of TPV
7	$1,235	$715	$975	73%
8	$1,350	$781	$1,041	75%
9	$1,486	$860	$1,120	77%
10	$1,650	$955	$1,215	79%
11	$1,850	$1,070	$1,330	80%
12	$2,100	$1,215	$1,475	82%
13	$2,421	$1,401	$1,661	84%
14	$2,850	$1,649	$1,909	86%
15	$3,450	$1,996	$2,256	88%

As shown above, the greater the growth rate assumed in the terminal value calculation, all else remaining constant, the greater the present value of the terminal value as a percentage of total present value.

The discounted cash flow model obviously is very sensitive to the amounts of income projected during the discrete projection period and the growth expected beyond the projection period. The reviewer should inquire whether the projections used were prepared during the normal course of business or in connection with a transaction for buyers or lenders (often optimistic) or for justifying the price to be paid (perhaps pessimistic).

If the projections were made in the normal course of business, the reviewer might inquire into the company's "track record" of meeting, failing to meet, or exceeding its projections. The reviewer might also inquire as to whether any *sensitivity analysis* was done—that is, whether the impact of changing certain variables in the assumptions was computed.

The Capitalization Model Versus the Market Multiples for Estimating Terminal Value

An alternative procedure to estimate the terminal value is to use estimated market multiples applied to some measure of the company's economic income projected for the year following the end of the discrete forecast period. An example would be to estimate net income for the year following the forecast period and use a price-to-earnings ratio to estimate the terminal value.

If valuing the entire invested capital rather than just the common equity (as discussed in a later section), then one might use a multiple of earnings before interest and taxes (EBIT), or a multiple of earnings before interest, taxes, depreciation, and amortization (EBITDA). This procedure is commonly used by investment bankers.

Although the market multiples procedure may be used to estimate terminal value, many in the business valuation community tend to prefer the income capitalization growth model, for the following reasons:

- A frequently used assumption is that market multiples will remain the same as on the effective valuation date, however, that is often not the case. Markets change, especially markets for specific industries. For example, if an industry is in a high-growth stage now, that fact is usually reflected in high market multiples. When the industry reaches a steadier state, market multiples are not likely to be as high. Even if the analyst assumes that multiples in a high-growth industry will decline, the level of multiples at any future date is hard to predict.
- Using market multiples brings an element of the market approach into the income approach, thus compromising the independence of the two approaches. The greater the impact of the terminal value on the estimated total present value, the greater the impact of the market approach influence on what started as an income approach if market multiples are used to estimate the terminal value.

This terminal value issue is critically important in the discounting method because the terminal value often accounts for over half the total value in the discounted cash flow method. If the analyst uses the constant growth model to estimate the terminal value, the reviewer can check to see whether the market multiples implied by the terminal value are reasonable. If the analyst uses market multiples to estimate the terminal value, the reviewer can check to see whether the capitalization rate implied by the terminal value is reasonable.

The Concept and Estimation of Discount Rates

From the formulas in the preceding sections, it should be apparent that the estimation of the discount rate has a major impact on the indicated present value. One should be suspicious of appraisals that fail to provide the estimation of the discount rate the detailed attention that it deserves. This section explains the concept of the discount rate and accepted procedures for estimating it.

The Concept of the Discount Rate

The discount rate is the expected *total rate of return* the investor requires to commit funds to the particular investment. It is market driven in that it represents the expected rates of return available in the market on other investments that are comparable in terms of risk.

The expected total rate of return includes two elements:

- Cash payouts
- Capital appreciation (or capital depreciation)

For example, consider a stock market investment opportunity for which the investor has the following expectations:

Stock price	$50
Annual dividend	$2
Expected annual price increase	10%

The expected appreciation would be \$5 per share (0.10 × \$50). Add that to the dividend of \$2, and the total expected return is \$7. On an investment of \$50, that is a total expected return of 14 percent (\$7 total return/\$50 purchase price = 0.14).

Such observed or expected total rates of return for various components of the market provide an empirical basis for estimating market-required total rates of return (discount rates) for various types of investments.

Elements of the Discount Rate: A Risk-Free Rate and a Premium for Risk

From a financial analysis perspective, the discount rate impounds within it the following elements:

- A risk-free rate of return, including the following:
    - A "real rate of return" for forgoing the use of money for some period of time
    - Expected rate of inflation over the life of the investment (The yield to maturity on U.S. government securities typically is used as a proxy for the risk-free rate, the implied assumption being that the U.S. government will not default on these obligations.)
- A premium for risk

Risk is defined as the degree of certainty or uncertainty of actually realizing the expected returns at the times and in the amounts expected. Because risk lies in the eye of the beholder and is not directly observable in the marketplace, financial analysts have developed various empirical procedures using market data to quantify the element of risk in the discount rate. Arguably, this quantification of the risk element is the single most challenging exercise in the discipline of valuation analysis. The next sections explain the procedures used for quantifying risk in the discount rate.

Estimating Discount Rates for Fixed-Income Securities

Unlike discount rates for equities, estimating discount rates for fixed-income securities is relatively easy because the expected return (yield to maturity) is specified for each publicly traded bond security in the daily financial press, and rating services provide guidelines for categorizing bonds and preferred stocks by their degree of risk.

The difference between the yield to maturity for any given bond and a Treasury bond of the same maturity represents the risk premium impounded into the market's required rate of return for that bond. Rating agencies (for example, Standard & Poor's and Moody's) publish risk ratings for most publicly traded bonds and the general criteria for each level of risk range. If the appraisal requires estimating the risk for the debt or preferred stock of a private company, the analyst compares the private company risk factors with one of the rating service's criteria for risk grades, estimates the risk grade for the private company, and observes the market's required rates of return for that risk grade.[4]

We are presenting the buildup model here before presenting the capital asset pricing model (CAPM) only because the buildup model is simpler; it is actually a simplified version of the capital asset pricing model. The buildup model implicitly reflects the simplifying assumption that sensitivity of returns for the subject company relative to returns for the market as a whole are about the same as for the typical public company in the market.

Estimating Equity Discount Rates: The Buildup Model

As the name suggests, the *buildup model* for estimating equity discount rates consists of a series of building blocks. Most analysts implement this procedure with four elements:

- The risk-free rate
- A general equity risk premium

- A size premium
- A specific company risk adjustment (usually an addition, but could be a subtraction)

The Risk-Free Rate

As noted earlier, the *risk-free rate* usually is a yield-to-maturity rate available on Treasury securities as of the effective valuation date. Analysts usually use one of three maturities: 30 days, 5 years, or 20 years. These maturities are used because they are the maturities for which Morningstar (Ibbotson Associates) has developed matching general equity risk premium series (see next section).

Analysts generally prefer the 20-year maturity. They recognize that it has an element of risk called *horizon risk*, or *interest rate risk*, meaning that the value of the principal will fluctuate with changing levels of interest rates, but investors generally accept this risk. The longer rates are preferable partly because they are more stable over time and less subject to short-term influences. Also, the longer maturity more closely matches the assumed long life of most businesses.

The Equity Risk Premium

The next building block is a general *equity risk premium.* This is the rate of return that investors expect from a portfolio of large public stocks (such as the Standard & Poor's 500) over and above the rate available on Treasury securities.

As noted earlier, Morningstar publishes three series of general equity risk premium data, based on 30-day, 5-year, or 20-year Treasury yields. If the analyst is using Morningstar data for the equity risk premium, the report should show which of the three maturity series he or she used, and the risk-free rate used should be for a maturity that matches the equity risk premium.

The Morningstar risk premium data are based on historical stock market returns compared with historical Treasury security yields. There are some major controversies about how these data should be used to estimate a general equity risk premium as of any given date, but the technical details of these controversies are beyond the scope of this book.[5]

The other important source of risk premiums is the *Duff & Phelps Risk Premium Report* (formerly known as the Standard & Poor's Corporate Value Consulting *Risk Premium Report*). Generally the Duff & Phelps report tends to adopt a lower equity risk premium when compared to the Morningstar's report because Duff & Phelps focuses on the time frame after 1963.[6]

The Size Premium

Extensive empirical studies have shown that smaller companies tend to have higher risk than larger companies. Although controversial, most observers believe this to be true. Because of this higher risk, such companies have a higher cost of capital. The incremental addition to the discount rate to reflect the company size component of risk is called the *size premium.*

Morningstar is also the primary purveyor of data on the historical magnitudes of the size effect in terms of how much should be added to the general equity risk premium to properly reflect the size effect in the discount rate.

Duff & Phelps is another provider of size premium data. Duff & Phelps's risk premium report uses eight different measures of size: market value of common equity, book value of common equity, five-year average net income, market value of invested capital, total assets, five-year average EBITDA, sales, and number of employees.

Specific Company Risk Adjustment

To the extent that the risk of the subject company differs from the average of the companies from which the size adjustment was derived, the last of the four building blocks in the buildup discount rate is a *specific company risk adjustment.*

Estimating this adjustment necessarily requires some subjective judgment on the part of the appraiser. The more the judgment is based on rigorous financial analysis, the more reliable the result is likely to be.

The analyst can use many ratios to compare the subject company to industry averages or to other specific companies, perhaps specific public companies chosen to be guideline companies in the market approach. If a market approach is used, financial ratios for the subject company can be compared with financial ratios for the guideline companies used in the market approach.

There are many qualitative factors that also might have an impact, such as recent actual or potential competition, quality and depth of management, condition of facilities, and countless other possibilities. It is important, however, not to double-count in the specific company risk premium factors that have already been reflected in the size premium.

Industry Risk Premiums

Morningstar introduced an alternative formula for the buildup model in the *SBBI Valuation Edition 2002 Yearbook*. The company included an industry risk premium in the buildup model to reflect the characteristics of the subject company's industry. Morningstar publishes this risk premium in *SBBI Valuation Edition Yearbook*.

Summary Illustration of the Equity Discount Rate Using the Buildup Model

The following is a typical presentation of the estimation of an equity discount rate by the buildup model (using Morningstar data):

Risk-free rate	4.3%[a]
Equity risk premium	7.1[b]
Size premium	2.7[c]
Specific company risk adjustment	2.0[d]
Equity discount rate	16.1%

Notes:

a. Yield on 20-year Treasury bonds as of valuation date.

b. Morningstar arithmetic mean equity risk premium for full period 1926 to 2006, from *Stocks, Bonds, Bills & Inflation* (SBBI) *2007 Valuation Edition*, p. 189.

c. Morningstar, SBBI 2007, nine largest, p. 137.

d. Analyst should have a supporting analysis in his or her valuation report.

Here is the other example illustrating the usage of an industry risk premium when calculating an equity discount rate (using Morningstar data):

Risk-free rate	4.3%[a]
Equity risk premium	7.1[b]
Size premium	2.7[c]
Industry risk premium	0.35[d]
Specific company risk adjustment	2.0[e]
Equity discount rate	16.45%

Notes:

a. Yield on 20-year Treasury bonds as of valuation date.

b. Morningstar arithmetic mean equity risk premium for full period 1926 to 2006, from *Stocks, Bonds, Bills & Inflation* (SBBI) *2007 Valuation Edition*, p. 189.

c. Morningstar, 2007 SBBI, nine largest, p. 137.

d. Morningstar, 2007 SBBI, p. 45 (Oil and Gas Field Services, SIC 138).

e. Analyst should have a supporting analysis in his or her valuation report.

The following is a typical presentation of the estimation of an equity discount rate by the buildup model (using Duff & Phelps data):

Risk-free rate	4.3%[a]
Equity risk premium (including size premium)	10.4[b]
Specific company risk adjustment	2.0[c]
Equity discount rate	16.7%

Notes:

a. Yield on 20-year Treasury bonds as of valuation date.

b. Duff & Phelps, *Risk Premium Report* 2007, smoothed equity risk premium for portfolio 20, Exhibit A-1, p. 26.

c. See analyst's valuation report for supporting analysis.

Estimating Equity Discount Rates: The Capital Asset Pricing Model

The capital asset pricing model (CAPM) today is considered by many to be the most theoretically correct model for estimating an equity discount rate. It has been theoretically challenged, but is still the model most commonly used by corporate finance practitioners.

The only difference between the capital asset pricing model and the buildup model is a modifier (coefficient) to the general equity risk premium called *beta*.

Definition of Beta

The coefficient called *beta* is a measure of market risk. It measures the sensitivity of returns on an individual security (or portfolio of securities) to returns on the market. The total return (dividends and capital appreciation) on the Standard & Poor's 500 stock composite average (S&P 500) is the most commonly used benchmark for returns on the market.

Beta measures the risk called *systematic risk* because it is the risk of the overall market. The theory is that market risk cannot be removed by holding a fully diversified portfolio of securities, and therefore it is unavoidable if investing in equities. A fundamental assumption of the CAPM is that the risk premium portion of a security's expected total return is a function of that security's systematic risk. (The risk that is *not* related to the market is called *unsystematic risk*.)

Computation of Beta

For a publicly traded security (or portfolio), beta is measured from market data, usually for the last three to five years. The computation of beta is a linear regression of the rate of return on a given security (or portfolio of securities) on the market return for a series of time periods. If returns for the subject security or portfolio go up and down about the same degree as the market, then beta equals 1.0. If the returns tend to be more volatile in response to market moves (that is, they go up more than the market when the market goes up and down more than the market when the market goes down), then beta is greater than 1.0. Conversely, if the returns tend to be less volatile in response to changes in market returns, then beta is less than 1.0.

Exhibit 15.3 shows schematically how the market-required rate of return increases as beta increases.

Exhibit 15.3

Schematic Diagram Illustrating Beta

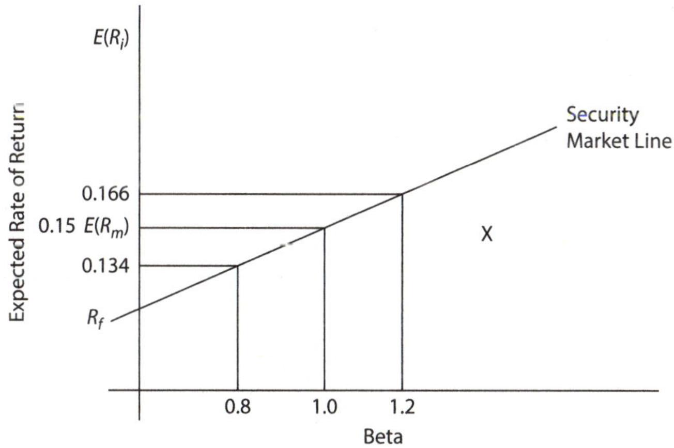

In this diagram:

$E(R_i)$	=	Expected return for the individual security
$E(R_m)$	=	Expected return on the market
R_f	=	Risk-free rate available as of the valuation date
X	=	The risk and return profile for a particular company

In a market in perfect equilibrium, all securities would fall on the security market line. If security *X* has a high beta (as shown in the diagram) and a security analyst expects the returns for that security to be as shown, the analyst would consider the security overpriced.

As this exhibit shows, the beta for the market as a whole is 1.0. Therefore, from a numerical standpoint, the beta has the following interpretations:

Beta > 1.0 When market rates of return move up or down, the rates of return for the subject tend to move in the same direction and with greater magnitude. For example, for a stock with no dividend, if the market is up 10%, the price of a stock with a beta of 1.2 would be expected to be up 12%. If the market is down 10%, the price of the same stock would be expected to be down 12%. Many high-tech companies are good examples of stocks with high betas.

Beta = 1.0 Fluctuations in rates of return for the subject tend to equal fluctuations in rates of return for the market.

Beta < 1.0 When market rates of return move up or down, rates of return for the subject tend to move up or down, but to a lesser extent. For example, for a stock with no dividend, if the market is up 10%, the price of a stock with a beta of 0.8 would be expected to be up 8%. The classic example of a low-beta stock would be a utility that has not diversified into more risky activities.

Negative beta (Rare) Rates of return for the subject tend to move in the opposite direction from changes in rates of return for the market. Stocks with negative betas are rare. A few gold-mining companies have had negative betas in the past.

Source: Shannon Pratt and Roger Grabowski, *Cost of Capital: Applications and Examples*, 3rd ed., Wiley, New York, 2008, pp. 81–82.

Betas for Privately Held Companies

Since a privately held company by definition does not have regular public market trading prices, such volatility in daily, weekly, or monthly returns cannot be measured directly. Therefore, analysts wishing to use the capital asset pricing model to estimate an equity discount rate for a private company must develop a proxy for the private company's beta.

The most common way of doing this is to observe betas of public companies in the same industry. The analyst then may use some average of the betas of those companies as a proxy for the beta of the private company. If the analyst also uses a public guideline company valuation method, the companies used in that method very likely would be the ones from which the betas are analyzed. Or the analyst might use industry average betas from *Morningstar*'s *Cost of Capital Yearbook and Quarterly Updates.*

Incorporating Beta into the Equity Risk Premium

To incorporate beta into the equity risk premium, one multiplies the general equity risk premium by the beta. To illustrate, we will use the general equity risk premium of 7.1 that we used in the illustration of the buildup model (using Morningstar data).

First, consider company *i*, whose returns are assumed to be less sensitive to changes in overall market returns than the average company and for which we have assigned a beta of 0.75:

$$0.75 \times 7.1 = 5.3 \text{ equity risk premium for company } i$$

Next, consider company *j*, whose systematic risk is estimated to be equal to the market as a whole, with a beta of 1.0:

$$1.0 \times 7.1 = 7.1 \text{ equity risk premium for company } j$$

Finally, consider company *k*, which is estimated to have 20 percent more volatility in returns in response to the overall market than the average company and therefore has a beta of 1.2:

$$1.2 \times 7.1 = 8.5 \text{ equity risk premium for company } k$$

The Size Premium in CAPM

The Morningstar studies show that small companies tend to have larger betas on average than big companies. However, the Morningstar studies also show that only some, not all, of the extra risk of smaller companies is captured by beta. Therefore, Morningstar publishes a series called *Size Premium in Excess of CAPM* for guidance for incorporating the size effect into the equity discount rate when using CAPM.

Specific Company Risk Adjustment in CAPM

To the extent that the company has risk factors that have not already been reflected in the general equity risk premium as modified by beta and the small company size premium, a further specific company risk adjustment could be warranted. Be careful to ensure that the analyst is not double-counting risk factors already captured by beta and the size premium. For example, are the subject company's weaknesses in management depth, geographical and product diversification, breadth of customer base, and other such elements any more limited than the companies from which the size factor was estimated?

Summary Illustration of the Equity Discount Rate Using CAPM

The following is a typical presentation of the estimation of an equity discount rate using the capital asset pricing model (using Morningstar data):

Risk-free rate	4.3[a]
Equity risk premium:	
General equity risk premium	7.1[b]
Beta × 1.3[c]	9.2
Size premium in excess of CAPM	2.7[d]
Specific company risk adjustment	1.0[e]
Equity discount rate	17.2%

Notes:

a. Yield on 20-year Treasury bonds as of valuation date.

b. Morningstar arithmetic mean equity risk premium for full period 1926 to 2006, from *Stocks, Bonds, Bills & Inflation* (SBBI) *2007 Valuation Edition*, p. 189.

c. Median beta for the group of guideline public companies as determined for the subject company.

d. Morningstar, SBBI 2007, p. 137.

e. See analyst's valuation report for supporting analysis.

Duff & Phelps also publishes data for CAPM, but it takes a slightly different approach from Morningstar's approach. The following is a typical presentation of the estimation of an equity discount rate using the capital asset pricing model (using Duff & Phelps data):

Risk-free rate	4.3[a]
Equity risk premium:	
General equity risk premium	4.9[b]
Beta × 1.3[c]	6.4
Size premium in excess of CAPM	4.4[d]
Specific company risk adjustment	1.0[e]
Equity discount rate	16.1%

Notes:

a. Yield on 20-year Treasury bonds as of valuation date.

b. Morningstar arithmetic mean equity risk premium for full period 1963 to 2006, from *Stocks, Bonds, Bills & Inflation* (SBBI) *2007 Valuation Edition*, p. 191.

c. Median beta for the group of guideline public companies as determined for the subject company.

d. Duff & Phelps, *Risk Premium Report* 2007, smoothed premium over CAPM for portfolio 20, Exhibit B-1, p. 34.

e. See analyst's valuation report for supporting analysis.

Although the CAPM is probably the most widely used procedure in corporate finance today for estimating the cost of equity capital, there is some controversy about the use of the beta factor. There are alternative models that purport to capture the risk associated with an equity as well or better, although they have not achieved wide usage.

The Concept and Estimation of Capitalization Rates

Capitalization rates, like discount rates, are utilized to determine value and can be computed using different methods.

The Concept of a Capitalization Rate

As noted earlier in this chapter, a *capitalization rate* is a divisor applied to a single number representing some type of economic income to derive an estimate of value. As such, unlike a discount rate, it does *not* represent the total annual rate of return expected by the investor over the life of the investment. It represents the *current* return, but it does not reflect the total return.

In the discounting method, all the changes in future expected returns are fully accounted for in the numerator of the discounting formula. In capitalizing, only a single number is used in the numerator, and *all future changes in the expected income are impounded into the capitalization rate.*

Elements of the Capitalization Rate

There are two basic elements impounded in a capitalization rate:

1. A discount rate, which represents the total annually compounded rate of return the investor requires over the life of the investment, reflecting the risk of the investment
2. An annualized expected rate of growth or decline in the amount of the economic income variable being capitalized

In respect to the e income approach, we specifically quantify each of these two elements. In the context of the market approach (next chapter), we simply observe the total capitalization rate for each of several possible measures of economic income, but we have no way of knowing for sure what portion of any observed capitalization rate represents required total rate of return and what portion represents expected changes in the variable being capitalized.

Estimating Equity Capitalization Rates

As suggested in the section above, the capitalization rate is simply the discount rate plus or minus the expected annually compounded rate of change in the variable being capitalized. In terms of a formula, this computation is as follows:

Formula 15.9

$$c = k - g$$

where

c = capitalization rate

k = discount rate (cost of capital or total required rate of return)

g = growth rate (in the variable being capitalized)

For an example, assume the following:

Discount rate	20%
Long-term sustainable growth rate	5%

Inserting these numbers in Formula 15.9 gives us the following:

Formula 15.10

$$0.20 - 0.05 = 0.15$$

It is important to note that the *growth rate* is assumed to be an *expected annualized rate in perpetuity.* The reasonableness of the rate used must be assessed with this requirement in mind. If this growth rate is overestimated, then the capitalization rate will be a lower number, which will result in an overestimated value.

The growth rate normally includes expected inflation. For example, if the company expected to maintain a physical volume increase of 3 percent with constant margins and expected price increases of 2 percent annually in line with expected inflation, the expected growth rate would be 5 percent. The capitalization model reflecting constant growth is sometimes referred to as the *Gordon growth model.*

Valuing Invested Capital Versus Valuing Equity

In Chapter 14, we said that an accepted procedure in any of the valuation approaches is to value all the *invested capital* and subtract the debt (and the value of preferred stock, if any) to get to the value of the common equity.

To use the procedure in the income approach, the numerator of the equation (the dollar amounts of expected returns) must include the returns available to all the invested capital—that is, the debt holders as well as the equity holders. The denominator (the discount or capitalization rate) must reflect a blending of the costs of each of the component costs of capital on the basis of their proportions in the capital structure, measured at market value. This blended rate is called the *weighted average cost of capital* (WACC).

The Concept of the Weighted Average Cost of Capital (WACC)

The *weighted average cost of capital* is the blended discount rate of all the capital structure components, each weighted at its pro rata portion of the total capital structure. It is critical that the weight assigned each component be *at market value, not at book value.* (Weighting the components at book value rather than at market value is a common error that can result in a significant misestimation of value.)

The Basic WACC Computation Model

The formula for the weighted average cost of capital is as follows:

Formula 15.11

$$WACC = (k_e \times W_e) + [k_d(pt)(1 - t) \times W_d]$$

where

WACC = weighted average cost of capital

W = weight (the percentage of each component of the company's total capital structure, measured at market value)

k_e = cost of equity capital (equity discount rate)

$k_{d(pt)}$ = cost of debt capital before tax (that is, before adjusting the cost for the tax deductibility of interest expense)

t = tax rate

Of course, if there is preferred stock or other components of the capital structure, there would need to be a component in the above formula for each capital structure component.

For an example of application of the above formula, assume the following:

Equity discount rate	20%
Percentage of equity in the capital structure (at market value)	60%
Cost of debt (pretax)	10%
Tax rate	30%
Percentage of debt in the capital structure	40%

Inserting these numbers in Formula 15.11 gives us the following:

Formula 15.12

$$\begin{aligned} \text{WACC} &= (0.20 \times 0.60) + [0.10(1 - 0.30) \times 0.40] \\ &= 0.12 + (0.07 \times 0.40) \\ &= 0.12 + 0.028 \\ &= 0.148, \text{ or } 14.8\% \end{aligned}$$

The above is often presented in tabular form:

Component	Cost	Weight	Weighted Cost
Equity	0.20	0.60	0.12
Debt	0.10(1 – 0.30)	0.40	0.028
Weighted average cost of capital			0.148

Derivation of Weights for the WACC

In the example above, the cost of equity is 20 percent, and the net cost of debt (after the tax effect) is only 7 percent. Such a large difference is not uncommon. Consequently, selection of the weights in the WACC can have a large bearing on the invested capital discount rate and thus on the indicated value. This is often a major area of controversy and one source of differences in value between appraisers.

The choice of weights may be different when one is valuing a controlling interest versus a minority interest. They may also be different under different standards of value. We will confine the discussion here to fair market value, but, for example, under investment value (value to a particular investor), that investor could select any weights desired.

Controlling Interests. Some would use the company's actual capital structure. However, for controlling interests, a good case can be made for using an industry average capital structure because one of the prerogatives of control ownership is to change the capital structure.

- One of the few sources that provides industry average capital structures at market value is *Morningstar*'s *Cost of Capital Yearbook and Quarterly Updates.* A common error is to use industry average capital structures at book value. Usually, book values have debt at close to market value but equity (based on depreciated historical costs) at considerably less than market value. This distorts the weights by overstating the debt proportion and understating the equity proportion, thus understating the invested capital discount rate and overstating the value.
- The data in *Morningstar*'s *Cost of Capital Yearbook and Quarterly Updates* are all from public companies. Private companies may have less access to the debt markets than public companies. Thus, it may be appropriate to assume a slightly higher proportion of equity for a private company.
- Changing the capital structure weights significantly can also change the cost of each component of the capital structure. As leverage (percentage) of debt is increased, risk is increased for both the debt and the equity, thus increasing the cost of each component. A common error is to hypothesize a much greater percentage of debt with no increase in the cost of debt or equity, thus lowering the computed WACC and reaching an unattainably inflated indicated value for the company.

Minority Interests. When valuing a minority interest at fair market value, the appraiser almost always uses the company's actual capital structure because the minority interest owner has no power to change the capital structure. At first glance this may seem like a dilemma because we have to weight the capital structure components at market value—which we do not yet know because that is what we are trying to determine. However, the dilemma is easily solved with modern computers using an *iterative process*—that is, testing different capital structures until one works out.[7]

Another source of weights for the capital structure, if using the market approach and/or the capital asset pricing model in the income approach, would be the capital structures of the guideline companies used. If the capital structures among the companies vary a great deal, this may be calculated by a procedure called *unlevering and relevering betas*, a topic that is beyond the scope of this book.[8]

The Preference for the Net Cash Flow in the Income Approach

The consensus among professional business appraisers and the corporate finance community is that net cash flow is the preferred measure of economic income to use in the income approach. There are good reasons for this:

- It matches with empirical data supporting the discount rate.
- There is a conceptual preference for net cash flow: it represents what the owner can take out and still expect to achieve the projected returns.
- It helps make the income approach discrete from the market approach because the market approach usually uses other income variables and usually not net cash flow.

Net Cash Flow Matches the Empirical Data

Both the Morningstar data and the Duff & Phelps data reflect *total return*, that is, dividends plus or minus capital appreciation or depreciation. (The data are based on public stocks, for which the dividends are distributed and the stock is in a liquid market, so the investor can sell the stock and realize the appreciation or depreciation.) This is tantamount to the appraisers' definition of *net cash flow.*

Net Cash Flow Is What You Get

One definition of net cash flow is the cash flow remaining after allowing for necessary capital expenditures and net working capital to support sales growth. In other words, it is what can be taken out of the company (at least by a control owner) without impairing the company's operations. This is the economic income variable that ultimately is of greatest importance to most investors.

Public companies look relatively more to net income than do private companies, but in the long run, net cash flow is the most essential ingredient to the success of public companies as well. This is an important conceptual reason for focusing on net cash flow in estimating value.

Use of Net Cash Flow Keeps the Income Approach Discrete

Appraisers like to be able to use two or more approaches to valuation to help increase the reliability of the valuation conclusion. To the extent that components of the different methods do not overlap, this increases the independence of one valuation method compared with another.

In spite of the preference for net cash flow in the income approach, it is almost never used in the market approach. This is because, for the comparative companies, we don't know whether two of the components of net cash flow—capital expenditures and additions to net working capital for any year—represent normalized amounts for those companies, and capitalizing abnormal figures would produce a distorted indication of value. Therefore, in the market approach we generally use every measure of economic income *except* net cash flow (for example, net income, pretax income, gross cash flow, EBIT, EBITDA, "discretionary earnings").

Thus, using net cash flow as the economic income variable in the income approach tends to make the income approach results more independent of the results from other valuation approaches.

The Midyear Discounting Convention[9]

The income approach procedures shown in previous sections implicitly assume that all the proceeds are received or distributed at the end of each year. Indeed, many businesses wait until the end of the year to assess cash availability and needs before deciding what to distribute to owners. Also, many have seasonal cash flow patterns.

If, however, it is more reasonable to assume that proceeds are received more or less evenly throughout the year, appraisers reflect this assumption with a mathematical procedure called the *midyear discounting convention.*[10]

The idea is that the effect of receiving proceeds more or less evenly throughout the year can be approximated by assuming that all the proceeds are received in the middle of each year, hence the term *midyear convention.* Since the assumption is that the cash flows will be realized earlier, the midyear convention procedure will always produce a higher indication of value than the assumption of receiving cash flows only at the end of each year. The way the mathematics work out, the higher the discount or capitalization rate, the greater the difference will be between the values indicated by the two alternative assumptions.

The Midyear Convention in the Capitalization Method

The midyear convention is accomplished in the capitalization method by a minor variation in the capitalization formula presented earlier.

The modification is made in the numerator of the capitalization formula. In Formula 15.12, we capitalized next year's economic income as follows:

$$PV = \frac{E_1}{c}$$

where

PV = present value

E_1 = expected economic income in the full period immediately following the effective valuation date

c = capitalization rate (as defined previously)

To introduce the midyear convention assumption, we multiply the E_1 above by 1 plus the discount rate (k), raised to the power of 0.5 (to reflect a half year). In other words, the expected income is multiplied by $(1 + k)^{0.5}$, resulting in the following formula[9]:

Formula 15.13

$$PV = \frac{E_1(1+k)^{0.5}}{c}$$

where

PV = present value

E_1 = expected economic income in the full period immediately following the effective valuation date

k = present value discount rate (cost of capital)

c = capitalization rate (as defined previously)

To illustrate the above with an example, assume the following:

$$E_1 = \$105$$
$$k = 20 \text{ percent}$$
$$c = 15 \text{ percent}$$
(20 percent less growth rate of 5 percent)

Inserting these numbers in Formula 15.13 gives us the following:

Formula 15.14

$$\begin{aligned} PV &= \frac{\$105(1+0.20)^{0.5}}{0.15} \\ &= \frac{\$105(1.09545)}{0.15} \\ &= \frac{\$115.02}{0.15} \\ &= \$766.82 \end{aligned}$$

Similarly, the Gordon growth model (Formula 15.3) can be modified to reflect the midyear convention by adding the same term in the numerator:

Formula 15.15

$$PV = \frac{E_0(1+g)(1+k)^{0.5}}{k-g}$$

where

PV = present value

E_0 = expected economic income in the full period immediately preceding the effective valuation date

g = expected long-term sustainable rate of growth in the economic income from the year immediately preceding the effective valuation date

k = present value discount rate (cost of capital)

To illustrate the above with an example, assume the following:

$$E_0 = \$100$$
$$g = 5 \text{ percent}$$
$$k = 20 \text{ percent}$$

Inserting these numbers in Formula 15.15 gives us the following:

Formula 15.16

$$\begin{aligned} \text{PV} &= \frac{\$100(1+0.05)(1+0.20)^{0.5}}{0.20-0.05} \\ &= \frac{\$100(1.05)(1.09545)}{0.15} \\ &= \$766.82 \end{aligned}$$

The Midyear Convention in the Discounting Method

To reflect the midyear convention in the discounting method, the number of periods by which each year's proceeds is discounted is reduced by a half year. In other words, each exponent in the denominator n is reduced by 0.5. The modified formula (modified from Formula 15.7) is as follows:

Formula 15.17

$$\text{PV} = \frac{E_1}{(1+k)^{0.5}} + \frac{E_2}{(1+k)^{1.5}} + \ldots + \frac{E_n}{(1+k)^{n-0.5}} + \frac{\dfrac{E_n(1+g)}{k-g}}{(1+k)^{n-0.5}}$$

where the variables are defined the same as in Formula 15.15.

For simplicity in an example, we will use only a three-year specific forecast period, and we will use the same assumed figures as in Formula 15.8:

Net cash flow year 1	\$100
Net cash flow year 2	\$130
Net cash flow year 3	\$150
Required rate of return (discount rate):	20%
Annually compounded growth in net cash flow beyond year 3	5%

Inserting these numbers in Formula 15.17 gives us the following:

Formula 15.18

$$\text{PV} = \frac{\$100}{(1+0.20)^{0.5}} + \frac{\$130}{(1+0.20)^{1.5}} + \frac{\$150}{(1+0.20)^{2.5}} + \frac{\frac{\$150(1+0.05)}{0.20-0.05}}{(1+0.20)^{2.5}}$$

$$= \frac{\$100}{1.10} + \rightarrow \frac{\$130}{1.31} + \frac{\$150}{1.58} + \frac{\frac{\$157.50}{0.15}}{1.58}$$

$$= \$90.91 + \rightarrow \$99.24 + \$94.94 + \$664.56$$

$$= \$949.65$$

Note that the above value is higher than the value from the year-end assumption—in this case \$949.65 compared with \$868.06 from Formula 15.8.

An alternative procedure is to reflect the midyear convention in the terminal value using the modified Gordon growth model (Formula 15.15), in which case the terminal value is discounted by n years instead of n - 0.5 years. This formula is written as follows:

Formula 15.19

$$\text{PV} = \frac{E_1}{(1+k)^{0.5}} + \frac{E_2}{(1+k)^{1.5}} + \ldots + \frac{E_n}{(1+k)^{n-0.5}} + \frac{\frac{E_n(1+g)(1+k)^{0.5}}{k-g}}{(1+k)^n}$$

where the variables are defined the same as in Formula 15.15. This will produce exactly the same result as Formula 15.17.

The difference in value between the year-end and the midyear conventions is equal to $(1 + k)^{0.5}$.

References

Basic Income Approach

Fishman, Jay E., Shannon P. Pratt, J. Clifford Griffith, et al. 2008. "Capitalized and Discounted Returns Methods." *PPC's Guide to Business Valuations.* Fort Worth, TX: Practitioners Publishing, pp. 5-1 to 5-113.

Hitchner, James R. 2006. "Income Approach" (ch. 4). In *Financial Valuation: Applications and Models,* 2nd ed. Hoboken, NJ: Wiley, pp. 97–150.

Pratt, Shannon. 2003. "The Income Approach: Cost of Capital," "The Income Approach: The Discounting Method," and "The Income Approach: The Capitalization Method." In *Business Valuation Body of Knowledge,* 2nd ed. Hoboken, NJ: Wiley, pp. 100–141.

Pratt, Shannon P., and Alina V. Niculita. 2007. "Income Approach: Discounted Future Economic Income Method" (ch. 9). In *Valuing a Business,* 5th ed. New York: McGraw-Hill Includes extensive bibliography and data references.

Pratt, Shannon P., and Roger J. Grabowski. 2008. *Cost of Capital: Applications and Examples,* 3rd ed. Hoboken, NJ: WIley.

Trugman, Gary. 2002. "The Income Approach" and "Discount Rates and Capitalization Rates." In *Understanding Business Valuation,* 2nd ed. New York: American Institute of Certified Public Accountants, pp. 281–322, 323–356.

Cost-of-Capital Data

Duff & Phelps LLC, 55 East 52nd Street, 31st Floor, New York, NY 10055, (212)871-2000: *Risk Premium Report,* published annually and available at http://www.bvresources.com and http://corporate.morningstar.com.

Morningstar (Ibbotson Associates), 225 North Michigan Avenue, Suite 700, Chicago, IL 60601, +1 (312)616-1620. Publishes three series of data dealing with cost of capital:

Stocks, Bonds, Bills & Inflation (SBBI), *Valuation Edition,* published annually. Provides equity risk premium series, small stock premium series, and other data to develop cost of equity capital.

Cost of Capital Yearbook and Quarterly Updates, published annually with quarterly updates. Contains cost of equity by both the CAPM and DCF procedures and the weighted average cost of capital by industry, as well as capital structure at market value by industry.

Beta Book, published semiannually. Several computations of beta for over 5,000 publicly traded stocks.

Morningstar Cost of Capital Center, online service for all of above data on a per inquiry basis, http://corporate.morningstar.com.

Chapter 16

The Market Approach

Market Approach Concept and Overview

The concept of the market approach in business appraisal is that valuation guidance can be found in transactions involving similar companies. It is the same technique as the more familiar appraisal of a house by analyzing sales of similar houses. However, "similar" businesses have far more differences among them than do similar houses, and the appraiser must carefully analyze the similarities and differences.

The market approach to business appraisal also has several dimensions that must be considered that are either not found at all or treated differently in the real estate appraisal comparative sales approach:

- Valuing controlling versus minority interests
- Valuing total invested capital versus direct valuation of equity
- Whether guideline transactions are sales of entire businesses or publicly traded minority interest stock market transactions

These possibilities are shown schematically in Exhibit 16.1.

Exhibit 16.1

Major Market Approach Business Valuation Scenarios

Valuing Controlling Interest	
Valuing total invested capital	Using sales of entire companies
	Using publicly traded guideline companies
Direct valuation of equity	Using sales of entire companies
	Using publicly traded guideline companies
Valuing Minority Interest	
Valuing total invested capital	Using sales of entire companies
	Using publicly traded guideline companies
Direct valuation of equity	Using sales of entire companies
	Using publicly traded guideline companies

Valuing Controlling Versus Minority Interests

In real estate appraisal, the valuation is virtually always that of a controlling (fee simple) interest in the property. After that, if valuing a partial interest, some minority discount may be applied to the fractional interest's pro rata portion of the fee simple interest value. In business appraisal, minority interests often are valued directly—that is, without ever addressing the question of what the company as a whole, on a controlling interest basis, might be worth. This is possible because there are thousands of public companies with minority shares actively traded every day.

The differences between minority and control value usually are considerably greater for businesses than for real estate. This is because owners of a fractional interest in real estate usually have the right to demand partition, thus converting their ownership interest to a controlling or fee simple interest. Owners of stock or partnership interests usually have no such right, leaving them at the mercy of policy decisions of the control owners.

If one starts with guideline sales of entire companies (merger and acquisition transactions) in the market approach (called the *transaction method*), then, if valuing a minority interest, it usually would be appropriate to make both a minority interest and a lack of marketability adjustment to the indicated control value. If one starts with publicly traded minority interest transactions in the market approach, then, if valuing a controlling interest, it may be appropriate to apply a control premium to the indicated value, and one might also consider a discount for lack of marketability.

However, control premiums certainly are *not* automatic when using publicly traded minority interest transactions to value a controlling interest.

Valuing Total Invested Capital Versus Direct Valuation of Equity

In real estate appraisal, property normally is appraised without regard to how much debt or other claims there may be against it. In business appraisal, if all components of the capital structure are appraised, it is usually called *value of invested capital* or *market value of invested capital* (MVIC). However, in business appraisal, the equity interest sometimes is valued directly without going through the step of estimating the value of the entire company, including debt and equity interests combined.

To get to a value for the equity, one can use market multiples of various levels of income available to equity owners (for example, price-to-earnings ratios). Alternatively, one can value the entire invested capital, including returns available to holders of interest-bearing debt and preferred stock, and then subtract the value of the senior securities to get to the value of the common equity.

Either procedure can be used for valuing either controlling or minority interests. However, the invested capital procedure tends to be preferred for valuing controlling interests, and the direct valuation of equity tends to be preferred for valuing minority interests. The reason for this preference is that a controlling interest holder can change the capital structure if that may enhance the value of the equity, while the minority interest owner does not have that option. However, if the subject and guideline companies have considerably diverse capital structures, eliminating the potential effects of that difference sometimes is a reason, and even a compelling reason to use the invested capital procedure even when valuing minority interests.

Using Sales of Entire Companies or Publicly Traded Guideline Companies

There are two commonly used types of market transactions:

- Sales of entire companies, or possibly controlling interests in companies. Some would divide this into two subcategories:
    - Companies that were publicly traded before the transaction
    - Companies that were privately owned before the transaction[1]
- Publicly traded company transactions (day-to-day transactions of minority interests in companies in the public stock markets).

Unfortunately, there are virtually no reliable data available on minority interest transactions in privately held companies. Therefore, if the appraiser is using the market approach to value a private company minority interest, he or she is forced to start with the above available data and adjust for the minority and marketability factors. If the standard of value is fair market value, the appraiser may consider eliminating or making adjustments for transactions that may have been representative of investment value rather than fair market value.

Fortunately, however, there have been huge improvements in recent years in the amount, quality, and ease of access to both public market transaction data and data on sales of entire companies, both public and private. This makes a good market approach valuation much more feasible today for many companies than it has been in the past.

Sources of Market Approach Data

As noted above, market data can be classified into two groups: (1) sales of entire companies or controlling interests of companies that were publicly traded or privately owned before the sale and (2) publicly traded company market transactions.

Public company data usually have the advantages of being more complete and more verifiable. On the other hand, if one is valuing a controlling interest, it may be preferable to start with controlling interest guideline transactions and not have to deal with the issue of a control premium.

Another reason to use private company controlling interest transactions in some cases is that there are many industries and professional practices that have few or no public companies.

Sales of Public Companies

If a public company is sold, required filings with the Securities and Exchange Commission (SEC) provide excellent data for implementing a market approach valuation. Since the transactions are not likely to be on the effective valuation date for the subject, the analyst should either explain adjustments for changes in market conditions between the transaction date and subject valuation effective date or explain why none are necessary.

There are many sources that valuation analysts use to locate sales of public companies. However, unlike currently traded stocks, there is not a single source that is totally comprehensive, so analysts often use several sources to search for transactions.

If one is relying on public company sales, it is preferable to use the actual SEC filing data rather than data summarized in secondary sources. Besides eliminating possible errors from secondary sources, original company filings usually provide more detail than secondary sources.

Sales of Private Companies

Data on sales of private companies usually are considerably more limited than data on sales of public companies. Unlike real estate transactions, for which data usually are required to be filed at the relevant government agency and made publicly available, there is no requirement for releasing any data on sales of privately owned companies. Therefore, unless the buyer is a public company and the purchase is of a sufficient size to require an SEC filing, the data services that collect private company transaction data usually gather them from the transaction intermediaries rather than directly from the companies sold. This usually means that the data for each individual transaction cannot be independently verified. While this is a limitation, the services have no reason to be biased. Furthermore, if valuing a private company or an interest in a private company, it often is considered more comparable to use private company rather than public company transactions as a starting point.

There are four major private sale transaction databases, all greatly expanded in recent years. These are listed and described briefly in the References section at the end of this chapter.

Guideline Public Company Data

Over 12,000 operating companies are required to file financial data with the SEC. The major reports are the following:

- 10-K: annual report
- 10-Q: quarterly report
- 8-K: special events report

There are also thousands of public companies that are not required to file with the SEC because either their number of stockholders or the amount of their assets falls below the SEC levels that require filing.

Since May 1996, all companies required to file with the SEC must do so electronically on the Electronic Data Gathering and Retrieval (EDGAR) system. All documents filed in the EDGAR system are in the public domain and may be retrieved at no charge through the Internet. There are also commercial systems available at reasonable charges that provide enhanced capabilities to manipulate the data. The data provide the information to do all of the market multiple calculations discussed in this chapter.

Since public transactions occur daily, the price information for public companies should be as of the effective date of the subject company valuation. Usually, the public company fundamental data (sales, earnings, and so on) should be as close to the valuation date as possible, or as close to the latest date available for the subject company as possible.

Developing Market Multiples for Valuation

As in the market approach in real estate appraisal, the market approach in business appraisal requires some "units of comparison." In real estate, for example, price per square foot is a common unit of comparison. In business valuation, however, physical units of comparison (for example, the number of board feet per year of manufacturing capacity) are much less common. The units of comparison usually are in some form of dollar measurement of various levels of income producing capacity or asset values.

In other words, the objective is to observe the transaction price and compute the multiple of that price times some relevant fundamental variables, such as sales, earnings, gross cash flow, net asset value, or others. The fundamental variables used in the market approach are defined and illustrated in Chapter 14. This chapter will present an example of the market approach using some of the most commonly encountered market multiples.

Invested Capital Multiples

When valuing the entire invested capital of a company (that is, equity and debt), the numerator of the market multiple is the *market value of invested capital* (MVIC). This is defined as the market value of all the common and preferred stock and interest-bearing debt. Technically, invested capital would include only long-term debt, including the current portion. However, more often than not, short-term interest-bearing debt is also included. One reason for this is that it often is difficult or even impossible, at least for the guideline companies, to determine how much of the interest expense is attributable to long-term versus short-term debt.

Many valuation analysts and almost all investment bankers subtract the cash and cash equivalents when they are defining and computing the market value of invested capital. This is to focus on the valuations of companies' operations without distortions of cash-rich versus cash-poor companies. If this is done for the guideline companies, then, of course, cash and equivalents for the subject company must be added back in after the multiples have been applied to estimate the company's value.

Because of these two ambiguities in computing the market value of invested capital, it is essential that the report or analysis that uses the market value of invested capital define how it is computed.

Since the numerator includes the market value of all invested capital, the denominator used to create the multiple must include all the returns available to all the invested capital. Usually, this means adding all the interest paid in addition to all the returns available to common equity. If there is preferred stock, the dividends on the preferred stock must also be included.

To recap from Chapter 14, the denominators typically used for invested capital multiples include the following:

- **Sales.** This is the only income statement denominator that can logically be used in either invested capital or equity market multiples. It is a more relevant multiple for invested capital than for equity because the multiples of the market value of the equity to sales can be significantly distorted by differences in capital structures among the companies.
- **Discretionary earnings.** This is the gross cash flow before interest, taxes, and all compensation to one owner-manager. Typically this is used only for small businesses and professional practices with one key owner-operator.
- **Earnings before interest, taxes, depreciation, and amortization (EBITDA).** A multiple of the EBITDA is the market multiple most preferred by acquirers for valuing companies under the market approach. It represents gross cash flow before taxes, and it eliminates the possibly distorting effect of differing depreciation policies among companies.
- **Earnings before interest and taxes (EBIT).** This is the second most frequently used invested capital market multiple.
- **Debt-free net income (DFNI).** A multiple of the EBIT is a multiple based on an estimation of what the after-tax net income to invested capital would be if there were no interest-bearing debt.
- **Debt-free cash flow (DFCF).** This is a multiple based on an estimate of what the after-tax gross cash flow available to invested capital would be if there were no interest-bearing debt.
- **Book value of invested capital.** When this multiple is used, it may refer to the total book value (BV) or only include the tangible book value. Intangibles usually are eliminated because the different methods of acquiring intangibles and accounting for them can distort comparisons between companies.

- **Adjusted book value of invested capital.** In some cases, this multiple can be used if it is possible to adjust values of major assets to market value for both the subject and guideline companies. Ideally, one would adjust all assets and liabilities to market value, but this may be impractical in most cases.

Equity Multiples

When valuing equity directly, the numerator of the market multiple is the market value of common equity, often simply referred to as "price." This may be expressed on the basis of the aggregate value of the common stock outstanding or on the basis of a per share value. Of course, the financial fundamental in the denominator must be expressed on the same basis.

Since the numerator is the market value of common equity, the denominator used to create the multiple must consist of returns at the common equity level (after deductions for interest and preferred dividends). To recap from Chapter 14, the denominators typically used for equity valuation multiples include the following:

- **Sales.** One should be careful using a multiple of sales for an equity valuation because:
  - It may be distorted due to different degrees of leverage among companies.
  - Used by itself, there is an implicit assumption that the subject and guideline companies have similar cost structures, which may or may not be true. (If earnings data are available for the guideline companies, the price-to-sales multiple can, and should be, adjusted to reflect differences in the companies' cost structures.)
  - It may be more appropriate for a control basis valuation than for a minority valuation on the theory that a control buyer may be able to bring the cost structure into line with industry averages after acquiring the customer base.

  - If sales is used in the denominator of an equity multiple (that is, stock price to sales), the level of the multiple should be justified by references to the relative return on sales between the subject and the guideline companies.
- **Gross cash flow (often just called *cash flow*).** The net income plus noncash charges is particularly helpful if the subject and guideline company have significantly different depreciation accounting policies.
- **Pretax income (net income before taxes).** Price-to-earnings ratios for public companies are reported on an after-tax basis. Be careful that the analyst has not used an after-tax P/E ratio and applied it to pretax earnings (a common error).
- **Dividends or withdrawals.** When valuing a controlling interest, the focus usually is on the capacity to pay dividends or withdrawals. However, when valuing a minority interest, the focus usually is on actual dividends or withdrawals since the minority owner cannot cause more to be paid.
- **Book value of equity.** Same comments apply as for the book value of invested capital.
- **Adjusted book value.** Same comments apply as for the adjusted book value of invested capital.

Time Periods for Company Financial Statement Data

Unless there is some special reason, balance sheet data normally should be the latest available as of the valuation date. However, if using guideline public company data, there usually are many options as to the possible time periods for income data:

- Latest fiscal year
- Latest 12 months
- Some number of years' simple average (such as 3, 5, 7, or 10 years, with 5 years the most common)

- Some number of years' weighted average (usually weighting the latest years based more on the theory that the most current results should be the most representative of future expectations)
- Estimates for the coming year (available for earnings, but generally not for other income variables, for several thousand public companies)

It is important that the time periods for which the guideline public company data are computed are the same as those used for the subject company. If the subject company had drastic changes in its operations (such as major new or discontinued product lines), it may be appropriate to go back only as far as the latest major change. The reviewer should be satisfied that the rationale for the time period or periods chosen makes sense in terms of developing a reasonable value for the subject by reference to the guideline companies.

If one is using sales of private companies for guideline multiples, usually only the latest year's data prior to the private company sale are available. While this is a limitation, it is often the case that the private companies sold were much more comparable to the subject than any public companies that may exist.

Criteria for Selecting Guideline Companies

One succinct quote summarizes the essence of the key characteristic that should be present in a guideline company:

> Do the underlying economics driving this comparable company match those that drive our company?[2]

In Revenue Ruling 59-60, the Internal Revenue Service (one of the strongest proponents of the guideline public company method) makes the following observation:

> Although the only restrictive requirement as to comparable corporations specified in the statute is that their lines of business be the same or similar, . . . it is obvious that consideration must be given to other relevant factors in order that the most valid comparison possible will be obtained.[3]

The most obvious criterion for comparability is the line of business. The next important criterion is (depending on circumstances) probably the markets served. For example, in valuing a manufacturer of electrical controls for sawmills, the most important criterion might not be manufacturers of electrical controls but manufacturers of equipment used in the forest products industry. In *Estate of Gallo*[4] (E.&J.Gallo Winery), in the absence of wine producers, appraisers on both sides expanded the line of business criteria to include brewers, distillers, soft-drink bottlers, and major consumer brand agricultural food producers. The tax court accepted this procedure.

Other criteria may include the following:

- Size
- Comparability of earnings patterns
- Position in industry
- Capital structure
- Maturity of company

One thing that all the selection criteria have in common is that they attempt to identify companies that are subject to the same risk factors as the subject company.

Once in a while the analyst has the luxury of lots of available guideline companies and can narrow the selection down to a few that are the most similar. More often it is necessary to broaden the criteria.

As noted earlier, it is useful to the reader of the valuation report if the appraiser states the criteria used and demonstrates that all companies that met the criteria were used, or if not, why certain ones that would appear to meet the criteria were rejected.

How Many Guideline Companies?

The more detailed and reliable the data for each company and the more similar the guideline companies are to the subject company, the fewer companies are needed. With public company data or with detailed private company data, analysts usually are comfortable with five to seven companies and sometimes as few as three.

However, in *Estate of Hall*[5] (Hallmark greeting cards), the tax court rejected a valuation based entirely on the only other good public company at the time, American Greetings, and accepted the analysis of a broad group of high market share consumer goods, such as Parker Pens. If there is only one excellent guideline company, the analyst certainly should use it, but generally he or she should not rely on it entirely.

Example of How to Develop Guideline Company Market Multiples

Exhibit 16.2 shows financial data for Marvel Corporation, selected as a guideline public company. Exhibit 16.3 develops four invested capital multiples for Marvel Corporation, using the information from Exhibit 16.2. Exhibit 16.4 develops five equity valuation multiples for Marvel Corporation, also using the information from Exhibit 16.2.

Deciding Where Subject Company Multiples Should Fall Relative to Observed Ranges

The appraiser will have developed valuation multiples for several guideline companies in the same manner as illustrated previously for the

Exhibit 16.2
Marvel Corporation Financial Data

Marvel Corporation Balance Sheet Assets

Current assets		
Cash		$ 1,500,000
Accounts receivable		2,500,000
Inventory		5,000,000
Total current assets		$ 9,000,000
Plant and equipment		
At cost	$24,000,000	
Less: accumulated depreciation	$20,000,000	
Net plant and equipment		4,000,000
Total assets		$13,000,000

Liabilities and Equity

Current liabilities		
accounts payable		$ 3,000,000
Long-term debt (including current portion)		6,000,000
Total liabilities		$ 9,000,000
Common equity (4,000,000 shares outstanding)	4,000,000	
Total liabilities and equity		$13,000,000

Marvel Corporation Income Statement

Sales	$40,000,000
Cost of goods sold	26,000,000
Gross margin	$14,000,000
Selling, general, and administrative expenses	10,000,000
Operating income, before taxes	$ 4,000,000
Interest expense	480,000
Income before taxes	$ 3,520,000
Income taxes	1,408,000
Net income	$ 2,112,000

Marvel Corporation Other Financial Data

The following data are derived from the statement of cash flows, footnotes to financial statements, and other available data:

1. The interest rate on the long-term debt is 8%.
2. The selling, general, and administrative expenses include depreciation of $1,000,000.
3. The market value of debt is about the same as the book value of debt.
4. The market price of the stock as of the valuation date is $6 per share.
5. The consensus forecast is that sales and earnings will grow at about 12% per year.

Exhibit 16.3

Marvel Corporation Invested Capital Valuation Multiples

Market Value of Invested Capital (MVIC)

Long-term debt	$6,000,000	20%
Equity: 4,000,000 shares @ $6	24,000,000	80%
Market value of invested capital	$30,000,000	100%

MVIC/Sales

$$\frac{\text{MVIC}}{\text{Sales}} = \frac{\$30{,}000{,}000}{\$40{,}000{,}000} = 0.75$$

MVIC/EBITDA

Operating income before taxes (pretax income plus interest expense)	$4,000,000
Plus: depreciation	1,000,000
Earnings before interest, taxes, depreciation, and amortization	$5,000,000

$$\frac{\text{MVIC}}{\text{EBITDA}} = \frac{\$30{,}000{,}000}{\$5{,}000{,}000} = 6.00$$

MVIC/EBIT

Operating income before taxes (pretax income plus interest expense)	$4,000,000

$$\frac{\text{MVIC}}{\text{EBIT}} = \frac{\$30{,}000{,}000}{\$4{,}000{,}000} = 7.50$$

MVIC/Book Value of Invested Capital

Book value of long-term debt	$ 6,000,000
Book value of equity	4,000,000
Book value of invested capital	$10,000,000

$$\frac{\text{MVIC}}{\text{BV of invested capital}} = \frac{\$30{,}000{,}000}{\$10{,}000{,}000} = 3.00$$

Marvel Corporation. For each variable, the appraiser must select a multiple to apply to the subject company's counterpart financial variable. An important step in evaluating the work of the appraiser is to evaluate how the multiple to be applied to each subject company financial variable was selected.

Exhibit 16.4
Marvel Corporation Common Equity Valuation Multiples

Note: When valuing equity directly, these multiples often are presented on a per share basis. The multiple should be exactly the same whether computed on a per share or aggregate common equity basis.

Market Value of Equity ("Price")

4,000,000 shares × $6 per share = $24,000,000

Price/Sales (Price/Revenue)

$$\frac{\text{Price}}{\text{Sales}} = \frac{\$24{,}000{,}000}{\$40{,}000{,}000} = 0.60$$

Price/Cash Flow (Price/Gross Cash Flow)

	Net income	$2,112,000
Plus:	Depreciation	1,000,000
	Cash flow (gross)	$3,112,000

$$\frac{\text{Price}}{\text{Cash flow}} = \frac{\$24{,}000{,}000}{\$3{,}112{,}000} = 7.71$$

Price/Pretax Income (Price/Pretax Earnings)

$$\frac{\text{Price}}{\text{Pretax income}} = \frac{\$24{,}000{,}000}{\$3{,}520{,}000} = 6.82$$

Price/Earnings (Price/Net Income)

$$\frac{\text{Price}}{\text{Net income}} = \frac{\$24{,}000{,}000}{\$2{,}112{,}000} = 11.36$$

Note: The term price-to-earnings (P/E) ratio, as used in the daily financial press, stock reporting services, and corporate finance, means the price to net income *after* taxes. A common error is to apply the P/E ratio to pretax income. The only condition under which this is justifiable is where it can be assumed that the effective tax rate is zero.

Price/Book Value

$$\frac{\text{Price}}{\text{Book value of equity}} = \frac{\$24{,}000{,}000}{\$4{,}000{,}000} = 6.00$$

The Relationship Between the Market Multiples and the Capitalization Rates Should Be Evaluated

A *multiple* in the market approach is like a *capitalization rate* in the income approach. A multiple is actually the reciprocal of a capitalization rate. That is, 1 divided by the multiple equals the capitalization rate. Conversely, 1 divided by the capitalization rate equals the multiple.

To illustrate, assume the following:

Guideline company price	$20 per share
Guideline company earnings	$ 1 per share

To compute the guideline company price-to-earnings multiple, one divides the price by the earnings:

Formula 16.1

$$\frac{\text{Price}}{\text{Earnings}} = \frac{\$20}{\$1} = 20$$

To convert the P/E multiple to a capitalization rate applicable to net income, one divides 1 by the P/E multiple:

Formula 16.2

$$\text{Cap rate} = \frac{1}{20} = 0.05$$

To convert the capitalization rate to a multiple, one divides 1 by the capitalization rate:

$$\text{P/E multiple} = \frac{1}{0.05} = 20$$

Multiplying by the P/E multiple or dividing by the capitalization rate should lead to the same result. For instance, if earnings equal $10 million, the value of the company will be $10 × 20 = $200 million, or $10/0.05 = $200 million.

The level of the multiple depends largely on two factors: *expected growth* and *risk*. In the income approach, the respective factors of risk and expected growth were quantified individually. However, in the market approach, multiples for company variables are observed in the market—that is, computed from market transaction data—and it is not possible to determine exactly how much any given company's multiple for any variable was influenced by expected growth and how much by perceived risk. Comparative analysis between the guideline and subject companies cannot separate these factors completely, but it can give some useful clues.

Multiples Selected Should Be Based on Comparative Analysis

Each multiple selected should be based on comparative analysis between the subject company and the guideline companies. This usually involves some combination of quantitative and qualitative analysis:

- **Quantitative analysis**. Exhibit 16.5 is a somewhat abbreviated example of typical comparative quantitative analysis.
- **Qualitative analysis.** Most of the qualitative factors the analyst would consider are those that bear on assessing risk. Just as higher risk requires a higher discount rate or capitalization rate in the income approach, higher risk augers for lower multiples in the market approach. Some of the common comparative qualitative factors to consider include the following:
  - Depth of management
  - Concentration versus breadth of customer base
  - Concentration versus breadth of product or service base
  - Concentration versus breadth of geographical operations
  - Comparative cost structure (Make sure, however, that the analyst has not double-counted this both here and in the quantitative analysis.)
  - Other effects of difference in size, such as buying power, supplier dependence, affordability of advertising, and similar factors[6]

Having done a careful comparative analysis, the expert may conclude the subject company is so comparable to the average of the guideline companies that every multiple for every variable should be

Exhibit 16.5

Widget Corporation and Guideline Companies Comparative Financial Analysis

Ratio	Marvel	Neon	Optimal	Premier	Quartz	Range	Median	Widget	Comment
Return on equity	0.528	0.150	0.700	0.300	0.900	0.150–0.900	0.528	0.700	Above median, but range very wide
Return on invested capital	0.240	0.100	0.400	0.200	0.500	0.100–0.500	0.240	0.228	Near median, but range very wide
Return on sales	0.053	0.030	0.080	0.090	0.040	0.030–0.090	0.053	0.070	Above median
Long-term debt to total capital (at book value)	0.60	0.67	0.032	0.40	0.50	0.32–0.67	0.50	0.75	Highly leveraged, above top of range
Current ratio	3.0	4.0	3.5	2.5	2.0	2.0–4.0	3.0	3.0	At median
Quick ratio	1.3	2.0	1.8	1.0	0.8	0.8–2.0	1.3	1.5	Near median
Times interest earned (EBIT/ interest expense)	8.3	2.0	9.8	5.0	4.0	2.0–9.8	5.0	2.3	Near bottom of range

Note: Ratio definitions and computations for the Widget Corporation are shown in Chapter 14, "Overview of Approaches, Methods, Procedures, and Terminology."

the median as observed among the guideline companies. If so, the expert should say so (not just apply median or average multiples without comment). More often than not, however, based on the comparative analysis, the expert will differentiate the subject from the guideline companies to result in a departure from average multiples for one or more variables. Reasons for selection of each multiple should be noted.

In some cases, the comparative financial analysis may indicate that the subject company is most like one, two, or a few of the guideline companies. In that case, the analyst may choose multiples close to those of the companies that appear to be more comparable to the subject than others.

Different Multiples May Be Higher or Lower Relative to Guideline Companies

We noted earlier that expected growth and risk are the two most important determinants of what multiple should be chosen for the subject company relative to the guideline companies, at least with respect to many of the variables. For example, higher leverage and lower coverage of interest obligations would be indications of higher risk.

These differences between the subject and guideline companies may lead to reductions of average multiples, the differentials chosen are sometimes referred to as *fundamental discounts*.

However, criteria for the selection of multiples may be influenced by factors other than just expected growth and risk. For example, price-to-sales multiples are heavily influenced by the return on sales. This is only logical since a company that earns more per dollar of sales is likely to sell for more per dollar of sales. Similarly, the return on invested capital and the return on equity influence the MVIC to book value of invested capital and the price to book value of equity valuation multiples. This also is logical because a company that earns more per dollar of book value is likely to sell for more per dollar of book value. Therefore, for example, a company with a very low return on equity may be operating very conservatively with a low degree of risk and deserve higher than average multiples for some or all income variables but a below average price-to-book value ratio.

Relative Weights to Accord Various Multiples

Some valuation multiples are clearly more important for some industries than for others. For example, the values of financial assets are very important for valuing financial institutions, whereas the asset values may have very little relevance for most service businesses and professional practices.

One clue to the relative importance of different valuation multiples in any given industry is the degree of central tendency versus dispersion of the multiples observed in the market for that industry. If multiples for a certain variable cluster in a narrow range, that tends to indicate that pricing of companies in that industry tends to depend more on that financial variable than on others. On the other hand, a very wide dispersion among observed multiples suggests that the particular multiple is not very important in that industry.

On the other hand, multiples with wide dispersions can be used if they can be explained. For example, a wide dispersion of price to book value often reflects a wide dispersion of return on equity. In this case, the multiple can be used if it reflects the level of the subject's return on equity relative to the guideline companies.

Another judgmental factor is the available data. If data to compute certain valuation multiples are not available for several companies among those chosen, the analyst may choose to put less weight on that valuation measure even if it might be considered more important if it were available for more companies.

Also, multiples for certain variables may be accorded little or no weight if they appear to be not very meaningful. For example, if an industry had such a bad year that earnings tended to be minimal, resulting in atypical P/E ratios, the P/E ratio on that year's earnings may be accorded no weight.

Example of a Valuation by Market Approach

Using the data from Exhibits 16.3 through 16.5, Exhibit 16.6 develops invested capital multiples to apply to Widget Corporation. Exhibit 16.7 develops an indicated value for the Widget Corporation using the invested capital procedure. Exhibit 16.8 develops equity multiples to apply to Widget Corporation.

Exhibit 16.9 develops an indicated value directly for Widget Corporation's equity. In this illustration, the rationale for the analyst's various choices is indicated briefly in the footnotes to the tables. In most reports, the rationale would be explained more fully in the text, exploring underlying relationships and explaining reasons for the appraiser's judgment. For example, while dispersion of observed multiples for the guideline companies is a useful quantitative observation, the analytical reasoning and judgment applied may be more important in assigning weights to variables in many cases.

Exhibit 16.6
Widget Corporation Guideline Company Invested Capital Multiples

	Market Value of Invested Capital (MVIC) to			
	Sales	**EBITDA**	**EBIT**	**Book Value**
Marvel	0.75	6.00	7.50	3.00
Neon	0.40	5.00	6.20	1.50
Optimal	0.80	5.50	6.90	6.00
Premier	0.90	6.00	8.00	2.00
Quartz	0.60	4.80	5.00	7.00
Mean	0.69	5.46	6.72	3.90
Median	0.75	5.50	6.90	3.00
Range	0.40–0.90	4.80–6.00	5.00–8.00	1.50–7.00
Coefficient of variation	0.283	.102	.175	.631
Multiple selected	0.80[a]	5.50[b]	6.90[c]	3.00[d]

Notes:

[a] Above the median because Widget's return on sales is above the median (Exhibit 16.5).

[b] At the median—Widget is quite comparable to the group.

[c] At the median—Widget is quite comparable to the group.

[d] At the median because Widget's return on invested capital is near the median (Exhibit 16.5).

Exhibit 16.7
Widget Corporation Valuation Using Invested Capital Multiples

	Sales	EBITDA	EBIT	Book Value	Weighted Value of Invested Capital
Widget Corporation fundamental (as computed for Widget Corporation in Chapter 14)	$10,000,000	$1,550,000	$1,300,000	$4,000,000	
Selected multiple (from Exhibit 16.6)	× 0.80	× 5.50	× 6.90	× 3.00	
Indicated value	$8,000,000	$8,525,000	$8,970,000	$12,000,000	
Weight	× 0.20[a]	× 0.50[b]	× 0.30[c]	× 0[d]	
Weighted value	$1,600,000	+ $4,262,500		+ $2,691,000	= $8,553,500
Less: long-term debt					3,000,000
Indicated value of common equity					$5,553,500

Notes:

[a] Deserves some consideration, but profitability ratios more important.

[b] Lowest coefficient variation (Exhibit 16.6)—the variable the industry considers most important.

[c] Next lowest coefficient (Exhibit 16.6).

[d] No weight. Coefficient of variation very wide, likely because of differences in historical costs and depreciation.

The various multiples within each group (invested capital and equity) produced similar results, but the direct equity procedure produced significantly higher values. The reason is that the company has benefited from a considerably higher degree of leverage than the guideline companies. Perhaps this risk should be reflected by equity multiples having greater discounts from the guideline medians than were actually used. The analyst in this case was cautiously optimistic and valued the equity at $5.7 million on the basis of a continued good outlook for the company. This value was based on an equal weighting

Exhibit 16.8
Widget Corporation Guideline Company Equity Multiples

	Market Value of Equity to				
	Sales	Cash Flow	Pretax Income	Net Income	Book Value
Marvel	0.60	7.71	6.82	11.36	6.00
Neon	0.30	6.20	5.52	7.78	2.50
Optimal	0.70	7.29	6.21	8.63	7.21
Premier	0.75	8.13	7.04	9.86	2.92
Quartz	0.50	6.83	4.55	6.28	7.50
Mean	0.57	7.23	6.03	8.78	5.23
Median	0.60	7.29	6.21	8.63	6.00
Range	0.30–75	6.2–8.13	4.55–7.04	6.28–11.36	2.5–7.5
Coefficient variation	0.314	0.104	0.169	0.221	0.453
Multiples selected	0.65[a]	7.0[b]	5.8[b]	7.5[b]	7.0[c]

Notes:
[a] Above the median because the Widget return on sales is above median (Exhibit 16.5).
[b] Slightly below the median because of the slightly higher risk (Exhibit 16.5).
[c] Above the median because of the above-average return on equity (Exhibit 16.5).

of the two indications of value from the equity and the invested capital procedures.

Prior Transactions, Offers, and Buy-Sell Agreements

In the following sections, we discuss the impact of considering prior transactions, offers to buy, and buy-sell agreements on the market approach because they sometimes provide some market evidence of value, and to some extent, they may be analyzed using some of the methods in the market approach.

Arm's-Length Negotiations

Whether considering a transaction, an offer, or an agreement, the first question is whether the indication of value it represented was negotiated on an arm's-length basis.

Exhibit 16.9
Widget Corporation Valuation Using Equity Multiples

	Sales	Cash Flow	Pretax Income	Net Income	Book Value	Weighted Value
Widget Corporation fundamental (as computed for Widget in Chapter 16)	$10,000,000	$ 950,000	$1,000,000	$ 700,000	$1,000,000	
Selected multiple (from Exhibit 16.8)	× 0.65	× 7.0	× 5.8	× 7.5	× 7.0	
Indicated value	$ 6,500,000	$6,650,000	$5,800,000	$5,250,000	$7,000,000	
Weight	× 0.20[a]	× 0.50[b]	× 0.15[c]	× 0.15[d]	× 0[e]	
Weighted value	$ 1,300,000	+ $3,325,000	+ $ 870,000	+ $ 787,500		= $6,282,500

Notes:

[a] Deserves some consideration, but profitability ratios are more important (also, the multiple of sales is considered in invested capital ratios where it may be a more meaningful multiple).

[b] Lowest coefficient of variation—clearly the variable the industry considers most important; similar to EBITDA in invested capital ratios.

[c and d] Approximately the industry average effective tax rates and equal coefficients of variation, so equal weight to each but combined, less than cash flow.

[e] Very wide coefficient of variation reflecting greatly different leverage and historical cost bases—not a good comparison with guideline companies.

If the negotiation was among unrelated parties, it usually is assumed to be at arm's length. Even among related parties, investigation may lead to the conclusion that there was an arm's-length negotiation, but ascertaining this may be problematic. If the degree of arm's-length negotiation cannot be ascertained, a valuation analyst may make a judgment as to whether or not it represented the fair market value at the time, in which case one can conclude that the parameters are controlling or at least useful guidance for valuation in the current transaction.

Prior Transactions

If reasonably arm's length, the prior transactions may be one of the best guides to market value. Such transactions may include the following:

- A prior purchase or sale of the entire company
- Sales of minority ownership interests
- Acquisitions of subsidiary companies by the subject company

Any such transactions can be analyzed to determine the valuation multiples discussed in this chapter that the transactions represented at the time. The relevance of the actual transaction should be judged based on the time since the transaction and the changes to the company, industry, and economy. Adjustments to the actual multiples should be made if appropriate based on changes in market conditions.

Offers to Buy

If the company received a bona fide offer to buy, it can be analyzed in the same way as a prior transaction. Such bona fide offers that can be used in this manner do occur, but they are rare and should be thoroughly investigated.

Inquiries about buying companies typically don't reach the stage of a bona fide offer that is never consummated. Even if an offer appears bona fide on the surface, inquiries should be made regarding escape clauses and prospective price changes based on due diligence and whether the buyer was legitimately willing and able to complete the transaction.

Buy-Sell Agreements

One of the most frequent controversies is the extent to which an existing buy-sell agreement should control or influence the value for any given transaction. This may ultimately be a legal determination, based on the purpose of the appraisal. For example, the buy-sell value may not be controlling for estate taxes if it fails to meet certain criteria, even though it is binding on the estate. In marital dissolutions, most courts have great discretion as to how much weight, if any, to accord the buy-sell agreement. One needs to refer to pertinent case law.

Alternative Definitions of Market Value in Some Fair Value Cases

In cases determining fair value for dissenting stockholder and minority oppression suits, courts tend to look at income value, asset value, and market value. In some cases, what they consider market value may be based only on past transactions.

If this is the case, then the multiples of income statement variables derived from the guideline public company method would be subsumed under the income value, and multiples of asset variables would be considered under the asset value.

References

Basic Market Approach

Fishman, Jay, et al. 2015. "Valuation Methods Based on Comparative Company Data." In *PPC's Guide to Business Valuations*. Ft. Worth, TX: Practioners Publishing Company, pp. 6-1 to 6-61.

Hitchner, James R. 2011. *Financial Valuation: Applications and Models*, 3rd ed. Hoboken, NJ: Wiley.

Pratt, Shannon P., and Alina V. Niculita. 2007. "Market Approach: Guideline Publicly Traded Company Method" and "Market Approach: Guideline Merged and Acquired Company Method." In *Valuing a Business*, 5th ed. New York: McGraw_Hill, pp. 261–330. Both chapters include a bibliography.

Trugman, Gary. 2003. "Guideline Public Company Method-Control or Minority Value?" *Shannon Pratt's Business Valuation Update*, December.

Private Company Sale Databases

Bizcomps, Post Office Box 97757, Las Vegas, NV 89193. (858) 457-0366. Provides price-to-sales and price-to-discretionary earnings ratios; average transactions over $400,000. Available online at www.BVResources.com.

Done Deals, Thomson PPC, Post Office Box 966, Fort Worth, TX 76101-0966. (800) 323-8724. Provides price-to-assets ratios, book value of equity figures, revenues, net income, and cash from operations; transactions $1 million to $1 billion, with about 79 percent of the selling companies' being privately owned.

IBA Market Database, Institute of Business Appraisers, Post Office Box 17410, Plantation, FL 33318. (954) 584-1144. Provides price-to-sales and price-to-discretionary earnings ratios; mostly small businesses and professional practices.

Pratt's Stats, Business Valuation Resources, 1000 SW Broadway, Suite 1200, Portland, OR 97205. (888) 287-8258. Provides six invested capital multiples already computed and information for most companies to compute all market valuation ratios discussed in this chapter; transaction sizes $50,000 to $16 billion. Available online at www.BVResources.com.

Public Company Transaction and Sale Data

Public company data fall into two categories, each of which has readily available sources of information far too extensive to list here:

- **Publicly traded securities.** There are over 20,000 publicly traded operating companies, the majority of which report data electronically to the Securities and Exchange Commission via the Electronic Data Gathering and Retrieval (EDGAR) system. This is accessible for free to the public. In addition, there are many services that publish summaries of the data filed, both electronically and in print, including Public Stats by Business Valuation Resources, Compustat and other Standard & Poor's products, Factiva, Mergent (previously Moody's), and Thomson Financial.
- **Acquisitions of public companies.** Several hundred public companies are acquired or "go private" every year. They are required to file the details of the transactions with the SEC, and those filings are also available for free to the public through EDGAR. In addition, many services publish summaries of such transaction data, including Mergerstat's *FactSet*, Business Valuation Resources' *Mergerstate/BVU's Control Premium Study*, and Thomson Financial's *SDC Platinum*. Details of the many information sources for publicly traded company data, public company acquisition, and going-private data are available in the *Business Valuation Directory*, published annually by Business Valuation Resources (BVR).

Chapter 17

The Asset-Based Approach

Basic Concept of the Asset-Based Approach

The basic concept of the asset-based approach is that if all the company's assets and liabilities are revalued to current values, then the difference between the assets and liabilities should equal the value of the equity.

The asset-based approach is generally assumed to produce a control basis value. From this value, if one is valuing a minority interest, it may be appropriate to adjust for factors such as minority interest and lack of marketability. If one is valuing a controlling interest, it may or may not be appropriate to deduct a discount for lack of marketability, although it would be a smaller discount than for a minority interest.

Discrete Versus Collective Revaluation

If each asset and liability is individually identified and valued, that method may be described differently using such terms as the *net asset value* (NAV) *method, adjusted net worth method, adjusted book value method, asset buildup method,* or *asset accumulation method.* For the purpose of this chapter, we will refer to the discrete revaluation of all assets as the *adjusted net asset value* (ANAV) *method.* The premise of value may be either going concern or liquidation.

In the collective revaluation of assets, the tangible assets, or at least the preponderance of them, are usually adjusted to current values, as discussed in subsequent sections of this chapter. The intangibles are then valued collectively by capitalizing any amount of return that the company achieves over and above a fair return on the tangible assets at their current values.[1] This method is called the *excess earnings method,* which assumes a going-concern premise of value.

In some cases, only a partial revaluation of assets is practical. There are too many variations on this possibility to go into details, and the reviewer is left to make the judgment as to whether the conclusions reached in a particular appraisal are adequately supported.

Steps in the Adjusted Net Asset Value Method

The five basic steps are as follows:

1. **Obtain or develop an accrual basis balance sheet.** If the entity does its accounting on a generally accepted accounting principles (GAAP) basis, developing this balance sheet requires only those adjustments necessary to conform to GAAP. If the company does its accounting on a cash basis, then adjustments to the accrual basis are necessary.
2. **Determine which assets and liabilities on the GAAP basis balance sheet require revaluation.**
3. **Identify any off–balance sheet actual or contingent assets or liabilities.** This could be an unlimited list, but some of the more common items include these:
   - Assets fully depreciated but still in service
   - Inventory or accounts receivable written off by accounting policy but still salable or collectible
   - Intellectual property developed internally and therefore expensed instead of capitalized
   - Workforce in place, systems, and similar elements of "going-concern value"
   - Goodwill

- Expected proceeds or costs related to existing or potential lawsuits
- Environmental liabilities
- Liability for corporate capital gains taxes on appreciated assets[2]

4. **Value the items identified in steps 2 and 3.** This may require appraisals by asset appraisers because appraising real estate and/or machinery and equipment would not be a skill possessed by most business appraisers.
5. **Construct a market value–based balance sheet using the adjusted values.** The net result of this should be the market value of the equity. In other words, the difference between the market value of the assets and the market value of the liabilities equals the market value of the equity.

Valuation Premises for Adjusting Balance Sheet Values

Generally speaking, each item will be valued on one of the following four premises of value:

1. **Value in continued use, as part of a going concern.** This usually means either *used-replacement cost*, including installation, or *replacement cost new* less depreciation, amortization, and/or adjustments for obsolescence.
2. **Value in place, as part of a mass assemblage of assets.** This would generally be used for a manufacturing plant in working order but not currently operating due to market conditions, bankruptcy, or any other reasons.
3. **Value in exchange, in an orderly liquidation.** This may be appropriate for all assets if an orderly liquidation is contemplated for the entire company. If the company is being valued as a going concern, an orderly liquidation premise may be appropriate for nonoperating or excess assets.

4. **Value in exchange, in a forced liquidation.** This may be appropriate if, for example, it was assumed that the assets would be sold piecemeal at auction.

Example of an Adjusted Net Asset Value Calculation

Exhibit 17.1 shows an example of an adjusted balance sheet resulting in an adjusted net asset value. There would be an explanation in either the

Exhibit 17.1
Alpha Company Adjusted Net Asset Value

Assets	**As Reported**	**Adjustments**	**As Adjusted**
Cash and marketable securities	$100,000	$ 30,000[a]	$130,000
Inventory	200,000	50,000[b]	250,000
Total current assets	$300,000		$380,000
Property and equipment	70,000		70,000
Land held for expansion	150,000	100,000[c]	250,000
Total assets	$520,000		$700,000
Liabilities & Equity			
Accounts payable	$ 50,000		$ 50,000
Long-term debt	200,000	−20,000[d]	180,000
Corporate taxes	______	30,000[e]	30,000
Total liabilities	$250,000		$260,000
Stockholders' equity	270,000		440,000
Total liabilities and equity	$520,000		$700,000

[a] To adjust to market prices as of the effective valuation date
[b] To adjust from LIFO to FIFO cost basis as of the effective valuation date
[c] To adjust land to appraised market value as of the effective valuation date
[d] To reduce the value of the long-term debt (with interest rate of 8%) to current market value (in light of current market interest rate of 10% on other comparable debt)
[e] To record the corporate tax liability on the difference between the assets' cost basis and current market value

text or footnotes for each item added to the balance sheet or adjusted from its original balance sheet value.

Breakup Value

Some companies may have two or more operating entities and possibly some nonoperating assets. The stock market tends to value such companies at less than the total of the value of each operating company plus the nonoperating assets.

In considering a possible acquisition of such a company, the acquirer might like to estimate what could be realized by selling each of the operating companies and the nonoperating assets separately. This is called the *breakup value.*

Studies have shown that conglomerates tend to sell at a discount of about 15 percent from their breakup values. Investors seem to prefer a "pure play" in an industry over a package of dissimilar companies or assets. One variation on the asset approach is to estimate a company's breakup value.

When Asset-Based Methods Are Used

The net asset value method is not used very often for valuation of operating entities, particularly in minority interest appraisals. The focus for operating entities tends to be more on the income approach, the market approach, or the excess earnings method.

However, there are a number of situations in which the courts do reach a valuation conclusion either entirely or partially on valuation by the asset-based approach. These may include but are not limited to the following:

- Start-up companies
- Holding companies, financial institutions, agricultural businesses, and other asset-intensive businesses

- Marital estate valuations of companies or practices in which all goodwill is personal and the state's case law does not consider personal goodwill a marital asset
- Companies that may not be financially viable as operating companies

For example, in one marital dissolution, the husband owned two start-up companies. The husband's lawyer moved to strike the testimony of the wife's expert, who used the discounted cash flow method even though the projections had been made by the husband. The trial court granted the motion and was upheld on appeal "because the expert's projections and opinion were overly speculative and by implication, unreliable," leaving only the testimony on asset value on which the trial court had based its conclusion.[3]

References

Fishman, Jay, et al. 2015. "Underlying Assets Methods," "Net Asset Value Method," and "Liquidation Value Method." In *PPC's Guide to Business Valuations.* Practitioners Publishing, Ft. Worth, TX pp. 7-1 to 7-18.

Hitchner, James R. 2011. "Asset Approach" (ch. 7). In *Financial Valuation: Applications and Models*, 3rd ed., Wiley, New York, pp. 309–364.

Pratt, Shannon P., and Alina V. Niculita. 2007. "Asset-Based Approach: Asset Accumulation Method." In *Valuing a Business*, 5th ed., McGraw-Hill, New York, pp. 349–380.

Trugman, Gary. 2012. "The Asset-Based Approach." In *Understanding Business Valuation*, 4th ed., American Institute of Certified Public Accountants, New York, pp. 387–408.

Chapter 18

Rules of Thumb

Rules of thumb should hardly ever be relied on as a primary appraisal method. Having said that, if there are valuation rules of thumb for an industry, especially if they are widely recognized, they can be useful in a number of ways: as a "sanity check" on a valuation arrived at through other methods; as a means to estimate a ballpark range of value; and within certain industries and in certain litigation contexts, as supporting evidence in court.

Rules of thumb are often classified within the market approach to business valuation because they are thought to have their origins in transactions in the industry. However, their actual origins can vary from pure folklore to (rarely) actual transaction studies.

Speaking to the relationship between rules of thumb and valuations, long-time appraiser Glenn Desmond cautions that valuations change over time in response to changing economic and industry conditions. Furthermore, at any given time, valuations may vary considerably from one locale to another.[1]

The General Nature of Rules of Thumb

Rules of thumb are usually expressed as multipliers. The most common is a multiple of revenues, such as "Many accounting practices sell for 0.75 to 1.25 times annual revenues." The other popular multiple for rules of thumb is a multiple of *discretionary earnings*, also called the *seller's discretionary cash flow* (SDCF), or *owner's cash flow* (OCF), earnings that may be defined, in certain applications, to reflect earnings of a business enterprise prior to the following items: income taxes, non-operating income and expenses, nonrecurring income and expenses, depreciation and amortization, interest expense or income, and the owner's total compensation for those services which could be provided by a sole owner-manager.[2]

Occasionally, one finds rules of thumb relating to some measure of physical volume. For example, a rule of thumb for taverns might be so many dollars for each keg of beer sold per month. Both the cable and cellular phone industries have been valued at *X* dollars per actual and/or potential subscriber.

To the extent that rules of thumb are used, they usually apply to small businesses and professional practices. They generally assume that the sale of the business would be on an asset basis rather than on a stock basis. It is generally assumed that the rule represents the transfer of the operating tangible and intangible assets but not the real estate or the current assets or liabilities (for example, cash, accounts receivable, inventory, or accounts payable). Often a *covenant not to compete* is included, and sometimes an employment agreement. A major problem with rules of thumb is that they are not clear as to exactly what business assets they purport to represent. Furthermore, they do nothing to deal with the essential valuation factors of relative risk and growth prospects.

Rules of Thumb are Not Cash Equivalent Prices

The rule of thumb values are intended to indicate face values of transactions, not necessarily (or even usually) cash equivalent values. That is, most of the businesses are sold on terms and not for cash. Normally, the seller receives a note for the balance, usually at a rate of interest below market rates for comparable credits and sometimes including contingencies. Thus, if such rules or transactions are used to develop fair market value (which assumes cash equivalency, as discussed in Chapter 13), adjustments need to be made accordingly.

Rule-of-Thumb Examples

Tom West's *The Business Reference Guide* includes an entire section on rules of thumb. Some of these rules of thumb, which are stated in terms of multiples of revenue, are shown in Exhibit 18.1. However, West also includes rules based on other parameters, particularly multiples of discretionary earnings (see Chapter 16 on the market approach).

Another source of rules of thumb is *101+ Practical Solutions for the Family Lawyer*, in which Harriet Cohen presents rules of thumb for valuing several types of businesses and professional practices.[3]

Checking Alleged Rules of Thumb Against Actual Transactions

If one wants to check an alleged rule of thumb against actual transactions, there are three databases that report ratios of price to discretionary earnings, as well as price to revenues, for actual completed sales of businesses. These are Bizcomps, the IBA Market Database, and Pratt's Stats. The last named also indicates whether a covenant not to compete or an employment agreement was involved, and if so, how much value was allocated to it. These databases are listed in the references at the end of the chapter.

Exhibit 18.1 includes data on multiples of revenue derived from actual transactions from the Pratt's Stats and Bizcomps databases. As can be seen from the exhibit, the actual multiples diverge quite a bit from the rules of thumb, proving that rules of thumb are not very reliable.

It is important to recognize that these rules of thumb and the transaction prices shown in both Pratt's Stats and Bizcomps represent face values of transactions, not cash equivalent values. They usually include

Exhibit 18.1
Rules of Thumb for Valuation

Occupation	2014 Business Reference Guide[a]	Actual Transactions from Pratt's Stats[b]	Actual Transactions from Bizcomps[c]
Accounting firms	75–125% of annual revenues *or* 9–15 times monthly net sales *or* 2–5 times the seller's SDE	Range: 56–161% m = 1.07 me = 1.06	Range: 37–132% m = 0.93 me = 1.00
Auto repair shops	25–30% of annual sales plus inventory *or* 1–2.5 times SDE plus inventory *or* 3 times SDE plus inventory *or* 3–3.5 times EBITDA	Range: 14–121% m = 0.47 me = 0.37	Range: 4–144% m = 0.39 me = 0.35
Beauty salons	35% of annual revenues plus inventory fixtures and equipment *or* 2 times SDE plus inventory *or* 4 times monthly sales plus inventory *or* 2.5 times EBIT	Range: 12–142% m = 0.44 me = 0.38	Range: 6–202% m = 0.40 me = 0.33
Dental practices	50–60% of annual sales plus inventory *or* 1.3–1.8 times SDE includes inventory *or* 4 times EBIT *or* 4–5 times EBITDA *or* 50–70 percent of annual collections (depending on managed care vs. fee for service)	Range: 13–189% m = 0.61 me = 0.60	N/A

Fast-food franchises	35–45% of annual sales plus inventory	Range: 7–161% m = 0.48 me = 0.42	Range: 8–204% m = 0.42 me = 0.39
Grocery stores	15–20% of annual sales plus inventory *or* 2–3 times SDE, plus fixtures, equipment, and inventory 3–3.5 times EBITDA	Range: 1–145% m = 0.31 me = 0.24	Range: 3–160% m = 0.29 me = 0.21
Restaurants (full service)	20–35% of annual sales plus inventory *or* 1–3 times SDE plus inventory *or* 2–3 times EBIT *or* 2.5–3 times EBITDA	Range: 3–83% m = 0.54 me = 0.59	Range: 10–73% m = 0.36 me = 0.32

m = mean; me = median; N/A = insufficient transactions for meaningful results; SDE = seller's discretionary earnings; EBIT = earnings before interest and taxes; EBITDA = earnings before interest, taxes, depreciation, and amortization.

[a] *Source:* From Tom West, *The 2014 Business Reference Guide.*

[b] *Source:* From Pratt's Stats, compiled by Business Valuation Resources, LLC.

[c] *Source:* From Bizcomps, distributed by Business Valuation Resources, LLC.

below-market seller financing and often include future payments that are contingent on future performance, such as retention of existing customers. Perhaps more important, the prices usually include values of noncompete covenants and employment agreements, that may or may not be considered part of the marital estate.

If the data are to be used for marital property settlements, we highly recommend that the parties' experts go to the actual transaction data now widely available to derive multiples based on recent transactions and to recompute the ratios after eliminating noncompete and employment agreements in jurisdictions where those agreements would not be considered marital property.

Also, most rules of thumb reflect the assumption that the seller will stay with the business for some period of time to assist in the transaction. To this extent, they implicitly imply some personal goodwill. There is a trend among states to separate personal from enterprise goodwill and to exclude personal goodwill from the marital estate.

Court Reactions to Rules of Thumb

Courts generally have been inclined to reject valuation opinions based on rules of thumb. One opinion, for example, contained the following language:

> [These] formulas . . . "are in reality the starting point of negotiation; and should not be confused with a valuation procedure." . . . Formulas based on gross billings are usually converted to a time payout of the purchase price and, as such, can be misleading because they are often negotiated more over the terms of payment than over the actual value of the business being acquired. . . . While "rules of thumb may be helpful to accountants or business people to gauge the overall fairness of a particular transaction," that is, whether it is "in the ballpark," they are not at all helpful to the Court in fixing a specific value on a specific economic enterprise in an ancillary proceeding. . . . A rule of thumb by definition

provides no theory. At best it is a guide or points out direction. At worst, it is nothing.[4]

However, rules of thumb have been accepted by courts in one form or another. In one case, the husband's expert simply utilized a rule-of-thumb multiplier of three to five times the husband's salary, then subtracted corporate debt to reach a final value. The trial court adopted this figure as opposed to the asset-based valuation presented by the wife's expert. The decision was appealed and upheld.[5]

References

Basic Rules of Thumb References

Cohen, Harriet N. 2003. "Using Rules of Thumb in Valuation." In *101+ Practical Solutions for the Family Lawyer*, 2nd ed., edited by Gregg Herman. Chicago: American Bar Association.

Desmond, Glenn M. 1993. *Handbook of Small Business Valuation Formulas and Rules of Thumb*, 3d ed., Valuation Press.

Feder, ed. 1997. "Courts' Use of Rules of Thumb to Value Assets." In *Valuation Strategies in Divorce*, 4th ed. pp. 450–453.

Fishman, Jay, et al. 2015. "Rules of Thumb" and "The Problem with Rules of Thumb in the Valuation of Closely-Held Entities." In *PPC's Guide to Business Valuations*. Practitioners Publishing, Fort Worth, TX pp. 7-40, 7-51 to 7-53.

Pratt, Shannon P., and Alina V. Niculita. 2007. "Formulas or Rules of Thumb." In *Valuing a Business*, 5th ed. McGraw-Hill, New York, pp. 319–320.

West, Tom. "Rules of Thumb." In *The Business Reference Guide 2014*, 24th ed. Business Brokerage Press, Westford, MA,

Transaction Databases with Price/Revenue and Price/Discretionary Earnings Ratios

Note: The following databases can be accessed through BVResources .com.

Bizcomps
Asset Business Appraisal
Post Office Box 97757
Las Vegas, NV 89193
(858) 457-0366

Pratt's Stats
Business Valuation Resources
1000 SW Broadway, Suite 1200
Portland, OR 97205
(888) 287-8258

IBA Market Database
Institute of Business Appraisers
Post Office Box 17410
Plantation, FL 33318
(954) 584-1144

Chapter 19

Valuations for Federal Tax Matters

There is more definitive precedential case law in the general area of valuations for federal tax purposes than for any other business valuation purpose. Some issues are well settled, but decisions on other issues continue to evolve. This chapter attempts to distinguish which issues are well settled, nearly settled, or still in flux.[1]

Even among tax issues that are well settled in principle, there is still room for argument about magnitudes, especially in such areas as discounts for minority interest and lack of marketability. There are also issues about which decisions seem to be conflicting (for example, discounts for lack of marketability for controlling interests). However, as Judge David Laro has explained:

> Each valuation case is unique. Although guidance can be obtained from earlier cases, one case is rarely on point with another, and a significant differentiation of the facts can usually be made.[2]

An understanding of valuations for federal tax purposes is also very important for valuations for many other purposes. Because of the extensive case law, IRS Revenue Rulings, and other literature, valuation principles and decisions for tax purposes are often cited in valuation reports and court decisions for other purposes.

Federal tax cases involving business valuations fall primarily into the following categories:

- Estate taxes
- Gift taxes
- Ordinary income and capital gains taxes
- Charitable contributions
- Transfer pricing

Although the standard of fair market value applies equally in all cases, the manner in which it applies can have extreme consequences, particularly for estate planning. While for gift tax purposes each transfer is valued individually, for estate tax purposes the entire amount in the estate is aggregated, regardless of the number of beneficiaries. For example, if an estate holds a 100 percent interest in a company, the interest will be valued as a 100 percent control interest, even if it is willed equally to three beneficiaries. But if three gifts of one-third interests are made, each will be valued as a minority interest, benefiting from the well-settled principle that the minority interest is discounted compared to a pro rata portion of the value as a whole.

Similarly, if the estate holds more than one class of security, the combined effect of all may be aggregated for the purpose of valuation,[3] but in some cases it is more appropriate to value only the subject voting shares, rather than valuing all voting shares of the company and deriving a pro rata value from that.[4]

Fair Market Value[5]

The standard of value for all federal tax cases is *fair market value*, defined by the Internal Revenue Service as follows:

> The price at which the property would change hands between a willing buyer and a willing seller, when the former is not under any

compulsion to buy and the latter is not under any compulsion to sell, both parties having reasonable knowledge of the relevant facts.[6]

There are many nuances to this definition, as discussed in a subsequent section. However, over several decades, the federal courts have developed seven standards that must be considered in determining fair market value:

1. The buyer and seller are both willing to engage in the transaction.
2. Neither the willing buyer nor the willing seller is under a compulsion to buy or sell the item in question.
3. The willing buyer and the willing seller are both hypothetical persons.
4. The hypothetical willing buyer and the hypothetical willing seller are both aware of all facts and circumstances involving the item in question.
5. The item is valued at its highest and best use, regardless of its current use.
6. The item is valued without regard to events occurring after the valuation date, unless the event was reasonably foreseeable at the valuation date or was relevant to the valuation.
7. The transaction is for cash and will be consummated within a reasonable commercial time frame.[7]

To this day, one of the most instructive cases on fair market value of closely held stock for federal tax purposes is *Central Trust Company v. United States*,[8] a lengthy, detailed discussion of valuation issues written over 50 years ago. Although the reader must recognize that the structure of markets and financial theory and evidence have advanced in quantum leaps since that decision, it is still the most comprehensive tax case discussion of basic valuation issues, well worth reading today. Other cases worth reviewing are *Foltz v. U.S. News and World Report*,[9] *Estate of Furman* (which is instructive reading in general),[10] and *Bank One Corporation v. Comm'r.*[11]

Fair Market Value Assumes Adequate Knowledge

Central Trust makes the point that "fair market value presupposes not only hypothetical willing buyers and sellers, but buyers and sellers who are informed and have adequate knowledge of the material facts affecting value."[12] As an example, in a 1999 case, Judge Laro rejected two sales proffered as evidence of fair market value, noting: "Neither seller was reasonably informed regarding the value of their stock. . . . Both took the offer . . . because it sounded like a good amount of money. Their testimony revealed that they were not knowledgeable sellers who aimed to realize the fair market value of their stock."[13]

Consideration Must Be Given to *Both* Buyer and Seller—and Both Must Be Hypothetical

A common problem in tax cases is that the expert will focus solely, or unduly, on the *buyer,* with no or inadequate consideration given to whether the value would be acceptable to a hypothetical willing seller. Instructive examples can be found in the decisions in *Estate of Kaufman v. Comm'r*[14] and *Moore v. Comm'r.*[15]

A transaction cannot take place at more than the highest price a willing buyer will pay. Fair market value assumes market conditions as they exist at the date of valuation. Therefore, if the seller is really willing, the implication is that he or she must accept what the market will bear at the valuation date. The existence of a market implies both buyers and sellers.[16] However, it can be difficult to determine the market for a closely held company. For example, some buyers might be interested in continuing the business as their own, whereas others might be interested in the business as an investment. There might also be other buyers who see the business as offering synergies with other acquisitions or assets.[17] Addressing this issue, some tax regulations require the value of the property be measured in the market where it would most likely be sold.[18] To comply with this requirement, the business appraiser should analyze the marketplace to identify the most likely pools of buyers. In any event, the "selection of the proper market for valuation purposes is a question of fact."[19] The expert or reviewer should be sure that the willing seller part of the hypothetical willing buyer/willing seller combination is not ignored.

Finally, both the seller and buyer must be hypothetical. In one case, the tax court's decision was reversed because, according to the court of appeals, it based its ruling on speculation and imaginary scenarios that identified particular buyers, rather than hypothetical buyers.[20]

Qualifications of Appraisers

While the quality of evidence is of primary importance, the tax court also is very interested in appraisers' qualifications in deciding on the relative weight to accord the respective experts' testimony. An instructive example can be found in the tax court's opinion on *Estate of Berg*, which included lengthy discussions of the experts' qualifications.[21] While failure to submit a report from a qualified appraiser can have significant negative financial consequences (as it did in *Estate of Berg*), submitting a report from a qualified appraiser can help shield the taxpayer even if the appraiser's report is not upheld; the tax court has on numerous occasions refused to impose the Section 6660 undervaluation penalty on the grounds that the taxpayer retained a qualified appraiser and submitted the amount shown on the return in good faith.

In *Kohler v. Comm'r*,[22] the tax court gave no weight to the opinions of the IRS's expert who, although a Chartered Financial Analyst (CFA) with a doctorate, was not credentialed in business valuation and did not provide a USPAP certification. The court also looked unfavorably at the expert's innovative, but unsupported, financial model. In *Estate of Thompson v. Comm'r*,[23] the tax court criticized the experts for both parties, finding that they were inexperienced and that their valuations generally lacked credibility. Conversely, in *Caracci v. Comm'r*,[24] the court rejected the taxpayer's attempt to challenge the IRS's expert's qualifications as "nonsensical and border[ing] on the frivolous" where the expert was a certified public accountant and principal in a business valuation firm that had conducted numerous business valuations. In *Estate of Josephine Thompson v. Comm'r*,[25] the tax court rejected both parties' valuations, and while declining to impose an underpayment penalty, it criticized the estate's decision to hire an accountant and lawyer from Alaska (the estate was in New York) with relatively little valuation experience.

Burden of Proof

For examinations commencing before July 22, 1998, if the IRS issued a notice of deficiency, the burden of proof was on the taxpayer to prove that the value claimed by the IRS was wrong[26]; see, for example, the opinion in *Estate of Kaufman*.[27]

For examinations commenced after July 22, 1998 (or, if no examination, court proceedings arising in connection with taxable periods beginning or occurring after July 22, 1998), the burden shifted to the IRS. *Kohler v. Comm'r*[28] is a particularly instructive instance of the estate and taxpayer successfully shifting the burden of proof to the IRS. In that case, at issue was a determination of the fair market value of stock of the company owned by the estate of Frederic C. Kohler on the alternate valuation date. The estate elected the alternate valuation date and filed its return with a $47.01 million appraisal. The IRS determined that the fair market value of the Kohler holdings on the alternate valuation date was $144.5 million. The parties stipulated that the value of the Kohler stock at issue in related gift tax cases would be calculated by reference to the value of the Kohler stock determined in the estate tax case. The parties also agreed that the per share value for the different classes of Kohler stock in each case would be determined by reference to an agreed formula that would take into account the value of the Kohler stock determined in the estate tax case. The tax court ruled that all the requirements for shifting the burden of proof were met. Although the IRS argued that the estate did not cooperate fully because it filed a motion to quash certain discovery requests, the court determined that the estate had legitimate concerns about providing confidential and proprietary business information that was possibly irrelevant absent a court order. Once the tax court denied the estate's motion to quash the summons, the estate provided the requested documents the respondent requested. Accordingly, the court found that the numerous exhibits that were part of the record belied the IRS argument, and the burden shifted to the IRS.

In *Estate of Josephine Thompson v. Comm'r,*[29] the Second Circuit confronted the issue of whether, once the taxpayer submitted a credible appraisal, the burden shifted to the IRS to prove the value after the tax court rejected the IRS's values, and whether, as a result, the tax court should have adopted the taxpayer's values. The Second Circuit determined that the allocation of the burden of proof does not require the tax court to adopt the taxpayer's valuation, however erroneous, whenever the court rejects the IRS's proposed value; the burden of disproving the taxpayer's valuation can be satisfied by evidence in the record that impeaches, undermines, or indicates error in the taxpayer's valuation. In this case, the IRS not only presented evidence in support of its valuation but also successfully rebutted the estate's valuation by identifying its errors and inconsistencies. The court reasoned that notwithstanding the allocation of the burden of proof in IRC Section 7491, the "Tax Court is not bound by the formulas and opinions proffered by expert witnesses. It may reach a determination of value based upon its own analysis of all the evidence in the record."

Adequate Disclosure of Gifts

A gift and its value must be adequately disclosed on a gift tax return in order to start the three-year statute of limitations on the assessment of gift tax.[30] On December 3, 1999, the Internal Revenue Service published final regulations pertaining to the adequate disclosure of gifts.[31] The regulations contain a list of what information must be included with the gift tax return in order for the gift to be deemed adequately disclosed. In response to extensive comments and concerns about the regulations as previously proposed, the IRS added a section to the regulations providing that a "qualified appraisal" may be submitted "in lieu of the information required" under one of the items in the list.[32]

Access to Sites, Management, and Records

It is clear that the tax court expects experts to have access to site visits, management interviews, and company records to the extent necessary for a thorough appraisal. In *Estate of Bruce v. Comm'r*, the court dryly commented:

> It is also noted that petitioner's counsel refused to allow respondent's expert an opportunity to visit PCBCED's warehouse and bottling plant. To the extent that this reflects counsel's attitude and approach towards Tax Court litigation, the Court suggests that this is not the way we conduct proceedings.[33]

In *Kohler v. Comm'r*,[34] one of the most instructive tax court cases, the court discredited an opinion based on a site visit that lasted under three hours because it did not provide the expert with adequate knowledge of the subject company, and the court lauded the opposing party's expert's detailed knowledge of the firm. In *Polack v. Comm'r*,[35] the court credited the expert's appraisal because it was based on a thorough site visit, with interviews of individuals at the company who were key to an understanding of the company's value.

Arm's-Length Transactions

The tax court will accord some weight to arm's-length sales of businesses or business interests, defined by *Black's Law Dictionary* as "a transaction between two unaffiliated and unrelated parties."[36]

For example, in *Estate of Bennett*, the court said, "Usually, in determining the value of untraded stock, one would look at actual arm's-length sales of such stock in the normal course of business within a reasonable time before or after the valuation date."[37] (Although the decision clearly articulated the principle, there were no such transactions in the *Bennett* case.) In *Morrissey v. Comm'r*,[38] the Ninth Circuit reversed the tax court's rejection of the taxpayer's evidence of actual sales near the valuation date. The appellate court concluded that because those actual sales had been arm's-length transactions, they presented the best evidence of fair market value.

Approaches to Value

The tax court expects all approaches to value to be considered. The relative weight it will accord to the various valuation approaches and methods generally depends on three factors:

1. The type of company
2. The quality of available evidence
3. Whether the company might be liquidated or continue as a going concern

The tax court tends to rely more on an asset approach for holding companies and on an income or market approach for operating companies. For hybrid companies, the court may weight the approaches to correspond to the degree to which the company has assets and earnings.[39] *Estate of Kaufman v. Comm'r*[40] is a useful caution; the tax court opinion in the case was critical of an expert for not considering an asset approach for a company for which most appraisers would have been very unlikely to have accorded the asset approach any weight at all.

Other cases are also instructive; in *Hess v. Comm'r*,[41] the court split the difference between the taxpayer's discounted cash flow (DCF) and guideline publicly traded company approach and the IRS's DCF, net asset value, prior transaction, and guideline publicly traded company approaches.

In *Estate of Leichter v. Comm'r*,[42] the issue of liquidation versus going concern was key. There, the expert opined that the company was worth less on a going-concern basis than in liquidation, but the court criticized the expert for not explaining why a hypothetical seller would choose not to liquidate under such circumstances.

The tax court's ultimate decisions, however, often are based on a single approach (in effect, a weight of 100 percent to one approach)—which is, more often than not, the market approach—or a blending of the results of two approaches.

Market Approach

The IRS and the tax court look very favorably on the market approach, which is heavily emphasized in Revenue Ruling 59-60. However, it is not uncommon for an expert's utilization of the market approach to be rejected if the court is not satisfied that the companies selected are comparable to the subject company.

For example, in *Estate of Brookshire*, two experts for the taxpayer and the IRS's expert all used the guideline public company method, among others. However, the court rejected the IRS's version of the guideline company method:

> Respondent's expert overstates the value of the Brookshire common stock because of his use of three companies as comparable companies that have significant sales in markets other than retail grocery and that are not comparable to Brookshire. The use of these companies distorts each of the valuation methods used by respondent's expert.[43]

Note that this is *not* a rejection of the guideline company method; the court accepted the guideline companies used by the taxpayer's experts.

Revenue Ruling 59-60 uses the language "the same or similar." Companies may be accepted as similar for reasons other than product or service line—for example, the markets into which they sell or their degree of brand dominance. In both *Estate of Gallo*[44] (Gallo wines) and *Estate of Hall*[45] (Hallmark greeting cards), the court relied entirely on the guideline publicly traded company method, even though there were no good public wine companies to use for *Gallo* and only one public greeting card company to use for *Hall*. In *Gallo*, the experts used breweries, distilleries, soft drink bottlers, and high brand recognition and market share food producers. In *Hall*, they used high brand recognition and market share consumer nondurable products companies, such as Parker Pen. In both cases, the court arrived at a value as if the stock were publicly traded, then applied a 36 percent discount for lack of marketability based on restricted stock and pre–initial public offering (pre-IPO) transaction study data. However, in *Estate of Heck v. Comm'r*,[46] the court rejected the use of a single comparable company where it was insufficiently similar to the subject company. The court said, "As similarity to the company to be valued decreases, the number of required comparables increases."

In *Hess v. Comm'r*,[47] the court upheld the comparison of the subject company to guideline companies solely on the basis of price-to-earning (P/E) ratios where the guideline companies were similar to the subject company and the guideline companies were properly adjusted.

Estate of Watts was a classic clash of opposing opinions on appropriate approaches to value—in that case, the taxpayer's reliance on the market approach and the IRS's reliance on the asset approach. Decedent's estate filed a valuation of $2,550,000 for a 15 percent interest in a timber growing and processing partnership. The notice of deficiency valued the interest at $20,006,000, based primarily on the liquidation value of the assets. At trial, the taxpayers' experts based their valuations on publicly traded companies that processed timber and held timberlands. Based on these companies, they presented valuation parameters such as price-to-earnings multiples, multiples of partnership interest value to book value and to adjusted net asset value, and capitalization of partnership withdrawals. Because the tax court did not accept the respondent's liquidation value approach, it relied on values provided by the business valuation experts (including a 35 percent discount for lack of marketability) and ultimately concluded the estate's value as originally filed of $2,550,000.[48]

Income Approach[49]

Both the IRS and the tax court have traditionally leaned more toward the market approach than the income approach. This is partly because of language in Revenue Ruling 59-60, written before the development of modern capital market theory, which evolved particularly in the 1960s. It is also partly because of concern about possible manipulation of both cash flow forecasts and discount rates in the discounted cash flow (DCF) method. The tax court has *rejected* the DCF method in cases in which it believed the model used by the expert was far too sensitive to minor changes in assumptions, such as the discount rate and/or the growth rate.[50] The court also rejected the income approach where the capital asset pricing model (CAPM) was used to value a small closely held company, as the CAPM does not address unsystematic risk.[51] The tax court has also been known to reach its conclusion by giving partial weight to a DCF method and partial weight to a market approach method.[52] Noteworthy decisions include those in *Estate of Jung*[53] and *Rakow v. Comm'r.*[54]

In *Estate of Lehmann v. Comm'r*,[55] the tax court accepted the DCF method for valuing an interest in a real estate partnership that owned a property with a hotel, noting: "The value of any interest in real property that has an income stream can be estimated by the DCF method. See *Estate of Bennett v. Comm'r.*"[56] (The court then took into consideration the minority, nonmarketable status of the partnership interest.)

Asset-Based Approach

Revenue Ruling 59-60 suggests that the asset approach should be accorded more weight for holding companies, while earnings-related methods should be accorded more weight for operating companies. For example, in *Estate of Jameson v. Comm'r*,[57] which involved the valuation of a controlling interest in a holding company the primary asset of which was timber, the tax court determined that the asset approach was appropriate since earnings were relatively low as compared to the fair market value of the assets. The IRS has tended to push this notion to the ultimate in the case of family limited partnerships, where they often have used the asset approach exclusively.[58]

Discounts[59]

Discounts for Lack of Marketability (Minority Blocks)

The principle that minority blocks of closely held stock are worth less, because of the lack of a ready market, than otherwise similar publicly held stock is thoroughly entrenched in tax court rulings. The argument is not whether, but how much?

There appear to be two long-term trends:

- The size of marketability discounts concluded has gradually increased.
- The court has increasingly emphasized reliance on empirical data in deciding on the size of the lack of marketability discount.

Gradually Increasing Marketability Discounts

In the 1980s, discounts purely for marketability reached 36 percent, the highest up to that time.[60] In the late 1990s there were several conclusions of a 40 percent lack of marketability discount.[61] In 2006, a 50 percent discount for lack of marketability (DLOM) was recognized.[62]

Increasing Reliance on Empirical Data

To some extent, the gradually increasing level of marketability discounts is attributable to the growing body of empirical data available to assist in quantifying such discounts and the tax court's increasing emphasis on that data. The relevant empirical data have for a long time been the *restricted stock studies* (sales of blocks of nonregistered or restricted stock of public companies) and the *pre-IPO studies* (transactions in stock of private companies that subsequently had successful initial public offerings). With time, these studies have been criticized for various deficiencies, and other ways of arriving at discounts for lack of marketability have been put forth, including the use of put options, put-call collars, regression analysis of the restricted stock studies, private placement studies, the Quantitative Marketability Discount Model (QMDM), and even analyses of stock illiquidity versus lack of marketability. All of these alternatives have their own weaknesses and flaws.

The restricted stock studies were first published starting in the early 1970s and include data going back to the late 1960s. They were recognized as valid evidence supporting discounts for lack of marketability in Revenue Ruling 77-287. The pre-IPO studies first appeared in the early 1980s, with data back to 1975. They were first introduced in *Estate of Gallo*[63] and also used in *Estate of Hall*.[64]

In the late 1990s, the tax court explicitly directed attention to *both* these lines of studies in reaching conclusions based on a discount for lack of marketability.[65] However, the court has not always accepted these data. Some criticisms of these studies are that they are dated, they have limited sample sizes, they are spread out over long periods of time, and they may have substantial standard errors in their estimates. In *Estate of Jelke v. Comm'r*[66] (affirmed as to the discount issue by 507 F.3d 1317 [11th Cir. 2007]), for example, the court rejected the use of restricted stock studies, determining they were insufficiently similar to the subject company as to size. A prevailing theme in tax court criticism of the application of restricted stock studies has been that many such uses unfairly exclude pertinent information about the company's specific industry; significant examples include *McCord v. Comm'r*,[67] *Estate of Kelly v. Comm'r*,[68] *Lappo v. Comm'r*,[69] *Peracchio v. Comm'r*,[70] *Estate of Deputy v. Comm'r*,[71] and *Janda v. Comm'r*.[72] Other questions as to the applicability of restricted stock studies were raised by *Temple v. United States*,[73] *Robertson v. United States*,[74] and *Estate of Green v. Comm'r*.[75] Although *Litman v. United States*[76] rejected a generalized use of restricted stock studies, the claims court expressed a preference for using individual transactions from the restricted stock studies rather than averages, a procedure that Shannon Pratt, one of the authors of this book, advocates and has used effectively many times.

A brief description of some of the other sources of empirical data supporting discounts for lack of marketability (or lack of liquidity) follows.[77]

Put Options. The put option method calculates a discount for lack of marketability by calculating the cost of locking in the current price to protect the downside risk of price movements while the security is illiquid. The price of the put provides market evidence of the price investors will pay to ensure marketability, and the formula for this model, as well as its key inputs (such as the risk-free rate and volatility) can be audited. The term of this model is more subjective. Potential criticisms of using this model are that it is a short-term, theoretical pricing model designed for liquid securities that is being applied to an illiquid security and that put options protect only against downside price movements. See *Estate of Gimbel v. Comm'r*[78] for an example of the tax court's rejecting this model in specific circumstances.

Put-Call Collars. A put-call collar locks in a security's price by selling away the upside while protecting against the downward price movements. This is done by buying a put option and selling a call option. Criticisms of this type of analysis are that the lack of a derivatives market in the subject security results in significantly understating the cost to execute this strategy for a privately held security and that cost information is not available and can result in significant subjective judgment. Where this analysis is feasible, it can be used to establish a floor for the discount. See *Litman v. United States*[79] and *Estate of Gimbel v. Comm'r*[80] for instances in which the tax court rejected the use of an option collar approach in specific circumstances, principally that there would not have been a market for such hedging contracts in their instances.

Regression Analysis. Francis Longstaff and others use regression analyses of restricted stock studies to provide a quantitative indication of the DLOM. The mathematical method and its inputs can be audited. The key drivers of this approach are duration and volatility. Criticisms include the fact that a key assumption—that an investor could perfectly time the market—may not be realistic. In contradistinction to the put-call collar approach, this approach can be used to establish a ceiling for the discount.

Liquidity Versus Marketability. Ashok Abbott differentiates between marketability and liquidity, defining *marketability* as relating to a security's registration (ease of transfer or salability) and *liquidity* as relating to the actual sale of the security (converting the asset to cash). Abbott postulates that the cost to trade becomes a critical factor, which most trading models overlook but "where the difference between marketability and liquidity become even more pronounced." According to Abbott, large blocks of stock are illiquid, so he uses the Black Scholes or Longstaff models to calculate "look back put" data as a way to reveal discounts from liquidity-related issues. He finds that, for the largest publicly traded companies (more than $100 billion), the liquidity discounts range from 4 percent for the smaller blocks of stock up to 12 percent for the larger blocks. But for smaller companies, a 25 percent block creates a discount of around 35 percent. Still, these companies are bigger than most in a valuation pool.[81]

Combined Minority and Lack of Marketability Discounts

Minority interest and marketability discounts are two different concepts, although there may be some overlap. The tax court has clearly articulated this distinction:

> Two conceptually distinct discounts are involved here, one for lack of marketability and the other for lack of control. The minority

> shareholder discount is designed to reflect the decreased value of shares that do not convey control of a closely held corporation. The lack of marketability discount, on the other hand, is designed to reflect the fact that there is no ready market for shares in a closely held corporation.[82]

In the majority of tax court cases in the 1980s and 1990s, minority and marketability factors were treated separately. However, more recent cases have combined the two factors in the final decision.[83]

Discounts for 50 Percent Interest

A 50 percent interest is neither controlling nor minority. In most cases, the court will allow some discount for lack of control and also some discount for lack of marketability. See particularly *Estate of Fleming v. Comm'r*[84] as one example.

Discounts for Lack of Marketability (Controlling Interests)

In many reported decisions, the tax court has recognized that discounts for lack of marketability for controlling interests in closely held companies are appropriate. The courts have used language such as the following:

> Even controlling shares in a nonpublic corporation suffer from lack of marketability because of the absence of a ready private placement market and the fact that flotation costs would have to be incurred if the corporation were to publicly offer its stock.[85]

The tax court has allowed discounts for lack of marketability for controlling interests up to 30 percent.[86] While *Estate of Cloutier*[87] is a particularly striking example of circumstances in which the tax court allowed no such discount, there are many more examples of the court allowing it, including *Estate of Dougherty*,[88] *Estate of Maggos v. Comm'r*,[89] and *Estate of Dunn v. Comm'r.*[90] There are many cases in the 10 to 15 percent range for discounts for lack of marketability for controlling interests[91]; *Estate of Bennett*[92] is a particularly useful example.

Discounts for Lack of Control (Minority Discount)

Discounts are applied to noncontrolling ownership interests. This type of discount is sometimes referred to as a *discount for lack of control* (DLOC) or *minority discount*. These discounts may be granted independently of, or in addition to, the discount for lack of marketability.

A particularly important (and still controversial) example is *Estate of Jelke v. Comm'r*,[93] in which the taxpayer's expert discounted the subject minority interest by 25 percent for lack of control, whereas the IRS's discounted it by 5 percent. The taxpayer's expert assumed that the company was most like a closed-end fund and it was not a widely traded investment fund holding publicly traded securities. Applying this assumption, the expert arrived at a 20 percent discount base and added an additional 5 percent discount because the subject company had fewer assets, paid fewer dividends, and posted lower short-term returns than the comparable funds. The IRS expert's analysis began with an average discount (8.61 percent) for closed-end funds and reduced this on the basis that the company outperformed the comparables used by the estate. The court adopted a 10 percent lack-of-control discount, finding that although the company was smaller than some of the comparables presented, it was well diversified, which reduced investment risk, and that investors in the company would base their investments on the company's history of good performance.

Other examples of such discounts include *Estate of Green v. Comm'r*[94] (17 percent), *Estate of Thompson v. Comm'r*[95] (15 percent), *Adams v. United States*[96] (20 percent—based on the taxpayer's expert providing "the lone specific analysis of the issues"), and *Robertson v. United States*[97] (19 percent—and noteworthy for the court's comment that the taxpayer's expert's use of the median was more appropriate than the average, which could be unduly influenced by outliers).

The experts for both sides in *Hess v. Comm'r*[98] agreed that a 15 percent DLOC applied, but the court criticized the taxpayer's expert for using a discount under the guideline public company method, concluding that such a discount is already included and inherent in that method. In *Temple v. United States*,[99] the court determined minority discounts in a range of 3.3 to 10.1 percent for limited partnerships holding publicly held marketable securities. The court arrived at this range by using closed-end funds data. The IRS's expert used all reporting closed-end funds and calculated the discount based on the mean of the reported discounts and premiums from net asset value. The taxpayer's expert used a limited universe of funds and computed the discount using the 75th percentile of the limited universe. The court preferred the IRS's expert's approach, finding it was more comprehensive.

Blockage

Blockage is a term used primarily in conjunction with publicly traded stock. It denotes a block of stock that is so large relative to the typical daily or weekly trading volume that it would require a long time to release it into the public market slowly enough to avoid depressing the price of the stock.

Blockage discounts tend to be relatively modest, often in the 3 to 10 percent range. However, sometimes the tax court denies the discount totally, sometimes even inexplicably.[100] At the other extreme, the tax court allowed a 25 percent blockage discount on a block of thinly traded public stock of Frederick's of Hollywood.[101] More typical is the *Estate of Foote*, for which the tax court concluded a 3.3 percent discount for blockage.[102] Nonetheless, unique facts and circumstances can lead to a higher discount.[103] In *Estate of Adams v. Comm'r*,[104] the court applied both a discount for lack of marketability and a blockage discount on the same block of stock.

Key Person Discount

Dependence on a key person introduces a risk of the consequences of the loss of that person's services in case of death, disability, or resignation. This risk is sometimes recognized through a separate discount for the key person factor.

In *Estate of Furman v. Comm'r,*[105] the tax court found the following:

> Where a corporation is substantially dependent upon the services of one person, and where that person would no longer be able to perform services for the corporation by reason of death or incapacity, an investor would expect some form of discount below fair market value when purchasing stock in the corporation to compensate for the loss of that key employee.

The court specifically cited *Estate of Huntsman v. Comm'r*, 66 T.C. 861, 1976 WL 3635 (1976); *Estate of Mitchell v. Comm'r*, 250 F.3d 696 (9th Circuit 2001); *Estate of Feldmar v. Comm'r*, T.C. Memo. 1988-429; and *Estate of Yeager v. Comm'r*, T.C. Memo. 1986-448. The court also made the important observation that while the company *could* have purchased key person life insurance, a minority shareholder could not *compel* the company to purchase such insurance, and in fact the company had had no such insurance in effect. The court went on to settle on a key person discount of 10 percent.

In *Estate of Mitchell v. Comm'r,*[106] the tax court applied a 10 percent key person discount but rejected a key person discount in *Estate of Renier v. Comm'r*[107] in which factual reasons supporting such a discount were absent from the valuation report.

Nonvoting Versus Voting Stock

If a company has nonvoting as well as voting stock outstanding, the nonvoting stock may be discounted compared to the value of the voting stock. For public companies that have both voting and nonvoting stock, the discount for nonvoting in most cases is quite small, often less than 5 percent, and that level of discount is often used for private companies and accepted by the IRS and the tax court.

In the unusual situation in which the voting stock that controls the company is only a tiny percentage of the total stock outstanding, voting control may be quite valuable, and it might be meaningless to measure the difference in value on the basis of a percentage discount. In the case of *Estate of Simplot*,[108] a tiny percentage of all the stock was voting stock, but it was owned by four parties, each a minority. The tax court placed a superpremium on the voting stock. On appeal, however, the Ninth Circuit reversed, finding that the tax court had based its ruling on speculation by creating a scenario in which a buyer would purchase a minority share of the voting stock but with time would be able to play a role in the company.[109]

Premiums

Premiums may be added to value for factors such as control, or a swing vote.

In *Estate of Simplot v. Comm'r*,[110] the decedent owned a minority interest in a small control block of stock. The tax court, adopting the IRS's position, attributed a 3 percent premium to the swing vote block and then took a 35 percent discount for lack of control from the decedent's pro rata share in that block. This resulted in a multi-million-dollar control premium on the noncontrolling interest in the control block. On appeal, the Ninth Circuit reversed, finding that a buyer of the block could never recover the premium. In accepting the taxpayer's application of a zero premium, the court decided that a controlling block of stock is not to be valued at a premium for estate tax purposes unless it can be shown that a purchaser of the block would be able to use it "in such a way to assure an increased economic advantage worth paying a premium for."

In *Estate of Maggos v. Comm'r*,[111] the decedent's controlling block of stock in a company was repurchased by the company without the benefit of a formal valuation. After applying a 25 percent DLOM, the court applied a 25 percent control premium based on average premiums paid in the industry at the time of purchase. However, in *Estate of Wright v. Comm'r*,[112] the court refused to apply a control premium asserted by the IRS's expert that was based on a hypothetical scenario in which other investors might purchase the decedent's block of stock.

Trapped-In Capital Gains Taxes

One of the most dramatic developments in tax court decisions, starting in 1998, was explicit recognition of liability for capital gains taxes on significantly appreciated property.

In cases arising before 1987, a corporation could liquidate its assets, distribute the proceeds, and dissolve within 12 months, and by so doing it could eliminate the payment of capital gains taxes at the corporate level. The Tax Reform Act of 1986 eliminated that option. Before 1986, at least partially relying on the tax-free liquidation option (known as the General Utilities Doctrine, named after a case that exercised the option), the tax court had steadfastly denied recognition of any trapped-in gains tax liability unless liquidation of the appreciated assets was clearly imminent.

After 1986 there were no C corporation gift or estate tax valuation cases clearly isolating this issue until the *Eisenberg*[113] case in 1997, when the tax court again denied recognition of capital gains liability as a factor diminishing value. In 1998, in *Estate of Davis*, the tax court decided as follows:

> We reject respondent's position that, as a matter of law, no discount or adjustment attributable to ADDI&C's built-in capital gains tax is allowable in the instant case. . . . We are convinced on the record in this case, and we find that, even though no liquidation of ADDI&C or sale of its assets was planned or contemplated on the valuation date, a hypothetical willing seller and a hypothetical willing buyer would not have agreed on that date on a price for each of the blocks of stock in question that took no account of ADDI&C's built-in capital gains tax.[114]

The court ultimately recognized a diminution in value equal to approximately half the trapped-in capital gains tax liability. Shortly following the *Davis* decision, the Second Circuit Court of Appeals, citing favorably *Estate of Davis*, reversed *Eisenberg*.[115]

In 1999, in *Estate of Simplot*, the tax court reached a decision that reflected a valuation deduction of 100 percent of the trapped-in capital gains tax on a block of stock owned by the company being valued.[116]

Another 1999 case, citing *Davis*, recognized the trapped-in capital gains tax liability of a company's timber. The court estimated the rate of growth, the rate of inflation, the capital gains tax rate, and the time period over which the timber would be cut. It discounted the estimated capital gains tax for each year to a present value, using an estimated equity cost of capital (discount rate). It then deducted the full present value of the capital gains liability thus estimated.[117]

The majority of cases that have followed, either at the tax court level or on appeal, have permitted discounts for trapped-in capital gains. The tax court in *Estate of Welch v. Comm'r*[118] denied such a discount but was reversed by the Sixth Circuit. In *Estate of Borgatello v. Comm'r*,[119] the tax court allowed a 24 percent discount for trapped-in capital gains on a controlling interest in a real estate holding company. The tax court in *Estate of Dunn v. Comm'r*[120] permitted only a 5 percent discount, but on appeal, the Fifth Circuit ruled that a dollar-for-dollar reduction, amounting to a 34 percent discount, had to be applied to the company's asset-based value. In *Estate of Jelke v. Comm'r*,[121] the tax court rejected a dollar-for-dollar reduction for trapped-in capital gains on a minority interest, reasoning that a hypothetical willing buyer of a minority interest would not adjust the purchase price to reflect the entire amount of the company's built-in capital gains tax liability and that a hypothetical seller would not accept that it was reduced for such liability. Finding the Fifth Circuit's approach in *Dunn* persuasive, the Eleventh Circuit reversed, essentially assuming that all company assets were sold in liquidation on the valuation date and that 100 percent of the trapped-in tax liability would be offset against the fair market value of the stock, dollar for dollar. The court thus rejected the tax court's distinction between a minority and controlling interest for purposes of the discount, noting that "whether or not a majority or minority interest is present is of no moment in an assumption of liquidation setting."

Cases that have rejected the discount for trapped-in capital gains have involved partnership interests, where the capital gains tax could have been avoided by an IRC Section 754 election. The courts in those cases have reasoned that a hypothetical buyer and seller would negotiate with the understanding that such an election would be made.[122]

Charitable Contributions

Regulation Section 1.170A-13(c) requires a summary appraisal by a qualified appraiser in conjunction with any charitable contribution in the form of a closely held business interest valued at over $5,000. The section defines a qualified appraiser as an individual who:

1. Holds himself or herself out to the public as an appraiser or who regularly performs appraisals
2. Is qualified to appraise property because of his or her qualifications
3. Is aware of the appraiser penalties associated with the overvaluation of charitable contributions under IRC Section 6701

Certain individuals, however, may not act as qualified appraisers, including:

1. The property's donor (or the taxpayer who claims the deduction)
2. The property's donee
3. A party to the property transfer transaction (with certain very specific exceptions)
4. Any person employed by, married to, or related to any of the above persons
5. An appraiser who regularly appraises for the donor, donee, or party to the transaction and does not perform a majority of his or her appraisals for other persons

6. An individual who would otherwise be a qualified appraiser, but the donor has knowledge of facts that would cause a reasonable person to expect the appraiser falsely to overstate the value of the donated property (for example, the donor and the appraiser make an agreement concerning the amount at which the property will be valued and the donor knows that such amount exceeds the fair market value of the property)

The IRS and the tax court enforce this requirement. In one case the IRS completely disallowed charitable deductions claimed in two years because the donor failed to comply with the appraisal requirement, even though the commissioner conceded that the values claimed as deductions were the same as the fair market value of the stock contributed. The tax court upheld the commissioner's determination. The court of appeals found that "Congress intended the qualified appraisal requirement to be mandatory." Accordingly, the taxpayer's failure to obtain an appraisal was fatal to any claim of deduction for his charitable contributions.[123]

In addition, other valuation issues arise in the charitable deduction context, such as the appropriate discounts to apply. For example, where shareholders owned a 45 percent interest in a corporation and simultaneously donated their interest in "lockstep" with the corporation's other minority shareholders, as part of a prearranged plan, the tax court reduced the IRS's proposed 22 percent minority discount to 10 percent but failed to explain why any minority discount was justified, since collectively 100 percent of the company was being transferred.[124]

With regard to contributions of qualified appreciated stock, an issue that can arise is whether on the transfer date market quotations with respect to the shares are readily available on an established securities market. In *Todd v. Comm'r*,[125] the stock at issue had not been listed on any exchange, and the taxpayer based the claimed deductions on subsequent sales of stock that occurred shortly after the contributions were made. The tax court disallowed the deductions, holding that the shares were not qualified appreciated stock on the transfer date. Therefore, the taxpayer was subject to substantiation requirements, which the taxpayer failed to provide. The case thus illustrates the importance of obtaining a formal appraisal when shares are not traded on an exchange.

Contingent Liabilities

The most common contingent liabilities are environmental liabilities (discovered or potential) and outcomes of lawsuits. The uncertainty, of course, makes it very difficult to quantify the impact on value of these contingencies at a moment in time. In a true market setting, the solution normally would be to create a reserve account in escrow pending resolution of the uncertainties, but in a tax setting, one must arrive at a specific number as of the effective valuation date.

A 1999 case involved a paint company that was considered a hazardous waste producer with potential environmental liability. The court allowed a 10 percent discount from the value indicated by the discounted cash flow method but no discount from the value indicated by the guideline public company method, on the theory that the guideline company stock market prices probably already reflected the potential environmental liability.[126] In *Estate of Mitchell v. Comm'r*[127] the tax court took a $1.5 million discount for a pending compensation lawsuit. In *Estate of Klauss v. Comm'r*[128] the court permitted a 10 percent discount for product liability and environmental claims.

One of the authors, Shannon Pratt, was involved in a case valuing three creosote plants on the shores of Puget Sound. The IRS and the company management agreed that the environmental damage was great enough that all three operations would potentially be shut down. But the company had been operating for ten years since the problems were known. The case was informally settled at an arbitrary 50 percent discount from the value that was reached by conventional approaches.

Subsequent Events and Information

The principle is clear that only events or information that were known or foreseeable as of the valuation date may be taken into consideration. Clear as the principle may be, the admissibility and relevance of post-valuation date information is often a major controversy.

Proximity of Financial Information to Valuation Date

If valuing stock late in a fiscal period, it usually is acceptable to use financial data as of the end of that period. The philosophy is that late in a fiscal period, the performance for the period would be reasonably foreseeable in most cases.

Useful examples can be found in *Rabenhorst v. Comm'r*[129] and *Central Trust v. Comm'r.*[130] A particularly relevant caution can be found in *Polack v. Comm'r*,[131] in which the taxpayer used unaudited financials for years subsequent to the valuation date to argue that actual results were significantly lower than projections provided by the IRS at trial. The Eighth Circuit did not admit these, saying that "post-transaction earnings would not have been known to a prospective purchaser" as of the valuation date.

Rulings on the "known and knowable" financial information in the circumstances of the decease of the taxpayer can be problematic, and the circumstances should be considered carefully. In *Okerlund v. United States*[132] the Federal Circuit affirmed the Court of Federal Claims' ruling that estate plan provisions requiring the purchase of stock upon decedent's death should not have been included in valuing the stock when decedent's death was untimely and unexpected. The court said that valuation must always be made as of the donative date relying primarily on ex ante information; ex post data should be used sparingly.

However, in *Estate of Noble v. Comm'r*[133] the court permitted the use of a post-death event to value minority shares in a bank. The estate presented as evidence of value an offer by the controlling shareholder to purchase the decedent's shares for $878,004 a few months after the date of death. However, the IRS presented evidence of the estate's sale of the shares to the bank for $1.1 million 10 months later. The court noted that there had not been any material change in circumstances between the sale date and the date of death. The court reasoned, "An event occurring after a valuation date, even if unforeseeable as of the valuation date, also may be probative of the earlier valuation to the extent that it is relevant to establishing the amount that a hypothetical willing buyer would have paid a hypothetical willing seller for the subject property as of the valuation date. . . . Unforeseeable subsequent events which fall within this latter category include evidence, such as we have here."[134]

Subsequent Sales

The tax court frequently relies on subsequent sales as evidence of value. The court distinguishes between subsequent sales that *affected* the value and those that are merely *evidence of value.*

A subsequent sale surfaced as an issue in *Estate of Jung* in an opinion released in November 1993. The matter involved the fair market value of a 20 percent interest in an operating company as of October 9, 1984. In mid-1986 the company was approached about selling its major operating assets, a transaction was completed on December 29, 1986, and the company was liquidated. The tax court explained its position as follows:

> Respondent contends that, in valuing Jung Corp. stock, this Court should consider the sale to Kendall, the other sales, and the ensuing liquidation of Jung Corp.
>
> Petitioner contends the 1986 sales and the liquidation are irrelevant because the sales and liquidation were unforeseeable at the valuation date.
>
> We agree in part with respondent and in part with petitioner.

A distinction may usefully be drawn between later-occurring events which affect fair market value as of the valuation date, and later-occurring events which may be taken into account as evidence of fair market value as of the valuation date.

If a prospective October 9, 1984, buyer and seller were likely to have foreseen the 1986 sale to Kendall, and the other activities leading to the liquidation, then those later-occurring events could affect what a willing buyer would pay and what a willing seller would demand as of October 9, 1984. We conclude, and we have found that, on October 9, 1984, Jung Corp. was not for sale, the sale to Kendall was not foreseeable, and the liquidation was not foreseeable. Accordingly, we conclude that those later-occurring events did not affect the October 9, 1984, fair market of decedent's stock. *Estate of Gilford v. Comm'r*, 88 T.C. 38, 51-55 (1987).

However, we have stated that "for purposes of determining fair market value, we believe it appropriate to consider sales of properties occurring subsequent to the valuation date if the properties involved are indeed comparable to the subject properties." *Estate of Thompson v. Comm'r*, 89 T.C. 619, 628-629 n. 7 (1987), *rev'd.* on other grounds 864 F.2d 1128 (4th Cir. 1989). To the same effect are, e.g., *Krapf v. United States*, 977 F.2d 1454, 1458-1460 (Fed. Cir. 1992); *Estate of Kaplin v. Comm'r*, 748 F.2d 1109, 1111 (6th Cir. 1984), *rev'g.* T.C. Memo. 1982-440 (1982); *Estate of Brown v. Comm'r*, 425 F.2d 1406, 1407 (5th Cir. 1970), *aff'g.* T.C. Memo. 1969-91 (1969). See *Estate of Jung v. Comm'r*, T.C. Memo. 1990-5 and cases cited therein.

Of course, appropriate adjustments must be made to take account of differences between the valuation date and the dates of the later-occurring events. . . . Although any such changes must be accounted for in determining the evidentiary weight to be given to the later-occurring events, those changes ordinarily are not justification for ignoring the later-occurring events (unless other comparables offer significantly better matches to the property being valued).

> When viewed in this light—as evidence of value rather than as something that affects value—later-occurring events are no more to be ignored than earlier-occurring events.
>
> Accordingly, we do not consider the sales and eventual liquidation as affecting the October 9, 1984, value of Jung Corp., but we do consider these events as evidence of the October 9, 1984, value.[135]

Ultimately, the tax court determined that some of the petitioner's higher indications of value were reconcilable with the subsequent sale.

In *Saltzman v. Comm'r*[136] a holding company sold its major asset, film rights, seven months after the valuation date at a much higher price than the taxpayer's expert had appraised the rights at as of the valuation date. The court relied on the sale value, discounted for the time value back to the effective valuation date. The court explained its position as follows:

> Generally, a sale of the property close in time to the valuation date is the best evidence of fair market value. *Estate of Spruill v. Comm'r*, 88 T.C. 1197, 1229, 1233 (1987); sec. 20.2031-1(b) Estate Tax Regs. A sale of the property after the valuation date is highly relevant evidence of value if there are no material changes in the interim. *Estate of Kaplin v. Comm'r*, 748 F.2d 1109, 1111 (6th Cir. 1984), *rev'g.* T.C. Memo. 1982-440 (sale 2 years after the valuation date). In contrast, material market changes following the valuation date may make a later sale price less probative or irrelevant in deciding the value on the valuation date. *Estate of Spruill v. Comm'r*, supra at 1233.[137]

The tax court also cited *Estate of Kaplin v. Comm'r* (748 F.2d 1109, 1111 [6th Cir. 1984], rev'g. T.C. Memo. 1982-440) and *Estate of Gilford* in this decision.

The most extreme case of the tax court's relying on a sale long after the effective valuation date is found in *Estate of Cidulka*.[138] The effective valuation date was January 25, 1982. Four years later (January 1986) the company, an outdoor advertising sign company, sold its assets to a major competitor for 2.89 times gross revenue. The tax court used this sale to conclude that the value of the stock should be 2.5 times the company's gross revenue for 1981 (the year prior to the effective valuation date).

In one case, the tax court relied on a January 1994 sale to value minority stock in an estate as of July 16, 1991. The estate tax return valued the stock at $35.20 per share, based on an update of an appraisal done in 1989. The 1994 sale took place at $75.15 per share. The tax court reduced the sale price by 30 percent, resulting in a value of $50.51 per share. The reason for the reduction was because the IRS offered no expert testimony, and the court rejected the taxpayer's expert's opinion for several reasons (highly instructive cautions for any professional dealing with a valuation in any way):

- He was unable to explain certain parts of the analysis contained in the reports.
- He arbitrarily applied a 35 percent marketability discount.
- He made no mention of a hypothetical seller.
- Whereas the 1989 report states that [taxpayer's expert] toured the facilities, there is nothing in his testimony or the 1991 report to suggest that he did likewise before preparing the 1991 report.
- The 1991 report does not adequately account for the fact that the company's 1991 earnings increased dramatically over the years covered by the 1989 report.
- The 1991 report does not adequately take into account that the company began paying dividends after the time covered by the 1989 report.
- The 1991 report refers to the financial data of publicly traded companies, yet never explains how those companies were selected, or in what respects their lines of business were similar to the subject company.[139]

The estate tax value filed might well have held up in court had it been adequately supported. In some other valuation context, such as family law, the case may have been remanded due to lack of adequate valuation evidence, but the tax court goes ahead and reaches a conclusion based on whatever it has before it.

In *Estate of Trompeter v. Comm'r*, the tax court relied on a redemption 16 months following the valuation date. Again the IRS offered no expert testimony, and the court rejected the taxpayer's expert's opinion as unpersuasive, noting, among other shortcomings, reliance on companies that were not comparable. The final determination of value was the redemption amount of $1,947,845, compared to $15,335 filed on the decedent's federal estate tax return. The court also upheld the fraud penalty under Section 6663(a).[140]

Buy-Sell Agreements

The value established by a buy-sell agreement may be controlling, may be ignored, or may be a factor to consider.

For buy-sell agreements entered into after October 8, 1990, a buy-sell price is binding for federal estate tax purposes if it meets all of the following criteria[141]:

- The price must be fixed or determinable as of a determinable date.
- The agreement must be binding on the parties both during life and after death.
- The agreement must have been entered into for a bona fide business reason.
- It must not be a substitute for testamentary disposition.
- The agreement must result in a fair market value for the subject business interest at the time the agreement is executed.
- Its terms must be comparable to similar arrangements entered into by persons in arm's-length transactions.

The tax court, in *Estate of Lauder v. Comm'r* (*Lauder II*),[142] adopted this test and ruled that the test's elements are conjunctive, meaning that all of them must be independently satisfied to give the buy-sell price dispositive effect.

Regulations Section 20.2031-2(h) provides the following:

> Such price will be disregarded in determining the value of the securities unless it is determined under the circumstances of the particular case that the agreement represents a *bona fide* business arrangement and not a device to pass the decedent's shares to the natural objects of his bounty for less than full and adequate consideration in money or money's worth.

In *Estate of Blount v. Comm'r*[143] the tax court disregarded a buy-sell agreement in determining the decedent's interest in a closely held company on the date of his death because the decedent had the unilateral ability to modify it, thus failing to satisfy the requirement that it be binding during life. The court also disregarded the agreement under IRC Section 2703, which requires that to be included in a valuation, a buy-sell agreement's terms must be "comparable to similar arrangements entered into by persons in an arm's length transaction." Here, the court concluded that the parties were "related" and had not engaged in arm's length bargaining. The Eleventh Circuit affirmed.

Interestingly in this case, there was a life insurance policy owned by the company that provided $3.1 million to pay off the mandated buyout of the shares. The tax court included the full amount of the insurance proceeds as nonoperating assets, and it also concluded that because the buy-sell agreement had been disregarded, the issue of whether the company's obligation under that agreement to redeem the decedent's stock should offset the proceeds was not before the court. As to the insurance proceeds, the Eleventh Circuit ruled that the tax court had erred because those proceeds had already been taken into account in the determination of net worth. The court noted that even when a buy-sell agreement is inoperative for establishing the value of the company for tax purposes, the agreement remains an enforceable liability against the valued company if state law fixes such an obligation—which it had in this case. Here, the insurance proceeds were offset dollar for dollar by the company's obligation to satisfy its contract with the decedent's estate. The court thus concluded that such nonoperating "assets" should not be included in the fair market valuation of a company where, as here, there was an enforceable contractual obligation that offset such assets.

In *Estate of True v. Comm'r*,[144] one issue was whether the book value price specified in the buy-sell agreements controlled estate and gift tax values of the subject interests in several family companies gifted and deeded to children. The analysis focused on the *Lauder II* factors. The court found that the fact that the children did not have independent legal or accounting advice, while not dispositive, reasonably suggested less than arm's length dealings. The court was critical that the companies' buy-sell agreements did not provide a mechanism for periodic review or adjustment to the tax book value formula. The court also considered an analysis under the *adequacy of consideration test*. This test requires that the formula price (1) be comparable to what persons with adverse interests dealing at arm's length would accept and (2) bear a reasonable relationship to fair market value. As the court said, "These standards must be applied with the heightened scrutiny imposed on intrafamily agreements restricting transfers of closely held businesses." The court concluded that "the True family buy-sell agreements do not satisfy the *Lauder II* test because they are substitutes for testamentary dispositions. As a result, under Section 2031 and the related regulations, the tax book value buy-sell agreement price does not control estate tax values of interests in the True companies at issue in the estate tax case." The court also determined that the buy-sell agreements were not controlling for the gift tax case. The Tenth Circuit affirmed.

An example of a case in which the buy-sell agreement price was controlling is *Hutchens Non-Marital Trust v. Comm'r*.[145] The court upheld the buy-sell price because it found that the negotiations had been at arm's length and in the ordinary course of business. In arriving at this decision, the court noted that a formal appraisal had been conducted and that each of the parties to the agreement had been individually represented by attorneys during negotiations. This case demonstrates the benefit of having an appraisal conducted after the buy-sell agreement has been entered into and also to aid in setting a buy-sell price or formula.

Weighting of Valuation Method Results

Revenue Ruling 59-60 is negative toward the idea of reconciling two or more indications of value by applying mathematical weights to each. Judge Laro discusses the issue as follows:

> In spite of this, some valuation practitioners apply weights to various factors in reaching their valuation conclusions because this allows them to clearly demonstrate the importance that they attach to various valuation considerations. This approach was used by the Tax Court in *Estate of Feldmar v. Comm'r.* T.C. Memo. 1988-429; *Estate of Titus v. Comm'r,* T.C. Memo 1989-466; *Estate of Campbell v. Comm'r,* T.C. Memo. 1991-615. The weighing of various methods, however, was squarely rejected by the Court in *Estate of Mueller v. Comm'r,* T.C. Memo. 1992-284.
>
> With what appears to be conflicting judicial positions on this issue, there is some concern about whether the weighing of factors is a proper method of appraisal.
>
> I believe that one should consider carefully all relevant factors but should not assign weights to each factor. However, practitioners may emphasize a few factors that could influence the ultimate valuation.[146]

Another case in which the court ultimately utilized an explicit percentage weighting of factors is the oft-quoted *Central Trust v. United States* in the U.S. Court of Claims. The court relied entirely on the guideline public company method and applied 50 percent of the weight to the price-to-earnings multiples, 30 percent to the dividend yield, and 20 percent to the price-to-book value multiple.[147] In *Hess v. Comm'r*,[148] the IRS's expert did not assign any weight to the discounted cash flow method because the company's future income was difficult to predict and because valuation conclusions were highly sensitive to small changes in assumptions. The tax court indicated that while less weight should be accorded to this method under such circumstances, it should nonetheless be considered in the valuation process. The court did not, however, specify an exact percentage of weight to be accorded to the method. In *Estate of Dunn v. Comm'r*,[149] the court indicated that weighting was a key issue. The IRS's expert accorded the asset approach a 100 percent weight, whereas the taxpayer's expert weighted the income and asset approaches equally given that no liquidation was planned. The tax court decided that the appropriate weight was 65 percent for the asset approach and 35 percent for the income approach, based on various factors, such as the depressed nature of the industry and the company's low profitability and high debt. On appeal, the Fifth Circuit determined that the likelihood of liquidation was a relevant factor for weighting and ruled that the earnings-based method should be weighted at 85 percent to reflect the low likelihood of liquidation.[150]

If the expert says, "I accorded more weight to *x* factor," the judge may ask, "Well, how *much* weight?" My colleagues and I have previously opined on this dilemma as follows:

> Despite this wording, the method has been used successfully in many gift and estate tax cases both in dealing with the IRS and in cases decided in court. The wording of Revenue Ruling 59-60 indicates concern that the averaging or weighted average method leaves room for omission of pertinent factors. However, it is possible to use the basic weighted average of factors procedure and still, at one stage or another, incorporate consideration of all the pertinent factors mentioned in Revenue Ruling 59-60. Of course,

> it is important to be careful to demonstrate in each case that all other pertinent factors were actively considered and reflected in the result to the appropriate extent.[151]

All this discussion leads to the conclusion that neither explicit nor implicit weighting of varying indications of value is clearly superior. If an explicit weighting is used, we suggest a disclaimer to the effect that there is not an empirical basis for the weighting; it is presented only to help the reader understand the analyst's thinking regarding relative importance.[152]

Pressure to Settle

The tax court has consistently urged taxpayers and the IRS to attempt to settle valuation disputes rather than bring them to trial. For example:

> Once again we must advise counsel that valuation cases such as this are better suited for the give and take of the settlement process than adjudication. See *Buffalo Tool & Die Manufacturing Co. v. Comm'r*, 74 T.C. 441, 451 (1980); *Messing v. Comm'r*, 48 T.C. 502, 512 (1967). It is quite clear from the record that the experts have not been permitted to meet to discuss their reports and attempt to resolve their differences. Furthermore, the Court concludes that counsel have failed to meaningfully confer with each other regarding settlement and stipulation as required by the Court's Standing Pre-trial Order. The result of this "Rambo" approach to Tax Court litigation is that the parties and the Court have had to spend considerable time and effort in trial, on briefs, and in opinion writing to resolve a question which clearly should have been settled.[153]

Similar opinions were expressed in *Estate of Furman v. Comm'r*,[154] citing both *Estate of Hall v. Comm'r* and *Messing v. Comm'r*.

References

Articles and Books

Bellatti, Robert M., and Shari L. West. 1999. *Estate Planning for Farms and Other Qualified Family-Owned Businesses.* Boston: Warren, Gorham & Lamont. Covers Section 2032A and Section 2057 special-use valuations.

Bogdanski, John. *Federal Tax Valuation,* 1996, Boston: Warren, Gorham & Lamont, plus annual supplements. Includes thousands of case citations with discussions.

Feld, Daniel E. 2002. *Estate and Gift Tax Digest,* 4th ed. Boston: Warren, Gorham & Lamont. Cites, and digests, cases and rulings.

Fishman, Jay, et al. Annual. "Estate and Gift Tax Valuations." In *PPC's Guide to Business Valuations.* Fort Worth, TX: Practitioners Publishing, pp. 10-1 to 10-75.

Howitt, Idelle A. 2002/2003. *Federal Tax Valuation Digest: Business Enterprise and Business Interests.* Boston: Warren, Gorham & Lamont. Summarizes most federal cases involving valuations of businesses and business interests from 1945 through the present. Each annual edition is cumulative.

Kasper, Larry J. 1997. "Federal Tax Valuations." In *Business Valuations, Advanced Topics.* Westport, CT: Greenwood Publishing, pp. 211–258.

Pratt, Shannon. 2003. "Tax Related Valuations." In *Business Valuation Body of Knowledge,* 2nd ed. New York: Wiley, pp. 309–314.

Pratt, Shannon P., and Alina V. Niculita. 2007. "Valuation for Estate and Gift Tax Purposes" and "Valuation for Income Tax Purposes." In *Valuing a Business,* 5th ed. New York: McGraw-Hill, pp. 627–660, 723–752.

Saltzman, Michael J. 2006. *IRS Practice and Procedure,* rev. 2nd ed. Boston: Warren, Gorham & Lamont. Covers the complete range of IRS procedures from rulings to collection of taxes.

Solomon, Lewis D., and Lewis J. Saret. 1998. "General Rules of Valuation: Tax Perspective." In *Valuation of Closely Held Businesses.* New York: Panel Publishers, pp. 67–104.

Trugman, Gary. 2002. "Revenue Ruling 59-60." In *Understanding Business Valuations*, 2nd ed. New York: American Institute of Certified Public Accountants (AICPA), pp. 409–448.

Websites

www.BVResources.com contains the BVLibrary.com. Contains full text of all case opinions in this chapter, all searchable by key word.

www.ustaxcourt.gov contains all appealable tax court opinions from January 3, 1999, to the present.

Chapter 20

Shareholder and Partner Disputes

Virtually all states have dissenting stockholder statutes. Dissenters' rights are triggered by major corporate actions, such as mergers, acquisitions, or liquidations, the criteria for which vary from state to state. Stockholders who dissent may not reverse the corporate action but are entitled to be paid the *fair value* of the shares immediately before the action has been put into effect, excluding any anticipatory appreciation or depreciation.

A growing number of states also have minority oppression statutes, many of which are based on the Model Business Corporation Act (MBCA), as revised.[1] Significantly, Delaware, considered a bellwether of corporate law, does not have a minority oppression statute, and the Delaware Supreme Court has refused to impose a remedy for minority shareholder oppression absent a pronouncement from the state's legislature.[2] Nonetheless, it is clear that a majority of states provide some form of relief for oppressed minority shareholders.[3]

Some states require that the collective minority seeking oppression relief own some minimum percentage of the total stock; others have no such requirement. Criteria required to trigger a finding of oppression or irreconcilable differences vary. In most states, oppressed owners may seek dissolution of the entity. Most states also provide for alternative remedies, particularly a compulsory buyout of the minority by the majority of the company at fair value.[4]

One line of cases requires a finding of wrongdoing by the controlling shareholder, such as self-dealing or repudiation of going-in corporate governance arrangements.[5] In such jurisdictions, the judicial scrutiny ordinarily takes the doctrinal form of an inquiry into whether the majority shareholder has breached a duty of "utmost good faith and loyalty" that is owed to the minority investor. Another line of cases defines *oppression* with reference to what a court determines to be the reasonable expectations of the minority shareholders. This "reasonable expectations test" is normally applicable only to founding shareholders and is based on expectations at formation.[6] Some states, such as Illinois, define *oppression* as "heavy-handed and overbearing or arbitrary conduct."[7] Especially in states that do not have an oppression dissolution statute, some courts have imposed a fiduciary duty between close corporation shareholders, and they have permitted a minority shareholder to bring a direct cause of action for breach of this duty. In the seminal decision of *Donahue v. Rodd Electrotype Co.*, the Massachusetts Supreme Judicial Court adopted such a standard:

> We hold that stockholders in the close corporation owe one another substantially the same fiduciary duty in the operation of the enterprise that partners owe to one another. In our previous decisions, we have defined the standard of duty owed by partners to one another as the "utmost good faith and loyalty." Stockholders in close corporations must discharge their management and stockholder responsibilities in conformity with this strict good faith standard. They may not act out of avarice, expediency or self-interest in derogation of their duty of loyalty to the other stockholders and to the corporation.[8]

Other courts have imposed a similar duty.[9] It is arguable that such a duty should be imposed in limited liability companies as well.[10]

Shareholder, limited liability company member, and partner suits involving valuation of interests arise in a variety of situations. The most common are these:

- Dissenting stockholder actions
- Suits for dissolution of a corporation, limited liability company, or partnership, usually based on a claim of minority oppression
- Breach of fiduciary duty (often coupled with minority oppression)

Although shareholder actions in all these categories are on the rise throughout the country, several states do not have precedential case law on many valuation issues. In deciding on issues, it is very common for states to quote case law from several different states.

Fair Value Standard in Most Dissent and Dissolution Suits

Stockholder appraisal rights are defined by state statute. The state statutes also designate the standard of value to be applied. A recent review of the state statutes relating to dissenting stockholder rights indicates that all states except California designate *fair value* or *fair cash value* as the standard of value (California's statute specifies *fair market value*). Most states have modeled their dissenting stockholder statutes after the Model Business Corporation Act. This act was revised in 1984 and became known as the Revised Model Business Corporation Act (RMBCA), which has had revisions through 2002. Until 1999, the RMBCA defined *fair value* as follows:

> The value of the shares immediately before the effectuation of the corporate action to which the shareholder objects, excluding any appreciation or depreciations in anticipation of the corporate action unless exclusion would be inequitable.

In 1999 the definition changed to:

> "Fair value" means the value of the corporation's shares determined:
> (i) immediately before the effectuation of the corporate action to which the shareholder objects;
> (ii) using customary and current valuation concepts and techniques generally employed for similar businesses in the context of the transaction requiring appraisal; and
> (iii) without discounting for lack of marketability or minority status except, if appropriate, for amendments to the articles pursuant to section 13.02(a)(5).[11]

The majority of states[12] use the pre-1999 definition, and only a handful have adopted the 1999 version. A minority of states uses the pre-1999 definition without the "unless exclusion would be inequitable" phrase, and some states omit this phrase but, in addition, add a clause that states that all relevant factors should be considered in determining value. Florida and Illinois use a hybrid of the pre-1999 and 1999 definitions.[13]

According to the official comment of the RMBCA, the definition of *fair value* leaves to the parties (and, ultimately, to the courts) the details by which fair value is to be determined within the broad outlines of the definition. As a result, interpretations of fair value vary considerably from state to state.

A typical and frequently quoted interpretation of the philosophy of fair value in a dissenting stockholder situation is the following:

> Fair value, in an appraisal context, measures "that which has been taken from [the shareholder], viz., his proportionate interest in a going concern." (*Source: Tri-Continental Corp. v. Battye*, Del. Supr. 74 A.2d 71, 72 [1950].)[14]

Delaware Block Rule Expanded

There is far more shareholder dispute litigation in Delaware than in any other state, primarily because so many corporations are incorporated in Delaware. This is particularly true of dissenting stockholder litigation. One of the results is that Delaware dissenting stockholder cases are quoted more than cases from any other state.

Before 1983, dissenting stockholder cases primarily used the Delaware Block Method. This method develops values in each of three categories: investment value, market value, and asset value. Mathematical weightings are then assigned to the indications of value from each of the three approaches (although the weight to one, or even two in extreme cases, could be zero), and the resulting weighted average is the concluded value.

The definitions of *investment value* and *market value* in this context are a little different from those discussed in the three basic approaches to value.

Investment value in the context of the Delaware Block Method means value based on expected earnings and/or dividends. It is akin to the value based on the income approach in the three basic approaches to value. It may be arrived at by discounted cash flow, capitalization of earnings, or capitalization of dividends. In this sense it mixes the traditional income approach and market approach in that it may derive capitalization rates by methods under either.

Market value, on the other hand, has historically been based on prior transactions in the subject company's securities. This contrasts with the traditional appraisal concept of market value as discussed in Chapter 14, where multiples of both income statement and balance sheet parameters based on comparable transactions are used.

The summary of a typical Delaware Block Method appraisal might look something like the following:

	Indicated Value per Share	**Weight**	**Weighted Value**
Capitalization of earnings	$10.00	30%	$3.00
Capitalization of dividends	$ 6.00	20%	1.20
Market value	$ 8.00	30%	2.40
Asset value	$15.00	20%	3.00
Weighted value per share			$9.60

However, a landmark case in 1983 said that the traditional factors considered under the Delaware Block Rule alone were not necessarily sufficient; instead, all relevant factors must be considered. In that particular case, the court specifically made the point that projections of future earnings were available and should be considered. The court also made the point that a determination of fair value "must include proof of value by any techniques or methods which are generally considered acceptable in the financial community."[15]

All Relevant Factors Must Be Considered

The interpretation of fair value is a subject of continued debate and is difficult to generalize. However, most states have embraced the notion that "all relevant factors should be considered."

Courts have treated *investment value* (defined in this context as value based on earning capacity) as the most important of the three elements. In fact, in one case the Delaware Court of Chancery stated that the discounted cash flow (DCF) model is "increasingly the model of choice for valuations in this court."[16] However, as noted earlier, one landmark case pointed out that *all* relevant factors must be considered,[17] and the Delaware Court of Chancery has rejected the DCF method where it finds that the projections or data underpinning the DCF analysis are inadequate.[18] Some courts have also indicated that a fair market value analysis may be a "relevant factor" that should be considered in determining fair value.[19]

Courts tend to rely heavily on expert reports and testimony in resolving fair value cases. Even in circumstances with diametrically opposed professional perspectives on the value of the entity in question, the courts typically accept certain portions of each expert's valuation and fashion their own conclusion.

Strategic Buyer Value Might Be Considered

The question frequently arises whether a "relevant factor" is what a company might be sold for if it were put "in play." The most likely buyer of many companies is another industry participant, who may be expected to pay more because of operational synergies or competitive advantages obtainable from the purchase. One difficulty is that any attempt to apply this standard requires some assumptions regarding the prospective buyer and is not limited to the operating characteristics of the company on a stand-alone basis.

Strategic buyer valuation also would seem to be in conflict with the language contained in most dissenters' rights statutes that appreciation in anticipation of the corporate action is not to be included. While the Delaware courts appear to have rejected this standard,[20] language in opinions from other states may be construed to permit consideration of strategic buyer values.[21] (In Canada, courts routinely include strategic value as an element of fair value in dissenting stockholder cases.) Some commentators also contend that not all synergies should be disregarded since only those synergies not available to a particular buyer may be indicative of investment value.[22]

Discounts or Premiums Are Often a Major Issue

The largest single issue in most shareholder and partner valuation disputes is whether discounts and/or premiums are applicable, and, if so, what should be the magnitude of such discounts and/or premiums. The most common issues involve minority discounts or control premiums and discounts for lack of marketability. Positions on these issues vary from state to state, and sometimes state case precedents change, so it is necessary to be aware of the latest precedential case law.

For example, not very many states have adopted the RMBCA, but even some of those that have not have refused minority and marketability discounts, citing the revision. Furthermore, case precedent often is different for dissenting stockholder actions than it is for dissolution actions.

Discounts for Lack of Marketability and Lack of Control

States often differ in their acceptance or rejection of discounting for lack of marketability and lack of control.

Discounts Left to Court's Discretion

Some states leave the question of applicability of both minority and marketability discounts to the court's or a jury's discretion.[23] For example, the Illinois Court of Appeals in *Jahn v. Kinderman* said with regard to such discounts that "the application of a discount was a matter for the discretion of the trial court."[24] These courts are reluctant to set a bright rule in the event that circumstances or justice require the application of a discount.

For example, in *Advanced Communication Design, Inc. v. Follett*,[25] the court indicated that it would only be fair and equitable to apply a marketability discount to the value of the company because there was no possibility that the company could achieve the liquidity necessary to compensate the departing shareholder. This was viewed as an extraordinary circumstance warranting the application of the discount. The American Law Institute (ALI) recognizes such extraordinary circumstances in the definition of *fair value* that it includes in its Principles of Corporate Governance.[26] It defines *fair value* thus:

> The value of the eligible holder's proportionate interest in the corporation, without any discount for minority status or, absent extraordinary circumstances, lack of marketability.

Extraordinary Circumstances

Other states also find the applicability of minority and marketability discounts to be a discretionary matter, but they require the court to consider whether extraordinary circumstances warrant the application of a discount for lack of marketability.[27] For example, the primary issue in two cases, decided the same day by the New Jersey Supreme

Court,[28] was whether a marketability discount should be applied in determining the fair value to be paid in shareholder suits.

In *Wheaton*, a statutory appraisal action, the court stated the following:

> The history and policy behind dissenters' right and appraisal statutes lead us to conclude that marketability discounts generally should not be applied when determining the "fair value" of dissenters' shares in a statutory appraisal action. Of course, there may be situations where equity compels another result. Those situations are best resolved by resort to the "extraordinary circumstances" exception in 2 ALI Principles, 7.22(a).

In *Balsamides*, in an oppressed shareholder action, the court stated the following:

> To secure "fair value" for Perle's stock, a marketability discount should be applied. To do otherwise would be unfair, particularly since Perle was the oppressor and Balsamides was the oppressed shareholder.

Rejection of Shareholder-Level Discounts

Delaware has consistently rejected the application of discounts. In *Cavalier Oil v. Harnett*,[29] the Delaware Supreme Court indicated that the objective of the appraisal outlined by the state's appraisal statute was to value the corporation itself rather than value a specific fraction of shares in the hands of one shareholder, and therefore, no shareholder-level discounts should be applied.

Of the states that have declared themselves on the issue of discounts in dissenters' rights actions, several follow the lead of Delaware and reject discounts for either minority interest or lack of marketability, either by statute[30] and/or case law.[31] For example, the Iowa Supreme Court affirmed a lower court valuation that rejected a discount for lack of marketability.[32] Another example is *Pueblo Bancorporation v. Lindoe*,

Inc.,[33] in which a divided Colorado Supreme Court affirmed a decision denying a lack of marketability discount when determining fair value under Colorado's dissenters' rights statute. The court noted that the trial court must first determine the value of the corporation as a going concern and the pro rata value of each outstanding share, and it said that discounts should not be applied except under extraordinary circumstances.

In *Brown v. Arp and Hammond Hardware Co.*,[34] the Wyoming Supreme Court, finding that the clear majority of courts have held that minority discounts do not apply when determining fair value in the appraisal context, ruled that it would join the majority and not permit such discounts.

The Kansas Supreme Court overruled a previous decision that allowed a minority discount in an action for appraisal: *Moore v. New Ammest, Inc.*[35] The court stated the following:

> In answering the certified question before us, we hold that minority and marketability discounts should not be applied when the fractional share resulted from a reverse stock split intended to eliminate a minority shareholder's interest in the corporation.[36]

We believe it is important to recognize that the applicability of this decision is limited to the narrow circumstances of the question put to the court: "when the fractional share resulted from a reverse stock split intended to eliminate the shareholder's interest in the corporation." There are many other actions where dissenters' rights are triggered even though the stockholders are not forced to be cashed out, a fact set that would seem to be very distinguishable from this case.

In Oregon, a marketability discount may be applied in a dissenters' case, but a minority discount may not (*Columbia Management Co. v. Wyss*, 94 Ore. App. 195, 765 P.2d 207 [1988]). However, in a minority oppression case (*Hayes v. Omstead & Associates, Inc.*, 21 P.3d 178 [Or. Ct. App. 2001]), neither discount is to be applied because the minority shareholder is entitled to recover his pro rata interest without regard to discounts applicable in other settings.

It is important to keep up on the current case law because states sometimes change their positions or take different positions from one case to another depending on the facts and circumstances of each. For example, a 1998 Montana Supreme Court dissenting stockholder case reversed a lower court decision that had accepted a 30 percent minority interest discount. Under the Montana Business Corporation Act, the Montana Supreme Court prohibited the consideration of a minority interest discount when establishing fair value.[37] This was in spite of the fact that a 1996 Montana Supreme Court minority oppression case allowed a 25 percent minority discount, stating that the stockholder "has not demonstrated to the satisfaction of this court that 'fair value' necessarily excluded an application of a minority discount."[38]

Discounts Permitted

Some states permit the application of shareholder-level discounts in determining fair value (or "fair cash value") in shareholder dissent and oppression cases. Some permit only the lack of marketability discount,[39] some permit only the lack of control discount,[40]and some permit both.[41]

Control Premiums

One of the most commonly cited cases regarding the use of a control premium is the Delaware Supreme Court case of *Rapid-American Corp. v. Harris.*[42] That case involved a statutory appraisal action contesting a merger. The state supreme court held that the trial court was required to add a control premium to the publicly traded equity value of a corporation's shares for each of the corporation's operating subsidiaries.

Hintmann v. Weber[43] is a case decided by the Delaware Court of Chancery after *Rapid-American.* The corporation was a holding company whose primary asset was 100 percent of the Fred Weber corporation's class A common stock, which represented approximately 90 percent of Fred Weber's value. Based on *Rapid-American*, the court decided that a control premium should be added to the value of Fred Weber's as a subsidiary of Weber Industries, Inc. The mean premium for publicly held companies in the 12 months ended June 30, 1992, was approximately 45 percent, and the median premium was about 55 percent. Because a portion of those premiums reflected post-merger values expected from synergies, the appraiser arbitrarily adjusted the premium down to 20 percent, which the court accepted.

Gilbert Matthews, currently an investment broker with Sutter Securities in San Francisco, has commented that, although this decision is well reasoned in accordance with case law, there are several errors of logic with respect to the control premium:

1. Discounted cash flow (DCF) value should represent the full value of the future cash flows of the business. Excluding synergies, a company cannot be worth a premium over the value of its future cash flows. Thus, it is improper and illogical to add a control premium to a DCF valuation.
2. The average premium in other transactions is not a relevant standard. It is biased upward by the fact that it includes purchases of companies that are undervalued in the market but excludes those that are overpriced.
3. Even if the average premium were relevant, it is calculated in relation to unaffected market value. Market price usually includes a minority discount, particularly for acquisition targets. The court applies it to a value that, in a Delaware appraisal, specifically excludes any minority discount.
4. The value of Weber Industries to any third party would not have been affected by its corporate structure. If Weber Industries had not been a holding company but had owned Fred Weber, Inc. as a division, *Rapid-American* would not have applied and there would have been no control premium added. This elevates form over substance.[44]

In a subsequent Delaware case, *Borruso v. Communications Telesystems International*,[45] the issue before the Court of Chancery was not whether a control premium should be applied but when it should be applied during the calculations. The court accepted one expert's methodology on this issue over the other expert's:

> I am persuaded that Petitioners' approach to the control premium is wrong. The observation that the comparable company method of analysis produces a minority equity value does not require that I change the methodology of that analysis. Rather, it requires only that I adjust the result derived from it to eliminate the implicit minority discount. Instead of adjusting the result, Huck undertook to alter, in a significant way, the methodology itself. Doing so, in my view, introduced an analytical distortion that, in this case, significantly overstates the value of the WXL equity. Neither Petitioners nor Huck has supplied authority in the valuation literature justifying this change in the accepted methodology. Because Huck's methodology is inconsistent with the methodology followed in *Harris v. Rapid-American Corp.*, 1992 Del. Ch. LEXIS 75, *9, Del. Ch., C.A. No. 6462, Chandler, V.C. (April 1, 1992), and because it is otherwise hard to square with the comparable company method, I will not adopt it.

In *Doft & Co. v. Travelocity.com, Inc.*,[46] the court, *sua sponte*, added a 30 percent control premium, saying, "The equity valuation produced in a comparable company analysis does not accurately reflect the intrinsic worth of a corporation on a going concern basis. Therefore, the Court, in appraising the fair value of the equity, 'must correct this minority trading discount by adding back a premium designed to correct it.'"

In a Maine dissenters' rights action involving a small, closely held business, the court permitted a control premium adjustment, concluding that the control premium could properly be used as an upward adjustment of the value of the subject company's shares when compared to similar companies in the industry.[47] The Iowa Supreme

Court has also held that in an appraisal action, a control premium may be considered in determining fair value if it is supported by the evidence.[48]

Other Discount Issues

Discounts for Trapped-In Capital Gains

Another frequently encountered issue is whether the value of a company with low-basis assets should be discounted due to the risk of tax liability if some or all of these assets are later sold. The U.S. Tax Court has reversed its prior position and approved a discount for such built-in capital gains.[49]

The Washington Court of Appeals in *Matthew G. Norton Co. v. Smyth*[50] rejected a bright-line rule rejecting a discount for trapped-in capital gains, reasoning that while discounts for such gains are not generally appropriate in dissenters' rights appraisal cases where no liquidation of the corporation is contemplated, such discounts might be appropriate at the corporate level if the business of the company is such that appreciated property is scheduled to be sold in the foreseeable future, in the normal course of business.

The Wyoming Supreme Court ruled that under the state's appraisal statute (pre-1999 RMBCA version), absent clear evidence that the company was undergoing liquidation, a discount for trapped-in capital gains would violate the purpose of the statute: to compensate dissenting shareholders for the "fair value" of their shares in a going concern.[51]

Lack of Entire Fairness in Broadening Remedies

The Delaware courts employ the concept of "entire fairness." This means *procedural fairness* as well as *substantive fairness* or *fair value.* If the transaction fails in terms of procedural fairness (*fair dealing*), the relief to the plaintiffs may go beyond just the fair value as adjudicated pursuant to dissenting stockholder statutes.

Procedural fairness is generally measured by two criteria: (1) independence and (2) competence and thoroughness.

Substantive fairness (*fair price*) also has two elements: (1) absolute fairness and (2) relative fairness.

Violations of the above criteria caused Delaware Vice Chancellor Jacobs to deny a motion for summary judgment to dismiss a class-action suit that allowed plaintiffs only the appraisal remedy. Among the facts cited by Judge Jacobs were these:

- The company obtained no fairness opinion at the time of the cash-out merger.
- The board did not establish an independent committee to safeguard the interests of the minority stockholders.
- There had been a series of private purchases at prices higher than the cash-out price, a fact that was undisclosed.

Judge Jacobs concluded that, since there was evidence that the entire fairness test was not met, "the Court must reject the defendants' argument that appraisal is the exclusive remedy."[52]

In another case, the Delaware Supreme Court found that "the Special Committee [of the board] chose as its financial advisor a bank which had lucrative past dealings with . . . related companies." Furthermore, the special committee's legal advisor was previously retained by two related companies. The court concluded that the special committee did not act in an independent and informed manner. Therefore, the case was remanded for a new fairness determination, with the burden of proof shifted to the defendants.[53]

A classic example of lack of fairness is found in *Ryan v. Tad's Enterprises*. First, the controlling stockholders arranged an asset sale of the corporation's major holding, a six-store New York restaurant chain, with employment and noncompete contracts of $1 million each. It then did a squeeze-out merger. One lawyer acted as a board member, represented the corporation in the transactions, and represented the controlling stockholders personally in negotiating their employment and noncompete agreements. The board did not retain any unaffiliated law firm, financial advisor, or other independent representative to represent or negotiate the merger on behalf of Tad's minority shareholders.

The opinion states, "Normally this court will defer to a decision involving the business judgment of a corporation's directors. . . . However, that presumption vanishes in cases where the minority shareholders are compelled to forfeit their shares in return for a value that is determined as a result of a bargaining process in which the controlling shareholder is in a position to influence both bargaining parties."[54] The dissenters ultimately were awarded $23.86 per share versus the $13.36 amount originally offered.

Another Delaware case finding a lack of entire fairness was *M.G. Bancorporation v. Le Beau*,[55] which found that the directors' failure to establish an independent committee of directors to represent the minority shareholders' interests, while on its own did not constitute evidence of unfair dealing, when combined with other pleaded facts could support a claim of unfair dealing. The court also found that the difference between the stock's $85 per share fair value and the $41 per share merger price, combined with the other pleaded unfairness claims, created an inference that the merger was the product of unfair dealing.

Lack of entire fairness usually occurs when control stockholders cause transactions that benefit them at the expense of other stockholders without independent oversight. The most common scenario is a transaction without an independent appraisal, often coupled with not having an independent committee of the board of directors to evaluate the transaction from the perspective of fairness to minority stockholders. Directors or controlling shareholders who stand on both sides of a transaction have the burden of establishing the transaction's entire fairness.[56]

In *Gesoff v. IIC Industries, Inc.*,[57] the class of minority shareholders argued that a going-private merger, intended by a foreign parent corporation to remove the minority shareholders of its U.S. subsidiary, was a product of unfair dealing, producing an unfair price for the subsidiary. Notwithstanding the defendants' argument that the merger was fair because any irregularities in the merger dealings did not affect the fairness of the merger price, the Delaware Court of Chancery found that the merger process was marked with grave examples of unfairness and led to a plainly unfair price for the going-private transaction. Consequently, the court awarded damages to the class and to those stockholders seeking appraisal based on the court's determination of fair value at the time of the merger—a figure significantly in excess of the consideration offered in the going-private transaction. In reaching its conclusion, the court determined that the process established by the defendants unilaterally imposed on the minority a price of the parent's own choosing, established a deceptive negotiation between the parties and left the minority's putative special committee almost entirely powerless against its parent.

Fair Value as Not Necessarily Fair Market Value

One thing that is clear is that virtually no court equates fair value with fair market value. In a New York case, the expert retained by the company based his valuation on a fair market value. The court stated, "The Standard on which [the expert's] valuation was based was Market value. . . . The statutory standard is much broader. . . . The Court *may give no weight* [emphasis added] to market value if the facts of the case so require."

The court also decided that the company's appraiser "was not independent in its evaluation and was unduly controlled and influenced by the petitioner to arrive at a low value."[58] Ultimately, the court rejected any minority and marketability discounts and awarded the dissenter $99 per share, as compared with the $32 per share originally offered.

In another example, the Colorado Supreme Court in *Pueblo Bancorporation v. Lindoe, Inc.*, said, "We are convinced that 'fair value' does not mean 'fair market value.'"[59] The New Jersey Supreme Court has expressed a similar sentiment,[60] as has a majority of courts in other jurisdictions.[61]

Other courts, however, have indicated that use of a fair market value analysis may inform the fair value standard of value where such an analysis is a "relevant factor," and that although the market value may be accorded little or no weight by a factfinder, the fair market value analysis may not be excluded and must be permitted at trial.[62] The Eleventh Circuit, while acknowledging that "fair value" and "fair market value" are not synonymous, has also indicated that they are not "mutually exclusive," so that when "potentially distorting corporate actions" such as a merger or sale are not at issue, fair market value may serve as an estimate of fair value.[63]

States Borrowing Other States' Precedents

When states lack precedential case law on an issue, they often look to other states for guidance. Thus, appraisers and lawyers often research cases in other states, especially states with similar statutory wording.

For example, in Utah's case of first impression under its dissenting stockholder statute, the appellate court cited case law from other states with similar statutes, including Iowa, Maryland, Maine, Delaware, and Massachusetts. Among its conclusions, it stated: "We agree with the courts cited above that a dissenting stockholder disclaims both the burden and the benefit of the disfavored corporate action.... Any effect of the sale must be excluded. . . . Fair value is not measured by any unique benefits that will accrue to the acquiring corporation."[64]

Before determining that "fair value" does not mean "fair market value," the Colorado Supreme Court conducted an extensive review of the law in other jurisdictions on this issue.[65]

Apparent inconsistencies are common in the field of fair value cases, often as a result of less than fully informed expert testimony. In a North Dakota case, it was alleged (and unrebutted) that an appraisal followed Delaware case law. However, it was apparent after reading what was done that the appraisal did not interpret the appraisal methodology as it is actually applied in Delaware.[66]

Timely Actions Essential

Courts usually hold assiduously to requirements for timeliness of filings and other procedural matters in dissenting stockholder actions. If the dissent is not filed within the statutory period, dissenters' rights are almost always considered waived.

When dissenters' rights actions are filed, most state statutes then require the corporation to commence a proceeding to determine the fair value of the shares within 60 days after receiving the demand. If it doesn't commence the proceeding within the 60 days, it must pay the dissenters the amount demanded.

In a Georgia case, for example (where the statute was based on the Model Business Corporations Act), the trial court awarded the dissenters the amount demanded because the corporation failed to initiate the valuation proceeding within the statutory period. The corporation appealed, and the trial court's judgment was affirmed.[67]

References

Brewer, Wilbur, Jr. "Minority Shareholder Rights." A 17-page paper on the rights of minority shareholders in closely held corporations, available on www.BVLibrary.com.

Cory, Jacques. 2004. *Business Ethics: The Ethical Revolution of Minority Shareholders*. New York: Springer.

Eggart, James. 2002. "Replacing the Sword with a Scalpel: The Case for a Bright-Line Rule Disallowing Application of Lack of Marketability Discounts in Shareholder Oppression Cases." *Arizona Law Review*, vol. 44, no. 1, pp. 213–246.

Emory, John D., Jr. 1996. "The Role of Discounts in Determining 'Fair Value' Under Wisconsin's Dissenters' Rights Statutes: The Case for Discounts." *Wisconsin Law Review, 1995*, no. 5 (March), pp. 1155–75. Although specifically oriented to Wisconsin, the article references statutes and cases throughout the United States.

Fishman, Jay E., Shannon P. Pratt, et al. 2009. "Fair Value under Shareholder Dissent and Minority Oppression Actions" (ch. 15). In *PPC's Guide to Business Valuations*, 19th ed. Fort Worth, TX: Practitioners Publishing.

Fishman, Jay, et al. 2008. "Fair Value Under Shareholder Dissent and Minority Oppression Actions." In *PPC's Guide to Business Valuations.* Fort Worth, TX: Practitioners Publishing, pp. 15-1 to 15-10.

Jacobs, Jack B. 1999. "Adjudicating Statutory Appraisal and Breach of Fiduciary Duty Valuations in the Delaware Court of Chancery," interview with Shannon Pratt. *Judges & Lawyers Business Valuation Update,* September, pp. 1, 3–4.

Malick, S. A. 2000. *Oppression of and Relief for Minority Shareholders: Cases and Commentaries.* Golden Books Centre, Selangor, Malaysia.

Mantese, Gerard V., and Ian Williamson. 2005. "Minority Shareholder Oppression: From Estes to Franchino." *Michigan Bar Journal,* August, pp. 16–20.

Minnesota Institute of Legal Education, Minneapolis. "Minority Shareholder Disputes." Several hundred pages of conference papers in three-ring binder. Although primarily oriented to Minnesota, the papers reflect national research on the issues.

Moll, Douglas K. 2005. "Minority Oppression and the Limited Liability Company: Learning (or Not) from Close Corporation History." *Wake Forest Law Review*, vol. 40, p. 883.

O'Neal, F. Hodge, and Robert B. Thompson. 1998. *O'Neal's Oppression of Minority Shareholders: Protecting Minority Rights in Squeeze-Outs, and Other Intracorporate Conflicts*, 2nd ed. St. Paul, MN: West Group.

Pratt, Shannon. 1999. "Shareholder Suit Valuation Criteria Vary from State to State." *Valuation Strategies*, January/February, pp. 12–15.

______. 2003. "Shareholder Buyouts and Disputes." In *Business Valuation Body of Knowledge*, 2nd ed. New York: Wiley, pp. 321–324.

Shartsis, Arthur, Jr. 1999. "Dissolution Actions Yield Less Than Fair Market Enterprise Value." *Judges & Lawyers Business Valuation Update*, January, p. 5.

Chapter 21

Marital Dissolution Valuations

While there are many reasons for which business valuations are performed, the various courts' positions on how a valuation should be performed are the least settled in the area of marital dissolution. This is especially true in terms of different approaches from one state to another, but there are also inconsistencies within states. Even when there is general agreement on broad approaches, the courts still take contradictory positions on many issues. Courts have a very high degree of discretion, into which appellate courts are reluctant to intrude.

Standard of Value for Marital Dissolutions

At the core of the differences among jurisdictions on how to value businesses or practices for marital dissolution is the appropriate standard of value. There can be many definitions (and interpretations of definitions) of value. Unfortunately, in most states, the definition of value for marital dissolution purposes is not clearly spelled out, leaving much room for interpretation. The lack of clear definitions and

Extensive work on this chapter was done by Noah J. Gordon, legal counsel for Shannon Pratt Valuations. Gordon is a regular contributor to valuation and legal publications.

interpretations challenges appraisers and lawyers to work together to assist the courts in creating some sound precedential case law that will clear up much of the existing confusion.

Family law courts sometimes use a *fair value* standard of value that can be inferred from the language and rulings in the case. When this standard is used, it usually is not intended to be synonymous with "fair value" as used in dissenting stockholder actions, although some marital dissolution decisions have expressly referred to the fair value standard used in shareholder oppression and appraisal actions. Rather, it usually means something akin to fair market value with some (usually not well defined) modifications. Some traits characteristic of fair value cases are that distributions are made on a pro rata share of enterprise value with no discounts[1]; there are no "shareholder-level discounts" such as discounts for lack of marketability or lack of control; some element of goodwill is included, but discounts are disallowed.

Some states, such as Florida, Hawaii, Illinois, Missouri, Pennsylvania, South Carolina, Texas, and Wisconsin, adhere quite strictly to the standard of *fair market value*, the price at which the property would change hands between well-informed, willing buyers and sellers on an arm's-length basis. Some states, such as Arkansas[2] and Louisiana,[3] mandate this standard by statute for the valuation of certain types of marital property. Those espousing the fair market value standard say that it is unfair to value the property that one spouse will receive at more than that spouse could actually realize in a sale. Other states adhere to the concept of *value to the owner*, reflecting whatever special circumstances may make the property more valuable to that owner than to someone else. Although the courts are not consistent in what they call this value, both business appraisers and real estate appraisers call it *investment value*.[4] States that have used an investment value standard of value include Arizona, California, Colorado, Kentucky, Michigan, Montana, Nevada, New Mexico, North Carolina, and Washington (however, such use has not precluded the application of other standards in these states). Depending on the owner's special circumstances, this value could be much higher than the value to other investors.[5] The rationale for this position is that if a sale is not imminent, the question of how much the property would bring is irrelevant. States do not have totally consistent positions on this critical issue.

The court, the lawyer, and the appraiser should all be wary that there are many case decisions in family law that use the term "fair market value" but then actually take positions that are not consistent with fair market value as defined in Chapter 1 and in the tax court case law. Therefore, when seeking precedential case law guidance, it is necessary to read the entire opinion to see what valuation procedures were actually accepted.

Business appraisers who have been active in valuations for marital dissolution have debated the issue of the appropriate standard of value. Alan Zipp advocates that the value should be "current value to the marital community in the hands of the present owner."[6] David Bishop and Steven Schroeder counter as follows:

> The relevant point to the court should be the amount the business assets could bring in cash or cash equivalent at the appropriate date. The point of whether or not the business or any other asset will actually be sold is beside the point. In fact, there is a sale of sorts which occurs within the dissolution. The net effect of the separation of marital assets is that each spouse purchases a (let's assume) 50 percent interest in certain assets from their spouse and pays for the purchase by selling back their 50 percent interest in other assets. The transfers occur and the marital assets are separated. The end result is not substantially different than when both spouses agree jointly to each sell a marital asset and divide the funds received. The primary difference is they are the buyers and sellers: there are no outside parties involved, and the mode of payment is the exchange of interests in the marital assets.[7]

Bishop and Schroeder make the point that marketability discounts should be recognized, as in the tax court, because one spouse usually gets liquid assets while the other lacks the flexibility and safety of being able to "cash out" readily. They also make the point that "underlying principles are much more consistent and broadly accepted" under the fair market value standard than they are in marital dissolutions not using fair market value. This sentiment has been echoed by others.[8]

If the standard of value is fair market value, then goodwill should be a marital asset only to the extent that it is transferable. Furthermore, if the state does not allow proceeds from future activities of the spouse (or restrictions on future activities) to be a factor in property division, then goodwill should have to be transferable without requiring either an employment agreement or a noncompete agreement in order for it to be given value for marital asset purposes. Most state statutes contain language to this effect, but case decisions often ignore it.

Typical of language among states using the fair market value standard is the following:

> When dividing and distributing the value of the property of the parties in a divorce case, the relevant value is, as a general rule, the fair market value (FMV) of the parties' interest therein on the relevant date. We define the FMV as being the amount at which an item would change hands from a willing seller to a willing buyer, neither being under any compulsion to buy or sell and both having reasonable knowledge of the relevant facts.
>
> We disagree with the position advanced by Wife, and In re *Marriage of Fleege*, 91 Wash. 2d 324, 588 P.2d 1136 (1979), that the relevant value of a sole professional business is its value to the professional who operates it. Other assets are, as a general rule, valued at their FMV. We know of no valid reason why sole professional businesses should not be valued at their FMVs.[9]

One of the states acclaiming fair market value as the standard of value in marital property distributions is Wisconsin.[10] Nevertheless, at least one Wisconsin case included goodwill in the value of an accounting practice, even clearly recognizing that the spouse would have to execute a noncompete covenant to realize that goodwill in a sale.[11]

If the standard were strictly fair market value of the practice, the value of the noncompete covenant should be separate property and carved out of the total value.

Premise of Value

A key issue regarding the premise of value is whether the business should be valued on a going-concern basis or on a liquidation basis. In *Sommers v. Sommers*,[12] the wife's expert valued the husband's orthodontic practice on a going-concern basis, whereas the husband's expert used a liquidation value. The trial court accepted the husband's valuation, but, on appeal, the North Dakota Supreme Court reversed, finding no evidence that the husband intended to sell the practice. In *Bausano v. Bausano*,[13] the husband's expert claimed that liquidation value was the appropriate premise of value because the company had operated at a loss in recent years.

The court rejected this approach and found the valuation of the wife's expert more credible because it used replacement value and valued the business as a going concern. The court found that the business had potential, especially since the husband had indicated that he was planning to focus his efforts on the business once the divorce was final. In *Hoverson v. Hoverson*,[14] the court rejected liquidation value for valuing a farm that had losses of about $1 million, finding that the assets had value to the farm as long as it continued in business. The court indicated that the business had to be valued as a going concern despite its current financial condition.

Appreciation: Active Versus Passive

Some states consider appreciation in a premarital asset as a marital asset, whereas others do not. Of the many states that do, some hold that whether the appreciation will be considered a marital asset depends on whether the increase will have resulted from the natural growth of the business (separate property) or from an individual's management skills (marital property).[15]

In some, the appreciation is marital if it results from either spouse's efforts.[16] Sometimes it is not clear whether appreciation has resulted from "active" efforts or merely market forces; if the latter, the appreciation will be held not to be a marital asset.[17] Also, courts have held that the party seeking to characterize appreciation as "active" must prove that marital efforts have resulted in the appreciation.[18]

Valuation Date

There are many possible dates that can be used for the valuation date in marital dissolutions. Many courts use the date of trial as the valuation date.[19] Some use a date as near as possible to the final divorce decree.[20] The effective date in some cases is the date the complaint was filed.[21] Some use the date of separation.[22] Also, trial courts may exercise discretion in determining valuation dates,[23] and when selecting a valuation date for marital dissolution purposes, the date can be different for different assets.[24]

Courts in some states have considerable discretion in choosing the valuation date. Where the valuation date is not set by law or not declared by the court, the valuation expert may need to be prepared to testify to a value as of two or more valuation dates.

Goodwill[25]

The classic concept of goodwill is the propensity of customers to return. If this propensity is due to the practitioner, it is often called *personal goodwill* or *professional goodwill.* If it is due to other factors (such as location) not dependent on the individual practitioners, it is often called *practice goodwill* or *enterprise goodwill.* Some definitions of goodwill include all intangible value, not just the persistence of the customer base.

A key issue in marital dissolution cases involving goodwill valuation is whether it is necessary to distinguish between personal goodwill and enterprise goodwill, and if such a distinction is necessary, which type of goodwill is a marital or distributable asset. A number of courts, but not a majority, make no distinction between personal and enterprise goodwill. These jurisdictions have taken the position that both personal and enterprise goodwill in a professional practice constitute marital property. A minority of courts have taken the position that neither personal nor enterprise goodwill in a professional practice constitutes marital property.

The majority of states differentiate between enterprise goodwill and personal goodwill. Courts in these states take the position that personal goodwill is not marital property but that enterprise goodwill is marital property. In many states, professional goodwill is an element of marital property value even if it is not transferable. Some states have not issued a decision on whether types of goodwill must be distinguished. For a comprehensive state-by-state guide of the treatment of goodwill in marital dissolution cases, see "Goodwill Hunting in Divorce."[26]

This section explores representative positions taken in various decisions on this issue. As you will see, the decisions sometimes seem to be inconsistent with the stated definition of value. It presents a challenge to the appraisers, lawyers, and courts to make the treatment of goodwill consistent with the espoused definition of value.

A case widely cited that details the factors to consider when calculating the value of professional goodwill in a divorce is the California case *Lopez v. Lopez*.[27] These factors are the following:

1. The age and health of the professional
2. The professional's demonstrated past earning power
3. The professional's reputation in the community for judgment, skill, and knowledge
4. The professional's comparative professional success

5. The nature and duration of the professional's practice, either as a sole proprietor or as a contributing member of a partnership or professional corporation[28]

An excellent summary and analysis of the extremes of various states' positions on goodwill in a professional practice as a marital asset is found in a decision by the supreme court of Missouri, sitting en banc and issuing the decision without dissent:

> The husbands in the consolidated cases are the sole partners in an oral surgery partnership. In *Hanson v. Hanson*, the Circuit Court of Boone County valued the partnership at $324,862, including $233,727, an amount characterized as "goodwill" by the parties. In *Graham v. Graham* the Circuit Court of Cole County, hearing virtually identical evidence, valued the same partnership at $90,280. . . .
>
> In addressing the question of the existence and value of goodwill in a professional context as marital property, the courts have not spoken with a uniform voice.
>
> In *Dugan v. Dugan*, 92 NJ 423, 457 A.2d 1 (1983), the New Jersey Supreme Court found that goodwill in the law practice of a sole practitioner is property subject to distribution in a dissolution action. The court recognized that reputation is "at the core" of any consideration of professional goodwill (457 A.2d at 6). While acknowledging that future earning capacity is not per se goodwill, the New Jersey justices noted that when "future earning capacity has been enhanced because reputation leads to probable future patronage from existing and potential clients, goodwill may exist and have value." Id. *Dugan* has been criticized, and properly so in our view, for its failure to distinguish between the reputation of the professional as an individual and the reputation of the professional practice as a business entity.
>
> *In the Matter of the Marriage of Fleege*, 91 Wash. 2d 324, 588 P.2d 1136 (banc 1979), the Washington Supreme Court defined the critical question as "not whether the goodwill of the practice could be

sold . . . but whether it [the goodwill] has value to [the practitioner]" (588 P.2d at 1138–39). In determining the value of such goodwill, *Fleege* outlined several factors for consideration: "The practitioner's age, health, past earning power, reputation in the community for judgment, skill and knowledge, and his comparative professional success" (588 P.2d at 1138). Each of these factors is, in our view, directly attributable to the professional as a person. For this reason, we find that the *Fleege* analysis is mired in the same mixture of personal reputation and entity reputation as is found in *Dugan.*

Several courts have refused to acknowledge professional goodwill as property. A leading case is *Holbrook v. Holbrook,* 103 Wis. 2d 327, 309 NW2d 343 (App. 1981). There the court refused to follow "the twisted and illogical path that other jurisdictions have made in dealing with the concept of professional goodwill in the context of divorce." The court continued, "If the concept of professional goodwill evanesces when one attempts to distinguish it from future earning capacity, . . . the goodwill or reputation of such a business accrues to the benefit of the owners only through increased salary," 309 NW2d at 354. See also *Powell v. Powell,* 231 Kans. 456 646 P.2d 218, 223 (1982). ("We are not persuaded that a professional practice such as Dr. Powell's has a goodwill value. The practice is personal to the practitioner. . . . It is totally dependent upon the professional.") *Nail v. Nail,* 486 SW2d 761 (Tex. 1972), reaches a similar result.

Between the opposing results reached in *Dugan* and *Holbrook,* several courts have attempted to chart a course which recognizes that goodwill is marital property, but only insofar as it exists independently of the individual professional's reputation. Characteristic of these cases is *Taylor v. Taylor,* 222 Neb. 721, 386 NW2d 851 (1986). There the Nebraska Supreme Court concluded that "goodwill must be a business asset with value independent of the presence or reputation of a particular individual, an asset which may be sold, transferred, conveyed, or pledged. . . . If a party produces appropriate evidence establishing salability or marketability of goodwill as a business asset of a professional practice, professional goodwill may be considered in determining the value of property in a marital estate to be divided in a dissolution proceeding" (*Taylor*, 386 NW2d at 858–859)....

As we have said, goodwill is recognized as property in this state; that recognition is not dependent on a traditional mercantile setting. Goodwill may exist in both commercial and professional entities. Irrespective of the setting in which it is found, the meaning of goodwill does not change. It is property which attaches to and is dependent upon an existing business entity; the reputation and skill of an individual entrepreneur—be he a professional or a traditional businessman—is not a component of the intangible asset we identify generally as goodwill.

With the caveats which follow, we hold that goodwill in a professional practice acquired during a marriage is marital property subject to division in a dissolution of marriage proceeding. We define goodwill within a professional setting to mean the value of the practice which exceeds its tangible assets and which is the result of the tendency of clients/patients to return to and recommend the practice irrespective of the reputation of the individual practitioner.

Professional goodwill may not be confused with future earning capacity. We have not declared future earning capacity to be marital property.

Proof of the existence of goodwill is particularly troublesome in a professional context. This difficulty is a product of the fact that the reputation of the individual practitioner and the goodwill of his enterprise are often inextricably interwoven. Because of the difficulties inherent in separating the reputation of the professional from that of his enterprise, evidence that other professionals are willing to pay for goodwill when acquiring a practice is, in our view, the only acceptable evidence of the existence of goodwill. Thus, as a matter of proof, the existence of goodwill is shown only when there is evidence of a recent actual sale of a similarly

> situated professional practice, an offer to purchase such a practice, or expert testimony and testimony of members of the subject profession as to the existence of goodwill in a similar practice in the relevant geographic and professional market. Absent such evidence, one can only speculate as to the existence of goodwill. Divisions of marital property may not be based on speculation as to the very existence of the property being divided....
>
> The fair market value method is most likely to avoid the "disturbing inequity in compelling a professional practitioner to pay a judicially determined value that could not be realized by a sale or another method of liquidating value" (*Holbrook*, 309 NW2d at 355). We therefore reject the notion advanced by some courts that goodwill may exist and be subject to division in a dissolution proceeding even though it may not be sold.[29]

A case representative of the majority position is *May v. May*.[30] In that case, the Virginia Supreme Court, ruling on an issue of first impression in that state, held that trial courts in marital dissolution cases must distinguish between personal and enterprise goodwill in a professional practice and that personal goodwill is not a marital asset but enterprise goodwill is. The court specifically noted that enterprise goodwill can exist in a professional practice that is operated as a sole proprietorship. The court also stated that this holding was consistent with its prior ruling that a professional degree or license is not marital property because it represents the future earning capacity of the professional spouse. Likewise, personal goodwill represents the future earning capacity of the professional spouse.

A case representative of the position that either personal goodwill or enterprise goodwill is a marital asset is *Stewart v. Stewart*,[31] in which the Idaho Supreme Court held that "where a professional business is an independent entity,... goodwill is calculable and divisible in divorce just as goodwill in any other business." In doing so, the court declined to enter the "morass" of trying to distinguish between the values attributable to a professional practice by virtue of the individual attributes of the professional and the value of the goodwill not attributable to those personal assets, valuing each separately and then dividing the latter but not the former. A strong dissent argued that because the majority had held that a professional's personal attributes—including knowledge, skill, reputation, and so on—are not divisible community property, the court should have required the parties to distinguish whether the husband's ability to earn above-average income was based on his personal attributes or "some other factor."[32]

Once a court has determined whether to distinguish between personal and enterprise goodwill, the issue becomes how to do so. Indiana's *Yoon v. Yoon*[33] exemplifies a case in which a court attempted to distinguish personal and enterprise goodwill in a professional corporation. The court ruled that to determine if any goodwill should be included in a marital estate, there must be a determination as to what portion of it is attributable to the individual and the value of that portion must be excluded from the estate. In its decision, the court made the following statement to explain that enterprise goodwill is subject to equitable distribution, whereas personal goodwill can affect only the relative distribution of property:

> Before including the goodwill of a self-employed business or professional practice in a marital estate, a court must determine that the goodwill is attributable to the business as opposed to the owner as an individual. If attributable to the individual, it is not a divisible asset and is properly considered only as future earning capacity that may affect the relative property division. In this respect, the future earning capacity of a self-employed person (or an owner of a business primarily dependent on the owner's services) is to be treated the same as the future earning capability and reputation of an employee.

On the basis of *Yoon, Bobrow v. Bobrow*[34] discussed the enterprise goodwill of the accounting firm Ernst & Young (E&Y). The husband, E&Y's global CEO, had a partnership interest in a division of the accounting firm E&Y. Although there was a partnership agreement limiting the owner's interest to the value of the capital account, thereby excluding goodwill, the husband conceded that the agreement applied only to a transaction of his partnership interest (resignation, retirement, or death). The court recognized that the assets of E&Y were not personal to the partner but, rather, belonged to the institution of which each partner had a share. These institutional assets included such intangible assets as E&Y's trade name; the entity's favorable business reputation and name recognition; methods and tools for conducting its business; and its relationships with suppliers. All these items were transferable to an outside purchaser.

This case, therefore, contrasted with *Yoon*, in which all these assets were associated with the doctor himself rather than the entity, and the court found that they could not be transferred to another individual. Ultimately, the court included the value of enterprise goodwill in valuing E&Y and awarded the wife a share of the value of the husband's partnership interest in E&Y based on his pro rata share of the value of the enterprise.

A method developed by David Wood that has been accepted in some courts to calculate the enterprise and personal components of goodwill in the valuation of a professional practice is called the *multi-attribute utility model* (MUM). This model involves several steps. First, the valuator sets forth an objective. Next, the valuator establishes "alternatives." An alternative is a "range of percentages" that will define the choices "in which the method will result." Each alternative is then assigned a "range." After the objective and the alternatives are set, the valuator must then define the "attributes," which are elements of goodwill to which the valuator must assign a value. Examples of attributes are personal reputation and business location.[35]

Another issue that may arise in valuing goodwill is the best method to do so. There are four major formulas that are used in valuing goodwill:

1. The straight capitalization accounting method
2. The capitalization of excess earnings method

3. The IRS variation of capitalized excess earnings method (based on Revenue Ruling 68-609The market value approach
4. The buy-sell agreement method[36]

Of these, the excess earnings method is the most commonly used; some courts find that the market value approach and buy-sell agreement methods are easily manipulated by the professional spouse. The capitalization of the excess earnings method focuses on the earning power of the business to determine what rate of return the predicted earnings will yield in light of the risks involved to attain them. Broadly put, the excess earnings approach is predicated on a comparison of the earnings of the spouse in question with that of a peer whose performance is average.

To make this comparison, courts may, among other things, determine the annual salary of a typical salaried employee who has had experience commensurate with the spouse who is the sole practitioner or sole owner-employee. Alternatively, courts may apply the similarly situated professional standard, under which reasonable compensation is based on the cost of hiring a nonowner outsider to perform the same average amount with which other people are normally compensated for performing similar services. Although not binding, compensation surveys may be used by experts and trial courts as guidelines for determining the reasonable compensation of a practitioner's peers. To be relevant, however, the surveys must account for similarly situated professional practices and practitioners.[37]

Other cases have clarified that personal goodwill and enterprise goodwill can be a part of going-concern value but that going-concern value and goodwill cannot be the same because the latter is subsumed within the former. Going-concern value is the intangible value attached to the physical assets of the business, including the business's fixtures, equipment, and its assemblage of personnel, as well as goodwill.[38]

Several courts, in attempting to determine what constitutes goodwill, have ruled that goodwill is indistinguishable from earning capacity, which is not a distributable asset.[39] Other courts have ruled that goodwill is separate from earning capacity where the professional's interest in a practice is transferable and separable from reputation.[40] In such instances, it must be proved that goodwill is separate from earning capacity to avoid double-counting the same asset. Still, other courts view goodwill as supplementing earning capacity, rather than merging with it.[41]

A related issue is whether enhanced earning capacity, which is an individual's ability to earn over and above what would be earned following a "normal" career path that results from enhancements, such as a degree, license, training, specialized knowledge, unique talent, and so on, should be considered goodwill that is a marital asset. Some states, such as New York[42] and New Jersey[43] recognize celebrity status or celebrity goodwill as marital property. This concept of goodwill is based on the enhanced earnings capacity of a celebrity. Only New York recognizes licenses or degrees as marital assets the value of which must be distributed.[44]

Another goodwill valuation issue is the degree to which goodwill inheres in a noncompete agreement. It is sometimes difficult to determine the value that should be assigned to a practice's goodwill and the value that should be assigned to a noncompete agreement.[45]

Yet another issue, discussed at greater length in a section that follows, is that of double-counting, or *double-dipping*. This issue arises when a court in a matrimonial dispute considers excess earnings (or other factors that assume continued involvement by the operating spouse) in determining the value of a business as well as in setting alimony. This issue arises more frequently in those jurisdictions that hold that personal goodwill is a marital asset.

The California Business and Professions Code Section 14100 defines goodwill as "the expectation of continued public patronage." However:

> The philosophy of the community property system is that a community interest can be acquired only during the time of the marriage. It would then be inconsistent with that philosophy to assign to any community interest the value of the postmarital efforts of either spouse (*In re Marriage of Fortier* [1973] 34 Cal.

App. 3d 384, 109 Cal. Rptr. 915). Since a community interest can only be acquired during the time of the marriage, the value of the goodwill must exist at the time of the dissolution, and that value must be established without dependence on the potential or continuing net income of the professional spouse (*In re Marriage of Fortier*, supra; *In re Marriage of Foster* (1974) 42 Cal. App. 3d 577 at 582, 117 Cal. Rptr. 49).[46]

A seemingly internal contradiction, which has also been referred to as the "market value of goodwill paradox"[47] is prevalent in family law case decisions. Courts espouse the position that the valuation of a business or practice should not be dependent on future efforts (or restrictions on future efforts) of the operating spouse. Having said this, the same courts often go on to accept appraisal methodology that, in fact, reflects earnings that could be achieved only if the operating spouse continued in the business or practice.[48]

Buy-Sell Agreements

A *buy-sell agreement* is a contract between an owner and the company, or between two or more owners, describing the conditions under which one party may (or must) sell his or her interest to the other. The agreement normally incorporates a price, or a mechanism for determining the price, for such a sale. As such, the buy-sell agreement price is the price that the spouse could realize on withdrawal from the partnership or corporation.

From the company's viewpoint, the agreement provides control over who will be involved in ownership. From the owner's viewpoint, the agreement usually provides liquidity if he or she leaves the company, or for the owner's estate in the event of death.

A frequent issue is whether a buy-sell agreement price is controlling for marital property valuation. Some courts hold that the price is controlling.[49] Others, especially in states where professional (personal) goodwill is a marital asset, find that the buy-sell agreement price generally is not binding. A Washington case is typical of this position:

> Professional goodwill has been recognized in Washington as intangible property subject to division in a marital dissolution (*Hall*, at 238–239, 692 P.2d 175). The important consideration is not whether the goodwill could be sold without the personal services of the professional, but whether it has value to him. *In re Marriage of Fleege*, 91 Wash. 2d 324, 327, 588 P.2d 1136 (1979) (goodwill of husband's solo dental practice was a community asset).
>
> Both parties cite cases from other jurisdictions as authority. Some cases hold the nonshareholder spouse should be bound by the buy-sell agreement or that the buy-sell agreement should at least be considered. *Hertz v. Hertz*, 99 N.M. 320, 657 P.2d 1169, 1174 (1983) (a nonshareholder spouse was bound by the goodwill valuation clause in corporate bylaws for purposes of establishing the valuation of corporate goodwill in a dissolution action. This ensured that the nonshareholder spouse did not receive a greater value than the shareholder.). See also *In re Marriage of Ondrasek*, 126 Wis. 2d 469, 377 NW2d 190, 192 (Ct. App. 1985) (in a dissolution, value of a partner's interest in a professional partnership is determined by the monetary consequences of that partner withdrawing from the business); *Holbrook v. Holbrook*, 103 Wis. 2d 327, 309 NW 2d 343, 355 (Ct. App. 1981) (capital account was the only value that should be assigned to a lawyer's partnership as an asset where lawyer was entitled to receive only his capital account value on withdrawal and any goodwill is reflected in his salary which can be considered in setting the family support award); and *Hanson v. Hanson*, 738 SW2d 429, 436 (Mo. 1987) (value of goodwill of professional practice, subject to division in dissolution proceeding, is determined by the price the practice would bring if sold on open, relevant market to qualified professional; under certain circumstances value may be established by buy-sell agreement).

Other courts have held that the nonshareholder spouse is not bound by the terms of the withdrawal agreement and in some cases, even where the nonshareholder spouse cosigned the withdrawal agreement. *In re Marriage of Slater*, 100 Cal. App. 3d 241, 160 Cal. Rptr. 686 (1979) (on theory withdrawal agreement was not signed for dissolution purposes); *Mitchell v. Mitchell*, 152 Ariz. 317, 732 P.2d 208, 210 (1987) (partnership agreement provided that no value was to be placed on goodwill of the firm; however, it did contain provisions for payments to a partner upon retirement or death which were not limited to the firm's tangible assets and accounts receivable, but included a share of net profits for a limited period. A buy-sell agreement had been considered in establishing the valuation of goodwill, but was not dispositive. At best it created a presumptive value which either spouse could rebut); *Stern v. Stern*, 66 N.J. 340, 331 A.2d 257, 260, 74 L.R.3d 613 (1975) (of the four payment plans found in the partnership agreement applicable to a partner who withdraws from a firm, becomes disabled, dies or retires, the formula applicable on a partner's death is presumptively the value to be used in dissolution; here, the partner was entitled to the value of his capital account plus a fixed sum appended to the partnership agreement which was revised quarterly). But cf. *Rogers v. Rogers*, 296 NW2d 849, 852–53 (Minn. 1980) (it was reversible error not to consider the terms of the buy-sell agreement which create contingencies that affect the value, such as the possibility the shareholder might die or be disabled before he realizes the full value of his interest).

Our state has not considered whether a buy-sell agreement not made in close proximity to a divorce is binding on the nonshareholder spouse in a dissolution action. *Hall* did not reach this issue but held that, at least in some circumstances, buy-sell agreements are not binding in a dissolution action. In light of *Hall* and *Fleege* (that it makes no difference whether the goodwill can be sold) we hold the court did not err in valuing goodwill even though it was assigned no value in the Brooks & Larson, P.S. corporation bylaws.[50]

In the above case, the spouse had practiced law for 4 years before the marriage and 13 years since. The court decided that the interest in the practice that the husband had bought (and that was subject to the buy-sell agreement) was separate property and that his goodwill (valued at $93,115 by the excess earnings method) was community property.

Sometimes a buy-sell price may be a factor to be considered but not as a completely controlling factor.[51] In one case the husband purchased stock, subject to a buy-sell agreement, for $65,567 from funds he borrowed from his mother. In three years, the stock paid $251,000 in dividends, and the buy-sell formula price increased to $82,000. In rejecting the trial court's valuation at the buy-sell price, the court of appeals explained:

> It is unreasonable to assume the value of the stock to Darrell was only what he could sell it to the company for, in light of the fact it was producing such generous dividends. It stretches the bounds of reasonableness to value a goose for slaughter price when it lays golden eggs.[52]

The appellate court declined to value the stock at $1.6 million, as claimed by the wife's expert based on capitalization of earnings, but it did award the wife an additional $40,000 representing her interest during the marriage.

One case that rejected a buy-sell agreement price as controlling the value of a minority interest noted the following:

- There was evidence that another family member had been bought out at a price that exceeded the value set by the buy-sell agreement.
- The buy-sell agreement was taken into consideration to some extent by the expert's reduction of 35 percent in value for minority interest and lack of marketability.[53]

Similarly, in another case where the stock was subject to a buy-sell agreement at book value, the court "decreased the unrestricted fair market value substantially more than it increased the book value to arrive at a valuation for purposes of the marriage dissolution."[54]

Another case summarized the most typical position:

> A majority of courts which have considered a buy-sell agreement in a closely held corporation setting the stock value for equitable distribution purposes has determined that such agreement should not be considered as binding, but rather should be weighed along with other factors in making a determination as to the value of such stock. E.g., *In re Marriage of Melnick*, 127 Ill. App. 3d 102, 82 Ill. Dec. 228, 468 N.E.2d 490 (1984); *In re Marriage of Moffatt*, 279 N.W.2d 15 (Iowa 1979); *Rogers v. Rogers*, 296 N.W.2d 849 (Minn. 1980); *Bowen v. Bowen*, 96 N.J. 36, 473 A.2d 73 (1984); *Amodio v. Amodio*, 70 N.Y.2d 5, 516 N.Y.S. 2d 923, 509 N.E.2d 936 (1987); *In the Matter of the Marriage of Belt*, 65 Ore. App. 606, 672 P.2d 1205 (1983); *Bosserman v. Bosserman*, 9 Va. App. 1, 384 S.E.2d 104 (1989); *Arneson v. Arneson*, 120 Wis. 2d 236, 355 N.W.2d 16 (Wis. Ct. App. 1984). It is apparent that buy-sell agreements in a closely held corporation can be manipulated by the shareholders to reflect an artificially low value. This is why caution should be exercised in accepting their value for equitable distribution purposes.[55]

In a Washington case involving a minority interest in an insurance agency, the court did find the buy-sell agreement price controlling. The court noted that the minority status was not likely to change, there was no evidence that the company was likely to be sold, and it was reasonable to conclude that if the husband were to sell his stock, he would do so subject to the buy-sell agreement formula.[56]

Buy-sell agreements involving key persons often are funded with life insurance benefits payable to the designated purchaser under the agreement, providing liquidity to exercise the buy-sell agreement in the case of the death of the owner of the interest. The amount of the "key man" insurance is sometimes presented as evidence of the partners' idea of the value of the interest. Such evidence could be supportive of an appraised value, at best, but it is certainly no substitute for an appraisal.

In almost any situation where a buy-sell agreement is taken into consideration, the extent to which the agreement was entered into on an arm's-length basis should also be considered.

Covenants Not to Compete

A *covenant not to compete* or *noncompete agreement* is a contract preventing an individual (or group of individuals) from competing with a given entity or person. In some cases, some partnerships or corporations require entering into a covenant not to compete as a condition of ownership. The covenant usually enhances the value of the entity by reducing the risk of certain individuals taking away business.

Treatment of an actual or prospective covenant not to compete is controversial. Most courts take the position that such a covenant restricts the postmarital activities of the spouse, and therefore is separate rather than marital property.[57] Others find that such covenants are marital property.[58] Still others hold that adjustments for hypothetical noncompete agreements are impermissible, even though comparable transactions include such agreements of similar duration, where the appraiser does not present evidence on the nature of such agreements or their impact on value.[59]

A covenant not to compete, by definition, restricts the postmarital efforts of the spouse. In most jurisdictions, this would be considered a nonmarital asset. If the analyst uses the market approach to value the business or practice and the comparable sales include covenants not to compete, it could be argued that the value of the covenants should be deducted from the comparable company or practice sales before they are used for comparison. However, most family law courts seem to ignore this factor.[60]

Minority and Marketability Discounts

A minority interest usually is worth significantly less than a pro rata share of the value of the entity as a whole. This is because a control owner can make many decisions that a minority owner can't—decisions that can affect both the value of the company as a whole and also the relative values of the controlling versus the minority interests.

Therefore, if the valuation methodology produces a controlling interest value, and the interest being valued is minority, a minority interest discount, also known as a *discount for lack of control* (DLOC), usually would be applied. Also, since minority interests usually are harder to sell than controlling interests, the minority interest discount might be compounded by also subtracting a *discount for lack of marketability* (DLOM).

A frequent issue is whether a minority discount should be applied (and if so, how much) if the interest owned is less than controlling.

In one case, an expert for the husband testified that a 15 percent minority discount was appropriate for a 50 percent interest. An expert for the wife testified that no minority discount was appropriate in a divorce settlement context because generally there is no change of ownership. The court rejected the wife's expert's opinion, with several references to decisions in other states:

> We reject [wife's expert's] view as a matter of law. The concept of value is keyed to the price that a prospective buyer would pay. *Moffitt v. Moffitt,* 813 P.2d 674 (Alaska 1991). Sherwin's testimony runs counter to this concept. We also note that courts in many jurisdictions have recognized that a minority discount is frequently appropriate in divorce proceedings. See *Arneson v. Arneson,* 120 Wis. 2d 236, 355 N.W.2d 16, 22 (App. 1984) (not clearly erroneous for trial court to apply minority discount); *In re Marriage of Jorgensen*, 180 Mont. 294, 590 P.2d 606, 610 (1979) (not an abuse of discretion to apply minority discount); *In re Marriage*

of Belt, 65 Ore. App. 606, 672 P.2d 1205, 1207–08 (1983) (trial court's valuation modified to include minority discount where the only credible evidence produced at trial favored discount); *In re Marriage of Reiling*, 66 Ore. App. 284, 673 P.2d 1360, 1364, 1365 (1983) (same); *In re Marriage of Hoak*, 364 N.W.2d 185, 192–93 (Iowa 1985) (no error to apply minority discount, but discount allowed by the trial court was too large and must be reduced); *Bowen v. Bowen*, 96 N.J. 36, 473 A.2d 73, 76–77, 81 (1984) (trial court should appoint independent expert to advise it in deciding whether to apply minority discount).[61]

In one case the minority interest discount was eliminated because the minority owner had a purchase right that would enable him to obtain control of the corporation sometime within the next 7 to 10 years.[62] There have been many marital dissolution cases that have accepted discounts for lack of control[63] and many that have not.[64]

As with discounts for lack of control, many courts in marital dissolution cases have accepted discounts for lack of marketability,[65] whereas many have not.[66] In one case, the court ruled that discounts for lack of marketability are not precluded as a matter of law in marital dissolution cases.[67]

Trapped-In Capital Gains Taxes[68]

In many cases the marital estate owns property that is worth more than its cost basis. In this case, if the marital estate (or one of the spouses) were to sell the property, it would be subject to paying federal capital gains taxes. This is a liability called *trapped-in capital gains.*

Whether to consider tax liabilities that would be triggered by the sale of assets is one of the most common issues in marital property divisions. For the most part, family law courts have been unwilling to make any allowance for trapped-in capital gains on appreciated property unless a sale of the property is imminent.[69] Since family law courts often take tax court positions into consideration, perhaps the tax court's sharp turnaround on this issue in 1998, directing reflection of trapped-in capital gains taxes in valuation will lead family law courts to give some consideration to this issue.

A Washington case is typical. The trial court adjusted the gross value of the parties' interest in a real estate partnership from $119,049 to $101,000 to reflect the capital gains tax that would be paid if it were sold. The court of appeals reversed. The court noted, "There is no Washington case specifically addressing whether capital gains tax consequences should be a factor in determining the value of marital assets." Thus the court looked to other states for precedent, citing cases in seven other states. The court then concluded:

> Courts have generally found that consideration of tax consequences is either required or at least appropriate where the consequences are immediate and specific and/or arise directly from the court's decree, but find they are not an appropriate consideration where speculation as to a party's future dealings with property awarded to him or her would be required. . . . We agree with the rule adopted by most jurisdictions. . . . Mr. Hay testified at trial that he had no plans to sell his partnership interest. . . . We remand to enable the trial court to consider the property division without regard to the capital gains tax consequences of a hypothetical sale of H&L Investments.[70]

The practice of reviewing decisions from other states is very common. Typical of a decision reached after doing this is that the court should consider potential tax consequences in valuing marital assets only if the following is true:

1. The recognition of a tax liability is required by dissolution or will occur within a short time.
2. The party's future dealings with the assets are definite enough that the court need not speculate.

3. The future consequences are definite enough that the court need not speculate, and the tax liability can be reasonably predicted.[71]

The courts usually factor in the tax consequences when it is clear that they will be triggered as part of the divorce action. However, a trial court ordered the husband to pay a mortgage, a car loan, and a cash judgment to the wife from the sale of at least one of two laundromats owned. The trial court reduced the marital estate by a $53,200 tax liability to be incurred on the sale of the laundromats. The trial court explained that although it did not specifically order the sale of the laundromats, sale was the only way that the husband could comply with the orders of the court. Nevertheless, the appellate court found that the sale of both laundromats was not an immediate consequence of the property disposition and that the trial court erred in reducing the marital estate by the amount of the tax liability.[72]

In an extreme denial of consideration of tax consequences, the property division mandated by the trial court had the effect of requiring the husband to liquidate his closely held business and turn the proceeds over to the wife to satisfy a cash award. Nevertheless, the court rejected the husband's argument that the stock should have been valued at its liquidation value rather than its going-concern value because of the tax consequences, reasoning that to follow this argument would universally prevent a court from valuing property at more than cost because of tax consequences.[73]

There are, however, cases in which the tax consequences on sale have been deducted in valuing the marital estate, even when no immediate sale was contemplated. For example, in one case it was concluded that it was proper to deduct the amount of capital gains tax that the husband would have to pay on the anticipated sale of limited partnership interests. The wife objected to reducing the value by the impounded taxes, claiming that they were "hypothetical, speculative, imaginary, unfair, and arbitrary." Evidence was introduced to show that the partnership was a tax shelter that would have lost its desirability in five to seven years and would probably be sold. The court concluded that the date of sale was not imaginary or hypothetical.

The court then offered an interesting broader statement that "*partnerships ought to be reduced by future capital gains taxes*" where the partnerships were investments that "*were only valuable as long as other investments were not more desirable*" and the husband "*was more likely to sell his interest in the partnerships than die owning them*" and would, therefore, incur a capital gains tax from the sale of the partnerships (emphasis added).[74] From the viewpoint of a financial analyst, it is reasonable to think that this reasoning should apply to *any* investment asset.

Another interesting decision upholding subtraction of capital gains tax involved a commercial building. The appellate court held that the trial court did not abuse its discretion in subtracting the capital gains tax that would be incurred on sale, even though there was no evidence that the property was going to be sold. The court found that experts for both parties attested to the property's fair market value and that the concept of fair market value assumes the sale of the property to an interested buyer. Thus, the court was reluctant to find any error by the trial court in presuming a sale of the real estate with its attendant tax consequences in order to value that marital asset.[75] In another case, where the husband would effectively have been forced to purchase the wife's shares in a company, the court permitted a credit for capital gains taxes.[76]

Some courts hold that tax consequences may be considered if the court determines that the property division award will force a party to sell the business to generate the cash needed to pay the court-imposed obligations.[77]

The holdings in these and similar cases suggest that if the sale of the assets is so remote a possibility as to eliminate consideration of the capital gains tax liability, the asset approach should not be the only primary valuation approach used. However, these holdings also suggest that perhaps an income approach would be more appropriate, or maybe an income approach blended with an asset-based approach.[78]

Adequacy of Evidence

Trial courts have wide discretion in deciding factual matters, such as value, but appellate courts expect trial courts to have an adequate evidentiary basis for reaching their conclusions of fact.[79] There is a considerable incidence of "expert" evidence at the trial court level being so inadequate that the appellate court has remanded the cases for new hearings and evidence on the value of a business or practice.[80]

This has usually meant that all the money and time spent on "experts" and the related lawyer fees have been wasted. This can be avoided if competent business valuation experts are retained to begin with, and the lawyer and expert work together to make a good record at trial—especially since courts tend to give significantly greater weight to the valuations of qualified, independent, business appraisers.[81] This also means that the attorney must obtain the full cooperation of, and disclosure from, the client.[82]

Access to Records

It is common for an operating spouse to resist access to the records necessary for the nonoperating spouse's expert to do a thorough valuation. Since the nonoperating spouse has a financial interest in the property, the lawyer can almost always get a court order compelling production of the information needed by the expert to do a thorough valuation. In a case that went all the way to the supreme court of Connecticut, a radiologist filed a motion to exclude the wife's expert's report and testimony because the report had not been produced prior to trial. The expert testified that the delay in preparing his report was attributable to a lack of cooperation on the part of the husband in failing to make the pertinent financial records available. In denying the motion, the court declared the following:

> If anybody is playing cat and mouse, it's the [husband].... It is virtually frivolous for the husband to suggest that the court abused

its broad discretion by failing to impose the sanction of excluding testimony because of delay in furnishing the report of an expert witness, after concluding that the delay was largely attributable to the husband's failure to comply with the order for disclosure of his financial records.[83]

Double-Dipping: A Persistent Problem

One of the most prevalent problems in family law cases involving a business or professional practice valuation is "double-dipping." By *double-dipping* we mean computing a value based, at least in part, on the spouse's future earnings for property division and then using the future earnings capacity as a basis for determining spousal support or alimony payments.

The potential for this problem arises when an income approach, an excess earnings method, or a market approach is used for the valuation. If these methods reflect an implication that the operating spouse will continue to operate, the value of that spouse's future efforts is impounded, at least to some extent, in the distributive value. If payments are then ordered out of the earnings from that spouse's efforts, double-counting is the potential result.

This problem is exacerbated in those jurisdictions that consider *personal goodwill* to be a marital asset. Personal goodwill is a function of future earning power resulting from persistence of patronage of the individual. If this value is fully reflected in the distributive asset, then this earning power is being used twice if it is the basis for future payments to the nonoperating spouse.

This problem can be avoided if the valuation methodology truly follows the philosophy of not being dependent on future efforts (or restrictions on efforts) of the operating spouse. However, as noted earlier, many court decisions espouse this philosophy, but they then accept a valuation methodology that actually incorporates an assumption of the operating spouse's continuing efforts, or restrictions on those efforts.

In *Steneken v. Steneken*,[84] the trial court determined that the husband's annual compensation was excessive, and the court normalized the compensation in determining the value of his company using the excess earnings method. The court then determined alimony using the husband's actual annual compensation which was $50,000 more. The husband argued that distributing his excess earnings as the goodwill portion of the value of his business, and also considering it for alimony purposes, was impermissible double-counting.

The New Jersey intermediate appellate court ruled that the value of the business was as of the date of dissolution and was based on past excess earnings, whereas the alimony determination was based on future income. The court also noted that even if this was double-counting, it was not banned by New Jersey law, which bans only the double-counting of pensions.

The New Jersey Supreme Court expressly rejected the premise that because alimony and equitable distribution are interrelated, a credit on one side of the ledger mandates a debit on the other side. Instead, the court focused on the "bedrock proposition" that all alimony awards and equitable distribution determinations must satisfy basic concepts of fairness and that, although clearly interrelated, the structural purposes of alimony and equitable distribution are different.

Accordingly, the court rejected the husband's assertions of double-counting, saying that the husband "mistakenly equates the statutory and decisional methodology applied in the calculation of alimony with a valuation methodology applied for equitable distribution purposes that requires that revenues and expenses, including salaries, be normalized so as to present a fair valuation of a going concern." The court concluded that it is not inequitable to use a valuation method that normalizes salary in an ongoing closely held corporation for equitable distribution purposes, and to use actual salary received in calculating alimony—the valuation methodology chosen for equitable distribution purposes should not alter the alimony award. According to the court, the "interplay of those two calculations does not constitute 'double counting.'" The ultimate judicial inquiry must be whether the ultimate result, both in toto as well as in its constituent parts, is fair under the circumstances and congruent with the standards set forth in the alimony and equitable distribution statutes. The court also rejected the distinction made by the appellate court between the fact that "valuation of the corporate asset was based on [the husband's] past earnings, not his future earnings," whereas "[the husband's] actual current and future compensation may be treated as income for alimony purposes."

Justice Long, in a dissenting opinion, agreed with the husband that the majority's holding would allow the impermissible double-counting of income (albeit not dollar for dollar). Justice Long's position was that the majority converted a certain amount of the husband's projected future income stream into an asset and then calculated the amount of alimony based on that asset. According to Justice Long, this was improper because "[o]nce a court converts a specific stream of income into an asset, that income may no longer be calculated into the maintenance formula and payout." Instead, Justice Long's solution would have used the appellate court's approach, which neither allows the unfettered dual use of a single income stream nor requires the use of the same figure for both calculations. "Rather, judges should be able to use the 'real' income for alimony and the 'normalized' income for the corporate valuation so long as the ultimate outcome recognizes that a single income source (the difference between the real and normalized income) played a part in both."

It is arguable that, to the extent the court used excess compensation as the basis for alimony, the court used that money twice: once to value the distributed value of the business and again to determine the amount of alimony—a classic case of double-dipping.

In *Sampson v. Sampson*[85] the value of the wife's insurance agency was offset in the husband's property distribution and then was counted as credit toward his alimony support obligations. The wife argued that this was double-counting. Because there were inconsistencies in the experts' reports concerning owner salary, the court was unable to determine whether double-counting had occurred, and it remanded the case for further factual determinations on this issue.

The court in *Champion v. Champion*,[86] noting that there is a split among jurisdictions on the issues of what constitutes double-dipping and whether it ought to be prohibited as a matter of law, rejected a claim of double-dipping and found the business to be both a marital asset and a source of income.

In *Keane v. Keane*,[87] New York's highest court held that the prohibition against double-counting applies only to intangible assets, such as professional licenses or goodwill, or the value of a service business, not income-producing tangible assets such as rental property.

In *Sander v. Sander*,[88] the court ruled that it is not double-counting to assign a value to a business, as well as to attribute gross income from that business to the spouse, without adjusting either. Where the trial court, in its discretion, valued the company at a value it would have to a buyer who would pay a manager's salary, the court's decision was upheld as both logical and supported by the record.

References

Bateman, Tracy A. 2000. *Divorce and Separation: Consideration of Tax Consequences in Distribution of Marital Property.* 9 A.L.R. 5th. Lawyers Cooperative Publishing, p. 568. Contains an exhaustive listing and discussion of cases involving consideration or lack of consideration of tax consequences in marital property settlements.

Business Valuation Resources (BVR), www.BVLibrary.com. Contains the complete text of all major state appellate decisions involving business valuation decisions, searchable by case name, keyword, and state. Also contains full texts of relevant laws and regulations and unpublished conference presentations.

Business Valuation Resources. 2007. *BVR's Guide to Fair Value in Shareholder Dissent, Oppression, and Marital Dissolution.* Portland, OR: Business Valuation Resources.

Business Valuation Resources. 2008. *BVR's Guide to* Personal v. Enterprise Goodwill. Portland, OR: Business Valuation Resources.

Feder, Robert D., ed. 1997. *Valuation Strategies in Divorce*, 4th ed. New York: Aspen Law & Business.

Fishman, Jay, et al. 2008. "Valuations for Divorce Engagements." In *PPC's Guide to Business Valuations.* Fort Worth, TX: Practitioners Publishing, pp. 12-1 to 12-49.

Goldberg, Barth, and Barry A. Schatz. 1984 plus 1999 supplement. *Valuation of Divorce Assets.* RM New York West Law, pp. 335–552 of the 1999 supplement and pages 443–485 of the 1984 volume are case summaries on the valuation of closely held corporations and partnerships; pages 176–217 of the 1999 supplement and 198–227 of the 1984 volume are on valuation of professional entities, goodwill, and license agreements.

Gold-Biken, Lynne Z., Steven A. Kolodny, Adam R. Koritzinsky, and Barbara A. Stark. 1994. *Divorce Practice Handbook.* Charlottesville, VA: Michie.

Kleeman, Robert E., Jr., James R. Alerding, and Benjamin D. Miller. 1999. *The Handbook for Divorce Valuations.* New York: Wiley.

Oldham, L. Thomas. 1999 edition. "The Closely Held Business." In *Divorce, Separation and the Distribution of Property.* pp. 10–1 to 10–5.

Pratt, Shannon. 2003. "Marital Dissolutions." In *Business Valuation Body of Knowledge*, 2nd ed. New York: Wiley, pp. 235–328.

Pratt, Shanon, and Alina V. Niculita, 2007. "Valuation for Marital Dissolution Purposes" and "Marital Dissolution Court Cases" (ch. 37 and 38). In *Valuing a Business*, 5th ed. New York: McGraw-Hill.

Chapter 22

Employee Stock Ownership Plans

> ESOPs are one of the most specialized and demanding areas of business valuation, and companies with or contemplating an ESOP are well advised to consult an appraiser with considerable experience in ESOP valuation.
>
> —*Shannon Pratt and Alina V. Niculita*

General Principles

An employee stock ownership plan (ESOP) is a qualified employee benefit plan that invests primarily in the common stock of the sponsoring corporation. ESOPs provide a means for employers to incentivize employees and provide liquidity to controlling shareholders, who in turn are able, in certain instances, to defer taxation on the gain from the sale to the ESOP.

This chapter is updated by the author from a chapter contributed by Kim Abello, an accredited senior appraiser at Duff & Phelps, to the first edition of "The Lawyer's Business Valuation Handbook: Understanding Financial Statements, Appraisal Reports, and Expert Testimony," by Shannon P. Pratt, American Bar Association, Chicago, 2000.

Becoming effective for the years beginning after December 31, 1997, the Internal Revenue Code (IRC) was amended to allow ESOPs to be shareholders in S corporations and to exempt the flow-through earnings to the ESOP from the unrelated business income tax (Section 1523 of the Tax Relief Act of 1997). This law allows the income of an S corporation to pass through to an ESOP, and because the ESOP is tax exempt, no tax is paid on the income.

Presently, ESOPs are available to only C and S corporations. While important operational differences exist between the two, it is significant to note that ESOPs provide controlling shareholders with an alternative means of creating a liquidity event other than an outright sale of assets or stock to strategic or financial buyers or the issuing of an IPO.

Valuation Principles

As a general rule professional appraisers involved in valuations for purposes of stock held by an ESOP follow many of the principles discussed in other parts of this book.

However, there are certain valuation considerations specific to ESOPs that require a modification of the general valuation theories. A complete understanding of ESOPs requires knowledge of valuation theory, the Employee Retirement Income Security Act (ERISA) of 1974, trust and fiduciary law, tax law, finance, and accounting issues. The discussion here will focus on the specific valuation factors affecting ESOPs.

Adequate Consideration

An ESOP is a qualified defined contribution plan under Section 401(a) of the Internal Revenue Code. ESOPs are subject to the requirements of ERISA, as amended, and pursuant to IRC, Section 4975(e)(7), also subject to regulations issued by the Treasury secretary (Treasury Reg. 54.4975-11 of the Excise Tax Regulations). Section 3(18) of ERISA generally states that an ESOP cannot pay more than "adequate consideration" when investing in qualifying employer securities. In the case of a stock that is publicly traded, the price in the public market represents adequate consideration.

Responsibility for the interpretation and enforcement of ERISA is divided among the Department of Labor (DOL), the Department of the Treasury (particularly the Internal Revenue Service), and the Pension Benefit Guarantee Corporation (PBGC). With respect to adequate consideration, the DOL issued the Proposed Regulation Relating to the Definition of Adequate Consideration on May 17, 1988.[1] Despite the passage of time, this regulation has not been finalized, yet it remains the most authoritative source of guidance on adequate consideration. The DOL's proposed regulations largely adopted the concepts of Revenue Ruling 59-60 for stock that is not publicly traded.

Internal and external ESOP plan trustees and fiduciaries must determine, in good faith pursuant to the terms of the plan, the fair market value of the stock. It is not enough for a fiduciary to rely in good faith on a third-party valuation to establish that adequate consideration was paid. A fiduciary must make his or her own prudent investigation of value and understand the underlying assumptions on which the valuation is made at the time the ESOP purchases the shares.[2] (Lawyers should inform the fiduciaries of this requirement. See *Howard v. Shay* and *Reich v. Valley National Bank of Arizona* later in this chapter.) This process establishes adequate consideration. The aforementioned DOL proposed regulation also defines fair market value. It defines it as the price at which property would change hands between a willing buyer and a willing seller when the former is not under any compulsion to buy and the latter is not under any compulsion to sell, and both parties are able, as well as willing, to trade and are well informed about the asset and the market for such asset.

When Appraisals Are Required

Pursuant to the Tax Reform Act of 1986, companies sponsoring ESOPs are required to have the ESOP stock valued by an independent appraiser at least annually for stock acquired after December 31, 1986. Valuation by an independent appraiser is not required in the case of employer securities that are readily tradable on an established securities market. An appraisal of ESOP stock is required at the following times:

1. When the ESOP makes its first acquisition of employer corporation stock
2. At least annually thereafter (although some companies routinely have their stock appraisals updated semiannually or quarterly)
3. Whenever there is a stock sale transaction with a controlling stockholder or member of a control group—that is, a transaction between the plan and a party-in-interest
4. If the ESOP sells out of its stock position[3]

Independence of Appraiser

Under Internal Revenue Code Section 401(a)(28)(C), the ESOP fiduciaries must employ an independent appraiser that meets the requirements of IRC Regulation Section 1.170A-13(c)(5), which defines independence with respect to appraisers for the valuation of donations to charities. The qualified independent appraiser, according to these regulations, meets the following qualifications, among others:

- Is not a party to the transaction, is not related to any party to the transaction, is not married to any person with a relationship to the transaction, is not regularly used by any of the parties to the transaction, and does not perform a majority of appraisals for these persons
- Holds himself or herself out to the public as an appraiser or performs appraisals on a regular basis
- Is qualified by background, experience, education, and memberships in professional associations to make appraisals of the type of property being valued

- Understands that an intentionally false or fraudulent overstatement of value may subject the valuation practitioner to a civil penalty
- Receives an appraisal fee that is not based on a percentage of the appraised value of the property

This independence requirement is specific to ESOP appraisals. It is intuitive that the appraiser needs to be independent, in this context, because the ESOP transaction typically involves a purchase by the ESOP of stock from a shareholder that may have the ability to control the selection of the appraiser. Internal Revenue Manual (IRM) 4.72.8.7.1, Employee Plans Technical Guidance, Valuation of Assets, Independent Appraiser Rules (September 1, 2006), addresses these independence requirements for audit purposes and lists the examination steps to be taken by IRS examiners. The appraiser should be familiar with these guidelines.

IRS Audit Guidelines

Internal Revenue Manual (IRM) 4.72.4, Employee Plans Technical Guidance, Employee Stock Ownership Plans (April 1, 2006), contains the IRS's examination guidelines for audits of leveraged ESOPs.[4] These guidelines can assist the appraiser in protecting an ESOP from attack by the IRS. The following are the salient ESOP valuation issues covered in these guidelines:

- The balance sheet on Form 5500 provides information such as whether investments are in employer securities, acquisition indebtedness and/or other liabilities (indicates leverage), and party-in-interest transactions. In smaller plans determine whether a valuation was made by adding the assets at the beginning of the year to the contributions and receipts less the disbursements during the year and comparing the total to the assets at the end of the year. If the total equals the assets at the end of the year, a valuation probably has not been made because the total reflects only the receipts and disbursements.

- When reviewing the income statement, note any noncash contributions because these may also indicate the acquisition of employer securities.
- Where stock is publicly traded, examine stock confirmation slips, trust receipt and disbursement accounts, and market records to verify the fair market value of security transactions.
- Where stock is not publicly traded and the transaction does not involve a disqualified person, the fair market value must be determined as of the plan's most recent valuation date. Examine the records used to value the stock at the last valuation date in order to determine whether the assigned value is comparable to the value of comparable non–publicly traded companies. See Regulation 54.4975–11(d)(5).
- Where stock is not publicly traded and the transaction involves a disqualified person, the fair market value must be determined as of the transaction date. Secure the appraisal report, if any, and use it as a basis for verifying the adequate consideration rules. If possible, request both the prior and subsequent appraisals for comparison purposes. If the appraisal method is not consistently applied, inquire as to the reason for the change. In addition, determine whether any projections used were reasonable estimates of what has actually occurred.
- *Note:* Particular attention should be given to subsequent events that could have been foreseen and that have an impact on value. See Revenue Ruling 59-60, 1959-1 C.B. 237. The independent appraisal will not in itself be a good faith determination. Also, examine the capital stock accounts of the employer to substantiate transactions of similar stock.
- Determine whether fair market value was paid for the stock. Look at the valuation report on the company's shares. See if the company that makes similar products has share prices that rise and fall with its earnings. If the company's earnings have fallen but the report says the price per share has risen, it may indicate

an incorrect valuation. Also check the correlation between earnings and stock price if there is no valuation report.

- Check the employer's audit report to see if the company's earnings have fallen after the valuation report was written. If they have, it is likely the shares' value should also have fallen. The plan fiduciary can no longer rely on the price per share from the valuation report because the facts on which it was based have changed.
- Ask to see documentation of the fiduciary's prudent investigation to ensure that the underlying assumptions have not changed since the last valuation.

There are other issues discussed in the examination guidelines that affect the review of the ESOP-exempt loan, the IRC Section 1042 rollover, the IRC Section 415 limitations, the Section 404(k) deduction for dividends paid on employer stock, the ESOP put option, voting rights, and other related issues. The appraiser should also be familiar with these guidelines if involved in the structuring of an ESOP transaction.[5]

Control Versus Minority Interest

Control premiums and minority interest discounts are often issues with ESOPs. There is some controversy over whether an ESOP that owns a controlling interest—that is, more than 50 percent—is really in control. Since the ultimate shareholder is the ESOP participant, it could be argued that the participant really owns the stock and is, therefore, typically a minority interest. Even though there is some controversy, the appraiser should remain consistent in the appraisals for a specific ESOP company.

The DOL proposed regulation provides some guidance on the ESOP's ability to pay a control premium. The regulation generally restricts the ESOP's payment of a control premium unless: (1) a third-party investor would pay a premium and (2) the ESOP receives voting control and control in fact (although the latter phrase is not defined). In addition, if the ESOP plans to purchase control over a period of time, the proposed regulation does allow the ESOP to pay the control price if there is an actual binding agreement obligating the employer to pass control within a reasonable time.

Lack of Marketability Discount

An ESOP company is required to provide a "put option" for distributions from the ESOP of employer stock that is not "readily tradable on an established market."[6] This put option is not binding on the ESOP.[7] The shares, however, may be put to the employer, and in such instances it creates what is referred to as the "repurchase obligation"—a future obligation on the part of the company to repurchase the shares from departing ESOP participants. Although some commentators suggest otherwise, current practice among a great majority of valuation professionals recognizes the fact that the ESOP's put option enhances the liquidity of the ESOP's stock and thus reduces, or in some cases even eliminates, the lack of marketability discount associated with the price the ESOP can pay.[8]

With respect to ESOP valuations, the proposed regulations state that the appraiser should consider the extent to which the put rights are enforceable, as well as the company's ability to meet its obligation with respect to these put rights (taking into account the company's financial strength and liquidity). To summarize, the following factors should be considered by the appraiser in selecting the magnitude of the lack of marketability discount:

- The provisions of the ESOP documents, including put rights
- The financial strength and solvency of the company
- The size of the block owned by the ESOP
- The company's liquidity from a balance sheet perspective
- The borrowing capacity of the business
- The repurchase liability and funding thereof
- The company's past repurchase of ESOP shares

- The form and timing of payment by the company to selling shareholders
- The overall priority of acknowledged and contingent financial claims that may conflict with achieving liquidity for the participants over time

Some commentators suggest that, since the put option and marketability enhancement do not exist until after the ESOP purchase, the ESOP cannot pay for the put in the initial ESOP purchase. Since marketability is less of an issue for a controlling interest shareholder, this controversy is limited to minority ESOPs. This issue has not been litigated or resolved as of the date of this writing. However, in actual transactions, most minority interest investors, recognizing the marketability limitations of their ownership, negotiate their exit vehicle at the time the investment is made. Thus a marketability discount is not considered in the estimate of fair market value either before or after the minority investment.

ESOP Financial Statement Adjustments

There are two specific financial statement adjustments typically made in the context of ESOP valuations. The first is recognition that the ESOP contributions may be in excess of normal employee benefit plan expenses. The second includes recognition of the additional tax benefits and leverage from any ESOP debt incurred as part of the initial purchase.

Because, in the case of leveraged ESOPs, the magnitude of the ESOP contributions is tied to the amount of the ESOP debt, this contribution may not be commensurate with normal employee benefit expense. The appraiser needs to have an understanding of the level of normal employer contributions both before the ESOP and once the ESOP debt is repaid. The typical income statement adjustment would eliminate the ESOP contribution as an expense (that is, add the amount back to earnings) and subtract the expected level of employee benefit expense. If the ESOP contributions were equivalent to the normal level of employee benefit expense, this adjustment would not be necessary. The objective is to arrive at a normalized level of earnings for the company's operations.

The second adjustment gives consideration to the tax benefits associated with the deductibility of the ESOP contributions used to pay the ESOP debt. The treatment of this item may vary from one case to another based on the valuation method employed. For example, debt-free methods provide for a subtraction of the ESOP debt from the market value of invested capital. However, as the ESOP debt payments are deductible, this debt is tax advantaged. Recognition of this can be quantified by calculating the present value of the tax savings created by this debt instrument and adding it back to the equity value.

In addition, the appraiser should consider the effect of the additional financial risk placed on the company after the ESOP transaction in subsequent annual valuations when deciding on discount or capitalization rates in the income approach to value and on valuation multiples in the market approach to value.

Repurchase Liability: Redemption or Recirculation

As previously mentioned, the put option received by the ESOP participants creates a repurchase obligation on the part of the company. The ESOP sponsor must decide whether to "redeem" or "recirculate" shares; this is a strategic decision.[9] A *redemption* is a direct acquisition by the company from the participant. A *recirculation* "involves the company repurchasing the shares from the participant and contributing those shares to the ESOP for redistribution to the remaining employees as part of a continuing benefit."[10]

Because participants' account balances grow over time, the repurchase liability becomes a more significant issue in more mature ESOPs. *Management of the repurchase obligation* by the company is the key concept. Repurchase liability studies help management to quantify and plan for the obligation so that major repurchases do not surprise management at a time when the company cannot afford the payment. In addition, plan design can help the company finance the obligation by establishing methods of distribution that provide flexibility.

The two primary variables affecting the obligation are the number of shares put to the company by participants in a year and the per share value at the time of the repurchase. This is an annual computation. However, management of an ESOP company needs to understand all the variables that affect this contribution now and in the future in order to manage the obligation effectively. Other factors affecting this obligation include the following:

- The amount of existing liquidity in the ESOP trust
- The percentage of stock held by the ESOP
- The demographics of the employee base (age, turnover, and actuarial determinations on life and disability)
- The ESOP plan provisions (vesting, eligibility, and so on)
- The ESOP plan distribution and diversification policy
- Structure of past and future ESOP transactions
- The company's borrowing limitations
- The growth in the value of the company's stock

The interaction of these factors is complex. However, a company must manage this obligation to protect future participants from dilution. It should also be noted that the rules differ for S corp ESOPs.

Relevant Case Law

Many issues involved in the valuation of ESOP shares are not settled. Also, the number of potential litigants that can contest the ESOP appraisal is significant.[11] Both the Internal Revenue Service and the Department of Labor are the enforcement agencies that monitor ESOPs in general and thus the appraisal. In addition, each participant (and often participants' spouses and/or beneficiaries) has rights with respect to the appraisal and valuation of his or her ESOP account.

The following is a discussion of some of the most significant cases affecting ESOP valuations today.

Charles S. Foltz v. U.S. News & World Report, Inc.[12]

This case involved the amount from the distributions received from 1973 through 1981 by the retirees of U.S. News & World Report, Inc. (U.S. News) from their profit-sharing plan (the Plan), which owned employer stock. Although not technically an ESOP, 100 percent of the stock was owned by employees. The initial purchase by the Plan was in 1962. The defendants in the case were U.S. News, certain company representatives, the Plan, and the appraiser. The stock value appreciated substantially from the 1975 price of $69 per share to $200 per share in 1980. The company was sold in 1984 for $2,842 per share. The court's decision involved the following valuation positions:

- A series of minority interest transactions did not mandate that the appraiser add a *control premium* for valuation purposes even if the ESOP eventually gained control. The court emphasized the fact that while the participants' combined interests represented a majority position, this did not entitle them to a pro rata percent of a control value.
- The 10 percent *discount for lack of marketability* applied by the appraiser was accepted in light of the fact that the company was under no obligation to repurchase the stock (there was no put option) and the company exercised the stock's call provision from time to time.
- U.S. News held some additional value in *nonoperating assets* that could not be reached by a minority shareholder. The court recognized that appraisals should give primary consideration to the earnings of the company and the shareholder's return on investment. Thus no additional emphasis was placed on the value of real estate.

- It was appropriate for the annual appraisals to consider the facts and circumstances known or perceived as of the appraisal date and not consider *subsequent events* that could not have been anticipated. The issue here was that employees who separated from the company before its sale did not participate in the appreciation realized upon the sale.

The court of appeals for the District of Columbia affirmed the U.S. News case on appeal, on all counts, on January 13, 1989.

Las Vegas Dodge, Inc. v. U.S.[13]

The IRS relied heavily on an asset-based method—that is, book value—in *Las Vegas Dodge, Inc. v. U.S.* The independent appraisal gave heavy emphasis to the earning power and dividend capacity of the company. The court found that the earnings-based method was more relevant, even though the appraisal considered a 20-year projection period, using the discounted cash flow (DCF) valuation method. The projections seemed reasonable in light of historical performance.

Howard v. Shay[14]

The *Howard v. Shay* case involved the ESOP of Pacific Architects and Engineers, Inc. (PAE). On November 9, 1988, the administrative committee of the PAE ESOP sold all the shares the ESOP held (about 37 percent of the total) to an irrevocable trust in connection with a termination of the plan. The stock value upon the sale was the highest it had ever been. Since the irrevocable trust was created by the controlling shareholder of PAE, some of the former ESOP participants alleged that the administrative committee engaged in self-dealing and sold the stock to the trust for less than fair market value. The following is a summary of the court's findings:

- The original court decision held that independent or neutral fiduciaries were not necessary in light of the fact that Arthur

Young was retained to render an independent appraisal and fairness opinion. However, in reversing the trial court, the Ninth Circuit Court of Appeals held that the mere fact that an independent appraisal was performed is an incomplete defense to a charge of imprudence, especially in cases in which there is a strong possibility of self-dealing. They found liability in the degree of care exercised by the ESOP trustees.

- There was nothing wrong with the appraisal procedures. In addition, the minority interest discount of 40 to 50 percent and marketability discount of 50 percent taken into account were reasonable under the circumstances. The ESOP participants did not have a put option (because all stock was acquired before 1986), and there was some concern over the company's ability to honor the repurchase obligation in the future. Support for these discounts in the form of market evidence in similar facts and circumstances was the overriding reason why the court accepted them.
- The Ninth Circuit Court decision added a fiduciary issue to the PAE case. It stated that "the fiduciary is required to make an honest, objective effort to read the valuation, understand it, and question the methods and assumptions that do not make sense." The court even suggested a second appraisal opinion if uncertainties remained.

On remand, the U.S. District Court reaffirmed its original decision concerning the valuation issues. However, based on the Ninth Circuit's decision finding a breach of fiduciary duty, the court granted the ESOP and/or any of the participants the right to buy back the original PAE shares at the tendered price. More important, the plaintiffs were awarded attorney's fees and costs, which amounted to about $4 million!

Reich v. Valley National Bank of Arizona[15]

Reich v. Valley National Bank of Arizona involves an action brought by the Department of Labor against Valley National Bank of Arizona for its participation as trustee in the Kroy, Inc., ESOP. The case could be characterized primarily as a trustee's fiduciary duty case rather than as a valuation case. The Kroy ESOP transaction involved an ESOP and other equity investors—that is, a multi-investor ESOP. The non-ESOP investor paid a per share price that was significantly less than the per share price paid by the ESOP. This involved a 1986 transaction in which Kroy was taken private in a management-led leveraged ESOP transaction. Some major points of the case were as follows:

- The fiduciary *must* be an active participant in the *negotiations* regarding the transaction price and terms.
- The *independent financial advisor* should be retained directly by the fiduciary.
- The *due diligence* of the company and security being purchased should be thorough, and the fiduciary should not rely on its advisor's due diligence.

The central issues were the following:

- The bank trustee approved the ESOP's investment without any due diligence or investigation of its own.
- The bank loan department had previously turned down its own investment in the ESOP debt of the leveraged buyout after its own diligence.
- The bank failed to disclose its reasons or documentation for the rejection of its participation in the leveraged buyout debt to its legal or financial advisor.
- The bank could not simply rely on the appraiser's report as a matter of law. In any event, the appraiser's report on its face raised questions that needed to be answered.

On September 20, 1994, the U.S. District Court for the Southern District of New York entered the settlement in the lawsuit against

Valley National Bank of Arizona. The settlement consisted of a reimbursement of principal and interest payments on the debt incurred in the ESOP's purchase to the Kroy ESOP.

Gary L. Eyler v. Commissioner[16]

In the *Eyler* case, Gary L. Eyler, the sole or majority shareholder of Continental Training Services (CTS), Inc., disputed the IRS's determination that he had engaged in a "prohibited transaction" with the CTS ESOP because the ESOP paid more than fair market value. Eyler was seeking to sell CTS and had decided to take the company public. The investment banker established a price for the initial public offering (IPO) of $13 to $16 per share in mid-1986 but failed to attract participants at this price. One month after the IPO failed in December 1986, Eyler sold stock to the ESOP at $14.50 per share. Seven of CTS's board members also purchased shares at $14.50 per share. In September 1986, two unrelated investigations for fraudulent practices were pending involving CTS.

The tax court's findings in the case were as follows:

- Eyler failed to establish that $14.50 was the fair market value of the CTS stock on the date of the transaction.
- The tax court agreed that a lack of marketability discount should have been applied to the value of CTS to reflect the hypothetical buyer's concern that there would not be a ready market available when the buyer, in turn, decided to sell.
- The purchases by the directors were related-party sales and did not reflect fair market value.
- Since the board members who approved the ESOP's purchase knew that many of the assumptions underlying the investment banker's IPO price had changed and they did not conduct any further investigation of the suggested price and did not obtain an independent appraisal, their actions did not rise to the level of prudence imposed on ERISA fiduciaries.

The appeals court affirmed the tax court and added that the fact that the IPO failed indicated that it did not reflect fair market value. In addition, the appeals court noted that the IPO would bring additional cash flow that would enhance market value that would not occur in an ESOP purchase. In fact, the ESOP required additional cash outlays in the form of employer contributions.

The appeals court also agreed with the tax court on the issue of marketability. It rejected the notion that the ESOP's put option reduced the lack of marketability discount because (1) the put option did not have a fixed price and (2) it could be paid out over five years under the terms of the ESOP. This aspect of the case has drawn attention to the lack of marketability discount in the ESOP context. Since it has been acceptable among ESOP valuation professionals to lower or even eliminate the marketability discount because of the ESOP's "put" right, this case raises some questions. This decision seems to be a situation (with respect to the marketability discount) of bad facts and thus a controversial result.

The conclusion regarding the related-party sales and the prudence of the fiduciaries was also affirmed by the appeals court.

Henry v. Champlain Enterprises[17]

The court in *Henry v. Champlain Enterprises* rejected the valuation by a nationally recognized appraisal firm of convertible preferred stock contributed to an ESOP on grounds that the valuation was biased. In addition, because the trustee failed to document that it had challenged some aspects of the valuation, the court found that the trustee had failed to prove it had not breached its fiduciary duties.

In 1994 the three owners of CommutAir, a closely held regional airline, wanted to establish an ESOP with a contribution of 30 percent of CommutAir's stock. CommutAir had been approached by two investment banking firms that provided CommutAir with written materials indicating that CommutAir had an equity value of between $140 million and $225 million. These offers were not pursued, but the CommutAir owners came to the conclusion, based on the offers, that their equity was worth $200 million. Accordingly, they wanted to sell their 30 percent stake for $60 million in a seller-financed transaction.

When they were ready to establish the ESOP, the owners hired U.S. Trust Co. (U.S. Trust), which routinely served as an ESOP trustee. U.S. Trust stressed the need for due diligence and an appraisal of the company, and Houlihan, Lokey, Howard, & Zukin (Houlihan) was retained for this purpose.

Based on a comparable company analysis and a discounted cash flow analysis, Houlihan initially determined that CommutAir was worth $180 million. Subsequently, it still concluded the ESOP was receiving "value in excess" as a result of the features of the convertible preferred stock. Ultimately, the stock sold for $60 million.

ESOP participants brought suit against CommutAir and U.S. Trust over the issue of whether the sale constituted a prohibited transaction under ERISA Section 406 and, if so, whether it qualified under the adequate consideration exception set forth by ERISA.

Both sides agreed that the primary component of the valuation would be to determine CommutAir's total equity value by employing the discounted cash flow method and the comparable guideline public company method. The plaintiff's expert concluded a total equity value of just under $106 million and opined that the convertible preferred stock should have been valued at $41.5 million. The expert criticized Houlihan's terminal growth rate, the use of certain financial measures, and the selection of above-the-median multiples used in the comparable company method (finding CommutAir to be at or below the comparable companies while Houlihan found them to be at or above the comparable companies).

The court found that while correct and in agreement on many issues, there was serious doubt about the overall credibility of both Houlihan and the plaintiff's expert. The court determined that Houlihan was not independent because it did not start with an open mind or independent approach to valuation. The court determined that the plaintiff's expert was hired to provide the lowest valuation conclusion possible to maximize the potential damages sustained by the ESOP. Based on their testimony, however, the trial court determined that the equity value of CommutAir in 1994 was $145 million and that, therefore, the fair market value of the stock purchased by the ESOP was $52.5 million.

As to the adequate consideration exception, the court found that U.S. Trust failed to prove that it had made a good faith, independent determination of fair market value. Specifically, the court questioned the reliability of management projections and the terminal value calculation, and, with respect to the comparable companies method, the court questioned the propriety of the selection of the comparable companies, the financial measures, and the multiples, and whether the most current information was used. The court concluded that U.S. Trust failed to address these areas of concern, noting that U.S. Trust "barely produced a shred of evidence that shows what Goldberg and Shea did." Accordingly, the court awarded the plaintiffs $7.75 million.

This case should serve as a warning to ESOP trustees to document their conduct and decision-making process. In this case, the trustee's failure to create such documentation seems to have given the court no choice but to find that the trustee failed to prove that it engaged in a good faith investigation of the merits of the transaction at issue. The court also found the appraisals in this case suspect, again serving as a reminder of how crucial it is for valuation experts to remain independent throughout the appraisal. In quoting from another case, the court emphasized that "little case law exists on valuation, so often a court's conclusion is determined by its evaluation of the credibility and background of the witnesses who performed the valuation."

Chao v. Hall Holding Co., Inc.[18]

In *Chao v. Hall Holding Co., Inc.*, the U.S. Department of Labor brought suit against Hall Holding and others on the grounds, among others, that the company breached its fiduciary duty by purchasing Hall Holding stock for the employee stock ownership plan without conducting a prudent and independent investigation to determine the stock's fair market value.

Goldman Financial Group, Inc. (GFGI), purchased Hall Chemical Co. (Hall Chemical) through Hall Holding Co. (Hall Holding). Hall Chemical was Hall Holding's primary asset, with Hall Holding owning 95 percent of Hall Chemical. The decision was made to create the Hall Chemical ESOP, and a valuation expert was hired to value Hall Chemical. However, the expert was not informed and never knew that the purpose of the valuation was to determine how much an ESOP should pay for Hall Chemical stock. The expert concluded that Hall Chemical was worth between $32.4 and $37.4 million, exclusive of debt.

Based on this valuation, Hall Chemical's president and vice president, who were also trustees of the ESOP, offered to and did purchase for the Hall Chemical ESOP 110 shares, or 9.9 percent, of Hall Holding stock for $3.5 million (the appraiser had not valued Hall Holding, however).

The district court, finding that Hall Holding stock should have been valued, conducted its own valuation. The court concluded that the fair market value of Hall Holding stock was $2,450,451. It arrived at this value by using the valuation expert's range of value for the Hall Chemical stock, subtracting a $13.6 million debt of Hall Holding and applying a 13 percent minority discount to account for the fact that the ESOP purchased only a minority interest (9.96 percent) in Hall Holding. The court also took into account the negative accounts receivable and liabilities of Hall Holding, applied a 5 percent marketability discount, and applied a 5 percent discount to reflect the president's 5 percent interest in Hall Chemical stock.

The court concluded that the trustees did not conduct a prudent and independent investigation to determine the fair market value of Hall Holding stock purchased by the Hall Chemical ESOP. The court also held that the ESOP was entitled to an award of $1,049,549, which represented the difference between the amount originally paid for the stock and the fair market value of the stock as determined by the court.

The Sixth Circuit affirmed the decision, concluding that the plan trustees had failed to prove that they had made a good faith inquiry into fair market value when (1) the trustees relied on a valuation by an individual who had valued the wrong company and who testified that, if had he been told that the valuation would be used for an employee stock ownership plan transaction, he would have made a different valuation; (2) the trustees generally were "unaware of what was going on"; (3) the trustees were not consulted on major decisions, such as the price to pay for the stock; (4) the trustees did not engage in any negotiation as to the price of the stock; (5) the trustees were more concerned with the return on the investment for the trust that had financed the stock purchase than for the plan; and (6) the trustees caused the plan to be charged several thousands of dollars simply to enable the trustees to communicate using round numbers.

This case serves as a valuable reminder that valuation professionals should make a detailed inquiry into the purpose of their valuation. Such inquiry in this case might have led the appraiser to discover that the valuation was for the purpose of establishing an ESOP, which might have led the appraiser to value the correct company for that purpose.

Keach v. U.S. Trust Co.

Keach v. U.S. Trust Co. has spawned over 20 reported decisions. Those of primary concern to valuators are a U.S. District Court case that decided whether a valuation firm hired by a company's board of directors has fiduciary liability to the company's ESOP,[19] and a U.S. Court of Appeals case that decided the liability of an ESOP's trustee in relying on a valuator's due diligence.[20]

The F&G ESOP began in 1988, when it purchased about 30 percent of F&G's stock from the company's founders. F&G's largest subsidiary conducted direct-mail sweepstakes promotions to its customers. In 1995, a leveraged purchase of a large number of F&G shares by the ESOP was proposed. At that time, F&G had been enjoying record profitability for several years and was forecast to continue this trend into the future.

On December 20, 1995, the ESOP, with U.S. Trust Company (U.S. Trust) acting as its trustee, purchased 3,589,743 shares of F&G stock from several F&G officers and directors at a price of $19.50 per share (the "ESOP II transaction"). F&G had retained Valuemetrics, Inc. (Valuemetrics) as its financial advisor. On September 30, 1995, Valuemetrics issued its first transaction memorandum to the F&G board of directors describing a proposed offer to sell 2,916,667 shares to the ESOP at $24 per share. U.S. Trust served as an independent trustee for the ESOP to consider the merits of the proposed transaction.

U.S. Trust, in turn, engaged Houlihan, Lokey, Howard, & Zukin (Houlihan) to assist in valuing the transaction and to render a written opinion to U.S. Trust as to whether the transaction was fair to the ESOP from a financial perspective.

Based on Houlihan's analysis, U.S. Trust determined that Valuemetrics' analysis was too optimistic in some respects. Houlihan prepared a new analysis reflecting a lower valuation range for the price of the F&G shares. U.S. Trust suggested a share price of $18.50; the final price of the transaction was $19.50.

For the next two years, F&G did enjoy record business; however, in 1998, in the wake of significantly increased sweepstakes regulation, its profits began to decline steadily until F&G declared bankruptcy in 2001. The ESOP participants sued after the value of F&G shares had reached less than 50 percent of their original purchase price.

In the district court case, the plaintiffs asserted that Valuemetrics was a fiduciary to the ESOP plan because it (1) exercised control over plan assets and (2) rendered investment advice with respect to the property of the plan. Valumetrics moved for a summary judgment, countering that it was not a fiduciary to the ESOP plan.

The district court agreed with Valumetrics. The court first observed that a showing of authority or control requires actual decision-making power, rather than the type of influence a professional advisor may have with respect to decisions made by trustees.

It was U.S. Trust, not Valuemetrics, that made the final decision and caused the ESOP to purchase the shares of stock, and it was U.S. Trust that had hired Houlihan as its own independent financial advisor for the transaction.

With regard to investment advice, the court stated that the record did not support a finding that Valuemetrics gave any investment advice to the ESOP regarding the transaction. In light of a Department of Labor advisory opinion indicating that appraising the value of closely held stock for an ESOP does not constitute the rendering of investment advice, the court held that Valuemetrics should not be a party to the action.

In the court of appeals case, one of the issues was whether Houlihan should have foreseen that within two years of its due diligence, the government would crack down on the company's sweepstakes promotions, and within three years, F&G would be bankrupt. The plaintiffs alleged that U.S. Trust had breached its fiduciary duty in relying on Houlihan's report. The district court had found that, rather than blindly accept the forecasts of F&G officers as to F&G's financial future, "U.S. Trust and Houlihan probed and challenged a number of assumptions in Valuemetrics' evaluation before developing their own independent evaluation that formed the basis for a price per share at closing that was almost 20 percent less than the selling shareholders' offering price."

The Seventh Circuit Court of Appeals agreed, saying, "When the record establishes that the overlooked matter was one that no one perceived to be a material concern at the time or to be outcome determinative, it cannot be said that the overall investigation was imprudent or in bad faith. ERISA's fiduciary duty of care 'requires prudence, not prescience.'" The court distinguished this case from that in *Chao v. Hall Holding Co.* (see the summary of the *Chao* case, above), saying that in the *Chao* case, the trustees failed to show they made a good faith inquiry into fair market value because, in part, they relied on a clearly inadequate valuation.

This case demonstrates that a thorough, independent valuation, conducted in light of all known facts at the time, will withstand ERISA's bad faith or breach of the duty of care claims. The case is also consistent with the principle that valuation professionals do not need to be "fortune tellers" to provide defensible valuations.

Armstrong v. LaSalle Bank National Association[21]

The U.S. Court of Appeals for the Seventh Circuit reversed the U.S. District Court's grant of summary judgment in favor of LaSalle serving as the ESOP trustee.

Issue. Did the ESOP trustee breach its fiduciary duty when the valuation of the company stock led to heavy losses to remaining ESOP participants?

Facts. LaSalle National Bank served as the ESOP trustee for Amstead Industries, Inc., a closely held manufacturer of railroad and other transportation equipment. Amstead's ESOP provided that it would redeem the shares of participants leaving the company in full and at once. In accordance with the terms of the plan, the price of Amstead ESOP shares was reset every September 30; an employee had until June 30 of the following year to decide whether to leave Amstead to redeem the vested shares at the September 30 value.

In August 1999, Amstead acquired Varlen Corporation for $800 million. Amstead financed the acquisition by borrowing $1 billion; the loan was unsecured and also enabled Amstead to refinance its previous debt. On September 30, 1999, a month after the acquisition, LaSalle hired a prominent valuation consulting firm to value the ESOP shares. This firm valued Amstead's stock at $184 per share, 32 percent higher than the previous September 30 value. This increase matched the amount by which the Dow Jones Index of 30 industrials had increased. LaSalle accepted this valuation report, apparently, assuming that Amstead was as good a performer as the average company in the index. At this juncture in time, Amstead's unused credit line was limited.

The ensuing year, 2000, redemptions turned out to be not 10 percent—the expected percentage—but 32 percent. The cost to Amstead to redeem the shares was $330 million. This created a liquidity problem and prompted Amstead to eliminate a departing employee's right to a lump sum distribution and make other changes adverse to the plaintiff class. In subsequent years, Amstead's stock was valued at a far lower amount. The facts revealed that the prominent valuation firm had failed to discount the shares for lack of marketability.

Held. The U.S. Court of Appeals, Seventh Circuit, acknowledged that judicial review of decisions of an ERISA trustee is deferential unless there is a conflict of interest. Yet, the court stated that "there are rules as to how much deference a court should give non-adjudicators, a pertinent example being the business-judgment rule, which decreases a light hand for a court asked to invalidate a business decision." Here, the court held that "a discretionary judgment cannot be upheld when discretion has not been exercised. "We cannot find in the record as now constituted any indication that LaSalle considered how best to balance the interests of the various participants in the ESOP in the novel circumstances created by Amstead's acquisition of Varlen. . . . A trustee who simply ignores changed circumstances [increases] the risk of loss to trust's beneficiaries is imprudent."

Summary

ESOP valuations are subject to more scrutiny than appraisals for other purposes mostly because they affect more people. There are over 10,000 ESOP companies in the United States covering about 20 million employees. Each of these employees has a personal stake in the valuation conclusions that are estimated at least annually. However, the subjective nature of valuation always leaves an opening for controversy and dispute.

The formal legal status of ESOPs was first established with the enactment in 1974 of the Employee Retirement Income Security Act (ERISA). However, ESOPs did not grow in popularity until the Tax Reduction Act of 1984, which enacted new, tax-favored positions for ESOPs. Thus, the evolution of the issues involved in ESOP valuation is relatively young.

As discussed, many issues are well settled, but continually growing case law still plays an important part in the formation of ESOP valuation practices.

References

Articles

Ackerman, David. 1999. "Technical Issues Under the New S Corporation ESOP Laws." *Journal of Employee Ownership Law and Finance*, Winter, pp. 3–19.

Austin, Douglas V. 2000. "Beware of Your ESOP." *Hoosier Banker*, vol. 84, no. 4, April 30, pp. 9–10.

Berka, Jack W. 1997. "An ESOP Update Review of Current Issues." Presentation to the International Conference of the American Society of Appraisers, June. Available at www.BVLibrary.com.

Buckley, Allen, Lynda M. Crouse, and Greg Kniesel. 2001. "S Corporation ESOPs in Dispositive Sales and Reorganization Transactions." *Valuation Strategies*, January/February, pp. 20–29, 46–48.

Etkind, Steven M., and Joseph E. Godfrey III. 2002. "ESOPs Rediscovered: Tax Advantages and Recyclable Refunding." *The CPA Journal*, vol. 72, no. 4, April 30, pp. 60–61.

Hirschfeld, Christopher. 2002. "ESOPs as an Estate Planning Vehicle for Business Owners." *Journal of Financial Planning*, vol. 15, no. 11, November 30, pp. 92–97.

Julius, J. Michael. 1998. "ESOP Appraisals and Non-ESOP Shareholders." *CPA Litigation Service Counselor*, July, pp. 9–10.

Kober, John A. 1999. "A Tool for Shareholder Liquidity, Estate Planning and Management Succession Planning." White paper available at www.BVLibrary.com.

Korschot, John. 2001. "Valuation Issues." *BV Papers*, December. Available at www.BVLibrary.com.

Kubersky, Andrew S. 1998. "Marketability Discounts and ESOP Acquisitions of Minority Share Interests." *Journal of Employee Ownership Law and Finance*, Fall, pp. 97–103.

Lannon, Allan L R. 1994. "Valuing Non-ESOP Shares in ESOP Companies—Some Empirical Evidence." *Business Valuation Review,* March, pp. 19-21.

Lippert-Gray, Carol. 2000. "An ESOP's Tale." *Financial Executive,* vol. 16, no. 1, February 28, pp. 40-42.

May, Richard C., Robert L. McDonald, and Brad Van Horn. 1994. "Valuation Issues in Leveraged ESOPs." *Journal of Employee Ownership Law and Finance,* Summer, pp. 61–82.

Miller, Karren L. 2000. "Using an ESOP to Let Go." *Central Penn Business Journal,* vol. 16, no. 23, June 9, p. 3.

Mueller, Susan L. 1998. "An Introduction to ESOP Appraisal Controversies." *Journal of Employee Ownership Law and Finance,* Winter, pp. 89–96.

Mueller, Susan L., and Judith C. Gehr. 1999. "Valuation Issues in Multi-Investor ESOP LBOs" (ch. 2). In *ESOP Valuation,* Scott S. Rodrick, ed. Oakland, CA: National Center for Employee Ownership.

Regnitz, Timothy J. 1999. "Understanding the ESOP Repurchase Obligation." *The Journal of Employee Ownership Law and Finance,* Winter, pp. 21–34.

Suhre, Karen K. 1998. "Should the ESOP-Owned Company Elect to Become an S Corporation?" *Benefits Law Journal,* Spring.

Tax Adviser. 2004. "To ESOP or Not to ESOP?" *Tax Adviser,* May.

Torolopoulos, Sam G. 2005. "Valuation of ESOP Shares: Opportunities and Challenges." *CPA Expert,* Fall, pp. 9–12.

Books

Ash, Merri E., Virginia J. Bartlett et al. 1996. *The ESOP Association Administration Handbook.* Washington, DC: ESOP Association.

Bernstein, Ron, David Binns, Marshal Hyman, and Martin Staubus. 2001. *Transitioning Ownership in the Private Company: The ESOP Solution.* La Jolla, CA: Foundation for Enterprise Development.

Brown, Karen W. 1993. "Payment of Control Premiums by ESOPs." *ESOP Report* (November/December), pp. 6–8.

Cook, Larry R. 2005. *Financial Valuation of Employee Stock Ownership Plan Shares*. Hoboken, NJ: Wiley.

ESOP Association. 1994. *Valuing ESOP Shares*, rev. ed. Washington, DC: ESOP Association.

———. 1997. *How the ESOP Really Works*. Washington, DC: ESOP Association.

———. 1998. *Report on Valuation Considerations for Leveraged ESOPs*. Washington, DC: ESOP Association.

———. 1999. *Structuring Leveraged ESOP Transactions*. Washington, DC: ESOP Association.

———. 2004. *ESOP Repurchase Obligations*. Washington, DC: ESOP Association.

———. 2005. *ESOP Accounting Standards*. Washington, DC: ESOP Association.

———. 2005. *An Introduction to ESOP Valuations*. Washington, DC: ESOP Association.

———. 2005. *The Ownership Advantage*. Washington, DC: ESOP Association.

———. 2005. *Valuing ESOP Shares*. Washington, DC: ESOP Association.

Frisch, Robert A. 2001. *ESOP: The Ultimate Instrument in Succession Planning*, 2nd ed. Hoboken, NJ: Wiley.

———. 2002. *ESOP Workbook: The Ultimate Instrument in Succession Planning*. Hoboken, NJ: Wiley.

Phillips, Perry. 2001. *Employee Share Ownership Plans: How to Design and Implement an ESOP in Canada*. Mississauga, Ontario: Wiley Canada.

Pratt, Shannon. 2003. "Employee Stock Ownership Plans." In *Business Valuation Body of Knowledge*, 2nd ed. New York: Wiley, pp. 315–320.

Pratt, Shannon P., and Alina V. Niculita. 2007. "Valuations for Employee Stock Ownership Plans." In *Valuing a Business*, 5th ed. New York: McGraw-Hill, pp. 809–836.

Rodrick, Scott S., ed. 2005. *Leveraged ESOPs and Employee Buyouts*. Oakland, CA: National Center for Employee Ownership.

———. 1999. *ESOP Valuation*. Oakland, CA: National Center for Employee Ownership.

Rosen, Corey. 2000. *Understanding ESOP Valuation.* Oakland, CA: National Center for Employee Ownership.

Rosen, Corey, John Case, and Martin Staubus. 2005. *Equity: Why Employee Ownership Is Good for Business.* Cambridge: Harvard Business School Press.

Smiley, Robert W., Ronald J. Gilbert, and David M. Binns. 1998. *Employee Stock Ownership Plans, 1998 Yearbook.* Boston: Warren, Gorham & Lamont of the RIA Group.

Smiley, Robert W., Jr., and Ronald J. Gilbert, eds. 1991. *Employee Stock Ownership Plans: Business Planning, Implementation, and Law and Taxation.* New York: Warren, Gorham & Lamont, supplemented annually.

Staubus, Martin, David Binns, and Ron Bernstein. 2005. *Transitioning Ownership in the Private Company: The ESOP Solution,* 2nd ed. La Jolla, CA: Beyster Institute.

Associations

ESOP Association
1726 M Street NW, Suite 501
Washington, DC 20036
(202) 293-2971 or (866) 366-3832
www.esopassociation.org

National Center for Employee Ownership
1736 Franklin Street, 8th Floor
Oakland, CA 94612
(510) 208-1300
www.nceo.org

Chapter 23

Analyzing the Business Appraisal: Example of an Appraisal of an Operating Company with Significant Real Assets

The business valuation of an operating company with significant real assets may necessitate the reliance on appraisal reports from other experts as well, such as real estate appraisers and/or machinery and equipment appraisers. These appraisers have their own standards and methodologies that the business valuation expert should be aware of. However, business valuation experts are not, nor should they be required to be, experts in the fields of other appraisal disciplines. Business appraisers should consult their own standards to make sure that they have followed all applicable rules for reliance on other appraisal reports.

Business valuation experts should communicate clearly their reliance on work done by other appraisers both prior to acceptance of an assignment and in the reporting of the assignment results. Business

---

Note: This chapter was contributed by Kimberly Linebarger, CFA, ASA, CVA, senior financial analyst with Shannon Pratt Valuations.

valuation experts should have a reasonable basis for believing that the appraisers performing any work relied upon are competent.

As with all business valuations, in the development of a business valuation of an operating company with significant real assets, the earnings power of the company is of utmost concern. While the asset approach may be highly relevant in the valuation of an operating company with significant real assets, the income approach and the market approach should also be considered. The business valuation expert should take into consideration the standard of value, the premise of value, and the ownership being considered. The asset approach is often considered more reasonable for the valuation of a controlling interest than for a minority interest as it indicates a value on a controlling interest basis. In any business valuation the facts and circumstances must be clearly outlined and considered.

June 1, 2013

Mr. John Heath, President
The Meat Processing Company
567 SW Processing Lane
Process City, WA 98621

Dear Mr. Heath:

We transmit herewith our report of the fair market value of a 100 percent equity interest in The Meat Processing Company as of December 31, 2012. It is our opinion that the fair market value of a 100 percent equity interest for estate planning purposes, as of December 31, 2012, was:

$3,289,000

This assignment was performed in accordance with the Uniform Standards of Professional Appraisal Practice (USPAP) as promulgated by the Appraisal Standards Board of the Appraisal Foundation, and it was done using conventional appraisal procedures. We appreciate the opportunity to have been of service to you in this matter.

Sincerely,

Josephine Brian, ASA Chairman and CEO	Tim Morgan, ASA Senior Manager

Expert Business Valuations, Inc.
The Meat Processing Company

Fair Market Value
of a 100 Percent Interest
as of December 31, 2012

Contents

I. Introduction

Description of the Assignment

Expert Business Valuations, Inc. ("us," "we," "our," or "EBV"), was retained by The Meat Processing Company ("MPC" or the "Company") to provide our opinion of the fair market value of the 100 percent interest in The Meat Processing Company, a Washington corporation, owned by John Heath as of December 31, 2012 (the "Valuation Date"), for estate planning purposes. The interest consists of 25,000 shares.

The results of our valuation analysis are summarized in this appraisal report (see also the valuation synthesis in Exhibit 23.1).

Purpose and Objective of the Analysis

EBV was retained for the purpose of providing an independent opinion of the fair market value of a 100 percent interest in the Company for estate planning purposes. The interest consists of 25,000 shares. Our analysis was conducted for this purpose only. No other purpose was intended nor should any other purpose be inferred.

Exhibit 23.1
The Meat Processing Company Valuation Synthesis as of December 31, 2012

	Indicated Value	Indicated Weight	Weighted Value
Income Approach			
Discounted Cash Flow Method	$32,67,193	20.0%	$6,53,439
Asset Approach			
Concluded Net Asset Value	$32,95,017	80.0%	$26,36,014
Concluded Value of Equity 100%, Control Rounded to the Nearest Thousand			$32,89,000

The objective of our analysis was to estimate the fair market value of the 100 percent controlling interest in The Meat Processing Company, owned by John Heath as of December 31, 2012.

Intended Use and Users of the Analysis

This report is submitted solely for the purpose stated above, and it is intended to be used by John Heath. This report may not be relied upon by any other than the intended user without EBV's prior written consent.

Standard and Premise of Value

The standard of value reflects an assumption as to who will be the buyer and who will be the seller in a hypothetical or actual sales transaction regarding the subject assets, properties, or business interest. There are numerous standards of value, with each having a very distinct definition and influence on a valuation engagement. One often-used standard of value is fair market value (FMV).

Fair market value is defined by the Internal Revenue Service in Revenue Ruling 59-60 as "the price at which the property would change hands between a willing buyer and a willing seller when the former is not under any compulsion to buy and the latter is not under any compulsion to sell, both parties having reasonable knowledge of relevant facts."[1]

The premise of value used in this appraisal is the going-concern value. *Going-concern value* is defined as the value of a business enterprise that is expected to continue to operate into the future.[2]

Brief Description of the Company[3]

The Meat Processing Company was founded in 1956 and was incorporated on December 23, 1976, in the state of Washington. The Company currently has one shareholder, John Heath, with 25,000 shares outstanding.

The Company's operations are located in Process City, Washington. The Company is principally involved in the manufacturing of meat products including the slaughtering, processing, and distribution of pork and beef. The Company's suppliers and customers are located mainly within the Pacific Northwest region of the United States, with most of the Company's suppliers located in Montana and most of the Company's customers located in Washington.

Scope of Work

In connection with this opinion, we have made such reviews, analyses, and inquiries as we have deemed necessary and appropriate under the circumstances. Among other things, we have done the following:

- Reviewed The Meat Processing Company tax returns and financial statements for the tax years ended December 2007 through 2012
- Reviewed various internal company documents, including, but not limited to, minutes from board of director meetings, fixed asset depreciation schedules, and employment agreements and compensation schedules
- Visited the Company headquarters in Process City, Washington
- Interviewed John Heath (president, shareholder) and Jacob Wood (vice president of operations) to discuss the operations, prospects, financial projections, financial condition, and capital structure of the Company
- Read several articles regarding the industry
- Considered the three approaches to value: asset approach, income approach, and market approach
- Considered adjustments to reflect relative control and unique risk characteristics associated with an investment in the subject interest
- Conducted other studies, analyses, and inquiries, as we deemed appropriate

References are footnoted throughout this report. A more comprehensive list of Company supplied documents is included in Appendix B. We assumed the accuracy and completeness of the financial and operational information and of other internal data provided to us. Unless otherwise noted in our analysis, information supplied by the Company has been accepted without further verification.

Economic, industry, and financial market data were obtained from various public and private sources and databases deemed, but not guaranteed, to be reliable. These data include the type of data reasonably and typically relied upon by valuation professionals for this type and other types of appraisal work.

Use of Specialists

The fair market value of the subject interest in the Company is partly dependent on the market value of the real property owned by the Company, as provided to us. We relied upon the expert report prepared by Scott Lloyd, MAI, of Real Estate Valuation, Inc., to ascertain the market value of land and structures owned by The Meat Processing Company as of December 31, 2012. We relied upon the expert report prepared by Jeremy Dryden of Machinery and Equipment Valuation, Inc., to ascertain the market value of machinery and automotive equipment owned by The Meat Processing Company as of December 31, 2012. Given their respective qualifications as outlined in their reports, we have a reasonable basis for believing that Scott Lloyd and Jeremy Dryden are competent to perform the appraisals provided by them. We have not verified the validity of the asset values, which we assume to be reliable, and which may have affected our assignment results.

Conclusion

Based on the analysis contained herein and our independent professional opinion, the fair market value of the 100 percent controlling interest in The Meat Processing Company, owned by John Heath as of December 31, 2012, was $3,289,000.

II. Company Analysis

Company Background

The Company was incorporated on December 23, 1976, in the state of Washington. The Company's history dates back to 1956 when the Company was started by Henry Heath. Henry Heath's son, John Heath, was hired as the general manager in 1984.

In 1992, John Heath purchased all the shares of the Company from Henry Heath. There have been no other transfers of stock in the history of the Company.

Operations, Suppliers, Products, and Customers

The Company is and has always been a meat packing company. Today the operations consist primarily of the slaughtering, processing, and delivery of hogs, cattle, and poultry meat products. The Company does not grow its own livestock. The Company has daily deliveries of livestock throughout the workweek from suppliers. Hogs and cattle are delivered two days each and poultry one day throughout the week. The animals are processed the following workday after delivery. The majority of the meat is never frozen but delivered to customers daily. The Company operates its own delivery trucks so as to control the end product and customer experience.

The Company's products include fresh, handcrafted meats from the Pacific Northwest region of the United States. Approximately 90 percent of the Company's livestock comes from growers located in Montana, and the remaining 10 percent from Washington. The Company does not have contracts with any of its vendors. However, the Company has long-standing relationships with the majority of its vendors and has worked with most of them since its inception.

The Company prides itself in producing fresh high-quality meat products. This allows the Company to charge a premium for its products and capture sales in the high-end local market grocery stores and restaurants. The majority of the Company's products are sold wholesale with a small amount sold case-ready (ready for supermarket display cases). The Company's customers are primarily retail and *purveyors*, defined as resellers of specialty foods such as gourmet meats. Retailers and purveyors make up approximately 50 percent of MPC's customer base (see table below). The Company's customers are slightly concentrated, with the top 10 customers representing approximately 30 percent of sales in the last fiscal year.

Sales Summary by Type of Customer, January 1 Through December 31, 2012

Type of Customer	Sales	Percent of Total Sales
Retail, grocery markets	$5,705,239	28.00
Purveyors	4,075,171	20.00
Restaurants	4,482,688	22.00
Specialty butchers	2,648,861	13.00
Sausage manufacturers	2,445,102	12.00
Private labels	1,018,793	5.00
Total	$20,375,854	

Competitors

Meat is largely a commodity; thus the profitability of individual companies depends on efficient operations and an effective distribution network. Large companies have economies of scale in production and distribution, while small companies can compete effectively in a local area or by producing unique products. MPC is a small meat processor that focuses on high-quality pork, beef, and poultry products. This has allowed it to successfully compete in the Pacific Northwest region. Management does not believe it has any current competitors actively trying to push the Company out of the market, and managers believe that as long as the MPC brand is not mismanaged, they will be able to maintain customers and sales.

There are numerous hog and cattle growers, processors, packers, and distributors located in and around Washington for which the Company's sales compete. These include the following:

- Western Meats (www.westernmeats.com) is located in Redmond, Washington, and it was acquired in 1989 by Harvest Meat Company. Management at MPC believes Western Meats is its main competitor. It is also one of MPC's customers.
- Northwest Specialty Meats (www.nwmeats.com) is located in Clarkston, Washington, and it processes a variety of meat products including pork and beef.
- Puget Sound Beef (www.pugetsoundbeef.com) is located in Lynnwood, Washington, and it processes and distributes cattle products.
- Trident Foods (www.trident-foods.com) is located in Graham, Washington, and it is a large producer of both cattle and hog products from the Northwest United States.

Members, Management, and Employees

Members

As of December 31, 2012, the Company had 25,000 common voting shares outstanding. As outlined previously, the Company has had one major change in ownership since inception, which occurred when the founder sold his shares to his son. The transfer was for an agreed upon price between family members and was not indicative of fair market value.

Management and Outside Counsel as of December 31, 2012

The Company's three directors are John Heath, Guy Johnston, and Christine Holiday.

Officers

- President: John Heath, hired February 2, 1984
- Vice president: Guy Johnston, hired October 28, 1985
- Secretary/treasurer: Christine Holiday, hired November 17, 2000

Management Structure

- President: John Heath
- Vice president of operations: Jacob Wood, hired January 1, 2003
- Plant manager: Jordan Robben, hired February 7, 2012
- Office manager/director of human resources: Frank Long, hired July 1, 1967
- Sales manager: Linda Peterson, hired September 1, 1972

Outside Advisors Include the Following

- Raymond Brownstone, attorney at law, 1600 NE Main Street, Seattle, WA 98707
- Stephen Thompson, certified public accountant, 4949 SW Meadows No. 475, Redmond, WA 98009

Employees

The Company's employee base is critical to its success. It has averaged between 75 and 115 employees over the last 10 years. The industry is characterized by lower than national wages, high injury and illness rates, and often the hiring of illegal immigrants as outlined by First Research in their industry analysis. In contrast to the industry, MPC's management prides itself on providing its employees with fair wages, a generous retirement savings matching plan, and safe working conditions, and it does not hire illegal immigrants. The attention to employees greatly contributes to the Company's low employee turnover rates at less than 10 percent per annum, low worker injury rates, and consistent production. These lead to lower expenses from workers' compensation claims and employee hiring and training costs and to higher revenues due to consistent products, all of which allow it to successfully compete in the high-quality meat products industry.

Some of the tasks performed by employees include management, various office positions, sales positions, kill floor and other production positions, sanitation, maintenance, and delivery drivers. The Company expects production employees to learn more than one station or task. The Company has implemented a comprehensive and ongoing training program and schedule for all employees. Employees' ongoing cross-training helps lower injury rates from repetitive motion, and it increases employees' awareness of the environment and other tasks being performed around them.

Key Employee Compensation

We researched the reasonableness of the compensation paid to John Heath, president. We looked at information from the 2011 to 2012 Northwest Executive Compensation Survey.

Since 1984, John Heath has been an integral driving force of the Company. Heath joined the Company as the general manager in 1984 after graduating from the University of Washington with a bachelor of science degree in commerce. In 1985, Heath joined the board of directors. He has held the title of president of the Company since 1994.

John Heath's salary of $300,000 is within a reasonable range of the median ($285,000) and mean ($325,000) wage data for chief executives in the Northwest. Given the data and Heath's extensive involvement in all aspects of the Company and his approximately 30 years of industry and management experience, we believe Heath's salary is warranted.

Strengths and Opportunities

- Well capitalized with adequate financial resources to fund operations
- Adequate facilities and assets to support current operations
- Successful and recognized brand name and high-quality products
- Efficient operations and distribution

- Stable employee base
- Established management team
- Mature industry

Weaknesses and Risks

- Significant exposure to risks associated with a catastrophic hog, cattle, or poultry disease
- Exposure to price fluctuations in the markets for hog, cattle, and poultry
- Lost sales due to substitute products from large competitors with economies of scale
- Significant government regulations
- High exposure to risk from animal mishandling by an employee
- Risk from difficult working conditions including worker injury claims and turnover
- Loss of key management personnel due to retirement and lack of a succession plan
- Need for significant capital expansion to support further abnormal growth
- Lack of geographic diversification

Financial Statements Analysis

The analysis of the financial statements should be looked at in conjunction with the exhibits and notes of the financials as presented in Exhibits 23.2 to 23.6. We have presented the balance sheets and income statements for fiscal years ended December 31, 2006, through 2012.

The financial statements are from accountant compiled financial statements. The Company prepares its financial statements on an accrual basis of accounting. We have not separately verified the data. We considered possible adjustments to the Company's historical financial statements, and we deemed none to be necessary.

Exhibit 23.2

The Meat Processing Company Historical Balance Sheets

	December 31							CAGR [5]
As of Date:	**2006**	**2007**	**2008**	**2009**	**2010**	**2011**	**2012**	**05-12**
	$	**$**	**$**	**$**	**$**	**$**	**$**	
Balance Sheets [1]								
Cash	2,84,213	1,37,888	2,79,071	3,03,589	3,74,255	7,59,651	5,07,429	10.1%
Accounts Receivable	6,04,889	6,44,917	5,71,363	6,32,524	6,54,230	7,39,488	8,65,495	6.2%
Other Receivables	8,640	13,521	7,946	9,411	8,568	6,856	6,481	−4.7%
Inventories	3,02,492	3,00,087	3,34,511	3,35,378	3,26,728	2,27,190	4,56,000	7.1%
Prepaid Expenses	1,49,435	1,49,190	1,34,548	1,43,422	1,47,212	1,25,974	1,36,928	−1.4%
Prepaid Income Taxes	1,300	19,620	3,048	2,647	4,774	3,515	38,977	76.3%
Current Assets	13,50,969	12,65,223	13,30,487	14,26,971	15,15,767	18,62,674	20,11,310	6.9%
Loan Costs, Net of Amortization	4,014	3,169	2,324	1,479	634			NM
Property, Plant and Equipment, Net	5,91,987	8,58,993	8,03,204	7,79,362	7,43,623	7,13,711	6,89,131	2.6%
Total Assets [2]	19,46,970	21,27,385	21,36,015	22,07,812	22,60,024	25,76,385	27,00,441	5.6%
Accounts Payable and Accrued Expenses	3,81,627	4,02,495	4,63,507	3,62,022	3,86,349	4,38,128	4,71,517	3.6%
Income Taxes Payable	24,337	0	1,344	88,818	629	63,867		−100.0%
Long-term Debt—Current	26,800	1,06,400	1,03,300	30,300	30,500	57,009	64,261	15.7%
Current Liabilities	4,32,764	5,08,895	5,68,151	4,81,140	4,17,478	5,59,004	5,35,778	3.6%
Long-term Debt—Non-current	4,12,087	4,63,181	3,58,063	3,28,140	2,97,982	2,36,468	1,77,034	−13.1%

Total Liabilities	8,44,851	9,72,076	9,26,214	8,09,280	7,15,460	7,95,472	7,12,812	−2.8%
Common Equity [3]	1,95,000	1,95,000	1,95,000	1,95,000	1,95,000	1,95,000	1,95,000	0.0%
Retained Earnings	9,07,119	9,60,309	10,14,801	12,03,532	13,49,564	15,85,913	17,92,629	12.0%
Total Equity Capital	11,02,119	11,55,309	12,09,801	13,98,532	15,44,564	17,80,913	19,87,629	10.3%
Total Liabilities and Equity [2]	19,46,970	21,27,385	21,36,015	22,07,812	22,60,024	25,76,385	27,00,441	5.6%
Working Capital [4]	*9,45,005*	*8,62,728*	*8,65,636*	*9,76,131*	*11,28,789*	*13,60,679*	*15,39,793*	8.5%
Change in Working Capital		*−82,277*	*2,908*	*1,10,495*	*1,52,658*	*2,31,890*	*1,79,114*	
Accumulated Depreciation	*21,25,491*	*22,13,734*	*22,87,945*	*24,32,177*	*24,43,925*	*25,36,703*	*26,77,245*	3.9%
Total Debt	*4,38,887*	*5,69,581*	*4,61,363*	*3,58,440*	*3,28,482*	*2,93,477*	*2,41,295*	−9.5%
Change in Debt		*1,30,694*	*−1,08,218*	*−1,02,923*	*−29,958*	*−35,005*	*−52,182*	

Notes:

[1] All financials are from accountant-compiled financial statements. The Company reports its financials on the income tax basis of accounting.

[2] Numbers may not add precisely due to rounding.

[3] Common stock: 25,000 shares outstanding.

[4] Working capital excludes long-term debt—current and notes payable.

[5] CAGR = compound annual growth rate; NM = not meaningful.

Exhibit 23.3

The Meat Processing Company Historical Common-Size Balance Sheets

	December 31							Integra [3]
As of Date:	**2006**	**2007**	**2008**	**2009**	**2010**	**2011**	**2012**	**2011**
Common-size								
Balance Sheets [1]								
Cash	14.60%	6.48%	13.07%	13.75%	16.56%	29.49%	18.79%	5.20%
Accounts Receivable	31.07%	30.32%	26.75%	28.65%	28.95%	28.70%	32.05%	15.00%
Other Receivables	0.44%	0.64%	0.37%	0.43%	0.38%	0.27%	0.24%	
Inventories	15.54%	14.11%	15.66%	15.19%	14.46%	8.82%	16.89%	16.60%
Prepaid Expenses	7.68%	7.01%	6.30%	6.50%	6.51%	4.89%	5.07%	
Prepaid Income Taxes	0.07%	0.92%	0.14%	0.12%	0.21%	0.14%	1.44%	
Current Assets	69.39%	59.47%	62.29%	64.63%	67.07%	72.30%	74.48%	40.30%
Loan Costs, Net of Amortization	0.21%	0.15%	0.11%	0.07%	0.03%			
Property, Plant and Equipment, Net	30.41%	40.38%	37.60%	35.30%	32.90%	27.70%	25.52%	49.50%
Total Assets [2]	100.00%	100.00%	100.00%	100.00%	100.00%	100.00%	100.00%	100.00%
Accounts Payable and Accrued Expenses	19.60%	18.92%	21.70%	16.40%	17.09%	17.01%	17.46%	10.90%
Income Taxes Payable	1.25%	0.00%	0.06%	4.02%	0.03%	2.48%		
Long-term Debt—Current	1.38%	5.00%	4.84%	1.37%	1.35%	2.21%	2.38%	4.90%
Current Liabilities	22.23%	23.92%	26.60%	21.79%	18.47%	21.70%	19.84%	23.80%
Long-term Debt—Non-current	21.17%	21.77%	16.76%	14.86%		9.18%	6.56%	23.30%

Total Liabilities	43.39%	45.69%	43.36%	36.66%	31.66%	30.88%	26.40%	51.60%
Common Equity	10.02%	9.17%	9.13%	8.83%	8.63%	7.57%	7.22%	
Retained Earnings	46.59%	45.14%	47.51%	54.51%	59.71%	61.56%	66.38%	
Total Equity Capital	56.61%	54.31%	56.64%	63.34%	68.34%	69.12%	73.60%	48.40%
Total Liabilities and Equity [2]	100.00%	100.00%	100.00%	100.00%	100.00%	100.00%	100.00%	100.00%
Working Capital	48.54%	40.55%	40.53%	44.21%	49.95%	52.81%	57.02%	21.36%
Total Debt	22.54%	26.77%	21.60%	16.24%	14.53%	11.39%	8.94%	28.40%
Accumulated Depreciation		104.06%	107.11%	110.16%	108.14%	98.46%	99.14%	52.30%

Notes:

[1] All financials are from accountant-compiled financial statements. The Company reports its financials on the income tax basis of accounting.

[2] Numbers may not add precisely due to rounding.

[3] *Source*: Data from Integra Information, *5-Year Industry Report*, SIC 2011: Meat Packing Plants, Sales Range $10 to $25 million.

Exhibit 23.4

The Meat Processing Company Historical Income Statements

	Fiscal Year Ended December 31							CAGR [5]
As of Date:	**2006**	**2007**	**2008**	**2009**	**2010**	**2011**	**2012**	**05-12**
	$	**$**	**$**	**$**	**$**	**$**	**$**	
Income Statements [1]								
Sales	**1,43,25,584**	**1,38,58,568**	**1,40,87,083**	**1,59,63,441**	**1,42,95,107**	**1,78,35,753**	**2,03,75,854**	6.0%
Cost of Goods Sold	1,25,94,829	1,20,53,557	1,22,49,624	1,39,47,649	1,23,43,292	1,56,84,258	1,78,65,458	6.0%
Gross Margin	17,30,755	18,05,011	18,37,459	20,15,792	19,51,815	21,51,495	25,10,396	6.4%
Operating Expenses	9,02,783	11,12,482	11,13,198	11,15,693	10,41,753	11,79,605	12,91,447	6.1%
Bad Debt		228	1,088	296	8,742	803		NM
Advertising	36,097	27,239	36,107	88,343	29,412	66,308	46,851	4.4%
Travel, Entertainment, and Education	17,263	10,312	14,548	28,195	13,674	16,257	33,432	11.6%
Life Insurance	26,239	30,879	24,689	23,475	23,619	21,581	25,257	−0.6%
Officer Salaries	2,85,147	2,85,147	2,86,013	3,03,558	3,00,961	3,00,961	3,00,000	0.8%
Total Operating Expense	12,67,529	14,66,287	14,75,643	15,59,560	14,18,161	15,85,515	16,96,987	5.0%
Income (Loss) from Operations	**4,63,226**	**3,38,724**	**3,61,816**	**4,56,232**	**5,33,654**	**5,65,980**	**8,13,409**	9.8%
Interest Income	6,205	11,600	9,296	6,301	771	178	202	−43.5%
Interest (Expense)	−43,484	−38,827	−52,908	−41,213	−25,455	−21,371	−12,274	−19.0%
Gain (Loss) on Sale of Assets	30,393	−6,502	10,000	1,500			18,200	−8.2%
Other Income (Expense)	7,604	6,987	3,131	2,373	3,047	6,453	2,024	−19.8%
Total Other Income (Expense)	718	−26,742	−30,481	−31,039	−21,637	−14,740	8,152	49.9%

Income (Loss) Before Taxes	4,63,944	3,11,982	3,31,335	4,25,193	5,12,017	5,51,240	8,21,561	10.0%
Provision (Credit) for Income Taxes [2]	53,827	31,006	33,364	1,22,268	1,54,605	1,53,001	2,25,523	27.0%
Income (Loss) After Taxes [3]	**4,10,117**	**2,80,976**	**2,97,971**	**3,02,925**	**3,57,412**	**3,98,239**	**5,96,038**	6.4%
EBITDA	6,22,008	4,54,687	4,89,491	6,18,362	5,78,374	6,71,065	10,64,483	9.4%
EBIT	5,07,428	3,50,809	3,84,243	4,66,406	5,37,472	5,72,611	8,33,835	8.6%
Depreciation & Amortization	1,14,580	1,03,878	1,05,248	1,51,956	40,902	98,454	2,30,648	12.4%
Capital Expenditures	1,91,880	3,19,452	1,30,649	1,74,277	13,855	89,489	2,39,326	NM
Operating Lease Expense [4]	2,500	3,654	3,322	3,373	3,414	2,210	4,245	9.2%
Stockholders' Distributions		2,27,786	2,43,479	1,14,194	2,11,380	1,61,890	3,89,322	NM

Notes:

[1] ll financials are from accountant-compiled financial statements. The Company reports its financials on the income tax basis of accounting.

[2] The Company is a C corporation.

[3] Numbers may not add precisely due to rounding.

[4] The Company has an operating lease associated with a copy machine.

[5] CAGR = compound annual growth rate; NM = not meaningful.

Exhibit 23.5

The Meat Processing Company Historical Common-Size Income Statements

	Fiscal Year Ended December 31							Integra [3]
As of Date:	**2006**	**2007**	**2008**	**2009**	**2010**	**2011**	**2012**	**2011**
Common-size								
Income Statements [1]								
Sales	100.00%	100.00%	100.00%	100.00%	100.00%	100.00%	100.00%	100.00%
Cost of Goods Sold	87.92%	86.98%	86.96%	87.37%	86.35%	87.94%	87.68%	80.20%
Gross Margin	12.08%	13.02%	13.04%	12.63%	13.65%	12.06%	12.32%	19.80%
Operating Expenses	6.30%	8.03%	7.90%	6.99%	7.29%	6.61%	6.34%	14.30%
Bad Debt		0.00%	0.01%	0.00%	0.06%	0.00%		
Advertising	0.25%	0.20%	0.26%	0.55%	0.21%	0.37%	0.23%	
Travel, Entertainment, and Education	0.12%	0.07%	0.10%	0.18%	0.10%	0.09%	0.16%	
Life Insurance	0.18%	0.22%	0.18%	0.15%	0.17%	0.12%	0.12%	
Officer Salaries	1.99%	2.06%	2.03%	1.90%	2.11%	1.69%	1.47%	1.20%
Total Operating Expense	8.85%	10.58%	10.48%	9.77%	9.92%	8.89%	8.33%	15.50%
Income (Loss) from Operations	3.23%	2.44%	2.57%	2.86%	3.73%	3.17%	3.99%	4.20%
Interest Income	0.06%	0.07%	0.04%	0.00%	0.04%	0.00%	0.00%	0.00%
Interest (Expense)	−0.37%	−0.38%	−0.29%	−0.16%	−0.29%	−0.12%	−0.06%	−0.60%
Gain (Loss) on Sale of Assets	0.21%	−0.05%	0.07%	0.01%			0.09%	
Other Income (Expense)	0.05%	0.05%	0.02%	0.01%	0.02%	0.04%	0.01%	
Total Other Income (Expense)	0.01%	−0.19%	−0.22%	−0.19%	−0.15%	−0.08%	0.04%	−0.60%
Income (Loss) Before Taxes	3.24%	2.25%	2.35%	2.66%	3.58%	3.09%	4.03%	3.70%
Provision (Credit) for Income Taxes	0.38%	0.22%	0.24%	0.77%	1.08%	0.86%	1.11%	1.40%

Income (Loss) After Taxes [2]	2.86%	2.03%	2.12%	1.90%	2.50%	2.23%	2.93%	2.30%
EBITDA	4.34%	3.28%	3.47%	3.87%	4.05%	3.76%	5.22%	6.30%
EBIT	3.54%	2.53%	2.73%	2.92%	3.76%	3.21%	4.09%	4.30%
Depreciation & Amortization	0.80%	0.75%	0.75%	0.95%	0.29%	0.55%	1.13%	2.03%
Capital Expenditures	1.34%	2.31%	0.93%	1.09%	0.10%	0.50%	1.17%	2.70%
Working Capital	6.60%	6.23%	6.14%	6.11%	7.90%	7.63%	7.56%	9.08%
Stockholders' Distributions	0.00%	1.64%	1.73%	0.72%	1.48%	0.91%	1.91%	
Taxes as a Percent of Income (Loss) Before Taxes	11.60%	9.94%	10.07%	28.76%	30.20%	27.76%	27.45%	38.00%

Notes:

[1] All financials are from accountant-compiled financial statements. The Company reports its financials on the income tax basis of accounting.

[2] Numbers may not add precisely due to rounding.

[3] *Source*: Data from Integra Information, *5-Year Industry Report*, SIC 2011: Meat Packing Plants, Sales Range $10 to $25 million.

Exhibit 23.6

The Meat Processing Company Historical Subject Company and Integra Rating Analysis

	Subject Company [1]						Integra [2]		
As of Date:	**2007**	**2008**	**2009**	**2010**	**2011**	**2012**	**2009**	**2010**	**2011**
Rates of Return									
Return on Equity (%, Pretax)	27.6%	28.0%	32.6%	34.8%	33.2%	43.6%	18.5%	20.7%	18.6%
Return on Equity (%, After Tax)	24.9%	25.2%	23.2%	24.3%	24.0%	31.6%	11.5%	12.8%	11.5%
Return on Assets (%, Pretax)	15.3%	15.5%	19.6%	22.9%	22.8%	31.1%	8.6%	9.5%	8.8%
Return on Assets (%, After Tax)	13.8%	14.0%	13.9%	16.0%	16.5%	22.6%	5.3%	5.9%	5.4%
Profitability Ratios									
Gross Margin (%)	13.0%	13.0%	12.6%	13.7%	12.1%	12.3%	19.9%	19.9%	19.8%
Operating Profit Margin (%)	2.4%	2.6%	2.9%	3.7%	3.2%	4.0%	4.2%	4.2%	4.2%
Pretax Margin (%)	2.3%	2.4%	2.7%	3.6%	3.1%	4.0%	3.6%	3.7%	3.7%
Net Profit Margin (%)	2.0%	2.1%	1.9%	2.5%	2.2%	2.9%	2.3%	2.3%	2.3%
Net Income/Earnings Before Tax	0.9	0.9	0.7	0.7	0.7	0.7	0.6	0.6	0.6
EBIT Margin	2.5%	2.7%	2.9%	3.8%	3.2%	4.1%	4.2%	4.3%	4.3%
Liquidity Indicators									
Cash Ratio	0.3	0.5	0.6	0.9	1.4	0.9	0.2	0.2	0.2
Quick Ratio	1.6	1.5	2.0	2.5	2.7	2.6	0.8	0.8	0.9
Current Ratio	2.5	2.3	3.0	3.6	3.3	3.8	1.7	1.6	1.7

Debt Management									
Current Liabilities to Total Equity	44.0%	47.0%	34.4%	27.0%	31.4%	27.0%	53.0%	54.2%	49.2%
Total Liabilities to Total Equity	0.8	0.8	0.6	0.5	0.4	0.4	1.2	1.2	1.1
Total Equity to Total Assets	0.5	0.6	0.6	0.7	0.7	0.7	0.5	0.5	0.5
Long-Term Debt to Total Assets	21.8%	16.8%	14.9%	13.2%	9.2%	6.6%	24.6%	24.6%	23.3%
Earnings Before Tax/ EBIT	0.9	0.9	0.9	1.0	1.0	1.0	0.9	0.9	0.9
Leverage Ratio	1.8	1.8	1.7	1.5	1.5	1.4	2.2	2.2	2.1
Asset Management									
Working Capital to Assets	15.3	16.3	17.3	13.6	14.3	14.1	0.2	0.2	0.2
Fixed Asset Turnover	19.1	16.9	20.2	18.8	24.5	29.0	4.9	5.3	4.8
Total Asset Turnover	6.8	6.6	7.3	6.4	7.4	7.7	2.4	2.6	2.4
Accounts Receivable Turnover	21.8	22.8	26.1	21.9	25.3	25.2	15.2	17.0	15.7
Inventory Turnover	40.0	38.6	41.6	37.3	56.6	52.3	11.0	12.3	11.4
Payables Turnover	30.7	28.4	33.8	33.0	37.8	39.8	16.5	18.5	17.0
Days of Sales Outstanding	16.8	16.0	14.0	16.7	14.4	14.5	24.0	21.5	23.2
Days of Inventory on Hand	9.1	9.5	8.8	9.8	6.4	7.0	33.2	29.7	32.0
Number of Days of Payables	11.9	12.9	10.8	11.1	9.7	9.2	22.1	19.8	21.4
Cash Conversion Cycle	14.0	12.6	11.9	15.4	11.2	12.3	35.2	31.4	33.8
Annual Growth Rates									
Revenue	−3.3%	1.6%	13.3%	−10.5%	24.8%	14.2%	−7.4%	14.4%	−1.4%
EBITDA	−26.9%	7.7%	26.3%	−6.5%	16.0%	58.6%	−8.6%	11.9%	−2.6%
Pretax Income	−32.8%	6.2%	28.3%	20.4%	7.7%	49.0%	−8.3%	11.3%	−2.3%

Notes:

[1] For multiples that are based on both an income statement and balance sheet item, an average of the current and prior year balance sheet item was utilized.

[2] *Source*: Data from Integra Information, *5-Year Industry Report*, SIC 2011: Meat Packing Plants, Sales Range $10 to $25 million.

Balance Sheet Analysis

Assets

- The Company's assets are principally composed of short-term assets, which account for 74 percent of its total assets as of December 31, 2012. This is a result of the Company's having a long history, and the majority of the Company's assets are fully depreciated. It also results from the Company's being principally involved in the slaughtering, processing, and distribution of fresh meat products, which results in a high percentage of total assets being cash, accounts receivable, and inventory.
- The book value of the Company's total assets increased from year to year from year-end 2006 at $1,946,970 to year-end 2012 at $2,700,441. This resulted in a compound annual growth rate of 5.6 percent over the time period. The increase can be mainly attributed to increases in cash, accounts receivable, and inventories.
- The Company also increased its property, plant, and equipment (PP&E) from $591,987 at year-end 2006 to $689,131 at year-end 2012. The Company has historically depreciated the majority of assets in the year acquired, which is not uncommon for a company the size of MPC. It also has a long history, and thus the majority of assets that were elected to be depreciated over a longer term are mostly fully depreciated. This leads to the Company's PP&E as a percentage of total assets of 25.5 percent at year-end 2012 being lower than industry indications as published by Integra of 49.5 percent for 2011.
- As a result of the Company's higher amount of accumulated depreciation as a percentage of fixed assets, comparison of asset percentages to industry indications is not necessarily useful because the Company's fixed assets are lower than if it had an amount of depreciation and depletion on a percentage basis in line with the industry.

Liabilities and Equity

- The bulk of the Company's current liabilities are accounts payable and accrued expenses, which were $381,627 at year-end 2006 and $471,517 at year-end 2012, or approximately 17.46 percent of total assets as of December 31, 2012. This is to be expected, as the Company operates in a high turnover environment, which will be further discussed in the ratio analysis.
- The Company's total long-term debt and notes payable has ranged from a high of $569,581 at year-end 2007 to a low of $241,295 at year-end 2012. Management of the Company does not project a need for further debt financing, and it plans on continuing to pay down debt into the foreseeable future.
- Member's equity increased from $1,102,119 at fiscal year-end 2006 to $1,987,629 at fiscal year-end 2012. The increase is due to debt reduction and reinvestment of net income into the Company to support growth of operations.
- Working capital, without inclusion of current long-term debt or notes payable, has increased from $945,005 at year-end 2006 to $1,539,793 at fiscal year-end 2012. Given that the majority of the company's assets are current assets and the high turnover in the Company's products, the increases in working capital are to be expected to support the growth in sales experienced over the time period analyzed.

Income Statement Analysis

- Revenues increased at a compound annual rate of 6 percent from $14,325,584 in 2006 to $20,375,854 in 2012. The majority of the growth was experienced between the fiscal years 2010 through 2012.
- Total cost of goods sold (COGS) increased during the seven-year period presented at a compound annual rate of 6 percent. As a percentage of total revenue, the costs of goods sold were

relatively consistent ranging from a low of 86.35 percent in 2010 to a high of 87.94 percent in 2011. This indicates that a vast majority of the Company's costs of goods sold are variable, which is expected given that management adjusts the prices of its products on an ongoing basis, at least monthly, which allows the Company's management to maintain tight control over its COGS.

- Total operating expenses increased during the seven-year period presented at a compound annual rate of 5 percent. As a percentage of total revenue, operating expenses have decreased from a high of 10.58 percent in 2007 to 8.33 percent for the 2012 fiscal year. The lower compound annual growth rate than that experienced in revenues or COGS indicates that at least some of the Company's operating expenses are fixed.
- Income from operations was 3.23 percent and 3.99 percent in fiscal years 2006 and 2012, respectively. This is below the Integra industry information for meat packing plants, at 4.2 percent. However, mainly due to the fixed nature of the operating expenses, income from operations has grown at a compound annual rate of 9.8 percent between 2006 and 2012, which is higher than the 6 percent growth in sales experienced over the same time frame for the Company.
- Income after taxes was approximately 2.86 percent of revenues, or on a dollar basis \$410,117, and 2.93 percent of revenues, or on a dollar basis \$596,038, in fiscal years 2006 and 2012, respectively.

Financial and Operating Ratio Analysis

Rates of Return

Rates of return ratios indicate what a company's overall performance is during the measurement period by combining measurements of profitability, efficiency, and financial leverage. Return on equity (ROE) focuses on return to the stockholders' investment, and return on assets (ROA) measures management's performance with regard to the company's asset base.

- As applied to the Company, both ratios show positive returns in each of the years from 2007 through 2012.
- As of fiscal year-end 2012, the Company's after-tax ROE stood at 31.6 percent, up from 24 percent in 2011, and 24.3 percent in 2010. This is greater than the average relative to the industry benchmarks of 11.5 and 12.8 percent in 2011 and 2010, respectively.
- As of fiscal year-end 2012, the Company's after-tax ROA stood at 22.6 percent, up from 16.5 percent in 2011. This is higher than the average relative to the industry benchmarks of 5.4 and 5.9 percent in 2011 and 2010, respectively. The higher Company ROA as compared to the industry is expected as a result of the Company's having a higher percentage of its assets fully depreciated.

Profitability

Profitability ratios indicate the profits and returns of the business as well as management performance over the measurement period. Often, profitability ratios help to determine where the industry is in its life cycle, and they are also good indicators of the level of market competition.

- As outlined in the income statement analysis section of this report, the Company has shown positive profitability over the time frame analyzed. During 2012, the Company's gross margin, operating profit margin, and net profit margin stood at 12.3, 4, and 2.9 percent of revenues, respectively. These were relatively close to the industry benchmarks of the same ratios for 2011 of 19.8, 4.2, and 2.3 percent, respectively.

Liquidity

Liquidity ratios indicate a company's ability to meet its short-term obligations. The cash ratio, quick ratio, and current ratio indicate the degree to which current liabilities are covered by current assets from the most liquid assets to inclusion of all the company's current assets. The higher the ratios, the better position the company is in to pay its short-term obligations.

- The Company's cash ratio, which measures the Company's ability to meet its current liabilities with only cash, was approximated at 0.9 times its current liabilities at December 31, 2012, and it was significantly better than industry indications of 0.2.
- The Company's quick ratio, which measures the Company's ability to meet its current liabilities with cash and accounts receivable, was approximately 2.6 times its current liabilities at December 31, 2012, and it was significantly better than industry indications of 0.9.
- The Company's current ratio, which measures the Company's ability to meet its current liabilities with all current assets, was approximated at 3.8 times its current liabilities at December 31, 2012, and it was significantly better than industry indications of 1.7.
- The Company's liquidity ratios indicate that the Company had sufficient liquidity to meet current obligations.

Debt Management

Debt management ratios indicate a company's ability to finance operations and its use of leverage or debt versus equity financing.

- The Company's current liabilities to total equity was 27 percent, and its total liabilities to total equity was 0.4 at year-end 2012. These were both lower then industry indications of 49.2 and 1.1 percent. This indicates that the Company has lower current and total liabilities as a percent of total equity then industry comparables.

- The Company's use of debt financing is lower than industry indications with long-term debt to total assets declining in each year from 2007 through 2012. Long-term debt to total assets was 6.6 percent as of year-end 2012. Industry indications were much higher at 23.3 percent.
- The lower debt financing versus equity financing is a positive sign from the viewpoint of the Company's being able to meet its debt obligations. It is of note that the Company does have a revolving line of credit currently set at $800,000 of which the company has not had any outstanding balance at the end of any of the years analyzed. Given the quick turnover nature of the Company operations, this revolving line of credit is critical to mitigate potential risks that would impact the Company's short-term sales and expenses.

Asset Management

It is important in any company to effectively manage assets. Turnover ratios indicate how efficiently a company is using its assets. The cash conversion cycle indicates how quickly a company is able to go from cash paid to cash received from operations; this is often referred to as a company's *net operating cycle,* and it can be a good indicator of company liquidity.

- Working capital to assets, fixed asset turnover, and total asset turnover were 14.1, 29, and 7.7, respectively, for fiscal year-end 2012. Working capital to assets, fixed asset turnover, and total asset turnover were all well above industry indications of 0.2, 4.8, and 2.4, respectively. Given the long history of the Company, this discrepancy with the industry could be highly impacted by differences in total depreciation, which are not necessarily good indicators of comparability.

- The Company's accounts receivable, inventory, and payables turnovers were 25.2, 52.3, and 39.8, respectively, for year-end 2012. All these turnover ratios are higher than industry indications, which is to be expected given the quick nature of the Company's operational cycle, which is highly impacted by its focus on delivery of fresh meat products.
- The Company's management has indicated that it receives credit terms from suppliers of 7 business days on average, and management also provides credit terms to customers of 7 business days with a customer no longer receiving product if payment is not received within 14 days. These quick payment terms are readily seen by a review of the Company's days of sales outstanding of 14.5 and number of days of payables of 9.2 for fiscal year 2012, which are both well below the industry indications of 23.2 and 21.4 for the 2011 year.
- The Company's days of inventory on hand also indicates the quick inventory turnover experienced by the Company as compared with the industry on average. The Company's days of inventory on hand for fiscal year-end 2012 was 7, while industry indications were 32. Again, this is expected given the focus on fresh, high-end meat products with a small amount of product being frozen and stored at the MPC facilities.
- The cash conversion cycle of the company was 12.3 days in 2012, which is well below industry indications as published by Integra of 33.8 days. This indicates that the Company is highly liquid and extremely susceptible to risk associated with disruptions in any portion of the Company's chain of operations from suppliers, internal operations, or customers.

Conclusion

Overall, the financial condition of the Company at the date of value was stable. The Company is well capitalized, and it has adequate liquidity to fund operations. The Company's management has access to quick debt financing if needed, which helps to mitigate risks associated with the quick net operating cycle of the Company. The Company has a long history and as a result higher accumulated depreciation of assets as compared to industry indications, which makes many of the balance sheet ratios poor indicators of comparability with industry indications. A time series analysis of the Company's balance sheet ratios indicates strong and relatively stable turnover ratios and a short net operating cycle over the period analyzed, which indicates decent and stable asset management by the Company.

Management does not anticipate any changes in operational needs in the foreseeable future beyond normal levels of repairs and replacement costs inherent in the business.

III. Economic Outlook

Note: This section is not shown for simplification of the example, but it should be included in any business valuation assignment.

IV. Industry Outlook

Note: This section is not shown for simplification of the example, but it should be included in any business valuation assignment.

V. Valuation Methodology

Selection of Approaches to Value

There are many methods and procedures that may be appropriate in the economic analysis and appraisal of private business interests. These methods and procedures typically fall into three general approaches to valuation analysis: the income approach, the market approach, and the asset approach.

We considered all three approaches to value, and we have relied on the discounted cash flow method (an income approach) and the net asset value method (an asset approach) in our estimate of the fair market value of the subject ownership interest.

Market Approach

In the application of the market approach, the value of a business is based upon the prices that investors are paying for similar interests in comparable "guideline" companies. The market approach includes the development of valuation multiples of market prices to various financial fundamentals of guideline companies that are then used to develop indications of value for the subject company. Consideration is given to adjustments for growth prospects, size, and specific company risks, as well as the quantity and quality of the market data.

In this case we were unable to find either guideline transacted companies or guideline publicly traded companies with a reasonable level of comparability to the subject company. Therefore we were unable to apply the market approach.

Adjustments and Reconciliation of Values

The adjustments were considered relative to the starting point of each valuation method. The discounted cash flow method and the net asset method each resulted in a controlling interest value. Therefore no adjustments to arrive at the level of value herein were necessary.

The values determined under each valuation method were reconciled and weighted based on our analysis of the quantity and quality of data available under each method.

VI. Income Approach to Value

The income approach is based on the premise that the value of the subject ownership interest is the present value of all the future expected economic income to be distributed to the Company's shareholders.

The two basic income approach methods are (1) the direct capitalization method and (2) the discounted cash flow method.

Discounting Model Versus the Capitalization Model

The difference between the discounting model and the capitalization model is how one treats anticipated changes in future income over time:

- In discounting, changes over time in the expected economic income stream are accounted for specifically in the terms of the numerator of the present value equation, which can be changed to reflect uneven projected economic income over time.
- In capitalizing, changes over time in the economic income are treated as a single average percentage change that is subtracted from the cost of capital in the denominator of the present value calculation.

When the same set of assumptions is used, the discounting model and capitalization model will produce an identical valuation conclusion. The discounting model is most often used when future economic income is variable for a discrete number of years until the company reaches a stable period of growth at which time a terminal value based on the capitalization model is employed. The underlying theory when only a capitalization model is used to arrive at a present value conclusion is that the company has already reached a stable or evenly growing normalized economic income.

Equity Versus the Invested Capital Procedures

There are two procedures that can be used under each method of the income approach discussed above, the capitalization method and the discounting method, and they are as follows:

1. **The Equity procedure.** Under this procedure, the equity is valued directly by estimating the net cash flows to equity and discounting them at the cost of the equity for the company.

2. **The Invested capital procedure.** Under this procedure, the equity is valued indirectly by first estimating the value of the total invested capital in the company and then subtracting the value of debt. To value the entire invested capital, one would estimate the net cash flows to invested capital and discount them at the weighted average cost of capital.

Valuation Analysis: Discounted Economic Income Method

In our analysis, we applied the discounted economic income method, and we utilized net cash flows to equity. Because the Company's debt was expected to change, and thus its net cash flow available to equity was expected to change, we did not use the capitalization method but rather utilized a discounted cash flow method to account for decreases in debt over the forecasted period. As a result, we calculated net cash flow to equity, and we discounted it at the cost of equity, as discussed below.

In the discounted economic income method, expected future returns from an investment in the form of cash flows are discounted to present value at an appropriate rate of return for the investment. Cash flows are forecasted for a discrete period of years and then projected to grow at a constant rate in perpetuity.

In our analysis, we utilized the midyear convention to estimate the present value of the cash flows beyond the Valuation Date. The midyear convention is a procedure under the discounting method that reflects that in a normal business—a nonseasonal business—the cash flows are received more or less equally throughout the year (as opposed to being received in a lump sum at the end of the year). This midyear convention results in a slightly higher value because the cash flows are assumed to be received faster.

Net Cash Flow to Equity

The methodology utilized within the income approach was the discounted net cash flows to equity method. The discounted net cash flow to equity method was based on cash flows that were available to equity holders of the Company (see Exhibit 23.7).

The discounted net cash flow to equity formula is as follows:

Net income (after taxes) available to equity
+ Noncash charges
− Capital expenditures
± Changes in working capital
± Changes in long-term debt
= Net cash flow to equity

The normalized cash flows to equity were determined as follows:

- **Net income.** To arrive at normalized cash flows, we utilized historical revenue and expense levels as well as management indications.
  - Projected revenues for fiscal years 2012 and beyond were forecasted to grow at a sustainable growth rate of 5.0 percent based on consensus estimates that the GDP would grow at 2.5 percent and that the rate of inflation would average 2.5 percent over the next 10 years, as published by the Federal Reserve Bank of Philadelphia.[4]
  - The costs of goods sold (COGS) were forecasted at 88 percent of revenues, and operating expenses were forecasted at 9 percent of revenues, based on the weighted average of the last two fiscal years. While the COGS are largely variable and operating expenses are mainly fixed, we believed that both would grow with the forecasted sales as the projected growth was tied to the GDP and inflation. This was indicative of a company growing at the rate of the general overall economy; thus employee and operating expenses would also grow at these levels.
  - Interest expense was forecasted based on the amortization schedule of the Company's current debt obligation.

Exhibit 23.7

The Meat Processing Company Discounting of Net Cash Flow to Equity as of December 31, 2012

	2013	2014	2015	2016	2017	Terminal Value
Forecasted Net Cash Flow to Equity [1, 2]	$2,50,191	$3,23,346	$3,94,688	$5,60,196	$5,12,723	$41,41,226
Present Value Factor [3]	0.92	0.78	0.66	0.56	0.47	0.47
Present Value of Net Cash Flow to Equity	$2,30,319	$2,52,258	$2,60,945	$3,13,872	$2,43,452	$19,66,346
Indicated Market Value of Equity Capital						**$32,67,193**
Assumptions:						
Value computed using a discount rate (k) of, as determined in Exhibit 23.8:						18.00%
Computed using the Gordon growth model assuming a growth rate (g) in perpetuity of [4]:						5.00%

Notes:

[1] See Exhibit 23.8 for the computation of forecasted net cash flow to equity.

[2] Terminal value cash flow: forecasted net cash 2,017 X (1 + growth rate) / (discount rate − growth rate).

[3] Includes midyear adjustment, calculated as 1/(1 + *k*)^(number of years −0.5).

[4] Growth rate calculated as the long-term inflation rate plus the GDP long-term rate of growth, 2.5% + 2.5%.

  - The Company is a C corporation with all taxes paid at the company level. The state and federal tax expense was forecasted at a combined rate of 28 percent for the forecasted period based on historical indications.
- Capital expenditures were forecasted based on discussions with management regarding anticipated levels and historical indications. Given that the Company did not anticipate any increase in capital expenditure beyond those needed to maintain current operations and levels of growth inherent in the general economy, we utilized the rounded average of capital expenses experienced in fiscal years 2006 through 2012. We utilized the longest time frame available because capital expenditures are a long-term investment and they are often are volatile from year to year based on a company's needs and its ability to finance expenditures. Based on our assumption of continued growth, capital expenditures were estimated to outpace noncash charges. The Company also has a history of aggressively depreciating capital expenditures. Thus, depreciation was forecast at 99 percent of forecasted capital expenditures.
- Required working capital levels were estimated at 7.5 percent of revenues based on historical indications. The change in the working capital was incorporated in the net cash flow to equity calculation.
- The Company was expected to continue to pay down debt until debt financing reached zero. The changes in debt were forecasted based on the amortization schedule of the Company's current debt obligation.

The forecasted net cash flows to equity are presented in Exhibit 23.8.

Discount Rate

The discount rate should match the economic income being converted into present value. For this reason, we used the Company's cost of equity when discounting cash flows to equity.

Exhibit 23.8

The Meat Processing Company Net Cash Flow to Equity as of December 31, 2012

	Historical					
As of Date:	**2010**		**2011**		**2012**	
	%	**$**	**%**	**$**	**%**	**$**
Revenues		$1,42,95,107		$1,78,35,753		$2,03,75,854
(−) Cost of Goods Sold	86.3%	$1,23,43,292	87.9%	$1,56,84,258	87.7%	$1,78,65,458
(−) Operating Expenses	9.9%	$14,18,161	8.9%	$15,85,515	8.3%	$16,96,987
(+) Other Expense (Income)	0.0%	($3,047)	0.0%	($6,453)	0.0%	($2,024)
Earnings Before Interest & Tax	3.8%	$5,36,701	3.2%	$5,72,433	4.0%	$8,15,433
(−) Interest Expense	0.2%	$25,455	0.1%	$21,371	0.1%	$12,274
Earnings Before Tax	3.6%	$5,11,246	3.1%	$5,51,062	3.9%	$8,03,159
(−) Tax (28 percent)	1.1%	$1,54,605	0.9%	$1,53,001	1.1%	$2,25,523
Net Income	2.5%	$3,56,641	2.2%	$3,98,061	2.8%	$5,77,636
(+) Depreciation	0.3%	$40,902	0.6%	$98,454	1.1%	$2,30,648
(−) Capital Expenditures	0.1%	$13,855	0.5%	$89,489	1.2%	$2,39,326
(−) Increase in Working Capital	1.1%	$1,52,658	1.3%	$2,31,890	0.9%	$1,79,114
(+/−) Changes in Long-Term Debt	−0.2%	($29,958)	−0.2%	($35,005)	−0.3%	($52,182)
EQUALS Net Cash Flow to Equity	1.4%	$2,01,072	0.8%	$1,40,131	1.7%	$3,37,662
Revenue Growth Rate		−10.5%		24.8%		14.2%
Working Capital		$11,28,789		$13,60,679		$15,39,793
Long-Term Debt		$3,28,482		$2,93,477		$2,41,295

Note:

Forecasts created by analyst with management input. See written analysis for further information.

Cost of Equity

The cost of equity was estimated using the build-up model relying on data as published by Duff & Phelps. Using the build-up model, the cost of equity was estimated using the following formula:

$$\text{Equity rate of return} = R_f + (R_m - R_f) + RP_s + RP_u$$

where

R_f = the risk-free rate

$(R_m - R_f)$ = general equity risk premium, computed as the difference between the expected market return (R_m) and the risk-free rate (R_f)

Forecasted									
2013		2014		2015		2016		2017	
%	$	%	$	%	$	%	$	%	$
	$2,28,20,956		$2,46,46,633		$2,58,78,965		$2,71,72,913		$2,85,31,559
88.0%	$2,00,82,442	88.0%	$2,16,89,037	88.0%	$2,27,73,489	88.0%	$2,39,12,163	88.0%	$2,51,07,772
9.0%	$20,53,886	9.0%	$22,18,197	9.0%	$23,29,107	8.3%	$22,63,075	9.0%	$25,67,840
0.0%	$0	0.0%	$0	0.0%	$0	0.0%	$0	0.0%	$0
3.0%	$6,84,629	3.0%	$7,39,399	3.0%	$7,76,369	3.7%	$9,97,675	3.0%	$8,55,947
0.1%	$14,000	0.0%	$12,000	0.0%	$8,000	0.0%	$5,000	0.0%	$0
2.9%	$6,70,629	3.0%	$7,27,399	3.0%	$7,68,369	3.7%	$9,92,675	3.0%	$8,55,947
0.8%	$1,87,776	0.8%	$2,03,672	0.8%	$2,15,143	1.0%	$2,77,949	0.8%	$2,39,665
2.1%	$4,82,853	2.1%	$5,23,727	2.1%	$5,53,226	2.6%	$7,14,726	2.2%	$6,16,282
0.7%	$1,64,340	0.7%	$1,64,340	0.6%	$1,64,340	0.6%	$1,64,340	0.6%	$1,64,340
0.7%	$1,66,000	0.7%	$1,66,000	0.6%	$1,66,000	0.6%	$1,66,000	0.6%	$1,66,000
0.8%	$1,71,779	0.6%	$1,36,926	0.4%	$92,425	0.4%	$97,046	0.4%	$1,01,898
-0.3%	($59,223)	-0.3%	($61,795)	-0.2%	($64,453)	-0.2%	($55,824)	0.0%	$0
1.1%	**$2,50,191**	1.3%	**$3,23,346**	1.5%	**$3,94,688**	2.1%	**$5,60,196**	1.8%	**$5,12,723**
	12.0%		8.0%		5.0%		5.0%		5.0%
	$17,11,572		$18,48,497		$19,40,922		$20,37,968		$21,39,867
	$1,82,072		$1,20,277		$55,824		$0		$0

RP_s = risk premium for small size

RP_u = risk premium attributable to the specific company or to the industry

As of the Valuation Date, the cost of equity was calculated as follows:

- **The risk-free rate.** This was based on the Duff & Phelps recommended forward-looking estimate.
- **General equity risk premium.** The indicated premium over the risk-free rate using the *Duff & Phelps Risk Premium Report 2012* was used as the equity risk premium.
- **Risk premium attributable to the specific industry.** Sufficient data for inclusion of a specific industry risk premium were not available.

- **Risk premium for small size.** The equity premium calculated from Duff & Phelps data for the build-up model already incorporated a size premium, so no additional premium was added to this model.
- **Risk premium attributable to the specific company.** Given our analysis of the Company at December 31, 2012, we did not believe that we had sufficient evidence to either increase or decrease the cost of equity for Company-specific risk factors.

The cost of equity as of December 31, 2012, was estimated to be 18.0 percent (see Exhibit 23.10.)

Terminal Value

In our analysis, the terminal value was equal to the present value of the cash flows attributable to the years beyond the discrete forecasted period (2013 to 2017). In calculating a terminal value, we applied the Gordon growth model, which is a perpetual growth model. This capitalization technique estimates value by assuming that subsequent cash flows will continue at a stable level of growth.

This model is defined as follows:

$$TV = CF_1/(k - g)$$

where

TV = terminal value

CF_1 = normalized cash flow in the terminal year

k = discount rate, in this case the cost of equity capital

g = expected long-term sustainable growth rate in perpetuity

The Gordon growth model is applied such that the normalized cash flow in the terminal year is discounted by a capitalization rate. The capitalization rate is determined by subtracting the expected long-term sustainable growth rate from the cost of equity capital. The indicated terminal value is then discounted back to present value.

Our analysis incorporated a long-term sustainable growth rate in perpetuity of 5 percent. This growth rate was based on discussions with management and long-term GDP and inflationary expectations.

Valuation Summary: Discounted Cash Flow Model

Based on the discounted net cash flow to equity model, the fair market value of the Company's equity on a controlling 100 percent interest basis was estimated as $3,267,193 as of December 31, 2012 (see Exhibit 23.7).

The discounted cash flow model is highly sensitive to its three main inputs: cash flow, the cost of capital, and the expected long-term sustainable growth rate. See Exhibit 23.9 for a sensitivity analysis based on changes to the discount rate and expected long-term sustainable growth rate.

Exhibits 23.7 to 23.10 present the details of the application of the discounted net cash flow to equity method as of December 31, 2012.

VII. Asset Approach to Value

The asset approach is most often applied in the valuation of companies for which tangible assets make up a significant portion of the company's value or for which the company is being valued for the purpose of liquidation.

Exhibit 23.9

The Meat Processing Company Income Approach Sensitivity Analysis as of December 31, 2012

		Long-Term Growth Rate				
		4.0%	4.5%	5.0%	5.5%	6.0%
Discount Rate	17.0%	$33,85,901	$34,61,359	$35,43,050	$36,31,784	$37,28,523
	17.5%	$32,58,194	$33,26,194	$33,99,581	$34,79,028	$35,65,325
	18.0%	$31,39,657	**$32,01,087**	$32,67,193	**$33,38,534**	$34,15,765
	18.5%	$30,29,341	$30,84,960	$31,44,652	$32,08,886	$32,78,207
	19.0%	$29,26,423	$29,76,884	$30,30,904	$30,88,879	$31,51,264
Value Range			$32,01,087	-	$33,38,534	

Exhibit 23.10

The Meat Processing Company Cost of Equity Computation Using Duff & Phelps Data

Buildup Model Using 2012 *Duff & Phelps Risk Premium Report*
Equity Risk Premiums over Risk-Free Rate and Size Premium: Using Guideline Portfolios

	Subject Company	**Indicated Smoothed Average Risk Premium**
Book Value of Equity [1]	$19,87,629	12.05%
5-Year Average Net Income [2]	$6,84,355	13.01%
Total Assets [3]	$27,00,441	12.65%
5-Year Average EBITDA [4]	$6,84,355	12.81%
Sales [5]	$2,03,75,854	11.90%
Number of Employees [6]	75	12.06%
	Average	**12.41%**
	Median	**12.36%**

Buildup Model Using Duff & Phelps Risk Premium Report	
Risk-Free Rate [7]	4.00%
PLUS Equity Risk Premium and Size Premium [8]	13.56%
PLUS Industry Premium [9]	0.00%
PLUS Company-Specific Risk Premium [10]	0.00%
Cost of Equity Buildup Model Using Duff & Phelps Data, Rounded	18.00%

Notes:

[1] *Source*: Data from the 25th portfolio for Companies Ranked by Book Value of Equity in the Duff & Phelps Report, Exhibit A-2.

[2] *Source*: Data from the 25th portfolio for Companies Ranked by Average Net Income in the Duff & Phelps Report, Exhibit A-3.

[3] *Source*: Data from the 25th portfolio for Companies Ranked by Total Assets in the Duff & Phelps Report, Exhibit A-5.

[4] *Source*: Data from the 25th portfolio for Companies Ranked by EBITDA in the Duff & Phelps Report, Exhibit A-6.

[5] *Source*: Data from the 25th portfolio for Companies Ranked by Sales in the Duff & Phelps Report, Exhibit A-7.

[6] *Source*: Data from the 25th portfolio for Companies Ranked by Number of Employees in the Duff & Phelps Report, Exhibit A-8.

[7] Coupon bond yield on U.S. Treasury with 20 years left to maturity as of March 9, 2012, was 2.83%, www.federalreserve.gov. We have utilized a 4% rate based on forward-looking estimates of the expected rate. See *Duff & Phelps Risk Premium Report 2012*, pp. 14 and 15.

[8] Median equity risk premium (ERP) and size premium from the Duff & Phelps data. This includes an adjustment for the ERP as outlined on page 17 of the *Duff & Phelps Report* (5.5% − 4.3% = 1.2%).

[9] Sufficient data were not available for estimation of an industry risk premium.

[10] Specific company premium estimated based on analyst research. See written analysis for further information.

In the asset approach, net asset value is estimated by restating the value of the assets and liabilities from historical cost to fair market value. Assets and liabilities can be valued either individually or collectively. Individual assets and liabilities of a business can be appraised using the cost, market, and income approaches to valuation.

The book value of equity is rarely an appropriate measure for most businesses because assets and liabilities are generally stated at historical cost and not market value. The book value may be an appropriate measure when an asset has been recently acquired and recorded at its fair market value or when an asset is being regularly tested for financial reporting purposes and shown at its fair market value.

The liquidation value of a business can be estimated using the asset approach, and it is computed as the fair market value of assets (net of liabilities) less estimated liquidation expenses. We did not consider the liquidation value of the Company because liquidation was not considered to be imminent or probable.

Assets and Liabilities Held

The following should be looked at in conjunction with the information in Exhibit 23.11.

Current Assets

As of December 31, 2012, the Company had total current assets of $2,011,310. This included cash and equivalents, accounts receivable, other receivables, inventories, prepaid expenses, and prepaid income taxes. The market value of current assets was estimated to be substantially equivalent to their carrying value. *Carrying value* is the value of an asset according to its balance sheet account balance, which is the original cost less any depreciation, amortization, or impairment costs. Current assets accounted for approximately 42 percent of the fair market value of total assets as of December 31, 2012.

Exhibit 23.11

The Meat Processing Company Asset Approach

	Net Book Value	Adjustment	Fair Market Value	As a Percentage of Total Assets
As of Date:	**December 31, 2012**		**December 31, 2012**	
	$	**$**	**$**	
Assets [1]				
Cash and Equivalents	5,07,429	0	5,07,429	10.5%
Accounts Receivable	8,65,495	0	8,65,495	18.0%
Other Receivable	6,481	0	6,481	0.1%
Inventories	4,56,000	0	4,56,000	9.5%
Prepaid Expenses	1,36,928	0	1,36,928	2.8%
Prepaid Income Taxes	38,977	0	38,977	0.8%
Total Current Assets	20,11,310	0	20,11,310	41.7%
Property				
Main Property Land	1,63,741			
Land Pasture	0			
Land Gaddis Property	0			
Land North Property	0			
Buildings and Improvements	4,60,132			
Total Property [2]	6,23,873	19,56,127	25,80,000	53.5%
Equipment and Other Assets				
Machinery & Equipment [3]	47,258	1,32,742	1,80,000	3.7%
Automotive Equipment [3]	18,000	32,000	50,000	1.0%
Computer Software	0	0	0	0.0%
Total Equipment and Other Assets	65,258	1,64,742	2,30,000	4.8%
Total Assets	**27,00,441**	21,20,869	**48,21,310**	100.0%

Liabilities [1]				
Accounts Payable and Accrued Expenses	4,71,517	0	4,71,517	9.8%
Current Liabilities	4,71,517	0	4,71,517	9.8%
Debt	2,41,295	0	2,41,295	5.0%
Total Liabilities	**7,12,812**	0	**7,12,812**	14.8%
Net Asset Value	**19,87,629**		**41,08,498**	85.2%
Indicated Net Asset Value			**41,08,498**	85.2%
Less: Tax Liability [4]			8,13,481	16.9%
Concluded Net Asset Value			**32,95,017**	68.3%

Notes:
[1] At book value unless noted otherwise.
[2] Real estate appraisal report of Powell Valuation, Inc., as of December 31, 2012.
[3] Appraisal report of Machinery and Equipment Valuation, Inc., as of December 31, 2012.
[4] Built-in gains on appreciated assets as calculated by the Company CPA.

Property Held

As of the Valuation Date, the Company had on its balance sheet various properties that had a total value estimated at $2,580,000 as provided in the real estate appraisal report of Scott Lloyd, MAI, Real Estate Valuation, Inc., as of December 31, 2012. Property held accounts for approximately 53 percent of the fair market value of total assets as of December 31, 2012.

Equipment and Other Assets Held

The Company had machinery and equipment in the amount of $47,258 at December 31, 2012. The value of the machinery and equipment was independently valued at $180,000. We utilized this amount as an estimate of the fair market value of the Company's machinery and equipment as of December 31, 2012. The fair market value of the automotive equipment was independently determined to be $50,000. Computer software was valued at its current carrying value. Equipment and other assets account for approximately 5 percent of the fair market value of total assets as of December 31, 2012.

Liabilities

As of December 31, 2012, the Company had total current liabilities of $471,517 which consisted of accounts payable and accrued expenses. As of December 31, 2012, the debt outstanding was $241,295. These liabilities were deemed to be substantially equivalent to their carrying values. Liabilities accounted for approximately 15 percent of the fair market value of the total assets as of December 31, 2012.

Built-In Gain Tax Liability

The value of the Company's operating assets under the asset approach was equal to its net asset value less its non-operating assets and the built-in tax liability associated with unrealized gains on the fair market value of assets owned as of the date of value. The built-in gain tax liability was estimated as calculated by the Company's CPA using

Washington State and federal tax rate schedules. The built-in gain tax liability was estimated at $813,481 (see Exhibit 23.11).

Valuation Summary: Asset Approach

As shown in Exhibit 23.11, the Company's adjusted net asset value (NAV) at December 31, 2012, was estimated as $3,295,017. The forego-ing NAV reflects a controlling interest in the equity of the Company.

VIII. Summary and Conclusion

The final step in the valuation process requires a review of each valuation approach and a reconciliation of these approaches to reach a final value conclusion. In a specific appraisal situation, the weight given to each approach depends on the valuation function and purpose, the value premise and definition, the quantity and quality of available data, and the reliability of the analysis.

The income approach was afforded a 20 percent weighting in the reconciliation of values. The income approach represented the amount a prudent investor would pay for the Company's expected future cash flows based on current market rates of return and the Company's specific risks. The value derived from the income approach appeared to be representative of the fair market value of the interest herein and the Company's ability to generate cash flow to a controlling equity owner.

The asset approach was accorded 80 percent weight in the reconciliation of value. The afforded weight was affected by the fact that the interest valued herein was a controlling interest and would thus have had complete control over the Company's assets as of the Valuation Date.

Based on our investigation and analyses, as described in this valuation report, it was our conclusion that the fair market value of a 100 percent controlling ownership interest in the Company for estate planning purposes as of December 31, 2012, was $3,289,000.

The valuation synthesis can be found in Exhibit 23.1.

Sales Summary by Customer Type
January 1 Through December 31, 2012

Type of Customer	Sales	Percent of Total Sales
Retail, grocery markets	57,05,239	28.00%
Purveyors	40,75,171	20.00%
Restaurants	44,82,688	22.00%
Specialty butchers	26,48,861	13.00%
Sausage manufacturers	24,45,102	12.00%
Private labels	10,18,793	5.00%
Total	2,03,75,854	

This conclusion is subject to the Statement of Contingent and Limiting Conditions found in Appendix D. We have no obligation to update this report or conclusion of value for information that comes to our attention after the date of this report.

Appendix A. List of Exhibits

Exhibit 23.9. The Meat Processing Company Income Approach Sensitivity Analysis as of December 31, 2012

Exhibit 23.10. The Meat Processing Company Cost of Equity Computation using Duff & Phelps Data

Exhibit 23.11. The Meat Processing Company Asset Approach

Appendix B. Company Source Document List

In connection with this opinion, we have made such reviews, analyses, and inquiries as we have deemed necessary and appropriate under the circumstances. We assumed the accuracy and completeness of the financial and operational information and of other internal data provided to us. Information supplied by the Company and its accountant has been accepted without further verification, unless otherwise noted in our analysis. The following is a list of the Company-supplied documents:

1. MPC, State of Washington Certificate of Incorporation and Articles of Incorporation, December 23, 1976
2. MPC, Inventory, Locker List, December 30, 2012
3. MPC, Annual Meetings, October 25, 2009 to 2012
4. MPC, Aged Trial Balances, Accounts Receivable, December 31, 2009 to 2012
5. MPC, Accounts Payable, December 31, 2009 to 2012
6. MPC, Depreciation Schedule, December 31, 2011 and 2012
7. MPC, Revolving Line of Credit Note Between MPC and BoA, July 1, 2011
8. MPC, Amortization Schedule of Loans, August 30, 2010
9. MPC, Financial Statements, Fiscal Years Ended December 31, 2016 through 2012
10. MPC, U.S. Corporation Income Tax Returns, 2006 Through 2012
11. MPC, Wage and Tax Statements, Dated 2007 to 2012

12. MPC, Compensation Backup Sheet, 2012
13. MPC, Sales Summaries, January Through December 2012
14. MPC, Marketing Brochure and Price List as of August 13, 2012
15. MPC, Employee Handbook, Revised August 2011
16. MPC, Training Plans: Monthly Schedules, Employee List Training Group Assignments, Total Man-Hours, and Training Calendars, 2011 through 2013
17. MPC, Employees List, December 11, 2012
18. Liberty Insurance, Workers' Compensation Injury & Loss Report, Policy Years 2010 Through 2012
19. Powell Valuation, Inc., Real Estate Appraisal Summary Report, Valuation Date as of December 31, 2012, March 12, 2013
20. Machinery and Equipment Valuation, Inc., Machinery and Equipment Appraisal Summary Report, Valuation Date as of December 31, 2012, April 9, 2013

Appendix C. Qualifications of Principal Appraisers

Josephine Brian, ASA

Josephine Brian is the chair and CEO of Expert Business Valuations, Inc. She has performed valuation assignments for the following purposes: transactions (acquisitions, divestitures, reorganizations, public offerings, public companies going private); taxation (federal income, gift, and estate and local ad valorem); financing (securitization, recapitalization, restructuring); litigation support and dispute resolution (including dissenting stockholder suits, damage cases, and corporate and marital dissolution cases); and management information and planning. She has also managed a variety of fairness opinion and solvency opinion engagements.

Education

Bachelor of arts, business administration, University of Washington

Professional Affiliations

Brian is an Accredited Senior Appraiser (ASA) of the American Society of Appraisers.

Tim Morgan, ASA

Tim Morgan is a senior manager for Expert Business Valuations, Inc. He is a case manager and works on various aspects of business valuation such as economic and industry analysis, financial statement analysis, and application of the three approaches to business valuation (income approach, market approach, and asset approach). He has managed or assisted on valuation projects for a variety of purposes including shareholder disputes, marital dissolutions, mergers and acquisitions, report reviews, damage actions, and estate matters.

Education

Bachelor of science, business administration with an emphasis in finance, University of San Diego

Professional Affiliations

Morgan is an Accredited Senior Appraiser (ASA) of the American Society of Appraisers.

Appendix D. Statement of Contingent and Limiting Conditions

This appraisal is made subject to the following general contingent and limiting conditions:

1. We assume no responsibility for the legal description or matters including legal or title considerations. Title to the subject business interests is assumed to be good unless otherwise stated.

2. The subject business interests are appraised free and clear of any or all liens or encumbrances unless otherwise stated. Except as specifically stated to the contrary in this report, we have relied on the representations of the owners, management, and other third parties concerning the value and useful condition of all equipment, real estate, and investments used in the business, as well as any other assets or liabilities. We have not attempted to confirm whether all assets of the business are free and clear of liens and encumbrances or whether the entity has good title to all assets.
3. We assume ownership and management actions that are consistent with the industry practices with respect to the subject business interests.
4. The conclusion of value arrived at herein is based on the assumption that the current level of management expertise and effectiveness will continue to be maintained and that the character and integrity of the enterprise through any sale, reorganization, exchange, or diminution of the owners' participation will not be materially or significantly changed.
5. The information furnished by others is believed to be reliable. However, we issue no warranty or other form of assurance regarding its accuracy.
6. Financial statements and other related information provided by the Company or its representatives, in the course of this engagement, have been accepted without any verification as fully and correctly reflecting the enterprise's business conditions and operating results for the respective periods. EBV has not audited, reviewed, or compiled the financial information provided to us, and, accordingly, we express no audit opinion or any other form or assurance on this information. Events and circumstances frequently do not occur as expected, and there will usually be differences between prospective financial information and actual results, and those differences may be material.

7. We assume no hidden or unapparent conditions regarding the subject business interests.
8. We assume that there is full compliance with all applicable federal, state, and local regulations and laws unless the lack of compliance is stated, defined, and considered in the appraisal report.
9. We assume that all required licenses, certificates of occupancy, consents, or legislative or administrative authority from any local, state, or national government, or private entity or organization have been or can be obtained or reviewed for any use on which the opinion contained in this report is based.
10. Unless otherwise stated in this report, we did not observe, and we have no knowledge of, the existence of hazardous materials with regard to the subject business interests beyond what it associated with current required licenses. However, we are not qualified to detect such substances. We assume no responsibility for such conditions or for any expertise required to discover them. Any person entitled to rely on this report, wishing to know whether such liabilities exist, or the scope and their effect on the value of the property, is encouraged to obtain a professional environmental assessment.
11. No effort has been made to determine the possible effect, if any, on the subject business due to future federal, state, or local legislation, including any environmental or ecological matters or interpretations thereof.
12. No change of any item in this appraisal report shall be made by anyone other than EBV, and we shall have no responsibility for any such unauthorized change.
13. Possession of this report does not carry with it the right of publication. It may not be used for any purpose by any person other than the client to whom it is addressed without our written consent, and, in any event, only with proper written qualifications and only in its entirety.
14. We, by reason of this opinion, are not required to furnish any further valuation materials, or to give testimony, or to be in

attendance in court with reference to the assets, properties, or business interests in question unless arrangements have been previously made in writing.

15. Neither all nor any part of the contents of this report (especially the conclusion of value, the identity of any valuation specialists, or the firm with which such valuation specialists are connected or any reference to any of their professional designations) shall be disseminated to the public through advertising, public relations, news, sales, or other media without prior written consent and approval of EBV.
16. The analyses, opinions, and conclusions presented in this report apply to this engagement only and may not be used out of the context presented herein. This report is valid only for the effective dates specified herein and only for the purposes specified herein.
17. Public information and industry and statistical information have been obtained from sources we believe to be reliable. However, we make no representation as to the accuracy or completeness of such information, and we have performed no procedures to corroborate the information.
18. We do not provide assurance on the achievability of the results forecasted by the Company because events and circumstances frequently do not occur as expected; differences between actual and expected results may be material; and achievement of the forecasted results is dependent on actions, plans, and assumptions of management.
19. This report and the conclusion of value arrived at herein are for the exclusive use of our client for the sole and specific purposes noted herein. They may not be used for any other purpose or by any other party for any purpose. Furthermore, the report and conclusion of value are not intended by the author and should not be construed by the reader to be investment advice in any manner whatsoever. The conclusion of value represents the

considered opinion of EBV, based on information furnished to it by the Company and other sources.

Appendix E. Appraisal Certification

We hereby certify the following statements regarding this appraisal:

1. We have personally inspected the business interests subject to the appraisals to the extent we deemed necessary to arrive at a professional opinion under this set of facts and circumstances.
2. We have no present or prospective future interest in the assets, properties, or business interests that are the subject of this appraisal project.
3. We have no personal interest or bias with respect to the subject matter of this project or the parties involved.
4. Our compensation for making the appraisal is in no way contingent upon the value reported or upon any predetermined value.
5. To the best of our knowledge and belief, the statements of facts contained in this appraisal, upon which the analyses, conclusions, and opinions expressed herein are based, are true and correct.
6. Our analyses, opinions, and conclusions were developed, and this communication has been prepared, in conformity with the Uniform Standards of Professional Appraisal Practice, as promulgated by the Appraisal Foundation.
7. The reported analyses, opinions, and conclusions were developed, and this communication has been prepared, in conformity with the requirements of the Code of Ethics and the Standards of Professional Appraisal Practice of the American Society of Appraisers and of the other professional organizations of which we are members.
8. As outlined in the Introduction of this report, the expert reports of Scott Lloyd, MAI, of Real Estate Valuation, Inc., and

Jeremy Dryden of Machinery and Equipment Valuation, Inc., were relied upon herein. No persons other than the individuals whose qualifications are included herein have provided significant professional assistance regarding these analyses, opinions, and conclusions set forth in this communication.

9. The reported analyses, opinions, and conclusions are limited only by the reported contingent and limiting conditions, and they represent our unbiased professional analyses, opinions, and conclusions.
10. Disclosure of the contents of this communication is subject to requirements of the American Society of Appraisers and the other professional organizations of which we are members related to review by their duly authorized representatives.
11. No services have been performed, as an appraiser or in any other capacity, regarding the property that is the subject of this report within the three-year period immediately preceding acceptance of this assignment.
12. The signatures of Josephine Brian, ASA, chair and CEO of EBV supervising this project, and Tim Morgan, ASA, senior manager with EBV, are incorporated in this certification by reference to their location on the transmittal letter at the beginning of this report.

Notes

Chapter 1

1. Appraisal Institute, *The Appraisal of Real Estate*, 14th ed., Appraisal Institute, Chicago, 2013, p. 82.
2. Ibid., p. 401.

Chapter 4

1. Emergency Wetlands Resources Act of 1986, 16 U.S.C.§§ 3901–3932, November 10, 1986, as amended 1988 and 1992, Office of the Law Revision Counsel, 2005.
2. L. M. Cowardin, V. Carter, F. C. Golet, and E. T. LaRoe, *Classification of Wetlands and Deepwater Habitats of the United States*, U.S. Department of the Interior, Fish and Wildlife Service, Washington, D.C., 1979, p. 131.
3. Ibid.
4. Ibid.
5. The regulatory text discussing this permitting program (40 CFR Parts 230-233) can be found at http://ecfr.gpoaccess.gov under "Title 40: Protection of the Environment."
6. U.S. Army Corps of Engineers, 2006.
7. Appraisal Institute, *The Dictionary of Real Estate Appraisal*, 4th ed., Appraisal Institute, Chicago, 2002.
8. Merriam-Webster, *Merriam-Webster's Collegiate Dictionary*, 11th ed., Merriam-Webster, Springfield, MA, 2003.
9. Appraisal Institute, *Dictionary of Real Estate Appraisal.*
10. Appraisal Institute, *Uniform Appraisal Standards for Federal Land Acquisitions*, Appraisal Institute, Chicago, 2000, p. 13.
11. *California Jury Instructions: Civil (Book of Approved Jury Instructions)*, 9th ed., BAJI 11.73, "Fair Market Value—Defined."

12. Appraisal Institute, *Uniform Appraisal Standards for Federal Land Acquisitions*, p. 47.
13. Appraisal Institute, *Uniform Appraisal Standards for Federal Land Acquisitions*, p. 18.

Chapter 5

1. Appraisal Institute, *The Dictionary of Real Estate Appraisal*, 4th ed., Appraisal Institute, Chicago, 2002.
2. Ibid.
3. Ibid.
4. The complete Freddie Mac Form 71A can be found at http://www.freddiemac.com/multifamily/mf_forms/pdf/f71a.pdf.

Chapter 7

1. Marshall & Swift Publications Company, *Marshall Valuation Service*, 2000 ed., Marshall & Swift Publications Company, Los Angeles, 2000.
2. Appraisal Institute, *The Dictionary of Real Estate Appraisal*, 4th ed., Appraisal Institute, Chicago, 2002.
3. Ibid.; and Marshall & Swift, *Marshall Valuation Service*, 2000 ed.
4. *West's Encyclopedia of American Law*, 2nd ed., Thompson Gale, Detroit, 2005.

Chapter 9

1. This information is used with permission and is similar to information found in John Lifflander, *Fundamentals of Industrial Valuation*, International Association of Assessing Officers (IAAO), Chicago, 2007.
2. Merriam-Webster, *Merriam-Webster's Collegiate Dictionary*, 11th ed., Merriam-Webster, Springfield, MA, 2003.
3. American Society of Appraisers, *Appraising Machinery and Equipment*, McGraw-Hill, New York, 1989, p. 97.
4. American Society of Appraisers, *Valuing Machinery and Equipment: The Fundamentals of Appraising Machinery and Technical Assets*, 2d ed., American Society of Appraisers, Herndon, VA, 2005.

Chapter 10

1. American Society of Appraisers, *Valuing Machinery and Equipment: The Fundamentals of Appraising Machinery and Technical Assets*, 2d ed., American Society of Appraisers, Herndon, VA, 2005, p. 68.

2. American Society of Appraisers, "Valuing Machinery and Equipment," Machinery and Technical Specialties Committee of the American Society of Appraisers, American Society of Appraisers, Herndon, VA, 2000, p. 5.
3. Ibid., p. 175.
4. John Lifflander, *Fundamentals of Industrial Valuation*, International Association of Assessing Officers, Kansas City, 2007, p. 134.
5. Ibid., pp. 127, 128.
6. Ibid., pp. 118–119.
7. Ibid., pp. 129–130.

Chapter 13

1. See, e.g., *Matter of Slant/Fin. Corp. v. The Chicago Corp.* (N.Y. Sup. Ct. Oct. 5, 1995), aff'd 236 A.D.2d 547, 654 N.Y.S.2d 627 (N.Y. App. Div. Feb. 18, 1997); and *Le Beau v. M.G. Bancorporation, Inc.*, 1998 Del. Ch. LEXIS 9, 1998 WL 44993 (Del. Ch. Jan. 29, 1998).
2. For a thorough discussion of definitions of value, see Jay Fishman et al., *Standards of Value: Theory and Applications*, 2nd ed., Wiley, New York, 2013.
3. 26 CFR 20.2031-3. See also Rev. Rul. 59-60.
4. For a thorough discussion of this issue, see Richard M. Wise, "The Effect of Special Interest Purchases on Fair Market Value in Canada," American Society of Appraisers, *Business Valuation Review*, vol. 22, no. 4 (December 2003), pp. 196–202.
5. Appraisal Foundation, Uniform Standards of Professional Appraisal Practice (USPAP), U-3, 2014, pp. 98–111.
6. *Pabst Brewing Co. v. Commissioner*, T.C. Memo. 1996-506 (1996).
7. SFAS 157, Fair Value Measurements.
8. For a complete listing of states' dissenters' rights statutes, see www.BVLibrary.com.
9. Alabama, Arizona, Arkansas, Colorado, Hawaii, Indiana, Kentucky, Massachusetts, Michigan, Missouri, Montana, Oregon, South Carolina, Vermont, Washington and, Wisconsin.
10. Connecticut, District of Columbia, Idaho, Iowa, Maine, Mississippi, Nevada, New Hampshire, North Carolina, South Dakota, Virginia, and West Virginia.
11. Georgia, New Mexico, Rhode Island, Tennessee, and Utah.
12. Delaware, Kansas, Oklahoma, and Pennsylvania.

13. See American Bar Association, Model Business Corporation Act 2007, 4th ed., 2008.
14. See, e.g., *Lawson Mardon Wheaton, Inc. v. Smith*, 160 N.J. 383, 734 A.2d 738 (1999); and *Balsamides v. Protameen Chemicals, Inc.*, 160 N.J. 352, 734 A.2d 721 (1999).
15. This section is excerpted from Shannon P. Pratt and Alina V. Niculita, *Valuing a Business*, 5th ed., New York, McGraw Hill, 2008.
16. Compare IFRS 3 defining *fair value* as "the amount for which an asset could be exchanged or a liability settled between knowledgeable, willing parties in an arm's-length transaction."
17. Scott Beauchene and Robert Duffy, "Getting Ready for 409A: Some Practical Considerations," *Business Valuation Update*, May 2007.
18. See Appraisal Institute, *The Appraisal of Real Estate 26*, 12th ed., The Appraisal Institute, Chicago 2001.
19. W. W. Cooper and Yuri Ijiri, eds., *Kohler's Dictionary for Accountants* 285, 6th ed., Prentice-Hall, Upper Saddle River, NJ, 1983. Reprinted by permission of Prentice-Hall.
20. Ibid., p. 228.
21. James H. Lorie, et al., *The Stock Market: Theories and Evidence*, 2nd ed., Irwin, Willowbrook, IL 1984.
22. American Society of Appraisers Business Valuation Standards 15, January 1995.
23. IPR&D generally refers to R&D acquired in an acquisition.
24. See, e.g., *Gaydos v. Gaydos*, 693 A.2d 1368 (Pa. Super. Ct. 1997).
25. IRC Section 2031.
26. *Active Wear, Inc. v. Parkdale Mills, Inc.*, 331 B.R. 669 (W.D. Va. 2005) (defining *fair market value* as the "value the debtor/bankrupt could receive for the property in a liquidation sale").
27. Prop. DOL Reg. §2510.3-18(b)(2)(ii) includes a two-part test: (1) the price paid must reflect the fair market value of the asset, and (2) the trustee/fiduciaries must conduct a careful and independent investigation of the circumstances prevailing at the time of the investment.
28. See, e.g., *Estate of Andrews v. Commissioner*, 79 T.C. 938 (1982).
29. Arthur J. Shartsis, "Dissolution Actions Yield Less than Fair Market Enterprise Value," *Judges & Lawyers Business Valuation Update*, January 1999, pp. 5–7.

30. Pratt and Niculita, *Valuing a Business*, p. 47.
31. Ibid.
32. See, e.g., *Foltz v. U.S. News & World Report, Inc.*, 106 F.R.D. 338 (D.C. Cir. 1984), appealed and affirmed.

Chapter 14

1. Additional guidance may be found in Shannon P. Pratt, *Business Valuation Body of Knowledge*, 2nd ed., Wiley, New York, 2003.
2. American Society of Appraisers Business Valuation Standards.

Chapter 15

1. Richard A. Brealey and Stewart C. Myers, *Principles of Corporate Finance*, 7th ed., McGraw-Hill Irwin, New York, 2003, p. 75.
2. See, e.g., *Guiffre v. Baker*, 1996 WL 535254, 1996 Ohio App. LEXIS 3673 (Ohio Ct. App. 1996); *Sergi v. Sergi*, 1996 WL 425914, 1996 Ohio App. LEXIS 3241 (Ohio Ct. App. 1996) (the courts in those cases accepted the DCF method over the excess earnings method); and *Howell v. Howell*, 523 S.E.2d 514 (Va. Ct. App. 2000).
3. See, e.g., *Shooltz v. Shooltz*, 498 S.E.2d 437 (Va. Ct. App. 1998).
4. For detailed procedures for analyzing and valuing debt instruments and preferred stock, see Shannon Pratt, with Alina Niculita, *Valuing a Business*, 5th ed., McGraw Hill, New York, 2007, pp. 547–562, 563–584.
5. For more detail about these and other Morningstar data and arguments regarding their use, see Michael W. Barad and Tara McDowell, "Using Morningstar Cost of Capital Data," in Shannon Pratt and Roger Grabowski, *Cost of Capital: Applications and Examples*, 3rd ed., Wiley, New York, 2008. See also *Stocks, Bonds, Bills & Inflation, Valuation Edition*, published annually by Morningstar.
6. In *Duff & Phelps LLC Risk Premium Report*, published annually and available at http://corporate.morningstar.com/ib/html/home.htm and www.bvresources.com.
7. The iterative process is described in Shannon Pratt and Roger Grabowski, *Cost of Capital: Applications and Examples*, 3rd ed., Wiley, New York, 2008. A shortcut for a reasonable estimate is presented by Frank Evans, "Debt and Equity Weightings in WACC," *CPA Expert*, Fall 1998, pp. 4–5, abstracted in *Shannon Pratt's Business Valuation Update*, March 1999, p. 11.

8. The formulas and examples are described in Pratt and Grabowski, *Cost of Capital*, app. 10A, p. 143.
9. Proof of the accuracy of this method is presented in Todd A. Kaltman, "Capitalization Using a Mid-Year Convention," *Business Valuation Review*, December 1995, pp. 178–182.
10. It is, of course, appropriate to make calculations adjusting for uneven but predictable cash flow patterns, for example, a toy retailer at Christmas or H&R Block in April, but such models usually are more complex to create.

Chapter 16

1. See Shannon Pratt and Roger Grabowski, "The Private Company Discount" (ch. 24), in *Cost of Capital: Applications and Examples*, 5th ed., John Wiley, New York., 2014.
2. Daniel W. Bielinski, "The Comparable Company Approach: Measuring the True Value of Privately Held Firms," *Corporate Cashflow Magazine*, October 1990, pp. 64–66.
3. Rev. Rul. 59-60, 1959-1 C.B. 237, Section 4(h).
4. *Estate of Gallo v. Commissioner*, 50 T.C.M. 470 (1985).
5. *Estate of Hall v. Commissioner*, 92 T.C. 312 (1989).
6. In "Bridging the Gap Between Public and Private Market Multiples," *Business Valuation Review*, September 1998, pp. 95–101, Richard W. Goeldner II suggests going as far as quantifying all these factors in terms of their impact on risk and potential future growth, and he suggests that it is not unreasonable for private company multiples to be half of observed public company multiples, or even less.

Chapter 17

1. Conceivably, certain intangibles, such as intellectual property, could be identified and valued separately, but in practice this is rarely done.
2. Tax cases have begun to recognize all or some portion of this liability. See, e.g., *Estate of Davis v. Commissioner*, 110 T.C. 530 (1998); *Eisenberg v. Commissioner*, T.C.M. 1997-483, 74 T.C.M. (CCH) 1046 (1997); and *Estate of Simplot v. Commissioner*, 112 T.C. No. 13, 1999 WL 152610 (1999). Family law courts have been reluctant to recognize this liability unless sale is imminent. See, e.g., *Granger v. Granger*, 579 N.E.2d 1319 (Ind. Ct.

App. 1991); *In re* Marriage of Hay, 907 P.2d 334 (Wash. Ct. App. 1995); and *Crooker v. Crooker*, 432 A.2d 1293 (Me. 1981).

3. *Shooltz v. Shooltz*, 27 Va. App. 264, 498 S.E.2d 437 (1998).

Chapter 18

1. Glenn Desmond, *Handbook of Small Business Valuation Formulas*, 3rd ed., Valuation Press, 1993, p. 3.
2. American Society of Appraisers, Business Valuation Standards.
3. Harriet Cohen, "Using Rules on Thumb in Valuation," in Gregg Herman, ed., *101+ Practical Solutions for the Family Lawyer*, 2d ed., American Bar Association, Chicago, 2003.
4. *Bostwick v. Bostwick*, 1991 WL 42628 (Del. Fam. Ct. 1991), quoted in Robert D. Feder, *Valuation Strategies in Divorce*, 4th ed., 1997, Wiley, New York, p. 451. See also, e.g., *Bolan v. Bolan*, 32 Ark. App. 65, 796 S.W.2d 358 (1990) and *Young v. Young*, 600 So. 2d 1140 (Fla. Dist. Ct. App. 1992).
5. *Carter v. Carter*, 1990 WL 145736 (Ohio App. 11 Dist. 1990).

Chapter 19

1. This chapter relies extensively on the work of Noah J. Gordon, legal counsel for Shannon Pratt Valuations, Inc. Gordon is a regular contributor to valuation and legal publications.
2. Hon. David Laro, "Judge Laro's Views on 'Fair Market Value,'" *Judges & Lawyers Business Valuation Update*, May 1999, pp. 1–3. Full text of address before the AICPA National Business Valuation Conference (November 17, 1998) available on www.BVLibrary.com.
3. *Ahmanson Foundation v. United States*, 674 F.2d 761 (9th Cir. 1981).
4. *Estate of Simplot v. Comm'r*, 249 F.3d 1191 (9th Cir. 2001).
5. For an extensive discussion on the nuances of fair market value in the federal tax valuation context, see Jay E. Fishman, Shannon P. Pratt, and William J. Morrison, *Standards of Value: Theory and Applications*, 2nd ed., Wiley, New York, 2013, pp. 36–79.
6. Rev. Rul. 59-60.
7. Hon. David Laro and Shannon P. Pratt, *Business Valuation and Federal Taxes: Procedure, Law, and Perspective*, Wiley, Hoboken, NJ, 2011, p. 9.
8. *Central Trust Co. v. United States*, 305 F.2d 393 (Ct. Cl. 1962).
9. *Foltz v. U.S. News and World Report, Inc.*, 106 F.R.D. 338 (D.C. Cir. 1984).
10. *Estate of Furman v. Comm'r*, T.C. Memo. 1998-157 (1998).

11. *Bank One Corporation v. Comm'r*, 120 T.C. 174, 2003 U.S. Tax Ct. LEXIS 13, 120 T.C. No. 11 (2003), rev'd and remanded 2006 U.S. App. LEXIS 20430 (7th Cir. 2006).
12. *Central Trust Co. v. United States*, 305 F.2d 393 (Ct. Cl. 1962).
13. *Estate of Kaufman v. Comm'r*, T.C. Memo. 1999-119 (1999).
14. *Moore v. Comm'r*, T.C. Memo. 1991-546 (1991).
15. *Estate of Lehmann v. Comm'r*, T.C. Memo. 1997-392 (1997).
16. See, e.g., *Walter v. Duffy*, 287 F. 41 (3d Cir. 1923).
17. Roger J. Grabowski, "Identifying Pool of Willing Buyers May Introduce Synergy to Fair Market Value," *Shannon Pratt's Business Valuation Update, Business Valuation Resources*, vol. 7, no. 4, April 2001.
18. See, e.g., IRS Treasury Regulations, Estate Tax Regulation § 20.2031-1; and IRS Treasury Regulations, Gift Tax Regulation 25.2512-1.
19. *Leibowitz v. Comm'r*, T.C. Memo. 1997-243 (1997).
20. *Estate of Simplot v. Comm'r*, 249 F.3d 1191 (9th Cir. 2001).
21. *Estate of Berg v. Comm'r*, T.C. Memo. 1991-279 (1991).
22. *Kohler v. Comm'r*, T.C. Memo. 2006-152 (2006).
23. *Estate of Thompson v. Comm'r*, T.C. Memo. 2004-174 (2004).
24. *Caracci v. Comm'r*, 118 T.C. 379, 118 T.C. No. 25, 2002 U.S. Tax Ct. LEXIS 25 (2002).
25. *Estate of Josephine Thompson v. Comm'r*, T.C. Memo. 2004-174 (2004), aff'd, 499 F.3d 129 (2d Cir. 2007).
26. Tax Ct. Rule 142.
27. *Estate of Kaufman v. Comm'r*, T.C. Memo. 1999-119 (1999).
28. *Kohler v. Comm'r*, T.C. Memo. 2006-152, 2006 Tax Ct. Memo. LEXIS 156 (2006).
29. *Estate of Josephine Thompson v. Comm'r*, 499 F.3d 129 (2d Cir. 2007).
30. IRC Section 6501(c)(9).
31. 64 Federal Register 67767 (December 3, 1999).
32. For a full discussion of the final regulations, see "IRS Adequate Disclosure Final Regulations Respond to Extensive Comments," *Judges & Lawyers Business Valuation Update*, January 2000, 1, pp. 4–5.
33. *Estate of Bruce v. Comm'r*, T.C. Memo. 1993-244 (1993).
34. *Kohler v. Comm'r*, T.C. Memo. 2006-152, 2006 Tax Ct. Memo. LEXIS 156 (2006).
35. *Polack v. Comm'r*, T.C. Memo. 2002-145, aff'd, 366 F.3d 608 (8th Cir. 2004).
36. *Black's Law Dictionary* 1726, 10th ed., Thomson West, New York, 2014.

37. *Estate of Bennett v. Comm'r*, T.C. Memo. 1993-34 (1993).
38. *Morrissey v. Comm'r*, 243 F.3d 1145 (9th Cir. 2001).
39. Shannon P. Pratt with Alina Niculita, *Valuing a Business: The Analysis and Appraisal of Closely Held Companies*, 5th ed., McGraw-Hill, New York, 2008, p. 663.
40. *Estate of Kaufman v. Comm'r*, T.C. Memo. 1999-119 (1999).
41. *Hess v. Comm'r*, T.C. Memo. 2003-251 (2003).
42. *Estate of Leichter v. Comm'r*, T.C. Memo. 2003-66 (2003).
43. *Estate of Brookshire v. Comm'r*, T.C. Memo. 1998-365 (1998).
44. *Estate of Gallo v. Comm'r*, T.C. Memo. 1985-363 (1985).
45. *Estate of Hall v. Comm'r*, 92 T.C. 312 (1989).
46. *Estate of Heck v. Comm'r*, T.C. Memo. 2002-34 (2002).
47. *Hess v. Comm'r*, T.C. Memo. 2003-251 (2003).
48. *Estate of Watts v. Comm'r*, T.C. Memo. 1985-595 (1985), aff'd, 823 F.3d 483 (11th Cir. 1987).
49. Shannon Pratt, *Cost of Capital* 157 (1998).
50. *Morton v. Comm'r*, T.C. Memo. 1997-166 (1997).
51. *Estate of Hendrickson v. Comm'r*, T.C. Memo. 1999-278,1999 Tax Ct. Memo. LEXIS 318 (1999).
52. *Estate of Freeman v. Comm'r*, T.C. Memo. 1996-372, 1996 WL 453872 (1996).
53. *Estate of Jung v. Comm'r*, 101 T.C. 412 (1993).
54. *Rakow v. Comm'r*, T.C. Memo. 1999-177.
55. *Estate of Lehmann v. Comm'r*, T.C. Memo. 1997-392 (1997).
56. *Estate of Bennett v. Comm'r*, T.C. Memo. 1993-34 (1993); and *Estate of Hatchett v. Comm'r*, T.C. Memo. 1989-637 (1989).
57. *Estate of Jameson v. Comm'r*, T.C. Memo. 1999-43 (1999), vacated and remanded by 267 F.3d 366 (5th Cir. 2001).
58. For a discussion of valuation and related tax issues with regard to family limited partnerships, see Shannon P. Pratt with Alina Niculita, *Valuing a Business: The Analysis and Appraisal of Closely Held Companies*, 5th ed., McGraw-Hill, New York, 2008, pp. 689–699.
59. For the most extensive sets of case citations and discussions of discounts and premiums in federal tax cases, see John A. Bodganski, Federal Tax Valuation 4–1 to 4–121, together with the 2000 Cumulative Supplement No. 1, 54–1 to 54–63. (1996).
60. See, e.g., *Estate of Gallo v. Comm'r*, T.C. Memo. 1985-363 (1985) (36%); and *Estate of Hall v. Comm'r*, 92 T.C. 312 (1989) (36%).

61. See, e.g., *Brookshire v. Comm'r*, T.C. Memo. 1998-365 (1998) (40%).
62. *Huber v. Comm'r*, T.C. Memo. 2006-96 (2006).
63. *Estate of Gallo v. Comm'r,* T.C. Memo. 1985-363 (1985).
64. *Estate of Hall v. Comm'r,* 92 T.C. 312 (1989).
65. See, e.g., *Mandelbaum v. Comm'r*, T.C. Memo. 1995-255 (1995); *Estate of Davis v. Comm'r*, 110 T.C. 530 (1998); *Estate of Williams v. Comm'r*, T.C. Memo. 1998-59 (1998); *Estate of Brookshire*, T.C. Memo. 1998-365 (1998); and *Okerlund v. United States*, 53 Fed. Cl. 341 (Fed. Ct. Cl. 2002), aff'd 365 F.3d 1044 (Fed. Cir. 2004).
66. *Estate of Jelke v. Comm'r*, T.C. Memo. 2005-131 (2005).
67. *McCord v. Comm'r*, 120 T.C. 358 (2003), rev'd, 461 F.3d 614 (5th Cir. 2006).
68. *Estate of Kelly v. Comm'r*, T.C. Memo. 2005-235 (2005).
69. *Lappo v. Comm'r*, T.C. Memo. 2003-258 (2003).
70. *Peracchio v. Comm'r*, T.C. Memo. 2003-280 (2003).
71. *Estate of Deputy v. Comm'r*, T.C. Memo. 2003-176 (2003).
72. *Janda v. Comm'r*, T.C. Memo. 2001-24 (2001).
73. *Temple v. United States*, 2006 U.S. Dist LEXIS 16171 (E.D. Tex. 2006).
74. *Robertson v. United States*, 2006 U.S. Dist. LEXIS 1167 (N.D. Tex. 2006).
75. *Estate of Green v. Comm'r*, T.C. Memo. 2003-384.
76. *Litman v. United States*, 78 Fed. Cl. 90 (Claims Ct. 2007).
77. For a discussion of these sources of empirical data supporting a discount for lack of marketability, see Scott Beauchene and Robert Duffy, "Getting Ready for 409A: Some Practical Considerations," *Business Valuation Update*, May 2007, pp. 1–5; and AICPA National Business Valuation Conference, December 2–4, 2007, Discounts for Lack of Marketability Panel—Who's on First, What's on Second, I Don't Know's on Third, Linda Trugman, Moderator, Mel H. Abraham, Z. Christopher Mercer, and Ronald L. Seigneur, Session No. 10.
78. *Estate of Gimbel v. Comm'r*, 2006 Tax Ct. Memo. LEXIS 274 (2006).
79. *Litman v. United States*, 78 Fed. Cl. 90 (Claims Ct. 2007).
80. *Estate of Gimbel v. Comm'r*, 2006 Tax Ct. Memo. LEXIS 274 (2006).
81. See Ashok Abbott, "Calculating the Cost of Liquidity in Current Markets," *Business Valuation Update*, vol. 14, no. 5, May 2008; and Ashok Abbott, "New Abbott Analysis Aids Valuators in Assessing Liquidity Discounts," *Business Valuation Update*, vol. 13, no. 11, November 2007.
82. *Estate of Andrews v. Comm'r*, 79 T.C. 938 (1982).

83. *Estate of Furman v. Comm'r*, T.C. Memo. 1998-157 (1998); *Estate of Magnin v. Comm'r*, T.C. Memo. 2001-31 (2001); *Estate of Mitchell v. Comm'r*, 250 F.3d 696 (9th Cir. 2001); *Estate of Janda v. Comm'r*, T.C. Memo. 2001-24 (2001); *Estate of Deputy v. Comm'r*, T.C. Memo. 2003-176 (2003); and *Temple v. United States*, 2006 U.S. Dist. LEXIS 16171 (E.D. Tex. 2006).
84. *Estate of Fleming v. Comm'r*, T.C. Memo. 1997-484 (1997).
85. *Estate of Andrews v. Comm'r*, 79 T.C. 938 (1982).
86. *Estate of Hendrickson v. Comm'r*, T.C. Memo. 1999-278,1999 Tax Ct. Memo. LEXIS 318 (1999).
87. *Estate of Cloutier v. Comm'r*, T.C. Memo. 1996-049 (1996).
88. *Estate of Dougherty v. Comm'r*, 59 T.C. 772 (1990).
89. *Estate of Maggos v. Comm'r*, T.C. Memo. 2000-129 (2000).
90. *Estate of Desmond v. Comm'r*, T.C. Memo. 1999-76 (1999).
91. See, e.g., *Estate of Dunn v. Comm'r*, T.C. Memo. 2000-12 (2000) rev'd on other grounds, 201 F.3d 339 (5th Cir. 2002)(15 percent); and *Temple v. United States*, 2006 U.S. Dist. LEXIS 16171 (E.D. Tex. 2006)(12.5 percent).
92. *Estate of Bennett v. Comm'r*, T.C. Memo. 1993-34 (1993).
93. *Estate of Jelke v. Comm'r*, T.C. Memo. 2005-131 (2005), rev'd 503 F.3d 1317 (11th Cir. 2007).
94. *Estate of Green v. Comm'r*, T.C. Memo. 2003-384 (2003).
95. *Estate of Thompson v. Comm'r*, T.C. Memo. 2004-174 (2004).
96. *Adams v. United States*, 2001 U.S. Dist. LEXIS 13092 (N.D. Tex. 2001).
97. *Robertson v. United States*, 2006 U.S. Dist. LEXIS 1167 (N.D. Tex. 2006).
98. *Hess v. Comm'r*, T.C. Memo. 2003-251 (2003).
99. *Temple v. United States*, 2006 U.S. Dist. LEXIS 16171 (E.D. Tex. 2006).
100. See, e.g., *Estate of Davis v. Comm'r*, 110 T.C. 530 (1998), where the court recognized in its decision that it probably would have taken five to six months to sell the stock without depressing the price, yet concluded that petitioner failed to satisfy the burden of proof that a blockage discount should be applied.
101. *Estate of Mellinger v. Comm'r*, 112 T.C. 26 (1999).
102. *Estate of Foote v. Comm'r*, T.C. Memo. 1999-37 (1999).
103. See, e.g., *Estate of Gimbel v. Comm'r*, 2006 Tax Ct. Memo LEXIS 274 (2006) (14.2 percent net discount rate for restricted and nonrestricted stock).
104. *Estate of Adams v. Comm'r*, T.C. Memo. 2002-80 (2002).

105. *Estate of Furman v. Comm'r,* T.C. Memo. 1998-157 (1998).
106. *Estate of Mitchell v. Comm'r,* T.C. Memo. 1997-461 (1997), vacated, 250 F.3d 696 (9th Cir. 2001).
107. *Estate of Renier v. Comm'r,* T.C. Memo. 2000-298 (2000).
108. *Estate of Simplot v. Comm'r,* 112 T.C. 130 (1999).
109. *Estate of Simplot v. Comm'r,* 249 F.3d 1191 (9th Cir. 2001).
110. *Estate of Simplot v. Comm'r,* 112 T.C. 13 (1999), rev'd, 249 F.3d 1191 (9th Cir. 2001).
111. *Estate of Maggos v. Comm'r,* T.C. Memo. 2000-129 (2000).
112. *Estate of Wright v. Comm'r,* T.C. Memo. 1997-53 (1997).
113. *Eisenberg v. Comm'r,* T.C. Memo. 1997-483 (1997).
114. *Estate of Davis v. Comm'r,* 110 T.C. 530 (1998).
115. *Eisenberg v. Comm'r,* 155 F.3d 50 (2d Cir. 1998).
116. *Estate of Simplot v. Comm'r,* 112 T.C. 130 (1999).
117. *Estate of Jameson v. Comm'r,* T.C. Memo. 1999-43 (1999).
118. *Estate of Welch v. Comm'r,* T.C. Memo. 1998-167 (1998) rev'd 208 F.3d 213 (6th Cir. 2000).
119. *Estate of Borgatello v. Comm'r,* T.C. Memo. 2000-264 (2000).
120. *Estate of Dunn v. Comm'r,* T.C. Memo. 2000-12 (2000), rev'd and remanded, 301 F.3d 339 (5th Cir. 2002).
121. *Estate of Jelke v. Comm'r,* T.C. Memo. 2005-131 (2005), rev'd 503 F.3d 1317 (11th Cir. 2007).
122. *Estate of Jones v. Comm'r,* 116 T.C. 121 (2001); and *Temple v. United States,* 2006 U.S. Dist. LEXIS 16171 (E.D. Tex. 2006).
123. *Hewitt v. Comm'r,* 166 F.3d 332 (4th Cir. 1998).
124. *Koblick v. Comm'r,* 2006 Tax Ct. Memo. LEXIS 63 (2006).
125. *Todd v. Comm'r,* 118 T.C. 354 (2002).
126. *Estate of Desmond v. Comm'r,* T.C. Memo. 1999-76 (1999).
127. *Estate of Mitchell v. Comm'r,* T.C. Memo. 1997-461 (1997), vacated, 250 F.3d 696 (9th Cir. 2001).
128. *Estate of Klauss v. Comm'r,* T.C. Memo. 2000-191 (2000).
129. *Rabenhorst v. Comm'r,* T.C. Memo. 1996-92 (1996).
130. *Central Trust v. United States,* 305 F.2d 393 (Ct. Cl. 1962).
131. *Polack v. Comm'r,* T.C. Memo. 2002-145 (2002), aff'd, 366 F.3d 608 (8th Cir. 2004).
132. *Okerlund v. United States,* 365 F.3d 1044 (Fed. Cir. 2004).
133. *Estate of Noble v. Comm'r,* T.C. Memo. 2005-2 (2005).

134. For an extensive list of notable subsequent events court cases, see Shannon P. Pratt with Alina Niculita, *Valuing a Business: The Analysis and Appraisal of Closely Held Companies*, 5th ed., McGraw-Hill, New York, 2008, ex. 28-1, p. 672.
135. *Estate of Jung v. Comm'r*, 101 T.C. 412 (1993).
136. *Saltzman v. Comm'r*, T.C. Memo. 1994-641, 68 T.C. Memo. (CCH) 1544 (1994).
137. Id.
138. *Estate of Cidulka v. Comm'r*, T.C. Memo. 1996-149, 71 T.C. Memo. (CCH) 2555 (1996).
139. *Estate of Scanlan v. Comm'r*, T.C. Memo. 1996-331 (1996).
140. *Estate of Trompeter v. Comm'r*, T.C. Memo. 1998-35 (1998).
141. IRC Section 2703.
142. *Estate of Lauder v. Comm'r* (Lauder II), T.C. Memo. 1992-736 (1992).
143. *Estate of Blount v. Comm'r*, T.C. Memo. 2004-116 (2004), aff'd 428 F.3d 1338 (11th Cir. 2005).
144. *Estate of True v. Comm'r*, T.C. Memo. 2001 167 (2001), aff'd 390 F.3d 1210 (10th Cir. 2004).
145. *Hutchens Non-Marital Trust v. Comm'r*, T.C. Memo. 1993-600 (1993).
146. Laro and Pratt, *Business Valuation and Federal Taxes: Procedure, Law, and Perspective.*
147. *Central Trust v. United States*, 305 F.2d 393 (Ct. Cl. 1962).
148. *Hess v. Comm'r*, T.C. Memo. 2003-251 (2003).
149. *Estate of Dunn v. Comm'r*, T.C. Memo. 2000-12 (2000) rev'd on other grounds, 201 F.3d 339 (5th Cir. 2002).
150. Other examples of express weighting are *Estate of Freeman v. Comm'r*, T.C. Memo. 1996-372 (1996) (court accepts IRS's 70 percent weighting of market approach and 30 percent of income approach, but the court accords no weight to taxpayer's value); and *Estate of Smith v. Comm'r*, T.C. Memo. 1999-368 (1999) (court accepts a 70/30 percent weighting to asset/income approaches, respectively).
151. Shannon Pratt et al., *Valuing a Business*, 3rd ed., Update to 5th Edition, 1996, p. 374.
152. For further discussion of this issue, see ch. "Weighting of Approaches," in David Laro and Shannon P. Pratt, *Business Valuation and Taxes: Procedure, Law, and Perspective*, Wiley, New York, 2005.
153. *Estate of Bruce v. Comm'r*, T.C. Memo. 1993-244 (1993).

154. *Estate of Furman v. Comm'r,* T.C. Memo. 1998-157 (1998). See also *Estate of Fleming v. Comm'r,* T.C. Memo. 1997-484 (1997); and *Buffalo Tool & Die Manufacturing Co. v. Comm'r*, 74 T.C. 441, 1980 WL 4569 (1980).

Chapter 20

1. See Model Bus. Corp. Act §14.30(2)(ii) (2002), available at http://www.abanet.org/buslaw/library/onlinepublications/mbca2002.pdf (providing that a shareholder may petition for dissolution when "the directors or those in control of the corporation have acted, are acting, or will act in a manner that is illegal, oppressive, or fraudulent").
2. *Nixon v. Blackwell,* 626 A.2d 1366, 1377 (Del. 1993).
3. See John H. Matheson and R. Kevin Maler, "A Simple Statutory Solution to Minority Oppression in the Closely Held Business," 91 *Minn. L. Rev.* 657, February 2007. (Based on its survey of the law in all 50 states, the article indicates that 20 states apply the reasonable expectations standard, 1 state uses reasonable expectations as a factor, and 12 states have adopted a fiduciary duty approach that, for the most part, is expansive and could be employed to reach the same result as the reasonable expectations standard.)
4. Id. at fn. 32 (indicating that about 40 states provide this remedy by statute or through case law).
5. See, for example, *Baker v. Commercial Body Builders,* 264 Ore. 614, 507 P.2d 387 (1973); and *Alaska Plastics, Inc. v. Coppock,* 621 P.2d 270 (Alas. 1980).
6. See, for example, *Landstrom v. Shaver,* 561 N.W.2d 1 (S.D. 1997); *Meiselman v. Meiselman,* 307 S.E.2d 551 (N.C. 1983); *Fox v. 7-L Bar Ranch Co.,* 645 P.2d 929 (Mont. 1982); *Mulenberg v. Bicon Corp.,* 669 A.2d 1382 (N.J. 1996); and *In re Kemp & Beatley, Inc.,* 473 N.E.2d 1173 (N.Y. 1984).
7. *Compton v. Paul K. Harding Realty Co.,* 285 N.E.2d 574 (Ill. Ct. App. 1972).
8. *Donahue v. Rodd Electrotype Co.,* 328 N.E.2d 505, 515 (Mass. 1975).
9. See, e.g., *Guy v. Duff & Phelps, Inc.,* 672 F. Supp. 1086, 1090 (N.D. Ill. 1987); *Orchard v. Covelli,* 590 F. Supp. 1548, 1556–59 (W.D. Pa. 1984); *W & W Equip. Co. v. Mink,* 568 N.E.2d 564, 570–571 (Ind. Ct. App. 1991); *Evans v. Blesi,* 345 N.W.2d 775, 779 (Minn. Ct. App. 1984); *Fought v. Morris,* 543 So. 2d 167, 170–171 (Miss. 1989); *Crosby v. Beam,* 548 N.E.2d 217, 220–221 (Ohio 1989); and *Estate of Schroer v. Stamco Supply, Inc.,* 482 N.E.2d 975, 981 (Ohio Ct. App. 1984).

10. See Douglas K. Moll, "Minority Oppression & The Limited Liability Company: Learning (or Not) from Close Corporation History," 40 *Wake Forest L Rev* 883, 925–940 (2005), which shows that the limitations imposed on limited liability companies by the new default withdrawal and dissolution provisions enacted after promulgation in late 1996 of the IRS "check the box" regulations (Treas Reg [26 CFR] §§ 301.7701-1 to 301.7701-3), were intentional and designed for estate and gift tax purposes "to minimize the tax value of an ownership interest" in an LLC "to reflect (1) that the interest is difficult to liquidate, and (2) that purchasers will generally pay less for illiquid positions." (40 *Wake Forest L Rev* at 936 [collecting authorities at 937–939].) "While perhaps accomplishing an estate tax goal, the elimination of default withdrawal and dissolution rights leaves minority members vulnerable to oppressive majority actions since the minority can no longer easily exit the venture with the value of its investment."
11. Model Business Corporation Act, § 13.01(4) (2002 ed.).
12. For a review of the standard of value for dissenters' rights and oppression actions in the 50 states, see Jay E. Fishman, Shannon P. Pratt, and William J. Morrison, *Standards of Value: Theory and Applications*, Wiley, New York, 2007, pp. 115–119. Please update this, Shannon says newer version out.
13. For a listing of states that have adopted some version of the RMBCA definition of fair value, see Jay E. Fishman, Shannon P. Pratt, et al., *PPC's Guide to Business Valuations,* 18th ed., Thomson Tax & Accounting, Houston, 2008, Ex. 15-1, "States That Have Adopted the RMBCA Definition of Fair Value," p. 15-5.
14. In *Matter of Shell Oil Co.*, 607 A.2d 1213 (Del. Sup. Ct. 1992).
15. *Weinberger v. UOP, Inc.*, 457 A.2d 701 (Del. 1983).
16. *Grimes v. Vitalink Communications Corp.*, 1997 Del. Ch. LEXIS 124, 1997 WL 538676 (Del. Ch. 1997). See also *Gholl v. eMachines, Inc.*, 2004 Del. Ch. LEXIS 171 (Del. Ch. 2004) ("This method is widely accepted in the financial community and has frequently been relied upon by this Court in appraisal actions"; *Andaloro v. PFPC Worldwide, Inc.*, 2005 Del. Ch. LEXIS 125 (Del. Ch. 2005) ("The DCF model of valuation is a standard one that gives life to the finance principle that firms should be valued based on the expected value of their future cash flows, discounted to present value in a manner that accounts for risk. The DCF method is frequently used in this

court and, I, like many others, prefer to give it great, and sometimes even exclusive, weight when it may be used responsibly"; *In re United States Cellular Operating Co.*, 2005 Del. Ch. LEXIS 1 (Del. Ch. 2005) ("While DCF analyses have become the dominant approach in appraisal proceedings . . . the ultimate selection of a valuation framework remains within the court's discretion."); *and In re PNB Holding Co.*, 2006 Del. Ch. LEXIS 158 (Del. Ch. 2006) (the court focused exclusively on the experts' DCF analyses); *Crescent/Mach I Partnership, L.P. v. Turner*, 2007 Del. Ch. LEXIS 63 (Del. Ch. 2007) (citing prior Delaware decisions, the court reiterated its preference for the DCF method and its general opinion that "other methodologies—all based on comparables of one form or another—are of limited value.")

17. *Weinberger v. UOP, Inc.*, 457 A.2d 701, 710 (Del. 1983).
18. See, e.g., *The Union Illinois 1995 Investment Limited Partnership v. Union Financial Group, Ltd.*, 847 A.2d 340 (Del. Ch. Dec. 19, 2003); *Doft & Co. v. Travelocity.com Inc.*, 2004 Del. Ch. LEXIS 75 (Del. Ch. 2004); *Finkelstein v. Liberty Digital, Inc.*, 2005 Del Ch. LEXIS 53 (Del. Ch. 2005); and *Highfields Capital, Ltd. v. AXA Financial, Inc.*, 2007 Del. Ch. LEXIS 126 (Del. Ch. 2007).
19. See *Bair v. Purcell*, 2008 U.S. Dist. LEXIS 6518 (M.D. Pa. 2008).
20. See, e.g., *Bell v. Kirby Lumber Corp.*, 413 A.2d 137 (Del. 1980); and *The Union Illinois 1995 Investment Limited Partnership v. Union Financial Group, Ltd.*, 847 A.2d 340 (Del. Ch. Dec. 19, 2003) (the fair value of the company's shares as of the merger date was the merger price minus any synergies).
21. See, e.g., *In re Valuation of Common Stock of McLoon Oil Co.*, 565 A.2d 997 (Me. 1989) ("Especially in fixing the appraisal remedy in a close corporation, the relevant inquiry is what is the highest price a single buyer would reasonably pay for the whole enterprise"); and *BNE Mass. Corp. v. Simms*, 588 N.E.2d 14 (Mass. App. Ct. 1992). The task assigned in *BNE Mass. Corp. v. Simms* under the appraisal statute was "not to reconstruct an 'intrinsic value' of each share of the enterprise but, rather, to determine what a willing buyer realistically would pay for the enterprise as a whole on the statutory valuation date. . . . Only in this fashion can minority stockholders be assured that insiders in control of a company, burdened by conflicting interests, may not purchase the enterprise at a price less than that obtainable in the marketplace of qualified buyers and avoid paying a full and fair price to the minority."

22. Jay E. Fishman, Shannon P. Pratt, and William J. Morrison, *Standards of Value: Theory and Applications*, 2nd ed., Wiley, New York, 2013, p. 122.
23. These states include *Alabama*—Ex parte Baron Service, Inc., 874 So.2d 545 (Ala. 2003); *California—Thompson v. Miller*, 2003 Cal. App. LEXIS 1489 (Cal. Ct. App. 2003); *Illinois—Jahn v. Kinderman*, 814 N.E.2d 116 (Ill. Ct. App. 2004); *Missouri—King v. F.T.J., Inc.*, 765 S.W.2d 301 (Mo. Ct. App. 1988); *Nevada—Steiner v. Benninghoff*, 5 F. Supp. 2d 1117 (1998); *New Mexico—McCauley v. Tom McCauley & Son, Inc.*, 724 P.2d 232 (N.M. Ct. App. 1986); and *North Carolina—Garlock v. Souteastern Gas & Power*, 2001 NCBC 10, 2001 NCBC LEXIS 9 (N.C. Super. 2001).
24. *Jahn v. Kinderman*, 814 N.E.2d 116 (Ill. Ct. App. 2004).
25. 615 N.W.2d 285, 292 (Minn. 2000)
26. American Law Institute, *Principles of Corporate Governance: Analysis and Recommendations*, American Law Institute, Philadelphia, 1992.
27. *Arizona—Pro Finish USA, Ltd. v. Johnson*, 63 P.3d 288 (Ariz. Ct. App. 2003); *Minnesota—Rain Forest Café, Inc. v. State of Wisconsin Inv. Bd.*, 677 N.W.2d 443 (Minn. Ct. App. 2004); *Advanced Communication Design, Inc. v. Follett*, 615 N.W.2d 285 (Minn. 2000); *New Jersey—Balsamides v. Protameen Chemicals, Inc.*, 734 A.2d 721 (N.J. 1999); *Lawson Mardon Wheaton, Inc. v. Smith*, 734 A.2d 738 (N.J. 1999); and *Utah—Hogle v. Zinetics Medical, Inc.*, 63 P.3d 80 (Utah 2002).
28. *Lawson Mardon Wheaton, Inc. v. Smith*, 734 A.2d 738 (N.J. 1999); and *Balsamides v. Protameen Chemicals Inc.*, 734 A.2d 721 (N.J., 1999).
29. *Cavalier Oil v. Harnett*, 564 A.2d 1137; 1989 Del. LEXIS 325 (Del. 1989).
30. *Connecticut*—Conn. Gen. Stat. § 33-855(4) (enacted 2002); *Florida*—Fla. Stat. §607.1301(4)(enacted 2006) (applies to corporations with 10 or fewer shareholders); *Idaho*—Idaho Code §30-1-1301 (enacted 2004); *Iowa*—Iowa Code § 490.1301(4) (enacted 2002); *Maine*—13-C Maine Rev. Stat. § 1301(4) (enacted 2003); *Mississippi*—Miss. Code Ann. § 79-4-13.01(4) (enacted 2007); *South Dakota*—S.D. Codified Laws § 47-1A-1301 (enacted 2005); *Virginia*—Va. Code Ann. § 13.1-729 (enacted 2005); and *West Virginia*—W. Va. Code § 31D-13-1301(4) (enacted 2002).
31. For a list of states and cases that reject discounts, see Jay E. Fishman, Shannon P. Pratt, and William J. Morrison, *Standards of Value: Theory and Applications*, Wiley, New York, 2007, ex. 3.7, "Cases Rejecting Discounts", pp. 139–142.
32. *Sieg Co. v. Kelly*, 568 N.W.2d 794 (Iowa 1997).

33. *Pueblo Bancorporation v. Lindoe, Inc.*, 37 P.3d 492 (Colo. 2003).
34. *Brown v. Arp and Hammond Hardware Co.*, 141 P.3d 673 (Wyo. 2006).
35. 630 P.2d 167 (Kan. 1981).
36. *Arnaud v. Stockgrowers State Bank of Ashland*, 992 P.2d 216, 1999 Kan. LEXIS 645 (1999).
37. *Hansen v. 75 Ranch Co.*, 957 P.2d 32 (Mont. 1998).
38. *McCann Ranch, Inc. v. Quigley-McCann*, 915 P.2d 239 (Mont. 1996).
39. See, e.g., *Ford v. Courier-Journal Job Printing Co.*, 639 S.W.2d 553, (Ky. Ct. App. 1982); and *In re Brooklyn Home Dialysis Training Center, Inc.*, 741 N.Y.S.2d 280 (N.Y. App. Div. 2002).
40. See, e.g., *Shopf v. Marina Del Ray Partnership*, 549 So. 2d 833 (La. 1989) (in determining "fair cash value," the "fair value" equivalent in Louisiana, the court permitted the application of a discount for lack of control to a 12 percent minority interest).
41. See, e.g., *English v. Atromick Int'l Inc.*, 2000 Ohio App. LEXIS 3580 (Ohio Ct. App. 2000). In determining "fair cash value," the "fair value" equivalent in Ohio, the court applied the willing buyer/willing seller approach and determined that both marketability and minority discounts were appropriate.
42. *Rapid-Americn Corp. v. Harris*, 603 A.2d 796 (Del. 1992).
43. *Hintmann v. Fred Weber, Inc.*, 1998 Del. Ch. LEXIS 26 1998 WL 853052 (Del. Ch. 1998).
44. Gilbert E. Matthews, "Delaware Court Adds Control Premium to Subsidiary Value," *Shannon Pratt's Business Valuation Update*, May 1998, at 9–10; and "A Review of Valuations in Delaware Appraisal Cases, 2004–2005," *Business Valuation Review*, vol. 25, no. 2 (Summer 2006).
45. *Borruso v. Communications Telesystems International*, 1999 Del. Ch. LEXIS 197 (1999).
46. *Doft & Co. v. Travelocity.com, Inc.*, 2004 Del. Ch. LEXIS 75 (Del. Ch. 2004).
47. *In re Valuation of Common Stock of Penobscot Shoe Company*, 2003 Me. Super. LEXIS 140 (Me. Super. 2003).
48. *Northwest Investment Corp. v. Wallace*, 2007 Iowa Sup. LEXIS 87 (Iowa 2007).
49. See *Estate of Davis v. Commissioner*, 110 TC 530 (T.C. 1998); *Estate of Jameson v. Commissioner*, T.C. Memo. 1999-43, 77 T.C.M. (CCH) 1383 (T.C. 1999); and *Estate of Eisenberg v. Commissioner*, T.C. Memo. 1997-483, 74 T.C.M. (CCH) 1046 (T.C. 1997).

50. *Matthew G. Norton Co. v. Smyth*, 112 Wn. App. 865, 51 P.3d 159 (Wash. Ct. App. 2002).
51. *Brown v. Arp and Hammond Hardware Co.*, 141 P.3d 673 (Wyo. 2006).
52. *Seagraves v. Urstadt Property Co.*, 1996 Del. Ch. LEXIS 36, 1996 WL 159626 (Del. Ch. 1996).
53. *Kahn v. Tremont Corp.*, 694 A.2d 422, 429 (Del. 1997).
54. *Ryan v. Tad's Enterprises*, 709 A.2d 682 (Del. Ch. 1996).
55. *M.G. Bancorporation v. Le Beau*, 737 A.2d 513 (Del. 1999).
56. *Weinberger v. UOP, Inc.*, 457 A.2d 701 (Del. 1983).
57. *Gesoff v. IIC Industries, Inc.*, 902 A.2d 1130 (Del. Ch. 2006).
58. *In re Slant/Fin Corp.*, 236 A.D.2d 547, 654 N.Y.S.2d 627 (N.Y. App. Div. 1997).
59. *Pueblo Bancorporation v. Lindoe, Inc.*, 63 P.3d 353 (Colo. 2003).
60. See *Lawson Mardon Wheaton, Inc., v. Smith*, 716 A.2d 550, 558 (N.J. Super. App. Div. 1998), aff'd, 734 A.2d 738 (N.J. 1999). "Fair Value carries with it the statutory purposes that shareholders be fairly compensated, which may or may not equate with the market's judgment about the stock's value. This is particularly appropriate in the close corporation setting where there is no ready market for the shares and consequently no Fair Market Value."
61. See, e.g., *Swope v. Seigel-Robert, Inc.*, 243 F.3d 486, 2001 U.S. App. LEXIS 2760 (8th Cir. 2001); *Wenzel v. Hopper & Galliher, P.C.*, 779 N.E.2d 30, (Ind. Ct. App. 2002); *First W. Bank Wall v. Olsen*, 2001 SD 16, 621 N.W.2d 611, (S.D. 2001); *Matthew G. Norton Co. v. Smyth*, 112 Wn. App. 865, 51 P.3d 159 (Wash. Ct. App. 2002); and *HMO-W, Inc. v. SSM Health Care Sys.*, 2000 WI 46, 234 Wis. 2d 707, 611 N.W.2d 250 (Wis. 2000).
62. *Bair v. Purcell*, 2008 U.S. Dist. LEXIS 6518 (M.D. Pa. 2008).
63. *Cox Enterprises, Inc. v. News-Journal Corp.*, 2007 U.S. App. LEXIS 29533 (11th Cir. 2007).
64. *Oakridge Energy Inc. v. Clifton*, 937 P.2d 130 (Utah 1997).
65. *Pueblo Bancorporation v. Lindoe, Inc.*, 63 P.3d 353 (Colo. 2003).
66. *Berens v. Ludwig*, 160 F.3d 1144 (7th Cir. 1998).
67. *Riddle-Bradley, Inc. v. Riddle*, 459 S.E.2d 576 (Ga. Ct. App. 1995).

Chapter 21

1. See, e.g., *Bobrow v. Bobrow*, State of Indiana, Hamilton Superior Court Case No. 29D01-0003-DR-166; *Howell v. Howell*, 1998 WL 972312 (Va. Cir. Ct. Sept. 4, 1998), aff'd 523 S.E.2d 514 (Va. Ct. App. 2000).

2. A.C.A. Section 9-12-315(4) (2008).
3. La. R.S. Section 9:2801-(1)(a) (2008).
4. See, e.g., *Golden v. Golden*, 270 Cal. App. 2d 401, 1969 Cal. App. LEXIS 1538 (Cal. Ct. App. 1969). In a community property state, the spouse's contribution to the intangible value of the other spouse's business is treated as an investment in stock.
5. For definitions and discussion of various standards of value, see Shannon Pratt and Alina V. Niculita, *Valuing a Business*, 5th ed., McGraw-Hill, New York, 2008, pp. 29–54, and Jay Fishman et al., *Standards of Valuation: Theory and Applications*, 2nd ed., John Wiley, New York, 2013, 2007.
6. Alan S. Zipp, "Business Valuation Standard for Divorce Is Different from Fair Market Value," *American Journal of Family Law*, Fall 1997, pp. 167–172; Alan S. Zipp, "Fair Value as a Basis for Business Valuation in Divorce," in ch. 5, "Fair Value in Marital Dissolution," *BVR's Guide to Fair Value in Shareholder Dissent, Oppression, and Marital Dissolution*, Business Valuation Resources, Portland, OR, 2007.
7. David M. Bishop and Steven F. Schroeder, "Business Valuation Standard of Value for Divorce Should Be Fair Market Value," *American Journal of Family Law*, Spring 1999, pp. 48–52.
8. See, e.g., Robert Kleeman, Jr., "Fair Value Versus Fair Market Value: Is There a Place for Fair Value in Marital Dissolution?" in ch. 5, "Fair Value in Marital Dissolution," *BVR's Guide to Fair Value in Shareholder Dissent, Oppression, and Marital Dissolution*, Business Valuation Resources, Portland, OR, 2007.
9. *Antolik v. Harvey*, 761 P.2d 305 (Haw. Ct. App. 1988).
10. *Liddle v. Liddle*, 410 N.W.2d 196, 199 (Wis. Ct. App. 1987), cited in *Sommerfield v. Sommerfield*, 454 N.W.2d 55 (Wis. Ct. App. 1990).
11. *Liddle v. Liddle.*
12. *Sommers v. Sommers*, 660 N.W.2d 586, 2003 ND 77 (N.D. 2003).
13. *Bausano v. Bausano*, 632 N.W.2d 123, 246 Wis.2d 987 (Wis. Ct. App. 2001).
14. *Hoverson v. Hoverson*, 629 N.W.2d 573, 2001 N.D. 124 (N.D. 2001).
15. See, e.g., *Baum v. Baum*, 584 P.2d 604 (Ariz. Ct. App. 1978).
16. See, e.g., *Brown v. Brown*, 913 S.W.2d 163 (Tenn. Ct. App. 1994).
17. See, e.g., *Scottson v. Scottson*, 1995 WL 550925 (Minn. Ct. App. 1995).
18. In *Conway v. Conway*, 1998 WL 865157 (N.C. Ct. App. 1998), the court ruled that to demonstrate active appreciation of separate property, there must be a showing of the value of the asset at the time of the acquisition; the

value of the asset at the time of separation; and the difference between the two values. Applying these criteria, the court determined that whereas marital efforts had led to the acquisition of a medical license, it did not result in the appreciation of the license's value. In *Deffenbaugh v. Deffenbaugh*, 877 S.W.2d 186 (Mo. Ct. App. 1994), the Missouri court held that where the husband failed to prove that his acumen and effort contributed to the appreciation in the wife's separate mutual fund shares, the appreciation was nonmarital property.

19. See, e.g., *Hargrave v. Hargrave*, 209 Cal. Rptr. 764, 769 (Cal. Ct. App. 1985); *Aufmuth v. Aufmuth*, 152 Cal. Rptr. 668, 670 (Cal. Ct. App. 1979); *Moffitt v. Moffitt*, 813 P.2d 674, 678 (Alaska 1991); *Ogard v. Ogard*, 808 P.2d 815, 818–819 (Alaska 1991); *Taylor v. Taylor*, 736 S.W.2d 388, 391 (Mo. 1987); and *Butler v. Butler*, No. 82077, 1998 WL 933354, at *2 (N.Y. App. Div. Dec. 30, 1998).
20. For example, *In re Marriage of Olinger*, 707 P.2d 64, 68 (Or. Ct. App. 1985); *Koch v. Koch*, 874 S.W.2d 571, 576 (Tenn. Ct. App. 1993); *Wilson v. Wilson*, 741 S.W.2d 640, 643 (Ark. 1987); *In re Marriage of Talty*, 623 N.E.2d 1041, 1046 (Ill. App. Ct. 1993); *In re Marriage of Thomas*, 608 N.E.2d 585, 587 (Ill. App. Ct. 1993); *In re Marriage of Lopez*, 841 P.2d 1122, 1125 (Mont. 1992); *In re Marriage of Swanson*, 716 P.2d 219, 222 (Mont. 1986); *Vivian v. Vivian*, 583 P.2d 1072, 1074 (Mont. 1978); *In re Marriage of Wagner*, 679 P.2d 753, 758 (Mont. 1984); *Dunn v. Dunn*, 802 P.2d 1314, 1320 (Utah Ct. App. 1990); *Sommerfield* 454 N.W.2d at 60; and *Skokos v. Skokos*, 40 S.W.3rd 768 (Ark. 2001).
21. *Mallett v. Mallett*, 473 S.E.2d 804, 810 (S.C. Ct. App. 1996); *Hickum v. Hickum*, 463 S.E.2d 321, 323 (S.C. Ct. App. 1995); *Hillebrand v. Hillebrand*, 546 A.2d 1047, 1049 (N.H. 1988); *Rosenberg v. Rosenberg*, 510 N.Y.S.2d 659, 662 (App. Div. 1987); *Muller v. Muller*, 456 N.Y.S.2d 918, 922 (Sup. Ct. 1982); and *Siegel v. Siegel*, 523 N.Y.S.2d 517, 520 (App. Div. 1987) (because possibility of dissipation of corporate assets existed). But see *Scharfman v. Scharfman*, 2005 N.Y. App. Div. LEXIS 6584 (N.Y. App. Div. 2005). The appellate court rejected the trial court's acceptance of the date of filing as the valuation date over the trial date where there was no evidence that the husband's efforts caused the appreciation in value of the marital property.
22. *Kilbourne v. Kilbourne*, 284 Cal. Rptr. 201, 204 (Cal. Ct. App. 1991); *Moffitt*, 813 P.2d at 678; *Ogard*, 808 P.2d at 818–819; *Richmond v. Richmond*, 779 P.2d 1211, 1214 (Alaska 1989); *Carlson v. Carlson*, 487 S.E.2d 784, 786 (N.C.

Ct. App. 1997); *Bergeland v. Bergeland*, 2000 Minn. App. LEXIS 952, 2000 WL 1239754 (Minn. Ct. App. 2000); *In re Marriage of Rubens*, 2003 Wash. App. LEXIS 1544 (Wash. Ct. App. 2003); and *Morton v. Morton*, 2005 M. Ch. App. LEXIS 1406 (Mich. Ct. App. 2005). But see, e.g., *Washington v. Washington*, 2005 Va. App. LEXIS 177 (Va. App. 2005) in which the court rejected the date of separation, instead of the date of evidentiary hearing, which occurred two years after the separation, where the husband's business increased in value over the two years but the husband did not present evidence that this increase was the result of his extraordinary efforts.

23. *Scalero v. Scalero*, 1998 WL 23845, at *3 (Ohio Ct. App. 1998); *Wallace v. Wallace*, 733 S.W.2d 102, 106 (Tenn. Ct. App. 1987); *Reese v. Reese*, 671 N.E.2d 187, 191 (Ind. Ct. App. 1996); and *Favell v. Favell*, 957 P.2d 556, 462 (Okla. Ct. App. 1997).
24. *Green v. Green*, 1998 WL 363840, at *3 (Ohio Ct. App. 1998); and *Quillen v. Quillen*, 671 N.E.2d 98 (Ind. 1996).
25. For an extensive discussion of goodwill valuation issues, see Noah J. Gordon, "Goodwill Valuation in the Courts," ch. 2, *BVR's Guide to Personal v. Enterprise Goodwill*, Business Valuation Resources, Portland, OR, 2008.
26. Available from Business Valuation Resources at www.bvlibrary.com.
27. *Lopez v. Lopez*, 38 Cal. App.3d 93, 113 Cal. Rptr. 58 (Cal. Ct. App. 1974).
28. For cases using similar factors, see, e.g., *In re Marriage of Fleege*, 91 Wash. 2d 324, 588 P.2d 1136 (Wash. 1979); and *Crosetto v. Crosetto*, 1996 WL 389337 (Wash. App. 1996).
29. *Hanson v. Hanson*, 738 S.W.2d 429 (Mo. 1987).
30. *May v. May*, 2003 W. Va. LEXIS 118 (W. Va. 2003). See also *Nowzaradan v. Nowzaradan*, 2007 Tex. App. LEXIS 1021 (Tex. App. 2007); *Thompson v. Thompson*, 576 So. 2d 267 (Fla. 1991).
31. *Stewart v. Stewart*, 2007 Ida. LEXIS 17 (Idaho 2007).
32. See also *Gaskill v. Robbins*, 2006 Ky. App. LEXIS 364 (Ky. Ct. App. 2006), in which the court ruled that it would be inequitable to hold that the form of the business enterprise can defeat the community's interest in professional goodwill since such a result ignores the contribution made by the nonprofessional spouse to the success of the professional; *Bunkers v. Bunkers*, 2007 Ohio App. LEXIS 523 (Ohio Ct. App. 2007), in which the court ruled that all goodwill of a solo practitioner is subject to equitable division in divorce.
33. *Yoon v. Yoon*, 711 N.E.2d 1265 (Ind. 1999).

34. State of Indiana, Hamilton Superior Court Cause No. 29D01-0003-DR-166.
35. *In re Marriage of Alexander,* 2006 Ill. App. LEXIS 836 (Ill. Ct. App. 2006); and *Neary v. Neary,* Case No. 06-DR-3254 (18th Cir., Seminole, Fla.).
36. See, e.g., *May v. May,* 2003 W. Va. LEXIS 118 (W. Va. 2003).
37. See, e.g., *In re* Marriage of Ackerman, 2006 Cal. App. LEXIS 2056 (Cal. Ct. App. 2006).
38. *Gaydos v. Gaydos,* 693 A.2d 1368 (Pa. Super. Ct. 1997).
39. See *Holbrook v. Holbrook,* 103 Wis. 2d 327, 309 N.W.2d 343, 1981 Wis. App. LEXIS 3322 (Wis. Ct. App. 1981): "The concept of professional goodwill evanesces when one attempts to distinguish it from future earning capacity"; *Donahue v. Donahue,* 299 S.C. 353, 384 S.E.2d 741 (S.C. 1989); and *Hickum v. Hickum,* 463 S.E.2d 321 (S.C. Ct. App. 1995).
40. *Peerenboom v. Peerenboom,* 433 N.W.2d 282 (Wis. Ct. App. 1988).
41. See, e.g., *In re* Bookout, 833 P.2d 800 (Colo. Ct. App. 1991), cert. denied, 846 P.2d 189 (Colo. 1993); and *In re* Hall, 103 Wn.2d 236, 692 P.2d 175 (Wash. 1984).
42. *Golub v. Golub,* 139 Misc. 2d 440, 527 N.Y.S.2d 946 (N.Y. Sup. Ct. 1988); and *Elkus v. Elkus,* 169 A.D.2d 134, 572 N.Y.S.2d 901 (N.Y. App. Div. 1991).
43. *Piscopo v. Piscopo,* 232 N.J. Super. 559, 557 A.2d 1040 (N.J. Super. Ct. 1989).
44. *O'Brien v. O'Brien,* 489 N.E.2d 712, 66 N.Y.2d 576, 498 N.Y.S.2d 743 (N.Y. 1985).
45. See, e.g., *In re* Marriage of Monaghan, 899 P.2d 841 (Wash. Ct. App. 1995), which held that a covenant not to compete is the personal property of the practitioner; *Kricsfeld v. Kricsfeld,* 588 N.W.2d 210, 8 Neb. App. 1 (Neb. Ct. App 1999), which held that a noncompete agreement is personal to the practitioner and can never be a marital asset; *Held v. Held,* 2005 Fla. App. LEXIS 14138 (Fla. Ct. App. 2005), which held that for the purpose of distinguishing enterprise goodwill from personal goodwill in the valuation of a business, there is no distinction between a "non-solicitation/non-piracy agreement" and a covenant not to compete, which is attributable to the personal reputation of the seller-spouse and not to the enterprise goodwill of the business; and *Sweere v. Gilbert-Sweere,* 534 N.W.2d 294, 1995 Minn. App. Lexis 912 (Minn. Ct. App. 1995), which held that to the extent that the purpose of a noncompete agreement is to prevent the spouse from interfering with the transfer of goodwill, the agreement is representative of marital goodwill.
46. *In re* Marriage of King, 197 Cal. Rptr. 716 (Cal. Ct. App. 1983).

47. Shannon Pratt with Alina Niculita, *Valuing a Business: The Analysis and Appraisal of Closely Held Companies,* McGraw-Hill, New York, 2008, pp. 971–972.
48. See Shannon Pratt, "Contradictions in Family Law Cases," *Judges & Lawyers Business Valuation Update*, December 1999, pp. 1, 4–5. See also, e.g., *Poore v. Poore*, 75 N.C. App. 414, 331 S.E.2d 266 (N.C. Ct. App. 1985), which lists as acceptable methods the following:
    - The price a willing buyer would pay
    - Capitalization of excess earnings
    - One year's average gross income
    - Evidence of sales of comparable practices

    All of these imply continued participation to some degree, or a noncompete agreement.
49. See, e.g., *Rosenberg v. Rosenberg*, 510 N.Y.S.2d 659, 662 (App. Div. 1987); *Hertz v. Hertz*, 657 P.2d 1169, 1174–75 (N.M. 1983); and *Johnson v. Johnson*, 771 P.2d 696, 698 (Utah Ct. App. 1989).
50. *In re* Marriage of Brooks, 756 P.2d 161 (Wash. Ct. App. 1988). See also *In re Matter of Overbey,* 2007 Wash. App. LEXIS 1651 (Wash. Ct. App. 2007), which continued this state's approach and indicated that a buy-sell agreement was not a binding separation contract, and that while the formula contained therein was relevant, it was not determinative of the company's value.
51. See, e.g., *In re* Marriage of Herlitzke, 2006 Wis. App. LEXIS 972 (Wis. Ct. App. 2006), which held that the buy-sell agreement may establish the fair market value of a partnership or S corporation, but it does not do so as a matter of law; *Herron v. Herron*, 2004 Ohio App. LEXIS 5209 (Ohio Ct. App. 2004), in which the court gave weight to the closely held company's buy-sell agreement because "[a]ny willing buyer would certainly take into account the buy/sell agreement before making any offer on the stock"; *R.V.K. v. L.L.K,* 2002 WL 31421572 (Tex. Ct. App. 2002); *Harmon v. Harmon*, 2000 WL 286718 (Tenn. Ct. App. 2000); and *Howell v. Howell*, 46 Va. Cir. 339; 1998 Va. Cir. LEXIS 256 (Va. Cir. Ct. 1998), aff'd, 31 Va. App. 332, 523 S.E.2d 514 (Va. Ct. App. 2000).
52. *In re* Marriage of Dieger, 584 N.W.2d 567 (Iowa Ct. App. 1998).
53. *Berenberg v. Berenberg*, 474 N.W.2d 843 (Minn. Ct. App. 1991).
54. *Lyon v. Lyon*, 439 N.W.2d 18 (Minn. 1989).

55. *Bettinger v. Bettinger*, 396 S.E.2d 709 (W. Va. 1990). See also *Barton v. Barton*, 2007 Ga. LEXIS 21 (Ga. 2007), in which the Georgia Supreme Court joined the clear majority of states on this issue and held that the value of stock set forth in a buy-sell agreement for a closely held corporation is not binding for purposes of property division in divorce proceedings. The court reasoned that "the buy-sell price in a closely held corporation can be manipulated and does not necessarily reflect true market value."
56. *In re* Marriage of Gillespie, 948 P.2d 1338 (Wash. Ct. App. 1997).
57. See, e.g., *In re* Marriage of Monaghan, 899 P.2d 841 (Wash. Ct. App. 1995), which said that the portion of the sale price attributable to covenant is the husband's separate property); *Kricsfeld v. Kricsfeld*, 588 N.W.2d 210, 1999 Neb. App. LEXIS 1 (Neb. Ct. App. 1999); *Ellerbe v. Ellerbe*, 323 S.C. 283, 473 S.E.2d 881 (S.C. Ct. App. 1996); *Cutsinger v. Cutsinger*, 917 S.W.2d 238 (Tenn. Ct. App. 1995), in which the court excluded monetary amounts for covenant not to compete from the purchase price of the chiropractic practice; *Hoeft v. Hoeft*, 74 Ohio App. 3d 809, 600 N.E.2d 746 (Ohio Ct. App. 1991), in which the court determined that while proceeds received for the sale of the husband's dental practice were marital property, monies received from a covenant not to compete were nonmarital; *Johnston v. Johnston*, 778 S.W.2d 674 (Mo. Ct. App. 1989), in which the covenant not to compete was properly excluded in the valuation of the dental practice; *Donahue v. Donahue*, 299 S.C. 353, 384 S.E.2d 741 (1989), which said that the goodwill of a professional practice is not subject to equitable distribution; and *Lucas v. Lucas*, 621 P.2d 500 (N.M. 1980), which said that the right to compete is a personal right and the separate property of its owner.
58. *Reese v. Reese*, 671 N.E.2d 187 (Ind. Ct. App. 1996); and *Sweere v. Gilbert-Sweere*, 534 N.W.2d 294, 1995 Minn. App. Lexis 912 (Minn. Ct. App. 1995), which said that to the extent that the purpose of a noncompete agreement is to prevent the spouse from interfering with the transfer of goodwill, the agreement is representative of marital goodwill.
59. *Duncan v. Duncan*, 90 Cal. App. 4th 617 (Cal. Ct. App. 2001).
60. The database Pratt's Stats (see ch. 3) shows how much was allocated to a covenant not to compete when one was involved in the sale of a business or practice.
61. *Hayes v. Hayes*, 756 P.2d 298 (Alaska, 1988).
62. *In re* Marriage of Harrington, 935 P.2d 1357 (Wash. Ct. App. 1997).

63. See, e.g., *Priebe v. Priebe*, 556 N.W.2d 78 (S.D. 1996) (40 percent); *In re* Marriage of DeCosse, 936 P.2d 821, 1997 WL 19374 (Mont. 1997) (20 percent); *Arneson v. Arneson*, 355 N.W. 2d 16 (Wis. Ct. App. 1984) (25 percent); *Rattee v. Rattee*, 767 A. 2d 415, 146 N.H. 44 (N.H. 2001); *L.R.M. v. R.K.M.*, 46 S.W.3d 24 (Mo. Ct. App. 2001) (32 percent combined discount); and *Anderson v. Anderson*, 2006 Tenn. App. LEXIS 592 (Tenn. App. 2006) (38.3 percent).
64. See, e.g., *Howell v. Howell*, 46 Va. Cir. 339, 1998 Va. Cir. LEXIS 256 (Va. Cir. Ct. 1998), aff'd, 31 Va. App. 332, 523 S.E.2d 514 (Va. Ct. App. 2000); *Oatey v. Oatey*, No. 67809, 67973 Ohio Ct. App., 1996 WL 200273 at *22 (Apr. 25, 1996); *Nardini v. Nardini*, 414 N.W. 2d 184, 189 (Minn. 1987); *Cross v. Cross*, 586 P.2d 547, 549 (Wyo. 1978); *Ferraro v. Ferraro*, 2000 WL 251678 (Va. Ct. App. 2000); *Brown v. Brown*, 348 N.J. Super. 466, 792 A.2d 463, 2002 N.J. Super. LEXIS 105 (N.J. Super. 2002), in which discounts were disallowed absent extraordinary circumstances; *Baltrusis v. Baltrusis*, 113 Wash. App. 1037 (Wash. Ct. App. 2002); and *Hanson v. Hanson*, 2005 Alas. LEXIS 166 (Alaska 2005), in which there was no discount where the majority spouse acquires the minority spouse's interest.
65. See, e.g., *In re* Marriage of Tofte, 895 P.2d 1387, 1392 (Or. Ct. App. 1995) (35 percent); *Ellis v. Ellis*, No. 77407 N.Y. App. Div., 1997 WL 35218 at *2 (Jan. 30, 1997) (25 percent); *Michael v. Michael*, 469 S.E.2d 14, 17 (W. Va. 1996) (25 percent); *Kapp v. Kapp*, 2005 Ohio App. LEXIS 6144 (Ohio App. 2005), in which the litigation contingency discount was accepted where proof of a pending lawsuit was presented; *Rattee v. Rattee*, 767 A.2d 415, 146 N.H. 44 (N.H. 2001); *L.R.M. v. R.K.M.*, 46 S.W.3d 24 (Mo. Ct. App. 2001) (32 percent combined discount); and *Collier v. Collier*, 790 So. 2d 759 (La. Ct. App. 2001) (25 percent combined discount for lack of marketability and contingent liabilities).
66. See, e.g., *Howell v. Howell* (no amount specified); *Neuman v. Neuman*, 842 P.2d 575, 579 (Wyo. 1992) (35 percent); *Hanson v. Hanson*, 86 P.3d 94, 192 Or. App. 422 (Or. Ct. App. 2004) (25 percent); *Brown v. Brown*, 348 N.J. Super. 466, 792 A.2d 463, 2002 N.J. Super. LEXIS 105 (N.J. Super. 2002); *Baltrusis v. Baltrusis*, 113 Wash. App. 1037 (Wash. Ct. App. 2002) (25 percent); *Ferraro v. Ferraro*, 2000 WL 251678 (Va. Ct. App. 2000); *Anderson v. Anderson*, 2006 Tenn. App. LEXIS 592 (Tenn. App. 2006) (10 percent for marketing costs associated with only a hypothetical sale of minority interest); *Hanson v. Hanson*, 2005 Alas. LEXIS 166 (Alaska 2005); *Kapp v. Kapp*, 2005 Ohio App.

LEXIS 6144 (Ohio App. 2005) (no discount for contingent transaction costs—broker, legal, accounting fees—where no sale is being contemplated); and *Bertuca v. Bertuca*, 2007 Tenn. App. LEXIS 690 (Tenn. Ct. App. 2007) (discount disallowed where a sale of the husband's interest was not "necessary or desirable").

67. *Erp v. Erp, 2007 Fla. App. LEXIS 18726 (Fla. Ct. App. 2007).*
68. Extensive references to treatment of tax consequences can be found in Tracy A. Bateman, *Divorce and Separation: Consideration of Tax Consequences in Distribution of Marital Property* 9, A.L.R. 5th, p. 568, 2000, Lawyers Cooperative Publishing.
69. See, e.g., *Buzanell v. Miller*, 590 S.E.2d 332, 162 N.C. App. 180, 2004 WL 26524 (N.C. Ct. App. 2004) (consideration of taxes too speculative); *In re* Marriage of Black, 2001 WL 57999 (Iowa Ct. App. 2001); *Guill v. Guill*, 2001 WL 770942 (Neb. Ct. App. 2001); *Skokos v. Skokos*, 40 S.W.3d 768, 344 Ark. 420 (Ark. 2001); *Kaiser v. Kaiser*, 555 N.W.2d 585 (N.D. 1996) (the deduction of hypothetical tax liabilities rejected); *In re* Marriage of Czapar, 232 Cal. App. 3d 1308, 284 Cal. Rptr. 41 (1991). It is improper to take into consideration the tax consequences of an order dividing a community asset unless the tax liability is immediate and specific and will arise in connection with the division of the community property.
70. *In re* Marriage of Hay, 907 P.2d 334 (Wash. Ct. App. 1995).
71. *Kaiser v. Kaiser*, 474 N.W.2d 63 (N.D. 1991).
72. *Granger v. Granger*, 579 N.E.2d 1319 (Ind. Ct. App. 1991).
73. *Bohl v. Bohl*, 657 P.2d 1106 (Kans. 1983). The court's reasoning seems flawed in that there is nothing inherent in valuing something at expected net liquidation proceeds that would always necessarily reduce that amount to or below cost. In any case, cost is historical and (except for its effect on taxes) irrelevant to the matter of monies available now or in the future.
74. *Liddle v. Liddle*, 410 N.W.2d 196 (Wis. Ct. App. 1987).
75. *Hogan v. Hogan*, 796 S.W.2d 400 (Mo. Ct. App. 1990).
76. *Hamilton v. Hamilton*, 2002 Ohio 2417 (Ohio Ct. App. 2002).
77. See, e.g., *Schuman v. Schuman*, 658 N.W.2d 30, 265 Neb. 459 (Neb. 2003).
78. See Shannon P. Pratt, "Trapped-In Capital Gains Affects Real-World Value," *Shannon Pratt's Business Valuation Update*, February 1996, pp. 1, 3.
79. See, e.g., *Zerbe v. Zerbe*, 2005 Ohio 1180 (Ohio Ct. App. 2005) ("A finding of value must be supported by competent, credible evidence. The court cannot take the two extremes presented by the evidence and choose a

value somewhere between those two extremes."); *Augoshe v. Lehman*, 2007 Fla. App. LEXIS 6367 (Fla. Ct. App. 2007) ("simply splitting the difference" between two divergent appraisals is an "improper method of valuation"); *In re* Marriage of Keener, 2007 Iowa Sup. LEXIS 13 (Iowa 2007) ("anecdotal evidence is simply an insufficient basis upon which to determine fair market value"); and *Pickard v. Pickard*, 2006 N.Y. App. Div. LEXIS 9961 (N.Y. App. Div. 2006) (the discount rate was rejected where the rate was selected arbitrarily without support for it).

80. See, e.g., *Crosetto v. Crosetto*, 918 P.2d 954 (Wash. App. Ct. 1996), in which the court said, "Because the trial court here did not state how it reached the valuation figure, we remand. . . ."
81. See, e.g., *In re* Marriage of Bidwell, 12 P.3d 76, 170 Or. App. 239 (Or. Ct. App. 2000) (the court accepted the wife's expert's opinion over the husband's because the husband had not presented expert evidence); *In re* Marriage of Gabriel, 2005 Cal. App. Unpub. LEXIS 8101 (Cal. Ct. App. 2005); *Miller v. Miller*, 14 S.W.3d 903, 70 Ark. App. 64 (Ark. Ct. App. 2000); *Ballas v. Ballas*, 2004 Ohio 5128, 2004 WL 2334329 (Ohio App. 7 Dist. 2004) (the expert's opinion was given greater weight than that of the business manager); *Dunn v. Dunn*, 2005 Miss. App. LEXIS 637 (Miss. Ct. App. 2005) (appeals by both spouses were unavailing where neither had hired a business valuation expert); and *Mace v. Mace*, 818 So. 2d 1130 (Miss. 2002) (where neither spouse hired a business valuation expert, the court recommended that they provide expert valuation evidence on remand).
82. See, e.g., *Weinstein v. Weinstein*, 2005 Conn. LEXIS 348 (Conn. 2005) (the husband's failure to disclose the true value of his company's intellectual property resulted in a finding of blatant and deliberate misrepresentation and reversal); and *Stribling v. Stribling*, 2005 Miss. App. LEXIS 58 (Miss. Ct. App. 2005) (where "a party fails to provide accurate information, or cooperate in the valuation of assets," the trial court is "entitled to proceed on the best information available").
83. *Eslami v. Eslami*, 591 A.2d 411 (Conn. 1991).
84. *Steneken v Steneken*, 843 A.2d 344 (N.J. App. 2004), aff'd, 873 A.2d 501, 183 N.J. 290 (N.J. 2005).
85. *Sampson v. Sampson*, 2004 Mass. App. LEXIS 1223 (Mass. App. Ct. 2004).
86. *Champion v. Champion*, 54 Mass. App. Ct. 215, 764 N.E.2d 898, 2002 Mass. App. LEXIS 363 (Mass. App. Ct. 2002).

87. *Keane v. Keane*, 2006 N.Y. LEXIS 3751 (N.Y. 2006).
88. *Sander v. Sander*, 2006 Conn. App. LEXIS 280 (Conn. Ct. App. 2006).

Chapter 22

1. Proposed DOL Reg. Section 2510.3-18(b)(1)(ii).
2. *Donovan v. Cunningham*, 716 F.2d 1455 (5th Cir. 1983). See also *Barker v. American Mobil Power Corporation*, 64 F.3d 1397 (9th Cir. 1995) and *Pugh v. Tribune*, Nos. 06-3898 and 06-3899 (7th Cir. 2008).
3. Shannon P. Pratt, and Alina V. Niculita, *Valuing a Business*, 5th ed., McGraw Hill, New York, 2007, p. 814.
4. This guideline considers changes enacted under the Small Business Job Protection Act of 1996 (SBJPA) P. L. 104–188 (see 4.4.2); the Taxpayer Relief Act of 1997 (TRA) P. L. 105–34 (see 4.2.7); the Economic Growth and Tax Relief Reconciliation Act of 2001 (EGTRRA) P.L. 107-16; and the American Job Creation Act of 2004 (AJCA) P.L. 108-173 (see 4.2.4). Additional guidance pertaining to the examination of both leveraged and nonleveraged ESOPs, including IRC Section 1042 transfers, the partial interest exclusion, and special rules pertaining to Sub S ESOPs can be found at http://www.irs.gov/ustreas/pub/irs-tege/epche80.
5. See ESOP Association, *Valuing ESOP Shares*, ESOP Association, Washington DC, 2005.
6. IRC Section 409(h)(1)(A) and (B).
7. Rev. Proc. 2004-14.
8. In *Armstrong v. LaSalle Bank National Association*, 446 F.3d 728 (7th Cir. 2006), Judge Posner reversed the trial court's award of summary judgment in favor of the defendant trustee's decision to accept a stock valuation that did not include a discount for lack of marketability. The decision appears to confirm the need to consider this discount, but not the extent.
9. *ESOP Valuation*, 3rd ed., NCEO, 2005, p. 74.
10. Ibid.
11. See *LaRue v. DeWolff, Boberg & Associates*, 552 U.S. __ (2008).
12. *Foltz v. U.S. News & World Report, Inc.*, 106 F.R.D. 338 (D.C. Cir. 1984), aff'd in part and vacated in part, remanded, 760 F.2d 1300 (D.C. Cir. 1985), on remand, 613 F. Supp. 634 (D.D.C. 1985) (distributions for 1973 through 1980); and *Richardson v. U.S. News & World Report, Inc.*, 623 F. Supp. 350 (D.C. Cir. 1985) (1981 distributions). (*Note:* This 80-page opinion is highly

instructive reading on both ESOP valuation issues and minority stock valuation issues in general.)

13. *Las Vegas Dodge v. United States*, 1985 U.S. Dist. LEXIS 21577 1985 WL 6366 (D. Nev. 1985).
14. *Howard v. Shay*, 1993 U.S. Dist. LEXIS 20153 (C.D. Cal. 1993), revised and remanded by 100 F.3d 1484 (9th Cir. Cal. 1996), cert. denied, 520 U.S. 1237 (1997).
15. *Reich v. Valley National Bank of Arizona*, 837 F. Supp. 1259, 1993 U.S. Dist. LEXIS 11837 (S.D.N.Y. 1993).
16. *Eyler v. Commissioner*, T.C. Memo. 1995-123 (T.C. 1995), aff'd 88 F.3d 445 (7th Cir. 1996).
17. *Henry v. Champlain Enterprises*, 334 F. Supp. 2d 252, 2004 U.S. Dist. LEXIS 18140 (N.D.N.Y. September 3, 2004).
18. *Chao v. Hall Holding Co., Inc.*, 285 F.3d 415, 2002 U.S. App. LEXIS 5929 (6th Cir. April 3, 2002).
19. 239 F. Supp. 2d 820, 2002 U.S. Dist. LEXIS 24829 (C.D. Ill. December 30, 2002).
20. 419 F.3d 626, 2005 U.S. App. LEXIS 17355 (7th Cir. August 17, 2005).
21. 446 F.3d 728 (7th Cir. 2006).

Chapter 23

1. Internal Revenue Service, IRS Revenue Ruling 59-60; American Society of Appraisers, ASA Business Valuation Standards, 2009, p. 27; Shannon P. Pratt with Alina V. Niculita, *Valuing a Business: The Analysis and Appraisal of Closely Held Businesses*, 5th ed., McGraw-Hill, New York, 2008, pp. 41–42.
2. American Society of Appraisers, ASA Business Valuation Standards, p. 28.
3. The Meat Processing Company (MPC), U.S. Corporation Income Tax Return, 2011, MPC website http://MPC.com/, and interviews with management.
4. Research Department, The Livingston Survey, Federal Reserve Bank of Philadelphia, December 12, 2012, p. 3.

Index